T0396309

Humanizing Online Teaching and Learning in Higher Education

Laura E. Gray
South College, USA

Shernette Dunn
Florida Atlantic University, USA

A volume in the Advances in Mobile and Distance
Learning (AMDL) Book Series

Published in the United States of America by
IGI Global
Information Science Reference (an imprint of IGI Global)
701 E. Chocolate Avenue
Hershey PA, USA 17033
Tel: 717-533-8845
Fax: 717-533-8661
E-mail: cust@igi-global.com
Web site: http://www.igi-global.com

Library of Congress Cataloging-in-Publication Data

Names: Gray, Laura E., 1970- editor. | Dunn, Shernette, 1981- editor.
Title: Humanizing online teaching and learning in higher education / Edited
   by Laura Gray, Shernette Dunn.
Description: Hershey, PA : Information Science Reference, [2024] | Includes
   bibliographical references and index. | Summary: "This book provides
   ready to use strategies to promote student engagement in online spaces
   using a variety of tools and strategies to promote student success and
   retention"-- Provided by publisher.
Identifiers: LCCN 2023055050 (print) | LCCN 2023055051 (ebook) | ISBN
   9798369307625 (hardcover) | ISBN 9798369307632 (ebook)
Subjects: LCSH: Education, Higher--Web-based instruction. | College
   teaching--Web-based instruction. | Motivation in education. | Engagement
   (Philosophy)
Classification: LCC LB2395.7 .H86 2024 (print) | LCC LB2395.7 (ebook) |
   DDC 378.1/7344678--dc23/eng/20231206
LC record available at https://lccn.loc.gov/2023055050
LC ebook record available at https://lccn.loc.gov/2023055051

This book is published in the IGI Global book series Advances in Mobile and Distance Learning (AMDL) (ISSN: 2327-1892; eISSN: 2327-1906)

British Cataloguing in Publication Data
A Cataloguing in Publication record for this book is available from the British Library.

For electronic access to this publication, please contact: eresources@igi-global.com.

Advances in Mobile and Distance Learning (AMDL) Book Series

Patricia Ordóñez de Pablos
Universidad de Oviedo, Spain

ISSN:2327-1892
EISSN:2327-1906

MISSION

Private and public institutions have made great strides in the fields of mobile and distance learning in recent years, providing greater learning opportunities outside of a traditional classroom setting. While the online learning revolution has allowed for greater learning opportunities, it has also presented numerous challenges for students and educators alike. As research advances, online educational settings can continue to develop and advance the technologies available for learners of all ages.

The **Advances in Mobile and Distance Learning** (AMDL) Book Series publishes research encompassing a variety of topics related to all facets of mobile and distance learning. This series aims to be an essential resource for the timeliest research to help advance the development of new educational technologies and pedagogy for use in online classrooms.

COVERAGE

- E-Books
- Ethical Considerations
- Administration and Organization
- Location-Based Integration
- Course Design
- Mobile Learning
- Cloud Computing in Schools
- Distance Learning
- Lifelong Learning
- Accreditation

IGI Global is currently accepting manuscripts for publication within this series. To submit a proposal for a volume in this series, please contact our Acquisition Editors at Acquisitions@igi-global.com or visit: http://www.igi-global.com/publish/.

Titles in this Series

For a list of additional titles in this series, please visit: http://www.igi-global.com/book-series/advances-mobile-distance-learning/37162

Designing Equitable and Accessible Online Learning Environments
Lydia Kyei-Blankson (Illinois State University, USA) Jared Keengwe (University of North Dakota, USA) and Esther Ntuli (Idaho State University, USA)
Information Science Reference • copyright 2024 • 295pp • H/C (ISBN: 9798369302682) • US $230.00 (our price)

Adjunct Faculty in Online Higher Education Best Practices for Teaching Adult Learners
Tanya McGlashing Tarbutton (Concordia University, Irvine, USA) and Lori Beth Doyle (Concordia University, Irvine, USA)
Information Science Reference • copyright 2024 • 389pp • H/C (ISBN: 9781668498552) • US $230.00 (our price)

Handbook of Research on Creating Motivational Online Environments for Students
Julie A. Bilodeau (Johnson & Wales University, USA) and Larry W. Hughes (Johnson & Wales University, USA)
Information Science Reference • copyright 2023 • 521pp • H/C (ISBN: 9781668445334) • US $270.00 (our price)

Emerging Trends and Historical Perspectives Surrounding Digital Transformation in Education Achieving Open and Blended Learning Environments
Nikleia Eteokleous (Frederick University, Cyprus) Despo Ktoridou (University of Nicosia, Cyprus) and Antonios Kafa (Open University of Cyprus, Cyprus)
Information Science Reference • copyright 2023 • 334pp • H/C (ISBN: 9781668444238) • US $240.00 (our price)

Comparative Research on Diversity in Virtual Learning Eastern vs. Western Perspectives
Zuheir Khlaif (An-Najah National University, Palestine) Mageswaran Sanmugam (Universiti Sains Malaysia, Malaysia) and Jamil Itmazi (Palestine Ahliya University, Palestine)
Information Science Reference • copyright 2023 • 322pp • H/C (ISBN: 9781668435953) • US $215.00 (our price)

Developing Curriculum for Emergency Remote Learning Environments
Susana Silva (School of Hospitality and Tourism, CEOS, CITUR, Polytechnic Institute of Porto, Portugal) Paula Peres (ISCAP, Polytechnic Institute of Porto, Portugal) and Cândida Silva (CITUR Algoritmi, School of Hospitality and Tourism, Polytechnic Institute of Porto, Portugal)
Information Science Reference • copyright 2023 • 334pp • H/C (ISBN: 9781668460719) • US $215.00 (our price)

Socioeconomic Inclusion During an Era of Online Education
Manuel B. Garcia (University of the Philippines, Diliman, Philippines)
Information Science Reference • copyright 2022 • 314pp • H/C (ISBN: 9781668443644) • US $215.00 (our price)

701 East Chocolate Avenue, Hershey, PA 17033, USA
Tel: 717-533-8845 x100 • Fax: 717-533-8661
E-Mail: cust@igi-global.com • www.igi-global.com

Table of Contents

Chapter 12

Lucas John Jensen, Georgia Southern University, USA
Jackie HeeYoung Kim, Georgia Southern University, USA

Chapter 13

Sunok Lee, Chonnam National University, South Korea
Daeun Kim, Chonnam National University, South Korea
Yura Jeong, Chonnam National University, South Korea
Jeeheon Ryu, Chonnam National University, South Korea

Detailed Table of Contents

Lacey D. Huffling, Georgia Southern University, USA
Allison Freed, University of Central Arkansas, USA
Heather C. Scott, Georgia Southern University, USA
Aerin Benavides, University of North Carolina at Greensboro, USA
Jodie L. Ward, Georgia Southern University, USA

Humanizing online professional development has become more important as schools, universities, and companies continue to shift to learning online. The purpose of the chapter is to chronicle the collaboration of four teacher educators' successes and failures in moving a two-hour face-to-face professional development to online (Real Science PD). The Real Science PD provided pedagogical methods to engage students in K-12 science standards by integrating online tools to examine local and global science issues for approximately 25 K-16 educators. The facilitators aligned the seven common features of effective PD with the principles of adult learning theory and humanizing pedagogy as they attempted to translate what they did face-to-face into an online setting. Findings indicated that humanizing online PD can be best understood with clear objectives, demonstration of relevance, opportunities for engagement, relevant classroom contexts, and by providing opportunities for participants to envision applying what they learned in their own classrooms.

Jim A. McCleskey, Western Governors University, USA
Rebecca M. Melton, Western Governors University, USA

The onset of COVID-19 brought about a significant transformation in higher education (HE), expediting an ongoing evolution and compelling institutions and educators to cultivate the necessary skills for effective online delivery and resource provision. Insights from student experiences during the spring of 2020 indicated that institutions faced challenges in their transitions, revealing deficiencies in crucial aspects such as online instructor presence, social interaction among instructors and students, and instructor immediacy. This chapter suggests instructional practices and technology approaches within HE from a community of inquiry (CoI) perspective to enhance student engagement and instructor presence. The trajectory of HE is persistently shifting towards advanced technology, aiming to expand, streamline, and enhance student engagement and interaction, all while introducing innovative methods to enhance instructor presence. The authors urge HE institutions to adopt and refine various techniques to elevate the student experience.

Chapter 3

Gerald Ardito, Manhattanville College, USA

This chapter will describe a graduate-level online teacher education course titled "CS for Teachers," which exposed novice teacher candidates to the key concepts of computational thinking, especially abstraction, mostly for the first time. This asynchronous online course was designed to introduce these teacher candidates to these concepts through increasingly challenging projects or "challenges" and to provide the highest levels of autonomy and freedom in meeting these challenges. Student-to-student and student-to-teacher interactions were examined to explore the content and tenor of such interactions throughout the course. This analysis revealed that during the hardest part of these challenges, student-to-student interactions dramatically increased and increasingly focused on asking for and providing support to one another in authentic and meaningful ways. Implications for teacher education are explored.

Chapter 4

Clara Hauth, Marymount University, USA
Jennifer Crystle, Marymount University, USA
Shannon L. Melideo, Marymount University, USA
Ruth Boyd, Marymount University, USA
Jennifer Thompson, Marymount University, USA

This chapter describes two of the best practices an asynchronous EdD program for educational leadership and organizational innovation program employs to humanize the online course space for its doctoral program. The researchers discuss the origins and development of the continuous weekly support (CWS) model and the lead doctoral faculty mentor (LDFM) program, which are two pillars of the student experience in the online doctoral program. A comprehensive analysis of the technological integrations, frequency of communication, and various messaging techniques are discussed. Additional data is shared regarding a thorough examination of the lead doctoral faculty mentor (LDFM) role, incorporating data from a recently completed institutional research project. The hope is that by sharing these practices, other institutions of higher education may modify and incorporate similar high-impact practices of their own, thereby increasing student persistence, retention, and degree completion, specifically in virtual program environments.

Chapter 5

Stuart K. White, Purdue University, USA
Qian Xu, Purdue University, USA
Anthony C. Robinso, Purdue University, USA
Weijian Yan, Purdue University, USA
Liu Dong, Purdue University, USA
Zhuo Zhang, Purdue University, USA
Adewole E. Babalola, Purdue University, USA
Adrie A. Koehler, Purdue University, USA

Asynchronous online discussions (AODs) are a primary way instructors design for interactions among students in online environments. However, many common challenges associated with AODs (e.g., self-doubt, poorly constructed question prompts, superficial posting) prevent students from benefitting fully from the experience. Furthermore, how instructional designers address these challenges has implications for how AODs are designed, facilitated, monitored, and evaluated. This chapter explores using an empathy-driven approach to overcome AOD challenges. Adopting an empathy-driven approach offers instructional designers opportunities to mitigate challenges with designing, facilitating, monitoring, and evaluating AODs in order to create a meaningful learning opportunity that fosters inclusivity, motivation, and engagement while reducing ambiguity. Specific strategies are shared for improving AODs by using an empathy-based approach.

Chapter 6

The technologically mediated context of online teaching and learning presents unique challenges that require making explicit the implicit human elements that may be taken for granted in face-to-face contexts. While empathy, the emotional (affective) and reflective (cognitive) process of relating to another's circumstance, has been effectively employed in other design fields, its application in instructional design has only recently emerged. Using a hybrid narrative literature review process, this chapter presents an investigation of empirical and conceptual applications of empathic analysis used in instructional design settings. The authors analyze various empathic tools and methods employed and offer examples and advice to instructional designers and researchers for incorporating the practices in their work as a means to humanize online learning at the earliest stages in the instructional design process.

Chapter 7

This chapter explores the importance of integrating culturally responsive teaching (CRT) principles into online education to enhance student engagement and success. It discusses the challenges of implementing culturally responsive practices in online learning environments. It encourages educational practitioners (including instructors, instructional designers, managers, and administrators) to engage in detailed planning and structured facilitation and to involve students in the process. The narrative invites reflection as it reviews the foundational works of scholars in culturally responsive pedagogy and teaching practices and outlines a framework for creating inclusive and culturally affirming learning environments. The literature suggests ways for educators to strategically utilize technology to foster inclusivity in online learning environments.

Chapter 8

This chapter outlines a rationale and best practices for humanizing online learning by implementing strategies for cultivating belonging. These strategies are rooted in the community of inquiry framework and the importance of intentionally cultivating students' social presence in order to enhance opportunities for cognitive presence and deep critical thinking. Culturally responsive teaching practices also guide these strategies for designing and facilitating inclusive online learning spaces where belonging is intentionally centered in the instructor's teaching presence. The strategies in this chapter include ways to design and develop courses with belonging in mind from the start as well as strategies for maintaining a sense of belonging and community throughout a course after it has been initially established.

Promoting human connections in online instruction can be challenging. Students may have technological barriers or may feel isolated or disconnected from their peers. Instructors must find ways to build rapport among students, encourage active learning, and personalize the learning process. This chapter explores the concept of humanizing online instruction by fostering human connections within virtual environments. Educational frameworks, digital tools, instructional strategies, and pedagogies are discussed that can facilitate this goal. Human connections are crucial for effective learning, and fostering these connections can lead to increased student engagement, mastery of content, and enhanced academic performance.

Using the three presences (teacher presence, cognitive presence, and social presence) of the community of inquiry framework as a guide to humanize the online environment, this chapter highlights strategies and tools that authentically engage graduate students to think, collaborate, and learn in a collaborative online environment. The authors discuss their journeys to teaching online from an in-person format. This chapter will give readers (faculty, instructors, and instructional designers) insight and ideas that will elevate their online teaching and improve student success through intentional engagement.

Chapter 11

This chapter explores the potential of artificial intelligence (AI) to personalize and humanize online education, transcending transactional learning. It emphasizes how AI, particularly generative large language models (LLM) utilizing natural language processing (NLP), can foster deeper, human-like interactions between students and educators. Moving away from traditional keyword-based searches, the chapter highlights how AI integrates with tools like search engines and research databases, transforming the way students and teachers think, research, and converse. Despite concerns over the potential dehumanizing impact of AI, the chapter argues that its capabilities can, in fact, actually facilitate continuous and creative engagement, while privileging understanding and creativity over rote memorization. These new generative tools can enhance, not challenge, the human element in online education and promote more authentic assessments in the process.

Chapter 12

Lucas John Jensen, Georgia Southern University, USA
Jackie HeeYoung Kim, Georgia Southern University, USA

Given ongoing issues with a lack of humanization in online classroom settings, this chapter shares insights gained through failed implementations of social media, the use of various multimedia introductions, and the utilization of a chatbot to humanize online classrooms. The chapter will discuss why participants did not feel a connection to each other when social networks were used in the classroom and how multimedia introductions built on Web 2.0 tools might increase relatedness among participants. Moreover, it discusses how AI-powered tools provide personalized assistance, such as meeting notes and summarizations, in promoting humanization, increased participation, and a sense of community. The chapter further highlights influential factors in both the failure and success of using multimedia introductions and AI-powered tools in the humanization of online learning, based on authors' experiences, backed by self-determination theory and social presence theory. This chapter concluded with guidelines on how to use these innovative tools to humanize online learning environments.

Chapter 13

Sunok Lee, Chonnam National University, South Korea
Daeun Kim, Chonnam National University, South Korea
Yura Jeong, Chonnam National University, South Korea
Jeeheon Ryu, Chonnam National University, South Korea

The concept of embodiment has been central to the design of extended reality (XR) technologies and is one of the keys to immersive learning. However, there is still a need for further conceptual frameworks to aid developers, practitioners, and educators in comprehending the various facets of embodiment and their impact on learning. This gap becomes apparent when examining the revised taxonomy that includes layers for interactive learning experiences in digital technologies. In this context, this chapter aims to address this deficiency by presenting a design case focused on a digital art application leveraging XR technology. By integrating sensorimotor information based on kinetic movements, the application aims to enrich the tactile painting experience within liberal arts education. Developed for Hololens2, the XR art application incorporates interactive elements such as avatars, narratives, multi-sensory features, and tools for creating artifacts. Throughout the chapter, the authors offer insights into the considerations taken during the interface and interaction design phases, particularly emphasizing the promotion of immersive engagement.

Foreword

I appreciate the opportunity to write the forward for *Humanizing Online Teaching and Learning in Higher Education*. A lot has changed regarding online learning in the past few years. While enrollments in online courses and programs consistently increased over the past two decades, the COVID-19 pandemic and the safety measures used to move education into some type of blended, remote, or fully online learning forced almost every instructor and student to experience teaching and learning online, many for the first time, almost overnight–essentially making online learning a household term. During this time, instructors' and students' experiences learning online differed from student to student, course to course, and institution to institution. Some had good experiences, but others did not (see Hodges et al., 2020; Stewart, 2021). This collective experience highlighted and even amplified a few things, some of which critics and proponents of online learning have been aware of for years and others that were new or unable to ignore.

Historically, online courses have a higher attrition rate than traditional in-person face-to-face courses. Researchers of online learning are quick to point out that attrition in online courses is influenced by multiple factors, including but not limited to course design, instructor facilitation, students' prior experience learning online, as well as numerous situational and socioeconomic factors, to name just a few (Shea & Bidjerano, 2014, 2018, 2019; Xu & Jaggars, 2011, 2013). One consistent finding suggests that one of the reasons *some* students are not successful with online learning is due to a lack of interaction and social presence, which in turn *can* result in a sense of isolation and loneliness and, ultimately, a feeling that what students are doing, learning, whether they login in or not, and even who they are might not ultimately matter.

These issues are not new. Distance educators, who turned to computer-mediated communication (CMC) to help instructors and students interact, wrote about their experiences interacting online, primarily with asynchronous text-based communication, in some classic books like Mason and Kaye's (1989) *Mindweave*, Harasim's (1990) *Online Education*, Eastmonds' (1995) *Alone but together, and* Palloff and Pratt's (1999) *Building Learning Communities in Cyberspace*. Other early adopters, building on research on communication, education, and psychology, investigated and developed frameworks to help guide the study and practice of online learning, with a specific focus on social interaction and collaboration. For instance, in the mid-1990s, Gunawardena (1995) was among the first to research the role of immediacy and social presence in online learning. A few years later, Garrison et al. (1999) developed the Community of Inquiry framework–which posits that a meaningful educational experience involves teaching presence, social presence, and cognitive presence) while Rovai (2002) began investigating how to create a sense of classroom community online. In different ways, each of these pioneers was interested in ways to make online learning social, engaging, meaningful, and memorable.

Often, to a fault, educators hold in-person, face-to-face educational experiences as the gold standard. We strive to mimic and recreate some idealized version of an in-person face-to-face course. But as McDonald (2002) reminded us over 20 years ago, "Is 'as good as face-to-face' as good as it gets?" In-person face-to-face courses are not inherently good, and online learning isn't inherently less than. Communicating online is indeed different, but that does not inherently make it worse or less effective. Decades of communication research, in particular, highlight that online communication isn't inherently antisocial, inefficient, or ineffective; rather, effectiveness depends on multiple situational factors such as who, why, when, and how one communicates (Lowenthal, 2010).

As a researcher whose research focuses on how people communicate online using emerging technologies—often concentrating on issues of presence, identity, and community, I have found that educators talk about humanizing online teaching and learning in different ways. Most conversations about humanizing online learning are in response to the belief or experience of teaching and learning online feeling unhuman, not human-like, dehumanizing, or lacking a human touch as if we are just interacting with a computer–pixels on a screen. In my experience, when instructors and researchers discuss humanizing online learning, they are essentially interested in human-centered and not computer-centered learning experiences. Some focus on how an instructor can add a "human touch" to their courses, whether that be through teaching presence (Jones et al., 2008; Kilgore & Lowenthal, 2015; McCarty, 2020; Parker et al., 2021) and/or instructor social presence (Li et al., 2022; Paciej-Woodruff, 2021; also see Richardson & Lowenthal, 2017), while others focus on how to develop a sense of connection and ultimately a sense of belongingness and community between instructor and student and students to students (Gilpin et al., 2023; Murtafi'ah & Pradita, 2023), and still others seem to take it a step further as

Michelle Pacansky-Brock has done in much of her work (see Pacansky-Brock et al., 2020). These individuals focus not only on issues of presence and connection but also important concepts such as empathy, accessibility, inclusion, trust, and agency (Pacansky-Brock, 2020).

Each chapter in this book focuses on the "who," "we," and "I" (i.e., the humans) involved in online learning, emphasizing the intrinsic social and emotional dimensions of education in their own way. This emphasis is not merely theoretical; it acknowledges the well-established understanding that learning, as a human activity, is deeply social and emotional. Through a focus on social presence and the development of connectedness, online educators leverage a substantial body of research that supports these practices. It is essential to recognize that online classrooms comprise individuals with distinct narratives, challenges, and ambitions, many seeking acknowledgment and visibility.

Thus, humanizing online learning often extends beyond simply the use of advanced technologies or pedagogical innovations; it requires the acknowledgment and appreciation of the diversity present in the learner population. This process necessitates a thoughtful approach to course design and facilitation, aiming to transform these courses into shared experiences that foster mutual learning from diverse perspectives.

Addressing the varied needs of students underscores the principle that not all learners will desire or need the same level of emotional engagement. However, it is universally accepted that all students benefit from an environment that supports their emotional well-being, even if not every interaction is intensely personal. The goal is to cultivate a space where students are recognized, respected, and valued for their individuality as well as their individual and collective contributions.

Empathy, diversity, and inclusivity principles should continue to guide us as we create online learning environments that are effective and enriching, promoting not just knowledge acquisition but also a sense of community and belonging. By doing so, we honor the individual and collective dimensions of online learning by making our courses both human and learner-centered.

Patrick R. Lowenthal
Boise State University, USA

REFERENCES

Eastmond, D. V. (1995). *Alone but together: Adult distance study through computer conferencing.* Hampton Press.

Garrison, D. R., Anderson, T., & Archer, W. (1999). Critical inquiry in a text-based environment: Computer conferencing in higher education. *The Internet and Higher Education, 2*(2-3), 87–105. doi:10.1016/S1096-7516(00)00016-6

Gilpin, S. A., Yoon, S. R., & Miller, J. L. (2023). Building community online: Moving toward humanization through relationship-focused technology use. *Online Learning : the Official Journal of the Online Learning Consortium, 27*(3), 133–154. doi:10.24059/olj.v27i3.3583

Gunawardena, C. N. (1995). Social presence theory and implications for interaction and collaborative learning in computer conferences. *International Journal of Educational Telecommunications, 1*(2), 147–166.

Harasim, L. M. (Ed.). (1990). *Online education: Perspectives on a new environment.* Greenwood Publishing.

Hodges, C. B., Moore, S., Lockee, B. B., Trust, T., & Bond, M. A. (2020). The difference between emergency remote teaching and online learning. *EDUCAUSE Review.* https://er.educause.edu/articles/2020/3/the-difference-between-emergency-remote-teaching-and-online-learning

Jones, P., Kolloff, M., & Kolloff, F. (2008). Students' perspectives on humanizing and establishing teacher presence in an online course. In K. McFerrin, R. Weber, R. Carlsen & D. Willis (Eds.), *Proceedings of SITE 2008-Society for Information Technology & Teacher Education International Conference* (pp. 460-465). Academic Press.

Kilgore, W., & Lowenthal, P. R. (2015). The Human Element MOOC: An experiment in social presence. In R. D. Wright (Ed.), *Student-teacher interaction in online learning environments* (pp. 389–407). IGI Global. doi:10.4018/978-1-4666-6461-6.ch017

Li, Q., Bañuelos, M., Liu, Y., & Xu, D. (2022). Online instruction for a humanized learning experience: Techniques used by college instructors. *Computers & Education, 189,* 104595. doi:10.1016/j.compedu.2022.104595

Mason, R., & Kaye, A. R. (Eds.). (1989). *Mindweave: Communication, computers, and distance education.* Pergamon Press.

McCarty, J. R. (2020). *Humanizing online learning: A phenomenological investigation of teaching presence* [Doctoral dissertation]. Frostburg State University.

McDonald, J. (2002). Is "as good as face-to-face" as good as it gets? *Journal of Asynchronous Learning Networks, 6*(2), 10–23.

Murtafi'ah, B., & Pradita, I. (2023). Social presence as means to humanizing online classroom. *Journal of Applied Research in Higher Education.*

Pacansky-Brock, M. (2020). *How to humanize your online class, version 2.0* [Infographic]. https://brocansky.com/humanizing/infographic2

Pacansky-Brock, M., Smedshammer, M., & Vincent-Layton, K. (2020). Humanizing online teaching to equitize higher education. *Current Issues in Education (Tempe, Ariz.), 21*(2). https://cie.asu.edu/ojs/index.php/cieatasu/article/view/1905

Paciej-Woodruff, A. (2021, March). The case for your face: teacher presence in asynchronous education courses. Stop feeling uncomfortable and start recording your face to humanize the online experience. In *Society for Information Technology & Teacher Education International Conference* (pp. 535-539). Association for the Advancement of Computing in Education (AACE).

Palloff, R. M., & Pratt, K. (1999). *Building learning communities in cyberspace: Effective strategies for the online classroom.* Jossey-Bass.

Parker, N., Mahler, B. P., & Edwards, M. (2021). Humanizing online learning experiences. *The Journal of Educators Online, 18*(2).

Richardson, J. C., & Lowenthal, P. (2017). Instructor social presence: Learners' needs and a neglected component of the community of inquiry framework. In A. Whiteside, A. Garrett Dikkers, & K. Swan (Eds.), *Social presence in online learning: Multiple perspectives on practice and research* (pp. 86–98). Stylus.

Rovai, A. P. (2002). Building sense of community at a distance. *International Review of Research in Open and Distance Learning, 3*(1), 1–16. doi:10.19173/irrodl.v3i1.79

Shea, P., & Bidjerano, T. (2014). Does online learning impede degree completion? A national study of community college students. *Computers & Education, 75,* 103–111. doi:10.1016/j.compedu.2014.02.009

Shea, P., & Bidjerano, T. (2018). Online course enrollment in community college and degree completion: The tipping point. *International Review of Research in Open and Distance Learning, 19*(2). Advance online publication. doi:10.19173/irrodl.v19i2.3460

Shea, P., & Bidjerano, T. (2019). Effects of online course load on degree completion, transfer, and dropout among community college students of the state university of New York. *Online Learning : the Official Journal of the Online Learning Consortium, 23*(4), 6–22. doi:10.24059/olj.v23i4.1364

Stewart, W. H. (2021). A global crash-course in teaching and learning online: A thematic review of empirical Emergency Remote Teaching (ERT) studies in higher education during Year 1 of COVID-19. *Open Praxis, 13*(1), 89-102.

Xu, D., & Jaggars, S. S. (2011). *Online and hybrid course enrollment and performance in Washington State community and technical colleges* (CCRC Working Paper No. 31). New York, NY: Columbia University, Teachers College, Community College Research Center.

Xu, D., & Jaggars, S. S. (2013). *Adaptability to online learning: Differences across types of students and academic subject areas* (CCRC Working Paper No. 54). New York, NY: Columbia University, Teachers College, Community College Research Center.

Preface

Welcome to the edited reference book *Humanizing Online Teaching and Learning in Higher Education*, which was meticulously curated by Laura E. Gray and Shernette Dunn. In the dynamic landscape of higher education, the surge in online learning brings with it a myriad of challenges and opportunities. As educators and stakeholders strive to meet the diverse needs of online learners, the human element emerges as a critical component for fostering engagement, success, and retention.

This book is a comprehensive resource designed for college professors, educational researchers, graduate students, policy makers, instructional designers, curriculum designers, college administration, educational technologists, developers, and all those invested in the evolving realm of online education. Through a thoughtful compilation of research-based strategies and practical tools, this volume aims to serve as a catalyst for humanizing the online learning environment.

OBJECTIVES OF THE BOOK

Ready-to-Use Strategies: Furnish practical strategies to promote student engagement in online spaces, utilizing a diverse array of tools to ensure student success and retention.

Research-Based Pedagogical Practices: Provide educators and stakeholders with research-based strategies that encompass educationally and culturally sound pedagogical practices. These practices can be seamlessly integrated into various subject matter courses, thereby enhancing the humanization of online courses.

Arsenal of Strategies for Higher Education Professionals: Equip higher education professionals with a rich arsenal of strategies and resources, empowering them to address the high attrition rates experienced by online learners in colleges and universities.

Professional Development Guide: Serve as a guide for colleges and universities in professional development opportunities for online faculty and staff, fostering a community of practitioners dedicated to humanizing the online learning experience.

Leveraging Instructional Technologies: Offer insights on leveraging various instructional technologies, including AI, to create engagement and promote deeper, relevant learning that connects students to the real world.

Book Chapters Overview

The book spans a diverse range of chapters, addressing key facets of humanizing online learning spaces:

ADA Compliance: Exploring the incorporation of ADA requirements in online spaces, adhering to federal and state laws.

Historical Perspectives: Analyzing the evolution of online learning in higher education, both within the U.S. and in an international context.

Research-Based Definition of Online Learning: Defining online learning and engagement through rigorous research, emphasizing the importance of evidence-based practices.

Using Augmented Reality and AI: Investigating the role of augmented reality and AI in promoting retention and success in online spaces, showcasing the transformative potential of technology.

Culturally Responsive Strategies: Unveiling culturally responsive strategies to enhance engagement and student success, underlining the significance of cultural inclusivity.

Combatting Attrition in STEM Courses: Examining methods to combat high attrition rates specifically in online STEM courses, emphasizing the critical need for retention strategies.

This book aspires to be a valuable resource for those dedicated to humanizing the online learning experience, fostering a collective commitment to student success in the ever-evolving landscape of higher education. The emphasis on research-based approaches underscores the commitment to advancing knowledge and improving outcomes in online education.

ORGANIZATION OF THE BOOK

Humanizing Online Professional Development: Moving Beyond Click and Tell

In this chapter, the authors delve into the crucial realm of humanizing online professional development, shedding light on successes and challenges faced by teacher educators. The focus centers on the transition of a face-to-face professional development program to an online format, specifically the Real Science PD initiative. The chapter narrates the experiences of four teacher educators, highlighting the alignment of effective professional development features with Adult Learning Theory and Humanizing Pedagogy. Findings emphasize the importance of clear objectives, relevance, engagement opportunities, and envisioning practical applications for participants, ultimately contributing to a nuanced understanding of humanizing online PD.

"Better Than Human?" in Partnership With AI: Enhancing Social Presence Through the Use of Technology

Examining the impact of COVID-19 on higher education, this chapter delves into the transformation it triggered and the challenges institutions faced in maintaining online faculty engagement. Drawing insights from student experiences during the pandemic, the authors advocate for optimal instructional practices and technology approaches within higher education to enhance student engagement, instructor immediacy, and online social presence. The chapter explores the persistent shift towards advanced technology in higher education, emphasizing the need for innovative methods to foster authentic engagement and elevate the student experience.

Cooperative Freedoms and Practical Inquiry in an Online Course for Teachers

This chapter presents a detailed exploration of a graduate-level online teacher education course, "CS for Teachers," focusing on introducing computational thinking concepts to novice teacher candidates. The asynchronous online format allows for autonomy and freedom, leading to increased student-to-student interactions during challenging phases. The analysis sheds light on the collaborative nature of student interactions and their focus on providing support to one another. The implications for teacher education are discussed, emphasizing the importance of autonomy and authentic interactions in online learning environments.

Humanizing the Online Doctoral Experience With High-Impact Faculty Engagement and Mentorship

This chapter unveils two best practices employed in an asynchronous EdD program for educational leadership and organizational innovation. The Continuous Weekly Support (CWS) Model and the Lead Doctoral Faculty Mentor (LDFM) program are examined in detail, providing insights into their technological integrations and impact on the student experience. The chapter aims to offer valuable practices for other institutions to enhance student persistence, retention, and degree completion in virtual program environments.

Empathy-Driven Instructional Design in Asynchronous Online Discussions

This chapter advocates for an empathy-driven approach in overcoming challenges associated with asynchronous online discussions (AODs). The authors explore how instructional designers can address self-doubt, question prompts, and superficial posting to create meaningful learning opportunities. By adopting an empath-driven approach, instructional designers can enhance inclusivity, motivation, and engagement in AODs, offering specific strategies to mitigate challenges and foster a positive learning environment.

Humanizing Instructional Design Through Empathic Analysis

Examining the technologically mediated context of online teaching and learning, this chapter introduces empathic analysis as a tool for instructional designers. The authors conduct a narrative literature review to explore empirical and conceptual applications of empathic analysis in instructional design settings. The chapter provides insights, examples, and advice for incorporating empathic practices in instructional design, emphasizing the importance of early-stage humanization in online learning.

Applying Culturally Responsive Strategies to Promote Engagement and Student Success in Online Courses

This chapter delves into the integration of Culturally Responsive Teaching (CRT) principles in online education to enhance student engagement and success. It addresses the challenges of implementing culturally responsive practices in online learning environments, advocating for detailed planning, structured facilitation, and student involvement. The chapter outlines a framework for creating inclusive and culturally affirming learning environments, strategically utilizing technology to foster inclusivity.

Strategies for Cultivating Belonging in Online Learning Spaces

This chapter outlines strategies rooted in the Community of Inquiry framework for humanizing online learning by cultivating a sense of belonging. It emphasizes intentional design for social presence, creating inclusive online learning spaces where belonging is centered. The strategies include considerations for initial course design as well as ongoing efforts to maintain a sense of belonging and community throughout a course.

Building Bridges: Fostering Human Connections Through Tools and Technology in Online Instruction

Addressing the challenge of promoting human connections in online instruction, this chapter explores frameworks, digital tools, instructional strategies, and pedagogies that facilitate humanizing online instruction. It emphasizes the crucial role of human connections in effective learning and discusses methods to build rapport among students, encourage active learning, and personalize the online learning process.

High Tech/High: Humanizing Teaching and Learning Online for More Effective Learning Experiences

Guided by the Community of Inquiry Framework, this chapter highlights strategies and tools to humanize the online environment, focusing on teacher presence, cognitive presence, and social presence. The authors share insights and ideas to elevate online teaching, providing readers with practical approaches to enhance student success through intentional engagement.

Leveraging AI to Personalize and Humanize Online Learning: Transforming Transactional Interactions Into Meaningful Engagements

Exploring the potential of Artificial Intelligence (AI) in online education, this chapter emphasizes the role of generative models using natural language processing (NLP) to foster human-like interactions. It discusses the transformative impact of AI on student-teacher interactions, challenging traditional approaches and highlighting the potential for authentic assessments. The chapter argues for the humanizing potential of AI in online education.

Humanizing Online Instruction With AI-Powered Chatbots and Multimedia Introduction: Empirical Advice for Online College Classrooms

Drawing on experiences and insights from failed and successful implementations, this chapter explores the use of multimedia introductions and AI-powered chatbots to humanize online classrooms. It discusses the challenges and successes in building connections among participants, providing empirical advice based on Self-Determination Theory and Social Presence Theory. The chapter concludes with guidelines for effectively utilizing these tools in the humanization online learning environments.

Exploring Embodied Learning and XR Technologies in Online Education

This chapter focuses on embodied learning in the context of extended reality (XR) technologies, presenting a design case centered around a digital art application. By incorporating kinetic-based sensorimotor information, the chapter aims to enhance the tangible painting experience in liberal arts education. The authors share insights into the considerations made during the design and development phases, emphasizing the potential impact of embodied learning on immersive engagement in online education.

IN SUMMARY

As we bring this edited reference book, *Humanizing Online Teaching and Learning in Higher Education*, to its conclusion, we reflect on the diverse and enriching insights shared by our esteemed contributors. The chapters within this volume collectively form a mosaic of strategies, experiences, and innovative approaches aimed at humanizing the online learning experience.

The journey through these chapters has been a profound exploration of the evolving landscape of higher education. From the historical overviews to the practical implementations of AI, gamification, and culturally responsive teaching, the authors have offered valuable perspectives on the intricate tapestry of humanizing online education. The central theme resonates: recognizing the human element as indispensable in fostering meaningful connections, engagement, and success in the virtual realm.

One of the key takeaways from this compilation is the importance of intentional design, empathy, and a holistic understanding of the diverse needs of online learners. The exploration of varied topics, from professional development and faculty engagement to the integration of emerging technologies, underscores the dynamic nature of the field and the ongoing commitment to enhancing the online educational experience.

Moreover, the emphasis on research-based practices and the inclusion of empirical evidence reaffirm the commitment to evidence-driven approaches in advancing online education. This not only bolsters the credibility of the strategies presented but also contributes to the scholarly discourse surrounding the humanization of online learning spaces.

As editors, our vision for this book was to serve as a beacon for educators, administrators, instructional designers, and all stakeholders invested in the vitality of online education. We believe that the collective wisdom shared within these pages can spark meaningful conversations, inspire transformative practices, and guide the continual evolution of online teaching and learning.

The chapters are not merely standalone contributions but threads woven into the larger narrative of reshaping higher education in a digital era. Whether through the exploration of AI's potential, the implementation of culturally responsive strategies, or the gamification of learning, each chapter contributes a unique perspective to the overarching goal of humanizing the online learning environment.

In closing, we extend our gratitude to the authors who generously shared their expertise and experiences, contributing to the creation of a comprehensive resource for educators and practitioners navigating

Preface

the complexities of online education. May this book inspire a continued commitment to humanizing online teaching and learning, fostering an inclusive, engaging, and successful educational journey for all learners in the digital age.

Laura E. Gray
South College, USA

Shernette D. Dunn
Florida Atlantic University, USA

xxiv

Chapter 1
Humanizing Online Professional Development:
Moving Beyond Click and Tell

Lacey D. Huffling
Georgia Southern University, USA

Allison Freed
University of Central Arkansas, USA

Heather C. Scott
Georgia Southern University, USA

Aerin Benavides
(iD) https://orcid.org/0000-0001-9876-0216
University of North Carolina at Greensboro, USA

Jodic L. Ward
Georgia Southern University, USA

ABSTRACT

Humanizing online professional development has become more important as schools, universities, and companies continue to shift to learning online. The purpose of the chapter is to chronicle the collaboration of four teacher educators' successes and failures in moving a two-hour face-to-face professional development to online (Real Science PD). The Real Science PD provided pedagogical methods to engage students in K-12 science standards by integrating online tools to examine local and global science issues for approximately 25 K-16 educators. The facilitators aligned the seven common features of effective PD with the principles of adult learning theory and humanizing pedagogy as they attempted to translate what they did face-to-face into an online setting. Findings indicated that humanizing online PD can be best understood with clear objectives, demonstration of relevance, opportunities for engagement, relevant classroom contexts, and by providing opportunities for participants to envision applying what they learned in their own classrooms.

DOI: 10.4018/979-8-3693-0762-5.ch001

Educational technology is rapidly changing; thus, the need for professional development workshops (PD) is paramount for educators to be exposed and have access to the latest tools for teaching and learning (Esterhuizen et al., 2013; Xie et al., 2021). Since the COVID-19 pandemic, PD has shifted even more online. These phenomena require PD facilitators to reflect upon how they design and implement professional learning in online spaces, or as Graham and colleagues (2014) discuss, reflect upon the physical layer (technology and delivery of the instruction) and the pedagogical layer (online learning strategies that aid in achieving learning objectives).

In their study of six instructional designers from four different institutions, Xie and colleagues discovered facilitator mindset shifts in regard to online professional learning and the COVID-19 pandemic went from expected isolation in online spaces to modeling community-building and belonging in online spaces; from monomodal instruction to multimodal instruction, and from performative learning strategies to performance-based assessments (p. 338). Yet, given the increased demand for online teacher PD (TPD), "general principles and guidelines relevant for in-person TPD are frequently assumed as applicable to online courses and programs without deeply considering whether specific research-based practices actually transfer well to online environments" (Lay et al., 2020).

Though online teacher professional development has rapidly expanded in the past ten years and even more so post-COVID, "research has not kept pace with the creation and delivery of online teacher professional development programs and courses" (Lay et al., 2020, p. 2). In their study comparing face-to-face and online teacher PD, Fishman and colleagues (2013) found teachers and students benefitted from both formats, with no significant difference between the two. Yet, there is still a lack of research regarding the design, implementation, and impact of online PD (Dede et al., 2009). As Moon and colleagues (2013) point out, even the Fishman and colleagues study showed gaps in the online professional development literature,

While the focus of the study was a comparison of two formats for delivery of PD, the design of the PD itself was somewhat under-specified. For example, there is not enough information in their article about specific design assumptions guiding PD learning goals, nor is there much detail about the specific nature of their evaluation measures. This is not intended to be critical, but to suggest that to take their findings as applicable to all online PD would be an overreach. (para 2)

In their meta-analysis of online teacher professional development over the last decade, Lay et al. (2020) used Grahm et al.'s (2014) framework of physical (technology) and pedagogical layers to ascertain best practices for online teacher professional development. Regarding the physical layer, aspects of navigability, technology support, duration, and additional research were paramount. Content, relevance, community building, and modeling instructional practices were highlighted for the pedagogical layer. "The field of oTPD [online teacher professional development) has taken what is known from the research into best practices in TPD [face-to-face teacher professional development] and oTPD and intentionally addressed improvements in both the physical and pedagogical layers" (Lay et al., 2020, p. 7). As online professional development becomes more accessible and convenient, additional work will need to take place to determine the best practices for effective online professional development.

The purpose of this book chapter is to chronicle our foray into translating an ongoing face-to-face PD that two of us have run the past 3 years (multiple summer sessions and follow-up academic year sessions) to a one-time two-hour online professional development so that others might learn from the successes and failures we experienced. We four authors are teacher educators who collaborate cross-institutionally in writing, research, and instruction. Most recently, the four of us came together to offer a two-hour online summer PD for K-16 educators, primarily from Arkansas, but including others from across the United States, on how to "Engage students in real science using simple virtual tools" (Freed et al., 2023). Coming together, we each brought different perspectives and experiences, yet we were all committed to providing an engaging and relevant PD that connected online learning to the human element that is often a part of on-going face-to-face learning.

By the human element of on-going face-to-face PD, we mean the natural sharing of self, recognition, and celebration of others' expertise, participation in hands-on learning, modeling best practices, and webs of collaboration that occur. Though we know from previous experience and research that these aspects can occur in online learning and are the tenets of robust online learning communities (Dias & Boulder, 2023; Farris, 2015; Ross, 2011; Scott & Scott, 2010), we wanted to explore what the possibilities are for developing these elements in short, one-time online PD offerings. Since professional learning workshops tend to be shorter in duration than university courses or the on-going face-to-face PD we do, we attempted to challenge ourselves to keep these tenets in mind when developing online PD, as we readily acknowledge it would be easy to fall into an information delivery model of instruction when time is constrained (Prestidge et al., 2023). This book chapter explores the successes and failures we experienced in our first attempt at translating the work we engage in with our K-12 colleagues in face-to-face settings into a short, one-time online workshop.

WHO WE ARE

In order to humanize ourselves, we provide a brief introduction that situates our past and present experiences with online PDs.

Lacey's entrance into online learning began as a doctoral student in an online semester-long class. Since then, she has attended many online PDs as a participant, where the structure of the PD was presented as a webinar/lecture, with a question and answer period at the end of the session. She never gave much thought to how to design online PDs as I designed, implemented, and researched face-to-face PD for science teachers.

In 2019, Lacey's interdisciplinary team received funding (National Academies of Sciences, Engineering, and Medicine Gulf Research Board Grant 2000009821) to conduct place-based, face-to-face PD in the Okefenokee Swamp. They traveled across the state in the spring to offer multiple full-day workshops to help prepare participants for the learning that would occur in the summer. That summer, they held a week-long workshop where participants and instructors lived, learned, and traveled together in a remote eco-lodge. Though they had prescribed activities and curriculum each day, they also had in-the-moment changes (like rainy days) or extra opportunities (frog call hikes at night) the participants requested. After the PD, they supported the teachers in curriculum design and were scheduled to observe classrooms in the Spring of 2020. However, the COVID-19 pandemic completely upended our plans.

The team had to quickly shift plans for the next round of PD as they could no longer meet face-to-face. Lacey experienced trepidation as she entered the realm of online PD, but she came away from the experience with an enriched view of what online PD could be and the constraints it removed from face-to-face PD (Scott & Huffling, 2022). Currently, her team has a new round of funding (National Academies of Sciences, Engineering, and Medicine Gulf Research Board grant GSURSF-SCON-10000690), and they purposefully chose to develop a hybrid PD model for their place-based work after reflecting upon the affordances of online learning during the pandemic.

Allison's transition from an in-person faculty position to a completely online position and realizing that more people can be impacted by PD online led Allison to offer more online PD sessions at her institution and with one of the state teacher education organizations. After experiencing successful online conferences during the COVID-19 pandemic, Allison coordinated with others in a state organization for teacher educators to create a grant-funded webinar series for teacher educators in-service and pre-service teachers in the state. She found that online methods provided an opportunity to maintain a connection with other members of the organization and a recruitment tool for gaining new members to our organization.

Heather was first introduced to online learning through taking a course during her doctoral program. She was also asked shortly after that to deliver a canned curriculum, online, short-term summer course, that was asynchronous and felt flat. The entrance into providing online PD for Heather and Lacey was necessitated by the COVID-19 pandemic when faced with either canceling a face-to-face immersive summer PD or moving it entirely online. Though completely online PD was foreign to them at the time, they trudged ahead, expecting mediocre results at best; however, the benefits of online learning for participants made them rethink their structure of PDs going forward (Scott & Huffling, 2022). Following the fully online PD in the summer of 2020, Heather and Lacey enrolled in an Online Learning Consortium course for teaching science labs online. They decided if this was the new method of expectation, they needed to learn more about it.

Aerin experienced the cancellation of scheduled in-person NSF-funded research in public schools during COVID-19 shutdowns. She had to imagine and design online, hands-on science and engineering for students logging in from home or after-school programs. She also developed an online teacher science outdoor learning PD for a community heritage language program. She views her failed attempts and successes as building blocks towards a future of overcoming hurdles to including hands-on activities in online instruction.

Positioning Ourselves

In our face-to-face and online university classes and face-to-face PD, our teaching philosophies rely heavily on humanizing PD; we value social interactions in the learning process (Vygotsky & Cole, 1978) and the creation of community (Pacansky-Brock et al., 2020) as a way to support a sense of belonging (Pacansky-Brock et al., 2023) and encourage vulnerability. In addition, we strive to continually keep our learners' needs central, whether it is K-12 colleagues or our university students engaging in professional learning (Xie et al., 2021). To implement our goals, we mindfully create a social environment, facilitate social interactions, and encourage participants and students to show up authentically (Dias & Boulder, 2023). In regard to PD, we assert that PD should be more than informing educators of pedagogical or technology tools rather, it should provide opportunities to experience and explore the tools being presented. Since we are working with educators, practicing best practices in humanizing online instruction is even more important. Modeling socially aware, interactive PD for teachers has the likelihood to impact their teaching at the K-16 level.

Before we begin discussing how we attempted to translate aspects of an on-going, face-to-face PD to a short, one-time online PD, we want to reiterate that this PD we collaborated on was our first attempt at hosting a short, one-time synchronous online PD. We were hoping in some ways, we could mirror what we are able to do in a face-to-face setting. However, we quickly realized we needed to reconceptualize our roles as PD facilitators in online spaces, and this book chapter attempts to capture our shifts in thinking regarding the professional learning we provide for teachers online, particularly in regard to engagement with technology. In the past, Heather and Lacey ran asynchronous PDs with opportunities for synchronous meetings, but these PDs were extended (summer and academic year) and ran more like a university course than a one-time PD session. Heather had experience with in-person PD sessions that were short but included interaction between the participants and the instructor. She has also led short online PD sessions about online teaching for educators, but never with a group of colleagues and never on the topic of citizen science. Aerin had most recently led an integrated place-based Science education and English education Peruvian PD, as a synchronous online collaboration between teachers in the USA and rural Peru, as part of a graduate-level teacher education course at her US university.

In the sections following, we will discuss the summer online PD (Citizen Science PD) we collaboratively developed and delivered for approximately 25 K-16 educators. We will reflect upon the encouragements and disappointments we experienced, and we will share a reflection template we have developed to aid us in the future that others can use or modify for their needs.

Context of Professional Development

The PD sessions we reference in our chapter were a College of Education virtual summer professional development series for teachers consisting of two months of two-hour PD sessions ranging from book groups to workshops using the newest technology tools. Attendance at the sessions resulted in state-approved PD hours that could be used for teacher licensure and license renewal. Various faculty members in the College of Education created sessions for teachers, and some faculty members invited authors and expert speakers in their fields. Other faculty collaborated with colleagues from the university and other universities to provide one-off PD workshops.

DESIGN OF THE CITIZEN SCIENCE PD

In designing our on-going, face-to-face PD, we utilized the seven features of effective PD (Darling-Hammond et al., 2017): 1) Disciplinary Content Focus, 2) Active Learning, 3) Collaboration, 4) Modeling Effective Practice, 5) Coaching and Expert Support, 6) Feedback and Reflection, and 7) Ongoing to shift face-to-face PD online. These were compiled by analyzing teacher PD studies that indicated a strong positive correlation between teacher PD, teaching practices, and student outcomes. Though this work was centered on content for K-12 learning environments, these seven features can also benefit faculty PD, particularly those teaching undergraduate students. As seen in Table 1, these aspects align with humanizing pedagogy (Mehta & Aguilera, 2020).

To begin our planning process for the Citizen Science PD, we analyzed ways in which we utilized the seven aspects of effective PD in our face-to-face workshops. We mapped the seven components to how we design PDs (Table 2), determining which aspects of the face-to-face PDs we wanted to try to keep or mimic in an online setting as we felt these aspects humanized participant learning. Some aspects of the PD were out of our control as we were facilitators of one PD session that was part of a larger summer PD series run by a university. For instance, the platform format (Zoom) was already selected by the institution, and we did not have access to participant information before the PD. Therefore, we could not contact participants before the workshop to invite them to co-design the learning workshop with us.

Table 1. Humanizing Pedagogy Aligned to Seven Features of Effective PD

Humanizing Pedagogy	Seven Features of Effective Teacher PD (Darling-Hammond et al., 2017)
Participant Voice and Inclusivity (Mehta & Aguilera, 2020)	"Incorporates active learning: Active learning engages teachers directly in designing and trying out teaching strategies, providing them an opportunity to engage in the same style of learning they are designing for their students. Such PD uses authentic artifacts, interactive activities, and other strategies to provide deeply embedded, highly contextualized professional learning. This approach moves away from traditional learning models and environments that are lecture based and have no direct connection to teachers' classrooms and students." (p. 7) "Supports collaboration: High-quality PD creates space for teachers to share ideas and collaborate in their learning, often in job-embedded contexts. By working collaboratively, teachers can create communities that positively change the culture and instruction of their entire grade level, department, school and/or district." (p. 7) "Is of sustained duration: Effective PD provides teachers with adequate time to learn, practice, implement, and reflect upon new strategies that facilitate changes in their practice." (p. 7)
Connection to Life Experience and Context Specific (Street, 2006)	"Provides coaching and expert support: Coaching and expert support involve the sharing of expertise about content and evidence-based practices, focused directly on teachers' individual needs.: (p. 7)
Participant Voice and Inclusivity (Mehta & Aguilera, 2020)	"Uses models of effective practice: Curricular models and modeling of instruction provide teachers with a clear vision of what best practices look like. Teachers may view models that include lesson plans, unit plans, sample student work, observations of peer teachers, and video or written cases of teaching." (p. 7) "Offers feedback and reflection: High-quality professional learning frequently provides built-in time for teachers to think about, receive input on, and make changes to their practice by facilitating reflection and soliciting feedback. Feedback and reflection both help teachers to thoughtfully move toward the expert visions of practice." (p.7)
Context Specific (Mehta & Aguilera, 2020)	"Is content focused - PD that focuses on teaching strategies associated with specific curriculum content supports teacher learning within teachers' classroom contexts. This element includes an intentional focus on discipline-specific curriculum development and pedagogies in areas such as mathematics, science, or literacy." (p. 7)

Note. We aligned the seven common features of effective PD with Humanizing Learning Pedagogy to ensure that we were developing the most effective PD that would be most beneficial to our K-12 colleagues.

Table 2. Seven PD Components Aligned to Desired Face-to-Face PD Aspects to Retain in Online Setting

PD Component	Face-to-Face PD Aspects We Wanted to Keep in an Online Setting
Objective/Purpose (Connects to disciplinary content focus and collaboration)	Have at least one facilitator of the disciplinary content focus Survey participants prior to PD to determine what learning outcomes participants were hoping the PD would address. Provide opportunities to use technology tools during PD Provide opportunities to self-reflect and collaborate outside the PD
Participant Voice (Connects to active learning, collaboration, and expertise/feedback)	Establish ourselves as educators and learners Establish every participant as a valued contributor Recognize and normalize the various levels of content and technology experience that exist when large groups come together
Connection/Engagement (Connects to active learning, collaboration, and ongoing)	Provide opportunities for social interaction Provide opportunities to interact with the instructors Provide ongoing support after the PD
Mirror Reality (Connects to disciplinary content focus, modeling effective practice, and expertise/feedback)	Provide at least one example of how this could be used in an elementary, middle grades, and secondary classroom Acknowledge the complexity of applying the newly learned teaching practices and technology tools
Hopes/Dreams (Connects to feedback and reflection and ongoing)	Provide opportunities for participants to envision the possibilities for student learning using what they learned Provide opportunities for participants to reflect on their learning

Note. For each identified PD component, we determined which pedagogical aspects of face-to-face PD we wanted to attempt to retain in the online environment. Identifying these retainable aspects helped us to frame the organization of the online PD.

The purpose of the Citizen Science PD was to provide pedagogical methods to engage students in science using authentic scientific contexts by integrating online tools to examine local and global science issues through Citizen Science. Citizen Science is the engagement of the general public to collect and/or analyze data for scientific purposes. For instance, the popular birding platform, eBird, which is a citizen project run by the Cornell Lab of Ornithology, enables participants to record their bird observations either on a mobile app or through a website. This allows participants to have an electronic archive of their birding adventures, and Cornell receives birding data from around the world to further advance the education, conservation, and research on bird diversity. The workshop was divided into 2 parts. Part 1 included: 1.) information on what citizen science is; 2.) a participant quiz following NPR's Wait, Wait, Don't Tell Me format to introduce the wide-ranging types of citizen science; 3.) how using citizen science in the classroom aligns with state and national science standards; 4.) a real-world example using Zooniverse (an online citizen science platform); 5.) time for participants to explore Zooniverse projects on their own; 6.) a share-out time of what participants discovered, and; 7.) a brief question and answer session.

The second part of the PD provided four breakout sessions, where participants could select one breakout session to attend (all breakout materials were shared at the conclusion of the PD), and time to create a preliminary individual or collective action plan for using what they learned in the PD to engage their students in authentic science experiences using citizen science. The four breakout sessions were: 1.) How do we find citizen science projects? This session focused on resources to help participants locate projects. Several portals that host multiple citizen science sites were explored, as well as how to select active projects. 2.) Local/community-based projects: this project highlighted designing your own schoolyard or local project, such as how to choose a location and other considerations such as student interest or maintenance of outdoor spaces; 3.) Data analysis skills and how to use Google Explore. This session modeled how to use the Explore feature in Google Sheets to conduct data analysis and graphing with student data; and 4.) Assessment when using citizen science. This session discussed several ideas for having students display their participation in citizen science projects, such as poster presentations. Single point rubrics were shared that could be used to assess the scientific poster. The session ended with another round of questions and answers. In the following sections, we will discuss our attempts at translating the face-to-face PD components we desired to keep to an online setting for the Citizen Science PD.

Objective/Purpose

In order to meet our disciplinary content focus objectives, we addressed K-12 science standards, and we were able to find examples to use from biology, ecology, chemistry, and physics with Zooniverse. The Zooniverse is an online platform that features citizen science projects across disciplines (e.g., sciences, arts, humanities). The four of us facilitating the workshop had varying grade-level teaching experiences, so we were also able to speak to different grade band requirements and the varying cognitive, emotional, and social aspects of the learners at different grade levels. Finally, part of the disciplinary content focus was acknowledging the complexity of the participants applying what they had learned to content that we may not have covered in depth or at all (e.g., physical sciences). Thus, we gave participants time at the end of the PD to work together in selected content areas to help them with transferring our examples to their specific contexts.

Unfortunately, we could not survey our participants prior to the PD to discern their goals/objectives for attending the PD or invite them to co-design the learning objectives with us as advocated by

Darling-Hammond and colleagues (2017). We did not have an opportunity to do this as we did not have participants' information prior to the PD. To compensate for this, we had participants write in on the Zoom chat or share with the larger group what they were hoping to achieve during our time together. We made a note of the desired learning outcomes participants shared, and one of us worked on adding additional resources for participants to explore on their own after the PD based on this information while others presented. The chat feature enabled us to simulate an activity we do in our face-to-face PDs, where we have participants write on sticky notes what they hope to learn in the PD, and then we categorize these together to see what themes emerge prior to starting the PD. If there are themes that emerge where participants have expertise to share, we design space within the PD for participants to lead mini-sessions to aid us all in our learning. This strategy is adapted from unconferences (Greenhill et al., 2008) and allows participants to co-design aspects of the PD. This again highlighted the tension we felt as instructors trying to implement what we see as best humanizing practices and what we find to be the constraints of online settings. Yet, we are committed to making small steps forward in our online teaching philosophies for one-time PDs.

During the first part of the PD, when we engaged students in an example of using a Zooniverse citizen science project to address Ecology standards, we had interactive points in the presentation where participants were able to take on the student role and answer questions or complete activities like a student would. Toward the end of the first part of the PD, we provided time for participants to further use the technology we introduced and to troubleshoot with us if they needed help. We called this Open Exploration of the Zooniverse, and participants were given 15 minutes to find and explore a project of interest. We left the main Zoom room open, and participants could choose to mute their audio and/or video during this time. They could also elect to write questions in the Zoom chat or request a break room to work with one of us. After the open exploration, participants were invited to share about projects they explored.

For the second part of PD, we designed an action plan template to guide participants in reflecting upon how to capture their initial ideas for integrating citizen science into their classroom (Figure 1).

Lastly, we designed a Google Form to share with participants to fill out their contact information and a statement indicating they gave us permission to contact them. There was an open-ended question for them to share other information with us they deemed relevant. The questions were set not to be required, so participants could elect what contact information they wanted to share.

Participant Voice

To elevate participant voice, we started the session by sharing a little about who we were and our experiences in K-12 settings. We also positioned ourselves as our learners along with the participants as we shared that one of our commitments is recognizing that as educators, we all have varying teaching experiences that establish shared expertise; thus, we invited participants to share their expertise throughout the PD as we welcomed opportunities for participants to share resources, ideas, or stories within the chat.

To further highlight the shared expertise, we built in questions within our session that allowed us all to stop, pause, reflect, and share. One example of this was at the beginning, where we had participants complete a Grab-A-Dot activity: Let's Find Out More About You! (Figure 2).

Participants then used their dot to fill out questions such as: What grade level do you teach? What content do you teach? Do you prefer squirrels, trees, frogs, or birds? What is your favorite science to learn? (Figure 3). We included a technology challenge for participants who were comfortable with the format and wanted to learn how to distinguish individual student dots, which enabled participants' active learning. The first two slides served as expertise maps to highlight for all participants the amount of teaching experience among us, and the final two slides were more to encourage social engagement. The

Figure 1. Action Plan Template
Note. We used this template for participants to provide an action plan in a format that allowed for easy feedback.

Citizen Science Action Plan

If you want feedback on your action plan, please place your file in this folder: Link to Group Google Folder

Technology help: How to copy a Google File

How to move Files in Google Folders

Want to continue to collaborate and learning together? Fill out the Connection Form: Link to Connection Form

Grade level	
Goals for using citizen science	
Lesson/Subject and Possible Standard Connections	
Citizen Science Tool(s)	
Outline of Project Idea	
Duration of Project	
Resources needed/available	
Possible Pitfalls to Look Out for	
Accountability Partners/Who can help?	

Grab-A-Dot activity was another face-to-face activity that we translated online. In our face-to-face PDs, we give participants actual dot stickers, and they walk around the room and put their dots on chart paper questions that we leave hanging up during the PD in order to remind ourselves and participants who is in the room. We often use these to draw out participants to share their expertise in different grade bands or subject areas. The "leaving up" of the posters is something we could not figure out how to translate

Figure 2. First Slide of the Grab-A-Dot activity: Let's Find Out More About You!
Note. This image captures the instruction slide we shared with participants for the Getting to Know You activity.

into an online space, which was unfortunate as we view this as another way to humanize the PD through participant voice and inclusivity (Mehta & Aguilera, 2020).

We acknowledge that the Grab-A-Dot activity is a surface-level activity for developing a culture of shared expertise as advocated by scholars (Zeichner et al, 2015). This often requires the trust of participants and a willingness to be vulnerable with others. Trust and vulnerability develop over time, which is one reason Hammond et al. (2017) found ongoing, sustained PD to be most effective. In our face-to-face PDs, we have much more time to develop relationships with our K-12 colleagues that afford opportunities for them to question, challenge, share, and celebrate our shared learning. This is another constraint for a one-time, short PD that we found challenging.

Though we had struggles, we did experience high success in the immediate relevance of the PD, evidenced by about a third of the participants sharing in the chat how they were already planning ways to implement the PD's teaching strategies into their fall classes. Participant engagement was also high,

Figure 3. Example of Grab-a-Dot Activity Question Slide
Note. This image is of one of the slides from the Getting to Know You activity. This demonstrates how some participants took the technology challenge of changing their dot color or the shape of their dot.

What Grade Level do you teach?	
Elementary Prek-2	● ○
Elementary 3-5	● ● ● ○ ● ● ● ●
6th Grade	● ●
7th Grade	● ● ● ● ●
8th Grade	● ● ●
9th Grade	● ● ● ●
10th Grade	●
11th Grade	○ ● ● ● ●
12th Grade	○ ●

with a participant evaluation rating of 4.86 out of 5. One participant suggested we make the PD session longer, stating, "This could be a longer PD, and I'd gladly participate." Another participant stated "The presenters made everything so engaging! We explored the sites introduced and even had specific breakout sessions depending on what we wanted to learn more about. This was such a great use of my time. I learned about many resources that I had no idea." Participants valued our use of an interactive presentation and our focus on collaboration, as a participant mentions, "The interactive presentation provided opportunities for practice and developing our own lessons through collaboration."

Connection/Engagement

Our collaborative efforts happened prior to the PD, during the PD, and after the PD. First, Allison reached out to Lacey, Heather, and Aerin to collaborate with her in developing the online PD. We bring different perspectives and experiences, and we have collaborated together successfully in the past. We also had prior collaborations with K-12 colleagues co-designing and implementing several of the learning activities we planned to share, so we not only had experience working with K-12 teachers and students, but we readily looked for opportunities to collaborate in such ways. We believe this form of collaboration is essential to stay connected to the disciplinary content.

We also had at least two of us monitoring the chat at all times to field questions or comments, so we could weave those into the natural flow of our conversation. We purposefully set aside time for our participants to try the learning activities. We left the large Zoom open so they could share in the chat as they worked through the activity, and we stayed online to field technology questions as the entire experience was using technology tools most participants had not used prior to the PD. In the large room, we were able to share our screens and allow participants to share their screens to facilitate learning how to use the technology.

During the PD, we shared ways in which we have collaborated with K-12 colleagues in the past and with each other. We asked participants to share ways they have engaged in successful collaborations. We developed four break-out rooms so participants could dive deeper into a learning topic and build a small group collaboration as contact information was exchanged. At the end of the PD, we provided a form for participants to fill out if they were interested in continuing to collaborate after the PD session. We had 22% of participants fill out the sheet and express a desire to receive information about future learning opportunities. They also wanted to share their contact information with each other so they could reach out and collaborate together.

Mirror Reality (Modeling Effective Practice)

Modeling effective practice was probably the most difficult aspect of translating a face-to-face PD to an online setting. Since the majority of our participants were themselves, face-to-face classroom teachers, we found it challenging to model what one would do in a face-to-face setting online. To compensate for this, we collaborated with fellow K-12 teachers prior to the PD and, thus, were able to provide relevant student examples of the activities/learning assessments we provided. This brought authenticity to content for our participants, as they acknowledged on the PD post-survey. One participant shared on the post-survey, "So many resources were provided that will be helpful in developing my own lessons using citizen science."

One aspect of the teaching realities our participants faced that we could model was the various levels of technology usage among the PD participants. Some of our participants were comfortable on various technology platforms and readily incorporated collaborative technology assignments into their classrooms, while others had limited access to classroom technology or were not as familiar with using collaborative educational technology like Google Suite for Education. This is where we were able to embrace Universal Design for Learning (UDL; CAST, 2018) principles, particularly in regard to action and expression. First, we openly recognized that we, as facilitators, had various levels of technology use, and we shared our own triumphs and pitfalls with incorporating technology into our classrooms. Second, we stated up front that we had prepared guided commentary and tutorial links on the learning activities we created to help address possible technology questions. We highlighted these in yellow on the learning activities to make it obvious to our participants where they could find assistance later when they went back to review the materials (see Figure 1 for an example). Even on the Citizen Science Action Template (Figure 1), we provided links to how to make a copy of the Action Plan and how to move the Action Plan file into the Feedback folder. We explained to participants that these practices could also be used with their students as even those overly familiar with technology can forget how to use certain features and might need a refresher. In addition to the embedded technology guidance, we created a Wakelet with all the resources we shared, and we had a special section within the Wakelet labeled Technology Assistance where we all housed all the technology helpful links. Finally, if we were unable to find a technology tutorial that fit our purposes, we prerecorded screencasts of ourselves explaining how to use the technology we shared. Participants were appreciative of having these to return to after the PD as reminders of the trips/tricks we had highlighted during the PD.

The ways in which we embraced a disciplinary content focus and encouraged shared expertise was in designing a scaffolded semester or year-long citizen science project about squirrels. In this learning example, participants could choose whether to start with technology (identifying squirrels through photos for an online citizen science project) or counting squirrels on their school grounds and reporting the numbers to an online citizen science database. Then, we gathered children's books about squirrels and introduced participants to behavior studies their students could design and run for the citizen science project, Project Squirrel (2018). In this way, we were using a model organism that mirrored the lived experiences of almost, if not all, kids within the areas our participants taught, as squirrels are one of the most common mammals in the United States and are found in urban, suburban, and rural areas.

Hopes/Dreams

In concluding any PD we offer, we desire to give time for participants to think about what they learned and imagine what they could do with what they have learned. Though it takes time out of the PD, we find it important for participants to be given time to pause and reflect. We set up this time by telling the participants we wanted them to brainstorm how they could apply the new strategies in a teaching situation that had no external or internal constraints (e.g., no time constraints, student issues, administrative questions, etc.). We encourage participants to make bullets, write on sticky notes, and/or draw/doodle their ideas. Then, we give time for participants to share in small groups, as sharing hopes/dreams can help move into action. We also have them write the names of two people at their school or their professional learning networks outside of their school with whom they can share their ideas. In order to facilitate this in the online setting, we developed the Citizen Science Action Plan template (Figure 1). This also served as a way for participants to share their ideas with us if they wanted us to give them feedback or offer resources for them. In order to facilitate the sharing process, we created a Google folder where participants could place their files. We left this open after the PD as well in case participants wanted more time to work on their action plans. On the template, we also included a link to a Google Form for participants to fill out if they wanted to continue receiving communication from us about future PDs, resources, and collaborative opportunities. Though we provided time for participants to develop an action plan for implementation and created a shared Google Drive for participants to place their action plans into if they wanted feedback, not a single participant shared a plan with us. However, seven participants did fill out a Google Form indicating they were interested in future collaborations.

REFLECTING BACK

In reflecting upon our experience in moving a face-to-face PD online, we found that we were able to humanize aspects of online learning. We attempted to make connections to participants' life experiences (Street, 2006) by inviting them to share their expertise in various formats. We elevated participant voice by providing multidimensional spaces for participants to share (e.g., through audio, chat, or the action plan), and participants had a choice in break-out sessions (Mehta & Aguilera, 2020). We attempted to be inclusive by providing context-specific examples for K-12 learning environments and science standards. We also tried to position ourselves as learners alongside our participants to attempt to portray that we were all on a learning journey together and each had knowledge to share. Though we felt our first online PD was successful, we still see several areas where we could push further to humanize online PD, and we still have questions about translating some human elements of face-to-face PD into an online setting.

First, we would like to have had more participants' voices. Online spaces are more difficult to manage in this regard, as the muting and unmuting of oneself can hinder participation. In a face-to-face setting, one does not have to remember to click a button in order to speak what has been called to her mind. This leads us to wonder if the actual finding of the mute button and clicking interrupts the flow of thought for the participant. Even though we did not hear many voices during the session, the chat feature allowed participants to participate and be active without using their physical voice. Features such as the chat function can give voice to students who typically do not speak up in group settings, but want to share their thinking and be engaged participants. We also found wait time online to be more difficult than in a face-to-face setting. We are not sure if this is due to having more experience with wait time in a face-to-face setting, but it has an aspect as instructors we felt could have been improved. Next time, we would ensure we each had a timer and agreed upon wait time for open-ended participant questions or participant share-out times.

Second, we felt relationships were more difficult to establish. In face-to-face PD settings, we usually have participants make nameplates, and we find that within the first 30 minutes, we typically know all participants' names. This creates a human connection as addressing people by name is one small way to be more inclusive. However, the small video tiles on the large Zoom screen were difficult to see, and we left the PD realizing we could not recall any name (other than two participants that some of us had known prior to the PD). Making it even more complicated was that some participants were not able to turn on their videos as they were in areas where Internet coverage was sparse, and the download and upload of videos made their Internet freeze, so their Zoom tiles were either a black screen with a name or a picture (which may or may not have been of them). This made the idea of ongoing collaborations difficult to imagine as when emailing participants we could not put names to faces or life experiences that were shared as it was difficult to recall the small images on the screen. Again, this may be due to our inexperience with trying to put names together with faces online. So, we are left wondering in what ways we could translate this to an online setting. In one of the online programs we teach in, we have students develop an About Me slide for faculty to learn about me, and we have found that it helps us make connections more readily to students, whom we never meet in person, and at the beginning of each semester, we re-share those slides with the spring program faculty. We could also create a spreadsheet or use a shareable document or platform (e.g., Padlet) where participants share their names and a picture of themselves, so we can reference back and become more familiar with them.

Third, the fact that no one shared an action plan surprised us. However, upon reflecting on this, we realize that much like we felt somewhat disconnected from participants as we were not in the same physical space, participants might have felt disconnected from us. Sharing one's work/ideas has an aspect of vulnerability, and it is difficult to be vulnerable with someone that you do not know. In a face-to-face setting, it is also easier to walk from participant to participant and have short conversations about their ideas as they reflect at the end of the PD. This aspect reminds us that there is not a one-to-one correlation between face-to-face and online teaching and learning, so there may be aspects of one that cannot and should not be translated to the other space. Furthermore, we question what our participants might have thought was the intent of us offering feedback with this assignment as we ponder the questions presented by Mehta and Aguilera (2020): "1.) From whose perspective are we defining and enacting 'humanizing' online pedagogies in our contexts? 2.)Toward what ends are we enacting and advocating for these approaches? And who benefits from these approaches?" (p. 113). We could ask similar questions of this assessment: 1.) From whose perspective did we define an action plan as a humanizing pedagogy? 2.) Who benefits from the assignment? Though we designed the action plan to benefit the participants, we now wonder if our feedback was more for their benefit or our own. If we would offer this PD again, we would offer it over two sessions, one day to get the information and try out the tools, and another day to establish small groups to create an action plan and collaborate for their next steps.

HUMANIZING ONLINE PD DESIGN TEMPLATE

To preserve the work we did in humanizing the Citizen Science PD, we developed a reflection template for us to use with future online PDs. We structured the template to include the PD components that we readily include as we design PDs, and then we developed questions that we, as facilitators, tend to ask ourselves or our co-collaborators as we go about creating the PD workshop. Finally, we included examples of ways we could humanize future online PDs. We share this template below as we hope others may find it useful. An editable version can also be downloaded for future use and is included in the reference list (Huffling et al., 2024)

CONCLUSION

Humanizing online PDs is more important than ever as schools, universities, and companies continue to shift to learning online. As we discovered with our foray into online PD, it is not possible to translate every aspect of face-to-face PD to an online PD, just like it is not possible in a semester-long class. However, there are ways that online PDs can still encourage participant voice and inclusivity (Mehta &

Table 3. Template for Humanizing Online PD Development

PD Component	Questions for Facilitator(s) to Consider	Examples of Ways to Humanize Online PD	Notes/ Thoughts
Objective/ Purpose	What are our expectations and how do we get there? What expectations might our participants bring? Who benefits from the objectives/purposes we are setting? Who potentially does not? How can we co-design objectives with our participants? How many discipline contexts do we need to address or provide examples of?	● Survey participants prior to PD to understand the learning objectives they have ● Focus groups help develop PD topics ● Develop a participant advisory board to help co-design the PD ● Survey representative group of the participant population to discover current needs and concerns. ● Rotate PD facilitators based on disciplines/contexts of participants ● Create database of discipline specific examples if multiple disciplines will be present	
Participant Voice	How will we establish all educators as contributors as well as learners? How can we support the various technology skills of participants?	● Survey participants' prior to workshop to understand the learning goals they have ● Invite participants to co-design workshop with us ● Survey participants' level of comfortability with online tools that will be highlighted ● Provide technology tutorial for each type of technology introduced ● Design advanced technology challenges for participants with working knowledge of technology ● Provide a breakout room for those who may need help with the technology ● Create collaborative online sharing space (e.g. Google Doc, Linoboard, Padlet, or Wakelet) for participants to share resources with each other ● Continue collaborative sharing space after the PD and keep adding resources	
Connection/ Engagement	How will we demonstrate the relevance/ usefulness of the teaching practice(s)? How will we provide opportunities for participants to interact with each other? With the instructors? How do we offer engaging and fun learning experiences in the PD?	● Discuss why strategies were selected to model during the PD (reveal the thought process behind the pedagogical design of the PD) ● Provide brief icebreaker activities at the beginning of the session. ● Create breakout rooms to help participants work together to learn and apply the material. ● Have participant choice within the PD (e.g. 10-15 minute breakout sessions to go deeper, get help, find a collaborative partner, etc...)	
Mirror Reality	How will we provide relevant examples of use in real classroom contexts? How will we acknowledge the complexity of applying the newly learned teaching practices?	● Use videos and own experiences as examples and models. ● Curate a database of online resources ● Ask prior participants and colleagues to share relevant examples	
Hope/ Dreams	How will we provide opportunities for participants to envision the possibilities for their lessons/classes using what they learned? How will we provide opportunities for participants to reflect on their learning? Are we able to provide support for ongoing collaborations or PD? If so, what level of support might we offer? If not, can we find other venues for participants to find this support?	● Allow for reflection using a public discussion platform (e.g., Padlet, Parlay, or Wakelet), the chat feature of a video conferencing software or a private platform. ● Get participants to brainstorm ideas using mind-mapping platforms. ● Ask participants to share contact information if interested in future collaboration. ● Survey participants on what the follow-up PD workshop should be ● Provide a list of venues where participants can continue their professional learning	

Note. For each identified PD component, we determined which pedagogical aspects of a face-to-face PD we wanted to retain in the online environment. Identifying these retainable aspects helped us to frame the organization of the

Aguilera, 2020), utilize and draw upon participants' life experiences (Street, 2006), and frame online learning within a context-specific domain (Mehta & Aguilera, 2020). We are encouraged by our first attempts and plan to continue in our efforts to humanize short, one-time online PD offerings as this a common learning space teachers engage in. Learning should be personal, and participants should feel they belong within the learning space. Online venues open up opportunities to reach participants who may not have ready access to PD in the areas where they live and work, and it allows for an intermingling of participants across geographic gradients, which provides more diverse life experiences to be shared.

REFERENCES

CAST. (2018). *Universal design for learning guidelines version 2.2* [graphic organizer]. CAST.

Darling-Hammond, L., Hyler, M. E., & Gardner, M. (2017). *Effective teacher professional development.* Learning Policy Institute. doi:10.54300/122.311

Dede, C. (2006). *Online professional development for teachers: Emerging models and methods.* Harvard Education Press.

Dias, B., & Boulder, T. (2023). Toward Humanizing Online Learning Spaces. *The Journal of Applied Instructional Design, 12*(4). https://edtechbooks.org/jaid_12_4/toward_humanizing_online_learning_spaces

Esterhuizen, H. D., Blignaut, S., & Ellis, S. (2013). Looking out and looking in: Exploring a case of faculty perceptions during e-learning staff development. *International Review of Research in Open and Distance Learning, 14*(3), 59–80. doi:10.19173/irrodl.v14i3.1358

Farris, S. (2015). Think "e" for engagement: Use technology tools to design personalized professional e-learning. *Journal of Staff Development, 36*(5), 54–58.

Fishman, B., Konstantopoulos, S., Kubitskey, B. W., Vath, R., Park, G., Johnson, H., & Edelson, D. C. (2013). Comparing the impact of online and face-to-face professional development in the context of curriculum implementation. *Journal of Teacher Education, 64*(5), 426–438. doi:10.1177/0022487113494413

Freed, A., Huffling, L. D., Benavides, A., & Scott, H. (2023). *Engage students in real science using simple virtual tools* [Interactive Webinar]. University of Central Arkansas summer professional development, Virtual. https://www.youtube.com/watch?v=2YaFtexWJZ0&list=PLMhw_-NyMrSzCIbLUB xhF6bG6RRfvhgDU&index=6

Graham, C. R., Henrie, C. R., & Gibbons, A. S. (2014). Developing models and theory for blended learning research. In A. G. Picciano, C. D. Dzuibun, & C. R. Graham (Eds.), *Blended Learning: Research Perspectives* (Vol. 2, pp. 13–33). Routledge.

Greenhill, K., & Wiebrands, C. (2008). The unconference: a new model for better professional communication. In *LIANZA Conference 2008: Poropitia Outside the Box*. LIANZA.

Huffling, L. D., Freed, A., Scott, H. C., Benavides, A., & Ward, J. L. (2024). *Template for Humanizing Online PD Development.* Department of Middle Grades and Secondary Education Faculty Publications, Paper 215. https://digitalcommons.georgiasouthern.edu/teach-secondary-facpubs/215

Lay, C. D., Allman, B., Cutri, R. M., & Kimmons, R. (2020). Examining a decade of research in online teacher professional development. *Frontiers in Education*, 5, 573129. doi:10.3389/feduc.2020.573129

Mehta, R., & Aguilera, E. (2020). A critical approach to humanizing pedagogies in online teaching and learning. *The International Journal of Information and Learning Technology*, *37*(3), 109–120. doi:10.1108/IJILT-10-2019-0099

Moon, J., Passmore, C., Reiser, B. J., & Michaels, S. (2014). Beyond comparisons of online versus face-to-face PD: Commentary in response to Fishman et al., "Comparing the impact of online and face-to-face professional development in the context of curriculum implementation". *Journal of Teacher Education*, *65*(2), 172–176. doi:10.1177/0022487113511497

Pacansky-Brock, M., Smedshammer, M., & Vincent-Layton, K. (2023). In search of belonging online: Achieving equity through transformative professional development. *Journal of Educational Research and Practice*, *12*(0), 39–64. doi:10.5590/JERAP.2022.12.0.04

Prestridge, S., Main, K., & Schmid, M. (2023). (2023). Identifying how classroom teachers develop presence online: Breaking the fourth wall in online learning. *Education and Information Technologies*. Advance online publication. doi:10.1007/s10639-023-11714-8 PMID:37361763

Project Squirrel. (2018). *Project Squirrel*. https://projectsquirrel.org/index.shtml

Ross, J. D. (2011). *Online professional development: Design, deliver, succeed!* Corwin Press.

Scott, D. E., & Scott, S. (2010). Innovation in the use of technology and teacher professional development. In A. D. Olofsson & J. O. Lindberg (Eds.), *Online learning communities and teacher professional development: Methods for improved education delivery* (pp. 169–189). Information Science Reference. doi:10.4018/978-1-60566-780-5.ch010

Scott, H., & Huffling, L. D. (2022). Going with the flow: Shifting Fface-to-Fface PD to Ffully Oonline in the Eera of COVID-19. *International Journal for the Scholarship of Teaching and Learning*, *16*(1), 6. doi:10.20429/ijsotl.2022.160106

Street, B. V. (2006). Autonomous and ideological models of literacy: Approaches from new literacy studies. *Media Anthropology Network*, *17*(1), 1–15.

Vygotsky, L. S., & Cole, M. (1978). *Mind in society: Development of higher psychological processes*. Harvard University Press. doi:10.2307/j.ctvjf9vz4

Xie, J. A. G., Rice, M. F., & Griswold, D. E. (2021). Instructional designers' shifting thinking about supporting teaching during and post-COVID-19. *Distance Education*, *42*(3), 331–351. doi:10.1080/01587919.2021.1956305

Zeichner, K., Payne, K. A., & Brayko, K. (2015). Democratizing teacher education. *Journal of Teacher Education*, 66(2), 122–135. doi:10.1177/0022487114560908

Chapter 2
"Better Than Human" in Partnership With AI:
Enhancing Social Presence Through the Use of Technology

Jim A. McCleskey

ⓘ https://orcid.org/0000-0002-7354-1823

Western Governors University, USA

Rebecca M. Melton

Western Governors University, USA

ABSTRACT

The onset of COVID-19 brought about a significant transformation in higher education (HE), expediting an ongoing evolution and compelling institutions and educators to cultivate the necessary skills for effective online delivery and resource provision. Insights from student experiences during the spring of 2020 indicated that institutions faced challenges in their transitions, revealing deficiencies in crucial aspects such as online instructor presence, social interaction among instructors and students, and instructor immediacy. This chapter suggests instructional practices and technology approaches within HE from a community of inquiry (CoI) perspective to enhance student engagement and instructor presence. The trajectory of HE is persistently shifting towards advanced technology, aiming to expand, streamline, and enhance student engagement and interaction, all while introducing innovative methods to enhance instructor presence. The authors urge HE institutions to adopt and refine various techniques to elevate the student experience.

The global eruption of COVID-19 proved to be an unprecedented disruptive force and leaving an enduring impact on various facets of contemporary life. While its repercussions persist, the focus has shifted toward forecasting and managing a response to a post-COVID-19 landscape. Despite differing opinions among experts about the aftermath of the virus, there is a unanimous consensus that a return to normalcy is improbable. A seismic paradigm shift occurred in the spring of 2020 with 86% of higher

DOI: 10.4018/979-8-3693-0762-5.ch002

education (HE) programs transitioning to online formats within a remarkably brief three-week period (Patch, 2020). This swift transition accelerated a pre-existing trend in the growth of online education signaling a broader movement away from traditional classroom instruction towards online modalities and incorporating *cutting-edge* technologies. Previous authors characterized this shift as "a digital disruption from within" (Thomas & Thorpe, 2018, p. 63).

STUDENTS' PERCEPTIONS OF ONLINE LEARNING

The post-Covid environment invited a moment of reflection on student opinions. In the aftermath of COVID, students expressed disappointment in their interactions with faculty and peers but maintained a positive outlook on their institutions' efforts to offer meaningful learning experiences (Patch, 2020). These sentiments continue to present an opportunity for HE educators and administrators to foster a more extensive community of care around students, assess the value of existing practices, and enhance online delivery methods. As the primary consumers of education, students play a pivotal role in transforming online education and interactions.

In 2020, a series of surveys illuminated students' perceptions of the quality of education during the COVID-19 pandemic. According to Patch (2020), 65% of students believed their universities effectively managed the crisis, but only 15% found online classes as practical as in-person ones. In a survey of 955 college students, Pinkus (2020) found that one-third expressed concerns about losing contact with instructors, while 31% were apprehensive about isolation from peers. Interestingly, Pinkus (2020) found that despite the counterintuitive nature of instructors often being alone in virtual meeting spaces during virtual office hours, 87% of students perceived these sessions as beneficial. Additional insights revealed video/chat conferencing as the second most preferred communication method with instructors and peers, with email ranking first for instructors and texting ranking first for peers (Pinkus, 2020).

In April 2020, a concise survey reported that 75% of students felt they were not receiving a quality e-learning experience from their HE institutions ("75% of College Students Unhappy…," 2020). A tophat. com survey of 3,000 students supported this sentiment, as 78% of the respondents rated the online class experience as unengaging, 75% expressed a desire for face-to-face interactions with peers and faculty, and 38% did not perceive value or enjoyment in synchronous online learning (Top Hat Staff, 2020).

McCleskey and Gruda (2020) surveyed 500 college students across diverse HE institutions. The results revealed that 45% of students felt they did not receive quality learning experiences from their respective universities or colleges. Additionally, the survey highlighted other concerns, with 59% of student respondents deeming online learning less effective than in-person learning, 17% expressing dissatisfaction with instructor preparation, 20% reported dissatisfaction with the quality of instruction, 26% noted dissatisfaction with the level of student engagement, and 22% indicated dissatisfaction with the overall learning experience in their recent courses (McCleskey & Gruda, 2020). These various surveys showed that students cared about instructor immediacy (ability to connect with students; Witt et al., 2004) and connections with their fellow students.

Online learning continued to expand post-COVID-19. In 2021, approximately 61% of undergraduate students enrolled in at least one online course, according to estimates (NCES, 2019). The World Economic Forum anticipates that global investment in online education will surpass $350 billion by 2025 (Li & Lalani, 2020).

Despite HE remaining a big business, educators and institutions focus on preserving a human touch in defining learner success. Their concerns revolve around course completion, degree attainment, degree costs, student debt, satisfaction, time required for degree completion, and ensuring equity (WGU, 2022). Post-graduation success may be defined by positive changes in salary, word-of-mouth referrals to the HE institution, or students returning for additional education at the same university (Kinzie & Kuh, 2017). However, these results directly result from an effective curriculum, supportive and timely instructor support, and the learner's persistence. While learning is fundamentally an internal process for the learner, HE faculty and administrators embrace the responsibility and the opportunity to create, enhance, implement, and consistently improve resources and approaches that influence the learning journey and, by extension, academic achievements.

This chapter reviews the Community of Inquiry framework of instructor presence along with example traits and behaviors of the three types of presence: *teaching*, *cognitive*, and *social*. Select technology applications and approaches will be reviewed with potential suggestions. Considerations and cautions presented here call attention to the essential nature of information and technology access.

ONLINE INSTRUCTOR PRESENCE: THE COMMUNITY OF INQUIRY

Instructor Presence

Research has shown that how instructors present themselves online impacts student engagement and outcomes (Garrison et al., 2000; Richardson et al., 2016). Sheridan and Kelly (2010) surveyed 299 undergraduate students about indicators of instructor presence. The top five factors they identified as impactful included making course requirements known, responding to learner needs, timely information and feedback, clear communication about critical due dates and deadlines, and clear expectations about discussion boards and how to learn course material (Sheridan & Kelly, 2010). Richardson (2016) pointed out that students prefer instructors who actively demonstrate a friendly and approachable presence, respond promptly, deliver relatable content, and tailor their tone to the students. Although this provides a brief set of considerations, the multi-faceted landscape of instructor presence may best be discussed within the well-documented Community of Inquiry framework (Garrison, 2000; Richardson et al., 2015). Garrison et al.'s (2007) Community of Inquiry (COI) framework (a constructivist paradigm) suggests that three types of presence impact student engagement in the online environment: cognitive presence, teaching presence, and social presence. Additionally, research has demonstrated that the intersection of the three spheres (see Figure 1 below) creates a space for a positive student experience and indicators for the learning process (Akyol et al., 2009; Singh et al., 2022). Research has shown the framework to be valid, efficient, and successful in brick-and-mortar and online environments (Berry, 2019; Dixson, 2015; Sanders & Lokey-Vega, 2020).

One sphere of the CoI is *cognitive presence* (Garrison, 2000). Garrison et al. (2001) defined cognitive presence as the ability to construct and confirm meaning through sustained reflection. Specific cognitive aspects of the course include assignments, lectures, and detailed feedback on performance (Sheridan & Kelly, 2010). Scholars have specified multiple actions instructors may take to impact *cognitive presence* including using scaffolding of content to encourage discussion, providing frequent opportunities for testing and feedback, and modeling and supporting divergent points of view (Richardson et al., 2009).

The second sphere of the CoI is *teaching presence*, defined as the design, facilitation, and direction of the class for optimal learning, and is a shared responsibility between the learner and instructor (Garrison et al., 2000). Effective *teaching presence* is orchestrated by the seamless integration of three key elements: design, facilitation, and direction, which collectively guide cognitive and social processes. Developing and supporting valuable instructional experiences is the central focus of *teaching presence* (Bangert, 2008; Garrison & Arbaugh, 2007). Scholars suggest that multiple behaviors impact learners' perception of *teaching presence,* including explaining how a course operates, communicating availability, sharing critical due dates, and providing information related to the course content (Richardson et al., 2015).

The third sphere of CoI is *social presence*. Scholars have suggested multiple definitions of *social presence*. As noted by Short et al. (1976), the earliest reference to social presence characterizes it as the prominence of an individual in mediated communication and the corresponding significance of the interaction. *Social presence* refers to the degree to which a person is perceived as a 'real person' in mediated communications (Gunwardena & Zittle, 1997). Aspects of the person that impact student perception may include personal characteristics, emotions, values, thoughts, and concerns (Garrison, 2000; Martin, 2019). Scholars have further defined *social presence* as the degree to which learners feel connected to one another (Garrison & Arbaugh, 2007; Richardson et al., 2015). Despite varying nomenclature, the commonality in social presence is its basis in interaction.

Scholars suggest multiple instructor behaviors impact learners' perception of social presence, including self-disclosure, expressing personal values and beliefs, providing pictures, using learners' names, and using the word *we* (Richardson et al., 2015). Fiock et al. (2021) emphasized that suggested indicators of social presence relate to one of three factors: student's emotional expression, open communication, and group cohesion (p. 138). Collaboration between learners and creating joint commitment to goals is a critical aspect of social presence, generating from and resulting in trust and group cohesion (Dixson, 2015; Garrison, 2000). Although primarily a perceptual phenomenon, deliberately cultivating social presence in online settings necessitates proactive efforts from instructors (Anagnostopoulos, 2005).

Studies have shown that each type of presence positively relates to students' perception of increased learning outcomes, student satisfaction, retention, and performance (Caskurla et al., 2017; Laylani, 2020). Gray and DiLoreto (2016) stated that student engagement correlates with student satisfaction, and many scholars believe that students perform well for teachers when they believe the teacher has their best interest in mind, as evidenced by instructor actions and behaviors (Martin, 2017; Richardson, 2016). In sum, instructors can rest assured that their actions toward students have weight and deserve attention.

Social Presence of Instructors

Existing literature indicates a positive correlation between increased social presence in online settings and enhanced learning outcomes, along with higher levels of student satisfaction (Hostetter & Busch, 2013; LaPointe & Gunawardena, 2004; Lee et al., 2011; Picciano, 2002; Swan et al., 2008). Social presence is also associated with comfort, reduced anxiety, emotional connections (Aragon, 2003), heightened peer social interaction, immediacy, and group cohesion (Sung & Mayer, 2012). Evidence supports the idea that social presence benefits students' learning, participation, retention, and motivation (Oh et al., 2018). Richardson and Swan (2003) found that social presence predicted higher student-perceived learning in online courses.

Recently, Daigle and Stuvland (2021) proposed that universities deliver high-quality digital experiences, both synchronous and asynchronous, and prioritize social presence in digital environments.

Figure 1. Elements of an online community of inquiry
(Garrison & Archer, 2007).

Fiock (2020) reviewed multiple peer-reviewed articles, identifying 65 instructional activities impacting social presence. Among the activities cataloged are the following: encouraging students to share their beliefs and experiences in an online discussion, developing icebreakers to allow students to learn about one another, and using audio/video feedback on assignments (Richardson et al., 2009). The authors encourage readers to review the complete list of instructional activities and their links to the three types of presence. Substantial evidence underscores the value of enhancing social presence. Professionals in HE should aim to understand how to effectively employ social presence in online educational settings, including what immediacy behaviors impact student engagement and outcomes.

Online Instructor Immediacy

Immediacy, denoting the instructor's ability to connect with students, correlates with positive learning outcomes (Witt et al., 2004). At the interpersonal level, immediacy behaviors include non-verbal actions such as nodding and making eye contact, while in the online environment, actions may include minimal encouragers such as 'uh-huh' or 'yes' that signify active listening (Comadena et al., 2007; Jahromi et al., 2016). In group facilitation, Thorpe's (2016) competencies for instructors include establishing group purpose, cultivating group culture, planning interactions, using collaboration tools, applying group processes, and engaging in reflective practice. Reflecting on practice involves soliciting feedback, acknowledging disparities, and finding an online facilitator voice to encourage student engagement (Thorpe, 2016).

Instructor techniques for enhancing immediacy include virtual student lounges, collaborative assignments, and student-led discussions (Martin & Bollinger, 2018). In addition, instructors can appear on camera and engage in video interactions with students to further foster immediacy and instructor presence (Ramlatchan & Watson, 2019). Ramlatchan and Watson (2020) explored factors like camera angles and eye contact in recorded sessions, finding that eye-level recordings with direct eye contact received superior feedback from students. Violanti et al. (2018) replicated research on immediacy behaviors, confirming their positive impact on student outcomes. In summary, immediacy is crucial for positive learning outcomes, and strategies like virtual lounges and reflective practices enhance instructors' presence. Factors like eye contact in recorded sessions also significantly influence student perceptions.

Social Presence and Instructor Immediacy

Hackman and Walker (1990) suggest that immediacy behaviors can convey social presence, impacting student learning and satisfaction. If being together and authentic is essential for social presence, it follows that being ready for communication is critical. Immediacy could be seen as the instructor's ability to communicate and the instructor's preparation to do so (Li, 2022).

Enhancing Instructor Immediacy and Presence

Johnson (2013) offers valuable insights to enhance instructor immediacy and presence through diverse recommendations. These insights include maintaining accessibility through various communication channels, sending personalized welcome messages, actively participating in student introductions, and incorporating emoticons. Additional tips involve personalized interactions, such as using students' names, reaching out to those facing challenges, fostering dialogues, actively moderating discussions, and cultivating a distinctive online voice with unique catchphrases. Continuous efforts to boost engagement and interactions with students are emphasized (Johnson, 2013).

Maintaining a human approach is another crucial aspect of online instructor immediacy. Bowen and Watson (2017) recommended the judicious use of humor. They encouraged instructors to adopt an approachable and authentic demeanor, build genuine connections by learning students' names, share personal anecdotes, and present themselves as more than just instructors (Bowen & Watson, 2017). Storytelling, leveraging current events or shared interests, provides relevant real-world examples in various online interactions; the use of blogs or social media posts may also connect the student to the instructor while connecting students to the relevancy of course content (Johnson, 2020; Singh et al., 2022). Richardson (2016) cautions that instructors carefully balance the personal approach with professionalism, using sharing as a strategic action.

Actively engaging students in synchronous online activities is another facet of immediacy and presence. Instructors can spontaneously call on students, encourage written reflections on course activities, and utilize whiteboards and cameras. Bowen and Watson (2017) advised instructors against predictable schedules with identical activities and suggested introducing variety to maintain freshness and engagement in online course meetings. These recommendations create less predictable, more enjoyable, and engaging online course experiences, reducing the likelihood of student multitasking (Bowen & Watson, 2017).

Facilitating Instructor Immediacy and Credibility

The literature highlights the connection between instructor immediacy and credibility (Ramlatchan & Watson, 2020). Credibility encompasses students' perceptions of the instructor's competence, trustworthiness, and positive attitude (Miller et al., 2014; Teven & McCroskey, 1997). Teven and McCroskey (1997) argue that students are more engaged when they sense instructor care, emphasizing the importance of instructors communicating in a caring manner, a fundamental aspect of credibility. Klebig et al. (2016) defined instructor credibility as demonstrations of "competence, caring, and trustworthiness" (p. 152) and noted that credibility positively relates to nonverbal immediacy (Ramlatchan & Watson, 2020; Miller et al., 2014).

Self-disclosure, involving conveying vulnerability, fosters shared experiences, contributes to student persistence (Cayanus & Martin, 2008), and correlates positively with participation and engagement. Instructor credibility is pivotal for successful engagement (Finn et al., 2009). Wombacher et al. (2017) discovered that online presence and credibility impact attitudes toward learning rather than directly affecting outcomes. Vallade and Kaufmann (2020) assert that instructor credibility is a critical factor influencing student outcomes, emphasizing competence, goodwill, and trustworthiness. Although evidence supports these relationships, further research is required to elucidate their nature. Evidence suggests that instructor self-disclosure, positive regard, friendliness, and intentional immediacy affect students' perceptions of credibility, cognitive learning, and affective learning (Vallade & Kaufmann, 2020). Further research is essential to comprehensively understand the intricate relationship between immediacy, credibility, and positive learning outcomes.

Learner to Learner Interaction

In online education, students prefer engaging with their peers, a choice linked to increased commitment and collaboration (NSSE, 2014; Patch, 2020; Pinkus, 2020; Theodosiou & Corbin, 2020). The importance of social interactions in the learning context of online courses emphasizes collaborative knowledge construction through activities, notably asynchronous discussions (Thomas & Thorpe, 2019). Positive correlations have been established between the frequency of posts by group facilitators, instructor engagement, and the ability to predict student engagement. It is notable that many students highly appreciate instructor-led discussions, viewing their instructors as authorities in the subject matter (Thomas & Thorpe, 2019).

Establishing student social presence emerges as a critical aspect, requiring the creation of a supportive climate that actively encourages participation (Kaufmann et al., 2016). In this dynamic, instructors play a crucial role, impacting student engagement positively or negatively, significantly influenced by student interactions (Thomas & Thorpe, 2019). The centrality of peer communication and collaboration in fostering online course engagement is evident, with these elements considered essential components (Cole et al., 2021). Therefore, the success of online education depends on the pivotal roles played by both instructors and students, with the effective utilization of technological resources emerging as another substantial contributing factor.

The anticipation of social presence and immediacy from instructors places a continual responsibility on educators to enhance their skill sets. Ongoing upskilling is imperative for HE instructors (Papanastasiou et al., 2019), and technology serves as a crucial link connecting students and instructors, reminiscent of traditional classroom interactions, office hours, or a leisurely walk across the campus quad.

Technological advancements foster increased engagement, enrich learning experiences, heighten focus and attention, and improve self-efficacy. Integrating technology into the virtual classroom sends a powerful message to students, signifying instructors' dedication to continuous learning, even if it involves navigating a learning curve while adapting to a new platform or program (Chen et al., 2021). Acknowledging instructor vulnerability and transparency contributes to an explicit embrace of instructional technology, further enhancing perceived presence and immediacy (Papanastasiou et al., 2019). Adopting technology within a community of care reinforces students' perception of the instructor's presence and immediacy, solidifying the interconnectedness of technology and effective teaching in the online educational landscape.

Technology as the Way Forward

From the simplest email and online discussion board methods to what Ouyang and Jiao (2021) describe as human-empowered AI in which the learner leads through real-time interaction with technology, AI continues to transform. Instructors contend with the evolving landscape of advanced HE technologies, exploring possibilities like live webinars, virtual classrooms, shared communications, and enhanced social presence and immediacy. Disruptive technologies such as AR/VR, Artificial Intelligence (AI), Internet-Based Learning (IBL) platforms, and Chatbots are rapidly expanding and poised to impact the HE online course room (Allen, 2020). Notably, Massive Open Online Courses (MOOCs) are excluded here for brevity, with Valverde-Berrocoso et al. (2020) providing a comprehensive review.

The widespread adoption of web-based virtual learning environments (VLEs) forms the foundation for these innovations, contributing to enhanced digital literacy, creative thinking, communication facilitation, improved collaboration, and refined problem-solving skills—integral components of 21st-century skills for active information transformation (Papanastasiou et al., 2019). As technology evolves, instructors have opportunities to leverage advanced tools for immersive and interactive learning experiences. For instance, live webinars and virtual classrooms serve as platforms for real-time engagement, fostering a sense of community in the virtual space. Shared communication tools facilitate seamless collaboration between students and instructors.

Emerging technologies like AR/VR and AI have the potential to revolutionize online learning (Lo, 2023). AR/VR creates immersive environments, allowing interactive exploration of subjects. AI personalizes learning experiences, offering adaptive content and feedback tailored to individual student needs (Chen et al., 2021; García-Peñalvo, 2023). Internet-based learning (IBL) platforms provide flexibility and accessibility for students to engage at their own pace. While these technologies offer exciting opportunities, they also pose challenges. Instructors must navigate learning curves, align technology with pedagogical goals, and address issues of equity and accessibility. Instructors' roles extend beyond traditional teaching to facilitating technology-enhanced learning experiences. As the HE technological landscape evolves, instructors must stay informed, embracing benefits while critically evaluating their impact on student engagement, learning outcomes, and overall educational experiences.

Internet-Based Learning Platforms *(IBLs)*

Internet-Based Learning (IBL) platforms encompass a variety of tools, including blogs, wikis, YouTube, and social media sites. Blogs, utilized by instructors and students, serve diverse purposes such as reflective writing, idea documentation, resource compilation, and fostering conversations (Yadav et al., 2017). They are crucial in connecting individuals within blended and hybrid learning environments. It is essential to distinguish between blogs, seen as personalized spaces, and discussion forums, which function as shared community spaces (Yadav et al., 2017).

Wikis, serving as collections of web pages for user-generated content, provide collaborative spaces for writing, idea sharing, and collective task engagement. This structure allows for observing task evolution over time, facilitating commentary and improvements within the shared space (Chu et al., 2017).

YouTube, known for its free accessibility, user-friendly format, and searchability, emerges as a valuable resource in educational settings. Instructors and students leverage YouTube to enhance engagement through rich content within blended learning environments (Yadav et al., 2017). The platform facilitates the creation of online communities, encourages video co-creation, and fosters interaction through the comments section. YouTube's increasing role significantly contributes to heightened student engagement and practical learning experiences (Orús et al., 2016).

Social Media and Social Networking Sites

Social networking platforms such as Facebook, Twitter, and LinkedIn serve as Internet-based learning (IBL) tools, fostering collaborative knowledge sharing among students (Yadav et al., 2017). Despite offering benefits, these platforms present challenges related to professional etiquette, communication issues, technical hurdles, and the need for instructor training. Instructors are encouraged to embrace digital tools in physical and virtual classrooms, aligning with students' preference for using personal devices for learning (Gierdowski, 2019).

E-books and reader apps provide convenient smartphone access to textbooks, challenging the necessity of restrictive technology policies in traditional and virtual settings (Figueras-Maz et al., 2021). Acknowledging the integral role of technology and social media in students' lives, their integration into education is crucial.

Research indicates that social media significantly contributes to online student engagement (George, 2017; Koranteng et al., 2019; Soffer & Yaron, 2017). The widespread use of social media shapes student collaboration, fostering active learning, improved communication, and information sharing among peers (Seifert, 2016; Cunha et al., 2016; Osatuyi, 2013). In HE, leveraging familiar platforms for content-related discussions offers advantages despite concerns about safety and security (Koranteng et al., 2019).

Popular social media applications in HE include creating Facebook pages, utilizing Groups for live discussions, employing Twitter (X) feeds as class message boards, allowing Instagram for assignments, establishing class blogs, and creating subject-specific, interest-based Facebook Groups (West, 2021). Given students' comfort with these platforms, the question arises whether instructors are similarly at ease employing this technology for student engagement. In addition to faculty use of social media for engagement, there is an opportunity for faculty to impact the clarity of information shared by students in formats such as Facebook or LinkedIn. For example, a new student may visit an FB group where multiple students have stated a course was easy to pass; instructors may message that every learner is different to encourage tailored learning techniques.

Augmented Reality/Virtual Reality and Virtual Representations of Instructors

Classroom 3.0, as envisioned by Fourtane (2021), represents a transformative shift in 21st-century HE, emphasizing the pivotal role of AR/VR and 3D technologies, including holograms, as essential tools for future educators. Integrating AR/VR in diverse disciplines, such as medicine and physical sciences, has notably provided hands-on skills instruction (Rajeswaran et al., 2018). Immersive Virtual Environments (IVEs) that incorporate formal lecture-based teaching introduce the Embodied Agent (EA), a customizable Professor Avatar that emulates instructors and highlights intricate social behaviors (Fitton et al., 2020). Previous research has indicated the positive effects of EAs on learning math and reducing math anxiety (Kim et al., 2017). However, pedagogical agents, which precede EAs or Professor Avatars, have shown mixed results in facilitating student learning (Schroeder & Adesope, 2015).

In HE settings, AR/VR positively correlates with student learning, satisfaction, memory preservation, learning motivation, and better investigative skills (Radu, 2014; Sotirou & Bogner, 2008). Ongoing initiatives are dedicated to integrating AR/VR through various learning approaches, underscoring its potential for enhancing retention, collaboration, satisfaction, performance, and engagement (Saltan & Arslan, 2017).

Impact of AR/VR on Immediacy and Presence

Integrating AR/VR, including avatars, has significantly elevated instructor social presence by incorporating non-verbal cues like eye contact, facial expressions, and gestures (Gautam et al., 2018; Makransky & Lilleholt, 2020). The real-time interaction within this environment enables students to pose questions and receive immediate acknowledgment and praise for their contributions (Suk & Laine, 2023). The projection of avatars onto the stage from various locations cultivates a sense of co-presence, prompting students to express that they felt as if they were together in person (Yuan & Gao, 2023). This collaborative setting may positively influence group problem-solving and learning outcomes. The speaker's nonverbal cues, including increased eye contact, gesturing, and facial expressions, were associated with students' perceptions of the instructor's communication competence.

Similarly, holographic videoconferencing (HVC) enhances social presence. Luévano, DeLara, and Castro (2015) reported that 93% of students in an accounting course with an HVC instructor experienced a presence comparable to their expectations of a live instructor. Attendees observed that maintaining attention during learning became more manageable with HVC, which enhanced enjoyment of the learning process and content.

Embedding VR in course learning has multiple uses. Scholars propose that VR use can facilitate teaching empathy. The innovative *Empathy Lens Project* at San Diego State University adopts a comprehensive strategy, utilizing virtual and immersive technologies to facilitate self-discovery and foster understanding of others (SDSU, 2023). Through the incorporation of VR technology, the Empathy Lens aims to enable individuals to gain insights into the thoughts and emotions of others, providing a unique and immersive experience. Through simulations, students acquire the opportunity to hear the inner thoughts of another individual, subsequently reflecting on differences in perspective and lived experiences in a particular situation (SDSU, 2023). Although the pilot originated in the university's diversity, equity, and inclusion efforts, empathy as a factor in social perceptiveness and active listening is a critical construct for universities with programs that train educators, leaders, medical professionals, and social workers for the workplace (O*Net, 2024). To be immersed in a scenario with multiple reactions from a second party may increase engagement and learning (SDSU, 2023). The authors suggested that instructors include themselves in at least one simulation, showing students increased vulnerability and modeling, thus increasing social presence.

Further, using A/R and V/R has improved nurses', teachers', and social workers' ability to gather behavioral data on a student or patient (Cipresso et al., 2018). Lee et al. (2022) have shown that interaction with simulated graphics in 3D models increased engagement and student grades in a biology undergraduate program. In coordination with Dreamscape, nine modules were crafted and implemented with 200 students; after 1.5 years, students achieved, on average, one letter grade higher and self-reported 15% higher engagement than the control group who did not utilize VR technology (Lee, et al., 2022). VR may have similar applications in engineering, art, and technology (Oje et al., 2023). Cipresso et al. (2018) observed that a stimulator capable of evaluating and boosting an individual's parasympathetic system can simulate internal bodily signals.

Imagine Anika, an undergraduate, is in a proctored exam in which she and the proctor are on video and audio. Could Anika's markers for test anxiety (increased heart rate; increased breathing) be projected on-screen, with the instructor's image alerting the student to implement some biofeedback? Even a couple minutes of deep breathing may induce calm, as evidenced in Navy Seals training with breathing techniques (Cleveland Clinic, 2021). Ma et al. (2017) found that after being trained in deep (diaphragmatic) breathing, participants could apply the technique, improve sustained attention and effect, and decrease cortisol levels. Students who effectively recognize and manage anxiety during testing sessions are expected to experience enhanced cognitive processing and performance, influenced by the instructor's demeanor affecting social presence and, consequently, student satisfaction and performance.

Career services departments may utilize A/R or V/R to simulate job interviews (Lee et al., 2022). Tailoring the session to factors such as job role, industry, and interview level (e.g., screening interview, interview with manager) or interview question type (e.g., behavioral, situational, even illegal questions) is possible (Virtual Speech, 2024). Perhaps these programs could expand to aid online learners with disabilities. Students with disabilities could practice discussing potential accommodations and handling varying employer objections or responses. Although this might be time-consuming for one student with one staff person at a time, if such sessions are available by A/R and V/R, many students could utilize the session with minimal staff intervention. The AI could provide feedback based on student responses, or that sensitive portion of the interaction could be human-to-human. Depending on staffing levels and bandwidth, instructors of Capstone courses may volunteer for the debriefing.

Further, A/R and V/R could be utilized in active shooter drills (Lee et al., 2022). Instructor and learner safety is paramount in the university setting. Whether the drills are part of students' teacher education modules during coursework or part of teacher professional development, the upfront cost of such practice cannot be compared with even one saved life through improved response time or methods. Social presence could be enhanced as the instructor plays the teacher's role in the classroom video, modeling appropriate behavior in the first module and then passing the teacher's role to the student.

Artificial Intelligence in Education

AI involves computers mimicking human cognitive tasks, especially learning and problem-solving (Baker & Smith, 2019). AI in HE, sometimes known as AIEd, has rapidly evolved, becoming a subfield of educational technology with diverse applications such as intelligent tutoring systems, assessment, evaluation, and profiling (Zawacki-Richter et al., 2019). Intelligent Tutoring Systems (ITSs) replicate personalized one-to-one tutoring, yielding positive learning outcomes (Kulik & Fletcher, 2016).

AIEd harnesses big data for just-in-time feedback and assessing student work, seamlessly integrating it into learning activities (Bahadir, 2016). Predictive algorithms estimate the likelihood of assignment failure or dropout, providing near real-time feedback valued by students and alleviating instructor workload. In online learning, AIEd's scalability is evident in automated assessments accommodating unlimited student enrollment.

AIEd includes subject-specific learning software, personalized learning management systems, and ITSs, extending beyond Computer Science to fields like mathematics, medicine, and reading comprehension (Duffy & Azevedo, 2015). It challenges conventional views on class size, pedagogy, and instructor roles, expanding rapidly with applications like math tutoring in China and gaining prominence in mainstream HE settings (Schiff, 2021; Hao, 2019; Nye, 2016). The evolving AIEd landscape offers insights into learner efficacy, positioning it as a game-changer in future learning research (Nye, 2016).

Regarding immediacy and presence, AIEd is integral to students' perceptions of online learning, aligning with the 24/7 responsiveness of asynchronous education. Instructors remain crucial, representing the university to students amid AIEd's pivotal role in shaping online education dynamics.

OpenAI and the Next Paradigm Shift

OpenAI's inaugural commercially viable product, ChatGPT, debuted in November 2022 (Lo, 2023). This language model, rooted in the GPT (Generative Pre-trained Transformer) architecture, specifically GPT-3.5, is a significant stride in natural language processing (Roumeliotis & Tselikas, 2023). ChatGPT, designed to emulate human-like text generation and engage in versatile conversations, has undergone training on a diverse range of internet text, enabling it to comprehend and produce contextually relevant responses. Interaction with ChatGPT involves users providing prompts or questions, with the model generating coherent and contextually appropriate responses (Lo, 2023). Positioned within OpenAI's broader non-profit mission to advance natural language processing and AI capabilities, ChatGPT facilitates sophisticated, context-aware interactions between users and AI systems.

Lo's (2023) rapid literature review delved into recent research on OpenAI, shedding light on ChatGPT's performance across academic domains. Although excelling in areas like economics and meeting expectations in programming, it needs to improve in subjects such as mathematics (Frieder et al., 2023). Despite its promise as a supportive tool for educators and a virtual tutor, aiding in content creation, guidance, query resolution, and collaboration, ChatGPT presents challenges, including generating inaccurate information and evading plagiarism detection (Ventayen, 2023).

Lo (2023) advocates for immediate actions to address these issues, urging a realignment of evaluation methodologies and institutional regulations in educational settings. Simultaneously, proposals for instructor training and student education aim to adeptly navigate and address the implications of ChatGPT's integration into the educational landscape (García-Peñalvo, 2023). OpenAI's recognition for advancements in AI and natural language processing underscores its impact on online teaching, holding the potential to enhance various facets of educational technology.

Content Generation and Personalization

Lo (2023) suggests that ChatGPT could be a valuable assistant for instructors and students. Instructors can categorize the functions of ChatGPT into teaching preparation, which involves tasks such as generating course materials and offering suggestions; performing language translation; and assessment, which includes tasks like generating assessment tasks and evaluating student performance (Wang et al., 2023). ChatGPT provided valuable suggestions for teaching preparation, as demonstrated by Megahed et al. (2023), who utilized ChatGPT to create a course syllabus, finding its teaching suggestions implementable with minimal modifications.

In sum, the language models developed by OpenAI, including ChatGPT, demonstrate exceptional proficiency in generating coherent and contextually relevant text. This proficiency holds great promise in education, enabling the creation of high-quality educational content. Additionally, these models produce personalized learning materials, adapting content based on individual student needs. This personalized approach accommodates diverse learning styles and preferences, enhancing the online teaching experience.

Other Applications of ChatGPT

Students grappling with essay writing and structuring may use ChatGPT to generate an example paper to learn about the structure. In doing so, instead of relying on content and questionable authenticity, learning focuses on applying the format or layout (Vos, 2023). Instructors may then offer support as the student begins their paper with the ChatGPT example, facilitating immediacy and social presence.

Second, instructors may ask ChatGPT to create a learning module on the ethical use of ChatGPT in their course (Englund et al., 2017). Such guidance would allow open discussion of policy and relevant industry uses and provide learners with practical and technical transferrable skills to employment (Pew Research, 2023). Employees must create and interpret company policies in multiple healthcare settings, leadership, and human resources positions (O*Net, 2024). Helping students avoid authenticity issues is a caring stance expected to increase social presence.

Third, instructors could guide students in critically evaluating ChatGPT's output (Greenfield, 2023). In that way, skills such as critical thinking and learning are enhanced rather than replaced by generative technology (Seo et al., 2021). Potential uses of ChatGPT in HE may be limited only by the creativity and time invested by humans to both glean information and foster AI's capabilities.

Automated Grading and Assessment

The sophistication of OpenAI's technology, particularly in language understanding, has the potential to impact the assessment and grading processes in online education significantly. According to McMurtrie (2023), artificial intelligence (AI) technologies, including ChatGPT, represent a crucial element in the future of education. One proposed strategy for improving assessment methods involves empowering educators with tools to use testing not only as an evaluative tool but also as a facilitator of learning itself. Automated grading systems powered by OpenAI's models can offer efficiency and personalization in feedback (Mhlanda, 2023). This advancement can streamline the evaluation process for educators while providing students with timely and constructive feedback tailored to their learning trajectories.

ChatGPT can formulate teaching methodologies, enhance student engagement and collaboration, and promote practical, experiential learning. Despite being considered a disruptive technology, ChatGPT presents a significant opportunity to revolutionize the educational system (Mhlanda, 2023; Seo et al., 2021).

Chatbots and Virtual Assistants

Chatbots, also known as conversational agents or dialogue systems, are applications simulating human conversation through text or voice, and they have gained attention in educational settings (Rudolph et al., 2023; Yin et al., 2020). Despite their existence since 1966 (Weizenbaum, 1966), recent AI advancements have significantly expanded their use. Examples like BookBuddy, which aids in English (Ruan et al., 2019), and StudBot, which handles Academic Advising questions (Vijayakumar et al., 2019), illustrate the versatility of Chatbots. Agents like Sammy, providing 24/7 tutoring for various courses (Gupta & Jagannath, 2019), contribute to student accessibility and engagement, playing a vital role in one-to-one dialogues, comprehension building, motivation enhancement, and collaborative learning (Tegos et al., 2019). Beyond mere responsiveness, these advanced models create a dynamic and interactive learning environment. Chatbots satisfy learner's desire for immediate response (van Wart et al., 2020). The strength of Chatbots lies in their ability to operate 24/7 asynchronously and, therefore, provide faster response time, meeting students' needs for immediacy and accessibility (Aivo, 2020). How can this technology be applied to increase the feeling of instructor and peer social presence in the learning environment? In a study by Hew et al. (2023), the constant availability of chatbots allowed for immediate responses and guidance, providing timely assistance to students. This constant availability stood in contrast to human teachers with limited office hours who could not match such instant availability. Additionally, adhering to the principles of multimedia use for learning (Mayer, 2017) and presenting learning content in a conversational format enhanced comprehension. As students set learning goals and engaged in listening tasks, their interaction with chatbots, resembling texting with friends, increased student engagement during online learning (Hew et al., 2023).

With the integration of natural language processing capabilities, chatbots powered by OpenAI's models excel at addressing student queries effectively (Hew et al., 2023). They deliver accurate and timely responses and engage in meaningful conversations. This functionality significantly enhances the overall responsiveness of the online educational experience. Integrating OpenAI's models into chatbots represents a transformative step toward creating more engaging, interactive, and student-centric online learning environments, aligning seamlessly with the evolving landscape of modern education. While concerns about academic integrity persist (King, 2023), and some scholars have raised the issue of whether these technologies may devalue the role of human educators (Kooli, 2023), it seems clear that these tools have arrived whether HE is ready or not. The future may be a two-tiered support system where students interact with AI-assisted tools for simple questions or initial support and then step up to an appointment with human instructors, tutors, and support services when additional support is needed.

Applications of Chatbots

Instructors may use chatbots to handle common questions from prospective students, offer initial guidance on accessing learning resources, or direct learners to a specific article recommended for an assignment (Seo et al., 2021). A human instructor addresses more complex guidance and instruction most effectively. In such situations, however, the chatbot could be programmed to "sort" by complexity, answering lower-priority issues and referring learners to instructors for higher complexity or higher-level items (Aivo, 2020; Seo et al., 2021). For efficiency, the bot could link the learner directly to an individual instructor's calendar to arrange the needed appointment or call the instructor's phone. The chatbot could offer the student options of communication mode, generating further student engagement and agency (Purdue, 2024). Chatbots for courses could be created with the picture and voice of the course instructor to increase social presence. Additional options to view/listen to the instructor biography or the course welcome could be included by the bot, which has also increased social presence (Fiock, 2020). Recent advancements in AI have received national news coverage as actors fought for (and won) creative control of their images and voices in the entertainment industry (Dalton, 2023).

The Associated Press (2023) explains that studios recognize the power of AI to utilize actors' past work (voice and image) to create new works, and studios must recognize that a singular contract for a movie only permits that movie's usage. The authors urge universities to balance the utility of voice and image with legal and ethical caution.

Other Applications of OpenAI in Education

Natural Language Interfaces for Learning Platforms

OpenAI's models contribute significantly to developing natural language interfaces and fostering intuitive interactions between students and online learning platforms (Mhlanda, 2023). This innovation has the potential to simplify the user experience, enabling students to communicate with educational technology using their natural language and, in turn, enhancing accessibility and engagement in online learning.

Language Translation Services

OpenAI's language models are pivotal in overcoming language barriers for globally reaching online courses (Mhlanda, 2023). By facilitating real-time language translation services, these models contribute to making educational content more accessible and inclusive for a diverse audience of students worldwide.

Enhanced Content Creation

The prowess of OpenAI's models extends to enhanced content curation, offering educators a valuable tool to analyze and summarize vast amounts of information (Mhlanda, 2023). By automating the process of sifting through educational resources, these models assist educators in efficiently finding relevant materials, saving time, and creating more engaging and effective learning materials.

Barriers to Equity, Access, and Fairness

Disparities in access to AI technologies may contribute to educational inequalities based on socioeconomic factors, race, and residence (Sanders & Scanlon, 2021). Often termed the *digital divide*, this phenomenon encompasses the opportunity gap created for those who do not have a phone, laptop, or affordable data plan (Sanders & Scanlon, 2021; vanDijk, 2006). According to the FCC in Sanders and Scanlon (2017), 26% of Americans in rural areas and 32% of people living on tribal lands had inadequate broadband access compared to only 1.5% in urban areas. Surprisingly, parts of large segments of metropolitan areas such as Chicago and Los Angeles face the same digital divide (Sanders & Scanlon, 2017). Research has shown that physical computer access positively relates to higher income, education, and professional occupation (vanDijk, 2006). Further, one in five adults solely access the Internet over their phone; these individuals are more likely to be Black or Hispanic (Pew Research, 2023). Some learning management system platforms may not be accessible, easily used, or visible in the telephone environment. Proctored exams may require a laptop or PC and a web camera to scan the learner's testing environment. Those with telephone only would be excluded. Beyond computer and Internet access affecting online learner enrollment, racial disparity prevails.

The National Center for Education Statistics (NCES; 2023) reports that of more than 14.9 million undergraduate online learners in 2021, 52.31% were White (7.8 million), whereas only 22.13% identified as Hispanic; 12.74% were Black, and 7.38% were of people of Asian descent. At the graduate level, disparities are more significant; of more than 2.8 million online learners, 60.49% were White, 13.59% were Black, 12.74% identified as people of Hispanic descent, and 9.06% were Asian. Would learners of varying races be more likely to attend online universities if most of their instructors, live or AR/VR, were part of their protected class, spoke their language, or understood their lived experiences?

Like the inequality between access based on socioeconomic, race, or residence, learners' skill levels in technology vary and may impact success in an online environment (Hargittai, 2002). Jessamyn West (2011) suggested a gap exists between people who can easily use technology and those who cannot (Sanders & Scanlon, 2021). Digital competence has multiple factors, including technical skills, the ability to deal with unexpected problems, and the aptitude to keep up with changing technology (Zhou et al., 2022; Sanders & Scanlon, 2021). VanDijk (2006) suggests that categories such as age, sex, intelligence, and personality relate to the ease of use of technology for learners. However, Hargittai (2002) found that learners matched by age, sex, and education level varied in success on a technology task based on digital skill alone. Some could complete a simple task of locating information online in less than 10 seconds, but it took others 7-14 minutes (Hargittai, 2002). Research suggests that many people learn digital skills through trial and error rather than formal education (vanDijk, 2006). Since specific segments do not have computer access to practice, HE institutions and instructors need to recognize and plan for significantly disparate digital skill levels in online learners.

Rawas (2023) noted ChatGPT's potential to enhance access to educational resources for students with disabilities or those unable to participate in conventional classroom settings. Faculty and university disability services should actively work to minimize technological disparities and promote equitable access to AI tools and educational resources as part of a commitment to universal access guidelines (Tlilli et al., 2023).

Although it is beyond the scope of this chapter to examine all these aspects, universities, and faculty must be aware of and collaborate to minimize technological disparities, promoting equitable access to AI tools. Seo et al. (2021) suggested that keeping humans in the loop of AI decision-making may balance using technology to improve student engagement and learning and the risk of over-standardization through AI prescribing acceptable responses and behaviors. Until AI is "perfect," like humans, its output will have biases.

Instructor Perceptions as a Potential Barrier

While many are excited about exploring novel technologies, some label specific instructors as "want nots" (van Dijk, 2006, p. 226). These individuals have no need, preference, or time for computers. Further, some avoid technology based on beliefs that connection is dangerous or surrenders some level of privacy. Zhao et al. (2006) postulate that the perception of time that the technology uses is compared, in the instructor's mind, to time saved, the effectiveness of the technology in reaching the outcome, and the perceived ease of use of the platform. Instructor time is a finite resource, and most are encumbered with regular teaching duties and administrative concerns and may serve as subject matter experts to produce or update curriculum. Therefore, time management impacts digital competency (Gkrimpizi et al., 2023; Lee et al., 2022; Mercader & Gairin, 2020; O'Doherty et al., 2018; Preisman, 2014). The added expectation of learning novel technologies may be seen as a burden, causing resistance to change or uncertainty; instructors see adequate IT support as critical for their success in the online environment (Gkrimpizi et al., 2023).

Transparency in AI Application

Transparency in communication about AI-generated content is imperative. Regular forums, workshops, and discussion groups facilitate ongoing dialogues among students and educators about the ethical and responsible use of AI. This commitment to transparency aids in the ethical and responsible deployment of ChatGPT in educational settings, ensuring that stakeholders comprehend the technology's functionalities and capabilities. Examples of transparent usage involve educating students about the technology's algorithms and data sources and elucidating the processes behind information processing and response generation. Instructors should communicate transparently about the role of AI in education, providing clear explanations of appropriate and inappropriate usage in academic work, tailored explanations by faculty in their courses, grading criteria, and the use of AI tools in assessments (Mhlanga, 2023; Rawas, 2023). Last, universities and educators should be clear about who is responsible if AI generates incorrect information, communicating this possibility and what process will be employed to determine consequences (Seo et al., 2021).

Academic Integrity

Rahman and Watanobe (2023) highlight the imperative for educators and institutions to recognize the potential risk of academic dishonesty in online exams facilitated by ChatGPT's ability to generate text resembling human writing. Integrating AI, particularly ChatGPT, in academic assessments raises concerns about the equity and credibility of online evaluations. Plagiarism and the authenticity of student contributions become focal points of apprehension. To maintain academic integrity, we urge faculty members to establish clear guidelines and communicate expectations regarding the ethical use of AI tools.

McMurtrie (2023) addressed the initial widespread concerns about ChatGPT's impact on essay assessments. Some instructors expressed apprehension that students might delegate their written assignments to ChatGPT, leveraging its ability to swiftly produce coherent prose without triggering plagiarism detection mechanisms. These apprehensions may arise from a reluctance to adopt new assessment methods, given that traditional written assignments might need to improve student engagement and effectiveness in assessing learning outcomes.

ChatGPT presents numerous promising opportunities in HE. However, ethical considerations and challenges must be acknowledged and addressed to ensure the responsible implementation of ChatGPT in academic settings. Students who utilize ChatGPT for application or case studies to generate their work run the risk of leaving the university without the competencies and skills expected of them in the workplace. It is essential to navigate the potential risks associated with academic integrity while embracing the transformative possibilities ChatGPT and other AIEd offer in HE.

Important Considerations

The increased utilization of emerging technologies such as AR/VR or AI enhances online presence, immediacy, and data-gathering capabilities. Instructors can utilize this information to identify gaps in individual and aggregate student learning with products such as Hobson's PAR and InsideTrack (Ji &

Han, 2019; Kinzie & Kuh, 2007). Institution-wide tools assist in monitoring attrition patterns, retention, and dropout risk, while various AIEd systems focus on profiling and prediction related to student outcomes (Kinzie & Kuh, 2007; Zawacki-Richter et al., 2019).

However, while technology offers online presence and instructor immediacy opportunities, caution is essential. The perception of distance and anonymity in particular social media formats may lead to oversharing of personal information (Williams, 2021). The increased use of social media necessitates clear expectations from the administration, considering both benefits and risks. Training becomes crucial for mastering novel technologies and understanding the privacy and professional behaviors associated with these modalities (Li & Lefevre, 2020).

FUTURE DIRECTIONS

Further exploration is essential to assess the effectiveness of emerging technologies, online methodologies, and activities promoting social presence, as well as the practices outlined in this manuscript. A central theme emphasized here is the critical role of evidence-based practices in online and virtual environments for sustained success in HE. It is imperative to subject novel technologies, tools, and practices to rigorous research and meaningful scholarly examination to remove barriers for students (Lee et al., 2022), match technology employed with institutional values (Kinzie & Kuh, 2017), and prudent stewardship of available financial resources in balance with attempts to manage student tuition costs during reduced public investment in education (Gkrimpizi et al., 2023; Lee et al., 2022).

Critical factors for HE success encompass online social presence, instructor presence, instructor immediacy, and the effective utilization of available technology. In a post-COVID-19 scenario, every HE professional must enhance their professional practices, emphasize student-centered engagement strategies, and make online synchronous and asynchronous education more authentic, personable, interactive, and rewarding for students. The landscape of HE is evolving, accelerated by the pandemic, prompting a focused examination of traditional approaches that have persisted for over a century, including conventional classroom structures, the instructor as a central figure, disengaged students, and technology platforms lagging industry standards and students' daily lives.

CONCLUSION

While this chapter does not provide definitive answers, it may serve as a starting point for essential questions, offering suggestions for improvement based on current literature and areas for instructors to explore for advancing online social presence, immediacy behaviors, and the integration of the next wave of HE technologies. AR/VR, educational assistants (EAs), and AI in education (AIEd), including OpenAI, social media sites, and chatbots, represent the upcoming wave of technology enhancing instructor immediacy and social presence.

The paradigm shifts in HE due to COVID-19 have imparted two crucial lessons. First, instructors' engagement with students, whether in person, virtually, synchronously, or asynchronously, remains integral to student satisfaction and meaningful learning outcomes. Second, effective technology utilization is indispensable for scaling HE delivery, fostering dynamic connections with students, enabling interactions, establishing an online social presence, and mastering essential 21st-century skills. HE has undergone irreversible changes and will not revert to its prior state. Embracing a HE landscape characterized by the need for heightened instructor social presence and integrating cutting-edge technological tools is the new normal, and HE must adapt accordingly.

REFERENCES

75% of College Students Unhappy with Quality of eLearning During Covid-19. (2020). https://oneclass.com/blog/featured/177356-7525-of-college-students-unhappy-with-quality-of-elearning-during-covid-19.en.html

Aivo. (2020). *How universities are using education chatbots to enhance the system.* Retrieved January 15, 2024, https://www.aivo.co/blog/how-universities-are-using-education-chatbots-to-enhance-the-system

Akyol, Z., Garrison, D., & Ozden, M. (2009). Online and blended communities of inquiry: Exploring the developmental and perceptional differences. *International Review of Research in Open and Distance Learning, 10*(6), 65–83. doi:10.19173/irrodl.v10i6.765

Allen, S. J. (2020). On the cutting edge or the chopping block? Fostering a digital mindset and tech literacy in business management education. *Journal of Management Education, 44*(3), 362–393. doi:10.1177/1052562920903077

Alyahyan, E., & Dustegor, D. (2020). Predicting academic success in higher education: Literature review and best practices. *International Journal of Educational Technology in Higher Education, 17*(3), 1–21. doi:10.1186/s41239-020-0177-7

Anagnostopoulos, D., Basmadjian, K. G., & McCrory, R. S. (2005). The decentered teacher and the construction of social space in the virtual classroom. *Teachers College Record, 107*(8), 1699–1729. doi:10.1111/j.1467-9620.2005.00539.x

Aragon, S. R. (2003). Creating social presence in online environments. *New Directions for Adult and Continuing Education, 100*(100), 57–68. doi:10.1002/ace.119

Bahadır, E. (2016). Using neural network and logistic regression analysis to predict prospective mathematics teachers' academic success upon entering graduate education. *Educational Sciences: Theory & Practice, 16*(3), 943–964. doi:10.12738/estp.2016.3.0214

Baker, T., & Smith, L. (2019). *Educ-AI-tion rebooted? Exploring the future of artificial intelligence in schools and colleges.* Retrieved from Nesta Foundation website: https://media.nesta.org.uk/documents/Future_of_AI_and_education_v5_WEB.pdf

Bangert, A. (2008). The influence of social presence and teaching presence on the quality of online critical inquiry. *Journal of Computing in Higher Education, 20*(1), 34–61. doi:10.1007/BF03033431

Beaudoin, M. F. (2015). Distance education leadership in the context of digital change. *Quarterly Review of Distance Education, 16*, 33–44.

Berry, S. (2019). Teaching to connect: Community-building strategies for the virtual classroom. *Online Learning, 23*(1), 164–183. doi:.v23i1.1425 doi:10.24059/olj

Bowen, J. A., & Watson, C. E. (2017). *Teaching Naked Techniques: A practical guide to designing better classes.* Jossey-Bass.

Caskurlu, S., Maeda, Y., Richardson, J., & Lu, J. (2020). A meta-analysis addressing the relationship between teaching presence and student's satisfaction and learning. *Computers & Education, 157,* 103966. doi:10.1016/j.compedu.2020.103966

Cayanus, J. L., & Martin, M. M. (2008). Teacher self-disclosure. Amount, relevance and negativity. *Communication Quarterly, 56*(3), 325–341. doi:10.1080/01463370802241492

Chen, C., Landa, S., Padilla, A., & Yur-Austin, J. (2021). Learners' experience and needs in online environments: Adopting agility in teaching. *Journal of Research in Innovative Teaching & Learning, 14*(1), 18–31. doi:10.1108/JRIT-11-2020-0073

Chu, S. K. W., Zhang, Y., Chen, K., Chan, C. K., Lee, C. W. Y., Zou, E., & Lau, W. (2017). The effectiveness of wikis for project-based learning in different disciplines in higher education. *The Internet and Higher Education, 33,* 49–60. doi:10.1016/j.iheduc.2017.01.005

Cipresso, P., Giglioli, I., Raya, M., & Rivan, G. (2018). The Past, Present, and Future of Virtual and Augmented Reality Research: A Network and Cluster Analysis of the Literature. *Frontiers in Psychology, 9,* 1–20. doi:10.3389/fpsyg.2018.02086 PMID:30459681

Cleveland Clinic. (2021). *How Box Breathing Can Help You Destress.* https://health.clevelandclinic.org/box-breathing-benefits

Cole, A. W., Lennon, L., & Weber, N. L. (2021). Student perceptions of online active learning practices and online learning climate predict online course engagement. *Interactive Learning Environments, 29*(5), 866–880. doi:10.1080/10494820.2019.1619593

Comadena, M. E., Hunt, S. K., & Simonds, C. J. (2007). The Effects of Teacher Clarity, Nonverbal Immediacy, and Caring on Student Motivation, Affective and Cognitive Learning. *Communication Research Reports, 24*(3), 241–248. doi:10.1080/08824090701446617

Cunha, F. R. Jr, van Kruistum, C., & van Oers, B. (2016). Teachers and Facebook: Using online groups to improve student's communication and engagement in education. *Communication Teacher, 30*(4), 228–241. doi:10.1080/17404622.2016.1219039

Daigle, D. T., & Stuvland, A. (2021). Social presence as best practice: The online classroom needs to feel real. *PS, Political Science & Politics, 54*(1), 182–183. doi:10.1017/S1049096520001614

Dalton, A. (2023). Hollywood actors' union board approves strike-ending deal as leaders tout money gains and AI rights. *WHYY.* Retrieved on January 15, 2024, https://whyy.org/articles/hollywood-actors-union-board-strike-ending-deal-money-gains-ai-rights/

David, F.D. (1989). Perceived usefulness, perceived ease of use and user acceptance of information technology. *MIS Quarterly, 13.*

Dixson, M. (2015). Measuring student engagement in the online course: The Online Student Engagement Scale. *Online Learning : the Official Journal of the Online Learning Consortium, 19*(4). Advance online publication. doi:10.24059/olj.v19i4.561

Duffy, M. C., & Azevedo, R. (2015). Motivation matters: Interactions between achievement goals and agent scaffolding for self-regulated learning within an intelligent tutoring system. *Computers in Human Behavior, 52*, 338–348. doi:10.1016/j.chb.2015.05.041

Englund, C., Olofsson, A., & Price, L. (2017). Teaching with technology in higher education: Understanding conceptual change and development in practice. *Higher Education Research & Development, 36*(1), 73–87. doi:10.1080/07294360.2016.1171300

Figueras-Maz, M., Grandío-Pérez, M.-M., & Mateus, J.-C. (2021). Students' perceptions on social media teaching tools in higher education settings. *Communicatio Socialis, 34*(1), 15–28. doi:10.15581/003.34.1.15-28

Finn, A. N., Schrodt, P., Witt, P. L., Elledge, N., Jernberg, K. A., & Larson, L. M. (2009). Meta-analytical review of teacher credibility and its associations with teacher behaviors and student outcomes. *Communication Education, 58*(4), 516–537. doi:10.1080/03634520903131154

Fiock, H. (2020). Designing a community of inquiry in online courses. *International Review of Research in Open and Distance Learning, 21*(1), 135–153. doi:10.19173/irrodl.v20i5.3985

Fiock, H., Maeda, Y., & Richardson, J. C. (2021). Instructor Impact on Differences in Teaching Presence Scores in Online Courses. *International Review of Research in Open and Distance Learning, 22*(3), 55–76. doi:10.19173/irrodl.v22i3.5456

Fitton, I. S., Finnegan, D. J., & Proulx, M. J. (2020). Immersive virtual environments and embodied agents for e-learning applications. *PeerJ. Computer Science, 6*, e315–e315. doi:10.7717/peerj-cs.315 PMID:33816966

Fourtane, S. (2021). *Classroom 3.0: Instructors Leveraging Augmented Reality, Holograms.* https://www.fierceeducation.com/best-practices/classroom-3-0-instructors-leveraging-augmented-reality-holograms?mkt_tok=Mjk0LU1RRi0wNTYAAAF8S27cvLN_H0BnxdROOkpqoe3kPO9pi4XL-wvifPXcyKmlP2BX6SiumorSRu_qzBcTTzCvUFtjc5SWu6qjPc9F-4X3ol5cAiNmKmolKekwTA8afj5odD3E&mrkid=144996160

Frieder, S., Pinchetti, L., Griffiths, R. R., Salvatori, T., Lukasiewicz, T., Petersen, P.C., Chevalier, A., Berner, J. (2023). Mathematical Capabilities of ChatGPT. *arXiv, 2301.13867.*

García-Peñalvo, F. J. (2023). The Perception of Artificial Intelligence in Educational Contexts after the Launch of ChatGPT: Disruption or Panic? *Education in the Knowledge Society, 24*, 1–9. doi:10.14201/eks.31279

Garrison, D., & Arbaugh, J. (2007). Researching the Community of Inquiry Framework: Review, issues, and future directions. *The Internet and Higher Education, 10*(3), 157–172. doi:10.1016/j.iheduc.2007.04.001

Garrison, D. R., Anderson, T., & Archer, W. (2000). Critical inquiry in a text-based environment: Computer conferencing in higher education. *The Internet and Higher Education, 2*(2), 87–105.

Garrison, D. R., Anderson, T., & Archer, W. (2001). Critical Thinking, Cognitive Presence, and Computer Conferencing in Distance Education. *American Journal of Distance Education, 15*, 7–23. doi:10.1080/08923640109527071

Gautam, A., Williams, D., Terry, K., Robinson, K., & Newbill, P. (2018). *Mirror Worlds: Examining the Affordance of a Next Generation Immersive Learning Environment*. Tech Trends.

George, B. H. (2017). A study of traditional discussion boards and social media within an Online landscape architecture course. *Review of Applied Socioeconomic Research*, *13*(1), 16–25.

Gierdowski, D. C. (2019). *ECAR Study of Undergraduate Students and Information Technology, 2019*. https://www.educause.edu/ecar/research-publications/ecar-study-of-undergraduate-students-and-information-technology/2019/technology-use-in-the-classroom

Gkrimpizi, T., Peristeras, V., & Magnisalis, I. (2023). Classification of Barriers to Digital Transformation in Higher Education Institutions: Systematic Literature Review. *Education Sciences*, *13*(7), 746. doi:10.3390/educsci13070746

Gray, J. & DiLoreto, M. (2016). The effects of student engagement, student satisfaction and perceived learning in online learning environments. *NCPEA International Journal of Educational Leadership*, *11*(1).

Greenfield, N. (2024). Facing Facts: ChatGPT can be a tool for critical thinking. *University World News*. Retrieved on January 15, 2024, https://www.universityworldnews.com/post.php?story=20230222131416630

Gunawardena, C. N., & Zittle, F. J. (1997). Social presence as a predictor of satisfaction with a computer-mediated conferencing environment. *American Journal of Distance Education*, *11*(3), 8–26. doi:10.1080/08923649709526970

Gupta, S., & Jagannath, K. (2019). Artificially intelligently (AI) tutors in the classroom: A need assessment study of designing chatbots to support student learning. *Twenty-third Pacific Asia Conference on Information Systems*.

Hackman, M. Z., & Walker, K. (1990). Instructional communication in the televised classroom: The effects of system design and teacher immediacy on student learning and satisfaction. *Communication Education*, *39*(3), 196–206. doi:10.1080/03634529009378802

Hao, K. (2019). *China has started a grand experiment in AI education. It could reshape how the world learns*. MIT Technology Review.

Hargittai, E. (2002). Second-Level Digital Divide: Differences in People's Online Skills. *First Monday*, *7*(4). Advance online publication. doi:10.5210/fm.v7i4.942

Hew, K. F., Huang, W., Du, J., & Jia, C. (2023). Using chatbots to support student goal setting and social presence in fully online activities: Learner engagement and perceptions. *Journal of Computing in Higher Education*, *35*(1), 40–68. doi:10.1007/s12528-022-09338-x PMID:36101883

Hostetter, C., & Busch, M. (2013). Community matters: Social presence and learning outcomes. *The Journal of Scholarship of Teaching and Learning*, *13*(1), 77–86.

Jahromi, V. K., Tabatabaee, S. S., Abdar, Z. E., & Rajabi, M. (2016). Active listening: The key to successful communication in hospital managers. *Electronic Physician*, *8*(3), 2123–2128. doi:10.19082/2123 PMID:27123221

Ji, Y., & Han, Y. (2019). Monitoring Indicators of the Flipped Classroom Learning Process based on Data Mining: Taking the Course of "Virtual Reality Technology" as an Example. *International Journal of Emerging Technologies in Learning*, *14*(3), 166–176. doi:10.3991/ijet.v14i03.10105

Johnson, A. (2013). *Excellent! Online Teaching: Effective strategies for a successful semester online.* Aaron Johnson.

Kaufmann, R., Sellnow, D. D., & Frisby, B. N. (2016). The development and validation of the online learning climate scale (OLCS). *Communication Education*, *65*(3), 307–321. doi:10.1080/03634523.2015.1101778

Kim, Y., Thayne, J., & Wei, Q. (2017). An embodied agent helps anxious students in Mathematics learning. *Educational Technology Research and Development*, *65*(1), 219–235. doi:10.1007/s11423-016-9476-z

King, M. R. (2023). A conversation on artificial intelligence, chatbots, and plagiarism in higher education. *Cellular and Molecular Bioengineering*, *16*(1), 1–2. doi:10.1007/s12195-022-00754-8 PMID:36660590

Kinzie, J., & Kuh, G. (2017). Reframing Student Success in College: Advancing Know-What and Know-How. *Change*, *49*(3), 19–27. doi:10.1080/00091383.2017.1321429

Klebig, B., Goldonowicz, J., Mendes, E., Miller, A. N., & Katt, J. (2016). The combined effects of instructor communicative behaviors, instructor credibility, and student personality traits on incivility in the college classroom. *Communication Research Reports*, *33*(2), 152–158. doi:10.1080/08824096.2016.1154837

Kooli, C. (2023). Chatbots in education and research: A critical examination of ethical implications and solutions. *Sustainability (Basel)*, *15*(7), 5614. doi:10.3390/su15075614

Koranteng, F. N., Wiafe, I., & Kuada, E. (2019). An empirical study of the relationship between social networking sites and students' engagement in higher education. *Journal of Educational Computing Research*, *57*(5), 1131–1159. doi:10.1177/0735633118787528

Kulik, J. A., & Fletcher, J. D. (2016). Effectiveness of intelligent tutoring systems: A meta-analytic review. *Review of Educational Research*, *86*(1), 42–78. doi:10.3102/0034654315581420

Lapointe, D. K., & Gunawardena, C. N. (2004). Developing, testing, and refining of a model to understand the relationship between peer interaction and learning outcomes in computer-mediated conferencing. *Distance Education*, *25*(1), 83–106. doi:10.1080/0158791042000212477

Lee, K. M., Jeong, E. J., Park, N., & Ryu, S. (2011). Effects of interactivity in educational games: A mediating role of social presence on learning outcomes. *International Journal of Human-Computer Interaction*, *27*(7), 620–633. doi:10.1080/10447318.2011.555302

Lee, N., Ray, R., Lai, S., & Tanner, B. (2022). *Ensuring equitable access to AR/VR in higher education.* The Brookings Institution. Retrieved on January 11, 2024, https://www.brookings.edu/articles/ensuring-equitable-access-to-ar-vr-in-higher-education/#:~:text=To%20improve%20student%20access%20to,of%20high%2Dspeed%20broadband%20networks

Li, C., & Lalani, F. (2020). The COVID-19 pandemic has changed the world forever: This is how. *World Economic Forum.* https://www.weforum.org/agenda/2020/04/coronavirus-education-global-covid19-online-digital-learning/

Li, F. (2022). "Are you There?": Teaching presence and interaction in large online classes. *Asian-Pacific Journal of Second and Foreign Language Education, 7*(1), 45. doi:10.1186/s40862-022-00180-3

Li, N., & LeFevre, D. (2020). Holographic teaching presence: Participant experiences of interactive synchronous seminars delivered via holographic videoconferencing. *Research in Learning Technology, 28*(0), 2265. doi:10.25304/rlt.v28.2265

Lo, C. K. (2023). What is the impact of ChatGPT on education? A rapid review of the literature. *Education Sciences, 13*(4), 410. doi:10.3390/educsci13040410

Luévano, E., DeLara, E. L., & Castro, J. E. (2015). Use of telepresence and holographic projection mobile device for college degree level. *Procedia Computer Science, 75,* 339–347. doi:10.1016/j.procs.2015.12.256

Ma, X., Yue, Z., Gong, Z., Duan, N., Shi, Y., Wei, G., & Li, Y. (2017). The effect of Diaphragmatic Breathing on Attention, Negative Affect and Stress in Healthy Adults. *Frontiers in Psychology, 8,* 874. doi:10.3389/fpsyg.2017.00874 PMID:28626434

Makransky, G., & Lilleholt, L. (2018). A structural equation modeling investigation of the emotional value of immersive virtual reality in education. *Educational Technology Research and Development, 66*(5), 1141–1164. doi:10.1007/s11423-018-9581-2

Martin, F., & Bolliger, D. U. (2018). Engagement matters: Student perceptions on the importance of engagement strategies in the online learning environment. *Online Learning : the Official Journal of the Online Learning Consortium, 22*(1), 205. doi:10.24059/olj.v22i1.1092

Martin, J. (2019). Building relationships and increasing engagement in the virtual classroom: Practical Tools for the Online Instructor. *The Journal of Educators Online, 16*(1). Advance online publication. doi:10.9743/jeo.2019.16.1.9

Mayer, R. E. (2017). Using multimedia for e-learning. *Journal of Computer Assisted Learning, 33*(5), 403–423. doi:10.1111/jcal.12197

McCleskey, J. A., & Gruda, D. (2021). The New Normal: Student Views of Higher Education During the COVID-19 Pandemic. *Southwest Academy of Management 2021 Virtual Conference.*

McKinney, P., & Sen, B. (2016). *The use of technology in group work: A situational analysis of students' reflective writing.* Education for Information.

McMurtrie, B. (2023, January 5). Teaching: Will ChatGPT change the way you teach? *The Chronicle of Higher Education.* https://www.chronicle.com/newsletter/teaching/2023-01-05

Megahed, F. M., Chen, Y., Ferris, J. A., Knoth, S., & Jones-Farmer, L. A. (2023). How generative AI models such as ChatGPT can be (mis)used in SPC practice, education, and research? An exploratory study. Quality Engineering, 1–29. doi:10.1080/08982112.2023.2206479

Mehrabian, A. (1971). *Silent messages: implicit communication of emotions and attitudes.* Wadsworth.

Mercader, C., & Gairin, J. (2020). University teachers' perception of barriers to the use of digital technologies: The importance of academic discipline. *International Journal of Educational Technology in Higher Education, 17*(1), 4. doi:10.1186/s41239-020-0182-x

MhlandaD. (2023). Open AI in Education, the Responsible and Ethical Use of ChatGPT Towards Lifelong Learning. SSRN. doi:10.2139/ssrn.4354422

Miller, A. N., Katt, J. A., Brown, T., & Sivo, S. A. (2014). The relationship of instructor self-disclosure, nonverbal immediacy, and credibility to student incivility in the college classroom. *Communication Education, 63*(1), 1–16. doi:10.1080/03634523.2013.835054

Miller, M., Hahs-Vaughn, D., & Zygouris-Coe, V. (2014). A confirmatory factor analysis of teaching presence within online professional development. *Online Learning : the Official Journal of the Online Learning Consortium, 18*(1). Advance online publication. doi:10.24059/olj.v18i1.333

National Center for Education Statistics. (2023). Undergraduate Enrollment. In *Condition of Education*. U.S. Department of Education, Institute of Education Sciences. Retrieved January 11, 2024, from https://nces.ed.gov/programs/coe/indicator/cha

Ngoc, H., Hoang, L., & Hung, V. (2020). Transforming education with emerging technologies in higher education: A systematic literature review. *International Journal of Higher Education, 9*(5), 252–258. doi:10.5430/ijhe.v9n5p252

NSSE. (2014). *Promoting student learning and institutional improvement: Lessons from NSSE at 13*. Indiana University for Postsecondary Research.

Nye, B. D. (2016). ITS, the end of the world as we know it: Transitioning AIED into a service-oriented ecosystem. *International Journal of Artificial Intelligence in Education, 26*(2), 756–770. doi:10.1007/s40593-016-0098-8

O*Net. (2024a). *Business Teachers, Postsecondary*. Retrieved on January 19, 2024, https://www.onetonline.org/link/summary/25-1011.00

O*Net. (2024b). *Chief Executives*. Retrieved on January 19, 2024, https://www.onetonline.org/link/summary/11-1011.00

O*Net. (2024c). *Child, Family, and School Social Workers*. Retrieved on January 19, 2024, https://www.onetonline.org/link/summary/21-1021.00

O*Net. (2024d). *Registered Nurse*. Retrieved on January 19, 2024, https://www.onetonline.org/link/summary/29-1141.00

O'Doherty, D., Dromey, M., Lougheed, J., Hannigan, A., Last, J., & McGrath, D. (2018). Barriers and solutions to online learning in medical education – an integrative review. *BMC Medical Education, 18*(130), 130. doi:10.1186/s12909-018-1240-0

Oh, C. S., Bailenson, J. N., & Welch, G. F. (2018). A Systematic Review of Social Presence: Definition, Antecedents, and Implications. *Frontiers in Robotics and AI, 5*, 5. doi:10.3389/frobt.2018.00114 PMID:33500993

Oje, A., Hunsum, N., & May, D. (2023). Virtual Reality assisted engineering education: a multimedia learning perspective. Computers & Education: X Reality, 3.

Orús, C., Barlés, M. J., Belanche, D., Casaló, L., Fraj, E., & Gurrea, R. (2016). The effects of learner-generated videos for YouTube on learning outcomes and satisfaction. *Computers & Education, 95*, 254–269. doi:10.1016/j.compedu.2016.01.007

Osatuyi, B. (2013). Information sharing on social media sites. *Computers in Human Behavior, 29*(6), 2622–2631. doi:10.1016/j.chb.2013.07.001

Ouyang, F., & Pengcheng, J. (2021). Artificial intelligence in education: The three paradigms. *Computers and Education: Artificial Intelligence, 2*, 1–6. doi:10.1016/j.caeai.2021.100020

Papanastasiou, G., Drigas, A., Skianis, C., Lytras, M., & Papanastasiou, E. (2019). Virtual and augmented reality effects on K-12, higher and tertiary education students' twenty-first century skills. *Virtual Reality (Waltham Cross), 23*(4), 425–436. doi:10.1007/s10055-018-0363-2

Patch, W. (2020). *Impact of Coronavirus on Students' Academic Progress and College Plans.* https://www.niche.com/about/enrollment-insights/impact-of-coronavirus-on-students-academic-progress-and-college-plans#college

Picciano, A. G. (2002). Beyond student perceptions: Issues of interaction, presence and performance in an online course. *Journal of Asynchronous Learning Networks, 6*(1), 21–40.

Pinkus, E. (2020). *SurveyMonkey poll: Distance learning for college students during the Coronavirus outbreak.* https://www.surveymonkey.com/curiosity/surveymonkey-poll-distance-learning-college-students-covid/

Poll, K., Widen, J., & Weller, S. (2014). Six Instructional Best Practices for Online Engagement and Retention. *Journal of Online Doctoral Education, 1*(1), 56–72.

Preisman, K. (2014). Teaching Presence in Online Education: From the Instructor's Point of View. *Online Learning : the Official Journal of the Online Learning Consortium, 18*(3), 1–16. doi:10.24059/olj.v18i3.446

Purdue University. (2024). *Student accountability in online environments.* Retrieved on January 15, 2024, https://onlineteachinghub.education.purdue.edu/wp-content/uploads/2022/11/student_accountability_in_online_environments_summary.pdf

Radu, I. (2014). Augmented reality in education: A meta-review and cross-media analysis. *Personal and Ubiquitous Computing, 18*(6), 1533–1543. doi:10.1007/s00779-013-0747-y

Rahman, M. M., & Watanobe, Y. (2023). ChatGPT for education and research: Opportunities, threats, and strategies. *Applied Sciences (Basel, Switzerland), 13*(9), 5783. doi:10.3390/app13095783

Rajeswaran, P., Hung, N., Kesavadas, T., Vozenilek, J., & Kumar, P. (2018). AirwayVR: learning endotracheal intubation in virtual reality. *2018 IEEE Conference on Virtual Reality and 3D User Interfaces (VR),* 669–670. 10.1109/VR.2018.8446075

Ramlatchan, M., & Watson, G. S. (2019). Enhancing instructor credibility and immediacy in online multimedia designs. *Educational Technology Research and Development, 68*(1), 511–528. doi:10.1007/s11423-019-09714-y

Ramlatchan, M., & Watson, G. S. (2020). Enhancing Instructor Credibility and Immediacy in the Design of Distance Learning Systems and Virtual Classroom Environments. *The Journal of Applied Instructional Design, 9*(2). Advance online publication. doi:10.51869/92mrgsw

Rawas, S. (2023). ChatGPT: Empowering lifelong learning in the digital age of higher education. *Education and Information Technologies*. Advance online publication. doi:10.1007/s10639-023-12114-8

Replication and extension in the online classroom. (2020). *Journal of Research on Technology in education, 1-17.* doi:10.1080/15391523.2020.1766389

Richardson, J., Koehler, A., Besser, E., Caskurlu, S., Lim, J., & Mueller, C. (2015). Conceptualizing and Investigating Instructor Presence in Online Learning Environments. *International Review of Research in Open and Distance Learning, 16*(3), 256–297. doi:10.19173/irrodl.v16i3.2123

Richardson, J., Koehler, A., Besser, E., Caskurlu, S., Lim, J., & Mueller, C. (2016). Instructor's perceptions of instructor presence in online learning environments. *International Review of Research in Open and Distance Learning, 17*(4), 82–104. doi:10.19173/irrodl.v17i4.2330

Richardson, J., & Swan, K. (2003). *An Examination of Social Presence in Online Courses in Relation to Students' Perceived Learning and Satisfaction* (Vol. 7). Research Gate.

Richardson, J. C., Ice, P., & Swan, K. (2009). *Tips and techniques for integrating social, teaching, & cognitive presence into your courses.* Poster session presented at the Conference on Distance Teaching & Learning, Madison, WI.

Roddy, C., Amiet, D. L., Chung, J., Holt, C., Shaw, L., McKenzie, S., Garivaldis, F., Lodge, J. M., & Mundy, M. E. (2017). Applying best practice online learning, teaching, and support to intensive online environments: An integrative review. *Frontiers in Education, 2*, 59. Advance online publication. doi:10.3389/feduc.2017.00059

Roumeliotis, K. I., & Tselikas, N. D. (2023). ChatGPT and open-AI models: A preliminary review. *Future Internet, 15*(6), 192. doi:10.3390/fi15060192

Ruan, S., Willis, A., Xu, Q., Davis, G. M., Jiang, L., Brunskill, E., & Landay, J. A. (2019). BookBuddy. *Proceedings of the Sixth (2019) ACM Conference on Learning @ Scale - L@S '19.*

Rudolph, J., Tan, S., & Tan, S. (2023). ChatGPT: Bullshit spewer or the end of traditional assessments in higher education? *Journal of Applied Learning and Teaching, 6*(1).

Saltan, F., & Arslan, Ö. (2017). The use of augmented reality in formal education: A scoping review. *Eurasia Journal of Mathematics, Science and Technology Education, 13*(2), 503–520.

San Diego State University (SDSU). (2023). *The Empathy Lens.* Retrieved on January 15, 2024, from https://its.sdsu.edu/innovation/empathy-lens

Sanders, C., & Scanlon, E. (2021). The digital divide is a human rights issue: Advancing social inclusion through social work advocacy. *Journal of Human Rights and Social Work, 6*(2), 130–143. doi:10.1007/s41134-020-00147-9 PMID:33758780

Sanders, K., & Lokey-Vega, A. (2020). K-12 Community of Inquiry: A case study of the applicability of the Community of Inquiry framework in the K-12 learning environment. *Journal of Online Learning Research, 6*(1), 35–56.

Schiff, D. (2021). Out of the laboratory and into the classroom: The future of artificial intelligence in education. *AI & Society, 36*(1), 331–348. doi:10.1007/s00146-020-01033-8 PMID:32836908

Schroeder, N. L., & Adesope, O. O. (2015). Impacts of pedagogical agent gender in an Accessible learning environment. *Journal of Educational Technology & Society, 18*(4), 401–411.

Seifert, T. (2016). Involvement, collaboration, and engagement—Social networks through a pedagogical lens. *Journal of Learning Design, 9*(2), 31–45. doi:10.5204/jld.v9i2.272

Seo, K., Tang, J., Roll, I., Fels, S., & Yoon, D. (2021). The impact of artificial intelligence on learner-instructor interaction in online learning. *International Journal of Educational Technology in Higher Education, 18*(1), 54. doi:10.1186/s41239-021-00292-9 PMID:34778540

Sheridan, K., & Kelly, M. (2010). The indicators of instructor presence that are important to students in online courses. *Journal of Online Learning and Teaching, 6*(4), 767–779.

Short, J., Williams, E., & Christie, B. (1976). *The Social Psychology of Telecommunications*. Wiley.

Singh, J., Singh, L., & Matthees, B. (2022). Establishing Social, Cognitive, and Teaching Presence in Online Learning-A Panacea in COVID-19 Pandemic, Post Vaccine and Post Pandemic Times. *Journal of Educational Technology Systems, 51*(1), 568–585. doi:10.1177/00472395221095169

Soffer, T., & Yaron, E. (2017). Perceived learning and students' perceptions toward using tablets for learning: The mediating role of perceived engagement among high school students. *Journal of Educational Computing Research, 55*(7), 951–973. doi:10.1177/0735633117689892

Sotirou, S., & Bogner, F. (2008). Visualizing the Invisible: Augmented Reality as an Innovative Science Education Scheme. *Advanced Science Letters, 1*(1), 114–122. doi:10.1166/asl.2008.012

Suk, H., & Laine, T. H. (2023). Influence of avatar facial appearance on users' perceived embodiment and presence in immersive virtual reality. *Electronics (Basel), 12*(3), 583. doi:10.3390/electronics12030583

Sung, E., & Mayer, R. E. (2012). Five facets of social presence in online distance education. *Computers in Human Behavior, 28*(5), 1738–1747. doi:10.1016/j.chb.2012.04.014

Swan, K. P., Richardson, J. C., Ice, P., Garrison, D. R., Cleveland-Innes, M., & Arbaugh, J. B. (2008). Validating a measurement tool of presence in online communities of inquiry. *E-Mentor, 2*(24), 1–12.

Tegos, S., Psathas, G., Tsiatsos, T., & Demetriadis, S. (2019, May 20–22). Designing Conversational Agent Interventions that Support Collaborative Chat Activities in MOOCs. *EMOOCs 2019: Work in Progress Papers of the Research, Experience and Business Tracks*. https://ceur-ws.org/Vol-2356/

Teven, J. J., & McCroskey, J. C. (1997). The relationship of perceived teacher caring with student learning and teacher evaluation. *Communication Education, 46*(1), 1–9. doi:10.1080/03634529709379069

Theodosiou, N. A., & Corbin, J. D. (2020). Redesign your in-person course for online: Creating connections and promoting engagement for better learning. *Ecology and Evolution, 10*(22), 12561–12572. doi:10.1002/ece3.6844 PMID:33250995

Thomas, G., & Thorpe, S. (2019). Enhancing the facilitation of online groups in higher education: A review of the literature on face-to-face and online group-facilitation. *Interactive Learning Environments, 27*(1), 62–71. doi:10.1080/10494820.2018.1451897

Thorpe, S. J. (2016). Online facilitator competencies for group facilitators. *Group Facilitation,* (13), 79.

Tlili, A., Shehata, B., Adarkwah, M. A., Bozkurt, A., Hickey, D. T., Huang, R., & Agyemang, B. (2023). What if the devil is my guardian angel: ChatGPT as a case study of using chatbots in education. *Smart Learning Environments, 10*(1), 15–24. doi:10.1186/s40561-023-00237-x

Top Hat Staff. (2020). *Adrift in a Pandemic: Survey of 3,089 Students Finds Uncertainty About Returning to College.* https://tophat.com/blog/adrift-in-a-pandemic-survey-infographic/

Vallade, J. I., & Kaufmann, R. (2020). *Instructor misbehavior and student outcomes.* Academic Press.

Valverde-Berrocoso, J., Garrido-Arroyo, M. C., Burgos-Videla, C., & Morales-Cevallos, M. B. (2020). Trends in educational research about e-learning: A systematic literature review (2009–2018). *Sustainability (Basel), 12*(12), 5153. doi:10.3390/su12125153

vanDijk, J. (2006). Digital divide research, achievements, and shortcomings. *Poetics, 34*(4-5), 221–235. doi:10.1016/j.poetic.2006.05.004

Ventayen, R. J. M. (2023, March). OpenAI ChatGPT Generated Results: Similarity Index of Artificial Intelligence-Based Contents. *SSRN 4332664.* https://ssrn.com/abstract=4332664

Vijayakumar, R., Bhuvaneshwari, B., Adith, S., & Deepika, M. (2019). AI-Based Student Bot for Academic Information System using Machine Learning. *International Journal of Scientific Research in Computer Science, Engineering, and Information Technology, 5*(2), 590–596. https://doi-org.ezproxy.liberty.edu/10.32628/CSEIT1952171

Violanti, M. T., Kelly, S. E., Garland, M. E., & Christen, S. (2018). Instructor clarity, humor, immediacy, and student learning: Replication and extension. *Communication Studies, 69*(3), 251–262. doi:10.1080/10510974.2018.1466718

Virtual Speech. (2024). *Job Interview Preparation.* Retrieved on January 14, 2024, from https://virtualspeech.com/courses/interview-vr

Vos, L. (2023). How to correctly use ChatGPT for essay writing. *E School News.* Retrieved on January 15, 2024, https://www.eschoolnews.com/digital-learning/2023/09/20/how-to-correctly-use-chatgpt-for-essay-writing/

WangX.GongZ.WangG.JiaJ.XuY.ZhaoJ.FanQ.WuS.HuW.LiX. (2023). ChatGPT Performs on the Chinese National Medical Licensing Examination. *Journal of Medical Systems.* doi:10.21203/rs.3.rs-2584079/v1

Watson, S., Sullivan, D., & Watson, K. (2023). Teaching Presence in Asynchronous Online Classes: It's Not Just a Façade. *Online Learning : the Official Journal of the Online Learning Consortium, 27*(2), 288–303. doi:10.24059/olj.v27i2.3231

Weizenbaum, J. (1966). ELIZA—A computer program for the study of natural language communication between man and machine. *Communications of the ACM, 9*(1), 36–45. doi:10.1145/365153.365168

West, C. (2021). *12 ways to use social media for education.* https://sproutsocial.com/insights/social-media-for-education/

Western Governors University. (2023). *Annual Report for 2022.* Retrieved on January 15, 2024, https://www.wgu.edu/about/annual-report.html

Williams, R. (2021). Concerns of Socially Interactive Technologies' Influence on Students: Digital Immigrant Teachers' Perspectives. *Ingenta Connect, 141*(3), 109–122.

Witt, P. L., Wheeless, L. R., & Allen, M. (2004). A meta-analytical review of the relationship between teacher immediacy and student learning. *Communication Monographs, 71*(2), 184–207. doi:10.1080/036452042000228054

Wombacher, K. A., Harris, C. J., Buckner, M. M., Frisby, B., & Limperos, A. M. (2017). The effects of computer-mediated communication anxiety on student perceptions of instructor behaviors, perceived learning, and quiz performance. *Communication Education, 66*(3), 299–312. doi:10.1080/03634523.2016.1221511

Xiao, M., Yue, Z., Gong, Z., Zhang, H., Duan, N., Shi, Y., Wei, G., & You-Fa, L. (2017). The Effect of Diaphragmatic Breathing on Attention, Negative Affect and Stress in Healthy Adults. *Frontiers in Psychology, 8*, 874. doi:10.3389/fpsyg.2017.00874 PMID:28626434

Yadav, R., Tiruwa, A., & Suri, P. K. (2017). Internet based learning (IBL) in higher education: A literature review. *Journal of International Education in Business, 10*(2), 102–129. doi:10.1108/JIEB-10-2016-0035

Yin, J., Goh, T., Yang, B., & Xiaobin, Y. (2021). Conversation technology with micro-learning: The impact of chatbot-based learning on students' learning motivation and performance. *Journal of Educational Computing Research, 59*(1), 154–177. doi:10.1177/0735633120952067

Yuan, Q., & Gao, Q. (2023). Being there, and being together: Avatar appearance and peer interaction in VR classrooms for video-based learning. *International Journal of Human-Computer Interaction,* 1-21. doi:10.1080/10447318.2023.2189818

Zawacki-Richter, O., Marín, V. I., Bond, M., & Gouverneur, F. (2019). Systematic review of research on artificial intelligence applications in higher education – where are the educators? *International Journal of Educational Technology in Higher Education, 16*(1), 1–27. doi:10.1186/s41239-019-0171-0

Zhang, Y., Stohr, C., Jamsvi, S., & Kabo, J. (2023). Considering the Community of Inquiry Framework in online engineering-a literature review. *Journal of Higher Education Theory and Practice*, *23*(6), 55–68.

Zhou, L., Xue, S., & Li, R. (2022). Extending the Technology Acceptance Model to explore students' intention to use an online education platform at a University in China. *SAGE Open*, *12*(1). doi:10.1177/21582440221085259

Chapter 3
Cooperative Freedoms and Practical Inquiry in an Online Course for Teachers

Gerald Ardito
Manhattanville College, USA

ABSTRACT

This chapter will describe a graduate-level online teacher education course titled "CS for Teachers," which exposed novice teacher candidates to the key concepts of computational thinking, especially abstraction, mostly for the first time. This asynchronous online course was designed to introduce these teacher candidates to these concepts through increasingly challenging projects or "challenges" and to provide the highest levels of autonomy and freedom in meeting these challenges. Student-to-student and student-to-teacher interactions were examined to explore the content and tenor of such interactions throughout the course. This analysis revealed that during the hardest part of these challenges, student-to student interactions dramatically increased and increasingly focused on asking for and providing support to one another in authentic and meaningful ways. Implications for teacher education are explored.

The intention of this book is to suggest ways in which online learning can be humanized. While the phrase "humanized" may have the appearance of being intuitively understandable, for this chapter, I am focusing on a case study which suggests possible ways of recognizing ways in which online learning that has been humanized through the presence or absence of degrees of cooperative freedoms, as defined by Paulsen (2003) and further developed by Dron & Anderson (2014). This chapter will describe a graduate level online teacher education course entitled "CS (Computer Science) for Teachers," which exposed novice teacher candidates in various licensure areas to the key concepts of computational thinking, especially abstraction, mostly for the first time. This asynchronous online course was designed to allow these teacher candidates to experience these concepts through projects of increasingly difficulty or "challenges" and to provide the highest levels of autonomy and freedom in the meeting of these challenges. Student-to-student and student-to-teacher interactions were examined to explore the content and tenor of such interactions throughout the course. This analysis revealed that during the hardest part of

DOI: 10.4018/979-8-3693-0762-5.ch003

these challenges, that student to student interactions dramatically increased and progressively focused on asking for and providing support to one another in authentic and meaningful ways. Implications for teacher education are explored.

CONCEPTUAL FRAMEWORK

The work described in this chapter was developed from a conceptual model that was shaped by two main components: the Community of Inquiry Model by Randy Garrison and his colleagues (Garrison, et al., 1999); and Jon Dron and Terry Anderson's work on Teaching Crowds and Cooperative Freedoms (Dron & Anderson, 2014); Dron, 2007).

Community of Inquiry

Inspired by the work of John Dewey (1959) and Charles Pierce (Klein, 2013), Randy Garrison and his colleagues developed the Community of Inquiry framework (Garrison, Anderson, & Archer, 1999). The Community of Inquiry framework is "a process model of online learning which views the online educational experience as arising from the interaction of three presences – social presence, cognitive presence, and teaching presence," (Swan, Garrison, & Richardson, 2009, p. 44). This model is depicted in Figure 1.

Figure 1. The Community of Inquiry Model
Note: This image was sourced from Wikimedia Commons and was created by Matt Bury, licensed under the Creative Commons Attribution-Share Alike 3.0 Unported license.

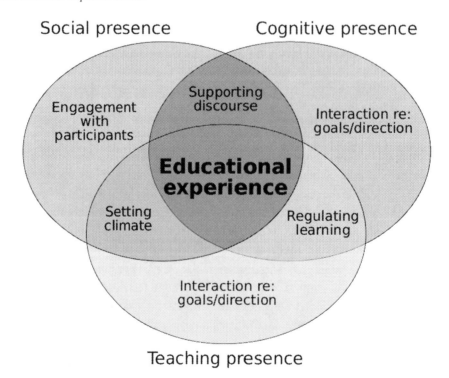

Garrison and his colleagues have further defined each of these presences. *Social presence* is "the degree to which participants in computer-mediated communication *feel* affectively connected one to another," (Swann, et al., 2009, p, 52). *Cognitive presence* is defined as the process of practical inquiry:

Practical inquiry begins with a triggering event in the form of an issue, problem or dilemma that needs resolution. As a result of this event, there is a natural shift to exploration, the search for relevant information that can provide insight into the challenge at hand. As ideas crystallize, there is a move into the third phase – integration -- in which connections are made and there is a search for a viable explanation. Finally, there is a selection and testing (through vicarious or direct application) of the most viable solution and resolution. (Swann, et all, 2009, pp. 50-51)

Teaching presence is defined as "as "the design, facilitation and direction of cognitive and social processes for the purpose of realizing personally meaningful and educationally worthwhile learning outcomes," (Swann, Garrison, and Richardson, 2009, p. 55).

In traditional learning environments, those that are typically teacher centered, the focus is usually on teaching presence (what is happening and how is it happening) and cognitive presence (what are we learning), with *social presence* loosely recognized and tolerated. For example much of the work in teacher education programs in classroom management, for example, focuses on the control of student-to-student interactions such as those teaching strategies that determine when students have or do not have opportunities to respond to the teacher or one another (Haydon, et al., 2012). These types of constraints on student social presence are quite common.

The real innovation of the work of Garrison and his colleagues was to describe and validate the interconnected whole formed by the intersections of these three presences. It was this innovation and intersection that influenced the work described in this chapter.

Cooperative Freedoms and Teaching Crowds

The work described in this chapter was also influenced by the work of Jon Dron and Terry Anderson, especially that detailed in their book *Teaching Crowds: Learning and Social Media* (Dron & Anderson, 2014). Their discussions of cooperative freedoms and designing social learning in social networking software Elgg are outlined in this section.

Cooperative Freedoms. Dron (2007) has described the nature of learning settings to require a balance between freedom and constraint. One framework for powerfully understanding this tension is that developed by Paulsen (2003). In his hexagon of cooperative freedoms, Paulsen (2003) identified 6 kinds of choices that might be available to a learner: *pace* (freedom to determine the rate at which one learns), *time* (freedom to determine when one learns) *place* (freedom to determine where one learns), *content* (freedom to determine what one learns), *medium* (freedom to choose the media used for learning), and *access* (freedom to learn regardless of qualifications or extrinsic obstacles).

Dron and Anderson extended and refined Paulsen's model with a focus on student autonomy. They did this by removing *access* and adding an additional five facets: *technology* (freedom to choose the tools and systems with which one learns); *method* (freedom to choose the pedagogical approach and pattern of learning); *relationship* (freedom to choose with whom one learns and how to engage with them); *delegation* (freedom to choose whether and when to choose or to allow someone else to make the choices, noting that this relates to the support aspect of autonomy); and *disclosure* (freedom to decide what and to whom it is revealed, noting that this relates to the level and extent of sharing with others). Their revised model of cooperative freedoms is depicted in Figure 2.

Teaching Crowds via Elgg. The second major inspiration for the work described in this chapter was the work of John Dron and Terry Anderson at Athabasca University. Their book, *Teaching Crowds*, described the development of a social network for the university which they referred to as Athabasca Landing. Their goal was to provide a setting in which each member of the University (professors, students, administrators, and staff) had an equal voice in a social community. As Dron and Anderson wrote:

While the early 2000s saw many social software systems emerge, from its inception Elgg had some distinguishing features that separated it from the crowd, at least partly due to its evolution within the context of research into online learning. Chief among these was an extremely fine-grained, bottom-up set of access controls. There is no single privacy setting that meets the needs of all potential users. What for one user is an inherent right to free expression and an important way to build social capital through creation of an online identity is for others an invasion of privacy. Moreover, these settings must be dynamic, as one blog message may be thoughtfully restricted to a circle of tight friends, or for a teacher, while the next might be addressed to a network, and a fourth meant for reading across the Internet. Thus, each user (and notably not just the teacher) should be afforded the capacity to set the permissions level on everything they create. (pp. 239-240)

Effectively, in Elgg, Dron and Anderson found a set of tools that could operationalize their insights about cooperative freedoms and how they could be combined to enhance the learning and engagement of students.

Figure 2. Decagon of Cooperative Freedoms
Note: This figure from Dron & Anderson, 2014) is used with permission.

What I took from their work was both the vision for a very open learning community as well as the specific application of Elgg social networking software to build an alternative to the Blackboard learning management system then at use at the university at which I was then teaching. The combination of conceptual framework for learning and the implementation of technological tools that could support that conceptual framework was tremendously empowering. My goal was to develop a learning setting in which I would be able to allow for the nuanced interrelationships described in the Community of Inquiry framework and to maximize the degrees of cooperative freedoms defined by Paulen and Dron & Anderson in order to provide the teachers and teacher candidates with whom I was working a learning environment more like the one I hoped they would design for their current and future students.

THE CASE STUDY

In this section, I will describe the course I designed, CS for Teachers, for teachers and teacher candidates enrolled in a graduate program in Educational Technology, and my implementation of Elgg social networking software for this course. The students were teachers and teacher candidates in ad variety of licensure areas seeking an additional license in Educational Technology in a Masters program.

CS (Computer Science) for Teachers, an asynchronous online course, focused on engaging these teachers and teacher candidates in a variety of learning activities that had several goals: 1) introduce course participants to the history of computer science in education, through reading and responding to influential texts readings (Read and Respond activity); 2) learn a programming language – HTML or Python – and maintain a learning log of their experiences in so doing (Learning Log activity; 3) programming robots to solve a set of increasingly difficult challenges (Robot Coding activity); and 4) reflecting on the process of learning in this open course design (Reflection activity).

Consistent with the work of Paulsen and Dron & Anderson, these activities were designed in ways to maximize the degrees of cooperative freedoms available to them as they were learning. The work of each activity specified the learning outcomes expected, but students were allowed to pursue those learning objectives in ways that were relevant, meaningful, and useful to them. Via the Elgg based social learning platform, course participants were encouraged to interact with each other in various ways. They could post blogs, photos, videos, and links, as well as comment on each other's posts. The platform emphasized openness and gave participants multiple options to express themselves and communicate through different media. Additionally, as mentioned by Dron & Anderson (2014), Elgg offered sophisticated and flexible security settings, allowing users to have fine-tuned control over everything that they shared.

In order to understand how these students responded to this unique course and its autonomy supportive design, student-to-student and student-to-instructor interactions were captured from the learning platform and analyzed using two different methods. The first, *social network analysis*, was used to investigate the types of social networks that formed within each of these four learning activities. The second, *textual content analysis*, was used to explore the content of what these students wrote in their interactions during each of the four learning activities.

We will begin by looking at some of the descriptive statistics from the interactions contained within each of the four learning activities. These are presented in Table 1.

These descriptive statistics reveal some trends regarding the patterns of interaction in the course as a whole and during the four key learning activities. First, students accounted for 83% of the total interactions that occurred during these four learning activities, contrasted with just 17% of the total interactions

Table 1. Descriptive statistics of interactions during each key learning activity in the course

Key Learning Activity	# Student Posts	% Student Posts	# Instructor Posts	% Instructor Posts	Total Posts
Learning Log	46	79%	12	21%	58
Read/Respond	130	87%	20	13%	150
Reflection	14	50%	14	50%	28
Robot Coding	151	86%	24	14%	175
Totals	341	83%	70	17%	411

belonging to the instructor. This is one way of identifying a student centered learning environment. Next, we can see that the most number of interactions occurred during the Robot Coding, the next most during the Read/Respond Activity, the next most during the Learning Lot activity, and the fewest occurred during the Reflection activity. This simple ranking of interaction frequency shows a strong positive relationship between the number of interactions and the degrees of cooperative freedom designed into each activity, with the Reflection activity (compose and post your reflection) having the least degrees of freedom and interaction, and the Robot Coding activity (write programs for your computer than meets each of the three challenges in any way that makes sense to you), having the highest degrees of freedom and interaction.

Social Network Analysis

Social network analysis examined the connections between course participants as derived from their interactions in this online course by analyzing closeness centrality, which measures relative proximity between nodes (in this case, students and their instructor) in a network (Borgatti, et al., 2009). Additionally, to improve the clarity of the social graphs, a Fruchterman and Reingold force-directed placement algorithm was employed (Fruchterman & Reingold, 1991). The visual representations of these social networks were created using SocNetV, a tool designed for social network visualization.

In general, social network graphs are either more centralized (one central node with connections between that node and each of the others) or more decentralized (there is no central node and each node has multiple connections with other nodes. Additionally, social network graphs are either less dense (fewer close connections between nodes) or more dense (more close connections between nodes).

The visualizations generated for each of the four key learning activities are displayed in Figures 3-6. ;; and A discussion of these visualizations are provided after Figure 6,

Figure 3 depicts the social network for the Read/Respond activity. This social graph identifies a set of two larger social networks within the larger class, as well as a couple of students who interacted only with the instructor.

Figure 4 depicts the social network for the Learning Log activity. This social graph depicts a set of smaller social networks comprised of about three students each within the larger class.

Figure 5 depicts the social network for the Robot Coding activity. This social graph depicts a far more complex social network that any of the other three.

Finally, Figure 6 depicts the social network for the Reflection activity. This social graph depicts, unlike the other three, interactions that primarily took place between each student and the instructor, with no student-to-student interactions.

We can see that the social graph for the Reflection learning activity is the most centralized and the least dense. This is a reflection of the fact that each student posted only one reflection which was com-

Figure 3. Social Network Graph for the Read/Respond Learning Activity

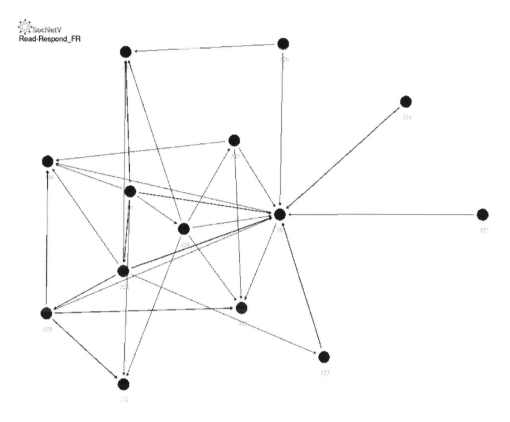

Figure 4. Social Network Graph for the Learning Log Learning Activity

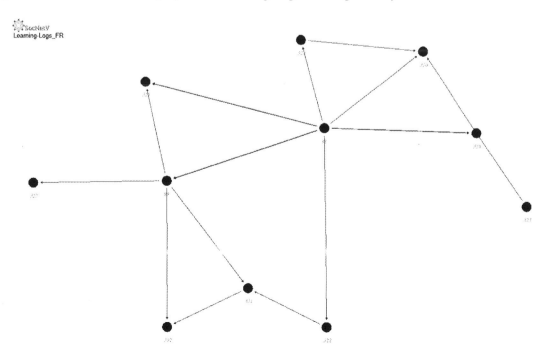

Figure 5. Social Network Graph for the Robot Coding Learning Activity

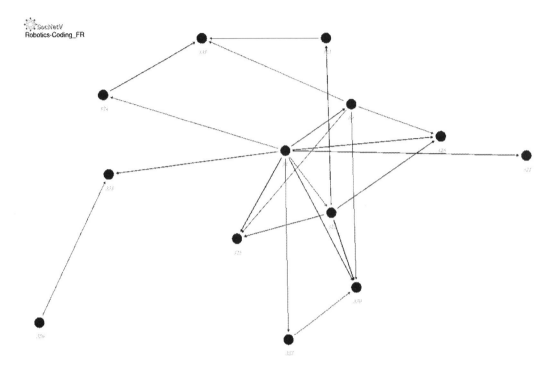

Figure 6. Social Network Graph for the Reflection Learning Activity

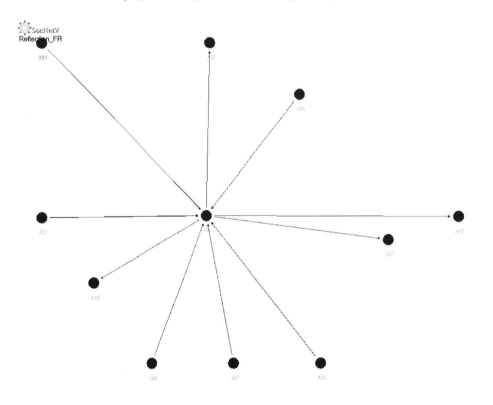

mented upon only only by the instructor. The social graph for the Learning Log activity is slightly less centralized and slightly more dense, reflecting that students posted their own work to which the instructor responded (as in the Reflection activity) and students to a limited degree responded to the work of one another. The social graph for the Read/Respond activity is still more decentralized and even more dense, reflecting on the discussion between students that took place as they interacted with the various texts (and one another). Finally, the social graph for the Robot Coding activity depicts the largest degree of decentralization along with the highest level of density, reflecting that students engaged in interactions with a larger number of their classmates. In fact, unlike in any of the other learning activities, as we shall discover below, these student interactions were largely comprised of requests for help from their classmates, and offers of help to their classmates, as they worked through the various robotics challenges.

Textual Content Analysis

There are many methods for performing textual content analysis, from various coding methods and schemes to the use of computational tools to "read" text based data (Dearing, 2023; Shaffer, 2017). For this case study, computations tools were use to examine word frequencies and other features of the course interactions in order to discern patterns that would shed further light on the ways that these patterns differed across the four key learning activities.

The first of these textual analyses was performed using a textual analysis software, Voyant-Tools (Sinclair & Rockwell, 2016). Voyant-Tools offers a wide variety of tools for investigating texts in all kinds of ways. For this analysis, I used the Trends tool, which visualizes the frequency of an-investigator selected set of terms within a document or across a set of documents. The result of this analysis is depicted in Figure 7. The terms examined for this visualization were ones very commonly used across the sets of interactions involving all four key learning activities, namely: *programming*, *learning*, and the wildcards *think**, *robot**, and *feel**. In the case of the wildcards, the analysis included any words that begin with the root. For example, *robot** included: *robot, robots,* and *robotics.* Since each form of the word in these wildcards are inherently related, they are legitimately and productively used here.

Some interesting patterns emerged from this visualization. First, despite the students reporting elsewhere various kinds of feelings (excitement, anxiety, and frustration), they rarely used any version of the term in their interactions. Second, the words *programming* and *learning* were used in the same ways across the four learning activities, strongly suggesting that they occurred together, as in the phrases *learning programming* or *learning to program.* Additionally, the relative frequencies of these two words peak during the Learning Logs activity in which students were learning to program, then falls during the Robot Coding activity (in which they were learning to program their robot, but not discussing it in those terms – more about this finding below), and then rises again in the Reflections activity as the students reflected upon their learning to program. Lastly, the term *think** is used most frequently during the Read-Respond learning activity, then dips across the Learning Log and Robot Coding activities, and then re-emerging during the Reflection activity. This pattern makes intuitive sense, as the students were reporting on how the authors they read thought about various topics, and then reflected on their own thinking as they reflected on their work during the course. It is worth noting that while they certainly were thinking during the Learning Logs and Robot Coding activities, they did not talk about having done so directly.

Other computational tools were used to perform additional textual analyses on the student interactions in this course. The R programming language was designed, and is extensively used, to achieve all

Figure 7. Voyant-Tools Assisted Analysis of Word Frequency Trends Across Course Interactions

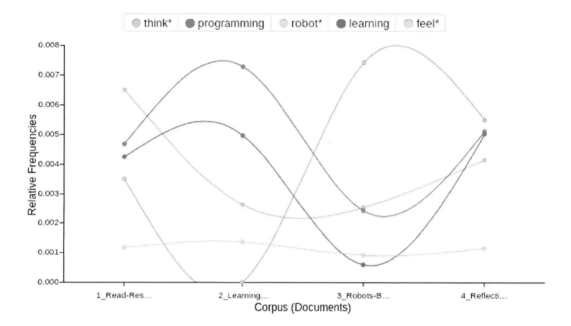

manner of statistical analyses. A group of tools have been developed to conduct textual analysis in R. These tools, referred to as *tidytools*, were used in this case study (Silge & Robinson, 2017).

Initially, I used tidytools to determine the term frequency (tf), or how often a term is used in a document. In this case, the document was the set of interactions for each of the four key learning activities. The visualizations for the term frequencies revealed in each of these learning activities are depicted in Figures 8 through 11. In each, the five most commonly used terms used in the interactions are represented.

These visualizations reveal an interesting pattern. In many ways, the five most common terms found in each of the four learning activities reflect the work designed for each, as well as the process the students were engaged in. For example, the texts assigned in the Read/Respond activity discussed the history of computer science in education, and so it is appropriate that the course interactions favored the terms *students* and *learning* (as in student learning), and *computers* and *science* (as in computer science). Additionally, the levels of frequency for each show a consistency of these ideas (terms) across the majority of all student interactions. This pattern also holds for the other learning activities. The Learning Log activity, in which the students learned either to code in HTML or Python is primarily represented by the terms *programming*, *learning*, *code*, and *python*, which we would expect, and *students*, which was used as applications to classrooms were discussed, such as: "What I'm finding that would be useful for students is the problem solving and creative thinking aspect of programming." The Robot Coding activity was represented by terms directly related to the work the students were doing: *robot*, *code*, *program*, and *mbot* (the type of robot with which they were working), and then time, which is often used to described their coding process, as in "I'm still working out the coding part because my bot seems to go rogue all the time."

The interesting symmetry of these findings suggests a coherence between the intended work of the course and experience of the course, as revealed through the student interactions both within each of the

Figure 8. Term Frequency for the Read/Respond Learning Activity

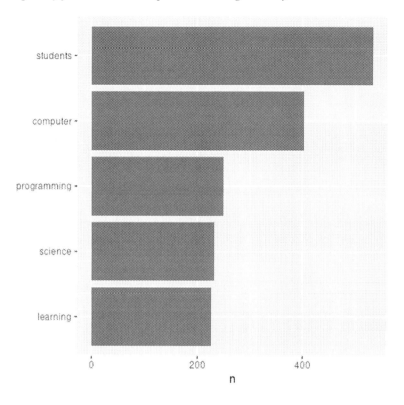

Figure 9. Term Frequency for the Learning Log Learning Activity

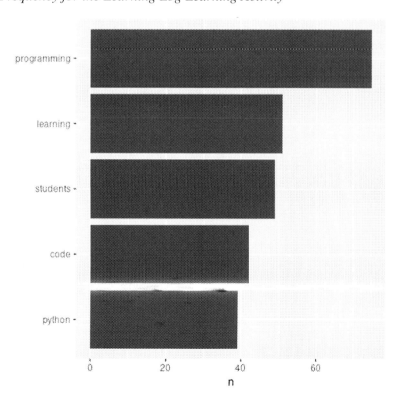

Figure 10. Term Frequency for the Robot Coding Learning Activity

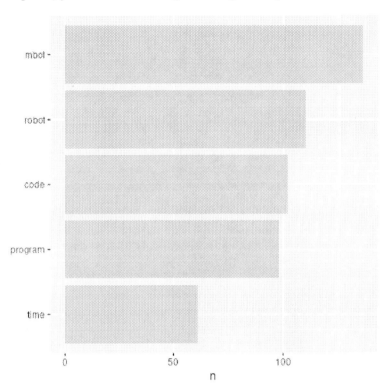

Figure 11. Term Frequency for the Reflection Learning Activity

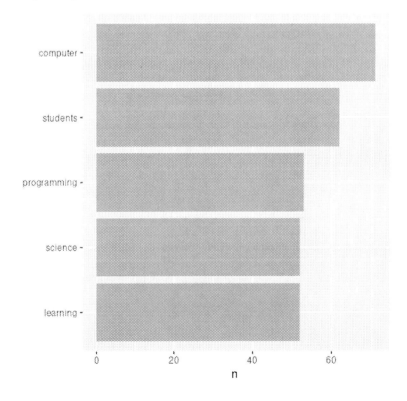

learning activities – the students were discussing most frequently those things that each of the learning activities were designed to address – as well as across the course as a whole. In some ways, I believe that this coherence is representative of a deeply human process of learning.

The tidytools were also used to explore another dimension of these four documents, inverse document frequency (idf), "which decreases the weight for commonly used words and increases the weight for words that are not used very much in a collection of documents. This can be combined with term frequency to calculate a term's *tf-idf* (the two quantities multiplied together), the frequency of a term adjusted for how rarely it is used" (Silge & Robinson, 2017, p. 31). This type of analysis allows us to discover the uniqueness of terms used in and across documents. The analysis of *tf-idf* for the interactions in each of the four learning activities in depicted in Figure 12.

This type of analysis provides interesting detail and color to our understanding of what is being addressed in the interactions associated with each of these learning activities. In the Read/Respond activity (upper right), we can see with much more granularity what the students were writing about. We can see a set of authors and key figures in computer science and education *papert, manovich,* and *kay*), key concepts (*digital, media, educational*), as well as process terms (*lack,* as in "Manovich focuses on the lack of change when it comes to the syntax in technology, similarly in education there is a lack of change when it comes to the students' knowledge"). We can also see more depth in the interactions around the Learning Logs activity in terms of both tools (*html, condition, language,* and *unix*) and process (missing,

Figure 12. Term Frequency/Inverse Term Frequency (tf-idf) for the Interactions in Each Learning Activity

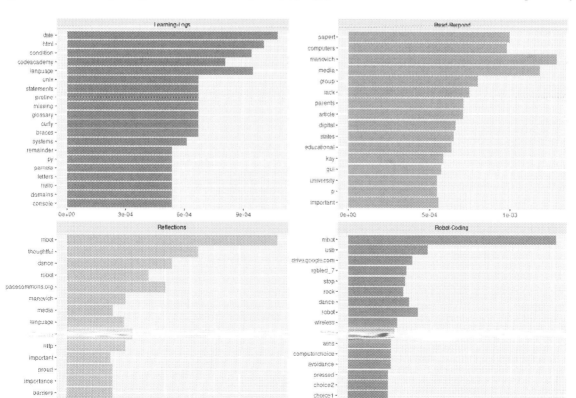

as in "I feel like an all star, because I spotted the missing *if* [statement] after an error message without being prompted," and date, as in "I noticed that the date was written with the year, month, then date. Why is that?"). In the Robot Coding activity, these terms reveal a much more rich world of the student experience as they programmed there robots, in operational terms such as *mbot, usb, robot, dance* (one of the challenges), *wireless,* and *wins* (referring to the robot race challenge), operational terms such as *mbot, usb,* and *robot,* as well as process terms such as *rgbled-7* (an operator in their coding); *rock, dance,* and *avoidance* (parts of the dance challenge); and *drive.google.com* (they shared their work via Google Docs). Finally, this analysis of the interactions in the Reflections activity expanded our understanding of the depth of their reflections in both concrete terms, such as *mbot, dance, robot,* and *manovich;* as well as process/feeling terms, such as *reflection, proud,* and *importance.*

In addition to the computationally guided textual content analysis, more traditional coding was done on these interactions data in order to discover trends and patterns in the ways that the instructor and students interacted with one another during these learning activities (Shaffer, 2017). In this case, a small set of codes was established to describe the nature of the ways that students responded to one another's work during the four key learning activities of the course. This code book is described in Table 2.

The codes were designed to capture two dimensions of student interaction: 1) the extent of the feedback left for one student by another; and 2) the degree of asking for/offering support by one student from another. The results of this coding are depicted in Table 3.

Table 2. Interaction Code Book

Code	Description	Example
FED	Student provided extended feedback to another student	Thanks for your thoughtful reflection. And I am particularly glad you had this experience.
AH	Student asked a question of another student	Did that come up automatically? I don't get that option and I cannot connect at all to my computer through the USB.
AQ	Student answered question asked by another student	Try opening your system preferences on your computer and under security, you can allow programs from untrusted sources

Table 3. Interaction Coding Results

Learning Activity	AQ	AQ %	AH	AH %	FED	FED %	Total
Read/Respond	1	4.5%	0	0.0%	52	53.1%	53
Learning Log	0	0.0%	2	15.4%	25	25.5%	27
Robot Coding	21	95.5%	11	84.6%	21	21.4%	53
Reflection	0	0.0%	0	0.0%	15	15.3%	15
Total	22		13		98		133

This coding made some patterns of interaction within and across the four learning activities visible. Students engaged in the highest amounts of extended feedback (FED) during the Read/Respond activity, and the least during the Reflection activity. This tracks with the course work in those activities as designed. During the Read/Response activity, students were invited and encouraged to interact with one another as they explored the various assigned texts, hence the increased levels of interactions. However, they were not specifically instructed to leave extended feedback for one another; this phenomenon emerged organically as the students posted their work. The Reflection activity was designed as a culminating experience for the course and was due right at the end of the term, hence the limited amount of feedback from other students. The only meaningful feedback in these interactions took place between the instructor and student on that student's final work. Sitting in between these two poles are the lowish levels of extended feedback during the Learning Log and Robot Coding activities. One thing of note is that about 15% of the coded interactions during the Learning Log activity were students asking questions (AH) about the programming work in HTML or Python. Since none of the students offered help during this, we can conclude that these questions were addressed by the instructor. It is worth noting that their programming work in this learning activity was individual in nature, both in terms of being and individual project and in the fact that they individually chose the programming language they wanted to learn.

This coding revealed something extremely interesting as occurring during the Robot Coding activity. During this activity, students were working to program their robots to meet challenges of increasing difficulty. In the first challenge, students worked to learn the basics of programming their robots. In the second challenge, they engaged in the Dance Challenge, during which they were asked to write a program that choreographed a dance performed by their robot, which included using data collected by one or more of the robots' sensors to trigger some of the dance. In the last challenge, the Dealer's Choice Challenge, the students were asked to go more deeply into what they had already learned about programming their robots and to design and meet a challenge of their own.

During this learning activity, we can see via the coding textual content analysis that a unique form of interaction has arisen. Instead of merely posting their work and even leaving extended feedback on one another's work, they consistently asked for help. 85% of their coded interactions fell into this AH category. More interestingly, the help they received came from other students. Almost 96% of the coded interactions during this learning activity involved students offering help to and answering questions from their colleagues (AQ). It is important to note that these interactions arose naturally; the students were never asked or encouraged to reach out to one another.

DISCUSSION AND IMPLICATIONS

The goal of this chapter has been to present a case study which I believe demonstrates that online learning can be humanized or at least made more open. This asynchronous online course, CS for Teachers, was taken by teachers and teacher candidates in a Masters program focused on educational technology. It is now time to discuss the findings of this case study and their implications for humanizing online learning. This discussion will focus on the course design, the social learning platform developed for this course, and the analysis of the interactions between students and their instructor during the course.

This course was designed to maximize the degrees of cooperative freedoms outlined by Paulsen (2003) and Dron & Anderson (2014). Students had a large degree of freedom in the areas of *pace, time, medium, place, relationship, disclosure, technology,* and *method.* They had a good degree of control as to where, when, how, with whom, and with which tools they engaged in the work of the course. They had less control over *content* and *delegation*, which were more tightly governed by the instructor.

Also fundamental to the design of the course was the use of Practical Inquiry, as articulated by Garrison, Anderson, & Archer (2001). The design of especially the Learning Log and Robot Coding activities met their criteria: Practical inquiry begins with a triggering event in the form of an issue, problem or dilemma that needs resolution. As a result of this event, there is a natural shift to exploration, the search for relevant information that can provide insight into the challenge at hand. As ideas crystallize, there is a move into the third phase – integration -- in which connections are made and there is a search for a viable explanation" (Swann, Garrison, and Richardson, 2009, pp. 50-51). It is important to note that this idea of inquiry was also central to the Read/Respond activity (as students were asked to engage powerfully and meaningfully with a variety of texts) and the Reflection activity (as student were asked to engage powerfully and meaningfully with their own learning in the course). However, these two activities were more cognitively focused and less "hands-on." This design component maps to both *teaching presence* (organization of the course) and *cognitive presence* (engagement in practical inquiry) as described by Garrison and his colleagues as part of the Community of Inquiry framework (Garrison, Anderson, & Archer, 1999).

The various analyses of the course interactions, in terms of both social network and textual content analyses, shed led light on the *social presence* in this course. The findings from the social network analysis demonstrate that during those activities in which there was the highest degree of practical inquiry, the Learning Log and Robot Coding activities, there were the densest and most decentralized social networks, and that the opposite was observed during the Read/Respond and Reflection activities, which involved practical inquiry but in different ways. In these two activities, the inquiry was primarily intellectual, as students responded to a set of text during the Read/Respond activity, and to their own learning in the Reflection activity. It is important to note that these distinct social networks arose organically and not as a result of instructor direction or behavior.

The findings from the various textual content analyses also provide insight into the students' *cognitive* and *social presence* in the course. The two sets of word frequency analyses, both term frequency and inverse term frequency (*tf-itf*), demonstrate that student interactions clearly and consistently reflected the cognitive nature and expectations for each learning experience. For example, the most frequent terms found in the Learning Log activity, in which the students learned either to code in HTML or Python were *programming, learning, code,* and *python.* Additionally, the *tf-idf* analyses revealed the depth, color, and nuance of this cognitive presence, as when both product and process terms were discovered in the interactions across each of the course learning activities.

Through this case study, we can identify the humannizing of online learning to encompass two key principles. The first is: work to increase the relative degrees of cooperative freedoms available to students in the course. The instructor and/or instructional designer can operationalize this principle by reviewing the decagon of cooperative freedoms developed by Dron & Anderson (and inspired by Paulsen's original hexagon) in order to identify opportunities to thoughtfully increase relative degrees of cooperative freedoms within the course where possible and practical. The second key principal is: work to increase the amount and degree of Practical Inquiry within the course. The instructor and/or instructional designer should make profitable use of the Community of Inquiry framework developed by Garrison and his colleagues in order to support higher levels of the social presence and cognitive presence available in the course. In this case study, this was primarily accomplished through the use of challenges (tasks of increasingly levels of complexity) which engaged the students deeply in the key concepts of skills of the course.

I strongly believe that the successful implementation of these two key principles – the degree of cooperative freedoms and a course design focused on practical inquiry – werefundamental to the emergence of the strong student-centered social presence that emerged in this course and that this social presence is essential to humanizing online learning.n my present work, I am continuing to deepen, refine, and extend these insights.

REFERENCES

Borgatti, S. P., Mehra, A., Brass, D. J., & Labianca, G. (2009). Network analysis in the social sciences. *Science*, *323*(5916), 892–895. doi:10.1126/science.1165821 PMID:19213908

Dearing, V. A. (2023). *Manual of textual analysis*. Univ of California Press. doi:10.2307/jj.8306194

Dewey, J. (1959). My pedagogic creed. In J. Dewey (Ed.), *Dewey on education* (pp. 19–32). Teachers College, Columbia University. (Original work published 1897)

Dron, J. (Ed.). (2007). *Control And constraint in e-learning: Choosing When to choose: choosing when to choose*. IGI Global. doi:10.4018/978-1-59904-390-6

Dron, J., & Anderson, T. (2014). *Teaching crowds: Learning and social media*. Athabasca University Press.

Fruchterman, T. M. J., & Reingold, E. M. (1991). Graph drawing by force-directed placement. *Software, Practice & Experience*, *21*(11), 1129–1164. doi:10.1002/spe.4380211102

Garrison, D. R., Anderson, T., & Archer, W. (1999). Critical inquiry in a text-based environment: Computer conferencing in higher education. *The Internet and Higher Education*, *2*(2-3), 87–105. doi:10.1016/S1096-7516(00)00016-6

Garrison, D. R., Anderson, T., & Archer, W. (2001). Critical thinking, cognitive presence, and computer conferencing in distance education. *American Journal of Distance Education*, *15*(1), 7–23. doi:10.1080/08923640109527071

Garrison, D. R., & Baynton, M. (1987). Beyond independence in distance education: The concept of control. *American Journal of Distance Education*, *1*(3), 3–15. doi:10.1080/08923648709526593

Haydon, T., Macsuga-Gage, A. S., Simonsen, B., & Hawkins, R. (2012). Opportunities to respond: A key component of effective instruction. *Beyond Behavior*, *22*(1), 23–31. doi:10.1177/107429561202200105

Klein, A. (2013). Who Is in the Community of Inquiry? *Transactions of the Charles S. Peirce Society*, *49*(3), 413–423.

Paulsen, M. F. (2003). *Online education and learning management systems: Global e-learning in a Scandinavian perspective*. NKI Forlaget.

Shaffer, D. (2017). *Quantitative ethnology*. Cathcart Press.

Silge, J., & Robinson, D. (2017). *Text mining with R: A tidy approach*. O'Reilly Media, Inc.

Sinclair, S., & Rockwell, G. (2016). *Voyant Tools.* https://voyant-tools.org/

Swan, K., Garrison, D. R., & Richardson, J. C. (2009). A constructivist approach to online learning: the Community of Inquiry framework. In C. R. Payne (Ed.), *Information Technology and Constructivism in Higher Education: Progressive Learning Frameworks* (pp. 43–57). IGI Global. doi:10.4018/978-1-60566-654-9.ch004

Chapter 4
Humanizing the Online Doctoral Experience With High-Impact Faculty Engagement and Mentorship

Clara Hauth
https://orcid.org/0000-0002-1104-8523
Marymount University, USA

Ruth Boyd
https://orcid.org/0000-0002-9483-3737
Marymount University, USA

Jennifer Crystle
https://orcid.org/0000-0002-9242-8906
Marymount University, USA

Jennifer Thompson
https://orcid.org/0009-0004-4169-8115
Marymount University, USA

Shannon L. Melideo
https://orcid.org/0009-0003-5880-4327
Marymount University, USA

ABSTRACT

This chapter describes two of the best practices an asynchronous EdD program for educational leadership and organizational innovation program employs to humanize the online course space for its doctoral program. The researchers discuss the origins and development of the continuous weekly support (CWS) model and the lead doctoral faculty mentor (LDFM) program, which are two pillars of the student experience in the online doctoral program. A comprehensive analysis of the technological integrations, frequency of communication, and various messaging techniques are discussed. Additional data is shared regarding a thorough examination of the lead doctoral faculty mentor (LDFM) role, incorporating data from a recently completed institutional research project. The hope is that by sharing these practices, other institutions of higher education may modify and incorporate similar high-impact practices of their own, thereby increasing student persistence, retention, and degree completion, specifically in virtual program environments.

DOI: 10.4018/979-8-3693-0762-5.ch004

Building and sustaining an engaging, interactive, and supportive environment for online adult learners can be daunting. Research reminds us that humanizing coursework and supporting students in an online program cannot be single-dimensional, but that it must be multi-faceted and consider the full scope of the student experience (Berry, 2017; Rockinson-Szapkiw et al., 2019). As noted by Kuh et al. (2010), leadership in higher education can make student success an institutional priority with a clearly established vision. In the design of Marymount University's online Doctor of Education (EdD) program for launch in Fall 2020, program leadership and faculty envisioned and designed multiple support structures to ensure doctoral students' success, specifically in the online environment. These supports included the establishment of student cohort groups, standardization of course design and mentorship support, and online community-building through synchronous office hours, teaching sessions, Learning Management System (LMS) tools, and social gatherings. Additionally, the program engages in a thorough matching process to provide each student with a Lead Doctoral Faculty Mentor (LDFM) who guides the doctoral student through the Dissertation in Practice (DiP) process. The LDFM is matched with the doctoral student early in their doctoral journey so that a collaborative mentor-mentee relationship may be established and honed throughout the program. This chapter describes in detail best practices the program employs to humanize the online course space and dissertation process. We discuss the origins and development of the Continuous Weekly Support (CWS) model and the LDFM program, which are two pillars of the student experience in the online doctoral program. First, an overview of online community-building strategies will be presented, along with research findings and a comprehensive analysis of the technological integrations, frequency of communication, and various messaging techniques used. Second, a thorough examination of the faculty mentor (LDFM) role will be examined, incorporating data from various institutional research projects. The hope is that by sharing these practices, other institutions of higher education may modify and incorporate similar high-impact practices of their own, thereby increasing student persistence, retention, and degree completion, specifically in virtual program environments.

BACKGROUND

Accredited by the Southern Associations of Colleges and Schools Commission on Colleges (SAC-SCOC), Marymount University awards doctoral, master's, bachelor's degrees, and non-degree seeking certificates. The School of Education launched the online Doctor of Education in Educational Leadership and Organizational Innovation in the fall semester of 2020. After enrolling an initial cohort of 42 students, the EdD program has grown to an enrollment of over 263 students for the Fall 2023 census. As the program has grown in enrollment, we also celebrate the diverse cohorts that we have been able to recruit, enroll, and retain in the program. As of the Fall 2023 enrollment reports, our student body is composed of individuals from thirty-seven states, Lebanon, and Japan. Beyond geographic diversity, we pride ourselves on the diversity of lived experiences, with students entrenched in career fields of education, business, non-profit, the arts, government, and healthcare.

Demographic data reveals the racial and ethnic diversity of our cohorts as well. According to Fall 2023 enrollment data, less than half (47.1%) of our student population identifies as white (*Figure 1*) and eighty percent identify as female (*Figure 2*).

This diversity, coupled with the socialization into academia (Gardner, 2010), offers opportunities for those in the program, including faculty, to continuously challenge their thinking while gaining and providing new perspectives alongside peers. Prioritizing and celebrating differing backgrounds of a

Figure 1. Marymount University EdD Program Race and Ethnicity (Cohorts 1-6)

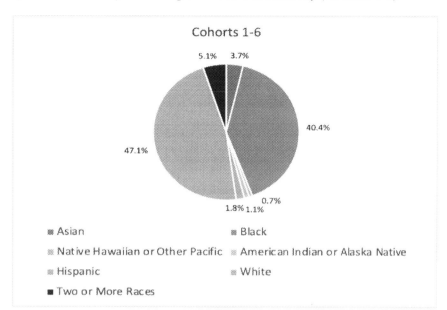

Figure 2. Marymount University EdD Program Gender (Cohorts 1-6)

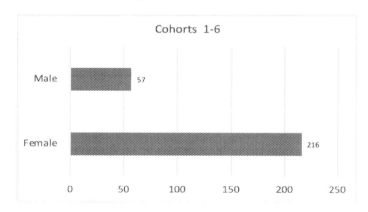

diverse student body works in conjunction with our CWS model to create a sense of community and belonging for the students in the doctoral program.

In 2021, a year after it officially launched, Marymount's EdD program was accepted into the Carnegie Project on the Education Doctorate (CPED). This affiliation enables the institution to collaborate within a consortium of over 130 colleges and schools of education to meet its mission - to accentuate the scholarly practice of professionals serving as organizational thought leaders, higher education professionals, and leaders in the fields of education, government, public service, non-profit, and for-profit sectors (Marymount University, 2021). The framework provided by CPED allows for the EdD program to develop its core supports through the alignment of the guiding principles (CPED, 2021). These core supports are further aided through the pre-constructed and standardized course design. Courses are developed and delivered asynchronously to allow students, most of whom are working professionals, to study at a pace that helps them balance other aspects of their lives and work. This asynchronous model is coupled with two to four recorded live synchronous content sessions, two cohort socials, and accessible faculty office hours for students. This course design enables faculty to offer individualized attention, participate in a high-touch process, and implement the CWS model.

Since the inception of the program, the LDFM program was designed to offer additional student touchpoints and scaffolded support through the progression of the research and dissertation process. The dissertation process can be lonely for online students (Roberts & Hyatt, 2018), especially if it is not scaffolded, integrated into coursework, and approached through effective mentorship practices. The sections below further detail both the online community building and the high-impact faculty mentorship program that come together to humanize the online doctoral student experience.

Providing Pillars of Support for Online Doctoral Students

In the online EdD in Educational Leadership and Organizational Innovation program, we strategically layered support structures to increase student engagement to maximize student persistence and completion. The program pairs the CWS model of online faculty with the support of the LDFM, and together these high-touch interactions humanize the online experience, creating multiple "safety-nets" to catch students who may be struggling to connect or who are failing to thrive in the online environment. According to Pacansky-Brock et al. (2020), the humanized online experience places faculty-student relationships at the center, and these identified layered faculty supports serve "as the connective tissue between students, engagement, and rigor" (p. 2). The pillars of high-touch faculty engagement and mentorship practices come together to humanize the online doctoral experience by integrating four interwoven principles: building trust, intentional presence, student awareness, and empathy (Pacansky-Brock, 2020).

Building on intentional engagement and presence, there is integrated support to ensure that students in the program stay informed, have the capability to plan by knowing what is on the horizon for them, and have designed avenues to access support for non-course related questions. As part of the framework for the program, the students are assigned an academic advisor who assists them with planning their courses from the beginning of the program. Students also have access to an in-depth review of what lies ahead through an interactive Student Support LMS course outlining the happenings of each semester. The administrative office also hosts weekly office hours so students have a dedicated time to reach someone live to answer any questions relating to their studies that are not course specific. These office hours and an open discussion board on the Student Support LMS site also help to humanize the online experience, as they serve as connection points for peers to gather and meet other doctoral students and candidates outside of their respective course sections and cohorts. Furthermore, students have the opportunity to engage in additional supplemental live online sessions and asynchronous modules through our program's Write Up! Institute. This is a place where students can gain practical advice to help them in their transformation from doctoral professionals to scholarly, and research-based practitioners (Azevedo et al., 2023).

Doctoral persistence and completion are already challenges in many traditional campus-based programs, and these setbacks can be further exacerbated in an online environment (Rigler et al., 2017). This chapter describes how each of these high-impact pillars support and frame the structure of the online doctoral experience (see *Figure 3*). Just as a structure cannot stand on a single pillar, student support must rely on multiple pillars to ensure a sound structural design for the online doctoral student experience.

Figure 3. Marymount University EdD Program Pillar Model

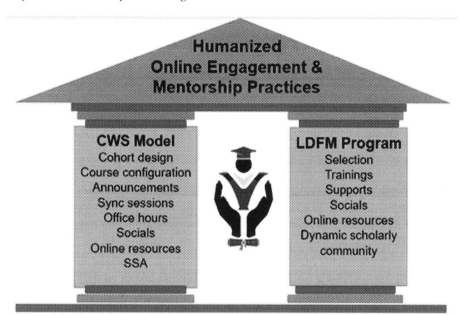

Continuous Weekly Support Model: Intentionality in Design

Effective community building in learning environments has long been touted as an impactful influence on student success (Brown & Burdsal, 2012; Kaufman, 2015; Kuh, 2001; Rilger et al., 2017). As online doctoral programs have emerged with vigor in the last 20 years, the academic community has found that virtual learners specifically need to develop this sense of community, whether participating in a synchronous or asynchronous format to help ensure successful completion of the degree. In fact, research has shown us that feelings of isolation, integration, and the paradox of learning alone, yet collaborating together, have contributed to the high attrition rate of 50-70% in online doctoral programs (Bawa, 2016; Heyman, 2010; Holder, 2007; Kuhn, 2015; Rovai, 2002; Smith, 2010; Terrell et al., 2009). Part-time doctoral students are at further risk of isolation and loneliness in their online studies due to the decreased nature of their weekly engagement as opposed to full-time candidates. Cultivating a community of learners requires time, extensive effort, and diligence.

Providing the environment for a healthy, successful community of online learners requires extensive forethought and planning. Garrison et al. (2001) first described the Community of Inquiry model as a conceptual framework that showcases how social, cognitive, and teaching presences can result in "...a worthwhile educational experience ..." We found these elements easily applicable to our online, asynchronous doctoral program. Awareness of and appreciation for the Community of Inquiry model served foundational to the humanizing of our EdD program curriculum content and experiences.

The first pillar contributing to the humanization of our online spaces is the CWS model. The impetus of CWS is to foster a sense of social belonging among online doctoral students, a crucial element to doctoral program engagement. Our goal is to provide opportunities for students to establish their social and cognitive presence, for teachers to build their teaching presence, and to strengthen student-student relationships as well as student-instructor relationships (Graham et al., 2023; Kumar et al,, 2011; Studebaker & Curtis, 2021). Our program is intentional about incorporating multiple andragogical strategies, including the use of LMS announcements and synchronous opportunities we termed sync sessions, socials, and office hours, in order to promote peer interaction and strengthen students' sense of community (Berry, 2017). It is important to note that our students are scheduled to take two courses per semester. The instructors of these companion courses collaboratively schedule these synchronous elements so that each week, a live, interactive element is available to students to further cultivate a sense of belonging.

Weekly Course Announcements

Faculty members create productive academic environments by providing consistent communication with students about course-level and program-level topics (Kumar et al., 2011). Prioritizing the use of the LMS announcement feature is an efficient means of directing asynchronous communication and is a small, yet essential first step, for faculty members in establishing their teaching presence each week (Garrison et al., 2001). This feature provides a one-stop-shop for students, as faculty post weekly announcements introducing the next lesson, provide reminders about synchronous meeting opportunities with their corresponding Zoom links, furnish templates for upcoming assignments, and offer encouragement for the upcoming week. In a recent survey, our current doctoral students said that they appreciated reminders of upcoming synchronous virtual opportunities in the announcements feature. In fact, 34% of those surveyed stated that this was the primary feature that made attendance at these events easy for them (Melideo, 2023).

Continuous Feedback

In the 1970s, Malcolm Knowles introduced his andragogical model, a process model in which the teacher acts as facilitator/change agent to involve adult learners, the principles of which continue to direct adult education today (Knowles et al., 1973). Contemporary research indicates that adult learners acknowledge immediacy behaviors, such as the timing of feedback, as crucial to their formative skill assessment and helpful to the establishment of social presence in an online setting (Bin Mubayrik, 2020; Dixson et al., 2017). The standardized course design within our program promotes this immediacy, as instructors provide personalized, weekly formative feedback to doctoral students. This continuity is appreciated by doctoral students; one stated that they "received the most impact from the professor's feedback and from [their] LDFM," while another indicated that they thought "the required interaction, [students'] responses to posts in weekly lessons" was the most powerful way in which they connected with classmates (Melideo, 2023).

Synchronous Sessions

In our program, synchronous sessions are offered two to three times per semester in each course. The scheduling of these sessions is coordinated so that conflicts between courses are avoided. Sync session attendance is always optional for the doctoral student; recordings are posted in the LMS shell so that they can be viewed by those unable to attend and for review by those in attendance. If multiple sections of a course are offered, their synchronous sessions are combined, allowing members of each section to interact with all members of their cohort. Facilitated by the course instructor(s), sync sessions enable faculty to establish their teaching presence and students to establish their social and cognitive presence

(Garrison et al., 2001; Kumar et al., 2011). Faculty members identify meaningful outcomes and extend understanding of recent course topics through direct instruction, encourage reflective thought, and bridge to upcoming concepts. They often divide students into digital breakout rooms, so that it is easier for individuals to establish their social presence within the cohort and to strengthen their cognitive presence by engaging in purposeful involvement, quality activities, reflection, and discussion with cohort members (Groen, 2021). In a recent survey of our doctoral students, 95% stated they attended some to all of available synchronous sessions (Melideo, 2023).

Office Hours

Course instructors are intentional in offering virtual office hours six times per semester. These synchronous meetings are offered as an optional, come-and-go opportunity for doctoral students. Although the faculty member remains online during the entirety of the hour, students may pop in for a quick question or just to say, "hi!" Typically, attendance during office hours is quite high, particularly in courses offered at the beginning of the program. Even if they don't have questions or concerns, cohort members seem to crave this social presence and engagement with one another, perhaps because it contributes to feelings of being "apart, but together," as stated by Graham et al. (2023, p. 304). Office hours are not recorded, in order to reflect the organic and individualized nature of traditional office hours, and if a doctoral student has a question or concern of a private nature, the instructor will establish a separate breakout room for that discussion. Office hours do not take the place of one-on-one advising appointments; rather, they serve as an extension, a built-in means of access to the professor. Our students have used these opportunities to their advantage. Melideo's (2023) survey indicated that 91% of 23 respondents attended at least a few office hours each semester.

Socials

Perhaps the highlight of each course are the two virtual social gatherings each semester. Although optional, and not video-recorded, socials provide an opportunity for cohorts to strengthen their social connections with one another. Socials are as the name implies, related to establishing friendly companionship. Since our students enroll in two companion courses each semester, socials include all sections of both courses, as well as all instructors. The faculty members collaborate to design a fun, interactive activity that helps us get to know one another better. For example, a recent social divided small groups into virtual breakout rooms, where they collaborated to design a playlist that corresponded to the emotions felt while writing their DiP. When the groups returned from the breakout rooms to share their playlist, we learned a lot about one another. Personalities shine through during these activities, and commonalities are established. Professors who are scheduled to teach the next two courses in the program sequence are invited to the last social of each semester, where they introduce themselves and give a short preview of upcoming courses to the students. Our students often comment on how much they enjoy the socials and how they contribute to their sense of connection to faculty and peers. When asked, "Since the beginning of the program, on average, how many virtual socials did you attend each semester?" 43% indicated that they attended at least one and 35% stated that they attended both (Melideo, 2023).

Online Community Building Study

This section of the chapter will explore the results of an IRB-approved, mixed methods study in which the researcher sought to determine what technological integrations, specific verbiage, frequency of communications, types of messaging, online interactions, and approaches best engaged doctoral students in order to help them build and sustain their learning communities. The methodology included two data collections and five distinct treatments of said data. A Qualtrics-created (Qualtrics, 2023) survey was administered to a cohort of mid-program part-time doctoral students to ascertain their input and beliefs related to community building in their program with ten quantitative and four qualitative questions. The survey distribution yielded a 37% response rate.

The first six quantitative survey items inquired about the frequency and purposes the doctoral students attended the CWS options of office hours, sync sessions, and socials. The results revealed 91% of the respondents attended at least a few office hours each semester. *Figure 4* demonstrates the doctoral students' purposes for attending scheduled office hours.

The live synchronous sessions were exceptionally well-attended, with 95% attending at least one live sync session per semester. We were particularly satisfied that attendance at the synchronous sessions was a priority for this cohort. *Figure 5* shares the doctoral students' purposes for attending scheduled sync sessions.

Figure 4. Doctoral Students' Motivations for Attending Office Hours

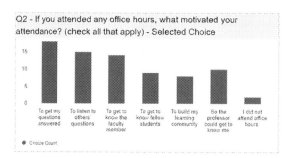

Figure 5. Marymount EdD Students' Motivations for Attending Sync Sessions

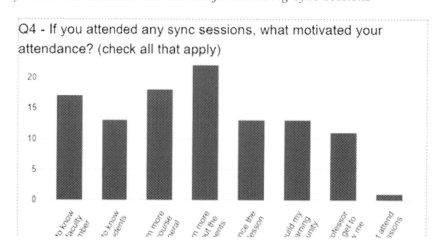

Making social connections appeared to be a priority for this cohort as 78% reported attending at least one social per semester. *Figure 6* shares the doctoral students' purposes for attending scheduled virtual socials.

The responses in the qualitative survey items revealed the doctoral students had a sincere appreciation for the efforts of the intentional program design and engaging faculty responses. Additionally, their efforts for building community via informal avenues such as student instigated social media, text, email, and telephone calls echoed Berry's (2017) research findings about the students' specific interest in socialization during their doctoral programs being different from traditional in-person programs.

To inform the continuous improvement of our online doctoral program, we elicit feedback from our students frequently. A recent survey by Melideo (2023), as indicated in Table 1, provides a sampling of students' views of the CWS model.

Humanizing Messaging in Weekly Course Announcements

Pacansky-Brock (2020) stressed the importance of building the faculty-student relationship in online educational contexts where, "...human connection is the antidote for the emotional disruption that prevents many students from performing to their full potential and in online courses, creating that connection is even more important." Qualitative results of Melideo's study (2023) demonstrated that online faculty are actively communicating with their students in endearing, motivational, and supportive means. The verbiage of the faculty's course announcements the students would have received thus far in their program was completed via the Delve Tool (Twenty to Nine LLC, 2023) to ascertain themes. Inductive thematic coding of every sentence from over 150 online course announcements authored by ten different professors was analyzed for themes. Every sentence of each announcement was coded for as many themes as were evident in the messaging. Out of the 18 codes, the most frequent preliminary themes emerged as follows: *directions/information, reminder, friendly greeting,* and *link provided.* Four unexpected and entirely thrilling themes surfaced: *cultural inclusivity, complimentary remark, grateful,* and *encouragement.* Utilizing hierarchical coding of the course announcements, academic *success, logistics,* and *humanizing content* surfaced with vigor. Textually through the weekly course announcements, the

Figure 6. Marymount EdD Students' Motivations for Attending Socials

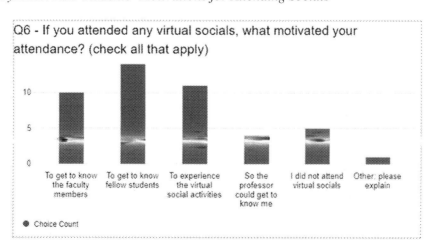

Table 1. Doctoral Students' Perception of Continuous Weekly Support Model

Item	Consensus of Responses	Sample Student Extended Responses
Whether you have or have not attended office hours, socials, and/or sync sessions, do you perceive the cultivated community engagement provided by the School of Education to be impactful in doctoral students' academic work?	87% affirmative	*The (school) has a strong sense of community that has helped to keep me motivated.* *It has motivated me to stick with it and I have a support group of peers who help each other out, encourage each other, and check in on one another.*
If you engaged with fellow doctoral students, what has been the most powerful way you found effective in connecting with classmates? If you have not engaged with fellow doctoral students outside of class assignments, please explain why.	Texting Phone calls Zoom meetings Social media connections	*I received the most impact from the professor's feedback and from my LDFM.* *I think the required interaction (responses to posts in weekly lessons) was another way [to garner feedback].*
What advice would you give to the newest cohort on cultivating their community engagement as they first enter the program?	Make peer connections Use synchronous connections	*Connect with people immediately. You all are in this journey together.* *Review coursework early and don't be afraid to ask tough questions from instructors and share thoughts with peers.*
What other information or ideas would you like to share with us to help cultivate community engagement in our doctoral program?	Informal and formal networks are desirable	*More opportunities for home groups where there is open sharing of feedback (but not group assignments* *I think offering an opportunity like Slack or Groupme outside of Canvas from the start that does not involve sharing phone numbers can help break down barriers and build community quicker.*

Note. Representative student feedback data taken from Melideo (2023).

online faculty have been intentionally laying a solid foundation upon which the "sense of community can make a significant impact on student success" (Byrd, 2016).

The Online Doctoral Student User Experience (UX)

As discussed in length earlier in the chapter, weekly course announcements are a means to efficiently deliver important information to all students in the courses simultaneously. The doctoral students' user experience (UX) throughout the entire program is of utmost importance to the faculty. An extensive heuristic examination of the internet links, attached document links, static and dynamic images, and videos from the weekly course announcements was executed using an adapted heuristic evaluation tool checklist. The static images appeared generally recognizable and understandable across generations and cultures. The static images and GIFs were fully functional and seemed to be intended as uplifting or humorous. The attached documents and videos were accessible and provided further research, additional course information, and professional development opportunities. Studying the ease and useability of the course announcements's content, at a cursory level, acknowledged additional, intentional humanizing efforts of the faculty.

The results of Melideo's mixed methods (2023) study supported the premises of social presence theory in that the online learning environment of our studied doctoral program provided a "warm, sociable, and personal interactions that lead to interpersonal relationships" (Whiteside et al, 2017). The messaging found in the faculty's weekly course announcements demonstrated Garrison et al. (2010) findings that faculty can create a warm and genuine atmosphere in online learning environments. The survey results demonstrated that the doctoral students acknowledged the efforts of the faculty to humanize the coursework and learning experiences overall.

Intentionality and Commitment

It has been our experience that, when provided multi-faceted and layered opportunities for peer- and instructor-interaction, online doctoral students are eager to use a variety of engagement tools and do so frequently, thus increasing their integration into the program (Berry, 2017; Rockinson-Szapkiw et al., 2019). The key seems to be intentionality and commitment - intentionality on the part of faculty members to communicate early and often through the LMS announcements, commitment to "hold sacred" the scheduled synchronous events for the semester, intentional design of instructional sync sessions to deepen understanding, and a commitment to humanize our online spaces by infusing them with engaging, interactive activities. It is also a commitment on the part of our students, who face great challenges in prioritizing their doctoral studies, while at the same time balancing work, home, and other responsibilities. We know that time management struggles can quickly emerge and have detrimental effects on their success (Graham et al., 2023). Providing students with multiple engagement opportunities throughout the semester enables them to "hold space" for themselves and their studies. As one student so eloquently stated: "Don't be afraid to put yourself out there. … if you feel isolated it's because you didn't put in the effort. There are so many opportunities to get to know your cohort and develop a sense of community."

High-Touch Online Faculty Mentorship

In addition to the CWS model, Marymount intentionally infused high-touch online faculty mentorship into the program design as another pillar to support the online student experience (see *Figure 3*). With the knowledge that doctoral student support cannot be single-dimensional, this mentorship pillar serves to complement and bolster the resources provided by the teaching faculty in the CWS model.

Historically, only half of all doctoral students complete their degree, and dissertation mentorship plays an important role in those who achieve program completion (Mullen, 2021). Doctoral students often note that a positive mentoring relationship with their dissertation chair, one in which advisors exhibit dispositions acknowledging daily struggles (balancing school, work, and family responsibilities) and promoting mentee proficiency, leads to increased intrinsic motivation of the doctoral student (Jameson & Torres, 2019). Mullen (2021) concurs, citing findings by Maddox (2017) that a leading cause of program disruption is "lack of advising and mentoring" (p. 140). Elmore (2021) also found that effective dissertation mentorship can help doctoral students overcome five common challenges of online doctoral learners, including "writing at a doctoral level, experiencing feelings of isolation, accessing online resources, establishing a professional and collegial relationship, and managing research" (p. 67).

The LDFM program was designed to meet the unique needs of the online doctoral student population, as they complete components of their dissertation research throughout research-embedded coursework. The LDFM program is unique in that it fosters high-touch mentorship, while also building a community of support and scholarship for both the LDFM and the student. While similar to a dissertation chair, the LDFM differs in that they are actively involved early and often in the student's process, providing coaching and encouragement from the earliest stages of theoretical and methodological development through the presentation of the final dissertation. The LDFM complements the faculty support that students receive in their coursework, providing an additional layer of guidance and communication as students conduct their research. Additionally, LDFMs become a part of a community of scholars and receive ongoing professional development and training throughout the course of the mentorship program. This portion of the chapter will detail the aspects of the LDFM program which help to humanize and personalize the online doctoral and mentorship experience including: early and personalized matching, intentional design, ongoing training and engagement, and inclusion and community building initiatives.

Early Matching and Ongoing Training

Since the inception of the EdD program, the LDFM program was designed to offer additional student touchpoints and scaffolded support through the progression of the research and dissertation process. The LDFM is matched with students at the start of their second year in the program. The timing of this match is intentional, as an early mentorship match allows LDFMs to build a strong foundation to cultivate the relationship over the course of five semesters, as students ideate, draft, and hone their research design and dissertation chapters. Scholars agree that quality mentorship is paramount to student success and persistence in doctoral programs, arguing that strong personal relationships, frequent touchpoints, and a sense of trust encourage student persistence and retention (Bair et al., 2004; Hoskins & Goldberg, 2005). By establishing trust early, LDFMs are able to engage with students on both a personal and professional level, closely monitor their research progress, and help students overcome the common hurdles and pitfalls that may lead to attrition.

In addition to intentional early matching, LDFMs also undergo intentionally designed and extensive onboarding and training in order to guide them in providing ongoing support to their doctoral mentees. As Saleem and Mehmood (2018) found, inadequate training at the institutional level often leads to gaps in quality advising for doctoral students. According to Lundine (2022), "[dissertation chairs] who are satisfied with the work and who feel adequately prepared to lead the dissertation process may increase doctoral students' success" (p. 16). As part of the LDFM program, dissertation mentors are invited to an initial information session prior to even applying for the role, allowing them a full understanding of the expectations, time commitment, and program culture and requirements. After completing their formal onboarding, LDFMs also undergo an initial orientation, as well as required semesterly training sessions, which provide an overview of how to support students in each respective semester. Training materials are centralized in the LMS, and LDFM coordinators regularly communicate announcements to LDFMs through this system. LDFMs are also invited to course sync sessions, welcomed to attend faculty office hours with their mentee, and encouraged to attend student support events to provide opportunities to engage in the mentee's learning and connect with the faculty teaching the courses. This ongoing engagement and communication addresses the training gaps that Saleem and Mehmood (2018) identified and helps our LDFMs feel more confident and prepared to support our doctoral students and candidates.

The impact of the training and engagement opportunities can be seen in program survey results. In a 2023 survey of LDFMs, 83.3% of mentors responded that they agree or strongly agree that they feel adequately prepared to answer their mentee's questions about their research. Similarly, 83.4% of mentors responded that they agree or strongly agree that they have a good understanding of the institutional processes and timeline for the DiP at Marymount University. These initial indicators demonstrate that a majority of our LDFMs feel prepared and supported in their mentorship of our online doctoral students, which according to Lundine (2022) can impact student persistence and success in their doctoral journeys.

CPED Framework to Guide the Design of the LDFM Role

The LDFM program at Marymount was designed with intention and attention to the framework and best practices provided by the Carnegie Project on the Education Doctorate (CPED, 2019). As part of their framework, CPED (2019) offers nine design concepts for building mentorship and advising programs, which we strategically leverage in order to humanize the online dissertation mentorship experience for students. Despite CPED's guidance, there are currently no universal set of standards in which committee chairs have to abide by and a severe lack of widely accepted standardized training practices for dissertation chairs. Yet the person designated in this role plays a critical part in the student's successful completion of their program (Begin & Gerard, 2013; Mullen, 2021). Beyond the assumed knowledge needed in writing and research methods (Hyatt & Williams, 2011), dissertation chairs and advisors need advanced skills in communication, relationship building, and teamwork (Riger, 2017). By intentionally infusing CPED's (2019) mentorship design principles throughout the onboarding and the extensive training of our dissertation mentors, the LDFMs in our program become well-acquainted with the expectations, standards of best practices for each semester, protocols, training materials and guidelines associated with the role. By employing the processes that promote knowledge construction and the dissemination of organizational knowledge (Lundine, 2022), the LDFM Leadership team provides each LDFM with a toolbox to best meet the current needs of their mentees on a semesterly basis. The scaffolded training structures for the LDFM community rooted in the CPED Framework for mentoring and advising (2019) have helped to re-designed the ambiguous role of "committee chair," "dissertation chair," or "dissertation supervisor" to provide the chairs with a safe space and platform to grow as mentors while simultaneously supporting their student's DiP.

Through continuous program review, assessment, and reflection, we aim to assess the ongoing alignment of the LDFM program with the CPED design principles (2019), as well as the impact that the mentorship has on student experience as it relates to feelings of support and connectedness to our high-touch and DiP-embedded program design. Several studies support using CPED's principles to guide EdD program design elements and assessment (Buss, 2018; Marotta, 2023; Crystle et al., 2023). In a recent program assessment, we conducted a thorough content analysis of our LDFM program materials to analyze the ways in which the program currently reflects the CPED principles, as well as opportunities for further alignment and improvement. Assessing this alignment helps us to understand the ways in which we are infusing best practices and further humanizing the dissertation mentorship process for our online student community.

Through the use of both inductive and deductive thematic coding, we conducted a thorough review of the EdD handbook, the LDFM position description, and the training materials in the LMS site for LDFMs to study the current alignment between the CPED Framework for mentoring and advising (2019) and the materials present to support the LDFM community. Three key themes were identified in CPED's framework: collaboration, responsive mentoring, and safe learning environments. Within each, subthemes emerged to include: mutual respect, open communication, knowledge construction, guidance and support, flexibility, support of professional passions, growth-oriented, dynamic learning, scaffolding, understanding needs of adult learners, peer-to-peer support, and community of learners.

In addition to analyzing this alignment with the CPED (2019) design principles for mentorship, we also drew on inductive coding to identify themes that extended beyond the CPED framework and were unique to the value, vision, and culture of the University, the EdD program, and the LDFM role. Further themes that emerged from the content analysis included: 1) focus on professional development, 2) accommodating nature, 3) empathy, and 4) collegial/non-hierarchical environment. The emergence of these themes reinforce and affirm the humanizing nature of the LDFM program design.

Empathy and socioemotional support have also been found to be an integral component to building and fostering the mentor-mentee relationship (Duffy et al., 2018); therefore, the emergence of the themes of empathy, accommodation, and collegial relationships help to affirm that we have built the LDFM program upon principles that foster positive and strong relationships between students and mentors. Additionally, the theme of professional development for mentors shows the program's investment and dedication to the support of our LDFM community. Findings from Duffy et al. (2018) emphasize the significance of support for online dissertation mentors and their ability to "lean on each other" (p. 69) by providing opportunities for connection, networking, and development. The networking and professional development opportunities embedded into our training content for LDFMs affirms our commitment to the student experience, as well as the experience for our online dissertation mentors.

Building a Diverse LDFM Community to Support Online Doctoral Student Success

The LDFM program was designed to meet the unique needs of the online doctoral student population as they complete components of their dissertation research throughout research-embedded coursework. According to Lundine (2022), the attrition, engagement, and retention of dissertation chairs can have a significant impact on doctoral student progress and persistence. Due to this relationship between the engagement and retention of faculty mentors and the engagement and retention of students, we have intentionally prioritized connection and community building within our LDFM program. As the size of our cohorts has increased, we have worked to systematize the recruitment, onboarding, and training of a diverse pool of LDFMs. While initially recruited internally and through word of mouth, the LDFM community has expanded to include over 90 scholars and experts from diverse fields including education, psychology, business, government, and healthcare, among others. Table 2 below demonstrates the exponential growth that the program has undergone to build a community of LDFMs to support our online doctoral students and candidates.

Along with this growth, we have been able to diversify our pool of LDFM candidates to better match and reflect the diversity of our doctoral students and candidates. Figure 7 shows a demographic breakdown of our LDFM community by gender, as well as race and ethnicity.

By expanding the role of LDFM beyond the faculty present at the University, we have been able to better mirror the diversity of the student body, not only in terms of race, gender, and ethnicity, but also

Table 2. Lead Doctoral Faculty Mentor Program Growth

Cohort	Students	LDFM (Total)	LDFMs - New Hires
Cohort 1	29	15	15
Cohort 2	42	18	8
Cohort 3	64	34	34
Cohort 4	30	20	15
Cohort 5	67	49	22
Total	232	86	94

Note. Data from Marymount University Assessments (2023).

Figure 7. Marymount LDFM Diversity by Race and Ethnicity

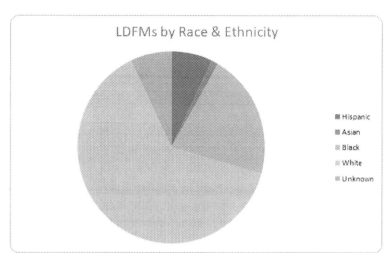

Figure 8. Marymount LDFM Diversity by Gender

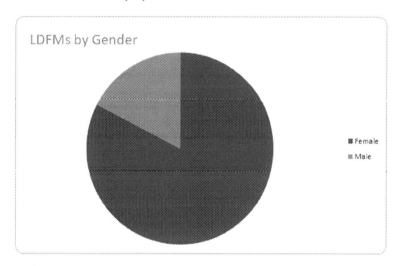

by research interest. This allows for stronger relational bonds between the student, the LDFM, the connection to their research, and therefore, the feeling of belonging in the program.

Such quick growth does not come without challenges. Onboarding new LDFMs required the development of many policies and procedures, as well as training materials, resources, and forms to monitor student progress. Additionally, assessment of some early attrition of newly hired LDFMs prompted us to update and clarify the position description, implement processes to better manage student and LDFM expectations, and bridge communication gaps between LDFMs and teaching faculty to streamline support for students. Despite the significant time associated with this human resources management, the EdD program has stayed true to our high touch and individualized approach, keeping the management of the LDFM program in-house, with faculty and staff LDFM coordinators leading the development of and taking a personalized approach to the onboarding and continued training of our LDFM community.

In addition to our commitment to training, communication, and engagement, the EdD program strives to build a sense of community and belonging for our LDFMs. As an example of this collegial approach, LDFM coordinators organize and lead "First Tuesday Happy Hour Drop-in Sessions" for the LDFM community. These informal monthly virtual touchpoints create a point of connection for LDFMs, as they are a space where they can share their experience, talk through challenges, and celebrate any wins with their mentee's progress. To maintain the integrity of these opportunities, these sessions are not recorded, similar to the student socials and office hours. These spaces also provide opportunities for spontaneous scholarly sharing and conversations, as LDFMs are able to share any of their own professional work, research, or publications. Previous research recognized that (Duffy et al., 2018), providing these collegial opportunities allows for mentors to have a "virtual 'water cooler'" space for emotional venting, idea sharing, and to mitigate feelings of isolation (p. 69). By humanizing the online experience for our online dissertation mentors, we in turn humanize the mentorship process for our doctoral students.

Another component of these community building initiatives is our commitment to the professional development of our LDFMs. While we offer training sessions that review the nuts and bolts of the program and the logistical components of the dissertation timeline, we also offer opportunities for scholarly conversations that extend beyond basic training and administration of the program. "Coaching Conversations" are professional development sessions which offer LDFMs an opportunity to engage in scholarly conversation on topics such as best practices in coaching and backward design in mentorship. Additionally, these sessions also offer methodological refreshers on quantitative and qualitative methods, where LDFMs can receive additional professional development on SPSS (IBM Corp., 2020), Delve (Twenty to Nine LLC, 2023), and other data analysis software. Furthermore, we extend many writing development opportunities to our LDFM community by giving them access to our in-person and virtual writing retreat and lab opportunities. These opportunities give LDFMs the opportunity to connect with students, faculty, and other LDFMs, while honing their own scholarship, writing, and mentorship skills. In a 2021 qualitative study, Studebaker and Curtis found that dissertation chairs played a pivotal role in helping students establish a sense of belonging. By offering these collegial opportunities for connection within the LDFM community, it is our hope that this culture of inclusion and belonging will engage LDFMs and trickle down to impact the belonging and success of our online student population.

To continually assess and improve our community building initiatives, we actively seek feedback from LDFMs to gauge their experience and ensure that they feel both valued and supported within our community. Select results from a survey of LDFMs from Cohorts 2, 3, and 4 are included below. Results of the survey demonstrate that many of our LDFMs are participating in our engagement opportunities, and that these initiatives are making an impact in establishing a culture of support and community for our LDFMs. Table 3 below demonstrates participation rates in our virtual engagement opportunities for LDFMs from Fall 2022 to Spring 2023.

Table 3. Participation Rates in LDFM Engagement Opportunities

Engagement Opportunity	Participation Rate (%)
Live Semester Training*	58.8
First Tuesdays Happy Hour Drop-in Session	54.2
Live Coaching Conversation*	45.8

Note: Writing retreat and lab opportunities were not assessed, as these were not developed and available at the time of the survey. *All semester trainings and Coaching Conversations are recorded, so this does not indicate asynchronous participation in these opportunities.

Qualitative responses further demonstrate the impact of these community building initiatives. One LDFM describes the benefit of one of the Coaching Conversations saying, "it was very useful in helping me to improve the quality of my interaction with different types of mentees." She goes on to mention that "the Drop-in Happy Hour sessions provided opportunities for me to understand what other mentors were doing and shared experiences helped provide new strategies for my own developing skills as a mentor." Other LDFMs commented on appreciating the informal nature of the happy hour sessions, as well as the timely nature of the semesterly training sessions. One mentor also commented on her appreciation for the accessibility of the recordings of each training, given differences in time zones and family and work obligations.

Additional survey questions were asked to gauge LDFM's sense of support and belonging within the university and EdD community. Results in Table 4 below demonstrate a strong sense of support and growing sense of community within our LDFM community.

While we recognize that there is still work to be done in building our LDFM community, we can see that our communication and engagement initiatives are having a positive impact on supporting our LDFMs, and as scholars have found, this community building can in turn significantly influence doctoral student's sense of belonging and program completion (Studebaker and Curtis, 2021; Lundine, 2022).

Humanizing the Dissertation Process & Personalizing the Match

A strong and diverse LDFM community provides us a strong foundation for humanizing the dissertation process and successfully supporting our students in their online doctoral journey. However, the individualized and high-touch nature of the LDFM program does not stop with our onboarding, orientation, and training, but extends to the comprehensive and personalized process we have in place to match students with their LDFMs.

As research reminds us, the dissertation mentor-mentee relationship is one of the most important relationships in the life of a doctoral student (Duffy et al., 2018; Doyle et al., 2016; Battaglia & Battaglia, 2016). Thus, the process of mentor-mentee selection and pairing has long been an important, yet understudied component of the doctoral student experience (Lovitts, 2001; Neale-McFall, 2011; Neale-McFall & Ward, 2015). In smaller, on-ground doctoral programs, students may be able to select their dissertation chair; however, as online accessibility aids to increase EdD enrollment numbers nationwide (Becker, 2022), it is increasingly common for universities to assign students to mentors in online graduate education (Duffy et al., 2018).

Table 4. Likert Questions on LDFM Support and Community Building

	Strongly Disagree	Disagree	Neutral	Agree	Strongly Agree
I feel supported by the Marymount faculty, staff, and LDFM coordinators.	—	—	4.2%	16.7%	79.2%
I feel respected by my Marymount mentees.	—	4.2%	4.2%	16.7%	75%
I feel like I am a part of the greater Marymount community.	—	8.3%	29.2%	29.2%	33.3%
I feel that I know where to go when I have questions.	—	—	8.3%	4.2%	87.5%
I feel that my questions are answered promptly by Marymount staff and LDFM coordinators.	—	—	—	8.3%	91.7%

Note. Survey data from Marymount LDFM received survey responses n=24.

At Marymount, we have taken intentional steps to humanize the way in which dissertation mentors are matched and assigned, seeking significant input from both the LDFM and the student mentee prior to the match. Prior to year two, we administer a survey to doctoral students to assess their professional background, research interests, and preliminary ideas around their research methodology. As a part of program assessment and improvement, we have added survey questions that ask the student about their working style, as well as possible barriers to progress with the dissertation process (i.e. family obligations, medical considerations, and work changes and transitions). These added survey components allow us to have a more holistic picture of the student's research journey, so that we are able to better assess and personalize their mentor match. In addition to student input, we have developed a systemized way of collecting information from LDFM candidates prior to our match process. Curriculum vitae (CV) are collected and coded as part of the matching process. In addition, in our most recent match process, we collected video recorded introductions from each LDFM, in which they detailed their research background and experience, as well as their motivations for serving as a dissertation mentor. These videos and the coded CVs allow us to make informed and individualized matches for each doctoral student in the cohort based upon research interests, LDFM experiences, and the consideration of student needs. The matching process is a multi-day collaborative process with collective input from the LDFM Leadership Team and faculty.

While the match process has become a point of pride for our program and continues to undergo process improvements, it certainly is not always perfect. Duffy et al. (2018) discuss the root causes and "challenges associated with the relationship deterioration" between dissertation mentor and mentee (p. 57). In the experience with our own match process, there are cases in which the mentor-mentee relationship may become strained or simply may not work out for various reasons, ranging from communication issues, working style differences, or mismatched expectations. In these cases, we have also worked to systematize and personalize the rematch process. We take the time to listen to and document input and concerns from both the mentor and mentee. Where appropriate and when mediation is possible, we offer a joint meeting between the LDFM and the student mentee to facilitate a productive dialogue to address concerns and discuss a path forward for success. In cases where a rematch is deemed necessary, we communicate changes with care and empathy. Typically, a conversation with the student is offered to glean additional information about their research topic and the type of support they need to be successful in the program. While a rematch is never the intent, we have managed to implement a process that considers the unique dynamics of the mentor-mentee relationship and is responsive to both the LDFM and student perspectives.

The success of our match process has been validated through quantitative and qualitative survey results that assess the doctoral student experience with the LDFM program. Quantitative findings reveal that students value the knowledge and expertise of their LDFM match. In a 2023 survey, 88.5% of students "Strongly Agreed" or "Agreed" that they valued their LDFM's "practical knowledge and understanding of research and inquiry." Additionally, 78.9% of students "Strongly Agreed" or "Agreed" that their LDFM had led them to a better understanding of the DiP timeline. This quantitative data provides a snapshot of the student experience and satisfaction with their LDFM.

However, qualitative data from these surveys is perhaps even more illustrative of the success of the LDFM matching process. Table 5 provides a sample of qualitative quotes representing student experiences with the LDFM program and process.

Table 5. Sample of Reported Doctoral Student Experiences With the LDFM Program and Processes

Student	Quote
Student A	"I truly appreciate this 1:1 relationship with my LDFM, because I feel I have a partner accompanying me through my EdD journey. I have developed friendships within my cohort but having this one person--my LDFM--to listen, encourage, support, guide me--gives me additional courage and strength."
Student B	"I'm very happy with the pairing of my LDFM, who has a background similar to my research. Although she is not MU staff, she has always been able to provide me with information with MU timelines and procedures. If she is unable to provide that during our meetings, she follows up in less than 24 hours with the information I was seeking. I am extremely happy with the support from my LDFM."
Student C	"This mentoring process has been vital to my success. The weekly meetings with my LDFM have been crucial to my success in this program and my ability to keep my head above water."
Student D	"[My LDFM is a] critical component of the process both for progress and morale. I appreciate her support greatly."
Student E	"My LDFM is amazing. Even if she doesn't know the answer she knows where to go or who to ask to get it. She's gone above and beyond dealing out the steps I need to take to be successful. She meets with me more than required and is one of my biggest cheerleaders. I am so thankful! I love the LDFM program. Some people in other doctoral programs have to pay a third party to get this kind of support."
Student F	"She is the perfect match for my style and personality. She also compliments areas of my DiP. It feels like I am being coached and mentored by a friend who genuinely cares about my wellbeing and success. Duplicate her: -) so others can experience her effective demeanor and excellence in mentoring and supporting graduate students."

Note. Survey data from Cohorts 2-4 (2023), n = 52.

Together, this qualitative data illustrates the human connection that students are building with their LDFMs throughout the program. The quotes provide evidence of the personal connection and rapport that is built and how this relationship boosts morale and encourages persistence in the program.

CONCLUSIONS AND IMPLICATIONS

In this chapter, we detailed the program components that have been intentionally designed and integrated within an online doctoral program to maximize student engagement, persistence, and success. Marymount's online EdD in Educational Leadership and Organizational Innovation program pairs a Continuous Weekly Support (CWS) model with high touch faculty mentorship to humanize the online doctoral experience and provide layered support structures for our adult learners. The CWS model includes weekly faculty announcements, ongoing feedback, and the opportunity for engagement through synchronous sessions, online office hours, and virtual socials. Melideo's (2023) mixed methods study revealed the importance of this continuous support and the opportunities for engagement, with 95% of student respondents reporting that they had attended at least one of the engagement opportunities. The study also revealed the importance of humanizing messaging in faculty communication, with survey results confirming that these efforts in community building positively impact the students' user experience (UX).

Ongoing program assessments have also underscored the importance of the Lead Doctoral Mentorship (LDFM) program and the humanizing nature of this one-on-one research support. We know that completion rates in doctoral programs is already low, and it is even lower for programs that are online (Bawa, 2016); therefore, human connection through the LDFM program helps to encourage student persistence, especially through the dissertation process. Early matching and ongoing training of our

LDFMs has proven to be particularly effective in building a strong LDFM community that, in turn, fosters students' success and completion.

Our program and our related research and assessments can offer many practical implications for educators and program administrators. First and foremost, our pillar model demonstrates the need for multiple layers of support for online students, especially at the doctoral level. While we detail two pillars here, our program offers many virtual supports that come together to positively impact the online student experience. Program research also highlights the importance of intentional design, human connection, and continuous support. Educators and administrators need to be intentional about community building, especially in an online program and at the doctoral level, where independent research can often be lonely and isolating. There are also practical implications for designing and implementing online mentorship programs, with attention to the importance of early and personalized matching. Our program assessments also shed light on the importance of continual and ongoing engagement of dissertation mentors in order to further enhance the research support that online doctoral students receive. While further research and assessment will of course be necessary, these preliminary takeaways have offered our program insight into what we are doing well, as well as areas of growth for supporting and humanizing the online experience for our online doctoral students.

Looking Forward

Henri Matisse eloquently shared that "Creativity Takes Courage." Our endeavors as leaders in humanizing online learning for doctoral students certainly echo Matisse's sentiments allowing for greater opportunities to create engaging, interactive, and supportive learning environments for all learners. Intentionality in building a sense of belonging is the most humanizing endeavor that online programs can hope to achieve. With our program and shared research we look toward the future and continual efforts to enhance the current program through open communication and sustained collaboration with all stakeholders in online learning at the doctoral level. Our efforts to create positive change in this arena using the pillar model demonstrates great hope for the future as we, as a community of learners, create changes in the way learning evolves in a growing online environment. A willingness to think outside of traditional lines, to reach out through multiple measures with extensive coaching and mentoring models has led the way in bringing about this change in online program development.

REFERENCES

Azevedo, P. C., Hauth, C., Macedonia, A., Marotta, J., & Thompson, J. (2023). Retreating: The gift of time and community to write [Research Presentation]. Carnegie Project on the Education Doctorate (CPED) Convening, Pensacola, FL.

Bair, C., Grant Haworth, J., & Sandfort, M. (2004). Doctoral student learning and development: A shared responsibility. *NASPA Journal, 41*(3), 709–727. doi:10.2202/1949-6605.1395

Battaglia, D., & Battaglia, J. (2016). Faculty mentoring in communication sciences and disorders: Case study of doctoral teaching practicum. *Academy of Educational Leadership Journal, 20*(3), 1–11.

Bawa, P. (2016). Retention in online courses: Exploring issues and solutions-A literature review. *SAGE Open, 6*(1), 1–11. doi:10.1177/2158244015621777

Becker, S. (2022, October 28). *Enrollment in this doctorate program is surging–here's why.* Fortune. https://fortune.com/education/articles/enrollment-in-this-doctorate-program-is-surging-heres-why/

Bégin, C., & Géarard, L. (2013). The role of supervisors in light of the experience of doctoral students. *Policy Futures in Education, 11*(3), 267–276. doi:10.2304/pfie.2013.11.3.267

Berry, S. (2017). Student support networks in online doctoral programs: Exploring nested communities. *International Journal of Doctoral Studies,* (12), 33-48. doi:10.28945/3676

Bin Mubayrik, H. F. (2020). New trends in formative-summative evaluations for adult education. *SAGE Open, 10*(3). Advance online publication. doi:10.1177/2158244020941006

Brown, S., & Burdsal, C. (2012). An exploration of sense of community and student success using the national survey of student engagement. *The Journal of General Education, 61*(4), 433–460. doi:10.5325/jgeneeduc.61.4.0433

Buss, R. R. (2018). How CPED guiding principles and design concepts influenced the development and implementation of an EdD program. *Impacting Education: Journal on Transforming Professional Practice, 3*(2). Advance online publication. doi:10.5195/ie.2018.57

Byrd, J. (2016). Understanding the online doctoral learning experience: Factors that contribute to students' sense of community. *The Journal of Educators Online, 13*(2), 102–135. doi:10.9743/JEO.2016.2.3

Carnegie Project on the Education Doctorate. (2019). *CPED Framework.* https://www.cpedinitiative.org/assets/images/cped_infographic_5.png

Corp, I. B. M. (2020). *IBM SPSS Statistics for Windows (Version 27.0)* [Computer software]. IBM Corp.

Crystle, J., Boyd, R., Melideo, S., & Hauth, C. (2024). *Faculty mentors' perceptions: Evidence of applied practitioner research by EdD candidates. In Impacting Education.* CPED.

Dixson, M. D., Greenwell, M. R., Rogers-Stacy, C., Weister, T., & Lauer, S. (2017). Nonverbal immediacy behaviors and online student engagement: Bringing past instructional research into the present virtual classroom. *Communication Education, 66*(1), 37–53. doi:10.1080/03634523.2016.1209222

Doyle, N., Jacobs, K., & Ryan, C. (2016). Faculty mentors' perspectives on e-mentoring postprofessional occupational therapy doctoral students. *Occupational Therapy International, 23*(4), 305–317. doi:10.1002/oti.1431 PMID:27250596

Duffy, J., Wickersham-Fish, L., Rademaker, L., & Wetzler, E. (2018). Using collaborative autoethnography to explore online doctoral mentoring: Finding empathy in mentor/protégé relationships. *American Journal of Qualitative Research, 2*(1), 57–76. doi:10.29333/ajqr/5794

Elmore, R. (2021). Reflections on mentoring online doctoral learners through the dissertation. *Christian Higher Education, 20*(1-2), 57-68.

Gardner, S. K. (2010). Keeping up with the Joneses: Socialization and culture in doctoral education at one striving institution. *The Journal of Higher Education, 81*(6), 658–679. doi:10.1080/00221546.20 10.11779076

Garrison, D. R., Anderson, T., & Archer, W. (2001). Critical thinking, cognitive presence, and computer conferencing in distance education. *American Journal of Distance Education, 15*(1), 1, 7–23. doi:10.1080/08923640109527071

Garrison, D. R., Anderson, T., & Archer, W. (2010). The first decade of the community of inquiry framework: A retrospective. *The Internet and Higher Education, 13*(1), 5–9. doi:10.1016/j.iheduc.2009.10.003

Graham, K., Rios, A., & Viruru, R. (2023). Constructing radical community: An ecological model for shifting from an EdD to a We-dD in online doctoral programs. *Higher Education, 85*(2), 301–323. doi:10.1007/s10734-022-00834-8 PMID:35287377

Groen, J. (2021). Student engagement in doctoral programs: Principal factors that facilitate learning. *New Directions for Teaching and Learning, 167*(167), 77–84. doi:10.1002/tl.20461

Heyman, E. (2010). *Overcoming student retention issues in higher education online program: A delphi study* [Doctoral dissertation]. ProQuest document ID:748309429.

Holder, B. (2007). An investigation of hope, academics, environment, and motivation as predictors of persistence in higher education online programs. *The Internet and Higher Education, 10*(4), 245–260. doi:10.1016/j.iheduc.2007.08.002

Hoskins, C., & Goldberg, A. (2005). Doctoral student persistence in counselor education programs: Student-program match. *Counselor Education and Supervision, 44*(3), 175–188. doi:10.1002/j.1556-6978.2005.tb01745.x

Hyatt, L., & Williams, P. E. (2011). 21st century competencies for doctoral leadership faculty. *Innovative Higher Education, 36*(1), 53–66. doi:10.1007/s10755-010-9157-5

Jameson, C., & Torres, K. (2019). Fostering motivation when virtually mentoring online doctoral students. *Journal of Educational Research and Practice, 9*(1). Advance online publication. doi:10.5590/JERAP.2019.09.1.23

Kauffman, H. (2015). A review of predictive factors of student success in and satisfaction with online learning. *Research in Learning Technology, 23*, 1–13. doi:10.3402/rlt.v23.26507

Knowles, M. S., Holton, E. F. III, Swanson, R. A., & Robinson, P. A. (1973). *The adult learner: A neglected species*. Gulf Publication Company.

Kuh, G. (2001, May - June). Assessing what really matters to student learning: Inside the national survey of student engagement. *Change, 33*(3), 10–17. https://www.jstor.org/stable/40165768. doi:10.1080/00091380109601795

Kuh, G. D., Kinzie, J., Schuh, J. H., & Whitt, E. J. (2010). *Student success in college: Creating conditions that matter*. Jossey-Bass.

Kuhn, D. (2015). Thinking together and alone. *Educational Researcher, 44*(1), 46–53. doi:10.3102/0013189X15569530

Kumar, S., Dawson, K., Black, E. W., Cavanaugh, C., & Sessums, C. D. (2011). Applying the community of inquiry framework to an online professional practice doctoral program. *International Review of Research in Open and Distance Learning, 12*(6), 126–142. doi:10.19173/irrodl.v12i6.978

Lovitts, B. E. (2001). *Leaving the ivory tower: The causes and consequences of departure from doctoral study.* Rowman & Littlefield.

Lundine, T. (2022). *How dissertation faculty leaders develop dissertation chairs using the knowledge creation process.* https://www.proquest.com/docview/2725223042?pq-origsite=gscholar&fromopenview=true

Maddox, S. (2017), *Did not finish: Doctoral attrition in higher education and student affairs* [Doctoral dissertation, University of Northern Colorado]. https://digscholarship.unco.edu/cgi/viewcontent.cgi?article=1434&context=dissertations

Marotta, J. A. (2023). It's time to make more room for program evaluation in the education doctorate program. *Impacting Education: Journal on Transforming Professional Practice, 8*(4), 50–56. doi:10.5195/ie.2023.335

Marymount University. (2021, September 1). Ed.D. in education leadership and organizational innovation handbook [Unpublished manuscript]. School of Education, Marymount University.

Melideo, S. (2023, July 3-5). *Constituting community: A heuristic examination of tools and opportunities for deepening connectivity and engagement of asynchronous doctoral students* [Paper presentation]. 15th annual International Conference on Education and New Learning Technologies, Palma de Mallorca, Spain. https://library.iated.org/view/MELIDEO2023CON

Mullen, C. A. (2021). Online doctoral mentoring in a pandemic: Help or hindrance to academic progress on dissertations? *International Journal of Mentoring and Coaching in Education, 10*(2), 139–157. doi:10.1108/IJMCE-06-2020-0029

Neale-McFall, C., & Ward, C. A. (2015). Factors contributing to counselor education doctoral students' satisfaction with their dissertation chairperson. *The Professional Counselor, 5*(1), 185. https://digitalcommons.wcupa.edu/cgi/viewcontent.cgi?article=1001&context=counsed_facpub

Neale-McFall, C. W. (2011). *Perceived satisfaction of counseling doctoral students with their dissertation chairperson: Examining selection criteria and chairperson behaviors* [Doctoral dissertation, Old Dominion University]. https://digitalcommons.odu.edu/cgi/viewcontent.cgi?article=1080&context=chs_etds

Pacansky-Brock, M. (2020). *How to humanize your online class, version 2.0* [Infographic]. https://brocansky.com/humanizing/infographic2

Pacansky-Brock, M., Smedshammer, M., & Vincent-Layton, K. (2020). Humanizing online teaching to equitize higher education. *Current Issues in Education (Tempe, Ariz.), 21*(2), 1–21.

Rigler, K. L., Jr., Bowlin, L. K., Sweat, K., Watts, S., & Throne, R. (2017). *Agency, socialization, and support: A critical review of doctoral student attrition* [Paper presentation]. International Conference on Doctoral Education, University of Central Florida. https://files.eric.ed.gov/fulltext/ED580853.pdf

Roberts, C., & Hyatt, L. (2018). *The dissertation journey* (3rd ed.). Corwin Press.

Rockinson-Szapkiw, A. J., Holmes, J., & Stephens, J. S. (2019). Identifying significant personal and program factors that predict online EdD students' program integration. *Online Learning : the Official Journal of the Online Learning Consortium, 23*(4), 313–335. doi:10.24059/olj.v23i4.1579

Rovai, A. P. (2002). Sense of community, perceived cognitive learning, and persistence in asynchronous learning networks. *The Internet and Higher Education, 5*(4), 319–332. doi:10.1016/S1096-7516(02)00130-6

Smith, B. (2010). *E-learning technologies: A comparative study of adult learners enrolled on blended and online campuses engaging in a virtual classroom* [Doctoral dissertation].

Studebaker, B., & Curtis, H. (2021). Building community in an online doctoral program. *Christian Higher Education, 20*(1–2), 15–27. doi:10.1080/15363759.2020.1852133

Student Engagement and Community-Building | Barnard Center for Engaged Pedagogy. (n.d.). https://cep.barnard.edu/student-engagement-and-community-building

Terrell, S. R., Snyder, M. M., & Dringus, L. P. (2009). The development, validation, and application of the doctoral student connectedness scale. *The Internet and Higher Education, 12*(2), 112–116. doi:10.1016/j.iheduc.2009.06.004

Twenty to Nine LLC. (2023). Delve [online qualitative analysis software]. Available from delvetool.com

Whiteside, A. L., Garrett, D. A., & Swan, K. (Eds.). (2017). *Social presence in online learning: Multiple perspectives on practice and research*. Stylus Publishing.

KEY TERMS AND DEFINITIONS

CPED: Carnegie Project on the Education Doctorate; an international network of Education Schools committed to advancing the design, rigor, and impact of the Professional Doctorate in Education.

CWS Model: Continuous Weekly Support; refers to a model of high-touch faculty support that combines various andragogical and engagement strategies to consistently engage students and humanize the online student experience.

DiP: Dissertation in Practice; a scholarly endeavor embedded into the EdD program that seeks to answer a Problem of Practice using original research conducted by the doctoral student.

LDFM: Lead Doctoral Faculty Mentor; refers to the individual who serves as the mentor and dissertation chair to guide the student through the process of their dissertation research and writing.

LMS: Learning Management System; the online system used to engage students, faculty, and LDFMs in learning and training experiences.

Chapter 5
Empathy–Driven Instructional Design in Asynchronous Online Discussions

Stuart K. White
https://orcid.org/0009-0000-3646-9183
Purdue University, USA

Qian Xu
https://orcid.org/0000-0002-8640-6372
Purdue University, USA

Anthony C. Ilobinso
Purdue University, USA

Weijian Yan
Purdue University, USA

Liu Dong
Purdue University, USA

Zhuo Zhang
https://orcid.org/0000-0003-3374-5650
Purdue University, USA

Adewole E. Babalola
https://orcid.org/0009-0006-0188-4911
Purdue University, USA

Adrie A. Koehler
Purdue University, USA

ABSTRACT

Asynchronous online discussions (AODs) are a primary way instructors design for interactions among students in online environments. However, many common challenges associated with AODs (e.g., self-doubt, poorly constructed question prompts, superficial posting) prevent students from benefitting fully from the experience. Furthermore, how instructional designers address these challenges has implications for how AODs are designed, facilitated, monitored, and evaluated. This chapter explores using an empathy-driven approach to overcome AOD challenges. Adopting an empathy-driven approach offers instructional designers opportunities to mitigate challenges with designing, facilitating, monitoring, and evaluating AODs in order to create a meaningful learning opportunity that fosters inclusivity, motivation, and engagement while reducing ambiguity. Specific strategies are shared for improving AODs by using an empathy-based approach.

INTRODUCTION

Over the past decade, online learning has experienced substantial growth. In 2012, approximately 25.9% of U.S. students at degree-granting postsecondary institutions enrolled in at least one online course

DOI: 10.4018/979-8-3693-0762-5.ch005

(Seaman et al., 2018), with this figure rising to 37.2% in 2019 (NCES, 2020). The COVID-19 pandemic further accelerated this trend, prompting approximately 1.5 billion global learners to pivot to remote education (UNESCO, 2021). As a result, online learning has become a fundamental instructional approach adopted by institutions of higher education as demand for both degree programs and continuing education increases (Broadbent & Poon, 2015; Koehler et al., 2022). This transition has been facilitated by technological advancements in education and communication, coupled with the accessibility, flexibility, and affordability that online platforms provide (Mukhtar et al., 2020).

Within online learning environments, learners are expected to share responsibility in shaping their learning experiences (Galustyan et al., 2019; Koehler et al., 2020; Moore, 2013), as online learning requires students to be self-directed and highly independent (Broadbent & Poon, 2015). Asynchronous online discussions (AODs) are a fundamental way instructional designers build interpersonal interactions within asynchronous learning environments. Hew and Cheung (2003) define AODs as "text-based human-to-human communication via computer networks that provide a platform for the participants to interact with one another to exchange ideas, insights and personal experiences" (p. 249). Furthermore, AODs have been found to be a productive approach to extending the learning experience beyond traditional class time and space (Xie et al., 2006), and instructors can leverage AODs as a means of encouraging students to take ownership of their learning within online courses (Koehler et al., 2020).

The aim of AODs is to emulate face-to-face discussions by fostering learner reflection, investigation, and application of course concepts while facilitating interactions among peers and instructors (Koehler et al., 2020; Loncar et al., 2014). Commonly, AODs consist of an initial prompt asking students to consider course content in an interactive way (e.g., role play, debate, consideration of readings followed by guiding questions and peer feedback) followed by peer responses and elaboration. While the goal of an AOD is to mimic the human-to-human interactions reminiscent of face-to-face classroom learning experiences, the reality is that AOD prompt planning and execution require slightly different skill sets on the part of instructors and instructional designers.

Though AODs have their flaws, two primary advantages of AODs include sustained access to past conversations and prolonged reflection time prior to posting, both of which support meaningful and thoughtful exchanges (Hew et al., 2010; Murphy & Coleman, 2004). Purposeful integration of discussion participation can promote careful construction of ideas through reflection and facilitate critical thinking competencies, such as analysis and synthesis (Newman et al., 1997). Moreover, an AOD forum can play an essential role when these discussions foster the formation of learning communities where learners are afforded a setting to safely exchange ideas and share perceptions (Garrison et al., 2001); promote students' perceived satisfaction with a learning experience (Caskurlu et al., 2020; Richardson et al., 2017); and facilitate learners' problem-solving skills by providing a space for exploring problems, analyzing causes, and creating solutions (Anderson et al., 2008; Koehler et al., 2020; Wu et al., 2013).

Although AODs can be a useful tool in online environments, much of their effectiveness depends on the way they are designed, facilitated, and managed (Ertmer & Koehler 2014, 2015). The likelihood of learners experiencing challenges increases when intentionality is missing from AOD design. Therefore, from an instructional design perspective, understanding the challenges that emerge when using AODs is important for overcoming potential barriers and increasing the probability of creating positive learning experiences (Reeve & Jang, 2022). Empathetic design is one approach for more fully understanding inherent challenges present in the design, facilitation, and management of AODs and overcoming these challenges equitably.

Empathy is one's ability to share the feelings of others (Davis, 1994; Page & Nowak, 2002; Weisz & Cikara, 2020) and genuinely acknowledge someone else's experience, even if they differ from one's own (Brown, 2021). Introducing empathy-driven strategies early in the instructional design process can ensure a deeper appreciation of learners' experiences, especially in the realm of online discussions. Empathy is a complex, dynamic, and multifaceted construct (Bayne et al., 2013), with overlapping dimensions and social functions (Cliffordson, 2002). Weisz and Cikara (2020) identify three foundational components of empathy: 1) affective - mirroring others' emotional states, 2) cognitive - understanding others' viewpoints and experiences, and 3) motivational - aspiring to enhance others' well-being or diminish their stress. These can be equated with experience sharing, perspective-taking, and empathetic concern, respectively.

Adopting an empathetic approach increases educators' and instructional designers' likelihood of creating learning experiences that resonate with users. This involves a deepened comprehension of users and their realities; combining cognitive, affective, and user-centered understanding; and translating this understanding into tailored educational offerings (Carroll & Mcbain, 2021; Tracey & Baaki, 2022; Wright & McCarthy, 2005). An empathetic approach is especially important when designing AODs, as it necessitates awareness of participants' self-perceptions, unique experiences, and varied viewpoints (Smeenk et al., 2018). In essence, when designing online learning experiences, instructional designers and educators need to project themselves into remote learning contexts and predict learners' engagement experiences in these contexts.

PURPOSE STATEMENT

AODs are extensively used in online courses. However, designing, facilitating, monitoring, and evaluating AODs comes with several challenges. To address these challenges and improve the design and use of AODs in online settings, new methods are needed to promote student engagement, facilitate meaningful collaboration and connection, and humanize the learning experience. Therefore, the purpose of this chapter is to explore the concept of an empathy-driven approach in designing, facilitating, monitoring, and evaluating AODs to offer designers and educators new methods for creating meaningful learning experiences. By adopting an empathy-driven approach, designers and educators can foster a more inclusive online learning environment and provide a more engaging and meaningful experience for learners. Additionally, we believe the outcomes of these efforts can have a positive impact on the instructional design process. This work is seen as contributing to the existing body of knowledge on the humanization of online learning by highlighting the potential benefits of employing an empathy lens in the design, development, and management of AODs.

To facilitate this discussion, we first consider common challenges with designing and implementing AODs. Next, we revisit these challenges using an empathy lens and identify strategies from this same lens that can be used to improve the process of designing, facilitating, monitoring, and evaluating AOD forum participation and content. To connect proposed ideas to the reviewed literature, we use a real-life AOD example to consider the challenges observed in the literature and the specific strategies we are sharing might be applied.

AOD CHALLENGES

Several elements influence students' continuous engagement in AODs. For instance, self-efficacious beliefs can deter their involvement due to feelings such as shyness, inferiority, intimidation, perfectionism (Koehler et al., 2020; 2022), lack of confidence (Aloni & Harrington, 2018; Xie, 2013), and self-doubt (Amichai-Hamburger et al., 2016). Additionally, the construction of AOD prompts can also influence students' abilities to fully participate in a discussion (Sadaf et al., 2011). Research suggests that question prompts targeting lower levels of Bloom's Taxonomy result in fewer responses from students than prompts higher on the scale (Ertmer et al., 2011). Moreover, if participants fail to perceive a discussion's relevance in their lives, their motivation may wane (Dennen, 2005; Hew & Cheung, 2014).

During ongoing discussions, participants' sense of belongingness can be affected if they do not receive timely feedback or positive affirmations (Nonnecke & Preece, 2000); fear judgment or ridicule, thereby not feeling psychologically safe (LaRose et al., 2001); or struggle to contribute because certain individuals monopolized the conversation (Murphy & Coleman, 2004). Other challenges include technophobia (avoidance of or dislike for technology), apathy, and surface-level contributions (Aloni & Harrington, 2018; Krasnova & Ananjev, 2015; Murphy & Coleman, 2004). Furthermore, the pacing and timing of AODs can alienate some students, causing them to feel disconnected from peers and course content (AlJeraisy et al., 2015), while learners' inability to socially regulate with their peers can negatively impact their overall experience (Hadwin & Oshige 2011; Shea et al., 2022).

Another challenge arises when students are unclear about the expectations of their AOD involvement. Simultaneously, instructors face significant challenges when assessing AOD participation (Liu, 2007). Current efforts for evaluating AODs typically either focus on indirect measures (e.g., how students react to assignments) or employ instrumental indicators (e.g., post length, frequency of post) instead of evaluating the actual learning that takes place (Calderon & Sood, 2020). Both approaches can be disconnected from students. To address these challenges, AOD designers and facilitators must motivate students to initially participate and revisit the AOD (Bradley et al., 2008); craft effective prompts to stimulate meaningful conversation and minimize confusion (Aloni & Harrington, 2018); guide and monitor discussions to foster depth, flow, belonging, and shared regulation (Aljeraisy et al., 2015; Krasnova & Ananjev, 2015); and devise methods to accurately evaluate both individual and collective outcomes (Hadwin & Oshige, 2011; Shea et al, 2022).

As Fandos-Herrera et al. (2023) noted, the development of high quality engaging AODs requires intentionality and planning by the designer or instructor, making allowances for learners' attitude and context-dependent empathetic behaviors as they navigate their duo roles both as "the discussed" and the "discussant." For designers and instructors to overcome these challenges and most effectively design and facilitate AODs, they must deeply understand what learners are experiencing by taking an empathetic approach to AOD design and management. In short, research suggests that an empathy-driven approach to the design, facilitation, monitoring, and evaluation of AOD forums can "facilitate ethical decision making and moral judgments; enhance short-term subjective well-being; strengthen relational bonds; allow people to better understand how others see them; and enhance prosocial and altruistic behavior" (Brown, 2021, p. 120).

USING AN EMPATHY APPROACH WITH AODS

Empathy and AOD Design

Razzouk and Shute (2012) describe design as a process combining existing needs for improvement "with a determination that some action must be taken to solve the problem[s]" (p. 330). The design of AODs includes structuring the initial prompt in such a way that the resulting conversation is aligned with established objectives and integrates specific activities (e.g., role play, debate) and interactions (e.g., pairs, small group) (Koehler, 2023; Rico & Ertmer, 2015). Moreover, appreciation of an empathy driven approach to design is essential for instructional designers and course instructors tasked with creating learning experiences to meet the needs/demands of diverse individuals and educational settings. Vann (2015) underscored the integral role of empathy throughout instructional design, emphasizing its potential to generate effective, learner-focused outcomes. This approach allows designers and educators to shift their perspective of the design process by viewing everything from analysis to evaluation through an empathetic lens (Parrish, 2006). Key benefits include improved planning for diverse learners by integrating varied learning approaches and preferences.

In an AOD context, designing with empathy preemptively addresses learner challenges like frustration, confusion, or apprehension, equipping designers to more holistically cater to both instructors and students, and fostering deeper, more impactful learning (Haag & Marsden, 2019; Vann, 2015). One powerful design strategy for constructing an AOD prompt that aligns with learner attributes and needs is the creation of personas (Stefaniak & Baaki, 2013). Pruitt and Grudin (2003) describe a persona as an abstract or pseudo representation of a character grounded in research-backed analysis of the target audience. Creating effective personas generally involves research-backed analysis—gathering data from sources like online analytics and user interviews to understand the target audience. Then, using segmentation, learners are grouped, and distinct personas are created for each segment (Pruitt & Grudin, 2003).

Rooting personas in the learners' lived experiences, can guide instructional designers in developing more engaging content strategies (Baaki et al. (2017). Conversely, unrepresentative personas might distance students from the educational content. Notably, when empathy-building techniques are woven into immersive simulations, they shepherd learners from initial disorientation to structured introspection (Engbers, 2019). With immersive role-playing, diverse viewpoints, defined participant roles, introspective exercises, and purposefully selected, relatable content, online discussions can champion empathetic engagement.

Another critical aspect of AOD design is creating prompts that clarify expectations and guide meaningful discourse. Ambiguous discussion prompts can perplex students, potentially discouraging active participation (Aloni & Harrington, 2018). Thompson et al. (2016) advocate for clear and precise prompts to facilitate social aspects of knowledge construction. Furthermore, Gilbert and Dabbagh (2005) assert that prompts cultivated with empathy, where learners are guided towards thoughtful input, can reinforce social knowledge construction in AOD spaces. This stresses the necessity for reflective prompt design, urging the exploration of tactics by which designers and instructors can stimulate critical, engaging discourse. Research suggests that discussion structure and prompt quality can significantly impact the depth and caliber of AOD interactions (Bradley et al., 2008; Garrison et al., 2001; Yang, 2002). Thus, empathetically considered design choices concerning AOD structure and format can amplify anticipated meaningful student interactions and realization of intended learning outcomes.

Osborne et al. (2018) emphasized that the efficacy of AODs hinges on students' understanding of performance expectations, which in turn supports their readiness to engage more meaningfully. Approaching AOD design through an empathetic lens can elevate the quality of student acquisition of knowledge/understanding and its subsequent application in real-world experiences. This is especially true when expectations regarding knowledge depth, engagement levels, interaction duration, and response length are transparently communicated to learners (Williams et al., 2015; Delahunty, 2018). Viewing the AOD design process through an empathetic lens transcends standard ID practice and encourages designers to foresee learner experiences, identifying potential instructional challenges (Parrish, 2006). The resulting immersive, thoughtful engagement with content by the designer in an effort to capture learner experiences resonates with Kouprie and Visser's (2009) empathetic design framework, mirroring the utilization of journey maps prevalent in user experience design (Endmann & Keßner, 2016). Such resultant design narratives or learner interaction accounts equip designers with nuanced insights that may be overlooked in traditional learner analysis.

Empathy and AOD Facilitation

When facilitating AODs, instructors prompt interaction among learners, helping them connect and support one another as they consider course content (Rovai, 2007) and foster understanding through clarifying and validating students' ideas, redirecting misconceptions, and pushing students to consider key content more fully (Ertmer & Koehler, 2015). Since their inception, AODs have been celebrated for offering learners and instructors an accessible social environment akin to in-person discussions with similar facilitation needs and expectations. The unique affordances of AODs not only bridge time and geographical gaps but also affords diverse participants the space to nurture critical thinking and contemplate ideas (Brooks & Jeong, 2006; Hew & Cheung, 2008; Wang, 2008). Effective AOD facilitation is "critical to maintaining the interest, motivation, and engagement of students" (Anderson et al., 2001, p. 7) and necessary if instructors want to achieve meaningful student interaction, learning, and content engagement (Rovai, 2007; An et al., 2009). Applying best practices in AOD facilitation fosters a positive and adaptable learning space which in turn serves as an indispensable tool for elevating student engagement, comprehension of course content, and understanding of relevance (Douglas et al.,2020)--practices clearly aligned with an empathy-based approach.

Krasnova and Ananjev (2015) highlighted four recurring issues in AODs: limited student contributions, superficial posts, rudimentary grammar constructions, and ill-suited vocabulary choices. Arguably, most impediments faced in conventional discussions may resurface in AODs—potentially amplified due to perceived lack of instructor oversight. Examples include learners not posting in online discussions because peers have already expressed similar thoughts, or a lack of creative insight. Factors such as long delays between interactions or rigid time limits can further hamper student engagement. Conversely, some students may view their classmates' contributions as subpar, diminishing their enthusiasm to engage across an AOD. Moreover, introverted learners may harbor inherent reservations within AODs, thus hesitating to immerse fully in the discussions or to share their insights.

Empathy-driven AOD facilitation establishes a roadmap detailing strategies that foster a more engaged AOD forum environment (De Lima et al., 2019). Considering many students are active social media users, a delay in AOD post response or feedback and perceptions of hostility in tone or comments may result in disengagement from AOD forums and possibly a broader disconnect from learning experiences (Hew et al., 2010). Empathy-driven approaches to AOD facilitation have the potential to surmount barriers to online student participation, especially when AOD forums risk becoming emotionally overwhelming. Employing an empathetic approach highlights the role instructors play in cultivating a positive AOD atmosphere. McDonagh (2006) suggests that when instructors approach facilitation from a framework of empathy, participants are aided in developing an innate ability to resonate with the emotions and cognitions of others, encompassing their motivations, emotional and mental models, values, priorities, preferences, and inner conflicts.

Adopting an empathetic stance during AOD facilitation can increase student ownership over the learning process, enhancing the quality of scholarly discourse (Woods & Bliss, 2016) and promoting discussion prompts that pique their interest (Du & Xu, 2010). Empathy-driven approaches to AOD facilitation can be achieved with different strategies. For example, instructors can model vulnerability by relating personal experiences while outlining participation requirements, deadlines, and evaluation processes (Ariely & Wertenbroch, 2002). Furthermore, viewing scaffolded support through an empathetic lens encourages the delivery of timely, constructive feedback in relation to AOD objectives and posting requirements in an insightful manner (Woods & Bliss, 2016). For instance, students are more inclined to engage in a peer review process if they are initially introduced to peers in a relaxed personalized manner (Du et al., 2005; St. Clair, 2015). Stephens and Jones (2015) advocate for commencing online courses with AOD sessions featuring open-ended, content-relevant questions. An empathy driven approach to facilitating AOD continued participation in course AODs can be done by refreshing memories of these introductions within subsequent AOD forums and fostering a sense of community and belonging.

Empathy and AOD Monitoring

Once an AOD is underway, an instructor should monitor how the conversation is progressing--whether prompts and strategies are working effectively; students are actively engaged and adhering to established forum protocols; practices are equitable and result in inclusive dialog—making adjustments accordingly (Ertmer & Koehler, 2018; Long & Koehler, 2021). The natural outgrowth of an empathetic approach to AOD facilitation is the application of an empathetic approach to AOD monitoring. A well-structured course with clear facilitation guidelines fosters meaningful student interactions as evidenced by the number of student postings and more extensive discussion threads. However, these improvements to AOD participation present challenges related to monitoring. This can lead instructors to focus on posts with shorter lengths and easily identifiable citations, both of which result in reduced student engagement (Gilbert & Dabbagh, 2005).

Empathy-driven monitoring may be as simple as well structured prompts with staggered deadlines for initial posts and subsequent responses (Black, 2005). Applying an empathy-driven process to monitoring involves deconstructing AODs into smaller "manageable units" (Akcaoglu & Lee, 2016; Aloni & Harrington, 2018), and establishing guidelines for tracking conversation flow (Jeong, 2004). Other empathetic approaches to AOD monitoring may manifest in the way instructors oversee AOD participation, promote thought progression, ensure AOD etiquette, and more. Furthermore, learners can and should share in this monitoring process. For instance, McKinney (2018) observed that utilizing an AOD monitoring evaluation rubric promoted metacognitive awareness in learners by setting clear expectations and fostering richer student responses.

The goal of an empathetic approach to AOD monitoring is to maintain learner motivation to revisit AOD forums and consider peer feedback. Effective AOD monitoring can support newcomers to online learning (Salmon, 2003) by alleviating anxiety, exemplifying optimal AOD engagement, and increasing the likelihood of future participation (Salmon, 2003; Woods & Bliss, 2016). Besides offering constructive feedback on AOD *content*, empathetic AOD monitoring includes just-in-time encouragement and feedback on *participation*, promoting continued participation and reinforcing the value of empathy-driven AOD facilitation. Additionally, instructors using empathy-driven monitoring approaches acknowledge and celebrate all learners' effort, thus increasing the likelihood of sustaining AOD interactions and preventing learners from withdrawing from participation due to perceived criticism of their content knowledge, feeling overlooked, or underappreciated (Rovai, 2007).

Xie (2013) suggested that specific and uplifting feedback bolsters students' self-efficacy beliefs. Thus, an empathetic AOD monitoring approach where instructors provide prompt, detailed, and affirming feedback, can significantly enhance learners' self-efficacy. Another strategy to promote effective monitoring is the forming of smaller student groups so that students feel integrated into the learning community, being more inclined to share ownership in the monitoring process. Instructors' burden of monitoring more discussion threads can be further reduced by assigning various roles, like facilitator, monitor, and/or peer-reviewer (Baran & Correia, 2009; Cheung, et al., 2008; Du et al., 2005).

Additionally, nurturing empathetic reflection skills through thought-provoking questions can support meaningful monitoring (Woods & Bliss, 2016). When applying an empathetic-approach to monitoring AODs, instructors can leverage diverse discussion formats (e.g., role play, debate, brainstorming, circle of voices, etc.) to stimulate learner reflection, critical thinking, and rich peer interactions. Additionally, effective AOD monitoring includes an instructor's awareness of a learning community and how prompts and strategies are working and then using this awareness to direct efforts behind the scene and make real-time adjustments. For instance, if an instructor notices a missing voice during a discussion, he can send an individual message to the student to check on their well-being. As another example, if an instructor realizes that a specific prompt is not working, she can adjust strategies to meet students where they are, based on what is needed (Long & Koehler, 2021; Watson et al., 2018).

When viewed together, empathetic facilitation and monitoring complement each other; the former encourages reflectiveness in discussion posting to enhance knowledge assimilation (Bye et al., 2009), while the latter consistently promotes clarity of posting guidelines. Empathy driven AOD monitoring enhances clarity within AOD posting norms, grading processes, and helps learners discern quality discussion criteria, allowing them to monitor their own performance (Gilbert & Dabbagh, 2005; Rovai, 2007), In short, empathetic monitoring requires a facilitator to be active and create an intentional presence in the discussion.

Empathy and AOD Evaluation

Evaluating AODs involves the formative process of judging the quality of students' postings and activity by providing feedback in alignment with established criteria (Rico & Ertmer, 2015). While AODs have become an essential instructional tool in distance education, a unified approach to evaluating learner participation remains elusive (Weltzer-Ward, 2010). Scholars such as Berner (2003), Klisc et al. (2009), and Laurillard (2002) suggest that integrating high quality assessments can foster active participation and enrich learning outcomes in AOD forums. Furthermore, studies by Leh (2002) and Seo (2007) suggest grade incentives might spur learners to engage more actively in AODs. Across these perspectives, gauging participation in AOD presents substantial challenges to both instructional designers and educators (Calderon & Sood, 2020; Liu, 2007). Current evaluation strategies for AODs tend to target indirect metrics (i.e., student reactions to tasks) or direct indicators (i.e., post length and frequency) and often overlook the assessment of genuine content knowledge acquisition and meaningful participation.

Using an empathetic approach to AOD evaluation enables designers and educators to enhance online discussion efficacy by leveraging both quantitative and qualitative assessment methods. As AOD design, facilitation, and monitoring evolve through an empathy-centric lens, the resulting evaluation tools are assumed to embody this same sensitivity. One common approach for quantitatively evaluating learner interaction during a discussion course involves tallying the posts learners generate (De Oliveira et al., 2021). While tallying posts alone does not offer an empathetic approach to discussion evaluation, this simplistic metric allows students to grasp fundamental participation standards, and pairing this metric with targeted course content or vocabulary allows learners to get a feel for the evaluative techniques employed by educators. Such content engagement tracking reportedly increases post submissions and equips instructors with insights into shifts in student engagement (Ding et al., 2018).

Solely relying on counting the quantity of posts or tracking the amount of content used does not ensure an equitable, insightful, and comprehensive AOD evaluation. These measures fail to consider the quality or depth of students' posts. Such a system can be perceived as biased by learners, and, consequently, they might deem it unfair and become disengaged in the discussion (Pereira Nunes et al., 2014; Shaul, 2007). Adopting an empathetic stance in AOD evaluation can address these concerns of perceived unfairness, fostering better communication between educators and learners regarding participation expectations.

Designers and instructors should consider integrating more qualitative methodologies for assessing AOD participation and quality. These evaluative tools can range from content analysis to grading rubrics aimed at gauging the depth and quality of learners' online discussion engagement. Embracing an empathetic approach through mixed methods evaluation ensures a nuanced assessment, promotes depth of content as well as length of post, and fosters development of a positive learning environment. However, qualitative approaches come with their own set of challenges (Shaul, 2007).

Framing discussion prompts to evoke responses indicative of higher-order and critical thinking skills (Bradley, 2008; Ertmer et al., 2011; Williams, 2015) can pose challenges for novice instructors and inexperienced online learners. An effective strategy to tackle this is the use of open-ended questions, with prompts designed to spur elaboration and showcase learners' understanding, rather than eliciting binary-style answers (Husain et al., 2012). These more qualitative evaluations can be inherently subjective as they are, contingent upon the instructor's interpretation of what constitutes a "quality" post. Sifting through every individual post to tease out learner meaning and intent can become burdensome, especially in classes with a large number of learners.

Open-ended prompts are important considerations when instructors are seeking to elicit responses aligned with higher-order thinking because they foster diverse responses, encompassing both established and evolving knowledge (Wasik, 2013). Moreover, open-ended discussion prompts resonate with Bloom's (1956) taxonomy and Andrews' (1980) typology (Ertmer et al., 2011). An empathetic approach to evaluation encourages designers and instructors to diversify AOD questions and develop evaluation rubrics to assess the depth of critical thinking in students' responses (Bradley et al., 2008; Ertmer, 2011). Content analysis serves as another evaluative technique, which, when integrated using an empathy-driven approach, can be useful in analyzing AOD transcripts (De Wever, 2006). Various studies have illustrated the use of pre-established evaluation tools for content analysis, with coding schemes focusing on grading rubrics for online discussions (De Wever, 2006; Solan & Linardopoulos, 2011; Weltzer-Ward, 2010). One such tool assesses student posts against a rubric that evaluates participation based on quantity, quality, relevance, and manner (Ho & Swan, 2007). Using predefined rubrics, significantly reduces the need for creating unique rubrics for each AOD thread. Additional empathy driven approaches to AOD evaluation include ungrading, self-assessment, and student-made rubrics as a means of promoting deep reflection on learning, respect resulting from shared decision-making, and self-regulation (Koehler & Meech, 2022).

A REAL-WORLD EXAMPLE CONNECTING RESEARCH TO PRACTICE

To more deeply understand an empathy-driven approach to AOD design and facilitation, consider the following learning context. Professor Plum teaches an undergraduate course on biology methods for individuals majoring in elementary education. Students within this course are pre-service teachers focusing on generalized elementary education, early childhood development, and elementary special education. Each semester, approximately 150 students enroll in the course. The course is designed to provide learning experiences directly applicable to next generation science standards (NGSS) for life science within K-6 classrooms. A secondary focus is to engage students with content from the perspective of future teachers, asking them to think like teachers when presenting content, developing possible resources, and evaluating educational contexts. This hybrid course uses a 50-50 split, requiring students to complete weekly in-person lab activities and collaborative online work, covering topics related to genetics, natural selection, evolution, and diversity.

Taft (2023) indicates that a typical life science AOD prompt for a course like this might as follows:

Sexual reproduction involves crossing-over to mix up genes. Is this a good thing or a bad thing? In the discussion this week explain one pro and one con to crossing-over. Overall, what is your opinion of crossing-over? Can evolution occur without it? After completing your initial post, return the discussion and comment on 3 peer posts.

While the goal may be to mimic the human-to-human interactions reminiscent of face-to-face classroom learning experiences, the reality is that discussion prompts written like this inhibit the expected exchange of ideas, insights, and person experiences looked for in a discussion dialog.

However, an AOD constructed using an empathy-driven approach to the design, facilitation, monitoring, and evaluation may look more like the following.

You just completed a unit covering genetics and now want to introduce students to the variety of organisms in the world around them. After sending home a coloring activity that contains a variety of different animals and plants you receive an email from a parent asking you why you are having students color pictures instead of learning. How do you respond? Include in your response a discussion of the use of different learning activities, age appropriateness of learning activities, and the learning value attached to a variety of learning experiences within a larger unit of instruction. After your initial post, create a communication thread with 2 or 3 peers where you take on the role of the parent and seek greater clarification to their posted response(s).

We consider these prompts using the four key aspects of AODs previously discussed.

Prompt Design

Comparison between the two life science AOD discussion prompts provide a good example of several empathy-driven design considerations. First, prior to designing the prompts, creation and application of a pre-service teacher persona to the construction of an AOD prompt leads the designer to connect pre-service teachers' current understanding, beliefs, and anticipated lived experience of the future teacher with both course content and science teaching methodology. Moreover, when AOD prompts are designed with empathy, it paves the way for instructors to articulate expectations (i.e., create a communication thread with 2 or 3 peers where you take on the role of the parent and seek greater clarification to their posted responses), enabling learners to mentally connect with content and their peers. The use of personas in instructional design contexts facilitates designers stepping into learners' shoes and fostering designers comprehending learner AOD experience. Furthermore, empathy-driven design practices aid in developing resources to guide instructors in offering AOD participation parameters that recognize varied learner viewpoints, encourage adaptive participation, and champion civil discourse (Wlodkowoski & Ginsberg, 2017).

Finally, revisiting the life science AOD prompt mentioned within the contextual setting and applying an empathetic lens we can identify areas for improvement. For example, this prompt is somewhat ambiguous and does not provide clear indications of the assignment's context or objectives. According to Thompson et al. (2016), this lack of clarity could potentially confuse students as they attempt to respond as "parents." The prompt could also be revised to provide more context, consider participant needs and expectations, and offer clearer post/response guidance aligning the prompt more closely with empathetic design principles. Additionally, students are tasked with assuming dual roles as both teachers and parents, providing them with an opportunity to immerse themselves in the experiences of both and bringing the task closer to home. The initial disorientation that may have occurred when considering the task purely in technical terms gradually gives way to structured introspection. As students reflect on the task through the lens of their current and prospective roles, they can engage more thoroughly and productively with the learning activity. Providing pre-service teachers an opportunity to engage in role playing parent-teacher interactions in an open, inviting, safe forum assists students develop important communication skills.

Facilitation

The course instructor (Professor Plum) engages with 10 random students during each AOD prompt, allowing the instructor to interact with all students' initial AOD post at some point during the semester and a variety of AOD prompt responders. Each teaching assistant (TA) is asked to engage in discussion threads associated with students assigned to their lab section. This serves two purposes - first, the instructor burden is shared by course TAs and second, all students get targeted just-in-time feedback on a regular basis. Moreover, student immersion into parent/teacher roles affords the instructor an opportunity to facilitate and model effective communication skill development, conflict resolution, and netiquette while preserving real-world educational role playing.

From an empathy-driven approach, instructors can facilitate this online discussion by first establishing clear guidelines related to participation and the frequency and quality of contributions. In addition, facilitators can remind peers to pose open-ended questions on students' posts to prompt thoughtful responses and promote continued discussion. An effective facilitation strategy is demonstrated by asking a student to respond to two or three peers' initial posts in this discussion thread. Instructors and TAs are then able to extend their reach of constructive feedback to a larger number of students' contributions, highlighting strengths, and providing guidance for improving interpersonal and content specific dialog. For example, both the instructor and TAs can acknowledge insightful comments and encourage students to explore their ideas further.

While actively engaging students with AODs may be easily accomplished in small course sizes, engaging students in courses with larger numbers may be more challenging. Hence, the number of students instructors engage with during any given discussion prompt may be limited by their available time. Additionally, empathy-driven approaches to AOD facilitation could be strengthened with different strategies. When instructors are willing to expose their vulnerability by relating personal strengths and weaknesses while outlining participation requirements, deadlines, and evaluation processes they can encourage students to share personal narratives and make course content more central to the dialog. Moreover, as instructors praise student willingness to share personal narratives of course content, connections between course concepts and real-world scenarios are solidified and understanding is enhanced (Powell & Murray, 2012).

Monitoring

Discussion prompts are set up so that someone initiates a conversation to which others provide feedback. To ensure this prompt strategy works effectively, Professor Plum sets up all discussion prompts so that responders must generate their initial response prior to accessing peer responses. This ensures students do not know how others are responding prior to constructing their response, supporting authentic give and take dialog. The inability of learners to construct their initial response using insight from previous responders, places all participants on an equal playing field. Another empathy-driven strategy associated with AOD monitoring is demonstrated by the formation of smaller student groups so that students feel integrated into the learning community. The larger course section is reduced to individual lab sections, allowing students to strengthen collaborative efforts and increase feelings of community. Instructors' burden of monitoring more discussion threads can be further reduced by grouping students from individual lab sections into lab groups of four to six. Participants are then assigned specific roles (e.g., facilitator, monitor, peer-reviewer). Thus, the instructor burden of monitoring all discussion threads is shared across the community of learners.

Evaluation

Looking at the second AOD prompt, Professor Plum is attempting to elicit student reactions to laboratory activities by asking students to respond to a specific number of posts, increasing their likelihood of meeting prompt content requirements. Furthermore, in the life science course, participants are evaluated on how well they engage in conversations within assumed roles. That is, students are evaluated based on addressing initial "parental concern," incorporation of different learning activities, and age appropriateness and value within the initial post. The discussion prompt requires responders to impersonate a stereotypical parent type (e.g., helicopter, ghost, hands-off, etc.), while the original post submitter is to remain in the role of the classroom teacher, in responding to parental comments. Finally, Professor Plum affords students 7 days (Sunday 12:01am to Saturday 11:59pm) to participate in the discussion. While discussion prompts remain open for student responses after the deadline, students are provided with a new discussion prompt each week. If students do not participate in a weekly discussion within the allotted time, they are assessed a 15% penalty, with students being allowed to make up incomplete AODs until the last day of the semester.

IMPLICATIONS OF EMPATHETIC DESIGN LENS

As instructional designers seek to understand AOD challenges using an empathetic approach to the design process they will reflect on the experiences of both AOD facilitators and participants. If instructional designers are going to move beyond instructor struggles with prompt creation, evaluation, and participant perceptions of relevance and "box checking" they must be willing to put themselves in others' shoes. This empathetic introspection provides the groundwork for examining AODs in a new light. An empathetic design lens can aid instructional designers in identifying recurring patterns of learner and instructor challenges, allowing them to assess preconceptions on learner and instructor experiences. Empathy-driven insights prompt conversations on effective AOD implementation, the significance of personas, and pedagogical best practices, among other topics. We assert that by embracing an empathetic design approach, designers and instructors can move beyond traditional methods and develop enhanced strategies for AOD forum design, facilitation, monitoring, and evaluation.

Several strategies for improving the design of AOD forums stand out within various empathy frameworks. First, there is emphasis on understanding user perspectives, which involves interacting with users (Kouprie & Visser, 2009), forging relationships with them (Carroll & Mcbain, 2021), stepping into the user's shoes (Dohrenwend, 2018), tuning in to the changing experiences (Dohrenwend, 2018), and acknowledging the vested interest students hold in their learning journey (Carroll & Mcbain, 2021). Second, examining the designer's viewpoint by identifying inherent biases (Carroll & Mcbain, 2021) and channeling personal experiences within the user context (Kouprie & Visser, 2009). Lastly, the integration of emotion in the design process is essential. This entails recognizing potential emotional reactions as the design unfolds (Dohrenwend, 2018) and leveraging raw data, like user photographs, to foster connections (Kouprie & Visser, 2009).

A central tenet of empathy-driven design is that genuine understanding mandates designers and instructors to connect with learners at a deeper level. This arises from the realization that educators and instructional designers' personal experiences shape their perception of content and influence their instructional strategies. In turn, empathy-driven design effectively tackles challenges associated with AOD prompt creation, the facilitation and monitoring of AODs, motivating participation, and evaluating responses within the AOD context.

Using an empathy-driven approach to design online discussions focuses on nurturing constructive, meaningful conversations that emphasize participants' emotional well-being and diverse viewpoints (Klapwijk & Van Doorn, 2015). Terry and Cain (2016) highlight that neglecting empathetic considerations can make learners feel their thoughts and contributions in AOD forums are undervalued. Consequently, designers and instructors should develop a deeper sensitivity to AOD usage, seeking to understand the situations and emotions that promote empathy.

By catering to both the cognitive and emotional (affective) facets of learners' experiences within the AOD context, instructors can more effectively discern learners' emotions towards and interpretations of AOD Forums (Kouprie & Visser, 2009). Such empathic forecasting plays an important role in

Table 1. Empathetic approaches for addressing key AOD challenges

AOD Phase	Key Challenges	Empathy-Informed Strategies
Design	Prompts containing language that lacks precision and clarity.	Create personas based on the lived experiences of the target learners. Craft prompts that address the preferences and understanding levels of these personas, using language that is clear and precise for the entire audience.
	Uncertain expectations regarding the level of involvement required.	Review the prompt from the learners' perspective to anticipate their thoughts about the clarity of the prompt and ensure they understand precisely what their participation will entail.
	Prompts crafted using language indicative of lower-order thinking skills.	Tailor the language in prompt construction to pose challenges that stimulate critical thinking among your target learner audience. Allow for varying levels of performance and scaffold learners' thinking through feedback cues that encourage higher-order cognitive engagement.
	Articulated prompts that highlight relevance to students' lives.	Construct prompts that connect with real-life scenarios, resonating with learners' experiences, interests, and daily lives. Offer opportunities for immersive simulations, consider diverse audience backgrounds, and purposefully select and design relatable content for learners.
Facilitation	Students lack self-confidence and/ or perceptions of subpar contributions, diminishing enthusiasm to persist in conversations.	Provide positive affirmations for students who have low self-confidence; pose open-ended, content-relevant questions for deep reflection; and create an opportunity for learners to introduce themselves in a relaxed personalized manner at the beginning of a class.
	Participants do not receive timely feedback; long delays between interactions.	Use scaffolds that encourage the delivery of timely, constructive feedback in relation to course grades.
	Students are unclear about the expectations of their involvement in the conversation.	Outline participation requirements, deadlines, and evaluation processes at the beginning of a class and allow these to be easily accessed by students.
	Students lack a sense of belonging, limited student contributions and/or superficial posts.	Draw on person details shared during introductions within subsequent AOD forums.
Monitoring	The conversation lacks a consistent flow over time	Stagger deadlines between initial post and response postings to allow targeted and timely feedback. Offer affirmation to individuals who are purposefully posting to promote others to participate in a similar way.
	Students feel disconnected from peers and uncertain about how to persist in the discussion.	Establish small sized groups of three to six individuals within discussion threads. Assign participant roles within discussion threads for self-monitoring and encouragement. E-mail individual students who are missing in the discussion to check on their well-being and offer support.
	Implemented prompts do not work as intended–students are confused, or prompts do not result in a robust discussion.	Reflect on where the problem is, making adjustments both in the moment using follow-up posts to redirect learners and for future implementations to fix mistakes.
Evaluations	The utilization of quantitative evaluation methods can lead to perceptions of unfairness among students and result in disengagement from posting activities.	Combine tallying number of posts generated with targeted course content vocabulary and tracking changes in post submissions for identifying shifts in student engagement.
	Limiting AOD assessments to purely quantitative data does not ensure an equitable, insightful, and comprehensive AOD evaluation.	Adopt qualitative methodologies, such as content analysis and grading rubrics, to assess the depth and quality of student engagement in online discussions. Blend empathetic evaluation with quantitative measures to foster a positive learning environment.
	Crafting discussion prompts that elicit higher-order and critical thinking can be challenging for new instructors and online learners.	Employing open-ended questions that encourage detailed responses and demonstrate learners' comprehension, rather than simple yes/no answers, is recommended.
	Evaluation standards can be vague and subjective, resulting in inconsistent assessments. Unclear criteria may leave students feeling lost and perceiving unfairness	Develop rubrics that measure depth of critical thinking and implement standardized tools for content analysis. Incorporate ungrading, self-assessment, and student-created rubrics to foster deep reflection, mutual respect through shared decision-making, and self-regulation.

design, bridging the gap between learners and the intended cognitive and emotional interactions with AOD forums and prompts (Tracey & Hutchinson, 2019). Empathetic design principles advocate for task assignments that match learners' abilities, avoiding overly simplistic or challenging tasks that might disengage them (Tracey & Baaki, 2022).

Adopting an empathetic design perspective in the creation, facilitation, and evaluation of AODs can deeply enhance both student and instructor experiences. By addressing primary AOD challenges such as prompt creation, facilitation and monitoring, motivation, and evaluation with an empathy-driven approach, there can be marked improvements in AOD forums. (See Table 1 for specific empathy-informed strategies aligned with common AOD challenges). When instructional designers integrate their personal experiences, they explore the challenges faced by both instructors and students, reshaping the approach to instructional resources, strategy implementations, and design evaluation principles. This not only offers a clearer direction for the design process but emphasizes the user's experience.

Integrating an empathy-driven approach to meet the unique experiences of designers and instructors shifts AOD design towards an "as-if" stance, promoting a deeper exploration of diverse learning experiences. When designers and instructors are immersed in the learners' real-world experiences, they become adept at understanding specific learning strategies. This improved understanding of learner experience ensures a fair balance in learning objectives, and the nurturing of a sense of community within the learning environment.

Given the proliferation of online education, the significance of incorporating an empathetic lens in the design and implementation of AODs has emerged as a pivotal determinant of pedagogical success. The ubiquity of AODs in contemporary online educational frameworks implies their critical role in fostering engagement, nurturing reflective and critical thought processes, and facilitating substantive interactions among participants. Nevertheless, the extant literature and our reflections indicate that the mere existence and integration of AODs do not guarantee efficacy. Rather, it is a nuanced, empathetic approach to their design, facilitation, monitoring, and evaluation that actualizes their full potential.

Grounded in our experiential insights and supported by comprehensive research, this paper underscores the need for empathy-driven approaches to AOD design beyond an abstract pedagogical ideal and as an indispensable, tangible tool for instructional design. By prioritizing empathy in the design process, educators and instructional designers are better poised to curate an online learning environment that is both receptive to the diverse exigencies of learners and conducive to fostering meaningful, authentic interactions. Beyond the operational dynamics of AODs, the integration of empathetic principles heralds a larger pedagogical imperative: the humanization of digital education.

As the trajectory of online education continues its upward trend, maintaining its intrinsic humanistic ethos becomes an imperative, not a choice. The empathetic paradigm offers a pragmatic framework for contemporary educational interventions, as well as presents an avenue for future academic exploration and pedagogical innovation. The academic community is thus beckoned to embrace and disseminate this empathy-centric approach, ensuring that as education evolves in the digital age, it remains tethered to the foundational human tenets of understanding, engagement, and transformative learning.

REFERENCES

Akcaoglu, M., & Lee, E. (2016). Increasing social presence in online learning through small group discussions. *The International Review of Research in Open and Distributed Learning, 17*(3).

AlJeraisy, M. N., Mohammad, H., Fayyoumi, A., & Alrashideh, W. (2015). Web 2.0 in education: The impact of discussion board on student performance and satisfaction. *Turkish Online Journal of Educational Technology-TOJET, 14*(2), 247–258.

Aloni, M., & Harrington, C. (2018). Research based practices for improving the effectiveness of asynchronous online discussion boards. *Scholarship of Teaching and Learning in Psychology, 4*(4), 271–289. doi:10.1037/stl0000121

Amichai-Hamburger, Y., Gazit, T., Bar-Ilan, J., Perez, O., Aharony, N., Bronstein, J., & Sarah Dyne, T. (2016). Psychological factors behind the lack of participation in online discussions. *Computers in Human Behavior, 55*, 268–277. doi:10.1016/j.chb.2015.09.009

An, H., Shin, S., & Lim, K. (2009). The effects of different instructor facilitation approaches on students' interactions during asynchronous online discussions. *Computers & Education, 53*(3), 749–760. doi:10.1016/j.compedu.2009.04.015

Anderson, T., Rourke, L., Garrison, D. R., & Archer, W. (2001). Assessing teaching presence in a computer conferencing environment. *Journal of Asynchronous Learning Networks, 5*(2), 1–17.

Anderson, W. L., Mitchell, S. M., & Osgood, M. P. (2008). Gauging the gaps in student problem-solving skills: Assessment of individual and group use of problem-solving strategies using online discussions. *CBE Life Sciences Education, 7*(2), 254–262. doi:10.1187/cbe.07-06-0037 PMID:18519617

Andrews, J. (1980). The verbal structure of teacher questions: Its impact on class discussion. POD Quarterly. *Journal of Professional and Organizational Development Network in Higher Education, 2*(3 & 4), 129–163.

Ariely, D., & Wertenbroch, K. (2002). Procrastination, deadlines, and performance: Self-control by precommitment. *Psychological Science, 13*(3), 219–224. doi:10.1111/1467-9280.00441 PMID:12009041

Baaki, J., Maddrell, J., & Stauffer, E. (2017). Designing authentic personas for open education resources designers. *International Journal of Designs for Learning, 8*(2), 110–122. doi:10.14434/ijdl.v8i2.22427

Baran, E., & Correia, A. P. (2009). Student-led facilitation strategies in online discussions. *Distance Education, 30*(3), 339–361. doi:10.1080/01587910903236510

Bayne, H., Neukrug, E., Hays, D., & Britton, B. (2013). A comprehensive model for optimizing empathy in person-centered care. *Patient Education and Counseling, 93*(2), 209–215. Advance online publication. doi:10.1016/j.pec.2013.05.016 PMID:23769885

Berner, R. T. (2003). *The benefits of bulletin board discussion in a literature of journalism course.* The Technology Source. Accessed Oct 2, 2023. http://technologysource.org/article/313/

Black, A. (2005). The use of asynchronous discussion: Creating a text of talk. *Contemporary Issues in Technology & Teacher Education, 5*(1), 5–24.

Bloom, B. (1956). *Taxonomy of educational objectives*. David McKay.

Bradley, M. E., Thom, L. R., Hayes, J., & Hay, C. (2008). Ask and you will receive: How question type influences quantity and quality of online discussions. *British Journal of Educational Technology, 39*(5), 888–900. doi:10.1111/j.1467-8535.2007.00804.x

Broadbent, J., & Poon, W. L. (2015). Self-regulated learning strategies & academic achievement in online higher education learning environments: A systematic review. *The Internet and Higher Education, 27*, 1–13. doi:10.1016/j.iheduc.2015.04.007

Brooks, D., & Jeong, A. (2006). The effects of pre-structuring discussion threads on group interaction and group performance in computer-supported collaborative argumentation. *Distance Education, 27*(3), 371–390. doi:10.1080/01587910600940448

Brown, B. (2021). *Atlas of the heart: Mapping meaningful connection and the language of human experience*. Random House.

Bye, L., Smith, S., & Rallis, H. M. (2009). Reflection using an online discussion forum: Impact on student learning and satisfaction. *Social Work Education, 28*(8), 841–855. doi:10.1080/02615470802641322

Calderon, O., & Sood, C. (2020). Evaluating learning outcomes of an asynchronous online discussion assignment: A post-priori content analysis. *Interactive Learning Environments, 28*(1), 3–17. doi:10.1080/10494820.2018.1510421

Carroll, M., & Mcbain, L. (2021). Where empathy meets learning: Exploring design abilities in K-12 classrooms. *Voices from the Middle, 29*(1), 14–17. doi:10.58680/vm202131424

Caskurlu, S., Maeda, Y., Richardson, J. C., & Lv, J. (2020). A meta-analysis addressing the relationship between teaching presence and students' satisfaction and learning. *Computers & Education, 157*, 103966. doi:10.1016/j.compedu.2020.103966

Cheung, W. S., Hew, K. F., & Ng, C. L. (2008). Toward an understanding of why students contribute in asynchronous online discussions. *Journal of Educational Computing Research, 38*(1), 29–50. doi:10.2190/EC.38.1.b

Cliffordson, C. (2002). The hierarchical structure of empathy: Dimensional organization and relations to social functioning. *Scandinavian Journal of Psychology, 43*(1), 49–59. doi:10.1111/1467-9450.00268 PMID:11885760

Davis, M. H. (1994). *Empathy: A social psychological approach*. Westview Press.

de Lima, D. P., Gerosa, M. A., & Conte, T. U., & de M. Netto, J. F. (2019). What to expect, and how to improve online discussion forums: The instructors' perspective. *Journal of Internet Services and Applications, 10*, 1–15. doi:10.1186/s13174-019-0120-0

De Oliveira, A. S., Silva, M. A. R., Da Silva, D., & Borges, R. C. (2021). Quality Assessment of Online Discussion Forums: Construction and Validation of a Scale That Values Student Perception. *Turkish Online Journal of Distance Education, 22*(4), 43–57. doi:10.17718/tojde.1002759

De Wever, B., Schellens, T., Valcke, M., & Van Keer, H. (2006). Content analysis schemes to analyze transcripts of online asynchronous discussion groups: A review. *Computers & Education*, *46*(1), 6–28. doi:10.1016/j.compedu.2005.04.005

Delahunty, J. (2018). Connecting to learn, learning to connect: Thinking together in asynchronous forum discussion. *Linguistics and Education*, *46*, 12–22. doi:10.1016/j.linged.2018.05.003

Dennen, V. P. (2005). From message posting to learning dialogues: Factors affecting learner participation in asynchronous discussion. *Distance Education*, *26*(1), 127–148. doi:10.1080/01587910500081376

Ding, L., Er, E., & Orey, M. (2018). An exploratory study of student engagement in gamified online discussions. *Computers & Education*, *120*, 213–226. doi:10.1016/j.compedu.2018.02.007

Dohrenwend, A. M. (2018). Defining empathy to better teach, measure, and understand its impact. *Academic Medicine*, *93*(12), 1754–1756. doi:10.1097/ACM.0000000000002427 PMID:30134271

Douglas, T., James, A., Earwaker, L., Mather, C., & Murray, S. (2020). Online discussion boards: Improving practice and student engagement by harnessing facilitator perceptions. *Journal of University Teaching & Learning Practice*, *17*(3), 7. doi:10.53761/1.17.3.7

Du, J., Havard, B., & Li, H. (2005). Dynamic online discussion: Task-oriented interaction for deep learning. *Educational Media International*, *42*(3), 207–218. doi:10.1080/09523980500161221

Du, J., & Xu, J. (2010). The quality of online discussion reported by graduate students. *Quarterly Review of Distance Education*, *11*(1), 13–24.

Endmann, A., & Keßner, D. (2016). User journey mapping–A method in user experience design. *i-com*, *15*(1), 105-110.

Engbers, R. (2019). Students' perceptions of interventions designed to foster empathy: An integrative review. *Nurse Education Today*, *86*, 104325. doi:10.1016/j.nedt.2019.104325 PMID:31926381

Ertmer, P. A., & Koehler, A. A. (2014). Online case discussions: Examining coverage of the afforded problem space. *Educational Technology Research and Development*, *62*(5), 617–636. Advance online publication. doi:10.1007/s11423-014-9350-9

Ertmer, P. A., & Koehler, A. A. (2015). Facilitated versus non-facilitated online case discussions: Comparing differences in problem space coverage. *Journal of Computing in Higher Education*, *27*(2), 69–93. doi:10.1007/s12528-015-9094-5

Ertmer, P. A., & Koehler, A. A. (2018). Facilitation strategies and problem space coverage: Comparing face-to-face and online case-based discussions. *Educational Technology Research and Development*, *66*(3), 639–670. doi:10.1007/s11423-017-9563-9

Ertmer, P. A., Sadaf, A., & Ertmer, D. (2011). Designing effective question prompts to facilitate critical thinking in online discussions. *Design Principles & Practices*, *5*(4), 1–10. doi:10.18848/1833-1874/CGP/v05i04/38121

Fandos-Herrera, C., Jiménez-Martínez, J., Orús, C., Pérez-Rueda, A., & Pina, J. M. (2023). The influence of personality on learning outcomes and attitudes: The case of discussants in the classroom. *International Journal of Management Education, 21*(1), 100754. doi:10.1016/j.ijme.2022.100754

Galustyan, O. V., Borovikova, Y. V., Polivaeva, N. P., Kodirov, B. R., & Zhirkova, G. P. (2019). Elearning within the field of andragogy. *International Journal of Emerging Technologies in Learning, 14*(9), 148–156. doi:10.3991/ijet.v14i09.10020

Garrison, D. R., Anderson, T., & Archer, W. (2001). Critical thinking, cognitive presence, and computer conferencing in distance education. *American Journal of Distance Education, 15*(1), 7–23. doi:10.1080/08923640109527071

Gilbert, P. K., & Dabbagh, N. (2005). How to structure online discussions for meaningful discourse: A case study. *British Journal of Educational Technology, 36*(1), 5–18. doi:10.1111/j.1467-8535.2005.00434.x

Haag, M., & Marsden, N. (2019). Exploring personas as a method to foster empathy in student IT design teams. *International Journal of Technology and Design Education, 29*(3), 565–582. doi:10.1007/s10798-018-9452-5

Hadwin, A., & Oshige, M. (2011). Self-regulation, coregulation, and socially shared regulation: Exploring perspectives of social in self-regulated learning theory. *Teachers College Record, 113*(2), 240–264. doi:10.1177/016146811111300204

Hew, K. F., & Cheung, W. S. (2003). Evaluating the participation and quality of thinking of pre-service teachers in an asynchronous online discussion environment: Part 1. *International Journal of Instructional Media, 30*(3), 247–262.

Hew, K. F., & Cheung, W. S. (2008). Attracting student participation in asynchronous online discussions: A case study of peer facilitation. *Computers & Education, 51*(3), 1111–1124. doi:10.1016/j.compedu.2007.11.002

Hew, K. F., & Cheung, W. S. (2014). *Student participation in online discussions: Challenges, solutions, and future research.* Springer Science & Business Media. doi:10.1007/978-1-4614-2370-6

Hew, K. F., Cheung, W. S., & Ng, C. S. L. (2010). Student contribution in asynchronous online discussion: A review of the research and empirical exploration. *Instructional Science, 38*(6), 571–606. doi:10.1007/s11251-008-9087-0

Ho, C. H., & Swan, K. (2007). Evaluating online conversation in an asynchronous learning environment: An application of Grice's cooperative principle. *The Internet and Higher Education, 10*(1), 3–14. doi:10.1016/j.iheduc.2006.11.002

Husain, H., Bais, B., Hussain, A., & Samad, S. A. (2012). How to construct open-ended questions. *Procedia: Social and Behavioral Sciences, 60*, 456–462. doi:10.1016/j.sbspro.2012.09.406

Jeong, A. C. (2004). The combined effects of response time and message content on growth patterns of discussion threads in computer-supported collaborative argumentation. *International Journal of E-Learning & Distance Education/Revue Internationale du e-learning et la formation à distance, 19*(1).

Klapwijk, R., & Van Doorn, F. (2015). Contextmapping in primary design and technology education: A fruitful method to develop empathy for and insight in user needs. *International Journal of Technology and Design Education, 25*(2), 151–167. doi:10.1007/s10798-014-9279-7

Klisc, C., McGill, T., & Hobbs, V. (2009). The effect of assessment on the outcomes of asynchronous online discussion as perceived by instructors. *Australasian Journal of Educational Technology, 25*(5). Advance online publication. doi:10.14742/ajet.1114

Koehler, A. A. (2023). Planning and facilitating case-based learning in online settings. In G. Quek (Ed.), *Designing technology-mediated case learning in higher education - a global perspective* (pp. 215–237). Springer.

Koehler, A. A., Cheng, Z., Fiock, H., Janakiraman, S., & Wang, H. (2020). Asynchronous online discussions during case-based learning: A problem-solving process. *Online Learning : the Official Journal of the Online Learning Consortium, 24*(4), 64–92. doi:10.24059/olj.v24i4.2332

Koehler, A. A., Cheng, Z., Fiock, H., Wang, H., Janakiraman, S., & Chartier, K. (2022). Examining students' use of online case-based discussions to support problem solving: Considering individual and collaborative experiences. *Computers & Education, 179*, 104407. Advance online publication. doi:10.1016/j.compedu.2021.104407

Koehler, A. A., & Meech, S. (2022). Ungrading learner participation in a student-centered learning experience. *TechTrends, 66*(1), 78–89. doi:10.1007/s11528-021-00682-w

Kouprie, M., & Visser, F. S. (2009). A framework for empathy in design: Stepping into and out of the user's life. *Journal of Engineering Design, 20*(5), 437–448. doi:10.1080/09544820902875033

Krasnova, T., & Ananjev, A. (2015). Students' perception of learning in the online discussion environment. *Mediterranean Journal of Social Sciences, 6*(6 S1), 202. DOI: doi:10.5901/mjss.2015.v6n6s1p202

LaRose, R., Mastro, D., & Eastin, M. S. (2001). Understanding Internet usage: A social-cognitive approach to uses and gratifications. *Social Science Computer Review, 19*(4), 395–413. doi:10.1177/089443930101900401

Laurillard, D. (2002). *Rethinking university teaching: A framework for the effective use of learning technologies* (2nd ed.). Routledge. doi:10.4324/9780203160329

Leh, A. (2002). Action research on hybrid courses and their online communities. *Educational Media International, 39*(1), 31–38. doi:10.1080/09523980210131204

Liu, S. (2007). Assessing Online Asynchronous Discussion in Online Courses: An Empirical Study. In *Proceedings of TCC 2007* (pp. 24-32). TCCHawaii.

Loncar, M., Barrett, N. E., & Liu, G. Z. (2014). Towards the refinement of forum and asynchronous online discussion in educational contexts worldwide: Trends and investigative approaches within a dominant research paradigm. *Computers & Education, 73*, 93–110. doi:10.1016/j.compedu.2013.12.007

Long, Y., & Koehler, A. A. (2021). Student participation and interaction in online case-based discussions: Comparing expert and novice facilitation. *Online Learning.* https://olj.onlinelearningconsortium.org/index.php/olj/article/view/2901

McDonagh, D. C. (2006). *Empathic design: emerging design research methodologies* [Doctoral dissertation]. Loughborough University.

McKinney, B. K. (2018). The impact of program-wide discussion board grading rubrics on students and faculty satisfaction. *Online Learning : the Official Journal of the Online Learning Consortium, 22*(2), 289–299. doi:10.24059/olj.v22i2.1386

Moore, M. G. (2013). The theory of transactional distance. In M. G. Moore (Ed.), *Handbook of Distance Education* (2nd ed., pp. 84–103). Routledge. doi:10.4324/9780203803738.ch5

Mukhtar, K., Javed, K., Arooj, M., & Sethi, A. (2020). Advantages, limitations and recommendations for online learning during COVID-19 pandemic era. *Pakistan Journal of Medical Sciences, 36*(COVID19-S4), S27.

Murphy, E., & Coleman, E. (2004). Graduate students' experiences of challenges in online asynchronous discussions. *Canadian Journal of Learning and Technology/La revue canadienne de l'apprentissage et de la technologie, 30*(2).

National Center for Education Statistics. (2020). *Table 311.15. Digest of Education Statistics (NCES 2017–094)*. Author.

Newman, D. R., Johnson, C., Webb, B., & Cochrane, C. (1997). Evaluating the quality of learning in computer supported cooperative learning. *Journal of the American Society for Information Science American Society for Information Science, 48*, 484-495. doi: 1097-4571 (199706)48:6<484::AID-ASI2>3.0.CO;2-Q. doi:10.1002/(SICI)

Nonnecke, B., & Preece, J. (2000, April). Lurker demographics: Counting the silent. In *Proceedings of the SIGCHI conference on Human factors in computing systems* (pp. 73-80). 10.1145/332040.332409

Osborne, D. M., Byrne, J. H., Massey, D. L., & Johnston, A. N. (2018). Use of online asynchronous discussion boards to engage students, enhance critical thinking, and foster staff-student/student-student collaboration: A mixed method study. *Nurse Education Today, 70*, 40–46. doi:10.1016/j.nedt.2018.08.014 PMID:30145533

Page, K., & Nowak, M. (2002). Empathy leads to fairness. *Bulletin of Mathematical Biology, 64*(6), 1101–1116. Advance online publication. doi:10.1006/bulm.2002.0321 PMID:12508533

Parrish, P. (2006). Design as storytelling. *TechTrends, 50*(4), 72–82. doi:10.1007/s11528-006-0072-7

Pereira Nunes, B., Kawase, R., Fetahu, B., Casanova, M. A., & de Campos, G. H. (2014). Educational forums at a glance: Topic extraction and selection. *Web Information Systems Engineering – WISE 2014*, 351–364. doi:10.1007/978-3-319-11746-1_25

Powell, R. M., & Murray, O. (2012). Using storytelling strategies to improve student comprehension in online classes. *The Journal of Effective Teaching, 12*(1), 46–52.

Pruitt, J., & Grudin, J. (2003, June). Personas: practice and theory. In *Proceedings of the 2003 conference on Designing for user experiences* (pp. 1-15). Academic Press.

Razzouk, R., & Shute, V. (2012). What is design thinking and why is it important? *Review of Educational Research, 82*(3), 330–348. doi:10.3102/0034654312457429

Reeve, J., & Jang, H. (2022). Agentic engagement. In *Handbook of research on student engagement* (pp. 95–107). Springer International Publishing. doi:10.1007/978-3-031-07853-8_5

Richardson, J. C., Maeda, Y., Lv, J., & Caskurlu, S. (2017). Social presence in relation to students' satisfaction and learning in the online environment: A meta-analysis. *Computers in Human Behavior, 71,* 402–417. doi:10.1016/j.chb.2017.02.001

Rico, R., & Ertmer, P. A. (2015). Examining the role of the instructor in problem-centered instruction. *TechTrends, 59*(4), 96–103. doi:10.1007/s11528-015-0876-4

Rovai, A. P. (2007). *Facilitating online discussions effectively. Internet and Higher Education, 10(1),* 77-88.

Sadaf, A., Richardson, J., & Ertnmer, P. (2011). Relationship between question prompts and critical thinking in online discussions. In *Annual Meeting of the Association for Educational Communications and Technology* (Vol. 10). Academic Press.

Salmon, G. (2003). *E-moderating: The Key to teaching and learning online.* Routledge.

Seaman, J. E., Allen, I. E., & Seaman, J. (2018). *Grade increase: Tracking distance education in the United States.* Babson Survey Research Group.

Seo, K. (2007). Utilizing peer moderating in online discussions: Addressing the controversy between teacher moderation and nonmoderation. *American Journal of Distance Education, 21*(1), 21–36. doi:10.1080/08923640701298688

Shaul, M. (2007). Assessing online discussion forum participation. *Information Communication Technologies,* 1459–1467. doi:10.4018/978-1-59904-949-6.ch099

Shea, P., Richardson, J., & Swan, K. (2022). Building bridges to advance the community of inquiry framework for online learning. *Educational Psychologist, 57*(3), 148–161. doi:10.1080/00461520.2022.2089989

Smeenk, W., Sturm, J., Terken, J., & Eggen, B. (2018). A systematic validation of the Empathetic Handover approach guided by five factors that foster empathy in design. *International Journal of CoCreation in Design and the Arts, 15*(4), 308–328. https://doi-org.ezproxy.lib.purdue.edu/10.1080/15710882.2018.1484490

Solan, A. M., & Linardopoulos, N. (2011). Development, implementation, and evaluation of a grading rubric for online discussions. *Journal of Online Learning and Teaching, 7*(4).

St. Clair, D. (2015). A simple suggestion for reducing first-time online student anxiety. *Journal of Online Learning and Teaching, 11*(1), 129–135.

Stefaniak, J. E., & Baaki, J. (2013). A layered approach to understanding your audience. *Performance Improvement, 52*(6), 5–9. doi:10.1002/pfi.21352

Stephens, M., & Jones, K. M. (2015). Emerging roles: Key insights from librarians in a massive open online course. *Journal of Library & Information Services in Distance Learning, 9*(1-2), 133–147. doi: 10.1080/1533290X.2014.946353

Taft, H. (2023, December 27). *Example biology discussion prompt*. Taft Portfolio, Blogspot. https://taftportfolio.blogspot.com/p/example-biology-discussion-prompts.html

Terry, C., & Cain, J. (2016). The emerging issue of digital empathy. *American Journal of Pharmaceutical Education, 80*(4), 58. Advance online publication. doi:10.5688/ajpe80458 PMID:27293225

Thompson, K., deNoyelles, A., Chen, B., & Futch, L. (2016). Create effective discussion prompts. In B. Chen & K. Thompson (Eds.), *Teaching Online Pedagogical Repository*. University of Central Florida Center for Distributed Learning. https://topr.online.ucf.edu/discussion-prompts/

Tracey, M. W., & Baaki, J. (2022). Empathy and empathic design for meaningful deliverables. *Educational Technology Research and Development, 70*(6), 2091–2116. doi:10.1007/s11423-022-10146-4

Tracey, M. W., & Hutchinson, A. (2019). Empathic design: Imagining the cognitive and emotional learner experience. *Educational Technology Research and Development, 67*(5), 1259–1272. doi:10.1007/s11423-019-09683-2

UNESCO. (2021). *Supporting learning recovery one year into COVID-19: The Global Education Coalition in action*. https://unesdoc.unesco.org/ark:/48223/pf0000376061

Vann, L. (2015). Demonstrating empathy: A phenomenological study of instructional designers making instructional strategy decisions for adult learners. *International Journal on Teaching and Learning in Higher Education, 29*, 233–244. https://files.eric.ed.gov/fulltext/EJ1146186.pdf

Wang, Q. Y. (2008). Student-facilitators' roles of moderating online discussions. *British Journal of Educational Technology, 39*(5), 859–874. doi:10.1111/j.1467-8535.2007.00781.x

Wasik, B. A., & Hindman, A. H. (2013). Realizing the promise of open-ended questions. *The Reading Teacher, 67*(4), 302–311. doi:10.1002/trtr.1218

Watson, S. L., Koehler, A. A., Ertmer, P. A., Rico, R., & Kim, W. (2018). An expert instructor's use of social congruence, cognitive congruence, and expertise in an online case-based instructional design course. *The Interdisciplinary Journal of Problem-Based Learning, 12*(1). Advance online publication. doi:10.7771/1541-5015.1633

Weisz, E., & Cikara, M. (2020). Strategic Regulation of Empathy. *Trends in Cognitive Sciences, 25*(3), 213–227. . doi:10.1016/j.tics.2020.12.002 PMID:33386247

Weltzer-Ward, L. (2011). Content analysis coding schemes for online asynchronous discussion. *Campus-Wide Information Systems, 28*(1), 56–74. doi:10.1108/10650741111097296

Williams, S. S., Jaramillo, A., & Pesko, J. C. (2015). Improving depth of thinking in online discussion boards. *Quarterly Review of Distance Education, 16*(3), 45.

Wlodkowski, R. J., & Ginsberg, M. B. (2017). *Enhancing adult motivation to learn: A comprehensive guide for teaching all adults*. John Wiley & Sons.

Woods, K., & Bliss, K. (2016). Facilitating successful online discussions. *The Journal of Effective Teaching*, *16*(2), 76–92.

Wright, P., & McCarthy, J. (2005). The value of the novel in designing for experience. In A. Pirhonen, C. Roast, P. Saariluoma, & H. Isom (Eds.), *Future interaction design* (pp. 9–30). Springer-Verlag. doi:10.1007/1-84628-089-3_2

Wu, S. Y., Hou, H. T., Hwang, W. Y., & Liu, E. Z. F. (2013). Analysis of learning behavior in problem-solving-based and project-based discussion activities within the seamless online learning integrated discussion (SOLID) system. *Journal of Educational Computing Research*, *49*(1), 61–82. doi:10.2190/EC.49.1.c

Xie, K. (2013). What do the numbers say? The influence of motivation and peer feedback on students' behaviour in online discussions. *British Journal of Educational Technology*, *44*(2), 288–301. doi:10.1111/j.1467-8535.2012.01291.x

Xie, K., DeBacker, T. K., & Ferguson, C. (2006). Extending the traditional classroom through online discussion: The role of student motivation. *Journal of Educational Computing Research*, *34*(1), 68–78. doi:10.2190/7BAK-EGAH-3MH1-K7C6

Yang, D., Richardson, J. C., French, B. F., & Lehman, J. D. (2011). The development of a content analysis model for assessing students' cognitive learning in asynchronous online discussions. *Educational Technology Research and Development*, *59*(1), 43–70. doi:10.1007/s11423-010-9166-1

KEY TERMS AND DEFINITIONS

Asynchronous Discussions: Online sharing of thoughts, perceptions, knowledge, and understanding using a post/response format that happens at different times.

Empathy: One's ability to share the feelings of others and genuinely acknowledge some else's experience, even if they differ from one's own.

Instructional Design: The systematic development of instructional material for the development of subject-matter knowledge, skills, and/or expertise.

Online Learning: Computer-based learning where students interact online synchronously and/or asynchronously to learn subject-matter content.

Technophobia: Avoidance of or dislike for technology.

Chapter 6
Humanizing Instructional Design Through Empathic Analysis

Sally Meech
https://orcid.org/0000-0002-4706-0794
Purdue University, USA

Adrie A. Koehler
Purdue University, USA

ABSTRACT

The technologically mediated context of online teaching and learning presents unique challenges that require making explicit the implicit human elements that may be taken for granted in face-to-face contexts. While empathy, the emotional (affective) and reflective (cognitive) process of relating to another's circumstance, has been effectively employed in other design fields, its application in instructional design has only recently emerged. Using a hybrid narrative literature review process, this chapter presents an investigation of empirical and conceptual applications of empathic analysis used in instructional design settings. The authors analyze various empathic tools and methods employed and offer examples and advice to instructional designers and researchers for incorporating the practices in their work as a means to humanize online learning at the earliest stages in the instructional design process.

BACKGROUND

The fundamental nature of instructional design (ID) has been debated in the field for decades, as exemplified by the "paradigm wars" (Willis, 1998, p. 6) among scholars such as Reigeluth (1996) and Merrill (1996). Simply stated, while some maintain that ID is systematic and process-oriented, necessitating a prescriptive approach to control for uncertainty, others embrace uncertainty and advocate for a humanized approach that more fully considers the "practices of people connected to the design of instruction – that is, designers, instructors, and students" (Wilson, 2013, p. 37). When considering the design of online

DOI: 10.4018/979-8-3693-0762-5.ch006

learning, humanization is especially pertinent as instructors and students experience unique environmental factors (e.g., reliance on technologically mediated communication). Thus, much like Wilson's (2013) call for a practice-centered approach to ID, a humanized approach to ID for online learning calls on instructional designers (IDs)[1] to incorporate perspectives, actions, and processes from other fields to design more effective instruction (Parrish, 2014). Designer empathy and tools for stimulating empathy for online learners in the design process are important elements for humanizing ID.

Empathy, the emotional (affective) response and reflective (cognitive) process of relating to another's circumstance (Devecchi & Guerrini, 2017), has been conceptualized as critical in ID (Glynn & Tolsma, 2017; Parrish, 2014) to help IDs understand their learners beyond demographic characteristics (Stefaniak & Baaki, 2013) and incorporate an understanding of a learner's lived, aesthetic experience (Gray, 2015). While understanding a learner's lived experience always involves designing for a "half-known" (Parrish, 2014, p. 264) conception of a learner, understanding online learners is even more difficult, as IDs often have no direct connection with learners (Lilley et al., 2012; Rapanta & Cantoni, 2014). Thus, expanding the ID process with new strategies and tools, while supported conceptually, is practically challenging for IDs developing online learning experiences. This chapter synthesizes literature related to empathic analysis in online ID, providing IDs and educators resources and insights useful for humanizing ID at the earliest stages of the design process.

Empathy and Empathic Design

There are multiple meanings associated with the term *empathy*. A contemporary perspective defines empathy as a psychological construct including affective and cognitive domains (Devecchi & Guerrini, 2017). Batson (2009), distinguishing among the different uses of the term *empathy*, suggested that five concepts relate to the question, "How do we know another's thoughts and feelings?" (Batson, 2009, p. 8): (a) imitating another's responses; (b) feeling as another feels; (c) projecting oneself into another's circumstance; (d) using what you know about others to imagine their thoughts and feelings; and (e) imagining how one would feel in another's circumstance.

Coming to know the thoughts and feelings of others is key to empathic design, a concept proposed by Leonard and Rayport (1997) as a way to develop more innovative solutions to design problems and "contribute to the flow of ideas" (Leonard & Rayport, 1997, p. 108). The tools and processes of empathic design help designers get closer to users and develop an understanding of the users' lifeworld, increasing the potential for meeting users' needs (Baaki & Maddrell, 2020; Nielsen, 2019). Empathic designers feel for the user through affective empathy and understand the user through cognitive empathy (Battarbee & Koskinen, 2005; Leonard & Rayport, 1997).

While descriptive details gleaned through research in the design process offer some information about potential users, observation allows a designer to intuit users' unarticulated wants and needs (Leonard & Rayport, 1997). Often, however, designers remain isolated from users, which leads to an absence of empathic understanding in the design process (Cooper, 2014). Thus, researchers and practitioners have developed ways to enhance empathic practices. Nielsen (2019), for example, detailed the process of developing and using research-based, narrative personas combined with user scenarios to enhance designer empathy. Kouprie and Visser (2009) developed a four-step empathic framework to help designers conceptualize and employ empathy in design practice. These are among the tools and methods that have recently been adopted and adapted in ID practice to enhance understanding of learners in the ID process.

Empathy and Instructional Design

As previously noted, scholars have advocated for developing a deeper understanding of learners and their learning experiences for effective ID. The analysis of learners and contexts is widely viewed as a critical component of the ID process (Baaki et al., 2017; Brinkerhoff & Koroghlanian, 2007; Parrish & Linder-VanBerschot, 2010; Stefaniak & Baaki, 2013). Traditionally, learner analysis has provided crucial information for shaping instructional strategies. Through learner analysis, IDs assess learners' entry skills, attitudes, motivations, abilities, preferences, attitudes, and group characteristics (Dick et al., 2015).

Despite its importance, the analysis process may often be undervalued or disregarded (Baaki, et al., 2017; Parrish & Linder-VanBerschot, 2010; Stefaniak & Baaki, 2013; Sugar, 2014). When a learner analysis is not completed, the results may be ineffective instruction (Asino et al., 2017; Brinkerhoff & Koroghlanian, 2007; Parrish, 2014) and may have an adverse impact on student success and satisfaction (Brinkerhoff & Koroghlanian, 2007). In addition, as ID problems have evolved, incorporating more complex social systems, an expanded analysis of the problem space has become necessary (Parrish, 2006).

Analysis for online learning adds an additional layer of complexity when IDs have little or no ability to interact with the target learners (Lilley et al., 2012; Rapanta & Cantoni, 2014). While demographic characteristics are often described, students' expectations (Brinkerhoff & Koroghlanian, 2007), identities (Dudek & Heiser, 2017), and interactions with instruction (Rapanta & Cantoni, 2014; Vann, 2017) are often not considered. Thus, designers are left with an inadequate understanding of learners (Lilley et al., 2012), and learners may be viewed as objects rather than individuals with "distinct agency, identity, and lived experience" (Gray, 2015, p. 201). This static conception may impact online learners' experiences and limit the effectiveness of instruction (Asino et al., 2017; Brinkerhoff & Koroghlanian, 2007; Parrish, 2014).

Empathy has been proposed as a way to expand analysis for ID in general (Glynn & Tolsma, 2017) and for online ID specifically (Parrish, 2014), helping IDs enhance their understanding of *who* learners are and not just *what* learners are (Stefaniak & Baaki, 2013), thereby reducing the distance between designers and learners (Kouprie & Visser, 2009). Empathic analysis is particularly relevant to online contexts because teaching and learning behaviors have distinct characteristics in such settings. For example, social presence, or the ability to perceive others as real and authentic others, may be taken for granted in an in-person instructional setting. In an online setting, however, developing social presence requires purposeful attention. Likewise, formative feedback in a physical classroom may often happen dynamically, while virtual settings require forethought and planning for feedback opportunities (Johnson & Nino, 2022). In other words, online learning requires making explicit many of the implicit characteristics of in-person teaching and learning (Lilley et al., 2012). Given these distinct characteristics, the intent of empathic approaches to analysis is to help IDs better anticipate the learning experience (Rapanta & Cantoni, 2014), develop a deeper understanding of learners (Baaki, et al., 2017), relate to learners (Kouprie & Visser, 2009), and become advocates for learners in the design process (Dudek & Heiser, 2017).

The purpose of this of this narrative literature review was to explore empathic analysis in online ID. Specifically, we first located examples of how empathic methods were used early in the design process to understand learners. Next, we analyzed the empathic analysis tools and methods being used across articles and identified common strategies. We describe these strategies and provide examples, while offering advice to IDs and researchers interested in using this approach in their own work. We see a major outcome of this research as the humanization of the ID process for developing online learning experiences.

METHOD

Narrative Literature Review Approach

This chapter summarizes and synthesizes literature at the intersection of learner analysis, online learning, and empathy for adult learners using a hybrid narrative literature review process. Literature reviews make important contributions to a field of study, providing collective evidence upon which researchers and practitioners can make decisions (Paré et al., 2015). While researcher bias in the selection and review of literature is a common criticism of literature reviews (Baumeister & Leary, 1997), systematic reviews generally have a narrow focus and aim to control bias through explicit, replicable criteria and documentation of research methods (Collins & Fauser, 2005). Unlike systematic reviews, narrative reviews generally cover a wider range of issues within a topic but are more prone to bias as they typically do not detail selection methods (Collins & Fauser, 2005). Adopting some of the bias control measures typically seen in systematic reviews can add methodological rigor and credibility to narrative reviews (Collins & Fauser, 2005; Ferrari, 2015; Green et al., 2006). Therefore, we adopted a hybrid narrative literature review process in which explicit methods are documented to research the emergent topic of empathic learner analysis.

Literature Selection and Criteria

A multi-stage process was used to select relevant articles (Figure 1). Education Source, ERIC, and Academic Search Complete databases were searched in March 2021 using the terms "instructional design" OR "instructional systems design" AND empath* in any field. A second search used the terms "instructional design" AND "learner analysis" AND "online learning" and related terms (e.g., distance learning). Limiters included publication in an academic journal and English language. Articles were selected for consideration if the primary focus was empathic approaches for learner analysis in the ID process. The initial search resulted in 100 articles. After duplicate articles were removed, 71 articles remained. Abstracts of the 71 articles were read in their entirety, and 16 articles preliminarily met the inclusion criteria of (a) a primary focus on instructional design and (b) discussion of empathic tools or practices for understanding learners. The 16 articles were reviewed in their entirety, and eight primary articles were determined to be relevant.

Limitations

The authors attempted to reduce bias in this review by employing a hybrid narrative literature review process but acknowledge that the use of specific search terms limited the scope, potentially excluding other relevant scholarship. The exclusive inclusion of peer-reviewed publications from scholarly database collections also limited the voices represented in the review. As empathic design is an emerging field of study, valuable insights may be gained from using additional search methods, such as engaging with practitioners, professional organizations, and practitioner-focused websites, that may broaden the scope of understanding and include voices that may otherwise be marginalized. Additionally, the strategies presented can be expanded upon and adapted to specific interests (e.g., cultural, economic, social, and political factors) using additional search terms to address unique considerations.

Figure 1. Literature Search Process

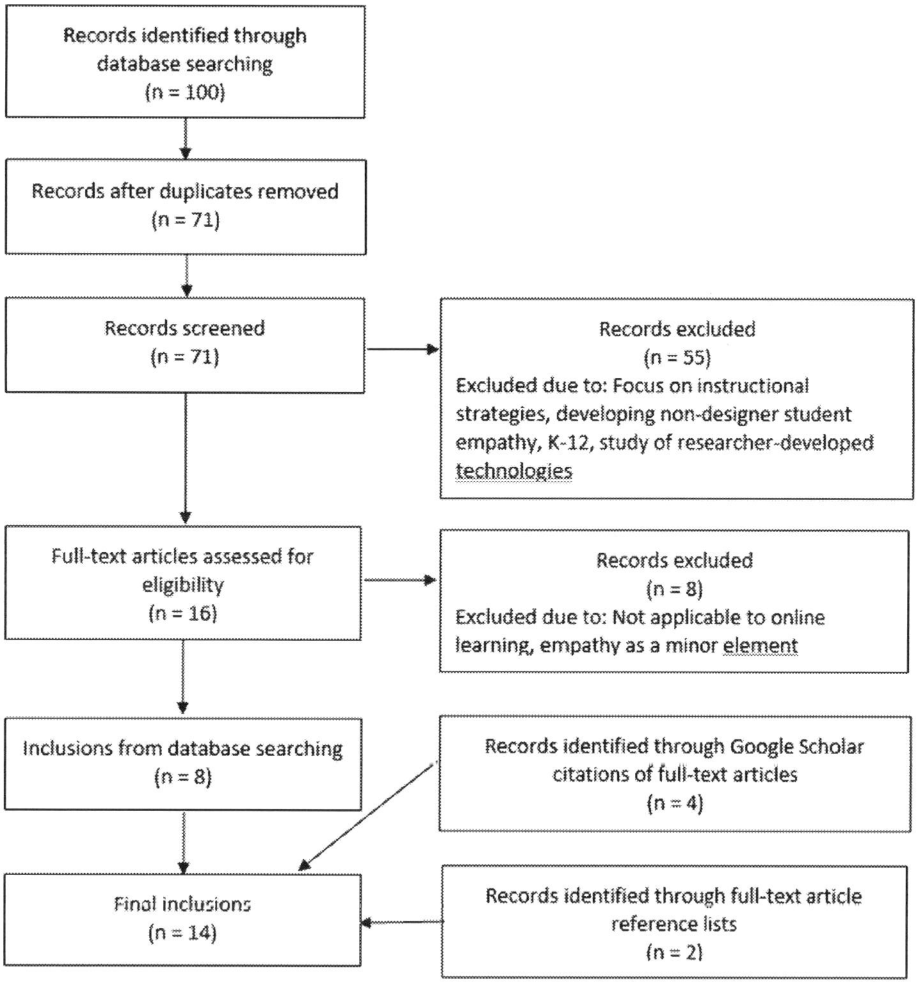

```
┌─────────────────────────┐
│ Records identified through│
│   database searching     │
│       (n = 100)          │
└─────────────────────────┘
            │
            ▼
┌─────────────────────────┐
│ Records after duplicates │
│        removed           │
│        (n = 71)          │
└─────────────────────────┘
            │
            ▼
┌─────────────────────────┐        ┌──────────────────────────────────┐
│   Records screened       │───────▶│      Records excluded              │
│        (n = 71)          │        │         (n = 55)                   │
└─────────────────────────┘        │ Excluded due to: Focus on          │
            │                       │ instructional strategies,          │
            │                       │ developing non-designer student    │
            │                       │ empathy, K-12, study of            │
            │                       │ researcher-developed technologies  │
            ▼                       └──────────────────────────────────┘
┌─────────────────────────┐        ┌──────────────────────────────────┐
│ Full-text articles       │───────▶│      Records excluded              │
│ assessed for eligibility │        │         (n = 8)                    │
│        (n = 16)          │        │ Excluded due to: Not applicable    │
└─────────────────────────┘        │ to online learning, empathy as a   │
            │                       │ minor element                      │
            │                       └──────────────────────────────────┘
            ▼
┌─────────────────────────┐        ┌──────────────────────────────────┐
│ Inclusions from database │        │ Records identified through Google  │
│ searching                │        │ Scholar citations of full-text     │
│        (n = 8)           │        │ articles                           │
└─────────────────────────┘        │         (n = 4)                    │
            │                       └──────────────────────────────────┘
            │                              │
            ▼                              ▼
┌─────────────────────────┐        ┌──────────────────────────────────┐
│   Final inclusions       │◀───────│ Records identified through         │
│        (n = 14)          │        │ full-text article reference lists  │
└─────────────────────────┘        │         (n = 2)                    │
                                    └──────────────────────────────────┘
```

TOOLS AND METHODS FOR EMPATHIC ANALYSIS

The 14 articles included in this study focused on various tools and methods for empathic analysis. Six articles focused on the use of personas (Baaki et al., 2017; Baaki & Maddrell, 2020; Haag & Marsden, 2018; Lilley et al., 2012; Stefaniak & Baaki, 2013; Williams van Rooij, 2012), five articles investigated perspective taking and projection through interviews with or observations of IDs (Matthews et al., 2017; Matthews & Yanchar, 2018; Rapanta & Cantoni, 2014; Tracey & Hutchinson, 2019; Vann, 2017), and three articles focused on applying alternative perspectives to enhance empathy (Dudek & Heiser, 2017; Parrish, 2006; Parrish, 2014) (see Appendix for a comprehensive table of all articles.)

Personas for Empathic Analysis

Direct contact with users is often impossible due to constraints such as distance (Baaki et al., 2017; Lilley et al., 2012) and limited resources (Stefaniak & Baaki, 2013). In such cases, creating personas can assist IDs in understanding the user experience and developing empathy for users (Baaki et al., 2017; Kouprie & Visser, 2009). Personas are research-based fictional profiles of individuals that help convey the needs, goals, attitudes, experiences, and other personal characteristics of larger groups. (Baaki et al., 2017; Lilley et al., 2012). Importantly, personas are not intended to look at the entire person, but rather to highlight the characteristics that are relevant to the context (e.g., the course being developed) so that all the project team members have the same understanding of the learners (Nielsen, 2019). In ID, personas provide a means for designers to focus on learners in the design process (Baaki et al., 2017; Lilley et al., 2012; Stefaniak & Baaki, 2013; Williams van Rooij, 2012).

Persona construction involves careful data collection and analysis. As an example, consider the case of an online degree program that has a policy of reviewing courses for potential redesign every three years. In constructing personas to better understand the student population, a designer should first begin by exploring what is currently known. This may include student data from past iterations of the course and discussions with instructors and other subject matter experts to help answer questions such as:

- What is the purpose of this course?
- Who has typically taken this course?
- What feedback have students given about the course?

From the information above, the designer could create ad hoc personas of students, which are written descriptions of typical students based on current knowledge (Lilley et al, 2012).

Second, the designer would engage in additional research, such as using surveys and/or interviews with past and current students, if possible, to generate a richer understanding of who the students are. At this stage, in addition to gathering specific demographic data, students may be asked questions such as:

- What were your motivations for taking this course?
- What are your short- and long-term goals?
- What knowledge, skills, and abilities do you have relative to the subject matter?
- Did you experience any challenges while taking this course?
- What did you learn and how have you applied it?
- What do you think about and expect from this course and online courses generally?
- How do you access and complete your course work?
- Are you a fulltime student or do you also work? If you work, please describe your job.
- What are your hobbies and interests outside of school and/or work?

After all data has been collected, the designer would analyze and combine details, discerning patterns, to create a set of data-driven personas, which typically include details such as a name, a picture, and a narrative description (Lilley et al, 2012).

While the persona construction process sounds fairly straightforward, humanizing analysis requires designers to actively and continually engage in reflexivity to monitor their decision-making and control for unconscious bias in persona creation. Bias is a concern at every step in the process, from the data sources used to the aggregation of data and selection of names and images that represent the personas (Nielsen, 2019). Designers who engage in persona construction should take care to have conversations with and get feedback from a diverse group in the process and products of their work. While a full discussion of bias in persona construction is beyond the scope of this chapter, the site Medium.com offers a useful, practitioner-focused article that reviews and gives examples of ten types of cognitive biases that may impact persona construction (Weave Media Team, 2023).

Table 1 provides an overview of studies that investigated the development or use of personas for empathic learner analysis.

Review of Studies Investigating Personas

The studies that investigated personas did so primarily because relying on traditional, demographic information about learners provides necessary but insufficient information to assist IDs in developing empathy for learners (Baaki et al., 2017; Stefaniak & Baaki, 2013). Haag and Marsden (2018) suggested that personas may act as a stepladder to invoke empathy in learner analysis and help IDs overcome ego-centric perspectives. Williams van Rooij (2012) noted that in other human-centered fields (e.g., healthcare, engineering, product and service design), empathy is considered integral to professional success, and often students are taught to use personas as a method to develop empathy. Adopting the use of personas as a tool to develop empathy in ID may help IDs develop a better understanding of learners, facilitate an effective design process, and meet user needs more successfully than by using traditional demographic information alone (Baaki et al., 2017).

Personas were also noted as a key to better understand who learners are (Lilley et al., 2012). Exploring who learners are helps develop a clearer view of individual learners and their environments (Stefaniak & Baaki, 2013). While demographic details are important, personas provide a richer sense of the lived experience of potential learners and help implicit information about learners become explicit (Lilley et al., 2012).

Despite the advantages, authors noted that personas have limitations. Among these are individual characteristics of IDs (Baaki & Maddrell, 2020; Haag & Marsden, 2018), time commitments (Baaki et al., 2017; Haag & Marsden, 2018; Lilley et al., 2012; Stefaniak & Baaki, 2013), IDs' agency (Stefaniak

Table 1. Studies Focused on Personas to Foster Empathy in Learner Analysis

Authors	Results/Observation	Observed Affordance	Potential Challenges
Baaki et al. (2017)	Authentic personas and empathy framework may help IDs understand and design for learners	Allows design decisions to be viewed from learners' perspectives	Time and stakeholder buy-in
Baaki, & Maddrell (2020)	IDs demonstrated empathy, connections with persona; persona influenced design conversations, design decisions	Provides context, motivation, and engagement for designers; reveals new design elements	Requires explicit commitment from IDs, time consuming
Haag & Marsden (2018)	Novice difficulty developing affective empathy, relating to personas unlike themselves, instead focused on cognitive empathy	Allows novice designers to develop cognitive empathy	Affective empathy with personas unlike self is more difficult than cognitive empathy for novices
Lilley et al. (2012)	Personas applied to instructional scenarios help designers make pedagogically sound choices based on who learners are	Allows designers to communicate about learners	Faculty resistance
Stefaniak & Baaki (2013)	Considering who learners are helped generate new instructional strategies, resulted in enthusiasm, effective problem solving, and project momentum	Surfaces instructional strategies that may have otherwise been unapparent	Limits in timelines and budgets
Williams van Rooij (2012)	Research-based personas, validated by surveys and usability testing, were key tool in design process	Enables designers to make appropriate design choices for users unlike themselves	Requires access to sample learners, stakeholders

& Baaki, 2013), and perceived value of the method by stakeholders (Lilley et al., 2012). Empathic learner analysis requires that designers possess motivation, affective abilities, and cognitive reasoning (Haag & Marsden, 2018). While Williams van Rooij (2012) noted that personas help novices remain focused on the intended audience for whom they are designing, Haag and Marsden (2018) found that novice designers may have difficulty relating affectively to users unlike themselves. This is consistent with other studies that contended that while empathic ID can be taught, it is a skill that is more often observed in expert IDs (Parrish, 2006; Rapanta & Cantoni, 2014; Tracey & Hutchinson, 2019; Vann, 2017).

Time is also a constraint in the use of personas. Not having or taking time is an initial obstacle in empathic design (Haag & Marsden, 2018), and developing personas is a time-consuming process for IDs (Baaki et al., 2017) and instructors (Lilley et al., 2012). Instructional designers also may lack agency in the use of personas, as decisions about ID projects are often made by stakeholders external to the design process. This limits the ability of IDs to use expanded analysis methods (Stefaniak & Baaki, 2013). Finally, stakeholders may not value personas. Lilley et al. (2012) noted that some instructors were skeptical and understood that although "the personas were representative of the student population, they already had a clear sense of who their learners were" (p. 12).

One important point of clarification is that different types of persona construction with varying levels of learner access were employed in the studies referenced. The use of personas has been studied extensively, and while a comprehensive review of persona research is beyond the scope of this chapter, Nielsen (2019) offers a useful resource for readers interested in more detailed information on their development and use. Readers should be aware that the type of persona construction, as well as the context of use, may have an impact on the affordances and challenges reported in each study.

Personas in Practice: Program Evaluation

Lilley et al. (2012) reported using personas to better understand the population of students in an online computing education program and enhance the design of the program's learning experiences. Using a three-step process (Figure 2) to develop a more in-depth perspective of who their learners were, the authors found distinct differences between Step 1 (ad hoc personas developed from program stakeholder perceptions) and Step 3 (research-based personas).

In step one, the ad hoc personas developed from program stakeholder input characterized students as primarily mature, fulltime professionals seeking to enhance their career prospects through an asynchronous, flexible online program. However, the eventual research-based personas painted a picture of a more diverse set of students. Briefly, the eventual five representative personas included (See Lilley et al., 2012 for complete persona descriptions):

- Tom, 40-year-old male, married with two children; fulltime professional seeking to earn his BSc to develop expertise; prefers learning independently, at his own pace when convenient for him
- Olufela, 28-year-old male, married with an infant; fulltime professional seeking to earn his BSc to enhance his external job prospects; has only a mobile device at home and values synchronous connections with the instructor
- Chloe, 21-year-old female, single and lives at home with her parents; former campus-based student who needs to complete the remainder of her BSc degree online due to a fulltime job offer; primarily uses mobile device and values interaction in online courses

Figure 2. Lilley et al.'s (2012) Persona Development Process

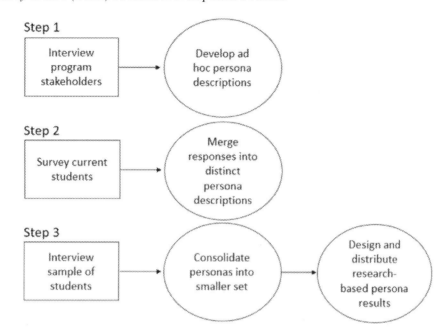

- Jean-Phillippe, 24-year-old male, single; fulltime professional; seeking BSc as a step toward an MS degree; does not have broadband connection at home and has concerns about feeling isolated in an online environment
- Shanice, 22-year-old female, single and lives at home with her parents; fulltime professional seeking to earn her BSc for internal career advancement; does not have broadband connection at home and desires a high level of support from instructors

In the above persona descriptions, Tom is most representative of the prevailing stakeholder perceptions, and the authors acknowledged that this accurately described their past student population. Using research-based personas, however, the authors were better able to understand new developments in their learner population. Contrary to stakeholder perceptions, humanizing the analysis process led to a more nuanced understanding of learners as individuals who valued instructor presence, synchronous interaction, and social involvement and also surfaced challenges faced by learners with diverse access to technology. The next step in the process was to determine how to use the research-based personas to inform the ID process.

Using the Community of Inquiry framework in designing their courses, the pedagogical structure of the program was informed by the personas, allowing the newly-recognized diverse set of learners to approach their learning in a customized fashion best suited to their needs – individually, cooperatively, or collaboratively. Lilley at al. (2012) described the design in the following way:

The framework presents a strong narrative strand to provide a coherent account of what learners are being asked to do by the tutor. It is present throughout the learning experience with the intention of maintaining the presence of the tutor even when they are not directly interacting with learners. (p. 11)

Beyond pedagogical aspects, the authors also noted that the personas influenced the technology used in the course implementation. Incorporating web-conferencing and online discussion forums were important to meet the needs of social interaction, while the use of audio or video with transcripts in place of text helped meet the needs of learners like Olufela and Chloe who represented the growing population of learners who primarily used mobile devices to engage in learning.

Lilley et al. (2012) demonstrated that personas can be an effective tool to evaluate and enhance online programs to meet the needs of diverse students. While the authors used data from actual learners in the program, research-based personas can use a variety of data sources. Baaki et al. (2017), for example, described how their design process incorporated results from similar projects, SME data and reviews, and research studies, thus the process is equally relevant to IDs with or without access to actual learners. In summary, the following questions and answers can help guide practitioners in using research-based personas for program evaluations:

1. Are there differences in ad hoc versus research-based personas? (see figure 2)
2. What student needs are being met by the current program/course design?
3. What student needs are not being adequately met?
4. What ID theory, model, or framework can guide the ID process to address unmet needs?
5. What changes can be made to the current program/course to address unmet needs?
6. What stakeholders need to be engaged/influenced to implement change?
7. What is the timeline and process to implement change?
8. What are the barriers to change and how can these be mitigated?
9. What resources are needed?
10. What steps can be taken to ensure a continual improvement cycle for meeting future student needs?

Research-based personas offer those involved in the ID process a way to better understand who their learners are. The suggestions in this section provide a useful guide for their construction and use.

Perspective Taking and Projection for Empathic Analysis

Design, as a creative endeavor, involves IDs engaging in a continual process of projection and reflection about learners as they develop learning experiences (Tracey & Hutchinson, 2019). Perspective taking is defined as using information and imagination to understand what another is thinking and feeling, while projection involves reflecting on one's own thoughts and experiences to relate to another's experience (Batson, 2009).

While the articles in this section offer practical ways for IDs to employ perspective taking and projection, designers focused on humanizing ID must take care to consider the limitations and potential bias inherent in the proposed processes. Van Boven and Loewenstein (2005), for example, discussed at length the concept of empathy gaps inherent in projection. The authors noted that social psychology research indicates that despite people's opinions about their abilities to bracket their perceptions, their social judgments tend to reflect their own attitudes, beliefs, and behaviors. This is partly due to overestimating the similarities between self and others and also due to contextual circumstances. In other words, a person's past experiences and how they are feeling in the moment both have an impact on their perceptions of others. It is important that designers take steps to explicitly surface their own experiences and current state when they engage in perspective taking and projection for ID.

Mehta and Gleason (2020) illuminated additional insights from the perspective of humanizing pedagogy. In a critique of Tracey and Hutchinson's (2019) article on empathic design, the authors proposed that perspective taking and projection may be "unintentionally aligned with political ideologies of colonization" (p. 88) that may "position others as less knowledgeable, less valuable, and less able to speak for themselves" (p. 89). While designers may approach the process with the intent to identify with learners, the results may reinforce harmful practices of othering, which objectifies and dehumanizes the people at the center of the design process. Given these perspectives, when possible, designers should strive to engage in participatory practices to co-construct experiences with learners, thereby empowering marginalized voices.

Five studies investigated empathic design through interviews with IDs or observations of designers-in-practice. Table 2 provides an overview of the studies, as well as affordances and challenges.

Review of Studies Investigating Perspective Taking and Projection

The studies in this section focused on developing an understanding of "the lived experiences of instructional designers" (Vann, 2017, p. 235) while designing for online learning. All articles contended that traditional methods of learner analysis are not sufficient or possible in many ID projects, and that IDs often encounter constraints or are limited in their ability to act upon empathic insights. The authors proposed that empathic approaches, such as perspective taking, may supplement traditional learner analysis for online learning.

Authors often used the analogy of being in the learners' shoes to represent perspective taking (Matthews et al., 2017; Matthews & Yanchar, 2018; Rapanta & Cantoni, 2014; Tracey & Hutchinson, 2019). Matthews and Yanchar (2018), for example, found that IDs attempted to make learning meaningful by imagining the concerns and thoughts of new college students, considering their potential struggles with

Table 2. Studies Focused on Empathic Practices of Instructional Designers

Authors	Results/Observation	Observed Affordance	Potential Challenges
Matthews & Yanchar (2018)	Absent formal learner analysis, IDs may imagine the learners' experience and project from their own experience to understand and empathize with learners	Imagining learner experience may help IDs design for learner engagement rather than control of the learner	May be driven by IDs values and approaches to design, not best practices
Matthews et al. (2017)	Empathy enacted through caring for the learner, using projection and perspective taking but IDs often constrained	Designers can employ empathy by keeping the learner in mind in the design process, investigating design ethnography resources, and employing empathic practices as possible in a design project	Lack of guidance for IDs for empathic practices; project constraints, complexity limit IDs agency
Rapanta & Cantoni (2014)	Provides insights into how and what type of discourse IDs use in design team meetings to anticipate learner experience	Multidisciplinary design team meetings provide context for anticipatory discourse that foregrounds empathy for users	IDs' ability to engage in empathetic discourse
Tracey & Hutchinson (2019)	IDs used empathic forecasting to imagine learners' cognitive and emotional experiences, aligned with learners' perceptions	Empathic forecasting is an important part of empathic design that enables IDs to connect with learners through imagination	More research needed to understand IDs construction, use, and awareness of empathic forecasting
Vann (2017)	Expert IDs considered empathy essential, believed it should guide instructional strategy decisions	Adopting the point of view of learners is a vital skill in ID practice that may support transformative learning for adults in online environments	Stakeholders' lack of buy-in, time, IDs limited influence, lack of engagement with learners

and goals for a particular course. These IDs "talked generally about empathy as the process of walking in the shoes of another" (Matthews et al., 2017, p. 489). Tracey and Hutchinson (2019) noted that "the instructional designers in this study stepped into the shoes of the learners" (p. 1270) which resulted in increased sensitivity to potential learner frustrations and significant alterations in the design. Rapanta and Cantoni (2014) concluded that "designers prefer to be 'in the users' shoes' rather than speaking on their own behalf" (pp. 773-774).

When very little is known about online learners, projecting is another way to invoke empathy (Matthews & Yanchar, 2018). Four articles observed projection, or IDs referencing their own experiences in relation to learners (Matthews et al., 2017; Matthews & Yanchar, 2018; Rapanta & Cantoni, 2014; Vann, 2017). Matthews et al. (2017) noted that "our participants' reflections on past learning experiences enabled them to see and understand learners that struggle" (p. 488). This was echoed by Vann (2017) who noted that IDs "often reflected on their own adult learning experiences to consider learners' viewpoints" (p. 236). Participants in another study "reported asking themselves questions intended to project themselves into their learners' situations" (Matthews & Yanchar, 2018, p. 155). Finally, Rapanta and Cantoni (2014) observed that during anticipatory discourse, IDs created imagined scenarios, often speaking from their own perspectives, to understand the learner's experience.

While these studies demonstrated that IDs value and use perspective taking and projection for learner analysis, Batson (2009) cautions that both may be misleading, especially with dissimilar others. In studying the use of personas, for example, Haag and Marsden (2018) demonstrated this concept empirically:

When personas are perceived as dissimilar, the information the persona holds for the design team is larger and the benefit of imagining the world form [sic] the persona's vantage point is bigger, but there is an empathy gap and effort and motivation is [sic] needed to get access to the persona's view of the world. (p. 5)

Thus, while perspective taking and projection in learner analysis are valued, the implementation is often complex and challenging (Rapanta & Cantoni, 2014; Vann, 2017), the effectiveness remains unknown (Rapanta & Cantoni, 2014), and more research is needed to develop best practices (Matthews et al., 2017; Matthews & Yanchar, 2018; Tracey & Hutchinson, 2019).

Perspective Taking and Projection in Practice: A Four-Step Framework, Empathy Mapping, and Empathic Forecasting

The field of ID is just beginning to embrace the affordances of well-established empathic practices in fields such as healthcare, engineering, and product and service design (Matthews et al., 2017; Williams van Rooij, 2012). The first application in this section offers a combination of two approaches to perspective-taking that, while referenced (e.g., Tracey & Hutchinson, 2019), were not foundational to any of the articles included in this review. Second, we describe an approach to projection, empathic forecasting, that is useful when designers have little to no data about their target learners.

Perspective Taking. Kouprie and Visser (2009) offered a four-step framework that is foundational for understanding the process of empathizing with learners. The framework can be used as the foundation for various design activities, such as empathy maps, to humanize learner analysis for online learning. The framework is based on the conceptual understanding of empathy as consisting of affective and cognitive components, where the former involves an immediate emotional response to and the latter an intellectual understanding of another person's experience. While theoretically separated, the two components represent the holistic way in which we understand and relate to others (see Figure 3). Understanding these components are foundational to using perspective taking and projection in empathic analysis for online ID.

The key actions of the framework involve stepping into another's life, immersing oneself in their experience, and then stepping out to gain perspective. Kouprie and Visser (2009) described this in four distinct steps:

1. Discovery: The designer connects with potential learners through data and other relevant resources and activities (e.g., research, observation, role play), invoking curiosity and the desire to explore and discover the learners' situations and experiences.
2. Immersion: The designer disconnects from their designer role to expand their knowledge about the learner, focusing on the learners' points of reference, keeping an open-minded and non-judgmental perspective.
3. Connection: The designer reflects on their own experiences to evoke understanding and make an emotional connection with the learner, revisiting their own perspectives that resonate with the learners' experiences.
4. Detachment: The designer detaches from their emotional connection with the learner and resumes their role as a designer with increased understanding about the learners to enable empathic design.

Figure 4 illustrates key actions in each step.

The steps are applicable to a number of potential ID analysis activities, such as providing the structure for design team meetings or creating role play activities. The key, as Kouprie and Visser (2009) noted, is in making the steps explicit to guide the selection of strategies and tools in the design process. One such tool this four-phase process can enable is empathy mapping.

Empathy maps are typically developed during the analysis stage of a project to document qualitative data about the user (i.e., learner), their goals, and what they see, say, do, and hear. This information is used to determine the learner's pains (e.g., obstacles and challenges) and gains (e.g., aspirations and

Figure 3. Affective and Cognitive Components of Empathy
Note. Adapted from "A framework for empathy in design: Stepping into and out of the user's life," by M. Kouprie and F. S. Visser, 2009. https://doi.org/10.1080/09544820902875033

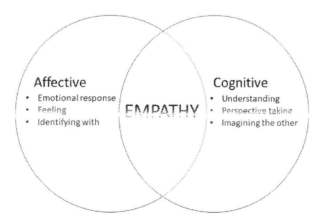

Figure 4. Kouprie and Visser's (2009) Four Phases of Empathy

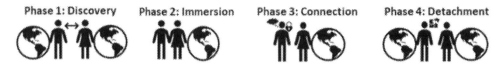

goals; Lammers, 2021). A useful resource is the empathy map canvas (Figure 5; available under creative commons license at https://gamestorming.com/empathy-map-canvas-006/). Once IDs are trained in using Kouprie and Visser's (2009) framework, they can use qualitative data to modify and populate the fields in the empathy map to create a common understanding about the learners, guiding the work of the ID team in humanizing the analysis process for online learners.

Projection. A distinct problem in analysis for online learning is that IDs often have no connection with the target learners and, even more problematic, often no access to data that can help them develop empathy for learners. In such cases, projection, or using their own experiences and perceptions, can help IDs humanize analysis for online learning activities. In their investigation documenting an ID team's process developing a virtual hospital activity for medical professionals, Tracey and Hutchinson (2019) documented ways in which the IDs on the team used empathic forecasting to anticipate the learners' experiences and how their actions changed the content of the course.

Empathic forecasting involves predicting another person's emotional state about future events (Tracey & Hutchinson, 2019). In their study, Tracey and Hutchinson (2019) investigated how IDs imagined the cognitive and emotional experiences of the learners during four design team meetings.

Figure 5. Empathy Map Canvas

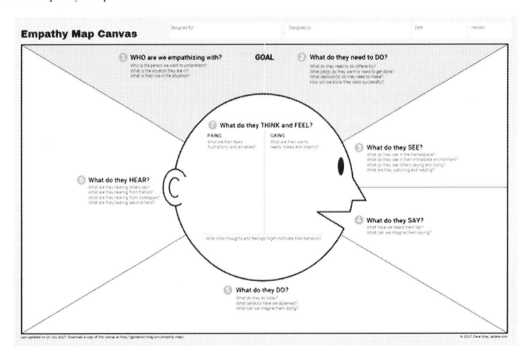

Their analysis of the meeting transcripts demonstrated key exchanges in which designers walked through an initial prototype of the design, projecting themselves as learners undergoing the learning experience. Results demonstrated that, in practice, designers projected themselves as a learner engaging with a course through:

- imagining themselves as a learner approaching the content for the first time;
- making explicit assumptions about learner actions;
- using think-aloud process while walking through a learning experience;
- verbalizing the learning objectives that align with learner actions;
- imagining learner apprehension and how to mitigate it;
- envisioning aspects of the learning experience that build learner confidence; and
- recognizing aspects of the learning experience that elicit learner excitement.

Tracey and Hutchinson (2019) reported that using empathic forecasting empowered the designers in the study to recognize key design problems and make significant changes to the initial learning experience design. These types of exchanges may be useful for ID teams as they use empathic analysis to humanize online learning throughout the design process.

Applying Alternative Perspectives for Empathic Analysis

Three articles focused on enhancing analysis and applying concepts from other fields. These authors viewed traditional learner analysis as restrictive and proposed non-traditional ID methods to enhance designer empathy. Table 3 provides an overview of the studies.

Review of Studies Investigating Alternative Perspectives

The traditional learner analysis process is "often a relatively superficial process, yielding only general characteristics" (Parrish, 2014, p. 265). Parrish (2006) proposed that a more complete conception of analysis would be analysis combined with synthesis. In other words, while in analysis disparate elements are discovered, synthesis involves combining the elements to create a cohesive whole. This combined analysis and synthesis process occurs throughout the design process and is aided by the creativity and imagination of IDs (Parrish, 2006). Expanded analysis allows IDs to understand "not

Table 3. Studies Offering Alternative Perspectives to Traditional Instructional Design Analysis

Authors	Results/Observation	Observed Affordance	Potential Challenges
Dudek & Heiser (2017)	Framework to help IDs understand, design for learners' identities	Multi-layered learner analysis helps IDs advocate for learners	Project constraints, stakeholder resistance, lack of ID models
Parrish (2014)	Guiding questions, design story techniques in analysis may make learner experience more tangible, detailed	Uncover unrealized constraints, enhance communication about potential learners	Uncertainty, complexity may prevent IDs from using approach
Parrish (2006)	Viewing design from learner experience perspective is a critical ID skill; learner experience stories use imagination, judgment, communication to bridge analysis and synthesis	Enhances traditional analysis, reveals constraints, provides shared vision, serves as formative evaluation when learner interaction not possible	Time to get to know learners' experience, develop and practice skills

only the cognitive processes of learners, but also their personalities, motivations, ambitions, desires and the things that frustrate these, [and] opens up to a fuller conception of how our designs fit into the learner's world" (p. 79).

Dudek and Heiser (2017) proposed a design framework that focuses on learner identity and noted that incorporating identity-centered principles into learner analysis adds additional layers of feedback that help designers more fully understand and advocate for learners in the design process. The proposed framework builds on understanding identity as the recognition of someone as a "certain kind of person" (Gee, 2000, p. 99) which can differ according to the context and in response to specific forces. Gee (2000) specified four perspectives that shape personal identity including nature (characteristics), institution (positions), discourse (traits) and affinity (experiences), each with distinct forces (e.g., authorities) and sources of power (e.g., institutions) that influence identity formation. Beyond individual identity, Dudek and Heiser (2017) also incorporated ideas from Schwalbe and Mason-Schrock's (1996) conception of the social construction of identity, referred to as subcultural identity. This group identity is formed through defining (social representation), coding (signifying rules), affirming (enacting and validating), and policing (enforcement). Using these two conceptualizations of identity as a guide, Dudek and Heiser (2017) proposed questions that foreground learner identity, including:

- What discourses do you ask your learners to draw upon?
- What explicit or implicit elements of identity are represented in the design?
- How will identity be used to support learning?
- Will learners experience believable self-representations in the design?

Using identity principles in the process of learner analysis and learner-focused design critique humanizes the ID process and encourages designers to be empathic advocates for learners.

A potential solution to the limitations of traditional analysis, suggested by the authors in this section, is an openness to influences outside of the ID field. Dudek and Heiser's (2017) identity-centered design is influenced by identity construction in sociology and user experience design in technology to help instructional designers better understand learners, especially in online settings (Dudek & Heiser, 2017). Parrish (2014) noted that expanding "cognition-oriented instructional design" (p. 263) involves drawing on influences from the "fringes" (p. 263) of ID as well disciplines focused on broader conceptions of experience, including other design fields and the arts. Relating design to narrative art, Parrish (2006) described using design stories to imagine and construct a fictional learner's journey as they engage in the designed experience. These influences can provide the dispositions and tools to help develop designer empathy (Parrish, 2014).

Alternative Perspectives in Practice: Questions to Guide Empathic Learner Analysis

Parrish (2014), drawing on the art of narrative, offered detailed recommendations for how IDs can create design stories to "complement traditional learner analysis and…stimulate more creative design considerations" (p. 267). His conceptions are founded on the belief that learning experiences are narrative in nature, and that empathy is a key component: "Empathy is the ability to see the narrative inherent in a situation and to understand how another perceives the situation participating in the narrative" (Parrish,

2014, p. 265). Traditional analysis can reveal general learner characteristics, but employing empathic practices can help designers develop a more nuanced understanding of learners.

Invoking the concept of the half-known world of learners, Parrish's (2014) recommendation that IDs incorporate alternative questions that can complement traditional analysis processes to provide deeper insights, stimulate creative design solutions, and surface alternative points of view can help humanize ID through empathic analysis. Parrish (2014) recommends that in employing the questions, IDs "try to imagine several responses for different types of learners. Then consider how you might adjust your design to accommodate, mitigate, or enhance what you discover in your responses" (p. 267). His alternative questions include:

- What will make learners say, "Wow! I wish I had known that before"?
- What are your learners most likely to forget, misunderstand, undervalue, resist, and fail to connect to?
- What will incite curiosity and make them want to come back?
- What will learners most likely skip or skim over, put off until the end, or feel is unnecessary?
- What do your learners feel they may fail to learn?
- What will learners want to share with their family or friends at dinner?
- What kind of learner might feel out of place or disenfranchised?
- In what learning experience did your learners previously struggle that may intimidate them now?
- What part of the learning experience will keep your learners awake at night?
- What related interests might be triggered in learners?
- What might learners want to explore more deeply than can be covered in this learning experience?
- What part of the instructional design will learners see as reflecting your own personality or personal biases?
- What part of your design DOES reflect your personal biases or past experiences?

While seemingly straightforward, Parrish's (2014) questions are not easy ones to answer. The questions require a certain humility in a designer – a willingness to step back from one's own perspectives and empathize with and design for unknown learners. The questions embody Wilson's (2013) practice-centered approach, wherein empathic analysis leads to "an elegant response to a learning need" (p. 39) in which designers are open to solutions that embrace the situational nature of ID rather than develop solutions based solely on theory or ideology. Adopting the mindset of an elegant response offers opportunities for IDs to humanize analysis for online learning.

CONCLUSION

Empathy is a way to reduce the distance between self and other, to walk in someone else's shoes, and to use the power of understanding, imagination, and emotion to help us relate to those who may be unlike ourselves. Using a narrative review process, this chapter detailed empathic strategies that IDs and researchers can use to humanize the ID process at the very early stages of design. Ideas included:

- developing personas to help designers understand the user experience and develop empathy for users (Baaki et al., 2017; Kouprie & Visser, 2009);
- engaging in perspective taking, or imagining what another is thinking and feeling, through questioning (Matthews & Yanchar, 2018), scenarios (Rapanta & Cantoni, 2014), or anticipatory discussions focused on learners' needs (Vann, 2017);
- using projection to reflect on one's own experiences and anticipate what learners may think or feel (Matthews & Yanchar, 2018) and consider the learner's point of view (Vann, 2017);
- adopting creativity or adapting ideas from the arts to understand the aesthetic experiences of the learner (Parrish, 2014); and
- using identity-centered principles to advocate for learners' unique identities.

Humanizing ID through empathy helps designers see instruction as not just a collection of learning outcomes but as an experience undergone by a learner. While the cognitive qualities of learning experiences have traditionally received much of the attention in ID literature, the aesthetic qualities are equally important (Parrish, 2014). Empathic instructional design is an effective means to enhance and humanize research and practice in the field of ID.

While the goal of empathic analysis is to reduce the distance between designers and online learners, understanding such methods could be enhanced by future research that focuses on specific applications and addresses potential challenges. For example, the research methods presented can be modified to specifically focus on technology-enhanced empathy (Neubauer et al., 2017), design thinking (Glynn & Tolsma, 2017), cultural analysis (Saxena, 2011), or identity-centered design (Dudek & Heiser, 2017). Additionally, studies that intentionally and critically focus on the potential challenges inherent in persona construction, perspective taking, and projection are also needed. Among the most salient issues relative to humanizing instructional design are designers' understandings of and abilities to demonstrate empathy (Haag & Marsden, 2018; Rapanta & Cantoni, 2014), unconscious bias in using empathic approaches (Dudek & Heiser, 2017; Saxena, 2011), and explicit attention to cultural differences (Asino, et. al., 2017; Parish & Linder-VanBerschot, 2010). Future studies are needed to help advance the understanding of humanizing online learning through the use of empathic analysis.

REFERENCES

Asino, T. I., Giacumo, L. A., & Chen, V. (2017). Culture as design "next": Theoretical frameworks to guide new design, development, and research of learning environments. *The Design Journal, 20*(1), 875–885. doi:10.1080/14606925.2017.1353033

Baaki, J., & Maddrell, J. (2020). Building empathy and developing instructional design experience and skills: A case study using personas to design open education resources. *The Journal of Applied Instructional Design, 9*(3), 1–14. https://edtechbooks.org/jaid_9_3/building_empathy

Baaki, J., Maddrell, J., & Stauffer, E. (2017). Designing authentic personas for open education resources designers. *International Journal of Designs for Learning, 8*(2), 110–122. doi:10.14434/ijdl.v8i2.22427

Batson, C. D. (2009). These things called empathy: Eight related but distinct phenomena. In J. Decety & W. Ickes (Eds.), *The social neuroscience of empathy* (pp. 3–15). The MIT Press. doi:10.7551/mitpress/9780262012973.003.0002

Battarbee, K., & Koskinen, I. (2005). Co-experience: User experience as interaction. *CoDesign, 1*(1), 5–18. doi:10.1080/15710880412331289917

Baumeister, R. F., & Leary, M. R. (1997). Writing narrative literature reviews. *Review of General Psychology, 1*(3), 311–320. doi:10.1037/1089-2680.1.3.311

Brinkerhoff, J., & Koroghlanian, C. M. (2007). Online students' expectations: Enhancing the fit between online students and course design. *Journal of Educational Computing Research, 36*(4), 383–393. doi:10.2190/R728-28W1-332K-U115

Collins, J. A., & Fauser, B. C. J. M. (2005). Balancing the strengths of systematic and narrative reviews. *Human Reproduction Update, 11*(2), 103–104. doi:10.1093/humupd/dmh058 PMID:15618290

Cooper, A., Reimann, R., Cronin, D., & Noessel, C. (2014). *About face: The essentials of interaction design* (4th ed.). John Wiley & Sons, Inc.

Devecchi, A., & Guerrini, L. (2017). Empathy and design. A new perspective. *The Design Journal, 20*(1), 4357–4364. doi:10.1080/14606925.2017.1352932

Dick, W., Carey, L., & Carey, J. O. (2015). *The systematic design of instruction* (8th ed.). Pearson.

Dudek, J., & Heiser, R. (2017). Elements, principles, and critical inquiry for identity-centered design of online environments. *International Journal of E-Learning and Distance Education, 2*(32), 1–18. https://www.ijede.ca/index.php/jde

Ferrari, R. (2015). Writing narrative style literature reviews. *Medical Writing, 24*(4), 230–235. doi:10.1179/2047480615Z.000000000329

Gee, J. P. (2000). Chapter 3: Identity as an analytic lens for research in education. *Review of Research in Education, 25*(1), 99–125. doi:10.3102/0091732X025001099

Glynn, K., & Tolsma, D. (2017). Design thinking meets ADDIE. *Learning and Development, 34*(1714), 1-20. https://www.td.org/td-at-work/design-thinking-meets-addie

Gray, C. M. (2015). Critiquing the role of the learner and context in aesthetic learning experiences. In B. Hokanson, G. Clinton, & M. Tracey (Eds.), The design of learning experience. Educational communications and technology: Issues and innovations (pp. 199-213). Springer International Publishing. doi:10.1007/978-3-319-16504-2_14

Green, B. N., Johnson, C. D., & Adams, A. (2006). Writing narrative literature reviews for peer-reviewed journals: Secrets of the trade. *Journal of Chiropractic Medicine, 5*(3), 101–117. doi:10.1016/S0899-3467(07)60142-6 PMID:19674681

Haag, M., & Marsden, N. (2018). Exploring personas as a method to foster empathy in student IT design teams. *International Journal of Technology and Design Education*. Advance online publication. doi:10.1007/s10798-018-9452-5

Johnson, A. L., & Nino, M. (2022). Gaining "empathy" for the online learner with instructional design and design thinking strategies (V). In E. Langran (Ed.), *Proceedings of Society for Information Technology & Teacher Education International Conference* (pp. 1304–1308). https://www.learntechlib.org/primary/p/220884/

Kouprie, M., & Visser, F. S. (2009). A framework for empathy in design: Stepping into an out of the user's life. *Journal of Engineering Design*, *20*(5), 437–448. doi:10.1080/09544820902875033

Lammers, J. (2021, June 17-18). *Empathy mapping: Bridging cultural and linguistic divides in international online education* [Symposium presentation]. Teaching Culturally and Linguistically Diverse International Students in Open or Online Learning Environments: A Research Symposium, Windsor, Ontario, Canada. https://scholar.uwindsor.ca/itos21/?_gl=1*1n7hgas*_ga*MTAyMTEyODQ1LjE2OTg2MDgxODY.*_ga_TMHVD0679R*MTY5ODYwODg3NS4xLjAuMTY5ODYwODg3NS42MC4wLjA

Leonard, D., & Rayport, J. F. (1997). Spark innovation through empathic design. *Harvard Business Review*, *75*(6), 102–108. PMID:10174792

Lilley, M., Pyper, A., & Attwood, S. (2012). Understanding the student experience through the use of personas. *Innovation in Teaching and Learning in Information and Computer Sciences*, *11*(1), 4–13. doi:10.11120/ital.2012.11010004

Matthews, M. T., Williams, G. S., Yanchar, S. C., & McDonald, J. K. (2017). Empathy in distance learning design practice. *TechTrends*, *61*(5), 486–493. doi:10.1007/s11528-017-0212-2

Matthews, M. T., & Yanchar, S. C. (2018). Instructional design as manipulation of, or cooperation with, learners? *TechTrends*, *62*(2), 152–157. doi:10.1007/s11528-017-0245-6

Mehta, R., & Gleason, B. (2021). Against empathy: Moving beyond colonizing practices in educational technology. *Educational Technology Research and Development*, *69*(1), 87–90. doi:10.1007/s11423-020-09901-2

Merrill, M. D. (1996). What new paradigm of ISD? *Educational Technology*, *36*(4), 57–58. https://www.jstor.org/stable/44428351

Neubauer, D., Paepcke-Hjeltness, V., Evans, P., Barnhart, B., & Finseth, T. (2017). Experiencing technology enabled empathy mapping. *The Design Journal*, *20*(1), S4683–S4689. doi:10.1080/14606925.2017.1352966

Nielsen, L. (2019). *Personas: User focused design* (2nd ed.). Springer. https://link.springer.com/content/pdf/10.1007/978-1-4471-7427-1.pdf doi:10.1007/978-1-4471-7427-1

Paré, G., Trudel, M. C., Jaana, M., & Kitsiou, S. (2015). Synthesizing information systems knowledge: A typology of literature reviews. *Information & Management*, *52*(2), 183–199. doi:10.1016/j.im.2014.08.008

Parrish, P. (2006). Design as storytelling. *TechTrends*, *50*(4), 72–82. doi:10.1007/s11528-006-0072-7

Parrish, P. (2014). Designing for the half-known world: Lessons for instructional designers from the craft of narrative fiction. In B. Hokanson & A. Gibbons (Eds.), *Design in educational technology: Design thinking, design process, and the design studio* (pp. 261–270). Springer International. doi:10.1007/978-3-319-00927-8_15

Parrish, P., & Linder-VanBerschot, J. (2010). Cultural dimensions of learning: Addressing the challenges of multicultural instruction. *International Review of Research in Open and Distance Learning, 11*(2), 1–19. doi:10.19173/irrodl.v11i2.809

Rapanta, C., & Cantoni, L. (2014). Being in the users' shoes: Anticipating experience while designing online courses. *British Journal of Educational Technology, 45*(5), 765–777. doi:10.1111/bjet.12102

Reigeluth, C. M. (1996). A new paradigm of ISD? *Educational Technology, 36*(3), 13–20. https://www.jstro.org/stable/44428335

Saxena, M. (2011). Learner analysis framework for globalized e-learning: A case study. *International Review of Research in Open and Distance Learning: A Case Study, 12*(5), 93-107. doi:10.19173/irrodl.v12i5.954

Schwalbe, M. L. & Mason Schrock, D. (1996). Identity work as group process. *Advances in Group Processes, 13*(113), 113-147. https://www.researchgate.net/publication/284293040_Identity_work_as_group_process

Stefaniak, J. E., & Baaki, J. (2013). A layered approach to understanding your audience. *Performance Improvement, 52*(6), 5–9. doi:10.1002/pfi.21352

Sugar, W. (2014). Analysis. In *Studies of ID practices: A review and synthesis of research on ID current practices.* Springer. doi:10.1007/978-3-319-03605-2_2

Tracey, M. W., & Hutchinson, A. (2019). Empathic design: Imagining the cognitive and emotional learner experience. *Educational Technology Research and Development, 67*(5), 1259–1272. doi:10.1007/s11423-019-09683-2

Van Boven, L., & Lowenstein, G. (2005). Empathy gaps in emotional perspective taking. In B. F. Malle & S. D. Hodges (Eds.), *Other minds: How humans bridge the divide between self and others* (pp. 284–297). The Guilford Press.

Vann, L. S. (2017). Demonstrating empathy: A phenomenological study of instructional designers making instructional strategy decisions for adult learners. *International Journal on Teaching and Learning in Higher Education, 29*(2), 233–244. http://www.isetl.org/ijtlhe/index.cfm

Weave Media Team. (2023, July 24). *Your user personas are biased.* https://medium.com/kubo/your-user-personas-are-biased-ac7280f9e222

Williams van Rooij, S. (2012). Research-based personas: Teaching empathy in professional education. *The Journal of Effective Teaching, 12*(3), 77–86.

Willis, J. (1998). Alternative instructional design paradigms: What's worth discussing and what isn't. *Educational Technology, 38*(3), 5–16. https://www.jstor.org/stable/44428983

Wilson, B. G. (2013). A practice-centered approach to instructional design. In J. M. Spector, B. B. Lockee, S. Smaldino, & M. Herring (Eds.), *Learning, problem solving, and mindtools: Essays in honor of David H. Jonassen* (pp. 35–54). Routledge.

APPENDIX

Summary of Research Investigating Empathic Learner Analysis

Author and Title	Context	Method/ Tool	Study Type and Sample	Data	Results/ Observation	Key Affordances	Primary Challenges
Baaki et al. (2017); Designing authentic personas for open education resources designers	Online adult learners, professional or informal settings	Personas	Design case; N/A	N/A	Authentic personas and empathy framework may help IDs understand and design for learners	Design decisions viewed from learners' perspectives	Time and stakeholder buy-in
Baaki & Maddrell (2020); Building empathy and developing instructional design experience and skills	Online adult learners, professional or informal settings	Personas	Case study; 37 designers, service-learning ID project	Participant reflections, discussion board data, & design artifacts	IDs demonstrated empathy. connections with persona; persona influenced design conversations, design decisions	Provides context, motivation, engagement for IDs, reveals design elements	Time, commitment from IDs
Dudek & Heiser (2017); Elements, principles, and critical inquiry for identity-centered design of online environments	Higher education, online	Design framework	Conceptual; N/A	N/A	Framework to help IDs understand, design for learners' identities	Multi-layered learner analysis helps IDs advocate for learners	Project constraints, stakeholder resistance, lack of ID models
Haag & Marsden (2018); Exploring personas as a method to foster empathy in student IT design teams	Higher education, applicable to online	Personas	Qualitative; 43 university students	Recording and transcription of 8 design meetings	Novice difficulty developing affective empathy, relating to personas unlike themselves, instead focused on cognitive empathy	Personas help novices develop cognitive empathy	Methods, training needed
Lilley et al. (2012); Understanding the student experience through the use of personas	Higher education, online	Personas	Design case; N/A	N/A	Personas applied to instructional scenarios help designers make pedagogically sound choices based on who learners are	Allows designers to communicate about learners	Faculty resistance
Matthews & Yanchar (2018); Instructional design as manipulation of, or cooperation with, learners?	Online adult learners, multiple sectors	Perspective taking, projection	Qualitative; IDs (n = 6), various U. S. sectors	3 semi-structured, in-depth interviews	Absent formal learner analysis, IDs may imagine the learners' experience and project from their own experience to understand and empathize with learners	Imagining learner experience may help IDs design for engagement rather than control	May be driven by IDs values and approaches to design rather than best practices
Matthews et al. (2017); Empathy in distance learning design practice	Online adult learners, multiple sectors	Perspective taking, projection	Qualitative; IDs (n = 6), various U. S. sectors	3 semi-structured, in-depth interviews	Empathy enacted through caring for the learner using projection and perspective taking but IDs often constrained	IDs can employ empathic practices to the extent possible in the context of a design project	Lack of empathic guidance, project constraints, perceived value

continued on following page

Table. Continued

Author and Title	Context	Method/Tool	Study Type and Sample	Data	Results/Observation	Key Affordances	Primary Challenges
Parrish (2014); Designing for the half-known world: Lessons for instructional designers from the craft of narrative fiction	Context agnostic, applicable to online	Storytelling	Conceptual; N/A	N/A	Guiding questions, design story techniques in analysis may make learner experience more tangible, detailed	Uncover unrealized constraints, enhance communication about potential learners	Uncertainty, complexity may prevent IDs from using approach
Parrish (2006); Design as storytelling	Context agnostic, applicable to online	Storytelling	Conceptual; N/A	N/A	Viewing design from learner experience perspective is a critical ID skill; learner experience stories use imagination, judgment, communication to bridge analysis and synthesis	Enhances traditional analysis, reveals constraints, provides shared vision, serves as formative evaluation when learner interaction not possible	Time to get to know learners' experience, develop and practice skills
Rapanta & Cantoni (2014); Being in the users' shoes: Anticipating experience while designing online courses	Higher education, online	Perspective taking, projection	Qualitative; Two ID teams, (n = 10, 3)	Recording and transcription of 15 design meetings	Provides insights into how and what type of discourse IDs use in design team meetings to anticipate learner experience	Multidisciplinary design team meetings provide context for anticipatory discourse, foregrounds empathy for users, improves design	IDs ability to engage in empathetic discourse
Stefaniak & Baaki (2013); A layered approach to understanding your audience	Adult learners, professional or informal settings, applicable to online	Personas	Conceptual; N/A	N/A	Considering who learners are helped generate new instructional strategies, resulted in enthusiasm, effective problem solving, and project momentum	Surfaces instructional strategies that may not otherwise be apparent	Timelines and budgets often limit learner analysis in ID projects
Tracey & Hutchinson (2019); Empathic design: Imagining the cognitive and emotional learner experience	Online adult learners, professional or informal settings	Perspective taking, projection	Exploratory mixed-methods; design team (n = 5-10), learners (n = 50)	Recording and transcription of 4 design meetings, learner surveys	IDs used empathic forecasting to imagine learners' cognitive and emotional experiences, aligned with learners' perceptions	Empathic forecasting enables IDs to connect with learners through imagination	Research needed to understand IDs construction, use, and awareness of empathic forecasting in ID
Vann (2017); Demonstrating empathy: A phenomenological study of instructional designers making instructional strategy decisions for adult learners	Higher education, online	Perspective taking, projection	Qualitative; IDs in various sectors (n = 6)	Intensive interviews	Expert IDs considered empathy essential, believed it should guide instructional strategy decisions	Adopting learner perspective is a vital skill in ID practice; may support transformative learning for adults in online learning	Stakeholders' lack of buy-in, time, IDs limited influence, lack of engagement with learners

continued on following page

Table. Continued

Author and Title	Context	Method/ Tool	Study Type and Sample	Data	Results/ Observation	Key Affordances	Primary Challenges
Williams van Rooij (2012); Research-based personas: Teaching empathy in professional education	Higher education, online	Personas	Design case	N/A	Research-based personas, validated by surveys and usability testing, were key tool in design process	Enables designers to make appropriate design choices for users unlike themselves	Requires engagement with sample learners and stakeholder validation

Chapter 7
Applying Culturally Responsive Strategies to Promote Engagement and Student Success in Online Courses

Florence Williams
ⓘ https://orcid.org/0000-0002-2169-7017
University of Central Florida, USA

ABSTRACT

This chapter explores the importance of integrating culturally responsive teaching (CRT) principles into online education to enhance student engagement and success. It discusses the challenges of implementing culturally responsive practices in online learning environments. It encourages educational practitioners (including instructors, instructional designers, managers, and administrators) to engage in detailed planning and structured facilitation and to involve students in the process. The narrative invites reflection as it reviews the foundational works of scholars in culturally responsive pedagogy and teaching practices and outlines a framework for creating inclusive and culturally affirming learning environments. The literature suggests ways for educators to strategically utilize technology to foster inclusivity in online learning environments.

INTRODUCTION

Imagine a world where access to higher education is determined not by merit or hard work, but by gender, ethnicity, aspects of diversity, institutional norms, or the zip code in which students live. While this may sound like a dystopian nightmare, the reality is that systemic inequalities and disparities in educational opportunities continue to plague our society, particularly in the age of online education. Creating humanized and culturally responsive learning environments is a significant challenge in higher education, regardless of the modality in which it is delivered. For many universities, creativity and innovation rather than culture provide the momentum for engaged classrooms and student success. In today's rapidly evolving educational landscape and

DOI: 10.4018/979-8-3693-0762-5.ch007

especially after the COVID-19 pandemic, online learning has emerged as a cornerstone of higher education. This shift brings with it the imperative to ensure that digital spaces not only disseminate information but also embrace the rich diversity of cultures and perspectives within our global learning community.

This chapter explores several tools and strategies that can be useful for integrating culturally responsive teaching principles into online education. Culturally responsive teaching is a pedagogical framework centered on leveraging the cultural backgrounds of students to inform and enhance their learning experiences (Ladson-Billings, 1995a). The significance of this approach lies in its capacity to create inclusive, humanized environments where each learner, irrespective of their cultural heritage, feels acknowledged, valued, and empowered. Addressing the challenges and limitations of online education therefore requires a multifaceted approach that prioritizes inclusivity and cultural responsiveness. We invite you to think about your classroom experiences and what made them memorable. In culturally responsive online teaching, the goal is to transfer skills and knowledge while promoting understanding of diverse perspectives and creating socially responsible learners.

Let's start with a question: What acceptance or resistance do you have to conformity, assimilation, or diversity, and what filters do these affiliations create for your reading and application of culturally responsive teaching principles? Consider writing these down beforehand. In the following sections of this chapter, we will review some *challenges faced in the online environment*, followed by an exploration of *culturally responsive pedagogy and teaching* based on *the foundational work of scholars*. We will introduce a *Culturally Responsive Online Education (CROE) framework* and discuss strategies for *fostering an inclusive environment online*. We wrap up the chapter with a *conclusion* of the discussions about promoting culturally responsive pedagogy and a call to action for implementation.

CHALLENGES FACED IN THE ONLINE ENVIRONMENT

The concept of "humanizing" online instruction is a significant area of focus in the discussion of culturally responsive teaching in online education. This approach involves creating a learning environment that prioritizes students' social and emotional needs, fostering a sense of community and belonging. However, implementing this approach in an online environment presents several challenges:

1. *Technological barriers:* Not all students have equal access to reliable internet and technology, which can hinder their ability to fully participate in online courses.
   a. *Digital literacy:* Beyond access to technology, there's also the challenge of digital literacy. Not all students have the necessary skills to navigate online learning platforms effectively, which can impact their learning experience in online classes.
   b. *Socioeconomic disparities:* The issue of technological barriers also highlights underlying socioeconomic disparities. Students from lower-income backgrounds may struggle more with access to reliable technology and the internet, potentially widening the achievement gap in higher education online classes.
2. *Lack of personal interaction:* The absence of face-to-face interaction can make it difficult to build strong relationships and a sense of community.
   a. *Nonverbal communication:* In traditional classrooms, nonverbal cues play a significant role in understanding and communication. The lack of these cues in online classes can lead to misunderstandings and make it harder for students and teachers to connect on a personal level.

    b.   *Collaborative learning:* Online classes often lack the spontaneous group discussions and collaborations that occur in physical classrooms. This absence can limit opportunities for peer learning and reduce the sense of community among students.

3.   *Engagement difficulties:* Keeping students engaged and motivated in a virtual environment can be challenging due to distractions and the impersonal nature of online learning.

    a.   *Self-discipline and time management:* In a virtual environment, students are required to have a higher degree of self-discipline and time management skills. The flexibility of online learning can sometimes lead to procrastination, making it harder for students to stay engaged and keep up with their coursework.

    b.   *Isolation and lack of immediate feedback:* Online classes can sometimes lead to feelings of isolation, as students may not receive immediate feedback or encouragement from their peers and instructors. This lack of real-time interaction can affect students' motivation and engagement levels in the course.

4.   *Cultural differences:* Online courses often attract a diverse group of students from diverse cultural backgrounds. Instructors may find it challenging to create content that is culturally sensitive and inclusive.

    a.   *Language barriers:* With students from diverse cultural backgrounds, language barriers can pose a significant challenge. Instructors need to ensure that their content is clear and comprehensible to nonnative speakers, which can be particularly challenging in an online setting.

    b.   *Cultural awareness training:* Instructors must undergo cultural awareness training to understand and respect cultural differences among students. This understanding can help them create a more inclusive and respectful online learning environment, fostering better communication and collaboration among students.

5.   *Assessment challenges:* Assessing student performance accurately and fairly in an online environment can be difficult due to issues like plagiarism and the impersonal nature of online tests.

    a.   *Integrity of online assessments:* The online nature of assessments can make it difficult to monitor academic integrity. Without the physical presence of an invigilator, students may be more tempted to use unauthorized resources during tests, leading to issues like plagiarism.

    b.   *Personalized feedback:* In a traditional classroom, instructors can provide immediate and personalized feedback based on their observations during assessments. However, in an online environment, this can be more challenging, potentially affecting the quality of feedback and students' learning outcomes.

Despite these challenges, the literature suggests that humanizing learning is particularly effective in promoting engagement and success in online courses, especially for students from historically marginalized groups. Kilgore (2016), in an analysis of methods for humanizing online instruction in business education, provides practical strategies for creating a sense of community. Kilgore proposes that online instructors prioritize building relationships with their students, using authentic and inclusive language, and creating opportunities for social interaction and community building. Kilgore's approach suggests that student perspectives should be respected in the co-creation of content online.

Adding to this, Pacansky-Brock (2020) has theorized a framework based on the principles of presence, empathy, awareness, and trust that directs faculty on how and why to humanize online courses. Pacansky-Brock et al. (2020) builds upon the discussion about humanizing online instruction and the importance of empathy and emotional connection in online teaching. The expanded research of Pacansky-Brock et al. (2022) presents a model for humanized online teaching using a theoretical framework influenced by Culturally Responsive Teaching (CRT), social presence, validation theory, and Universal Design for Learning (UDL). Working with twelve faculty members from Cal State, the researchers collated a list of strategies for building community. They found that valuing an emotional connection and prioritizing students' emotional needs were essential for success. They concluded that humanizing online instruction is critical for promoting engagement and encourages success, particularly for students from historically marginalized groups.

Furthermore, Mehta and Aguilera (2020), in a qualitative study involving the perspectives of undergraduate online students in vignettes, examined the impact of a humanized pedagogical approach on student engagement in online courses. Similar to Pacansky-Brock et al. (2022), they emphasize the importance of prioritizing students' social and emotional needs in higher education online and have developed a framework for humanizing online instruction that focuses on building relationships, establishing trust, and fostering a sense of community. Supporting the ideology of humanizing, Parker et al. (2021) reviewed fifteen articles and provided practical strategies for creating inclusive virtual spaces that empower students and support efficacy and autonomy. The combined research suggests that a humanizing approach in online instruction not only fosters a sense of community and belonging but also empowers students, thereby enhancing their learning experience and success.

Culturally Responsive Pedagogy and Teaching: Foundational Work of Scholars

To understand cultural responsiveness practitioners can draw from seminal scholarship such as the pivotal work of Ladson-Billings (1995a, b), which introduces a theory of culturally relevant pedagogy. Ladson-Billings' work introduced the anthropological debate of matching teaching with community culture by integrating students' cultural backgrounds to support culturally appropriate pedagogy. This theoretical exploration centers the principle of culturally responsive pedagogy in the literature and establishes the core principles underlying this transformative culturally responsive approach by (1) identifying students' strengths, (2) creating culturally supportive environments, (3) adjusting existing curriculum, and (4) deepening practitioner understanding of cultural inclusion. Additionally, Gay's (2002, 2018) theoretical exploration of culturally responsive teaching supports the work done by Ladson-Billings and provides a robust foundation for understanding the preparation and practical applications of culturally responsive pedagogy and practices in educational settings. Ladson-Billings (2021a) has expanded on earlier theory by providing examples for how to ensure academic, cultural, and social success for students in culturally centered pedagogical settings.

As we navigate the higher education space, it is vital to acknowledge the challenges inherent in integrating culturally responsive approaches in online learning environments. Primarily, online faculty grapple with issues of digital accessibility (Bong & Chen, 2021). Their research on the use of information and communication technology, with a group of students with disabilities enrolled in online courses, outlines the benefits of technology while identifying the need to understand how to incorporate digital accessibility. Advocating the need for ensuring broad cultural representation in virtual spaces, Broderick (2020) interviewed students from diverse backgrounds enrolled in online courses. He presents strategies for addressing key challenges, including the views of underserved populations, by assessing the climate and culture around diversity and inclusion. García-Morales et al. (2021) conducted a study on the impact of culturally responsive teaching on student engagement and academic performance in online courses. The study involved a sample of sixty-seven students who were enrolled in an online course at a Spanish university. Their findings focus on the challenges and opportunities posed by the transformation of higher education in the wake of the COVID-19 pandemic with a control group and an experimental group as it relates to digital accessibility.

Digital accessibility refers to acknowledging the importance of cultural and social identity, removing barriers to ensure equal access, and adapting teaching strategies for effective virtual engagement. Experts review the role of online learning in building resilient educational systems for the future, with a focus on the opportunities and challenges presented by the increasing use of digital technologies in education (Dumford & Miller, 2018; Kanwar, 2021). However, within these challenges there are myriad opportunities, harnessed through the strategic use of technology, incorporating and honoring diverse cultural practices through universal learning design, and devising and implementing innovative techniques to foster inclusivity and remove cultural conformity in academic settings (Borrego, E., 2017; Kieran & Anderson, 2019; Ladson-Billings, 2021a, b).

An expansive body of literature continues to contribute to the discourse on Culturally Responsive Teaching. Emerging research, such as Pitchford et al. (2020) and Tatum (2021), has examined the intersectionality of language, culture, and identity within educational settings. Tatum's work emphasizes the importance of not just acknowledging cultural diversity but actively sustaining and promoting it within the learning environment. Furthermore, the work of Pitchford et al. provides insights into the importance of multicultural education, offering educators practical approaches to connect culture with academic processes. As culturally responsive pedagogy continues to evolve, this expanding body of literature from diverse voices enriches the understanding of how educators can authentically engage with students from various cultural backgrounds in the pursuit of meaningful and equitable learning experiences. Indeed, we rely on the broader literature on culturally responsive teaching (Broderick, 2020; Bollinger & Halupa, 2019; Day & Beard, 2019; Fuentes et al., 2021; Gay, 2018; Kieran & Anderson, 2019; Lopez-Littleton & Blessett, 2015) and culturally relevant pedagogy (DeCuir & Dixon, 2004; Ladson-Billings, 2023; Lindo, 2020) that builds on these seminal works to support our understanding of the practice. Lindo urges educators to foster cultural competence and culturally sustaining pedagogy in providing high-quality learning experiences for exceptional children. However, integrating a culturally responsive approach in online learning environments presents several challenges, such as ensuring digital accessibility, cultural representation in virtual spaces, using computer-based technology to teach foundational skills, and adapting teaching strategies for effective virtual engagement. Despite these challenges, technology can be strategically used to foster inclusivity. The literature is replete with interventions that are culturally responsive and address the unique challenges faced by these students (Brown et al., 2019; Borrego, M. L., 2022; Martin et al., 2019), thereby providing numerous opportunities for cultural inclusivity.

The research on cultural responsiveness and inclusivity indicates that this pedagogical method has gained significant attention in recent years in K–12 and higher education classrooms. Attempts have been made in universities all over the Western world to incorporate culturally responsive strategies into digital environments for more than two decades, with varied rates of success. Leaning in on the research of Geneva Gay (2002), Will and Najarro (2022) describe culturally responsive pedagogy as "using students' customs, characteristics, experience, and perspectives as tools for better classroom instruction" (p. 1). They consider the cultural response in education as the "kind of teaching that helps students [to] see themselves and their communities as belonging in schools and other academic spaces, leading to more engagement and success" (p. 1). Supporting the notion of student-focused curricula, Hernandez et al. (2019) advocate for deeper learning opportunities, an approach to education that seeks to engage students in more meaningful and authentic learning experiences, with a focus on equity and social justice. Mensa (2021), in supporting cultural relevance for STEAM (science, technology, engineering, arts, and mathematics) approaches, suggests that "culturally relevant pedagogy and culturally responsive teaching offer additional benefits for academic success in the science classroom that is not measured on tests. For example, due to the nature of science learning, students work together, teach each other, and share different perspectives as they engage in science" (p. 2). Similarly, Muhammad (2023) provides a guide to culturally and historically responsive curricula and instructions to address the cultural backgrounds and experiences of students in the classroom. She discusses a model for advancing curriculum, instruction, and leadership through culturally responsive education that supports their inclusion and belonging in educational spaces. Muhammad invites educators to facilitate truth-telling, which allows students to share their perspectives freely and without fear of judgment in the learning community.

Figure 1 illustrates how the culturally relevant approach is centered around cultural awareness, which is influenced by cultural competence and critical consciousness. These elements collectively contribute to student achievement, emphasizing the importance of integrating students' cultural backgrounds into the learning environment for a more inclusive and effective educational experience. In the context of culturally relevant pedagogy, critical consciousness plays a pivotal role in student achievement by fostering an understanding and questioning of societal and cultural norms. Student curiosity and interrogation thereby empower students to actively engage in their learning and apply it to their cultural contexts. This idea suggests that cultural competence, critical consciousness, and cultural awareness work synergistically to enhance the educational experience and success of students in an inclusive online learning environment.

Figure 1. Components of Culturally Relevant Pedagogy

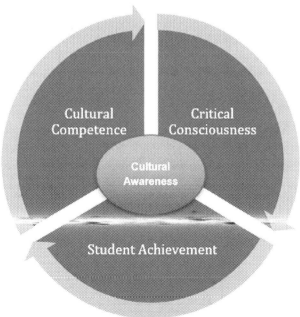

At the core of Culturally Relevant Pedagogy (figure 1.1) is the cultivation of cultural awareness among both educators and students. This cultural awareness involves recognizing the diverse backgrounds, experiences, and perspectives that learners bring to the educational setting (Abacioglu et al., 2020). By fostering an environment where cultural differences are acknowledged and valued, instructors create a space in which students feel seen and respected (Gay, 2002). Fuentes et al. (2021) also urge practitioners to foster a culture of respect through explicit engagement and intent in their practice. To foster an inclusive classroom environment, practitioners must engage students using their lived experiences and worldviews in the development of critical consciousness. In other words, the students' folklore and cultural practices must form the foundation or at the least be incorporated into curricula at each level of the system to drive overall student achievement.

Inclusivity lies at the heart of culturally responsive practices. It involves actively working to create a classroom environment that is welcoming and affirming for all students, regardless of their cultural or ethnic backgrounds. This includes strategies such as inclusive language, fair and equitable participation opportunities, and promoting mutual respect among students (Ladson-Billings, 1995a, b). Online learning is so deeply integrated into the higher education process that students can meet through the modality they choose for their learning. Williams (2021) posits that to be successful, culturally responsive strategies should incorporate detailed course planning in advance and structured facilitation that involves the student in the process. Williams' research found ways to ensure improvements in the inclusion of culture and identity for different contexts in online courseware through intentional inclusion practices (differentiated instruction, gender-sensitive content, and assessment flexibility). It is therefore incumbent on faculty and training professionals to find the sweet spot in digital environments that supports authentic engagement and keeps students coming back to their chosen digital modalities. There is a sense of urgency for educators to collaborate on the choice of good online delivery practices and implementation for use. Bueno (2020) suggest policies that provide the parameters for the adoption and integration of flexible learning and teaching approaches that align with institutional learning and teaching policies. Ideas of flexibility, responsiveness, and responsibility remain critical in higher education. As universities recognize "place" as relevant, they should work to implement technology that supports place through culturally responsive strategies. Gayon and Tan (2021) explore the experiences of higher education teachers in implementing flexible learning and teaching approaches that seek to provide students with more choice and control over their educational experiences.

Ali (2020) discusses the necessity of online and remote learning. Ali posits that universities worldwide are consistently moving towards online learning or e-learning. He suggests that, apart from resources, staff readiness, confidence, student accessibility, and motivation play crucial functions in digital learning environments. Santos et al. (2020) contribute to the debate surrounding readiness for flexible learning, which seeks to provide students with more choice and control over their educational experiences. During the pandemic, it was disconcerting to see the inequities across institutions and the inability to pivot to provide culturally responsive opportunities through technology. Pacansky-Brock et al. (2020, 2022) focus on understanding and addressing the diverse cultural backgrounds and experiences of students in the classroom and provide practical guidance for humanizing online courses, with a focus on building community, creating engaging content, and giving personalized feedback to students. The infographic and narrative together identify four interwoven principles for humanized online learning that include empathy, awareness, presence, and trust. Pacansky-Brock asks, "If our personal narratives reveal these adjectives as essential traits for meaningful teacher-student relationships, why aren't they characteristics that college professors strive to portray?" (2022, p. 5). Her discussion of cultural influences on relationships identifies culture as an iceberg with invisible attributes at the portion below the waterline. Acknowledging that online classes hold the potential to expand college access to diverse populations, Pacansky-Brock et al. (2022) discuss the need for institutions to provide transformative professional development opportunities for educators to achieve equity in online learning environments. The research also proposes techniques for humanizing the online class that make the process responsive for the students. Humanized and responsive curricula seek to identify and manage process approaches that support the design of quality online programs with students at the center. In a culturally responsive environment, higher education faculty can engage students in the design process, empowering them to find answers and provide feedback on their learning. An invitational design introduces active learning engagement, community awareness, and authentic assessment. A culturally responsive approach in online higher education classrooms incorporates students' cultural identities and lived experiences into the online environment as tools for effective instruction. These tools consider strategies, pedagogical needs, and opportunities for sustained engagement for all students.

Central to cultural responsiveness is the integration of curriculum and instructional materials that reflect the experiences, histories, and contributions of diverse cultural groups. This not only engages students on a personal level but also provides them with a broader and more accurate understanding of the world (Gay, 2015). Educators might consider using the idea of Culturally Responsive Teaching to respond to the question, How can practitioners (including instructors, instructional designers, managers, and administrators) create interactive learning experiences to facilitate cultural diversity and learning preferences?

Culturally Responsive Teaching can be distilled into the core principle of inclusivity. Craig and Kuykendall (2020) using a combination of empirical evidence and experiences, outline the essence of this foundational concept as a means for emphasizing the active cultivation of a learning space that warmly embraces every student, irrespective of their cultural or ethnic heritage. The authors suggest that faculty should practice anonymous grading to mitigate the negative bias of grading on students. To reduce time in downloading and uploading papers, faculty might use the affordance of their learning management systems to anonymize student submissions during the grading process. The research of Ladson-Billings (1995b) underlines that inclusivity is not a passive endeavor, but demands deliberate efforts to create an environment where every student feels valued and affirmed.

Mensa (2021) affirms that, collectively, culturally relevant pedagogy and culturally responsive teaching have common features and are often used interchangeably. The confluence of these practices suggests that educators must be aware of the tenets of culturally responsive teaching to adopt the practice with fidelity. For example, figure 1.2 represents a progression of transformative stages, starting from "Validating" and moving through "Comprehensive" and "Multidimensional." These processes lead to a second sequence of stages: "Empowering," "Transformative," and finally, "Emancipatory." Each stage signifies a step in the development or transformation process of the culturally responsive teaching approach. Online faculty members who aim to incorporate these principles into their practice should align the intersections of student identity by validating cultural experiences at the start of the process. The arrows indicate the direction of progression, suggesting a journey of growth and empowerment that is supported by the teacher.

The culturally responsive teaching approach builds on the idea of culturally relevant pedagogy and provides strategic engagement options for the educator. The approach (figure 1.2) incorporates engaged learning techniques that are validating, comprehensive, multidimensional, empowering, transformative, and emancipatory. Significant findings from research by Graham (2020) emphasized inclusive education,

Figure 2. The Culturally Responsive Teaching Approach

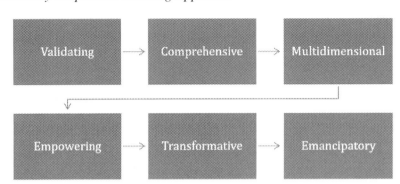

which seeks to ensure that all students have access to high-quality learning experiences, regardless of their backgrounds or abilities. Tamtik and Guenter (2019) provide a policy analysis of equity, diversity, and inclusion strategies in Canadian universities, with a focus on the progress that has been made and the challenges that remain. Their work highlights the pivotal role of language in cultivating inclusivity through the acknowledgment of diversity. Inclusive language, as a strategy, plays a crucial part in setting the tone of the classroom. Graham's research supports earlier findings from Ladson-Billings, which makes the case for culturally relevant pedagogy as a necessary approach to education that addresses the cultural backgrounds and experiences of students. The findings demonstrate that consciously using language that acknowledges and respects diverse perspectives can foster an environment where all students feel seen and heard. This linguistic approach goes beyond mere words; it establishes an atmosphere of respect and understanding (Ladson-Billings, 1995b). In concert with these suggestions, Howard (2021) believes that culturally responsive pedagogy can adopt the social contexts and experiences of students in the classroom to expand educational opportunities culturally.

Equitable participation opportunities emerge as another key aspect in the search for inclusivity. Studies have shown that providing equal opportunities for every student to engage actively in the learning process not only enhances academic achievement but also reinforces a sense of belonging. Through structured activities and collaborative learning experiences, students are given the chance to contribute meaningfully, transcending barriers that may arise from differing cultural backgrounds (Ladson-Billings, 1995a, b).

Moreover, promoting mutual respect among students has been identified as a fundamental strategy for fostering an inclusive classroom environment. Research affirms that creating a culture of respect, where students honor and appreciate each other's perspectives, leads to a more harmonious and enriching learning experience. This not only enhances the social dynamics of the classroom but also lays a solid foundation for collaborative learning and constructive dialogue (Gay, 2018; García-Morales et al., 2021; Ladson-Billings, 1995a, b, 2021a, b, 2023). Gay (2015) outlines the challenges and opportunities presented by the increasing diversity of students in schools. Building on this premise, Gay (2018) later provides an overview of the theory, research, and practice of culturally responsive teaching, which seeks to address the cultural backgrounds and experiences of students in delivery.

The foundation of culturally responsive practices lies in the active cultivation of inclusivity within the classroom. Research findings underscore that this endeavor demands intentional efforts, encompassing the use of inclusive language, the provision of equitable participation opportunities, and the promotion of mutual respect among students. The lack of face-to-face interaction can make it more difficult to establish a sense of community and create a safe space for students to share their perspectives. As such, the intentional creation of netiquette guidelines and honor codes that support respect and inclusion may be required for successful integration. While these principles are not without inherent challenges, by incorporating specific strategies, educators can create a classroom environment that not only nurtures academic growth but also cultivates a sense of belonging and affirmation for every student.

To address the challenges of integrating culturally responsive pedagogy into online learning environments, educators can consider the integrating techniques that could help alleviate the challenges of achieving equity. One answer is to select those strategies that meet the needs of the diverse learners in your specific context. Online teaching faculty members who seek to incorporate cultural competence and address student diversity might use the strategies outlined in table 1.1 as a foundation for building a toolbox. The table utilizes a descriptive narrative that incorporates strategies and implementation principles as a starting point for culturally responsive engagement. Some general references are listed for additional guidance for those who would like to develop a better understanding of the underlying principles.

The strategy of incorporating diverse perspectives is aimed at enhancing students' understanding of diverse cultural backgrounds. This approach, supported by Abacioglu et al. (2020) and Bolliger and Halupa (2019), involves the inclusion of multiple perspectives and voices in online courses. This might be achieved by inviting experts and guest speakers for specific topics so that students can see themselves reflected in the field of study. If experts are unavailable, faculty can achieve comparable results by using videos and multimedia resources to include perspectives and increase interaction.

Fostering collaboration can build a sense of community and foster cross-cultural understanding among students. As suggested by Ali (2020), E. P. Bonner (2014), M. L. Borrego (2022), and Broderick (2020), this involves encouraging students to work together on group projects. Some collaboration is possible through promoting the use of discussion boards for interactive learning and incorporating team-based learning activities in the curriculum.

Providing training for faculty is crucial to enhance their ability to foster an inclusive and culturally diverse learning environment. As highlighted by Bong and Chen (2021), F. A. Bonner (2013), E. Borrego (2017), Craig and Kuykendall (2020), Cruz et al. (2020), and Day and Beard (2019), faculty members should receive training on how to create and foster an inclusive online learning environment.

Re-evaluating course design is a strategy that involves reviewing the course design to ensure that it is accessible to all students. This could involve adjusting the course structure, content, or assessment methods, as suggested by Ali (2020), Bong and Chen (2021), Bueno (2020), and Castro and Tumibay (2021).

Utilizing technology involves using technology to create inclusive and culturally affirming environments. This could involve providing translation services or incorporating virtual reality experiences that highlight diverse cultures, as suggested by Abacioglu et al. (2020), Bolliger and Halupa (2019), and Broderick (2020).

Encouraging feedback might involve encouraging students to provide feedback on their learning experiences. This can help identify areas where culture could be further integrated into online courses, as suggested by E. P. Bonner (2014), M. L. Borrego (2022), and Craig and Kuykendall (2020).

Including participation and reflection opportunities could incorporate opportunities for participation and reflection into the course design. This could include discussion forums, reflective journals, or peer review activities, as suggested by Ali (2020), E. P. Bonner (2014), and M. L. Borrego (2022).

Table 1. Implementing Culturally Responsive Strategies in Online Teaching*

Strategies	Implementation Principles	Related References
Incorporate diverse perspectives	- Incorporate multiple perspectives and voices. - Include experts and invite guest speakers. - Use videos to provide visual or auditory experiences. - Use multimedia resources to increase interaction.	- (Abacioglu et al., 2020) - (Bolliger & Halupa, 2019) - (Brown et al., 2019) - (DeCuir & Dixson, 2004)
Foster collaboration	- Encourage students to work together on group projects. - Promote the use of discussion boards for interactive learning. - Incorporate team-based learning activities in the curriculum.	- (Ali, 2020) - (Bonner, E. P., 2014) - (Borrego, M. L., 2022) - (Broderick, 2020)
Provide training for faculty	- Train faculty on the effective use of online tools. - Guide faculty on how to engage students in online discussions. - Help faculty learn how to adapt traditional teaching methods to online environments. - Include training on how to handle technical issues online.	- (Bong & Chen, 2021) - (Bonner, F. A., 2013) - (Borrego, E., 2017) - (Craig & Kuykendall, 2020) - (Cruz et al., 2020) - (Day & Beard, 2019)
Re-evaluate course design	- Course design should be reviewed to ensure that it is accessible to all students. - Adjust the course structure. - Adjust the course content. - Adjust the assessment methods.	- (Ali, 2020) - (Bong & Chen, 2021) - (Bueno, 2020) - (Castro & Tumibay, 2021)
Utilize technology	- Technology can be used to create inclusive and culturally affirming environments. - Provide translation services. - Incorporate virtual reality experiences that highlight diverse cultures.	- (Abacioglu et al., 2020) - (Bolliger & Halupa, 2019) - (Broderick, 2020)
Encourage feedback	- Encourage students to provide feedback on their learning experiences. - Ask students to share what they found helpful. - Request suggestions on areas for improvement. - Use student feedback to integrate culture into online courses.	- (Bonner, E. P., 2014) - (Borrego, M. L., 2022) - (Craig & Kuykendall, 2020)
Include opportunities for participation and reflection	- Include discussion forums as part of the course. - Add reflective journals to the course activities. - Incorporate peer review activities into the course structure.	- (Ali, 2020) - (Bonner, E. P., 2014) - (Borrego, M. L., 2022)
Foster a culture of respect	- Use language that acknowledges and respects diverse perspectives. - Establish guidelines for respectful communication.	- (Bonner, F. A., 2013) - (Borrego, E., 2017) - (Cruz et al., 2020) - (Day & Beard, 2019)

* The table outlines strategies and implementation principles for culturally responsive teaching online. References are matched based on the general themes and topics they cover in the literature, and may not directly address every aspect of the strategies or implementation principles.

Fostering a culture of respect is a strategy that involves fostering a culture of respect in the online classroom. This could involve using language that acknowledges and respects diverse perspectives, and setting clear expectations for respectful communication, as suggested by F. A. Bonner (2013), E. Borrego (2017), Cruz et al. (2020), and Day and Beard (2019).

A Theoretical Framework for Culturally Responsive Online Education (CROE)

Culturally Responsive Teaching can serve as the critical foundational framework for the design and implementation of online education that is inclusive, engaging, and responsive to the diverse needs of learners. The Culturally Responsive Online Education (CROE) framework is built upon key principles and strategies that incorporate the threads of engagement, inclusivity, responsiveness, collaboration, authenticity, and learning functions into a cohesive whole that supports inclusivity and a sense of belonging online. These principles help alleviate imposter syndrome and support autonomy and efficacy.

The foundational principles of the frame outline the needs and benefits of cultural awareness and recognition, cultivating an inclusive environment, and authentic cultural integration. Considering the classroom as a space and place for meaningful negotiation, it considers several implementation strategies and outlines the benefits of intentionally integrating students' culture into higher education online curricular and classroom practices. The approach is practical rather than prescriptive in order to allow flexibility and contextual implementation. Educators can consistently apply the foundations and strategies toward the related benefits as outlined in table 1.2.

Foundations of the Culturally Responsive Online Education (CROE) Framework

Cultural Awareness and Recognition

The first pillar of CROE is built upon fostering cultural awareness and recognition. Educators, inspired by research insights, actively engage in recognizing and understanding the diverse cultural backgrounds of their students. Faculty should work on these principles by understanding cultural diversity, promoting inclusivity, recognizing cultural bias, and encouraging cultural exchange in the online classroom. These ideas require continuous learning and adaptation on the part of both the teacher and the learners.

· *Understanding Cultural Diversity:* The first step in fostering cultural awareness and recognition is understanding the concept of cultural diversity. This involves recognizing that each student comes from a unique cultural background that influences their learning style and perspective. Educators should be trained to understand these differences and adapt their teaching methods accordingly.
· *Promoting Inclusivity:* The CROE framework emphasizes the importance of creating an inclusive online learning environment. This means ensuring that all students, regardless of their cultural background, feel valued and included. Educators can achieve this by incorporating diverse cultural perspectives into their teaching materials and discussions.
· *Recognizing Cultural Bias:* It's crucial for educators to recognize their own cultural biases and how these may impact their teaching. By acknowledging these biases, educators can work towards providing a more balanced and fair learning experience for all students.

Table 2. Culturally Responsive Online Education (CROE) Framework*

Foundations	Strategies	Benefits
Cultural awareness and recognition	- Multimodal interaction and engagement - Flexible and equitable assessment	- Improved academic performance - Supports social-emotional development
Inclusive environment cultivation	- Collaborative and global learning - Interactive learning platforms	- Increased student engagement
Authentic cultural integration	- Flexible and equitable assessment - Continuous reflection and adaptation	- Enhanced cultural understanding - Promotes critical thinking

* The table outlines the foundations, strategies, and benefits of the proposed Culturally Responsive Online Education (CROE) framework.

· *Encouraging Cultural Exchange:* The CROE framework encourages educators to facilitate cultural exchange among students. This could involve creating opportunities for students to share their cultural experiences and learn from each other. Such exchanges can enrich the learning experience and promote mutual understanding and respect among students.

· *Continuous Learning and Adaptation:* The process of fostering cultural awareness and recognition is ongoing. Educators should continuously seek to learn more about unfamiliar cultures and adapt their teaching methods as they gain new insights. This commitment to continuous learning and adaptation is a key principle of the CROE framework.

Inclusive Environment Cultivation

Drawing from the principles for fostering inclusive classroom environments, the second pillar emphasizes the cultivation of an inclusive online environment. Inclusive language, equitable participation opportunities, and the promotion of mutual respect form the basis of this principle.

· The use of inclusive language is crucial in cultivating an inclusive online environment. This involves avoiding language that could be perceived as biased, discriminatory, or offensive. Educators should be trained to use language that respects and acknowledges all students' cultural backgrounds.

· The CROE framework emphasizes the importance of providing equitable participation opportunities for all students. This means ensuring that all students, regardless of their cultural background, have equal opportunities to participate in online discussions, group projects, and other learning activities. Strategies to promote equitable participation could include clear guidelines for online discussions, flexible assignment options, and anonymous peer review processes.

· Promoting mutual respect among students is another key principle of the CROE framework. Educators can foster mutual respect by setting clear expectations for respectful online interactions, addressing disrespectful behavior promptly, and modeling respectful communication in their interactions with students.

· Incorporating culturally relevant content into the curriculum can help cultivate an inclusive online environment. This involves selecting readings, examples, and learning materials that reflect the diverse cultural backgrounds of the students.

· Ensuring that all learning materials are accessible to students with different learning needs is another important aspect of cultivating an inclusive online environment. This could involve providing transcripts for video content, using clear and simple language in written materials, and ensuring that online platforms and resources are compatible with assistive technologies.

Authentic Cultural Integration

The integration of culturally relevant content serves as the third foundational principle. This involves the infusion of authentic cultural narratives, histories, and contributions into the curriculum to provide a more accurate understanding of the world.

· Infusion of cultural narratives involves incorporating stories, anecdotes, and experiences from various cultures into the curriculum. These narratives can provide students with a more personal and relatable understanding of diverse cultures.
· Understanding the history of distinct cultures is crucial for a comprehensive worldview. The curriculum should include historical events, traditions, and customs from various cultures to provide a broader perspective.
· Every culture has made significant contributions to various fields such as science, arts, literature, and more. Highlighting these contributions can foster respect and appreciation for unfamiliar cultures.
· It's important to ensure that the cultural content integrated into the curriculum is authentic and accurate. This involves careful research and consultation with cultural experts or community members.
· Cultures are dynamic and constantly evolving. Therefore, the culturally relevant content in the curriculum should be regularly updated to reflect current contexts and realities.

The Culturally Responsive Online Education (CROE) Framework presents a comprehensive approach to creating an inclusive, culturally sensitive, and globally aware online learning environment.

Strategies for Implementation

Multimodal Interaction and Engagement

The strategy of multimodal interaction for engagement, as discussed in the section on engaging diverse learning styles, serves as a key element in CROE. By designing interactive learning modules that cater to diverse learning preferences, educators ensure that the learning experience is engaging and accessible.

Flexible and Equitable Assessment

Aligning with the principles of inclusivity and recognition of diverse learning styles, CROE advocates for flexible and equitable assessment methods. This approach, supported by literature from M. L. Borrego (2022), ensures that assessments accommodate the varied ways students demonstrate understanding.

Collaborative and Global Learning

Building upon the collaborative spirit emphasized in the section on collaboration, CROE encourages collaborative and global learning experiences. Virtual teams that connect students from diverse cultural backgrounds, as proposed by F. A. Bonner (2013), foster a sense of shared learning and understanding.

Interactive Learning Platforms

The use of interactive learning platforms, highlighted in the discussion on engaging diverse learning styles, serves as a pivotal strategy in CROE. These platforms offer spaces for diverse forms of interaction, including discussions, quizzes, and collaborative projects (Bolliger & Halupa, 2019).

Continuous Reflection and Adaptation

Critical reflection, as suggested in the section on learning functions, forms the third pillar of the CROE framework. Teaching faculty and instructional designers engage in continuous reflection on their teaching practices, the inclusivity of their courses, and the responsiveness of their strategies to diverse student needs.

Benefits of Implementing the (CROE) Framework for Inclusion and Belonging

1. *Improved academic performance:* Cultural inclusion has been shown to improve academic outcomes for students from diverse cultural backgrounds. When students see themselves reflected in the curriculum and feel valued, they are more likely to engage with the material and perform better academically.
2. *Increased student engagement:* Students' cultural practices create a sense of belonging and community in the classroom, which leads to increased student engagement. When students feel that their voices are heard and their perspectives are valued, they are more likely to participate in class discussions and activities.
3. *Enhanced cultural understanding:* Cultural inclusion helps students to develop a deeper understanding of diverse cultures and perspectives. This understanding can lead to greater empathy and respect for others, which is an important skill in today's diverse society.
4. *Promotes critical thinking:* The inclusion of students' experiences encourages them to think critically about their cultural biases and assumptions. This leads to a deeper understanding of the complexity of cultural identities and promotes a more nuanced approach to cultural differences.
5. *Supports social-emotional development:* When culture is integrated into curricula it creates a safe and inclusive learning environment that supports students' social-emotional development. When students feel valued and respected, they are more likely to feel safe to take academic risks and express themselves creatively.

The Culturally Responsive Online Education (CROE) framework integrates foundational principles of inclusion and a sense of belonging, implementation strategies, and a commitment to continuous reflection and adaptation. In applying this framework, educators not only enhance the online learning experience but also contribute to the development of culturally competent and globally engaged learners. The principles of CROE are dynamic, recognizing the evolving nature of educational contexts and the ongoing journey toward a more inclusive and culturally responsive online education. Overall, the benefits of cultural inclusion are numerous and can have a positive impact on humanizing online learning for all students, regardless of their cultural background.

The Culturally Responsive Online Education (CROE) framework provides educators with a comprehensive approach that embodies the principles of validation, comprehensiveness, multidimensionality, empowerment, and transformation, rooted in emancipatory pedagogy. CROE encourages educators to actively validate and recognize the diverse cultural backgrounds of students, creating an inclusive and empowering online environment. By infusing authentic cultural narratives into the curriculum and leveraging interactive platforms, the framework ensures a comprehensive learning experience that resonates with diverse learning styles. The multidimensional nature of CROE is evident in its encouragement of flexible assessments, collaborative global learning, and continuous critical reflection. Ultimately, CROE seeks not only to enhance the online learning experience but also to empower learners by fostering a transformative and emancipatory educational journey, transcending cultural and societal barriers, and encouraging engagement among all learners.

The adoption of culturally responsive strategies in online learning within the higher education milieu is not merely an option for humanizing learning but a fundamental necessity because of the diversification of academia. As clarified in the literature and discussions, the foundational principles of Culturally Responsive Teaching underscore the critical importance of acknowledging and valuing the diverse cultural backgrounds of students. Success in higher education is not solely measured by academic achievement but also by the cultivation of inclusive and affirming learning environments that resonate with the multifaceted identities of students. The utilization of principles of inclusion has been shown to enhance humanized environments, fostering student engagement, satisfaction, and overall academic success. When educators intentionally integrate culturally relevant content, validate diverse perspectives, and employ inclusive instructional strategies, students are more likely to persist in their academic journey and also to develop a deeper understanding of course material by examining it through a lens that reflects their own experiences.

Furthermore, the success of culturally responsive strategies extends beyond academic outcomes. By promoting a sense of belonging and empowerment, inclusion practices and culturally responsive strategies contribute to the holistic development of students, preparing them to navigate an increasingly interconnected and diverse global society. Studies have indicated that students exposed to culturally responsive pedagogy demonstrate higher levels of cultural competence, empathy, and critical thinking skills. This equips them with the tools needed for successful careers and also positions them as socially responsible and culturally aware contributors to their communities and the wider world. By its very nature, the integration of culturally responsive strategies is an essential pedagogical choice and serves as an investment in the success, well-being, and enriched perspectives of the next generation of global citizens.

Fostering an Inclusive Environment Online

As with inclusive language, the deliberate infusion of curriculum and instructional materials with the rich tapestry of experiences, life histories, and contributions from various cultural groups strengthens and expands Culturally Responsive Teaching. For instance, in a science class, teachers can use culturally relevant examples to explain scientific concepts. In a literature class, teachers can incorporate diverse voices and perspectives into the curriculum. Educators should seek to incorporate cultural responsiveness into assessments, allowing students to demonstrate their knowledge in ways that align with their cultural backgrounds. This initiative-taking integration serves a dual purpose—it not only forges a personal connection with students but also expands their perspective, offering a more comprehensive and accurate portrayal of the global community (Gay, 2002, 2018).

Building on the pioneering research of Geneva Gay (2002), which provided practical guidance for teachers looking for ways to prepare themselves for culturally responsive teaching, scholars have continued to emphasize the critical importance of culturally relevant content in educational settings. Tatum (2019, 2021), continuing the work in conversations about race from 1997, underscores the fact that providing students with a curriculum that reflects their own experiences and the experiences of others is essential for promoting a sense of belonging and academic engagement. Tatum argues that when students see themselves reflected in the curriculum, it validates their identities and fosters a greater sense of self-worth.

Controversial discussions surrounding the incorporation of culturally relevant content often revolve around the question of academic rigor and the potential for bias. Scholars urge education practitioners to move beyond compliance with legal requirements and broaden the discussion to include a wider range of learners to facilitate student achievement on a wider scale. Lowenthal et al. (2020), Hernández et al. (2019), and Pitchford et al. (2020) argue that there may be a tendency to dilute academic standards to make content more accessible or relatable to students from diverse backgrounds. Additionally, there is ongoing debate about which cultural perspectives designers should prioritize as well as concerns about the potential for misrepresentation or oversimplification of complex cultural narratives. Academia is influenced by individual achievement and the creation of stereotypes of what academic rigor should look like. These debates highlight the need for careful consideration and ongoing dialogue as practitioners develop and implement culturally relevant curricula. Incorporating culturally responsive teaching strategies in online assessments and evaluations is not without challenges. Depending on the content and assessment selected there might be issues related to access and equity in online learning, such as unequal access to technology and resources, which can further marginalize students from underrepresented groups. Educators who wish to make shifts in their teaching must understand the complexities of implementing culturally responsive teaching in online learning environments. One answer to overcoming these complexities might be to get buy-in from leadership to provide the needed technology infrastructure. Pitchford's work outlines practical principles for implementing authentic learning experiences in higher education toward the development of transformational learning that connects students with real-world problems and challenges.

In navigating these discussions and selections, it is important to strike a balance that honors the students' diverse experiences while maintaining the integrity and rigor of academic content. Research and ongoing dialogue on the literature in this area by Castro and Tumibay (2021) serve as valuable resources in shaping effective practices for incorporating culturally relevant content in education. By engaging in critical pedagogy, educators can create learning experiences that resonate with students on a personal level, while equipping them with a broader and more nuanced understanding of the world.

Mensah (2021), in focusing on the confluence between culturally relevant pedagogy and culturally responsive teaching, posits that "culturally relevant and culturally responsive pedagogies are concerned with liberatory teaching so that instruction and learners gain an understanding of the social, political, and historical knowledge to challenge and critique society and even what and how they are learning" (p. 3). They suggest that a commitment to Culturally Responsive Teaching extends to recognizing and addressing diverse learning styles, ensuring that educational experiences resonate with every student. Mensah's approach builds on the principles of inclusivity and authenticity, and examines strategies that cater to the varied ways in which students process information. Students from diverse cultural backgrounds depend on a distinct set of experiences for foundational knowledge. Designers and faculty can incorporate cultural responsiveness into assessments, thereby allowing students to demonstrate their knowledge in ways that align with their cultural backgrounds.

In alignment with the principle of multimodal interaction for engagement, Ladson-Billings (2023) and Gay (2018) assert that diverse learning styles benefit from a variety of instructional approaches. Designing learning modules that integrate multimedia elements—videos, podcasts, and interactive simulations—not only caters to varied learning preferences but also aligns with the need for authentic, culturally relevant content. Recognizing diverse cultural learning preferences requires a nuanced approach to assessments. M. L. Borrego (2022) and Martin et al. (2019) suggest incorporating flexible assessment methods, allowing students to demonstrate understanding through various formats, including written assignments, oral presentations, or multimedia projects. This approach aligns with the overarching goal of promoting equitable participation opportunities, as discussed in the section on fostering inclusive classroom environments.

Equity practices also encourage the creation of personalized learning pathways for students from diverse cultural backgrounds. Echoing the collaborative spirit emphasized in the section on collaboration, E. P. Bonner (2014) proposes personalized learning pathways that cater to individual learning styles. The approach suggested by Bonner recognizes that students bring unique strengths and preferences to the virtual classroom, and tailoring content and activities to align with these individual traits can enhance both engagement and comprehension. While these ideas are not new, active and interactive learning strategies and tools support the development of students' cultural competence and sense of belonging.

Expanding on the use of technology for inclusivity, Brown et al. (2019) and Bolliger and Halupa (2019) highlight the effectiveness of interactive learning platforms. Bolliger and Halupa's study focused on how students perceive engagement, transactional distance, and outcomes in online courses. The authors posit that these factors could be influenced by the ineffective use of online platforms for engagement. Conversely, Brown et al. suggest that online platforms, through features such as discussion forums, quizzes, and collaborative spaces, provide opportunities for students to engage with course content in ways that suit their learning styles, fostering a sense of autonomy in the learning process. Taken together, engaging diverse learning styles within a culturally responsive online learning environment involves a thoughtful integration of multimedia content, flexible assessment methods, personalized learning pathways, and interactive platforms. By drawing insights from various sources, educators can tailor their approach to accommodate the diverse ways in which students absorb and process information, enhancing the effectiveness and inclusivity of the online learning experience.

CONCLUSION

Humanizing online education through culturally responsive approaches supports personalized learning. While we have identified challenges in applying culturally sensitive approaches in virtual settings, foundational contributions to humanized online learning may lead to improved teaching methods in the virtual environment. Furthermore, the CROE framework for constructing learning environments that acknowledge cultural diversity and inclusivity provides practical strategies for educators to utilize technology effectively in fostering inclusiveness within online learning spaces.

As we move forward in the rapidly evolving higher education online arena, we must prioritize the needs of all students, regardless of their cultural backgrounds or other unique circumstances. By incorporating culturally responsive principles into online education, we can create transformative learning environments that empower students from all backgrounds to reach their full potential. We invite practitioners to experiment with Culturally Responsive Teaching practices in their online courses and to explore the many resources and strategies available for creating inclusive and humanizing virtual spaces. Together, we can work towards a future in which online education is truly accessible, empowering, and transformative for all learners.

These principles encourage the use of intentional design and the creation of culturally relevant materials and activities to engage students effectively. Institutions that invest in creating supportive and inclusive learning environments will thrive better than those that rely on traditional methods for their market share. The return on the investment of students' tuition dollars must be realized through accessible technology, a safe and supportive environment, and resources that promote academic success. Encouraging student engagement through collaboration, discussion, and feedback in respectful ways can also foster a sense of community and belonging in the classroom and at the institution as a whole. By implementing these strategies, instructional designers, faculty, and by extension higher education institutions can better incorporate student success into their policies and practices and create a more positive and beneficial learning experience for all.

REFERENCES

Abacioglu, C. S., Volman, M., & Fischer, A. H. (2020). Teachers' multicultural attitudes and perspective-taking abilities as factors in culturally responsive teaching. *The British Journal of Educational Psychology*, *90*(3), 736–752. doi:10.1111/bjep.12328 PMID:31814111

Ali, W. (2020). Online and remote learning in higher education institutes: A necessity in light of COVID-19 pandemic. *Higher Education Studies*, *10*(3), 16–25. doi:10.5539/hes.v10n3p16

Bolliger, D. U., & Halupa, C. (2019). Culturally Responsive Teaching in online learning environments: A faculty development intervention. *The Internet and Higher Education*, *40*, 11–19.

Bong, W. K., & Chen, W. (2021). Increasing faculty's competence in digital accessibility for inclusive education: A systematic literature review. *International Journal of Inclusive Education*, *25*, 1–17. doi:10.1080/13603116.2021.1937344

Bonner, E. P. (2014). Investigating practices of highly successful mathematics teachers of traditionally underserved students. *Educational Studies in Mathematics*, *86*(3), 377–399. doi:10.1007/s10649-014-9533-7

Bonner, F. A. (2013). *The role of faculty in multicultural initiatives: A critical policy analysis of teaching and learning*. Stylus Publishing.

Borrego, E. (2017). *Cultural competence for public managers: Managing diversity in today's world*. Routledge. doi:10.4324/9781315095219

Borrego, M. L. (2022). *The relationship between culturally engaging campus environments and sense of belonging among Hispanic students* [Unpublished doctoral dissertation]. University of Miami.

Broderick, M. (2020). Representation in 21st century online higher education: How the online learning culture serves diverse students. In *Socioeconomics, diversity, and the politics of online education* (pp. 165–183). IGI Global. doi:10.4018/978-1-7998-3583-7.ch010

Brown, B. A., Boda, P., Lemmi, C., & Monroe, X. (2019). Moving culturally relevant pedagogy from theory to practice: Exploring teachers' application of culturally relevant education in science and mathematics. *Urban Education*, *54*(6), 775–803. doi:10.1177/0042085918794802

Bueno, D. C. (2020). *The "New Normal": Consolidated plans, practices, policies, and procedures on flexible instructional management and supervision*. Graduate school for Professional Advancement and Continuing Education (G-SPACE), Columban College Inc.

Castro, M. D. B., & Tumibay, G. M. (2021). A literature review: Efficacy of online learning courses for higher education institution using meta-analysis. *Education and Information Technologies*, *26*(2), 1367–1385. doi:10.1007/s10639-019-10027-z

Craig, L., & Kuykendall, L. (2020). Fostering an inclusive classroom environment with evidence-based approaches. *Industrial and Organizational Psychology: Perspectives on Science and Practice*, *13*(4), 482–486. doi:10.1017/iop.2020.85

Cruz, R. A., Manchanda, S., Firestone, A. R., & Rodl, J. E. (2020). An examination of teachers' culturally responsive teaching self-efficacy. *Teacher Education and Special Education*, *43*(3), 197–214. doi:10.1177/0888406419875194

Day, L., & Beard, K. V. (2019). Meaningful inclusion of diverse voices: The case for culturally responsive teaching in nursing education. *Journal of Professional Nursing*, *35*(4), 277–281. doi:10.1016/j.profnurs.2019.01.002 PMID:31345507

DeCuir, J. T., & Dixson, A. D. (2004). So when it comes out, they aren't that surprised that it is there: Using Critical Race Theory as a tool of analysis of race and racism in education. *Educational Researcher*, *33*(5), 26–31. doi:10.3102/0013189X033005026

Dumford, A. D., & Miller, A. L. (2018). Online learning in higher education: Exploring advantages and disadvantages for engagement. *Journal of Computing in Higher Education*, *30*(3), 452–465. doi:10.1007/s12528-018-9179-z

Fuentes, M. A., Zelaya, D. G., & Madsen, J. W. (2021). Rethinking the course syllabus: Considerations for promoting equity, diversity, and inclusion. *Teaching of Psychology*, *48*(1), 69–79. doi:10.1177/0098628320959979

García-Morales, V. J., Garrido-Moreno, A., & Martín-Rojas, R. (2021). The transformation of higher education after the COVID disruption: Emerging challenges in an online learning scenario. *Frontiers in Psychology*, *12*, 616059. doi:10.3389/fpsyg.2021.616059 PMID:33643144

Gay, G. (2002). Preparing for culturally responsive teaching. *Journal of Teacher Education*, *53*(2), 106–116. doi:10.1177/0022487102053002003

Gay, G. (2015). The what, why, and how of culturally responsive teaching: International mandates, challenges, and opportunities. *Multicultural Education Review*, *7*(3), 123–139. doi:10.1080/2005615X.2015.1072079

Gay, G. (2018). *Culturally responsive teaching: Theory, research, and practice*. Teachers College Press.

Gayon, R., & Tan, D. (2021). Experiences of higher education institution (HEI) teachers in the implementation of flexible learning. *Science International (Lahore)*, *33*(1), 47–52.

Graham, L. (Ed.). (2020). *Inclusive education for the 21st century: Theory, policy, and practice*. Routledge. doi:10.4324/9781003116073

Hernández, L. E., Darling-Hammond, L., Adams, J., & Bradley, K. (2019). *Deeper Learning networks: Taking student-centered learning and equity to scale. Deeper Learning Networks Series*. Learning Policy Institute.

Howard, T. C. (2021). Culturally responsive pedagogy. In J. A. Banks (Ed.), *Transforming Multicultural Education Policy and Practice: Expanding Educational Opportunity* (p. 137). Teachers College Press.

Kanwar, A. (2021). *Building resilient education systems for the future: Role of ODL.* http://hdl.handle.net/11599/3869

Kieran, L., & Anderson, C. (2019). Connecting universal design for learning with culturally responsive teaching. *Education and Urban Society*, *51*(9), 1202–1216. doi:10.1177/0013124518785012

Kilgore, W. (2016). Humanizing online instruction in undergraduate business education. In *Humanizing Online Teaching and Learning*. https://pressbooks.pub/humanmooc/

Ladson-Billings, G. (1995a). Toward a theory of culturally relevant pedagogy. *American Educational Research Journal*, *32*(3), 465–491. doi:10.3102/00028312032003465

Ladson-Billings, G. (1995b). But that's just good teaching! The case for culturally relevant pedagogy. *Theory into Practice*, *34*(3), 159–165. doi:10.1080/00405849509543675

Ladson-Billings, G. (2021a). *Culturally relevant pedagogy: Asking a different question*. Teachers College Press.

Ladson-Billings, G. (2021b). I'm here for the hard re-set: Post-pandemic pedagogy to preserve our culture. *Equity & Excellence in Education*, *54*(1), 68–78. doi:10.1080/10665684.2020.1863883

Ladson-Billings, G. (2023). "Yes, but how do we do it?": Practicing culturally relevant pedagogy. In *White teachers/diverse classrooms* (pp. 33–46). Routledge. doi:10.4324/9781003448709-6

Lindo, E. J. (2020). Committed to advancing cultural competence and culturally sustaining pedagogy. *Teaching Exceptional Children*, *53*(1), 10–11. doi:10.1177/0040059920945644

Lopez-Littleton, V., & Blessett, B. (2015). A framework for integrating cultural competency into the curriculum of public administration programs. *Journal of Public Affairs Education*, *21*(4), 557–574. doi:10.1080/15236803.2015.12002220

Lowenthal, P. R., Humphrey, M., Conley, Q., Dunlap, J. C., Greear, K., Lowenthal, A., & Giacumo, L. A. (2020). Creating accessible and inclusive online learning: Moving beyond compliance and broadening the discussion. *Quarterly Review of Distance Education*, *21*(2), 1–22.

Martin, J. P., Choe, N. H., Halter, J., Foster, M., Froyd, J., Borrego, M., & Winterer, E. R. (2019). Interventions supporting baccalaureate achievement of Latinx STEM students matriculating at 2-year institutions: A systematic review. *Journal of Research in Science Teaching*, *56*(4), 440–464. doi:10.1002/tea.21485

Mehta, R., & Aguilera, E. (2020). A critical approach to humanizing pedagogies in online teaching and learning. *The International Journal of Information and Learning Technology*, *37*(3), 109–120. doi:10.1108/IJILT-10-2019-0099

Mensah, F. M. (2021). Culturally relevant and culturally responsive. *Science and Children*, *58*(4), 10–13. doi:10.1080/00368148.2021.12291647

Muhammad, G. (2023). *Unearthing joy: A guide to culturally and historically responsive curriculum and instruction*. Scholastic.

Pacansky-Brock, M., (2020). *How and why to humanize your online course*. Academic Press.

Pacansky-Brock, M. (2022). Reflections on inclusive teaching. *Journal of Educational Research and Practice*, *12*(0), 1. doi:10.5590/JERAP.2022.12.0.01

Pacansky-Brock, M., Smedshammer, M., & Vincent-Layton, K. (2020). Humanizing online teaching to equitize higher education. *Current Issues in Education (Tempe, Ariz.)*, *21*(2). https://cie.asu.edu/ojs/index.php/cieatasu/article/view/1905

Pacansky-Brock, M., Smedshammer, M., & Vincent-Layton, K. (2022). In search of belonging online: Achieving equity through transformative professional development. *Journal of Educational Research and Practice*, *12*, 4.

Parker, N., Mahler, B. P., & Edwards, M. (2021). Humanizing online learning experiences. *The Journal of Educators Online*, *18*(2), 119–129.

Pitchford, A., Owen, D., & Stevens, E. (2020). *A handbook for authentic learning in higher education: Transformational learning through real-world experiences*. Routledge. doi:10.4324/9780429242854

Santos, J. P., Abana, E. C., Tindowen, D. J. C., Mendezabal, M. J. N., & Pattaguan, E. J. P. (2020). *Perceptions and readiness of USL stakeholders on flexible learning*. http://119.92.172.179/papers/dafun/dafun_vol3_s2020_p3.pdf

Tamtik, M., & Guenter, M. (2019). Policy analysis of equity, diversity, and inclusion strategies in Canadian universities–How far have we come? *Canadian Journal of Higher Education*, *49*(3), 41–56. doi:10.47678/cjhe.v49i3.188529

Tatum, B. D. (2019). Together and alone? The challenge of talking about racism on campus. *Daedalus*, *148*(4), 79–93. doi:10.1162/daed_a_01761

Tatum, B. D. (2021). What is racism anyway? In S. M. McClure & C. A. Harris (Eds.), *Getting real about race* (p. 17). SAGE.

Will, M., & Najarro, I. (2022). What is culturally responsive teaching? *Education Week*, *41*(33), 16–18. https://www.edweek.org/teaching-learning/culturally-responsive-teaching-culturally-responsive-pedagogy/2022/04

Williams, F. (2021). Flexible learning design: A turning point for resilient adult education. *Journal of Adult Education in Tanzania*, *23*(1), 165–191.

Chapter 8
Strategies for Cultivating Belonging in Online Learning Spaces

Jessica Herring Watson

(iD) https://orcid.org/0000-0001-5393-389X
University of Central Arkansas, USA

Noël Gieringer
University of Central Arkansas, USA

Michael S. Mills
University of Central Arkansas, USA

ABSTRACT

This chapter outlines a rationale and best practices for humanizing online learning by implementing strategies for cultivating belonging. These strategies are rooted in the community of inquiry framework and the importance of intentionally cultivating students' social presence in order to enhance opportunities for cognitive presence and deep critical thinking. Culturally responsive teaching practices also guide these strategies for designing and facilitating inclusive online learning spaces where belonging is intentionally centered in the instructor's teaching presence. The strategies in this chapter include ways to design and develop courses with belonging in mind from the start as well as strategies for maintaining a sense of belonging and community throughout a course after it has been initially established.

INTRODUCTION

As online education continues to evolve, so does our understanding of how best to create meaningful and effective learning experiences. This understanding requires us to consider not only the content we deliver but also the environment in which it is delivered. In this chapter, we consider this through the lens of the Community of Inquiry (CoI) framework (Garrison et al., 2000), a model that suggests

DOI: 10.4018/979-8-3693-0762-5.ch008

effective online learning experiences are framed by an interplay of cognitive, social, and teaching presence. Within this discussion, we will explore how students build and validate their understanding through introspective reflection and thoughtful dialogue (i.e., cognitive presence), how students project their personal characteristics into the online community (i.e., social presence), and how the design and facilitation of cognitive and social presences are integrated to realize meaningful learning outcomes (i.e., teaching presence).

This exploration serves a dual purpose: It underlines the importance of creating a human connection within the digital learning environment and introduces the idea of cultivating a sense of belonging among students. Such a sense of belonging can significantly enhance student engagement (Chiu, 2022), persistence (Peacock et al., 2020), and overall learning experience (Peacock & Cowan, 2019).

We will further discuss how the sense of belonging can be integrated into course design and maintained throughout the learning journey. The aim is to provide educators and course designers with practical strategies for creating online learning experiences that are engaging, supportive, and ultimately, more effective. The discussion will have less emphasis on content itself and more on creating an online space that feels welcoming, inclusive, and engaging. By bringing in principles from the CoI framework and the concept of belonging, rooted in culturally responsive teaching practices, we hope to paint a clear picture of how online education can be both rigorous and deeply humanized. Through this lens, we can begin to refine our approach to online course design and delivery.

CONCEPTUAL FRAMEWORK

Community of Inquiry (CoI)

The online learning best practices in this chapter are guided by the principles of Garrison et al.'s Community of Inquiry. The CoI framework was developed by Garrison et al. (2000/2010) to describe the educational experience in online coursework, with particular regard to text-based discussion forums. However, CoI has since been applied to many aspects of online teaching and learning across disciplines and educational levels throughout the empirical literature over the past two decades (Kim & Gurvitch, 2020). For example, La Fleur and Dlamini (2022) used the CoI framework to examine how K-12 teachers create technology-enhanced, learner-centric classroom environments and how engagement with professional development informs their work. The CoI framework has also been used as a learning design model to inform online instructional design decisions (Nolan-Grant, 2019), as a framework to examine students' perceptions of online project-based learning (Guo et al., 2022), and as a system of support for developing blended learning designs (Wicks et al., 2015). Essentially, the framework can be used at any point in the instructional design process, serving as a guide for online learning design decisions and as a reflective framework through which to view an existing design and determine its effectiveness.

The theoretical foundation of this framework is aligned with the work of John Dewey and is constructivist in nature (Garrison & Arbaugh, 2007). According to Garrison et al. (2000/2010), there are three essential elements, or constructs, within the CoI framework that must be effectively balanced for meaningful online learning to occur. These essential elements of the educational experience are cognitive presence, social presence, and teaching presence (Garrison et al., 2000/2010; Garrison & Arbaugh, 2007). Within the CoI framework, each of the three essential constructs is clearly defined. In more recent years, Shea et al. (2022) have called for the addition of a fourth construct: learner presence. However, for the purposes of this chapter and the following recommendations and best practices, we have chosen to focus on Garrison et al.'s (2000) original three constructs, which are defined and described in the following sections.

Cognitive Presence

Cognitive presence is defined as "the extent to which learners are able to construct and confirm meaning through sustained reflection and discourse" (Garrison & Arbaugh, 2007, p. 161). Cognitive presence is strongly linked to the processes of critical thinking and inquiry, both trademarks of higher order thinking skills (Garrison, et al., 2000). In their research, Garrison et al. (2000) found that there are certain affordances to well-designed, collaborative online learning spaces that promote higher order thinking (Garrison et al., 2000). Cognitive presence online is activated because students have time to reflect upon and research the questions posed before formulating their initial responses, improving the overall quality of the thinking that is articulated in students' interactions.

Social Presence

Social presence is defined as "the ability of participants in the Community of Inquiry to project themselves socially and emotionally as 'real people' through the medium of communication being used" (Garrison et al., 2000, p. 94). Garrison et al. (2000) found that participants were more willing to commit to deep critical thinking in online discussion forums when they felt as if they were part of a true community; thus, social presence is necessary for learners to achieve cognitive presence. Social presence is developed through "familiarity, skills, motivation, organizational commitment, activities, and length of time in using the media" (e.g., length of time in engaging with online course components) (Garrison et al., 2000, p. 95).

Ultimately, centering students' social presence in the online space is what humanizes the online learning experience and moves it beyond the transactional toward the affirming and transformative. Social presence within the online learning experience can be intentionally structured and continually supported by the instructor, which then increases cognitive presence because students feel safe to take learning risks within the space. For this reason, teaching presence is the third essential construct of the Community of Inquiry framework.

Teaching Presence

Teaching presence is defined as "the design, facilitation, and direction of cognitive and social processes for the purpose of realizing personally meaningful and educationally worthwhile learning outcomes" (Garrison & Arbaugh, 2007, p. 163). Essentially, teaching presence is the glue that binds the CoI together. While a group of learners may be able to motivate and facilitate some critical thinking on their own, the presence of an instructor who can curate quality resources, facilitate authentic social connection, and guide deep critical discourse is what shifts a collaborative online learning space toward a true CoI (Garrison et al., 2000/2010; Garrison & Arbaugh, 2007). The interaction of the three constructs of CoI – teaching, social, and cognitive presences – is illustrated in Figure 1.

Figure 1. Community of Inquiry Framework
Note. Adapted from "Critical inquiry in a text-based environment: Computer conferencing in higher education," by D.R. Garrison, T. Anderson., and W. Archer, 2000, The Internet and Higher Education, 2(2-3), p. 88.

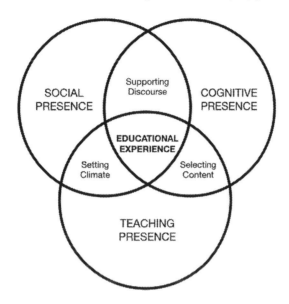

Culturally Responsive Teaching

All three constructs of CoI must work in conjunction with one another for highly effective learning to take place online. However, instructors cannot fully step into their teaching presence to cultivate the social presence that is necessary for deep, authentic learning (i.e., cognitive presence) if they are not also attune to the need to provide a culturally responsive and affirming learning space that supports all learners (Gay, 2010; Gay, 2018; Ladson-Billings, 1995; Martin et al., 2017; Paris & Alim, 2014). Thus, the best practices described in this chapter are also rooted in the concepts of culturally responsive teaching and culturally relevant pedagogy (Gay, 2010; 2018; Ladson-Billings, 1995). Gay (2010) defined culturally responsive teaching as "using the cultural knowledge, prior experiences, frames of reference and performance styles of ethnically diverse students to make learning encounters more relevant to and effective for them" (p. 31). Culturally responsive teachers align their instructional practices with the following tenets:

- Holding high expectations for all learners of all backgrounds;
- Engaging students by integrating diverse cultural knowledge, experiences, and contributions into instruction;
- Educating the whole learner (i.e., academically, socially, emotionally, politically);
- Embracing an asset-based, or strengths-based, approach to instruction and assessment;
- Adopting a critical stance toward educational systems and structures that replaces oppressive educational practices with transformative practices. (Gay, 2010; Aronson & Laughter, 2016)

While Gay's (2010; 2018) work focuses on teaching practice, Ladson-Billings' (1995) culturally relevant pedagogy focuses on the ideas, dispositions and attitudes, in short, the pedagogies, that underlie those teaching practices (Aronson & Laughter, 2016). Thus, the two approaches to teaching complement one another by providing a framework for teachers to create a space of belonging, engagement, and empowerment for all learners.

Gloria Ladson-Billings (1995) reminds practitioners that culturally relevant practices are "just good teaching" (p. 484). All learners benefit when their backgrounds are affirmed, when their lived experiences are connected to course concepts in meaningful ways, and when the instructor cultivates an online learning space that promotes respect and demonstrates high expectations for all learners.

BEST PRACTICES

The following sections describe and provide examples of teaching best practices that are rooted in both CoI and culturally responsive teaching. The practices are organized into two main categories: (1) Building Belonging into Course Design and (2) Maintaining Belonging throughout the Learning Experience. Because each of these strategies leverages the interplay of the three "presences" in CoI and aligns with the tenets of culturally responsive teaching as described above, connections to these frameworks are highlighted throughout the narrative. A summary of the strategies and their connections to CoI and culturally responsive teaching is also provided in tables following each main section of strategies.

Building Belonging Into Course Design

It is imperative to design a course with belonging in mind from the start. A few ways to lay the foundation for belonging include a course structure that shows the instructor is available to the students, a plan to gain students' insights and set shared class norms, prompt-driven introduction activities, and genuine attempts to learn about students' lives with interest and curiosity.

Practices for Showing Availability

Instructors can enhance their teaching presence online by building opportunities for connection and demonstrating availability to address students' questions and concerns within the learning management system (LMS) (Yengin et al., 2010). For example, providing flexible and easily accessible scheduling options for students to engage with the course instructor can be helpful and takes into consideration the varying communication preferences of students in the course. Figure 2 illustrates how one might promote teacher/student engagement through individual meetings. The language of the post is student-focused and serves as an invitation to reach out with questions and concerns or to discuss course concepts further. The scheduling link embedded in the post makes it simple to schedule meetings for both the student and instructor and can be automated to initiate reminders to meeting participants before the scheduled meeting time. Scheduling apps that allow this flexibility include Calendly and YCBM (You Can Book Me).

Demonstrating instructor availability and openness to feedback can also take the form of designated time within online synchronous class meetings; often, this is time set aside at the beginning or end of pre-scheduled course meetings when students are likely already logged in to learn. Thus, this option allows the instructor to meet students where they are, provide teaching presence, and, by doing so, enhance the social presence among learners through discussion of questions, concerns, or feedback. Finally, an instructor might host virtual "office hours" to supplement online, asynchronous instruction.

Figure 2. LMS post to encourage teacher/student engagement

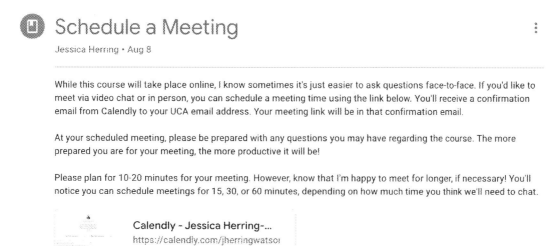

These opportunities for engagement between the instructor and learners support teaching presence in the Community of Inquiry and demonstrate the instructor's focus on being present and engaged with the needs and experiences of students (Martin et al., 2022).

Setting Shared Class Norms and Gathering Student Insight

In online education spaces, cultivating a sense of belonging and community is a priority in developing successful learning experiences and is grounded in the practice of setting shared class norms, which involves gathering crucial insights from students to construct a foundation of mutual respect and understanding.

The preliminary stage in building a cohesive online learning community is to guide learners in establishing a set of shared class norms, in alignment with the idea of "setting climate" that intersects both teaching and social presence in the CoI. This process is instrumental in shaping an environment where each member, despite not sharing a physical space, feels an ingrained sense of belonging and accountability towards the collective goals of the group. This participatory approach to norm-setting encourages students to voice their expectations, concerns, and aspirations, thereby laying the groundwork for a classroom culture that is both inclusive and representative of its diverse membership.

Supporting discourse, which is vital in any learning environment, takes on an even greater significance in the virtual classroom and serves as a tool to foster a sense of community and connection among students who may be geographically dispersed. Encouraging open discussions from the outset allows students to actively participate in shaping the guidelines that will govern their interactions throughout the course, promoting a sense of agency and vested interest in the well-being of the community.

Furthermore, integrating student insights into the creation of shared class norms opens up avenues for a richer, more nuanced understanding of the various factors that influence the dynamics of online learning, enabling the educator to tailor the instructional design and communication strategies to better suit the needs and preferences of the students, thereby enhancing the overall effectiveness and impact of the learning experience.

In this context, students are not merely passive recipients of knowledge, but active contributors in the crafting of a learning community that respects and celebrates diverse viewpoints and approaches to learning in alignment with a culturally responsive teaching approach that promotes respect for diverse viewpoints and models high expectations for all students (Gay, 2018). By giving students a voice in setting the norms, we are fostering a democratic space where students feel valued and heard, paving the way for a more harmonious and collaborative learning journey.

In practice, the instructor can initiate the process of collective norm setting with a simple set of questions:

- What are your expectations for our time together?
- What are your expectations for the instructor in this course? How might the instructor best support your learning in this course?
- What are expectations for yourself and other students in this course? How can we create the best conditions for everyone to benefit from the learning environment?

These questions can be used during synchronous learning time or to launch an asynchronous discussion in which students voice their opinions about the most important collective guidelines for the group to follow. At the start of a new course, when students are still establishing their own sense of social presence, it may be helpful to use polling software, such as Mentimeter, Slido, or Poll Everywhere, for students to submit their ideas anonymously.

Often students will voice similar ideas, and the instructor can synthesize this information into a set of shared class norms. An important next step is to confirm the shared norms as a group, creating open space for discussion and revision, if necessary. An example of shared norms developed by a group of students in an online undergraduate course is provided in Figure 3.

To demonstrate our shared value of and commitment to the class norms, it is important to post them in the LMS for all course participants to see and revisit, as necessary. Prioritizing their location in the LMS serves as a visual reminder that we have all agreed to abide by these shared class norms.

Figure 3. Example of student-generated class norms

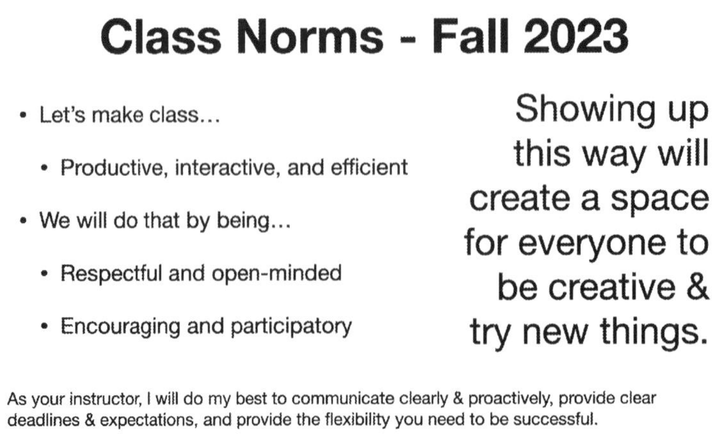

Class Norms - Fall 2023

- Let's make class...
  - Productive, interactive, and efficient
- We will do that by being...
  - Respectful and open-minded
  - Encouraging and participatory

Showing up this way will create a space for everyone to be creative & try new things.

As your instructor, I will do my best to communicate clearly & proactively, provide clear deadlines & expectations, and provide the flexibility you need to be successful.

Prompt-Driven Introduction Activities

Introduction activities continue the discourse through various prompts where students are able to begin getting to know one another. It is important to offer opportunities for connection among the learners before expecting collaboration in an academic context (Peacock et al., 2020). Connection can stem from more surface-level commonalities like favorite books and movies into deeper similarities like personality traits and preferred learning modalities.

Introduction activities align significantly with the CoI model by encouraging an atmosphere of social presence, where students can express themselves openly while forming interpersonal relationships. As they delve into discussions concerning favorite books or movies, or even identifying similar personality traits and preferred learning modalities, they gradually construct a network of mutual understanding and respect. This forms a conducive environment for fostering cognitive presence, where critical thinking and meaningful reflection can take place later during academic collaboration (Shea et al., 2022).

To facilitate these introductory interactions seamlessly, educators can again utilize various online polling tools, such as Mentimeter, Poll Everywhere, and Slido. These tools not only support the creation of instant surveys but also foster an inclusive learning environment by featuring different styles of questions ranging from multiple-choice to open-ended. Particularly, the word cloud feature embedded in these polling tools acts as a visual representation of the conversation, highlighting commonalities among learners by displaying the most frequent responses in larger text. This enables students to identify shared interests and ideas swiftly and can increase their sense of belonging within the community. This aligns with the CoI's emphasis on nurturing social presence by cultivating interpersonal relationships and open communication as a prerequisite to cognitive presence and increased academic rigor.

Within the arsenal of these tools, Slido stands out as an interactive platform that enhances both the teaching and learning experience. Its diverse range of features, including quizzes and sliding scale polls, facilitates an engaging learning environment where students can actively participate and share their insights. Furthermore, Slido's integration capabilities with presentation tools such as Google Slides and PowerPoint simplify the instructional process, allowing educators to focus more on fostering a nurturing, inclusive space, aligning with the teaching presence aspect of the CoI framework.

In initiating these engagements, even simple ice-breaker questions like "What is your favorite season?" can play a pivotal role. These light-hearted inquiries serve as gateways to deeper, meaningful conversations, where students can progressively build trust and camaraderie. As they transition from sharing personal preferences to academic collaboration, they embark on a journey of intellectual exploration, where collective knowledge and diverse perspectives are harnessed, epitomizing the essence of the cognitive presence component in the CoI framework.

Learning About Students' Lives With Genuine, Sincere Interest

Showing students that they are valued individually is imperative for a sense of belonging, and ultimately, for long-term learning. While ice-breaker questions like "What is your favorite movie?" may seem simple, these easy to discuss questions can open the door to more vulnerable, deeper conversations.

One approach to showing interest in your students is to commit time in each online class meeting to check in and attempt connection. This can be as simple as starting class with a reference to one of the many "National Holidays" for an icebreaker question. This could be asking about students' favorite book on National Read-a-Book Day or asking about a favorite pet on National Pet Appreciation Day.

The precedent of checking in with a question like this every day shows you always make time for your students. They can share responses verbally or through the chat function in an online meeting. You can even put students into a quick breakout room to share this conversation, laying the foundation for students to collaborate in breakout rooms related to the course content later.

A second way to enhance your teaching presence by displaying your dedication to getting to know your students is making time at the end of each class to talk with them less formally. A clearly established practice of leaving five minutes at the end of class for informal questions and discussion shows your willingness to connect and helps to establish and model social presence for all participants. The instructor can offer to stay on for those needing to ask questions and dismiss students otherwise at this five-minute mark. These moments can allow an uncomfortable or shy student to feel more comfortable turning on their camera or microphone and connecting in a smaller group or one-on-one with the instructor. The student might need to tell you something about why their work is late or missing, why they will miss an upcoming class, or something else they might feel hesitant to share in the larger group. Even if you offer the whole group opportunities to ask questions, some students will prefer a moment like this to ask a question they feel uncertain about.

Finally, some students may feel most comfortable at the outset of a course, when they are still establishing their social presence, communicating directly with the instructor in a format that feels more individualized. Using online survey tools such as Google Forms or Qualtrics, or survey software built into your LMS, can provide a one-on-one avenue to learn more about students' lives, build rapport, and determine how students' interests, lived experiences, and priorities can be integrated into course content in alignment with culturally responsive teaching practices that connect in-school learning and out-of-school living (Gay, 2018). You might provide prompts like the following:

- Describe something not school-related that you are most proud of.
- If you could take a course to learn about anything, what would it be and why?
- Describe a school assignment you did especially well on. What did you do to make it so successful?
- Is there anything you would like me to know that would help me support your success this semester?

It is critically important to reply to what students share in response to these questions. Even simple feedback or expressing appreciation for students' responses indicates that they hold a valuable space in the learning environment. Making connections to shared experiences or interests can also demonstrate to students that we are all welcome to bring our whole selves to the learning space. An example of how this feedback might look is provided in Figure 4 below.

Creating Space for Humanity Through Video

Another way to build space for belonging from the start is to integrate opportunities for multimodal learning (e.g., video in addition to text-based content) throughout the course design. This can be applied to both content delivery and assignments that provide students with choices in how they express their understanding. Through the effective utilization of online tools for video recording and the employment of techniques and policies that foster rapport during online class meetings, it becomes possible to connect on a human level, irrespective of the physical distance that separates us.

Figure 4. Example of feedback to student survey responses

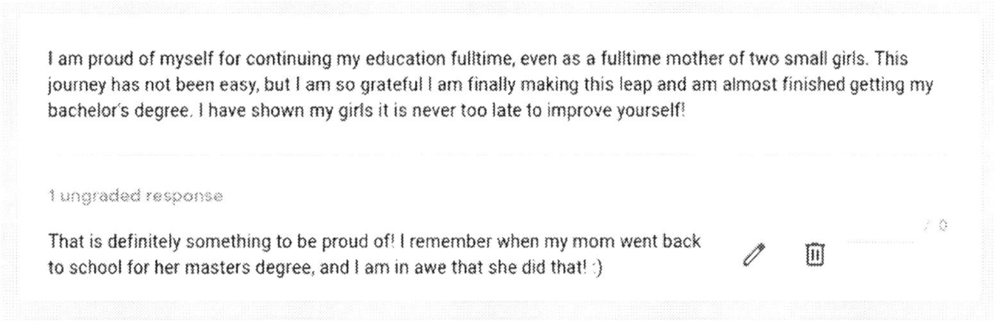

> I am proud of myself for continuing my education fulltime, even as a fulltime mother of two small girls. This journey has not been easy, but I am so grateful I am finally making this leap and am almost finished getting my bachelor's degree. I have shown my girls it is never too late to improve yourself!
>
> 1 ungraded response
>
> That is definitely something to be proud of! I remember when my mom went back to school for her masters degree, and I am in awe that she did that! :)

Instructor-created video. Embedding instructor-created video is a helpful strategy for humanizing teaching presence in the often text-heavy design of online courses. In order to enhance teaching presence, instructors can create weekly overview videos or videos to launch each new module in the course. We have also created "project tours" to launch project-based learning in online courses by guiding students through project instructions and rubrics. Tools such as Loom and Screencastify, among other screen recording tools, provide the option to guide students through the components of an upcoming module or project while also using a picture-in-picture video feature. Clark & Mayer's (2016) multimedia and personalization principles highlight that students learn best with both words and images; students can attend more actively to online content when an instructor avatar or likeness is present in the media. It is also important when creating videos, like the one provided in Figure 5 below, to use a conversational, friendly tone. Conversing with students in these videos, rather than focusing on a perfect, polished final product, humanizes online instructors to their students and has actually been shown to increase student attention and engagement (Clark & Mayer, 2016).

Student-created video. Technology also offers many affordances for students to create video to represent their thinking and learning. The opportunity for students to show what they know through a variety of multimedia tools rather than only through written text can enhance both social and cognitive presence, as it allows for students to personalize their understanding of course content and ensures that the medium of their submission does not create a barrier to their ability to show what they have learned (CAST, 2018). Providing students with choices for how they represent their learning aligns with the culturally responsive teaching principle of engaging students in multidimensional tasks (Woodley et al., 2017) as well as Universal Design for Learning (UDL) principles that promote greater accessibility within learning materials and tasks. This could look like providing students with the choice to complete a reflection in writing or video (see Figure 6). Instructors could also integrate the use of video-based discussion boards, such as Flip (formerly Flipgrid), for students to see one another and connect with experts and other learners beyond those enrolled in the course, thus expanding and enhancing the learning community.

Practices for video use in synchronous meetings. While encouraging students to join synchronous class sessions with video enabled can help everyone note facial expressions and read nonverbal cues more readily, there are some important considerations to keep in mind when determining whether or not a "cameras on" policy is best for cultivating students' sense of belonging in the online learning space. Primarily, it is important to recognize that not all learners have full control over their physical space when engaging in synchronous class sessions. For example, some students may not have access to wi-fi strong

Figure 5. Example of a picture-in-picture structure for weekly overview videos

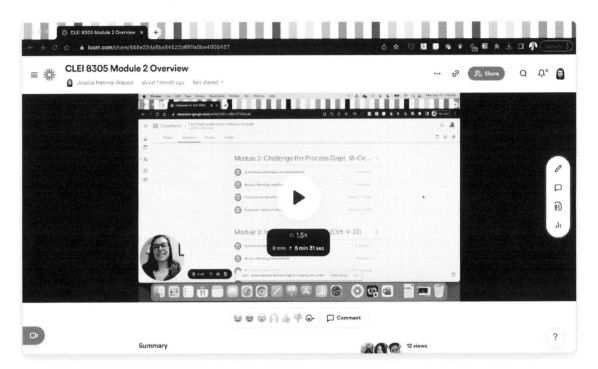

Figure 6. Example instructions for providing choice in assignment medium

CLEI 8303: Reflection 1

For this reflection, you will be asked to detail your experience as a learner and leader and the role of mindsets on those experiences. Think of this as a personal, reflective narrative. However, you should reference Module 1 readings/resources to support your narrative with professional literature. You may also cite additional literature not provided to you in the course LMS. When you include references to other texts, please cite them in APA 7 format, both parenthetically and in a reference list following your reflection.

You can either create a video reflection or a written reflection (less than 1000 words). If you choose a video reflection format, please also attach a reference list and cite your sources verbally. Regardless of format, you need to explain what your personal experiences have been.

Use the following questions to guide you:
- In what area(s) of your life have you demonstrated a fixed mindset?
- In what area(s) of your life have you demonstrated a growth mindset?
- In what area(s) of your life have you demonstrated a mixed mindset?
- How has reviewing Anderson's Mindset Continuum changed your thinking about mindset and its components?
- How can self-awareness of our mindsets influence our ability to learn and to lead others by establishing a learning culture? Can you think of a leader, either formal or informal, in your life who has done this successfully?

enough to support a "cameras on" policy, or they may not have access to a quiet, distraction-free space from which to join class (Moses, 2020). To assume that all learners have access to these affordances is to operate from a position of relative privilege.

Additionally, we should always consider students' right to privacy when determining the best policy for camera use in synchronous class meetings. We want to ensure that our underlying goal in encouraging students to join meetings with video enabled is to invite engagement and interaction, not to fall into patterns of surveillance and policing student behavior (Gleason & Heath, 2021). At times, students may feel more comfortable turning on their cameras only when in small groups for breakout rooms or partner work. Creating space for students to make their own choices regarding camera use shows them your care for them as a learner and your understanding of potential constraints within their physical learning space.

Fortunately, there are alternatives to "cameras on" policies that can still create space for students to represent their authentic selves. The instructor can encourage all students to create their own digital avatars to use as profile pictures when using video conferencing software for synchronous meetings. There are many tools available for creating such avatars. Two common tools are the "Memoji" feature that is built into messaging on Apple devices (see an example in Figure 7 below) and Bitmoji. Both tools allow individuals to create cartoon avatars of themselves with many options for personalization and integration of one's interests and appearance.

Alternatively, the instructor can encourage students to choose a favorite photo of themselves for their profile pictures, perhaps photos that include beloved pets or show students engaging in a favorite hobby or pastime. Creating or selecting a profile image might even serve as an introductory activity or discussion board in an online course; students could share their profile images, as well as brief paragraphs, describing why they have chosen that particular representation of themselves for the course. In this way, students can express themselves within the synchronous class space in the way that feels most comfortable to them and provides an opportunity for rapport and community building. This strategy aligns with the culturally responsive teaching practice of celebrating and integrating students' authentic identities and lived experiences in the learning space (Gay, 2018; Woodley et al., 2017) while also intentionally encouraging students to develop their social presence.

Figure 7. Example of a Memoji avatar

Table 1 provides a summary of these best practices for building belonging into course design and aligns each practice to the constructs of CoI and tenets of culturally responsive teaching.

Maintaining Belonging Throughout the Learning Experience

After building a course with the constructs of a Community of Inquiry and culturally responsive teaching practices in mind, the instructor must continue cultivating belonging throughout the entire course. The following sections provide suggestions from our own teaching practices that have been successful, including checking in with students consistently, revisiting shared class norms, building on the community established early in the course, and fostering equity and inclusion.

Checking in Consistently

Just as we find it valuable to learn about our students' lives and interests when a course begins, it is equally important to continue that dialogue throughout a semester or academic year. Consistent two-way communication is critical in building effective educator-student relationships, making students feel acknowledged and involved in their learning process (Govindaraju & Seruji, 2022).

By leveraging tools like Google Forms and Mentimeter, educators can distribute periodic anonymous surveys, offering students an avenue to provide feedback about the ongoing dynamics and developments of the course. This strategy encourages students to voice any concerns or opinions freely, fostering a transparent and inclusive channel of communication between instructors and the class. Instructors can use this feedback to continuously improve their courses based on student needs. For example, if an assignment or unit of study received feedback of being confusing to students, the instructor should adjust

Table 1. Summary of Best Practices for Building Belonging into Course Design

	Community of Inquiry Presences	Culturally Responsive Teaching Tenets
Practices for showing availability	● Teaching Presence ● Social Presence	● Educating the whole learner (i.e., academically, socially, emotionally, politically)
Setting shared class norms & gathering student insight	● Teaching Presence ● Social Presence ● Cognitive Presence	● Holding high expectations for all learners of all backgrounds ● Engaging students by integrating diverse cultural knowledge, experiences, and contributions into instruction ● Educating the whole learner ● Adopting a critical stance toward educational systems and structures that replaces oppressive educational practices with transformative practices.
Prompt-driven introduction activities	● Social Presence	● Engaging students by integrating diverse cultural knowledge, experiences, and contributions into instruction ● Educating the whole learner
Learning about students' lives with genuine, sincere interest	● Teaching Presence ● Social Presence	● Engaging students by integrating diverse cultural knowledge, experiences, and contributions into instruction ● Educating the whole learner ● Embracing an asset-based, or strengths-based, approach to instruction and assessment
Creating space for humanity through video (instructor & student created)	● Teaching Presence ● Social Presence ● Cognitive Presence	● Engaging students by integrating diverse cultural knowledge, experiences, and contributions into instruction ● Educating the whole learner

the next assignment or unit to add clarity such as an example or a video description to complement a written assignment.

These tools are more than just feedback mechanisms; they allow educators to swiftly gauge a student's comprehension of the material, as well as the general mood and comfort level of the class. Building in these checks for understanding is imperative as a formative assessment tool before leading up to a summative assessment. Not only will instructors gain insight about their students' learning, but students can gain confidence and clarity about the style of assessment in the course and whether or not they are growing towards the course's learning objectives. Tools for checking in on students' learning and state of mind play a pivotal role in cultivating an environment where students, regardless of their backgrounds or perspectives, feel empowered to share their insights without apprehension. Furthermore, maintaining these open channels of communication nurtures a cohesive classroom community where each student can feel valued and heard, fostering a sense of belonging and mutual respect that contributes to social presence. This proactive approach serves as a catalyst in enhancing the quality of education and promoting a more equitable learning experience.

Checking in with students consistently can become a standardized practice by building it into the course structure. When major projects are coming up, a new topic or unit is about to begin, or feedback has recently been shared, these are opportune times to require or strongly encourage one-on-one meetings with the instructor. These meetings, though required, should be conversational and open for any questions students or instructors might have, concerns the instructor may have about a student, or information a student wants to share. The effort it takes to schedule and attend these meetings with students can be rewarded with powerful insights that would otherwise go unspoken and unnoticed.

Revisiting Shared Class Norms

Reassessing the class norms initially set forth by the learning community is a vital step in maintaining a positive and respectful classroom atmosphere. This becomes particularly significant before undertaking major assessments or delving into subjects that necessitate a heightened level of empathy and, perhaps, vulnerability from students. Periodically revisiting the norms established at the beginning of a course encourages continuity and coherence in a dynamic learning environment and can be facilitated through regular discussions or reflective exercises where students can express how they are embodying the norms in their behaviors and interactions. This ongoing practice helps in fostering a culture of mutual respect and understanding, where norms are not just rules but become integral values that guide the learning community. In a more specific sense, there are several ways in which revisiting norms can be valuable (or even essential):

- When addressing sensitive topics about which students may feel heightened emotions or strong, deeply held opinions
- When launching a student-driven discussion strategy, such as Socratic Seminar in a synchronous session
- When entering small-group breakout sessions, in which the instructor cannot be universally present
- When the instructor notices that one or more students are engaging in behaviors out of alignment with the shared class norms

Revisiting the class norms may look like a brief reminder at the beginning of an activity of our shared commitments and how they can be applied to the activity or dialogue at hand. However, it might require a deeper discussion of whether the shared class norms need to be revised to better support the work of the group. Reminding students that we are constantly changing, growing, and learning, and thus, may need to adjust our shared commitments to reflect those changes, is an important component of humanizing the online space.

Moderating Sensitive Discussions. Before venturing into discussions surrounding sensitive or potentially controversial topics, revisiting the established class norms serves as a prudent step in fostering a respectful and empathic atmosphere for dialogue (Rovai, 2007). This foundational practice is vital in ensuring that students approach the subject matter with an acute sensitivity and a heightened sense of understanding, fully acknowledging the diverse tapestry of perspectives and lived experiences that their peers may bring to the table.

By reiterating the shared class norms, educators facilitate an environment where every voice is valued, thereby protecting the social presence that students have built in the online space and nurturing a safe haven for open discussion. This not only encourages students to communicate with empathy and respect but also fosters a deeper, personal connection with the content at hand, allowing for a more complex and nuanced exploration of the topic that enhances students' cognitive presence.

Moreover, this practice plays a crucial role in developing a culture of inclusivity within the classroom, where students are conditioned to tread carefully and considerately when navigating delicate subjects. It promotes an environment where individuals are more likely to listen actively, to respond thoughtfully, and to engage in a manner that is both considerate and constructive.

Ultimately, the proactive review of shared class norms before embarking on sensitive discussions is a vital component of teaching presence that helps to foster a classroom climate that is conducive to richer and more nuanced dialogues. It creates a setting where students feel respected, heard, and encouraged to share, thereby enhancing the depth and quality of classroom discussions and promoting a learning community where empathy and respect are fundamental values (Gay, 2018).

Facilitating Conflict Resolution. Shared class norms also serve as a pivotal tool in navigating and resolving conflicts in a constructive manner. In the face of disagreements or conflicts, which are inevitable in any dynamic learning environment, revisiting these established norms can act as a guiding framework that helps in structuring the conversation in a manner that respects and values the diverse viewpoints of all parties involved. Turning to the class norms during these moments emphasizes a communal commitment to maintaining a respectful and inclusive dialogue that honors the diversity of the group (Gay, 2018, Woodley et al., 2017), rather than devolving into divisive arguments. This approach not only ensures that discussions remain focused and respectful but also assists in uncovering underlying issues or misunderstandings that might be at the root of the conflict.

Furthermore, this structured approach to conflict resolution does more than just mediate disputes; it encourages a deeper level of dialogue and understanding among students. It prompts individuals to actively listen to each other, fostering empathy and a willingness to see issues from multiple perspectives. This, in turn, facilitates a more harmonious and collaborative learning environment, where students are encouraged to learn from one another and grow together as a cohesive unit. Thus, shared class norms become more than just guidelines; they evolve into a living, breathing framework that nurtures a culture of respect and understanding (Johnson & Johnson, 1996).

Promoting Reflective Practice. Encouraging students to periodically assess their adherence to shared class norms through reflective practices can be a powerful catalyst for fostering a deeper, more personal connection with the community's agreed-upon values and standards. This commitment to self-assessment can take various forms, including individual journaling exercises or collaborative small group discussions, by which students are given the opportunity to candidly evaluate their growth and evolving understanding of the norms as the course unfolds.

Engaging in these reflective practices not only aids in the internalization of the shared class norms but also sparks an intrinsic motivation to uphold them. As students document their journey or share their experiences within groups, they begin to notice the nuances of their development, appreciating positive changes and recognizing areas where further growth is possible. This continuous cycle of reflection and dialogue encourages a proactive stance towards personal development and adherence to the community standards, promoting a mature and empathic learning environment.

Moreover, this reflective process serves as a nurturing ground where students can cultivate a deeper personal connection with the norms. It transforms them from being mere guidelines to living principles that students embody in their interactions and engagements within the community. The reflection becomes a tool for fostering empathy and understanding, as students are encouraged to not only introspect on their actions but also appreciate the diverse perspectives and contributions of their peers (Gay, 2018).

By fostering such an environment, educators pave the way for a learning community that thrives on mutual respect and collaborative growth. It nurtures students who are not only cognizant of their learning journey but also empathically attuned to the experiences of their peers, fostering a learning space where empathy, understanding, and personal growth are at the forefront, guided by the collective endeavor to uphold and enrich the community's norms (Portman, 2020).

Maintaining an Adaptive Learning Environment. As the class progresses, it is not uncommon to witness a significant evolution in students' perspectives and understanding. This evolution, which is both a testament to their growth and a reflection of the course's dynamic nature, necessitates the establishment of a responsive feedback loop. This loop facilitates necessary dialogue by which students can actively suggest modifications or additions to the existing class norms. Doing so transforms the learning environment into a space that is not static but rather one that is adaptive and responsive, constantly attuned to the changing needs and insights of the class participants (Henry, 2008).

The initiation of this feedback loop is more than just a tool for adaptation; it is a gesture of respect towards the ever-changing nature of group dynamics. It places trust in the students, allowing them to have an active stake in shaping their learning community. This, in turn, fosters a classroom culture that not only grows but evolves harmoniously to better suit the needs and comfort levels of all participants. Moreover, it encourages students to be more personally invested in their learning journey, as they recognize that their voices are not only heard but valued. This democratic approach to learning nudges the community towards a model of collective responsibility, where each member is keenly aware of their role in fostering a positive, respectful, and enriching learning environment. Through this collaborative endeavor, the course transforms into a living entity, continually adapting and flourishing, driven by the shared experiences and collective wisdom of its members.

In practice, establishing a feedback loop with students can take many forms. It could take the form of an asynchronous discussion board that remains open throughout the length of the course and acts as a "suggestion box" where students can submit questions and feedback for course and assignment structures. Feedback can also be intentionally sought through direct communication between the instructor and individual students. For example, the instructor can schedule emails to each student in the course to seek feedback about what is working well and what could be adjusted to better serve students' needs at regular intervals (e.g., at midterm or quarterly through an academic year). Figure 8 illustrates how a midterm check-in email might look. Some students may prefer to provide feedback anonymously, rather than attaching their names to their feedback. In that case, online tools such as Survey Monkey, Google Forms, or Qualtrics could be used to gather feedback on the instructor's teaching presence, both in terms of course design and structure and in terms of instructor engagement within the learning community. The most important factor in this strategy is that the instructor acts on the feedback that is provided, demonstrating that they value student engagement and feedback and actively seek to design an online learning environment that adapts to learners' needs and preferences.

Figure 8. Midterm check-in email example

EDDL 7312 Midterm Check-in
10 messages

Jessica Herring <jherring@uca.edu>   Wed, Oct 19, 2022 at 8:30 AM

Good morning!

Since we're just about to midterm for the semester, I wanted to send an email to check in and see how things are going for you in the course. If you have any feedback about what's working well and how I can continue to make EDDL 7312: Digital Age Professional Learning more user-friendly, I'd love to hear it.

Please let me know if there is anything I can do to better support you in your learning. I hope you have a great day!

Regards,

Jessica Herring-Watson, Ed.D.
Assistant Professor
Department of Teaching & Learning
College of Education
University of Central Arkansas
she/her/hers
🍎 **Distinguished Educator**

My work day may look different than your work day, so I may send emails outside of typical daytime office hours. Please do not feel any pressure to respond outside of your own work schedule.

                                                                Wed, Oct 19, 2022 at 8:37 AM
To: Jessica Herring <jherring@uca.edu>

Good morning! Thanks for checking in with me. I'm really enjoying the class so far I'm looking forward to my professional development! It has really helped me add a new light to my online classroom also.
[Quoted text hidden]

                                                                Wed, Oct 19, 2022 at 8:52 AM
To: Jessica Herring <jherring@uca.edu>

It was great!
[Quoted text hidden]

                                                                Wed, Oct 19, 2022 at 9:52 AM
To: Jessica Herring <jherring@uca.edu>

Thank you for checking in! I have enjoyed the class so far and feel that I have already been able to apply what I've learned in my professional life. You have been a great instructor and this experience has been a confidence booster for me as I enter the Ed.S program. I appreciate all your help and feedback, and I hope you have a great day!
[Quoted text hidden]

Building Community

Periodically revisiting the shared class norms not only serves as a gentle reminder of the communal ethos inherent in the learning process but also underscores the principle that the classroom is not merely a space for individual learning, but a vibrant community where collective goals are pursued with a shared spirit of cooperation and mutual respect (Palloff & Pratt, 2007). This conscious reinforcement of communal principles works as a catalyst in fostering positive relationships among students, enhancing social presence, and nurturing a sense of camaraderie and unity. It creates an environment where students are motivated to uplift each other, sharing knowledge, insights, and help organically, thus engendering a culture of mutual support.

By encouraging students to view each other not as competitors but as collaborators through assignment design and discussion facilitation, the instructor inculcates a sense of responsibility and accountability among learners. This shift in perspective creates a fertile ground for a vibrant and cohesive learning community where students are more likely to thrive in both their social and cognitive presence.

Furthermore, fostering a sense of community can serve to enhance the overall classroom experience, as it aids in breaking down barriers and dispelling feelings of isolation that can sometimes permeate online learning spaces (Cole et al., 2021). This proactive approach thus contributes to building a learning environment that is not only cohesive but also genuinely supportive and nurturing.

In practice, consistently building community can be augmented by offering dedicated forums within the LMS where students can engage in deeper discussions and reflections on course concepts. These platforms can act as a safe space for critical thinking, where students can pose questions, analyze information, and synthesize insights collaboratively. Instructors can proactively facilitate these discussions and enhance students' cognitive presence by posing thought-provoking questions, encouraging students to connect theory with practice, and offering timely feedback that nudges students towards higher-order thinking. Additionally, the instructor might initiate activities that require students to work together in groups, thereby nurturing a sense of camaraderie and mutual respect. These activities could involve collaborative projects, peer reviews, or discussion groups where students can share their experiences and perspectives, thereby enriching the learning environment with diverse viewpoints. By emphasizing the collaborative aspects of the educational journey, we pave the way for a more enriching, inclusive, and engaging learning experience, where students are inspired to work hand in hand towards common goals, fostering a community that is bound by respect, empathy, and a shared commitment to learning and growth.

Table 2 provides a summary of strategies for maintaining belonging throughout the learning experience and aligns each strategy to the constructs of CoI and tenets of culturally responsive teaching.

Fostering Equity and Inclusion

Ultimately, all of the best practices described above are designed to humanize the online learning environment and foster equity and inclusion. Facilitating open discourse, intentionally creating opportunities for all participants to represent themselves authentically, and navigating continuous adjustment of the course structure and norms cultivates a learning community where students are actively engaged in reflecting upon and appreciating the diverse viewpoints, needs, and cultural backgrounds of their peers, fostering a sense of community enriched by its multifaceted membership (Gay, 2018; Salazar et al., 2017).

Table 2. Summary of Best Practices for Maintaining Belonging throughout the Learning Experience

	Community of Inquiry Presences	**Culturally Responsive Teaching Tenets**
Checking in consistently	● Teaching Presence ● Social Presence ● Cognitive Presence	● Educating the whole learner (i.e., academically, socially, emotionally, politically) ● Adopting a critical stance toward educational systems and structures that replaces oppressive educational practices with transformative practices
Revisiting shared class norms	● Teaching Presence ● Social Presence ● Cognitive Presence	● Holding high expectations for all learners of all backgrounds ● Engaging students by integrating diverse cultural knowledge, experiences, and contributions into instruction ● Educating the whole learner ● Adopting a critical stance toward educational systems and structures that replaces oppressive educational practices with transformative practices
Moderating sensitive discussions	● Teaching Presence ● Social Presence ● Cognitive Presence	● Holding high expectations for all learners of all backgrounds ● Educating the whole learner
Facilitating conflict resolution	● Teaching Presence ● Social Presence ● Cognitive Presence	● Holding high expectations for all learners of all backgrounds ● Engaging students by integrating diverse cultural knowledge, experiences, and contributions into instruction ● Educating the whole learner
Promoting reflective practice	● Social Presence ● Cognitive Presence	● Holding high expectations for all learners of all backgrounds ● Adopting a critical stance toward educational systems and structures that replaces oppressive educational practices with transformative practices
Maintaining an adaptive learning environment	● Teaching Presence	● Embracing an asset-based, or strengths-based, approach to instruction and assessment ● Adopting a critical stance toward educational systems and structures that replaces oppressive educational practices with transformative practices
Building community	● Social Presence ● Cognitive Presence	● Holding high expectations for all learners of all backgrounds ● Engaging students by integrating diverse cultural knowledge, experiences, and contributions into instruction ● Educating the whole learner ● Embracing an asset-based, or strengths-based, approach to instruction and assessment

This proactive stance, which advocates for regular reflection and dialogue, serves as a catalyst in identifying and dismantling any inadvertent barriers to participation that might have surfaced. In doing so, it ensures that the classroom transcends being a mere physical or virtual space, evolving instead into a nurturing community of inquiry where each student feels valued, respected, and genuinely included.

This dynamic approach promotes a more responsive and adaptive learning environment. It encourages students to become advocates for both themselves and their peers, fostering a culture of empathy and understanding. This collaborative atmosphere further assists in breaking down pre-existing stereotypes and biases, paving the way for more enriched and nuanced discourse. In addition, this works to establish a classroom where inclusivity is not just a term but a lived experience. It encourages students to take personal agency within the classroom culture, fostering a sense of responsibility towards creating and maintaining a space that cherishes diversity in all its forms. By nurturing a conscious and continual focus on equity and inclusion through course design, development, and facilitation, we are fostering a learning environment that is vibrant, respectful, and harmonious, where all students have the opportunity to thrive, feeling truly valued and included in every aspect of the educational process.

CONCLUSION

In this chapter, we aimed to explore how online course design can emphasize the creation of meaningful learning environments through the lens of the Community of Inquiry framework and culturally responsive teaching practices. The discussion focused on the value of helping students construct understanding through reflection and dialogue while projecting their unique identities to humanize their online presence while maintaining a strong emphasis on harmonizing the social and cognitive aspects to ensure learning outcomes are being met.

Moreover, we have emphasized the critical role of fostering genuine human connections and a sense of belonging in online education. This not only elevates student engagement but also enhances the overall quality of the learning experience. Throughout our discussion, we have outlined specific strategies to weave a sense of belonging into course designs. This requires a focused effort to cultivate a welcoming and inclusive space that still maintains high standards for achieving learning goals, a balance that proves to be significant for the individuals interacting in any digital platform.

This approach acknowledges the vital role that community plays in the online educational landscape, aiming to foster a space where students not only learn but also feel seen and valued. These methods, we believe, foster a learning environment where engagement is not just about participation but is rooted in meaningful and respectful interaction, thus paving the way for a richer and more fruitful educational experience. Creating space for humanity in the online environment echoes the profound insight of Maya Angelou, who often shared, "I've learned that people will forget what you said, people will forget what you did, but people will never forget how you made them feel." This principle guides us as we emphasize the importance of showing up as a real person in an online learning environment, encouraging our students to do the same.

REFERENCES

Aronson, B., & Laughter, J. (2016). The theory and practice of culturally relevant education: A synthesis of research across content areas. *Review of Educational Research*, *86*(1), 163–206. doi:10.3102/0034654315582066

CAST. (2018). *Universal Design for Learning Guidelines Version 2.2.* http://udlguidelines.cast.org

Chiu, T. K. F. (2022). Applying the self-determination theory (SDT) to explain student engagement in online learning during the COVID-19 pandemic. *Journal of Research on Technology in Education*, *54*(sup1, S1), S14–S30. doi:10.1080/15391523.2021.1891998

Clark, R. C., & Mayer, R. E. (2016). e-Learning and the science of instruction: Proven guidelines for consumers and designers of multimedia learning. Wiley.

Cole, A. W., Lennon, L., & Weber, N. L. (2021). Student perceptions of online active learning practices and online learning climate predict online course engagement. *Interactive Learning Environments*, *29*(5), 866–880. doi:10.1080/10494820.2019.1619593

Garrison, D. R., Anderson, T., & Archer, W. (2000). Critical inquiry in a text-based environment: Computer conferencing in higher education. *The Internet and Higher Education, 2*(2-3), 87–105. doi:10.1016/S1096-7516(00)00016-6

Garrison, D. R., Anderson, T., & Archer, W. (2010). The first decade of the community of inquiry framework: A retrospective. *The Internet and Higher Education, 13*(1-2), 5–9. doi:10.1016/j.iheduc.2009.10.003

Garrison, D. R., & Arbaugh, J. B. (2007). Researching the community of inquiry framework: Review, issues, and future directions. *The Internet and Higher Education, 10*(3), 157–172. doi:10.1016/j.iheduc.2007.04.001

Gay, G. (2010). *Culturally responsive teaching: Theory, research, and practice* (2nd ed.). Teachers College Press.

Gay, G. (2018). *Culturally responsive teaching: Theory, research, and practice* (3rd ed.). Teachers College Press.

Gleason, B., & Heath, M. K. (2021). Injustice embedded in Google Classroom and Google Meet: A techno-ethical audit of remote educational technologies. *Italian Journal of Educational Technology, 29*(2), 26–41. doi:10.17471/2499-4324/1209

Govindaraju, V., & Seruji, Z. (2022). Interpersonal communication and relationship: A conceptual review between educators and undergraduate students. *Multicultural Education, 8*(6), 30–37.

Guo, P., Ren, D., & Admiraal, W. (2022). The community of inquiry perspective on teachers' role and students' evaluations of online project-based learning. *Online Learning : the Official Journal of the Online Learning Consortium, 26*(4), 259–280. doi:10.24059/olj.v26i4.3193

Henry, D. (2008). Changing classroom social settings through attention to norms. *Toward positive youth development: Transforming schools and community programs*, 40-57. doi:10.1093/acprof:oso/9780195327892.003.0003

Johnson, D., & Johnson, R. (1996). Conflict resolution and peer mediation programs in elementary and secondary schools: A review of the research. *Review of Educational Research, 66*(4), 459–506. doi:10.3102/00346543066004459

Kim, G., & Gurvitch, R. (2020). Online education research adopting the community of inquiry framework: A systematic review. *Quest, 72*(4), 395–409. doi:10.1080/00336297.2020.1761843

La Fleur, J., & Dlamini, R. (2022). Towards learner-centric pedagogies: Technology-enhanced teaching and learning in the 21st century classroom. *Journal of Education (University of KwaZulu-Natal)*, (88), 4-20. doi:10.17159/2520-9868/i88a01

Ladson-Billings, G. (1995). Toward a theory of culturally relevant pedagogy. *American Educational Research Journal, 32*(3), 465–491. doi:10.3102/00028312032003465

Martin, F., Pirbhai-Illich, F., & Pete, S. (2017). Beyond culturally responsive pedagogy: Decolonizing teacher education. In F. Pirbhai-Illich, S. Pete, & F. Martin (Eds.), *Culturally responsive pedagogy: Working towards decolonization, indigeneity and interculturalism* (pp. 235–256). Palgrave. doi:10.1007/978-3-319-46328-5_11

Martin, F., Wu, T., Wan, L., & Xie, K. (2022). A meta-analysis on the community of inquiry presences and learning outcomes in online and blended learning environments. *Online Learning : the Official Journal of the Online Learning Consortium, 26*(1), 325–359. doi:10.24059/olj.v26i1.2604

Moses, T. (2020, August 17). *5 reasons to let students keep their cameras off during Zoom classes*. The Conversation. https://theconversation.com/5-reasons-to-let-students-keep-their-cameras-off-during-zoom-classes-144111

Nolan-Grant, C. R. (2019). The community of inquiry framework as learning design model: A case study in postgraduate online education. *Research in Learning Technology, 27*(0). Advance online publication. doi:10.25304/rlt.v27.2240

Palloff, R., & Pratt, K. (2007). *Building online learning communities: Effective strategies for the virtual classroom*. Wiley.

Paris, D., & Alim, H. (2014). What are we seeking to sustain through culturally sustaining pedagogy? A loving critique forward. *Harvard Educational Review, 84*(1), 85–100. doi:10.17763/haer.84.1.982l873k2ht16m77

Peacock, S., & Cowan, J. (2019). Promoting sense of belonging in online learning communities of inquiry at accredited courses. *Online Learning : the Official Journal of the Online Learning Consortium, 23*(2), 67–81. doi:10.24059/olj.v23i2.1488

Peacock, S., Cowan, J., Irvine, L., & Williams, J. (2020). An exploration into the importance of a sense of belonging for online learners. *International Review of Research in Open and Distance Learning, 21*(2), 18–35. doi:10.19173/irrodl.v20i5.4539

Portman, S. (2020). Reflective journaling: A portal into the virtues of daily writing. *The Reading Teacher, 73*(5), 597–602. doi:10.1002/trtr.1877

Rovai, A. (2007). Facilitating online discussions effectively. *The Internet and Higher Education, 10*(1), 77–88. doi:10.1016/j.iheduc.2006.10.001

Salazar, M., Norton, A., & Tuitt, F. (2017). Weaving promising practices for inclusive excellence into the higher education classroom. *To Improve the Academy, 28*(1), 208–226. doi:10.1002/j.2334-4822.2010.tb00604.x

Shea, P., Richardson, J., & Swan, K. (2022). Building bridges to advance the community of inquiry framework for online learning. *Educational Psychologist, 57*(3), 148–161. doi:10.1080/00461520.2022.2089989

Wicks, D. A., Craft, B. B., Mason, G. N., Gritter, K., & Bolding, K. (2015). An investigation into the community of inquiry of blended classrooms by a faculty learning community. *The Internet and Higher Education, 25*, 53–62. doi:10.1016/j.iheduc.2014.12.001

Woodley, X., Hernandez, C., Parra, J., & Negash, B. (2017). Celebrating difference: Best practices in culturally responsive teaching online. *TechTrends, 61*(5), 470–478. doi:10.1007/s11528-017-0207-z

Yengin, İ., Karahoca, D., Karahoca, A., & Yücel, A. (2010). Roles of teachers in e-learning: How to engage students & how to get free e-learning and the future. *Procedia: Social and Behavioral Sciences*, 2(2), 5775–5787. doi:10.1016/j.sbspro.2010.03.942

Chapter 9

Building Bridges:
Fostering Human Connections Through Tools and Technology in Online Instruction

Jana Gerard
Southeast Missouri State University, USA

Trudy Giasi
Valle Catholic Schools, USA

ABSTRACT

Promoting human connections in online instruction can be challenging. Students may have technological barriers or may feel isolated or disconnected from their peers. Instructors must find ways to build rapport among students, encourage active learning, and personalize the learning process. This chapter explores the concept of humanizing online instruction by fostering human connections within virtual environments. Educational frameworks, digital tools, instructional strategies, and pedagogies are discussed that can facilitate this goal. Human connections are crucial for effective learning, and fostering these connections can lead to increased student engagement, mastery of content, and enhanced academic performance.

INTRODUCTION

Human connections are crucial in online instruction. Students are more invested in their own learning when they feel connected to both their peers and their instructors which leads to increased participation, better understanding of content, and enhanced academic performance. Working collaboratively on projects and assignments allows students to learn from each other's perspectives while enhancing problem-solving skills and critical thinking. Online instruction can be isolating but fostering human connections promotes a greater sense of belonging which can reduce stress and anxiety while improving retention rates. Through thoughtful and intentional planning, instructors can build a sense of trust and

DOI: 10.4018/979-8-3693-0762-5.ch009

rapport among their online learners while promoting inclusivity and diversity, as well as encouraging critical thinking and the development of social and emotional intelligence.

Challenges

There are challenges to building human connections in online learning. Students may have technological barriers that can include unstable connections to the Internet, device limitations, or lack of access to software needed for learning. The lack of physical presence can cause feelings of isolation and reduce opportunities for informal and spontaneous conversations with peers that occur naturally in face-to-face learning environments. Often, online instruction is primarily text-based which limits opportunities to build relationships among peers and reduces empathy. Online instruction also poses pedagogical challenges for instructors. It can be difficult to build rapport with students and traditional online instruction promotes passive learning as there can be limited opportunity for collaborative learning activities. Unlike face-to-face instruction, online instruction can add the additional challenges of having students in multiple countries and time zones which can lead to misunderstandings and inadvertent cultural insensitivity.

Purpose and Structure of the Chapter

The advent of technology and the rapid growth of online education have transformed the landscape of higher education. While these advancements have brought numerous benefits, there is a growing concern that the human element of teaching and learning is being diluted in the virtual realm. To address this issue, online instructors can ground teaching in various frameworks, pedagogies, and digital tools that can enhance human connections in online teaching and learning environments.

FRAMEWORKS FOR HUMANIZING ONLINE EDUCATION

This section delves into the multifaceted domain of humanizing online education, with a particular focus on frameworks that bridge the gap between technological advancements and the essential human connections that underpin effective learning. The grounding of pedagogy and the use of digital tools within these frameworks provide a student-centered structure that can provide flexibility in the learning to meet the individual needs of students, allows for individual voices to be acknowledged within an online learning environment, and promotes engagement, interaction, and collaboration among students in meaningful ways.

Technology Pedagogy and Content Knowledge (TPACK)

The Technology Pedagogy and Content Knowledge (TPACK) framework provides a comprehensive approach to effective teaching with technology. In online teaching, TPACK becomes even more relevant as instructors navigate the challenges and opportunities presented by digital learning environments. The framework emphasizes the intersection of three essential components: technological knowledge, pedagogical knowledge, and content knowledge, see Figure 1 (Mishra & Koehler, 2006).

- Technological Knowledge (TK): At the core of TPACK lies technological knowledge, emphasizing the importance of instructors' familiarity and proficiency with digital tools. In the context of online learning, this extends beyond basic technical skills to a deeper understanding of the diverse technologies available. From learning management systems to collaborative platforms, instructors can leverage these tools strategically to enhance the educational experience (Harris et. al, 2009).

- Pedagogical Knowledge (PK): Online instruction demands a profound understanding of pedagogical principles that transcend traditional classroom boundaries. Instructors can adapt their teaching methods to the digital realm, considering factors such as asynchronous learning, student engagement, and the incorporation of multimedia resources. Pedagogical knowledge in the online context is about creating an inclusive and interactive virtual space that fosters active learning (Harris et. al, 2009).

- Content Knowledge (CK): TPACK recognizes the importance of content knowledge in driving effective teaching and learning. In the online environment, instructors must not only possess deep subject matter expertise but also the ability to translate and present this knowledge in a manner conducive to the digital world. Content knowledge is the foundation upon which technology and pedagogy converge, ensuring that the educational content is rigorous and relevant (Harris et. al, 2009).

Instructors using the TPACK model can employ digital tools thoughtfully, design engaging and interactive learning experiences, and deliver content with a human touch. The transmission of information coincides with the creation of a virtual community where students feel connected, supported, and motivated to learn (Koehler & Mishra, 2009).

Universal Design for Learning (UDL)

UDL serves as a foundational framework for creating inclusive online learning experiences that cater to diverse learners. By offering multiple means of student engagement, information representation, and student action and expression, instructors can ensure that learners with different abilities and learning styles can access and participate in the course content effectively, see Figure 2. At its core, UDL is rooted in the principles of inclusivity and accessibility (CAST, 2018). In the online realm, UDL aims to design learning experiences that consider the varied needs, preferences, and abilities of a diverse student population.

- Multiple Means of Representation: UDL encourages instructors to provide content in various formats, acknowledging that learners have different ways of perceiving and comprehending information. In the online setting, this translates to the incorporation of multimedia, varied text formats, and alternative resources. By offering content through diverse means, instructors ensure that the virtual classroom is accessible to a broad spectrum of learners, fostering a sense of inclusivity.

- Multiple Means of Engagement: To cultivate human connections in the online learning environment, UDL emphasizes providing multiple pathways for student engagement. This involves incorporating interactive elements, collaborative projects, and fostering a sense of community through discussion forums. By acknowledging and accommodating different interests and motivational triggers, instructors create a virtual space where students are not just passive recipients of information but active participants in their learning journey.

Figure 1. Technology Pedagogy and Content Knowledge (TPACK) Venn Diagram

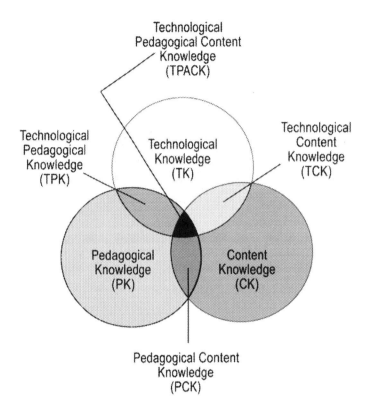

- Multiple Means of Expression: In the virtual realm, UDL encourages students to express their understanding in diverse ways. This could involve offering choices in assessment methods, allowing for multimedia presentations, or providing alternative formats for assignments. By recognizing and valuing the diverse ways in which students can demonstrate their thinking and knowledge, UDL promotes a sense of autonomy and individuality, fostering a more personalized and humanized learning experience.

The versatile nature of digital tools enables the incorporation of diverse formats and adaptable options into the learning process. Instructors have the flexibility to present information in various formats, such as combining text, visuals, and audio. Additionally, they can integrate features that empower users to choose how they consume information, such as enabling text-to-speech for simultaneous reading and listening. Students, in turn, can utilize these tools to create multimedia content and express themselves in diverse and multimodal ways.

Technology-based environments not only provide engagement but also offer instructors the opportunity to deliver authentic and relevant learning experiences, fostering interaction and collaboration. Consequently, online learning environments that inherently rely on digital tools for delivery and instruction present numerous possibilities for implementing Universal Design for Learning (UDL). By incorporating UDL guidelines into the instructional design process, instructors can strategically integrate digital delivery formats, digital tools, and instructional strategies to create inclusive online learning experiences.

Figure 2. Three Pillars of Universal Design for Learning (UDL)

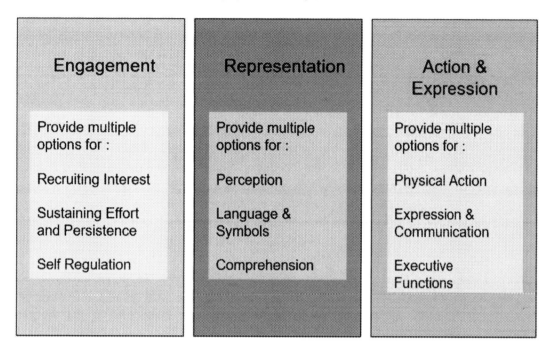

Connectivism

Connectivism emphasizes the role of networks and connections in learning. In online teaching, instructors can capitalize on the power of social networks and online communities to facilitate collaborative learning, knowledge sharing, and social interactions among students (Siemens, 2005). At its essence, connectivism is a learning theory that recognizes the changing nature of knowledge and the evolving role of instructors and learners in the digital age (Harasim, 2017). Developed in response to the dynamic, networked environment of the internet, connectivism posits that learning is not confined to individual minds but is distributed across networks (Hendricks, 2019). In the context of online education, connectivism becomes a powerful tool for fostering human connections by leveraging the potential of digital networks.

- Learning in Networks: Connectivism asserts that learning is a process of connecting specialized nodes or information sources. In the online classroom, this translates to acknowledging and embracing the diverse sources of information available, including peers, online communities, and resources beyond traditional textbooks. By fostering a networked approach to learning, connectivism emphasizes the collaborative and social nature of knowledge creation, enriching the human connections within the digital learning space.
- Role of Technology in Connectivism: Digital tools and technologies are not just facilitators but integral components of connectivism. Social media, collaborative platforms, simulations, gamification, virtual reality, and online multimedia discussion forums become the conduits through which learners connect, share, and co-create knowledge. Instructors, in turn, serve as guides in navigating this vast network, helping learners develop the skills to critically evaluate and filter information in the digital domain.

Connectivism places a premium on learners' ability to navigate, evaluate, and contribute to digital networks. It emphasizes the development of skills such as critical thinking, information literacy, and effective communication in online environments. By empowering learners as active participants in their networked learning journey, connectivism fosters a sense of agency and connection, transcending the limitations of physical distance.

Constructivist Learning Theories and Models

Constructivist learning theories and models encourage active learning, critical thinking, and problem-solving (Papert & Harel, 1991). Integrating these approaches into online instruction can promote deep learning experiences and foster meaningful connections between learners and the subject matter.

- Social Learning Theory: At the heart of Social Learning Theory is the idea that learning is a social endeavor, driven by interaction and collaboration (Bandura, 1977). In online instruction, this translates to the utilization of collaborative tools, discourse through multi-media discussion forums, and group tasks or projects. By fostering a community of learners who actively share and co-construct knowledge, Social Learning Theory enhances the social fabric of the virtual classroom, creating an environment where human connections thrive through dialogue and collective exploration.
- Discovery Learning: Discovery Learning places emphasis on students actively discovering and exploring knowledge, often through hands-on experiences (Bruner, 1961). In the online setting, this involves creating interactive simulations, virtual labs, and multimedia resources that encourage self-directed exploration. Questions are open-ended, concepts are scaffolded from familiar concepts to new concepts, and self-reflection is encouraged. By providing opportunities for independent discovery, learners engage in a more personalized and immersive learning experience, strengthening their connection to the subject matter.
- Inquiry-based Learning: In the realm of online education, inquiry-based learning prompts students to ask questions, seek answers, and explore solutions independently or collaboratively (Herman & Pinard, 2015). Virtual environments provide fertile ground for the creation of inquiry-driven modules, research projects, and problem-solving activities (Lin & Tallman, 2006). Through the pursuit of answers to real-world questions, students not only deepen their understanding but also forge connections between theory and application, fostering a sense of relevance and engagement (Dewey, 1910).
- Problem-Based Learning (PBL): Problem-based learning is rooted in presenting learners with real-world problems, encouraging them to collaboratively work towards solutions. In the online context, this involves case studies, virtual scenarios, and collaborative problem-solving platforms. By immersing students in authentic challenges, PBL not only enhances critical thinking skills but also creates a sense of shared purpose and connection among learners as they collectively tackle complex issues (Savery, 2006).

Digital Competence: Fluency, Literacy, and Citizenship

Instructors need to possess digital competence to effectively leverage technology in online teaching (Kolomitz & Cabellon, 2016). This involves understanding various digital tools, platforms, and applications, and using them proficiently to enhance the learning experience. To be digitally competent, instructors must be digitally fluent, digitally literate, and be strong digital citizens, see Figure 3 (Center for Digital Dannelse, 2023).

Digital Fluency. Digital fluency transcends mere technological proficiency. It embodies a comprehensive understanding of how to effectively and ethically leverage digital tools for communication, collaboration, and knowledge creation. In the context of online education, digital fluency becomes a bridge between the technical capabilities of digital tools and the human-centric objectives of meaningful teaching and learning experiences. Digital fluency equips instructors and learners with the skills to communicate and collaborate seamlessly in the online environment. This involves not only mastering the use of communication tools but also understanding the nuances of virtual interactions. Digital fluency enables the creation of a virtual community where communication is clear, collaboration is dynamic, and the human connection is actively fostered. Beyond proficiency, digital fluency involves the strategic and adaptive integration of a diverse array of digital tools. From learning management systems to collaborative platforms, instructors fluent in digital tools can select, implement, and customize technologies to enhance the human-centric aspects of their teaching. This adaptive integration ensures that technology serves as an enabler, not a barrier, in fostering connections.

Digital Literacy. Digital fluency goes hand-in-hand with digital literacy—the ability to assess and analyze information in the digital domain. Instructors and learners fluent in digital literacy can navigate the vast online landscape, critically evaluate resources, and distinguish between credible and unreliable information. This not only strengthens the educational content but also fosters a culture of trust and reliability in the virtual learning environment. Digital literacy enhances communication in the online classroom. Whether through emails, discussion forums, or collaborative platforms, individuals fluent in digital communication can express ideas clearly, engage in meaningful dialogue, and build a sense of community. Effective communication skills are essential for humanizing the virtual learning space and maintaining a sense of connection among participants. A digitally literate individual is adaptable in navigating a variety of digital tools and platforms. This adaptability is crucial in the ever-evolving landscape of online education, where new technologies continually emerge. Instructors and learners proficient in digital literacy can confidently integrate diverse tools, ensuring that technology serves as an enabler rather than a barrier to human connection.

Digital Citizenship. Digital citizenship encapsulates a comprehensive set of ethical and responsible behaviors in the digital space. Rooted in the principles of respect, responsibility, and empathy, digital citizenship serves as a cornerstone for building bridges between technology and the human aspects of education. At the core of digital citizenship lies the commitment to ethical conduct in the online context. Instructors and learners, as responsible digital citizens, understand the implications of their online actions, including the importance of respecting privacy, citing sources appropriately, and engaging in civil and constructive online discourse. These ethical considerations form the foundation for maintaining a positive and inclusive virtual learning community. A crucial facet of digital citizenship is awareness of cybersecurity. Instructors and learners understand the importance of safeguarding their digital identities, protecting personal information, and adopting secure online practices. Cybersecurity literacy fosters a secure and trustworthy online learning environment, instilling confidence in participants and contributing to a sense of safety in the virtual realm. Digital citizenship extends beyond individual responsibility to embrace a sense of global connectedness. Instructors and learners appreciate the diversity of perspectives in the digital world, engage in cross-cultural communication, and contribute positively to global digital communities. This interconnectedness fosters a broader understanding of the human experience and enriches the virtual learning environment with a tapestry of global perspectives.

ISTE Standards

The ISTE Standards for Students, developed by the International Society for Technology in Education (ISTE), are a set of guidelines and principles designed to promote effective and innovative integration of technology in education (International Society for Technology in Education, 2023). These standards provide a framework for instructors to leverage technology and digital tools to enhance teaching and learning experiences both in traditional classroom settings and in online environments. Rooted in the principles of effective technology integration, these standards provide a framework for fostering human connections by emphasizing the responsible and purposeful use of technology in education. This involves developing digital-age skills such as creativity, critical thinking, communication and collaboration. Student agency and ownership is encouraged and instructors enhance the human element in online learning, turning students into active participants in their educational journey.

- Digital Citizenship: A key pillar of the ISTE Standards is the promotion of digital citizenship. Instructors using these standards guide learners to become responsible, ethical, and respectful digital citizens. This emphasis on digital ethics and responsible online behavior contributes to a positive and inclusive virtual learning community, reinforcing the human connections that are vital for meaningful learning experiences.
- Knowledge Constructor: ISTE Standards emphasize the role of learners as knowledge constructors. In the online environment, this involves leveraging digital tools to gather, evaluate, and synthesize information. By cultivating the ability to critically assess and contribute to digital content,

Figure 3. Digital Competence Venn Diagram

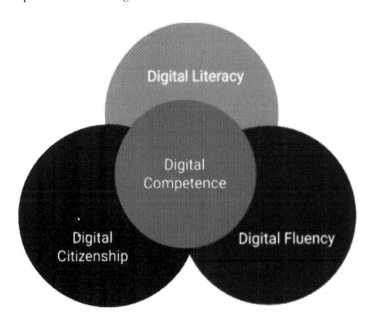

instructors enhance the human dimension of education, emphasizing the collaborative nature of knowledge construction in virtual classrooms.

- Innovative Designer: The ISTE Standards highlight the importance of cultivating an innovative mindset. Instructors are encouraged to design and implement digital learning experiences that promote creativity, problem-solving, and exploration. This approach not only enhances the quality of online education but also fosters a culture of innovation and adaptability, contributing to a dynamic and humanized virtual learning environment.

The ISTE Standards provide a roadmap for instructors to navigate the digital landscape with purpose, ensuring that technology is not a barrier but a bridge to meaningful human connections. By aligning with the ISTE Standards, instructors can infuse the online learning environment with a sense of purpose, responsibility, and innovation, creating a human-centric educational experience that transcends the virtual realm. The ISTE Standards thus become instrumental in building bridges that connect learners, instructors, and knowledge in the digital age.

DIGITAL TOOLS FOR HUMANIZING ONLINE INSTRUCTION

Technology enhances instruction by providing various ways to present information, such as videos, audio recordings, and interactive simulations, accommodating different learning preferences (Sutton & DeSantis, 2017). It also enables students to express their understanding through written essays, multimedia presentations, podcasts, or interactive websites, promoting personalized and strengths-based learning. Moreover, technology fosters inclusive learning environments by offering assistive technologies for students with disabilities and designing accessible online platforms for seamless navigation and interaction with course materials.

Digital Tools for Collaboration

Digitally based tools focused on collaboration help to recreate the dynamics of face-to-face discussions, promoting engagement and social interaction. Suites of collaborative technology-based tools exist to facilitate real-time collaboration, allowing instructors and learners to co-create documents, presentations, and spreadsheets, enhancing a sense of collective engagement (Google Workspace - Google Docs, Sheets, Slides, Sites, etc.). Some technology platforms serve as a centralized hub for communication and collaboration (e.g. Microsoft Teams). Features may include file sharing, video conferencing, and collaborative document editing. Virtual spaces are created where students and instructors can connect, share resources, and engage in discussions. Other systems assist instructors with managing and monitoring students' devices during class. Although focused on device management, it can also foster a collaborative environment where instructors can share content and guide students through their learning journey.

Learning Management Systems (LMS), provide comprehensive tools for course management, content delivery, and collaboration (e.g. Moodle, Canvas, and Blackboard). These platforms offer discussion forums, assignment submissions, and collaborative spaces, creating a centralized hub for the online learning community.

Other platforms like Dropbox, OneDrive, and Box enable users to share and collaborate on documents, files, and resources. This fosters a collaborative space where instructors and learners can co-author content, exchange ideas, and collectively contribute to the learning experience.

Digital curation tools (e.g. Google Keep and Wakelet) allow users to collect, organize, and share content. These tools support collaborative curation, enabling instructors and students to curate and share resources, fostering a sense of shared knowledge. Reference management tools promote and facilitate collaborative research (e.g. Zotero). They enable users to collect, organize, cite, and share research materials, promoting collaborative scholarly endeavors.

Digital whiteboarding tools (e.g. Miro, FigJam, and Explain Everything) provide virtual whiteboards where users can collaborate in real-time. These platforms are particularly useful for brainstorming, ideation, and collaborative problem-solving. Mind mapping tools (e.g. MindMeister and XMind) offer collaborative environments for visualizing ideas and concepts. These tools promote collective brainstorming and knowledge mapping. Figma is a collaborative design tool that allows users to create, prototype, and collaborate on designs in real-time. It is particularly valuable for courses involving design, creativity, and collaborative projects.

Blogging platforms and discussion boards, whether integrated into an LMS or standalone tools, provide spaces for written reflections, discussions, and collaborative writing. These platforms facilitate ongoing dialogue, enabling learners to express their thoughts and engage in meaningful conversations.

Practical Applications

- Encourage collaborative document creation, real-time editing, and synchronous video meetings for virtual class sessions or group projects.
- Assign collaborative writing projects, allowing students to collectively create and edit documents, promoting active engagement.
- Leverage team-based platforms for seamless communication, collaborative document editing, and organizing virtual meetings for interactive discussions.
- Centralize course content, assignments, and communication within a Learning Management System fostering an organized and easily accessible virtual learning environment.
- Establish centralized repositories for course materials, facilitating easy access to shared resources and promoting collaborative knowledge-building.
- Encourage students to use a tool for collaborative note-taking, idea-sharing, and task management.
- Foster collaborative content curation, allowing students to share resources related to course topics.
- Facilitate collaborative research projects, enabling students to collectively manage and cite sources.
- Enhance creativity and engagement through collaborative idea-sharing and brainstorming exercises.
- Facilitate real-time collaborative drawing, diagramming, and problem-solving activities.
- Encourage collaborative mind mapping for visualizing complex concepts and fostering collective understanding.
- Integrate blogging or discussion board assignments, promoting reflective writing and collaborative dialogue.

Audio Tools

Digital audio tools (e.g. GarageBand, Audacity, VoiceThread, Anchor, Vocaroo, a device's internal voice recorder, etc.) allow instructors and students to convey information utilizing tone, intonation, and vocal expression to create a more engaging and relatable learning experience. Audio tools, such as podcasts and voice recordings, can add a personal touch to online courses or distance learning environments. These tools enable instructors to provide audio feedback, facilitate discussions, and create a sense of presence. Audio content accommodates diverse learning styles and is accessible to learners with different abilities, offering an inclusive approach to content delivery. Integrating audio tools alongside other instructional materials supports multimodal learning, catering to varied preferences and enhancing overall comprehension. Digital audio tools provide flexibility for asynchronous learning, allowing students to engage with content at their own pace. The human voice carries emotional nuances, fostering a sense of connection and community even in virtual spaces, and contributing to a more human-centric learning experience.

Practical Applications

- Facilitate quick and easy voice recordings for assignments, reflections, or short audio discussions.
- Foster collaborative discussions by allowing students to comment on course content using their voices.
- Integrate voice-based discussions, allowing students to express themselves verbally and engage in interactive conversations.
- Record narrative-style lectures to provide a more engaging and personal touch to course content, allowing students to connect with the instructor's voice.
- Create and edit podcast-style audio content, record lectures, or facilitate audio discussions.
- Assign podcast creation projects where students explore and present topics, encouraging creativity, research skills, and effective communication.
- Enable students to create and edit audio projects, such as narrated presentations or musical compositions.
- Provide audio feedback on assignments, offering a more nuanced and personalized approach that can enhance understanding and connection.
- Invite guest speakers or conduct interviews using audio tools, creating authentic learning experiences and exposing students to diverse perspectives.
- Facilitate collaborative storytelling projects, where students contribute to a collective narrative using their voices, fostering teamwork and creativity.

Video Tools

Digital video tools provide a dynamic means to convey information, engage learners, and cultivate a sense of presence in the virtual classroom. Video is a versatile medium and allows instructors to use video for pre-recorded lectures, video discussions, demonstrations, storytelling, interactive activities, and collaborative projects.

Video discussion platforms (e.g. Flip) provide a space for asynchronous video discussions and is a tool that can transform asynchronous communication into a vibrant video-based conversation. Instructors and students can share thoughts, ideas, and responses through short video clips, creating a virtual space that transcends the limitations of text-based interactions. This approach adds a personal touch to online discussions, providing individuals with a means to express themselves authentically, thereby fostering a sense of community.

Video conferencing has emerged as a cornerstone technology, revolutionizing the way individuals communicate, collaborate, and conduct meetings or engage in distance learning in the digital age. This powerful tool transcends geographical boundaries, bringing people together in a virtual space for face-to-face interactions. Video conferencing allows participants to see and hear each other in real-time, creating a more immersive and interactive communication experience compared to traditional methods. Presenters can share their screens, documents, or multimedia content, facilitating collaborative discussions and enabling dynamic presentations. Many video conferencing platforms offer chat and messaging features, allowing participants to communicate via text in parallel with the video meeting. The ability to record video conferences enables participants to revisit discussions, review content, and share information with those not present. Some platforms offer virtual background options, allowing users to customize their surroundings and maintain a professional appearance, regardless of their physical location. Video conferencing platforms prioritize security and privacy, implementing features like meeting passwords, waiting rooms, and encryption to safeguard sensitive information. Common video conferencing platforms include Zoom, Microsoft Teams, Google Meet, Cisco Webex, Skype, and FaceTime.

Video hosting sites (e.g. YouTube, Kaltura, Vimeo) provide a platform for course video management, video storage, organization, creation of interactive quizzes within videos, sharing options, playlist curation, conducting live sessions, or hosting private discussions. Video hosting sites use streaming technology, enabling users to watch videos in real time without the need to download the entire file. This facilitates a seamless viewing experience. Videos hosted on these platforms are typically accessible globally, allowing users from different locations to view and share content. Users can often choose the quality settings for their videos, accommodating different internet speeds and device capabilities.

Practical Applications

- Flipped Classroom Approach: Use digital video for content delivery, allowing students to engage with lectures at their own pace. Reserve synchronous class time for discussions, collaborative activities, and deeper exploration of concepts.
- Assign video prompts for discussions, reflections, or collaborative projects. Encourage students to respond to each other's videos, creating a rich tapestry of diverse perspectives and human connections.
- Conduct virtual classes, facilitate group discussions, and record sessions for asynchronous access.
- Host and manage course videos, and enhance engagement with interactive elements.
- Share instructional videos, conduct live sessions, and curate playlists for organized content delivery.
- Embed quizzes, polls, or reflective questions within videos to gauge student understanding and promote active engagement.
- Assign video projects or presentations, encouraging students to create and share their insights, fostering a sense of ownership and creativity.
- Conduct virtual office hours through video conferencing tools, providing a platform for personalized interactions and addressing individual concerns.

- Leverage video conferencing tools to bring guest speakers or industry experts into the virtual classroom, enhancing the learning experience with real-world insights.
- Encourage active participation through features like polls, Q&A sessions, and breakout rooms, fostering collaboration and preventing participant disengagement.
- Encourage collaborative projects where students create and share videos, promoting teamwork and communication skills.
- Ensure that video content is accessible to all students by providing captions, transcripts, and alternative formats. Consider the diversity of learning needs within the class.
- Use video messages to communicate important announcements, updates, or motivational messages, fostering a sense of connection and community.
- Integrate digital storytelling through video projects, allowing students to express themselves creatively and share their unique perspectives.
- Have a support system in place to assist participants with technical issues promptly, ensuring a smooth experience.

Interactive Technology Tools

Interactive technology tools, such as gamification elements and augmented/virtual reality, enhance learner engagement and create a more dynamic and enjoyable online learning environment. Gamification tools (e.g. Kahoot!, Blooket, Gimkit, Quizziz, Classcraft, Labster) inject elements of game design into course design and educational activities, transforming the learning experience into an engaging and interactive journey that fosters mutual goal achievement and problem-solving. These tools provide options for instructors to create gamified quizzes and competitions, experimental or design challenges, learning tasks, or role-playing simulations.

Augmented Reality (AR) is a technology that overlays digital information, such as images, sounds, or text, onto the real-world environment. AR enhances the user's perception of the real world by providing additional context or information through the use of devices like smartphones, tablets, or AR glasses. Virtual Reality (VR) is a technology that immerses users in a computer-generated environment, isolating them from the physical world. VR typically involves the use of a headset or other devices that create a completely virtual experience. Augmented Reality/Virtual Reality (AR/VR) tools (e.g. Z Space, ClassVR, JigSpace, 360° video, YouTube) allow students to interact with virtual objects and engage with content in new ways which can build a stronger understanding of complex concepts while promoting shared experiences.

Practical Applications

- Create game-based collaborative activities related to course content
- Integrate exploration of 3D models, simulations, or specific places or environments using immersive technologies
- Create or integrate virtual field trips for student exploration
- Utilize AR-enhanced textbooks that can display additional multimedia content when viewed through a mobile device or AR glasses. Students can access 3D models, videos, or supplementary information related to the material.

- Gather feedback from students on the tools and how they are being used and be willing to change tools when needed.
- Encourage students to use the tools to create their own learning content and share with fellow learners to enhance engagement and collaboration.
- Use the data provided by the tools to track student progress and identify areas for student improvement

Digital Assessment Tools

The evolution of online education has prompted a reevaluation of assessment strategies to ensure they not only measure academic progress but also contribute to the human connections that are integral to effective learning experiences. Digital assessment tools, including online quizzes and automated grading systems, streamline the assessment process and provide timely feedback to learners, promoting a sense of progress and achievement. Digital assessment tools enable prompt feedback, fostering a more responsive learning environment and enhancing student engagement with course content. Assessments can be tailored to diverse learning needs and preferences, allowing for a more personalized approach to evaluation through adaptive technologies. Collaboration occurs through tools that support group assessments, promoting teamwork and communication skills.

Collaborative commenting tools or features (e.g. Google Doc comments, Microsoft Word comments, VoiceThread, Flip) enable instructors and peers to provide immediate feedback. Students can engage with content and provide comments in writing, through voice, or other means. Annotation tools or features (e.g. Kami, Annotate, Hypothesis) can be used for collaborative reading and annotation, encouraging students to engage in shared discussions within digital texts.

Integrating performance-based assessment into online learning experiences as a means of assessment and evaluation requires students to demonstrate or apply their knowledge, skills, and strategies by creating a response or product or doing a task. Performance-based assessments often simulate real-world scenarios, tasks, or projects. This relevance to actual situations helps students see the practical application of their learning, creating a connection between academic concepts and real-life experiences (Linn et al., 1991). Many performance-based assessments involve collaborative projects or tasks. Group work fosters interaction, communication, and teamwork, allowing students to build connections with their peers as they collectively work towards a common goal. In performance-based assessments, instructors often provide personalized and detailed feedback based on the actual work produced. This one-on-one feedback establishes a direct connection between the instructor and the student, addressing specific strengths and areas for improvement.

Performance-based assessments often emphasize the process of learning and problem-solving rather than just the final result. This focus on the journey encourages a deeper understanding of the subject matter and allows for a more nuanced connection between the student, their work, and the learning process. Diverse talents and skills are acknowledged and celebrated among students. Allowing individuals to showcase their strengths in different ways, creates a more inclusive learning environment where each student's unique abilities are recognized and valued. Through performance-based assessments, students engage in authentic communication. When students are engaged in presenting findings, defending a position, or collaborating on a project, these activities mirror real-world interactions, contributing to the development of effective communication skills and establishing connections between individuals.

Digital portfolios (e.g. Google Sites, Seesaw) can be used as a documentation tool to showcase and share student work through an online platform.

Plagiarism detection and feedback tools (e.g. Turnitin) help to ensure academic integrity and provide detailed feedback on written assignments. Quiz creation tools (e.g. Canvas quizzes, Google Form quizzes) can be integrated within learning management systems, and offer a range of question types. Game-based learning platforms (e.g. Kahoot, Gimkit, Quizlet, Quizizz) include engaging and interactive assessments, promoting a competitive yet collaborative atmosphere. Peer assessment platforms (e.g. Peergrade) allow students to review one another's work and provide meaningful feedback. Students upload their work (written, videos, graphics, etc.) and then provide feedback based on the feedback rubric created by the instructor.

Digital rubrics (e.g. Turnitin, Rubistar, LMS rubric creators) provide a platform for instructors to create and use digital rubrics for streamlined assessments and grading. Rubrics can be customized for various types of assessments including formative, summative, and performance-based assessments. Performance-based assessment allows for personalized and constructive feedback tailored to each student's unique strengths and areas for improvement. Instructors can provide written, video, or audio comments to provide personalized feedback. This not only aids in academic growth but also establishes a connection between instructors and students, demonstrating a genuine interest in their individual progress.

Digital data gathering and analysis tools provide instructors with valuable data on student performance, along with interpretation and analysis capabilities, enabling them to identify areas of strength and weakness and tailor instruction accordingly. These features are often embedded in other platforms or tools (e.g. LMS, quiz or survey tools).

Practical Applications

- Integrate various types of assessments, including quizzes, essays, projects, and peer reviews, to accommodate different learning preferences and skills.
- Use digital tools to facilitate reflective assessments, encouraging students to articulate their learning journey, challenges faced, and insights gained.
- Incorporate collaborative assessments that require group work and discussion, fostering teamwork and interpersonal skills.
- Leverage the quiz tool for formative and summative assessments, providing a seamless experience within the LMS.
- Clearly communicate assessment expectations, guidelines, and assessment criteria to ensure transparency and fairness in the evaluation process.
- Encourage the incorporation of multimedia elements, such as videos, podcasts, or interactive presentations, to allow students to showcase their understanding in diverse ways.
- Leverage digital tools for formative assessments to gauge ongoing student understanding, enabling instructors to adjust their teaching strategies in real-time.
- Foster collaborative learning by assigning group annotation projects. Students work together to analyze and annotate a document, encouraging shared understanding and critical thinking.
- Have students maintain digital portfolios as reflective journals. They can showcase their achievements, discuss challenges, and articulate their learning journey.
- Incorporate self-assessment components in assignments. Encourage students to use the digital rubrics to evaluate their work before submitting, promoting metacognition and accountability.

- Leverage LMS analytics to identify areas where students may need additional support. Implement adaptive learning paths, providing targeted resources or alternative content based on individual performance.
- Use analytics to assess the effectiveness of instructional strategies. Analyze student engagement, completion rates, and assessment outcomes to make informed decisions for continuous improvement.

Tools for Digital Portfolios and Documentation

Digital portfolios and documentation tools (e.g. Google Sites, Squarespace, Wix, Wordpress) allow learners to showcase their work, progress, and achievements. They enable learners to reflect on their growth and learning journey while facilitating feedback and interactions with peers and instructors. Students can curate portfolios that reflect their unique learning experiences, providing a personalized narrative that goes beyond grades and standardized assessments. Portfolios encourage reflective practice, prompting students to think critically about their learning, articulate their goals, and track their progress over time. Beyond academic achievements, portfolios allow students to showcase a diverse range of talents, including projects, presentations, and extracurricular activities. Digital portfolios allow students to store multiple demonstrations of learning. These portfolios can contain video, audio, text, images, and multimedia which allows students to show skills beyond the standard text resume.

Documentation tools complement digital portfolios by providing a structured way to capture and organize evidence of learning, achievements, and reflections. Digital note-taking platforms (e.g. OneNote, Evernote, or Notion) can be used for organizing class notes, research findings, and insights. These tools facilitate organization and retrieval of information for later use in assignments or portfolio creation. Collaborative documentation platforms (Google Workspace or Microsoft 365) can be used for group projects and collaborative research and enable real-time collaboration, teamwork and shared knowledge creation.

Practical Applications

- Have students create a website as a digital portfolio which they can continue to build as they progress through their coursework. This becomes a tool they can use in job interviews or graduate school applications as a comprehensive record of created content, coursework, and digital skills.
- Integrate digital portfolios into the curriculum by aligning them with specific learning objectives. Clearly communicate the purpose and expectations to students, emphasizing the connection between portfolio creation and their overall learning experience.
- Foster a sense of community and collaboration by incorporating peer review into the portfolio creation process. Encourage students to provide constructive feedback on their peers' portfolios, promoting a supportive learning environment.
- Implement digital documentation tools that allow students to maintain ongoing progress journals. These journals serve as a space for students to document their thoughts, challenges, and successes throughout the course, creating a narrative of their learning journey.
- Integrate prompts or templates within documentation tools to guide students in reflective writing. This structured approach helps students delve deeper into their learning experiences, making the documentation process more intentional and meaningful.

- Embrace tools that support a variety of media, including text, images, and multimedia elements. This allows students to document their experiences in a rich and expressive manner, providing a more comprehensive view of their achievements.

Digital Tools for Visual Creation and Presentation

One avenue that holds immense potential is the integration of digital tools for visual creation and presentation. These tools not only enhance the educational experience but also provide a means for human expression and collaboration. Visual creation and presentation tools enable learners to express their ideas creatively. By incorporating visuals, infographics, and multimedia presentations, instructors can make the learning experience more engaging and memorable. Creation tools (e.g. Canva, Adobe Spark, Prezi, Google Slides, Microsoft PowerPoint, Keynote, Genial.ly, Powtoon, etc.) have various features and functions for creating content. These platforms often offer customizable templates, data visualization tools, real-time audience engagement, and styling options. By tapping into the creative potential of students and providing platforms for expression and collaboration, these tools become catalysts for meaningful engagement, enhancing the overall quality of the online learning experience.

Practical Applications

- Have students create digital images to represent concepts.
- Incorporate infographics into learning materials and allow students to create infographics to demonstrate learning.
- Use multimedia presentations to model and share content through a variety of means, such as audio, video, text, and images.
- Introduce students to multiple tools for creating multimedia. Allow students to experiment with these tools to create their own content. Assign multimedia projects to students and encourage them to incorporate a variety of modes to creatively express their ideas.
- Provide clear guidelines and expectations for visual assignments. Ensure that students understand the learning objectives and the role of visual tools in enhancing their understanding and expression of course content.
- Incorporate opportunities for peer feedback on visual creations.
- Ensure that selected tools and assignments are accessible to all students, considering various learning needs and abilities. Choose tools with features that support accessibility.
- Integrate reflective activities and discussions around visual creations. Encourage students to share the thought processes behind their designs.

Artificial Intelligence (AI)

As the landscape of higher education undergoes a profound transformation propelled by technology, one of the most revolutionary forces at play is Artificial Intelligence (AI) (Hacker, et. al, 2023). While concerns persist about the potential dilution of the human element in online learning, AI presents a unique opportunity to not only enhance educational processes but also to foster meaningful human connections. Adaptive learning systems powered by AI (e.g. DreamBox, Knewton, Smart Sparrow) analyze student performance data to tailor educational content based on individual needs. This personalization promotes a more student-centric approach, addressing diverse learning styles and pacing. Intelligent Tutoring Systems (e.g. Cognii, Cerego, Squirrel AI) utilize AI algorithms to provide personalized guidance, feedback, and support. These systems simulate one-on-one interactions, enhancing the learning experience for each student. Natural Language Processing (NLP) (e.g. Google Cloud Natural Language API, IBM Watson, NLTK) enables AI systems to understand and respond to human language. In education, this technology facilitates improved communication between students, instructors, and digital interfaces. Predictive analytics in education (e.g. LMS Learning Analytics, RapidMiner, Brightspace Insights) leverages AI to analyze historical data and identify patterns. This enables instructors to anticipate students' needs, facilitating proactive interventions.

Practical Applications

- Leverage AI-generated insights to understand students' strengths, weaknesses, and learning preferences.
- Implement AI-powered feedback systems that offer real-time insights into student progress.
- Integrate intelligent tutoring systems to provide additional support outside regular class hours.
- Use AI for adaptive assessments that tailor questions based on individual student performance.
- Implement AI-driven chatbots to provide instant support for common queries related to course content, assignments, and technical issues.
- Use predictive analytics to identify students at risk of falling behind. Implement early intervention strategies, such as targeted resources, additional support, or personalized feedback, to prevent academic challenges. Leverage insights from predictive analytics to optimize course design.
- Integrate virtual labs with AI assistance. Labster combines simulations with virtual tutors powered by AI, providing students with guidance and feedback during experiments.
- Enhance online discussions with AI-powered features. AI can analyze discussions to identify key points, summarize content, and suggest relevant resources.

Social Media

Social media refers to a set of online platforms and technologies that enable individuals and communities to create, share, and exchange information, ideas, and multimedia content in virtual spaces. These platforms provide a digital environment for users to connect, communicate, and engage with each other in real-time or asynchronously. Social media has become an integral part of contemporary communication, shaping how people interact, share experiences, and access information (Deaton, 2015). Integrating social media platforms into virtual learning environments can foster community building, networking, and knowledge sharing among learners. Social media can also serve as a platform for ongoing discussions and collaboration. Social media sites (e.g. Instagram, Facebook, Twitter, WhatsApp, YouTube, Pinterest, TikTok, Snapchat, Reddit, Tumblr, Quora) can be used for real-time discussions, visual storytelling, instant communication, collaborative video projects, collaborative resource boards, creative assignments, project collaboration, timely updates, threaded discussions, video discussions, Q&A, collaborative knowledge sharing, reflective blogging, brainstorming, or book clubs. The visual nature of social media sites adds a personal touch, allowing students to express themselves creatively and fostering a deeper connection with course content. Professional networking sites (e.g. LinkedIn) can be used for networking within and beyond the academic community. Students can develop a professional online presence to showcase their academic and professional endeavors.

Practical Applications

- Establish course-specific hashtags and schedule regular online chats.
- Establish a social media group for a virtual book club within the course. Assign readings related to the course content and facilitate discussions.
- Pose discussion prompts, and have students respond with short video clips.
- Create a class-specific social media account to share brief updates and reminders.
- Assign prompts on a social media platform for threaded discussions organized around specific topics, making it easy for students to engage in focused conversations, share resources, and seek help from peers.
- Assign periodic blog posts where students can share reflections on course content, insights gained, and connections to real-world applications.
- Create a class-specific online professional networking group where students can connect, share achievements, and engage in discussions related to the course content.
- Encourage students to share photos and short videos depicting their learning experiences, projects, or reflections.
- Actively participate in social media discussions to model desired behaviors, provide guidance, and foster a sense of instructor presence.
- Incorporate reflective activities where students can share their experiences and insights gained through social media interactions.
- Emphasize the importance of privacy and set guidelines regarding the sharing of personal information on public platforms.

Data Literacy

Data literacy refers to the ability to understand, interpret, and communicate information presented in the form of data. It involves a set of skills and competencies that allow individuals to effectively navigate, analyze, and draw meaningful insights from data. In a rapidly evolving digital landscape, data literacy is increasingly recognized as a crucial skill set in various professional, academic, and personal contexts. Instructors can incorporate data-driven activities into online instruction to enhance critical thinking and problem-solving abilities.

Technology-based data literacy tools facilitate the creation of accessible learning materials that cater to diverse learning styles and abilities. Interactive platforms for visualizing and sharing data (e.g. Tableau Public) allow students to create interactive dashboards, making data exploration more accessible and engaging. Collaboration tools (e.g. Google Sheets or Microsoft Excel Online) allow real-time collaboration on data analysis. Students can work on datasets together, provide feedback, and collectively analyze data. Data visualization platforms (e.g. Datawrapper, Tableau, Power BI, Looker Studio-formerly Google Data Studio) provide students with options for translating and transforming data into visual formats allowing users to grasp patterns, trends, and insights in data.

Practical Applications

- Provide multiple resources to students for digital literacy training. Coursera, Khan Academy, and the Google for Education Teacher Center have pre-built data literacy courses and modules.
- Embed data exploration into existing lessons to utilize real-world data sets to encourage critical thinking and illustrate key concepts.
- Assign learning tasks that require students to collect, analyze, and interpret data.
- Update data tools and resources often as these tools have frequent updates and changes. Be prepared to adapt your approach to data literacy instruction to change as new technologies emerge.

PEDAGOGY AND INSTRUCTIONAL STRATEGIES

Tech for You, Tech for Us

The Tech for You, Tech for Us approach is a powerful strategy for transitioning from fluency to application in utilizing technology. This approach focuses on two key aspects: leveraging technology as a learner and harnessing it within professional roles. As learners, instructors can explore and engage with various technological tools and platforms that align with interests and goals, deepening fluency and understanding. By actively using technology to enhance learning experiences, valuable insights into the potential applications of technology are gained. Simultaneously, as professionals, instructors should seek opportunities to integrate technology into work processes and projects. This involves identifying ways in which technology can optimize efficiency, improve collaboration, or address specific challenges in instructors' respective fields. By taking a dual perspective on technology integration, as both learners and professionals, instructors can bridge the gap between fluency and practical application, unlocking its transformative power in their personal and work lives.

Substitution, Augmentation, Modification, and Redefinition (SAMR) Model

The Substitution, Augmentation, Modification, and Redefinition (SAMR) model provides a roadmap for integrating technology in a meaningful way, see Figure 4. Instructors can leverage SAMR to elevate traditional teaching methods through technology, thus fostering a more engaging and interactive online learning environment (Hamilton et al., 2016). Examples of substitution can include the use of virtual classrooms or video conferencing to replace the traditional classroom or the use of collaborative documents such as Google Docs or Padlet to encourage students to work together in real-time on projects or assignments. Instructors can augment technology, leveraging tools like interactive whiteboards, live polls, and breakout rooms to boost engagement and social interaction.

Instructional modifications can include the use of student-created multimedia projects to help students enhance their creativity and connect with a wider audience as well as online simulations, virtual escape rooms, or role-playing activities that encourage communication and collaboration while boosting problem-solving skills. Technology can redefine online instruction through the use of virtual field trips that allow students to explore different cultures, natural environments, or historical sites while promoting global awareness and creating shared experiences to foster connection. Instructors can build online communities through social media tools that allow students to raise awareness about social justice issues, connect with other experts in their field, or collaborate with a wider global audience. Instructors can also use technology to create online environments for peer mentoring or tutoring and sharing of knowledge among students which also encourages students to build relationships with each other.

Discourse: TAG Framework

The Transactive Goal-Oriented Approach (TAG) framework emphasizes collaborative learning through discourse (Fitzsimons & Finkel, 2018). By incorporating meaningful discussions and interactions in online courses, instructors can build a sense of community and enhance the human connection between learners. The TAG format gives respondents to submissions a framework to provide responses that enhance learning and promote constructive discussion. While there are multiple ways to incorporate transactive learning in online instruction an uncomplicated approach is to include three components for discussion responses. These components are: **T**ell the submitter what you liked about their submission, **A**sk a thoughtful question about their submission, and **G**ive positive suggestions to expand their critical thinking. Examples of TAG responses include: "Your idea about XXX was creative ...", I wonder if ...", I am confused by ...".

Providing Options and Choices

Offering learners options and choices in their learning journey empowers them to take ownership of their education. By providing varied pathways to access content and demonstrate understanding, instructors can cater to individual learning preferences and increase engagement. Meaningful connections can be created through shared interests and experiences which builds a sense of community among learners. When students have ownership of their learning, it allows them to feel more comfortable expressing themselves which leads to greater participation and greater participation contributes to a richer understanding of content and a deeper learning experience. Further, providing learners with multiple means to engage with learning as well as multiple ways to demonstrate learning support the key principles of accessibility and inclusivity of the UDL framework (CAST, 2018). There are multiple ways to offer learners options and choices in online instruction including choice boards, differentiated activities, personalized projects, and student-led discussions.

Figure 4. Substitution Augmentation Modification Redefinition (SAMR) Model

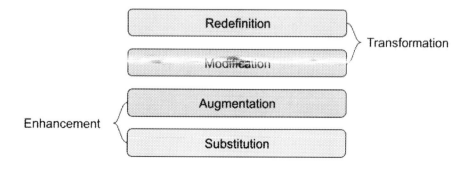

Reflection

Reflection is a powerful tool for deepening learning and self-awareness. Incorporating reflective practices in online instruction encourages learners to connect their experiences to course content and fosters a deeper understanding of the subject matter. When learners articulate their thoughts and feelings they increase their communication skills while having time to consider their learning challenges and successes. Reflections can be text, audio, video, or multimedia which also allows learners to practice creativity skills and deepen their digital fluency and digital literacy skills. By allowing learners to incorporate poetry, visual art, music composition, or kinesthetic composition into reflection students are encouraged to express themselves in diverse ways and connect to other learners through shared experiences. To promote meaningful reflection, provide clear guidelines and prompts for reflection, give constructive and timely feedback on student reflections, and model reflective practices by sharing reflections. Reflection also causes learners to think about their thinking, or metacognition, which reinforces not only their content knowledge but also their ability to apply this knowledge to new situations (Silver et al., 2023).

STRATEGIES FOR TECHNOLOGY IMPLEMENTATION IN THE CLASSROOM

1. Clear Communication: Communicate expectations for tool usage, guidelines for collaboration, and the role of each tool in the course.
2. Access: Ensure that participants have the necessary technology, a stable internet connection, and have tested their settings before classes. Explore options for loaning or providing equipment if needed. Recognize potential bandwidth limitations and offer alternatives such as lower-quality audio options or providing transcripts for those facing connectivity challenges.
3. Training Sessions: Conduct training sessions or provide resources to ensure students and instructors are comfortable with the selected tools.
4. Consistency Across Platforms: Aim for consistency in tool usage to avoid confusion. Choose tools that integrate well with each other for seamless collaboration.
5. Assessment Criteria: Clearly define how collaborative efforts will be assessed, ensuring alignment with course objectives.
6. Feedback Mechanisms: Establish effective feedback mechanisms within collaboration tools to facilitate ongoing communication and improvement.
7. Accessibility Considerations: Ensure that chosen tools are accessible to all students, considering different learning needs and abilities.
8. Continuous Improvement: Regularly solicit feedback from students regarding the effectiveness of digital tools and adjust your strategies accordingly.
9. Digital Citizenship: Model, inform, establish guidelines, and hold students accountable for using technology safely and appropriately. Address privacy concerns by establishing guidelines for creating and sharing digital content, ensuring that students feel comfortable participating in activities.

REFERENCES

Bandura, A. (1977). *Social learning theory*. General Learning Press.

Bruner, J. S. (1961). The act of discovery. *Harvard Educational Review, 31*(1), 21–32.

CAST. (2018). *Universal design for learning guidelines version 2.2*. http://udlguidelines.cast.org

Center for Digital Dannelse. (2023). *The digital competence wheel*. https://digital-competence.eu/dc/en/front/what-is-digital-competence/#:~:text=Digital%20competence%20is%20a%20combination,to%20the%20use%20of%20technology

Deaton, S. (2015). Social learning theory in the age of social media: Implications for educational practitioners. *Journal of Educational Technology, 12*(1), 1–6.

Dewey, J. (1910). *How we think*. D.C. Heath and Company. doi:10.1037/10903-000

Fitzsimons, G. M., & Finkel, E. J. (2018). Transactive-goal-dynamics theory: A discipline-wide perspective. *Current Directions in Psychological Science, 27*(5), 332–338. doi:10.1177/0963721417754199

Hacker, P., Engel, A., & Mauer, M. (2023). Regulating ChatGPT and other large generative AI models. *2023 ACM Conference on Fairness, Accountability, and Transparency,* 1112-1123. 10.1145/3593013.3594067

Hamilton, E. R., Rosenberg, J. M., & Akcaoglu, M. (2016). The substitution augmentation modification redefinition (SAMR) model: A critical review and suggestions for its use. *TechTrends, 60*(5), 433–441. doi:10.1007/s11528-016-0091-y

Harasim, L. (2017). *Learning theory and online technologies*. Routledge. doi:10.4324/9781315716831

Harris, J., Mishra, P., & Koehler, M. (2009). Teachers' technological pedagogical content knowledge and learning activity types: Curriculum-based technology integration reframed. *Journal of Research on Technology in Education, 41*(1), 393–416. doi:10.1080/15391523.2009.10782536

Hendricks, G. P. (2019). Connectivism as a learning theory and its relation to open distance education. *Progressio, 41*(1). Advance online publication. doi:10.25159/2663-5895/4773

Herman, W., & Pinard, M. (2015). *Critically examining inquiry-based learning: John Dewey in theory, history, and practice*. doi:10.1108/S2055-36412015000000301

International Society for Technology in Education. (2023). *ISTE standards for students*. https://iste.org/standards/students

Koehler, M. J., & Mishra, P. (2009). What is technological pedagogical content knowledge? *Contemporary Issues in Technology & Teacher Education, 9*(1), 60–70. https://www.learntechlib.org/primary/p/29544/

Kolomitz, K., & Cabellon, E. T. (2016). A strategic necessity: Building senior leadership's fluency in digital technology. *New Directions for Student Services, 2016*(155), 47–57. doi:10.1002/ss.20182

Lin, J., & Tallman, J. (2006). A theoretical framework for online inquiry-based learning. In C. Crawford, R. Carlsen, K. McFerrin, J. Price, R. Weber & D. Willis (Eds.), *Proceedings of SITE 2006--Society for Information Technology & Teacher Education International Conference* (pp. 967-974). Association for the Advancement of Computing in Education (AACE).

Linn, R. L., Baker, E. L., & Dunbar, S. B. (1991). Complex, performance-based assessment: Expectations and validation criteria. *Educational Researcher, 20*(8), 15–21. doi:10.2307/1176232

Mishra, P., & Koehler, M. (2006). Technological pedagogical content knowledge: A framework for teacher knowledge. *Teachers College Record, 108*(6), 1017–1054. doi:10.1111/j.1467-9620.2006.00684.x

Papert, S., & Harel, I. (Eds.). (1991). *Constructionism*. Ablex Publishing.

Savery, J. R. (2006). Overview of problem-based learning: Definitions and distinctions. *The Interdisciplinary Journal of Problem-Based Learning, 1*(1), 9–20. doi:10.7771/1541-5015.1002

Siemens, G. (2005). Connectivism: A learning theory for the digital age. *International Journal of Instructional Technology and Distance Learning, 2*(1).

Silver, N., Kaplan, M., LaVaque-Manty, D., & Meizlish, D. (Eds.). (2023). *Using reflection and metacognition to improve student learning: Across the disciplines, across the academy*. Taylor & Francis.

Sutton, K. K., & DeSantis, J. (2017). Beyond change blindness: Embracing the technology revolution in higher education. *Innovations in Education and Teaching International, 54*(3), 223–228. doi:10.1080/14703297.2016.1174592

Chapter 10
High Tech/High Touch:
Humanizing Teaching and Learning Online for More Effective Learning Experiences

Allison Freed
University of Central Arkansas, USA

Lacey D. Huffling
Georgia Southern University, USA

Heather C. Scott
Georgia Southern University, USA

Aerin W. Benavides
(iD) https://orcid.org/0000-0001-9876-0216
University of North Carolina at Greensboro, USA

ABSTRACT

Using the three presences (teacher presence, cognitive presence, and social presence) of the community of inquiry framework as a guide to humanize the online environment, this chapter highlights strategies and tools that authentically engage graduate students to think, collaborate, and learn in a collaborative online environment. The authors discuss their journeys to teaching online from an in-person format. This chapter will give readers (faculty, instructors, and instructional designers) insight and ideas that will elevate their online teaching and improve student success through intentional engagement.

In recent years, online learning has become an increasingly more viable course delivery method. Most postsecondary students taking advantage of online courses are first-generation college students from historically marginalized backgrounds. However, online learning can feel and be more isolating to students; instructors are not provided with the in-the-moment student feedback for adapting as instructors in face-to-face environments are provided with (Dias & Boulder, 2023). Instructors must be more forward-thinking, mindful, and intentional about instructional delivery and design, student expectations,

DOI: 10.4018/979-8-3693-0762-5.ch010

and goals for the course in order for the course to be accessible to all students. As instruction moves to blended and online environments, instructors are advised to be conscious of the risks of bias and continuing educational inequities that already exist in in-person classrooms (Mehta & Aguilera, 2020). As Pacansky-Brock and colleagues (2020) discuss, online learning has become increasingly popular for students of Color, making it more important to humanize the traditionally White-centric curriculum and delivery.

With more and more linguistically and culturally diverse students learning online in higher education settings, it has been found to be imperative to create a learning environment that fosters a sense of community (Pacansky-Brock et al., 2020), as learning is a social endeavor that must involve social interactions (Vygotsky & Cole, 1978). The online environment can achieve social learning and relational teaching through the use of pedagogical methods chosen by the instructor that, in essence, humanize the curriculum (Dias & Boulder, 2023). Humanizing the curriculum for inclusion and belonging requires a thoughtful analysis of the context surrounding the course structure, content, students, and instructors (Mehta & Aguilera, 2020). According to Pacansky-Brock et al. (2020), affective and cognitive barriers are removed from the online curriculum in a humanized online environment to create a more equitable and supportive learning space for all students.

Technology can provide instructors with the tools necessary to enact inclusive, equitable education in an online setting. This is where a new perspective of *high tech/high touch* comes into play. *High tech/ high touch* was originally a cognitive dichotomy proposed by Naisbitt and Bisesi (1982), which helped establish a base for global society's nascent intellectual understanding of the new use of computer technology to replace humans. What was lacking in this initial vision was imagining learning spaces by people and for people–a partnership of sorts of technological tools and a highly intentional human touch that would incorporate the strengths of both in seamless collaboration. This can also be referred to as online instruction 'humanizing' our virtual spaces (Dias & Boulder, 2023; Mehta & Aguilera, 2020). We find high touch and high tech can work together as instructors create a humanized online environment using technology to support interactions and learning. Teachers can utilize the technology tools available to online instructors to provide high-touch environments, build trust, allow instructors to interact with students regularly, build rapport that will support students through difficult situations, and provide them with the connection needed to succeed in online classes.

BACKGROUND

Knowing how important context is and how much it matters in online learning, we first want to humanize ourselves by providing the reader with context around our experiences as online instructors before we discuss how we can work to situate online teaching and learning by using humanizing pedagogies. In the next few paragraphs, we will describe our path toward humanizing online instruction, share our journey towards more accessible online learning, and introduce who our learners are, typically.

We are graduate-level course professors teaching in online graduate programs. In these graduate programs, students either learn to integrate technology and become online teachers or work toward middle grades and secondary initial teaching certification. One of us (Allison) teaches in an Instructional Technology Graduate program, and the other two (Lacey and Heather) teach in a Master of Arts in Teaching (MAT) program. Our students come to us as working adults, some transitioning to education as a second career, others wanting to advance their skills in the classrooms, some already join us with many technology skills and strategies, and some participate with little to no prior technology skills; some have never taken an online class before. However, they all come with life experience, a professional identity, and experiences that we realize may surpass us and/or our course preparation as experienced university professors.

Allison's journey to teaching online started as an in-person high school science teacher and outdoor adventure educator, which after graduate school led to her work as an undergraduate professor at a small liberal arts university—where in-person student-professor interactions and relationships were required and essential to student success. When instruction shifted to an online format, markedly at the beginning of the pandemic, Allison shifted to online teaching for the first time. Her initial thoughts with reference to online course planning were to keep the same format and structure of her already existing in-person class. Over time, she realized that students needed additional support to what she had been offering in order to thrive in an online environment. She also needed to provide instructions on accessing and using the online course technology necessary for her students to succeed in the online course. Throughout the transition from in-person to online instruction, using what she had learned from her experiences with students from high school to undergraduate instruction, she focused on community building and promoting social contact with her students. Fast forward a few years, and she is teaching experienced teachers whom she may never physically meet how to mindfully use technology to enhance student learning in a completely online environment. This transition from in-person to online teacher education includes a newly developed mindset and personal identity shift for her students in order for them to move accessible social learning experiences and community building to an online environment.

Lacey's journey began as an in-person high school science teacher who experienced first-hand how blended in-person/online learning environments provided opportunities for students silent in the face-to-face classroom to contribute to an online learning space. As a doctoral student, she took one fully online course centered around discussion boards, which were the only form of peer interaction. Realizing the imminent importance of online education, Lacey elected to take one of the first doctoral courses on teaching online, but this course was taught in person. Although many theoretical frameworks were explored in the course, the pedagogical application was not a direct model for online teaching, and online pedagogies were not as readily available due to the course delivery method. It was not until she attained her first appointment in higher education that she began teaching fully online courses. Her first online courses were for a Masters in Education program with students already teaching in a K-12 classroom for several years. Yet, she still taught some face-to-face courses in the MAT program, which is considered an initial teacher licensure program, even though most students were Teachers of Record. Prior to the pandemic, the in-person MAT had already shifted to be completely online. Lacey has spent the past four years developing and attempting to further humanize her online MAT courses. She has struggled with trying to teach online students who will go on to be in-person teachers. As opposed to Lacey's early online teaching course, her course model is online, yet her students will need to teach in person, without a live model by the instructor for this included in the coursework. And, like Allison, she realizes the identity and mindset shifts she is undertaking to reconcile her pedagogical struggles and seek answers to her questions.

Heather's journey began as an in-person high school science teacher who later moved into higher education, working with an MAT program that still taught face-to-face, providing initial certification for middle and secondary teachers. Her first experience with online learning was a personal learning experience as a student in a doctoral program. Shortly after experiencing online learning as a student, she was asked to teach a fully online, asynchronous class with a canned (detailed and pre-established) curriculum in the summer. Fast forward several years to just prior to the COVID pandemic era, and the MAT program she was teaching was gradually moving towards an online program in order to reach out to more students state-wide. However, when COVID entered the scene, the shift to fully online happened much faster, and MAT faculty scrambled to determine what that would mean for their courses. While some of the courses shifted to an online environment more easily, the faculty for the content methods courses (such as science methods courses) felt a little more resistant - finding that thinking about how to model pedagogy in a meaningful way for preservice teachers was a challenge.

Before we begin discussing implementing the Community of Inquiry (CoI) Framework to humanize our online courses, we first want to say that we do not use all of the strategies and technology tools for all our online courses simultaneously. We are also a few years into our development as online instructors and would not expect a new online instructor to use all of the tools we mention in the following paragraphs. In addition, technology is ever-changing, meaning that the tools we describe in this chapter may become outdated, so we will describe the purpose of the tools as well as their names. Students are also changing in their adoption of technology and will change in their willingness and capacity to use certain technologies. Teaching online requires instructors to be adaptable, flexible, curious, and open-minded. These skills are required if the goal is to humanize the curriculum and keep students engaged and at the forefront of course design.

THEORETICAL FRAMEWORK: COMMUNITY OF INQUIRY MODEL

Using 1.) what we understand to be true about teaching and learning and 2.) our personal teaching philosophies, we have utilized the CoI (Garrison et al., 1999) model as a framework within which to organize and make decisions about our online courses in order to humanize the curriculum and delivery of our online courses. The framework is most appealing because it focuses on the teachers' touch, their impact on cognitive presence, and the importance of social interactions they establish in the learning environment. Social exchanges, collaboration, and community are all essential to academic success, even if a course is online.

CoI is a model of online learning that emphasizes the importance of three presences: teacher, social, and cognitive presence for effective learning in an online environment (Garrison et al., 1999). The framework was developed using social constructivism and Dewey's educational philosophy as the theoretical foundations, positing that collaboration facilitated by an instructor increases critical thinking (Castellanos-Reyes, 2020). Figure 1 outlines our understanding of the CoI model and how the model facilitates humanizing online learning.

Teacher Presence

The online instructor and teacher presence are essential factors for designing a humanized curriculum. Figure 1 highlights the connection between teacher presence and social and cognitive presence in facilitating collaborative, rigorous, humanized curriculum using technology. Anderson and colleagues (2001) determined that teacher presence is important to student success in online settings. Teacher presence includes the designing, developing, and facilitating learning experiences (via their choices of technological tools), activities, and assessments (Darby and Lang, 2019; Foick et al., 2021; Garrison et al., 1999). There is increasing awareness that a well-organized online course has significant impacts on

Figure 1. Humanizing Online Teaching and Learning in a CoI
Note. Using the three presences (teacher presence, cognitive presence, and social presence) of the Community of Inquiry Framework as a guide (Garrison et al., 1999), this diagram shows that the teacher, through personal touch, presence, and design, facilitates social presence and cognitive presence, which creates a context in which connectedness and collaboration are facilitated, which in turn helps facilitate critical thinking. These facilitate humanized learning online in creative ways through the use of technological tools.

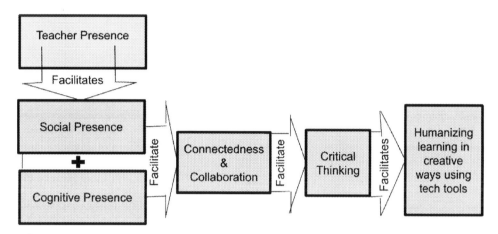

the accessibility of the course for all students (Alon et al., 2023; Edmunds et al., 2020). According to the CoI framework (Garrison et al., 1999), teachers serve as the guide and leader of the course objectives, leading the students through the course content and providing feedback. The teaching decisions made in an online course help students navigate the content, manage difficult tasks, and assist students in being successful learners (Fiock et al., 2021). To manage the cognitive and social presence within the online environment, instructors must manage how students interact with each other, how they interact with the instructor, and how students will engage with the course content.

Teacher presence facilitates the learning environment's cognitive and social components (Anderson et al., 2001). Teachers take on their role as facilitators by building and creating experiences for students to engage with the content and each other to create a more humanized online environment. According to Stone and Springer (2019), connecting with students through video introductions, welcome icebreakers, facilitated discussions, and timely feedback on assignments lets students know that their instructor is present in the online learning process. Students know that there is a human interacting with their assignments and that they care about their learning. Teacher presence improves the overall quality of the online learning experience in a number of ways. Stone and Springer (2019) have shown that teacher presence improves students' overall success by helping them connect with the university, prepares them for academic success through clear and consistent feedback, short videos assisting students on how to use the learning management systems (e.g., technology, in the case of online courses), and encouraging and engaging students with peer-to-peer interactions regularly.

Course design and delivery are another essential aspect of teacher presence (Stone & Springer, 2019). Online course delivery and design differ from in-person delivery, and we have found online courses require different thinking on the part of the instructor. As online instructors, we must consider how our asynchronous and synchronous delivery will be interpreted by our students. The learning activities and assessments are important to consider when developing online courses, but so is how students will communicate with each other both synchronously and asynchronously. Inclusive teacher presence requires that online instructors provide clear and concise instructions in multiple ways (verbal and written). These instructions must also be provided in multiple accessible locations.

Guiding Questions

Questions we considered when evaluating and planning teacher presence online: 1) How can we facilitate learning through collaboration? 2) How can we use technology tools to create a learning environment where social interactions, critical thinking, and academic discourse are elevated? 3) How can we initiate inquiry-based thinking in the assignments created for class? 4) When and how do we give feedback to students? 5) How does the teacher create an online learning environment where students can solve problems, think critically, and do all this while working with others?

Examples in Practice

For example, we used Loom (Loom, n.d.), an online video-sharing platform, to provide tutorials on how to use technology in our course, provide feedback on assignments, share about the modules for each week, and share announcements. Loom allows students to respond to questions asked during the presentation, or students can ask questions during the recording, allowing for back-and-forth conversations asynchronously. Using Loom, we engage with students by providing comments on the videos produced by Loom. We provide students with a walk-through of our feedback on major assignments using the Loom screenshare feature while we talk through our feedback. In an attempt to humanize the process of student feedback and to show we value student voice in designing the curriculum (Mehta & Aguilera, 2020), we encouraged students to provide us with feedback in a myriad of ways, including surveys, office hours discussions, and cogenerative dialogue groups (Emdin, 2016).

We also developed feedback books for students. We shared these as Google Spreadsheets with a one-point rubric (Fluckiger, 2010) on each tab, where we provided feedback on assignments throughout the semester. Students could make comments and ask questions using the comment feature, and they could tag us to ensure we received the message. This provided one place where feedback was stored and an opportunity for students to track their improvement over the course of the semester. Teacher presence was also established as we developed learning pathway options for students as they worked on a Plan-Do-Study-Act project. Students could determine which time of the semester was better for their data collection and select the Learning Pathway to complete course assignments based on those dates. Finally, during our program orientation, we developed the initial teacher presence for all instructors in the program by providing students with technology assistance and break-out sessions during the Zoom orientation. We have asynchronous parts of the orientation that students complete to review the technology that will be used throughout the program. However, student comfortability with technology varies, so we keep the Zoom room open in case students have questions or a student can request a private room where we walk them through the technologies.

Another way we show inclusive teacher presence is through the use of choice boards. We provide them with a variety of choices in how they show their understanding of course content or how they present their final projects by giving students choices in how they show their learning. For instance, we allow students to present their work using a traditional slideshow, interactive video, podcast, or written infographic representing their findings. The choices allowed students to feel empowered to share their learning in the most appropriate and beneficial way possible.

Cognitive Presence

Cognitive presence is understood in CoI as the extent to which students can be critical thinkers (Garrison et al., 1999; Castellanos-Reyes, 2020), solve problems, reflect, think, and act using the discourse of the subject matter. Courses designed by instructors with a robust cognitive presence ask students to construct meaning by engaging in reflection, connecting content to prior experience or subject areas, and being open to new perspectives (Darby & Lang, 2019). In order for deep learning, critical thinking, and knowledge construction to occur in online courses, the instructor must structure the interactions in a way that emphasizes structured discourse (Garrison & Cleveland-Innes, 2005; Wu & Hiltz, 2004). Online instructors play an important role in developing cognitive presence through the creation of engaging questions that elicit personally relevant, thoughtful student responses and meaningful discussions. This is key to initiating cognitive presence (Garrison & Clevland-Innes, 2005; Kanuka et al., 2004).

We, as instructors, created a strong cognitive presence in our online graduate classes by using resources such as Harvard's Project Zero Thinking Routines (Project Zero, 2023) and Zaretta Hammond's *Culturally Responsive Teaching and The Brain* (2014) to facilitate deep, critical thinking throughout the course using technology tools to encourage it. As course instructors, we strategically used discussion board platforms and other platforms such as Canva and Padlet to allow our students to frequently reflect, think critically, and accessibly show their understanding using technological tools creatively. These activities give students a course-wide public forum to express their understanding while allowing their peers to ask questions, support, and extend cognitively upon the posts, thus further establishing deeper critical thinking, perspective-taking, and reflection.

Guiding Questions

Questions we reflect upon when planning and designing our online teaching cognitive presence are as follows: 1.) How do we create an environment where students deeply engage with the learning material? 2.) How do we create assessments and learning activities that help us to engage students based on their cultural backgrounds? 3.) How do students use technology tools to show their learning and reflect on it? 4.) How do we encourage students to engage with their local and global communities using the course content?

Examples in Practice

We utilized Perusall, an online social learning reading platform, to help engage students in article and textbook reading by posing questions students had to respond to embedded within the text and by requiring them to reference other readings. Students in the course were encouraged to tag peers and instructors as they posed questions and engaged with the text. Perusall allowed students to engage with each other around content and cognitive knowledge development. Through this process of learning socially, students could more deeply engage and reflect meaningfully on their learning in their responses to others.

Another idea we used for furthering cognitive engagement included the Hammond (2015) text, *Culturally Responsive Teaching and the Brain*, which our online program uses over two semesters. As students are invited into discussions around the text through Perusall, they also complete assignments that connect what they are reading in the text and their classroom experiences. For example, they read about Climbing out of the Gap, a reference to the academic achievement gap recognized in most American K-12 schools, and then they write a reflective paper about how they are encouraging their students to be independent learners in their own classrooms. Hammond also addresses the neuroscience of learning in this text. Students select specific instructional strategies when writing lesson plans that can be justified as cognitively beneficial with evidence from the neuroscience of learning. At the end of the semester, students prepare a presentation of learning (screencast) that provides an analogy to neuroscience, instructional strategies, and cultural preparedness for learning to be a culturally prepared teacher.

In addition, our online students developed and implemented personalized professional learning plans in which they read pedagogical articles, listened to podcasts, explored new educational technology, and analyzed teaching resources based on personal teaching and learning goals they had set. This professional learning plan became the basis for a plan-do-study-act (PDSA) project where students implemented a strategy in their class for four weeks, collected data on the 4-week implementation, and reported back to their peers. Students used the results of this project to develop an academic conference proposal and presentation for their respective content area teaching organization (e.g., National Science Teaching Association).

We also engaged students cognitively through a video idea pitch assignment to begin a semester. We asked students to create a short one to two-minute video of a unit plan idea that would entice other students to vote for their idea to continue to use this idea throughout the semester. The instructors' planning group considered the idea as a great way to engage students in creativity while simultaneously providing them with choices. However, some students did not appreciate the assignment and pushed back on completing it. We provided scaffolding and model videos to help students through this more ambiguous assignment. However, students felt pushed out of their comfort zone, perhaps more than they were ready for. We can ask when it is okay to allow pushback and how much we should allow without changing the assignment. Is it humanizing to allow students to experience productive struggle out of their comfort zone? Would we need to explain that they will be pushed out of their comfort zone ahead of time and that we have set up models and supports to help them through the experience? Table 1 outlines additional ways we utilized technology tools for greater impact using the CoI framework.

Social Presence

Social presence is defined as the ability of the learner to feel connected to other students and their teachers (Swan & Ice, 2010; Castellanos-Reyes, 2020). A strong social presence included in course design by the instructor allows students to show up as their authentic selves, interact with others, trust their instructor, and collaborate often (Hammond, 2014; Pacansky-Brock et al., 2020). We knew how important social interactions were in creating strong academic communities in person, so we sought and found ways to bring students together online.

The instructor-student relationship is essential to humanizing and "serves as the connective tissue between students, engagement, and rigor" (Pacansky-Brock et al., 2020, p. 2). Connecting with students who have unique needs, experiences, and assets creates an environment where students feel they can trust their instructor and feel that they belong to a community of learners (Pacansky-Brock et al., 2020). In a study that examined the best and worst online and face-to-face undergraduate classes, Glazier and colleagues (2021) found the instructors who taught the best online classes were engaged and caring, building a sense of rapport with their students (Glazier, 2021).

To create a social presence in our online classes, we created assignments that encouraged students to interact in real time via video conferencing software. The meetings were set up to create a community of practice (Lave & Wenger, 1996), where they discussed the course topics, shared ways to improve their teaching, and learned about themselves through the process. In addition, we used Flip, Parley, Wakelet, and Padlet to create spaces for students to share using video to discuss topics, introduce themselves, and create an active presence in the online space. Another important component for creating a social presence in our courses was to require virtual office hours visits, which were one-to-one online. These visits were essential in building rapport (Glazier, 2021), creating a community of learners, and for us as instructors to relate to our students, humanize ourselves, individualize instruction, and get buy-in for making an effort to be a part of a community and take the time to build relationships with other students and their faculty instructor.

Guiding Questions

The questions we used as instructors to determine how the task and technology encourage social presence and interaction were: 1) How can we be present as instructors in our courses? 2) How can we cultivate a community of learners in our online classroom? We work with working adults who have multiple other responsibilities, so we struggle with requiring intensive peer-to-peer interactions. 3) What is the balance between requiring student social interactions and not overburdening students to engage in ways they may find inauthentic or not desire as they push back that they chose online learning so that it would be asynchronous and self-paced?

Examples in Practice

To align our classes with professional teacher standards and create a stronger social presence among students, we implemented Communities of Practice or Critical Friends Groups (Lave & Wenger, 1996) assignments throughout the semester. During our online classes, we ask students to interact with each other to share ideas, discuss content, get feedback, and complete shared assignments. In doing this, students created small groups that became a network for them as they navigated the online course and completed assignments. Students were provided guidance and feedback from their instructors and peers, creating an environment focused on connection and shared learning. Students were graded as a group and asked to complete mini-check-ins about group members as a way of helping assess the group's productivity.

Another way we establish a social presence is through required office hours visits for all students. In theory, office hours and face-to-face virtual meetings with instructors have great potential for establishing connections and relationships with students. These meetings also provide students with the support they may need to succeed in online courses (Mehta & Aguilera, 2020; Pacansky-Brock et al., 2020). However, requiring students to visit us during office hours adds time to student and teacher schedules. Since our students are at the graduate level, many have full-time jobs and other commitments outside class time. This time requirement creates barriers to having the time necessary to maintain face-to-face interactions and requires us as instructors to find other creative ways to engage students in creating personal connections with us, such as cogenerative dialogues.

In order to encourage students to engage in authentic dialogue (Dias & Boulder, 2023) and have a say in how the course is structured, executed, and organized, we encouraged students to participate in

Cogenerative Dialogues (Emdin, 2016). Cogenerative dialogues are where the teacher meets with a "focus group of students on a weekly basis to generate and deliberate suggestions for improved opportunities—and a more responsive environment—for student learning" (Beltramo, 2018, p. 9). The conversations in these dialogues focus on questions such as how activities and the classroom environment supported and/or impeded student learning. What related improvements should be made to bolster student engagement and learning? (Beltramo, 2018; Emdin, 2007). Cogenerative dialogues bolster student voices in their learning by interacting with their instructor and other peers interested in providing feedback to their instructors. According to Beltramo (2018), cogenerative dialogues create supportive, humanized student environments by giving teachers insights into culturally responsive and inclusive practices that align with student interests. These focus group sessions build students' social capacity by co-constructing learning environments that serve their unique needs.

Using a platform in addition to course platform(s) such as Discord, an online communication venue, has also shown promise in encouraging ongoing asynchronous communication throughout the course. Discord is an instant messaging social communication platform that allows text messaging, file sharing, and voice calls (Discord, 2023). Students engage with instructors and each other to pose questions, get information, find group members, and engage with content outside of the course LMS. We have used this platform and engaged students by posing questions and asking for responses to continue the social engagement process throughout the semester in an environment that is not officially a course venue.

Peer observations and reviews further enable us to develop a social presence in our courses. Students can record video snippets of their classroom instruction based on the pedagogical strategies we have discussed in class. Then, they share their videos in small groups or as a partner activity. They provide feedback based on prompts that we provide them, depending upon the pedagogical strategy they are learning. Students also conduct peer reviews of a 3-minute Thesis activity, which is the cumulative project for their MAT. In this activity, students provided three glows (items their peer did well), one grow (an item that could be improved), and one question that the project elicited. Student feedback for the courses in which these peer interactions are embedded has been highly rated, and more than 75% of students have commented on how they appreciated viewing each other's work.

REFLECTIONS

In developing online instruction, we found that the transition from in-person teaching to online had its challenges and the solutions had their ups and downs. We were more successful when we were committed to our educational values and teaching philosophy during the transition. We all are strongly tied to social constructivism and value collaborative projects and connections, believing and using supporting evidence that we learn more effectively when we learn together. Many of the strategies we embraced in an online setting provided us with a way to humanize our curriculum, maintain our social presence, and continue to ask students to collaborate despite the distance. For instance, we used technology platforms such as Flip and Perusall that assisted us and our students in maintaining their presence with others while interacting with the material asynchronously.

Cognitively, students are engaged with the content of our courses through the use of Thinking Routines (Project Zero, 2023). Students engage with the course material individually and collaboratively. Our course designs allowed for deeper engagement of the learning material through video and online discussions and synchronous meetings with small groups.

Table 1. Connecting CoI model to tools and strategies for online teaching and learning

CoI Element	Questions to Consider	Example Tools/High Tech (Beyond Your Learning Management System (LMS))	Example Strategies/High Touch
Social Presence	How can I be present as an instructor in my course? How can I cultivate a community of learners in my online classroom?	Video conferencing tools (e.g., Flip) Interactive discussion platforms (e.g., Parlay) Video conferencing software (e.g., Zoom, Google Meet, Webex, Teams) Curation and communication tools (e.g., Wakelet or Padlet) Instant messaging and file sharing tools (e.g., Discord) Group Collaboration Assignments	Video/Audio Discussions Discussion Board Office Hours Requirements Use these to help students introduce themselves, engage with others, share resources, etc. It provides a back channel for students to communicate with each other, ask questions, and share resources. Opportunities for students to engage with each other to form communities of practice (Lave & Wenger, 1996), safe places to ask questions and receive feedback.
Teacher Presence	How can I facilitate learning through collaboration? How can I use the technology tools to create a learning environment where social interactions, critical thinking, and academic discourse are elevated? How can I initiate inquiry-based thinking in the assignments created for class? When and how do I give feedback to students?	Screencasting and presentation platform (e.g., Loom) Choice Boards Discussion Boards Curation and communication tools (e.g., Wakelet or Padlet)	Use Loom to share your screen, presentation, and directions. It also shows your face and audio. Students can engage by adding comments to your video. Provide a space to share screencasts for the technology we use. Provide students with the chance to feel autonomous and to showcase their learning in the way that they feel most comfortable or competent. You show that you value their choices and independence. Engage frequently with students in discussion forums. Provide a place to put resources to support learning.
Cognitive Presence	How do I create an environment where students deeply engage with the learning material? How do students use technology tools to show their learning and reflect on their learning? How do we encourage students to engage with their local and global communities using the course content?	Project Zero Thinking Routines (Project Zero, 2023) Video conferencing software (e.g., Zoom, Google Meet, Webex, Teams) Interactive presentation creation and sharing tools (e.g., Nearpod or Peardeck) Graphic design and communication tool (e.g., Canva) Curation and communication tools (e.g., Wakelet or Padlet)	Used to create thinking routines and strategies for your students to use throughout your course. These can be used in a variety of settings using a variety of tools. Virtual check-ins and office hours Used to create interactive presentations involving student engagement, problem-solving, and student interactions. Provides students with creative ways to show their learning, including infographics, brand messaging, presentations, and websites. Pose questions and ask students to engage with the platform by adding comments, pictures, gifs, links, and resources.

Note. This table describes the questions asked to select technology tools for the three presences in the CoI framework.

To continue the ongoing collaboration into a hybrid space outside the online course platform, we preserved our presence as teachers by using platforms like Loom and video conferencing software to provide feedback on student work and share content and presentations with students. We were mindful of our choices of technology use as we learned how students engaged with the technology platforms we put forth. We adjusted how we used them and taught our students to use the platforms, being conscious of the level of technology experience our students may have had as they navigated our courses.

The transition from being an in-person instructor to an online instructor who purposefully provides students with ways to connect with other students and us is an ongoing process. We reflect on our teaching in various ways. We do so by assessing how students perform on assessments and evaluations and reflecting upon how we thought the courses went. In addition, we continuously engage in professional learning that helps bring us closer to humanizing online teaching practices that engage students in active learning through collaborative projects. Through the transition, we have continuously checked in with each other and with our biases around online teaching and how we believe online learning is a valuable tool for learning from everywhere. We strive to continue to provide engaging, inclusive, and connected learning environments where students feel they can be authentically human.

Knowing online instruction requires certain technological skills that in-person instructors do not need to succeed, we continuously reflect on our work to transition and become more effective online teachers. We engage in professional learning provided by our institutions, the International Society of Technology in Education (ISTE), and other communities focused on online teaching and learning. After each semester, we reflect on our practice by reviewing student evaluations, student grades, and feedback. We value and expect continuous improvement and tweaking of our classes each semester.

CONCLUSION

Humanizing online courses is vital to the success of the increasingly diverse student body taking online classes. The CoI framework is a valuable model for organizing, planning, and implementing humanized online instruction. To prepare for highly connected collaboration and critical thinking, instructors must use technology to facilitate their course's social and cognitive presence. Using CoI as a reflective tool allowed us to establish norms for our teaching that lead to engaged, collaborative learning using technology. The CoI model gave us a roadmap for transitioning our instruction from in-person to online by considering the technology tools we used to implement learning activities and peer-to-peer interactions. We will continue to use the model to reflect and adjust our instruction moving forward.

Next Steps and Lingering Questions

As we have analyzed our teaching practices through the humanizing lens, we have become aware of the need to use Universal Design for Learning (UDL) (CAST, 2018). The goals of UDL are to make instruction more readily available to students with various learning needs (Dell et al., 2015). The UDL approach utilizes the need to provide all students with positive learning experiences online through the use of supportive strategies (Novak & Thibodeau, 2016). UDL-focused course designers aim to "support learner differences by providing multiple and flexible modes of presentation, expression, and engagement" (Dell et al., 2015, p. 172). Overall, UDL enhances instruction for all learners in online environments. We want to be more systematic in using UDL practices to enhance the learning environment, including multiple representations in expressing knowledge and skills, engaging students, and expressing action and expression (CAST, 2018) in our assignments and modules. We are finding more ways to implement UDL systematically throughout our online curriculum.

There are a number of opportunities for using artificial intelligence in online learning environments (Roll et al., 2018; Seo et al., 2021). AI has the potential to personalize learning, automate instructor feedback and responses, provide supplemental instruction to students in need, and support instructors in finding strategies for continuing to humanize their online instructors (Seo et al., 2021). As AI continues to flourish and advance, we want to leverage it to enhance our instruction and the environments we create in online settings. We are experimenting with AI as a tool for humanizing our instruction. In addition, we are encouraging our students to implement AI as they brainstorm, prepare materials, and create materials for their own classes. We believe AI has the potential to humanize our instruction in new ways that will enhance the learning experience for our students.

We continue to grapple with providing students with engaging, sometimes difficult, uncomfortable tasks to get them outside their educational comfort zone while maintaining our commitment to humanizing our curriculum. We wonder if a curriculum can still be considered humanized while allowing students to participate in productive struggle, as referenced by Trinter & Hughes (2021) (Heibert & Grouws, 2007). Productive struggle is a common construct used in mathematics instruction, but it can be utilized when considering any task that requires students to work to learn a concept. We want to be more mindful of humanizing the cognitive dissonance that happens when students are asked to learn new concepts or try new strategies (Trinter & Hughes 2021). As we reflect, we continue to question the impact of productive struggle in humanizing online course curricula. If a student is in a productive struggle, how can we inclusively engage with students as humans? When is educational discomfort going too far? How can we continue to push students cognitively without letting go of compassion and care?

The CoI Framework (Garrison et al., 1999) is a seminal model many online instructors use to organize and implement online courses. As we continue to use CoI, we wonder about the role of the students and the technology in creating an online environment that leads to engaging interactive learning. Online communities also include students' courses and the technology tools used to learn, process, or communicate information. In order to strengthen the model, we posit that more emphasis should be placed on the role that students and technology play in creating a cognitively engaging collaborative learning environment in online settings.

REFERENCES

Alon, L., Sung, S., Cho, J., & Kizilcec, R. F. (2023). From emergency to sustainable online learning: Changes and disparities in undergraduate course grades and experiences in the context of COVID-19. *Computers & Education, 203,* 104870. doi:10.1016/j.compedu.2023.104870

Anderson, T., Rourke, L., Garrison, D. R., & Archer, W. (2001). Journal of asynchronous learning networks. *Journal of Asynchronous Learning Networks, 5*(2), 1–17. doi:10.24059/olj.v5i2.1875

Beltramo, J. L. (2018). Developing Mutual Accountability between Teachers and Students through Participation in Cogenerative Dialogues. *International Journal of Student Voice, 3*(1). https://ijsv.psu.edu/?article=developing-mutual-accountability-between-teachers-and-students-throughparticipation-in-cogenerative-dialogues

CAST. (2018). *Universal Design for Learning Guidelines version 2.2.* Retrieved from http://udlguidelines.cast.org

Castellanos-Reyes, D. (2020). Years of the Community of Inquiry Framework. *TechTrends, 64*(4), 557–560. doi:10.1007/s11528-020-00491-7

Darby, F., & Lang, J. M. (2019). *Small teaching online: Applying learning science in online classes.* John Wiley & Sons.

Dell, C. A., Dell, T. F., & Blackwell, T. L. (2015). Applying universal design for learning in online courses: Pedagogical and practical considerations. *The Journal of Educators Online, 12*(2), 166–192. doi:10.9743/JEO.2015.2.1

Dias, B., & Boulder, T. (2023). Toward Humanizing Online Learning Spaces. *The Journal of Applied Instructional Design, 12*(4). https://edtechbooks.org/jaid_12_4/toward_humanizing_online_learning_spaces

Discord. (2023, November 26). https://discord.com/

Edmunds, J. A., Gicheva, D., Thrift, B., & Hull, M. (2021). High tech, high touch: The impact of an online course intervention on academic performance and persistence in higher education. *The Internet and Higher Education, 49*, 100790. Advance online publication. doi:10.1016/j.iheduc.2020.100790

Emdin, C. (2007). Exploring the contexts of urban science classrooms: Part 1: Investigating corporate and communal practice. *Cultural Studies of Science Education, 2*(2), 319–350. doi:10.1007/s11422-007-9055-z

Emdin, C. (2016). *For White folks who teach in the hood... and the rest of y'all too: Reality pedagogy and urban education.* Beacon Press.

Fiock, H., Maeda, Y., & Richardson, J. C. (2021). Instructor impact on differences in teaching presence scores in online courses. *International Review of Research in Open and Distance Learning, 22*(3), 55–76. doi:10.19173/irrodl.v22i3.5456

Fluckiger, J. (2010). Single Point Rubric: A Tool for Responsible Student Self-Assessment. *Teacher Education Faculty Publications,* 5. https://digitalcommons.unomaha.edu/tedfacpub/5

Garrison, D. R., Anderson, T., & Archer, W. (1999). Critical inquiry in a text-based environment: Computer conferencing in higher education. *The Internet and Higher Education, 2*(2-3), 87–105. doi:10.1016/S1096-7516(00)00016-6

Garrison, D. R., & Cleveland-Innes, M. (2005). Facilitating cognitive presence in online learning: Interaction is not enough. *American Journal of Distance Education, 19*(3), 133–148. doi:10.1207/s15389286ajde1903_2

Glazier, R. A. (2021). *Connecting in the online classroom: Building rapport between teachers and students.* JHU Press. doi:10.1353/book.98266

Hammond, Z. (2014). *Culturally responsive teaching and the brain: Promoting authentic engagement and rigor among culturally and linguistically diverse students.* Corwin Press.

Hiebert, J., & Grouws, D. A. (2007). The effects of classroom mathematics teaching on students' learning. Second handbook of research on mathematics teaching and learning, 1(1), 371-404.

Kanuka, H., & Garrison, D. R. (2004). Cognitive presence in online learning. *Journal of Computing in Higher Education, 15*(2), 21–39. doi:10.1007/BF02940928

Lave, J., & Wenger, E. (1996). *Communities of practice.* doi:10.1007/978-3-642-28036-8_644

Loom. (n.d.). *Free screen recorder for Mac and PC.* https://www.loom.com/

Mehta, R., & Aguilera, E. (2020). A critical approach to humanizing pedagogies in online teaching and learning. *The International Journal of Information and Learning Technology, 37*(3), 109–120. doi:10.1108/IJILT-10-2019-0099

Naisbitt, J., & Bisesi, M. (1983). Megatrends: Ten new directions transforming our lives. *Sloan Management Review, 24*(4), 69. doi:10.1016/0007-6813(83)90036-8

Novak, K., & Thibodeau, T. (2016). *UDL in the cloud: How to design and deliver online education using universal design for learning.* CAST Professional Publishing.

Pacansky-Brock, M., Smedshammer, M., & Vincent-Layton, K. (2020). Humanizing online teaching to equitize higher education. *Current Issues in Education (Tempe, Ariz.), 21*(2).

Project Zero. (2023, July 12). *Project Zero's Thinking Routine Toolbox.* https://pz.harvard.edu/thinking-routines

Roll, I., Russell, D. M., & Gašević, D. (2018). Learning at scale. *International Journal of Artificial Intelligence in Education, 28*(4), 471–477. doi:10.1007/s40593-018-0170-7

Seo, K., Tang, J., Roll, I., Fels, S., & Yoon, D. (2021). The impact of artificial intelligence on learner–instructor interaction in online learning. *International Journal of Educational Technology in Higher Education, 18*(1), 1–23. doi:10.1186/s41239-021-00292-9 PMID:34778540

Stone, C., & Springer, M. (2019). Interactivity, connectedness and teacher-presence': Engaging and retaining students online. *Australian Journal of Adult Learning, 59*(2), 146–169.

Swan, K., & Ice, P. (2010). The community of inquiry framework ten years later: Introduction to the special issue. *The Internet and Higher Education, 13*(1–2), 1–4. doi:10.1016/j.iheduc.2009.11.003

Trinter, C. P. & Hughes, H. E. (2021) Teachers as Curriculum Designers: Inviting Teachers into the Productive Struggle. *RMLE Online, 44*(3), 1-16. doi:10.1080/19404476.2021.1878417

Vygotsky, L. S., & Cole, M. (1978). *Mind in society: Development of higher psychological processes.* Harvard University Press.

Wu, D., & Hiltz, S. R. (2004). Predicting learning from asynchronous online discussions. *Journal of Asynchronous Learning Networks, 8*(2), 139–152. https://doi.og/10.1142/S1609945104000115

Chapter 11

Leveraging AI to Personalize and Humanize Online Learning:
Transforming Transactional Interactions Into Meaningful Engagements

James Hutson

 https://orcid.org/0000-0002-0578-6052
Lindenwood University, USA

Daniel Plate

 https://orcid.org/0000-0002-1238-5425
Lindenwood University, USA

ABSTRACT

This chapter explores the potential of artificial intelligence (AI) to personalize and humanize online education, transcending transactional learning. It emphasizes how AI, particularly generative large language models (LLM) utilizing natural language processing (NLP), can foster deeper, human-like interactions between students and educators. Moving away from traditional keyword-based searches, the chapter highlights how AI integrates with tools like search engines and research databases, transforming the way students and teachers think, research, and converse. Despite concerns over the potential dehumanizing impact of AI, the chapter argues that its capabilities can, in fact, actually facilitate continuous and creative engagement, while privileging understanding and creativity over rote memorization. These new generative tools can enhance, not challenge, the human element in online education and promote more authentic assessments in the process.

INTRODUCTION

The global shift towards online education has reached an unprecedented scale, a trend only accelerated by the COVID-19 pandemic that saw temporary closures affecting 70% of the global student population (Vlasova, 2022). In the post-pandemic era, a 2021 survey revealed that 73% of students wanted to take

DOI: 10.4018/979-8-3693-0762-5.ch011

some courses fully online, reflecting a change in attitudes and acceptance of online learning (McKenzie, 2021). By 2023, this sentiment had grown stronger, with 79% of online students and graduates strongly affirming the value of their online degrees (White, 2023). With such a demand on the part of students, the global e-learning market, already on an impressive growth trajectory, is expected to reach $336.98 billion by 2026 (Patra & Sahu, 2020). Moreover, the reasons cited in favor of online and distance education have remained consistent since before the pandemic. For instance, a 2019 survey identified affordability, reputation, and quick paths to degrees as key factors driving students to online programs (Singh & Sharma, 2021). Fast forward to 2023, and the prevalence of online education has continued to expand dramatically, reflecting not only the technology-driven revolution in learning but also the evolving needs and preferences of students (Alenezi, 2023).

In the shifting sands of education, where learning management systems (LMS) have increasingly replaced physical classrooms, the integration of digital platforms within the educational landscape has seen a notable surge. This chapter aims to explore the multifaceted implications of this transition, particularly focusing on how it has expanded opportunities for personalized learning while also raising questions about maintaining quality and integrity in education. Indeed, the rapid progression of technology has led to more sophisticated virtual learning environments (Hutson, Steffes, & Weber, 2023), educators are continually innovating with content delivery methods (Lytras et al., 2022), and there is a notable shift towards flexible learning modalities aligning with student preferences (Addae, 2022; Alanzi & Alhalafawy, 2022; Armellini et al., 2022). Despite the entrenched nature of online classes in the higher education framework, this chapter scrutinizes the remaining concerns about their quality and integrity, with a particular emphasis on overcoming the impersonal nature of online learning to ensure a richer, more engaging educational experience. As we delve into the strategies and tools that can humanize online learning, including the potential of emotionally intelligent AI, the aim is to provide a comprehensive guide for educators to navigate and enhance the digital learning landscape.

While the embrace of online education within higher education institutions has been extensive and growing, this trend has not been without its share of criticisms and challenges. Concerns persist over the quality and rigor of online instruction. Skeptics question whether the depth and rigor of traditional classroom experiences can be maintained in an online format, particularly in subjects that typically require hands-on practice and in-person mentoring (Malik & Zhu 2023; May et al., 2022). Such critiques were especially pronounced with the unprecedented and unexpected move to online and distance education during the pandemic (Pozo-Rico et al., 2020; Sutiah et al., 2020; Whalen, 2020). One of the main concerns over the quality and rigor of online learning is the issue of cheating and academic integrity. The remote nature of this learning modality creates opportunities for academic misconduct such as cheating and plagiarism, leading to implementation of plagiarism detecting software such as Turnitin and exam proctoring with live services such as ProctorU (Adzima, 2020; Janke et al., 2021; Noorbehbahani et al., 2022). However, these concerns over quality, rigor, and academic integrity have often resulted in the focus of online education design, development, and deployment being on creating a controlled environment rather than fostering authentic learning experiences, thus potentially stifling innovation and limiting opportunities for deeper engagement and understanding (Rippy & Munoz, 2021).

Moreover, online education has been criticized for creating impersonal and isolated experiences that can fundamentally alter the nature of learning interactions (Azmat & Ahmad, 2022; Evans et al., 2023). Standard online interactions often consist of scheduled video conferences, asynchronous discussion boards, written assignments, and automated assessments (Fun et al., 2022). These interactions, while efficient, often lack the spontaneity, nuance, and richness of face-to-face encounters (Gherheș et al., 2021).

In some cases, this model has led to a transactional approach to education, where learning is reduced to a series of disconnected tasks rather than a cohesive and engaging experience (Stöhr et al., 2020). Without the immediacy and authenticity of physical presence, barriers to genuine student-to-student and student-to-instructor interactions might emerge, creating a sterile environment that can feel more akin to completing a checklist than participating in a vibrant learning community. Such situations impact not only learning outcomes but also the overall satisfaction, motivation, and well-being of students within the educational experience.

While online education will only become more prevalent for the factors outlined above, recent technological advances, particularly in the realm of artificial intelligence (AI), may be leveraged to address the impersonal and dehumanizing experiences that can result from standard online course design and engagement, thus opening new pathways for individualized and impactful learner-focused education within the virtual learning environment. The transformative potential of the most recent generation of AI in education is truly groundbreaking, especially through the utilization of natural language processing (NLP) and large language models (LLM) like Bard, Llama, Claude, and ChatGPT. Natural Language Processing, or NLP, is a branch of AI that focuses on the interaction between computers and humans through natural language. Essentially, the technology allows machines to understand and respond to text or voice data in a way that is natural for humans. This means computers can read text, hear speech, interpret it, understand sentiment and even generate text that humans can understand. Imagine the possibilities in an educational setting: a computer can read a student essay and offer suggestions, or understand a question posed by a student and provide the correct answer or resources.

Building on this, large language models (LLM) like Gemini, Bard, Llama, Claude, and ChatGPT represent the cutting edge of this technology. These models have been trained on vast swathes of text data, allowing them to generate responses that can mimic human-like understanding and writing. They can compose essays, answer questions, and even create poetry or code. The capability of these models to understand context and nuance in language makes them powerful tools for personalizing learning. For example, they can provide feedback on student assignments that is tailored to the student's writing style or level of understanding, engage in back-and-forth conversations to clarify concepts, or adapt materials to suit different learning preferences.

This generation of AI is not just about automating tasks but enriching the educational experience. This chapter sets forth an argument that, contrary to concerns of dehumanization, the capabilities of AI tools can augment and deepen the human dimension of online education. It can make learning more accessible, engaging, and tailored to individual needs, helping students and educators alike navigate the complexities of education in the digital age. As these technologies continue to evolve, the potential for personalized and human-centered learning environments becomes increasingly attainable. Amidst a rapidly changing educational landscape that often defaults to transactional interactions, AI stands as a beacon for a more enriched, engaging, and human-centric learning experience. Through the shift from keyword-based search strategies to conversational inquiry, the integration of generative AI into tools such as Scite, Consensus, Elicit, and JSTOR has initiated a more engaging and human-like approach to research and learning. Scite, Consensus, Elicit, and JSTOR are transforming the landscape of research and learning into a more engaging and intuitive experience. Scite revolutionizes citation analysis by showing how research is supported or contradicted, providing deeper insight into the quality of work. Consensus enhances collaborative efforts with structured decision-making tools. Elicit uses AI to streamline literature reviews, helping users quickly find relevant studies, while JSTOR remains an invaluable digital library offering a wealth of academic resources. Together, these tools are not just digitizing education but enriching it, making academic research more accessible, insightful, and tailored to the evolving needs of learners and educators alike.

Furthermore, the ability of AI to continuously learn from historical data and user interactions opens the door to personalized learning pathways, heralding a significant transformation in pedagogical methods across educational levels. The generative abilities of these new tools can also expand access to education for underserved communities and individuals with learning disabilities through individualized learning pathways and tutoring, fostering a more inclusive educational environment (Kim et al., 2020). At the same time, proficiency in interaction with AI tools is evolving as a vital career skill. Techniques such as prompt engineering and generation have already risen as some of the top skills essential for maintaining an industrial competitive edge (Tangermann, 2023). Thus, these generative tools represent not just an innovative approach to teaching and learning but also a key aspect of future personal and professional development for students. Equipping them with these tools should stand as a fundamental goal for educators. Therefore, not only can AI help personalize online education, but in doing so provides learners with indispensable skills in all industries.

By transcending the transactional limitations of traditional online learning, AI can facilitate real-time conversations, allowing students to engage and practice dialogues with virtual entities, simulating peer or instructor interactions. This immediate feedback loop can challenge assumptions and nurture critical and creative thinking skills. For example, AI-driven virtual debates can be designed to sharpen argumentative abilities, encouraging students to think from different perspectives. LLM can be trained to adopt different emotional states, personalities and personas, allowing for a dynamic and highly customizable learning experience. Complex problem-solving exercises, aided by AI, can simulate real-world scenarios, pushing learners to develop innovative solutions. Personalized learning pathways, constructed through an understanding of individual learning styles and needs, allow for targeted growth in specific areas. These tools reflect a paradigm where learning becomes a dynamic, continuous, and creative process, fostering a more connected educational environment. In contributing to the evolving discourse on the future of online education, this chapter illustrates how generative technologies not only complement but also significantly enhance the human element of learning. Therefore, AI should not be viewed merely as a sterile, mechanistic tool; rather, it serves as an empowering ally, infusing the educational landscape with life, empathy, and innovation for the future. This perspective underscores the potential of AI in transforming learning experiences, making them more engaging, personalized, and effective.

PERSONALIZING ONLINE LEARNING

A new era in education has dawned, marked by the robust and versatile capabilities of generative AI like ChatGPT. This era is characterized by the unprecedented ability to leverage these advanced tools for personalized learning, providing real-time feedback, and assisting with administrative tasks, thereby transforming the educational experience. Montagnino (2023) has noted that "Today's educators are pioneers in classrooms where artificial intelligence (AI) is part of daily conversations and students are exploring new ways to write, research, brainstorm, analyze, and complete assignments." These new use cases have coincided with a period of unprecedented disruption in the field. In the wake of the global pandemic of 2020, several interconnected factors have led to the growing demand for more affordable, flexible, and personalized educational options in higher education. One the one hand, pressure has been increasing to modernize academic programs, incorporating career-oriented structures that align with job market demands, enhancing the employability of graduates (Bishop, 2019; Shulock & Offenstein, 2012), while, simultaneously, the need for debt-free education has led institutions to explore alternative funding models to alleviate financial burdens on students (Jones et al., 2020). Alongside this, the emphasis on inclusivity and support services, though often increasing tuition when handled by human agents, aims to create a welcoming environment for all students, enhancing retention and contributing to personalized education (Braumberger, 2021: Counselman Carpenter et al., 2020). Lastly, intensified competition and a focus on tangible results have led to the adoption of data-driven approaches, emphasizing measurable outcomes, thus underlining the need for educational experiences that are not only accessible and adaptable but also in direct alignment with societal and economic demands (Teng et al., 2023; Wingard, 2019).

The disruptive trends impacting higher education institutions appear to present conflicting demands to decision-makers. On one side, there is a call for increased individualized support, greater accessibility, tailored learning experiences, and tangible outcomes like job placement for graduates. Conversely, the push for more affordable college degrees requires innovative solutions, diverging from the traditional approach of hiring additional faculty and support staff to meet students' diverse needs. Fortuitously, these seemingly opposing trends align with the rapid emergence and adoption of generative AI tools, the quickest uptake of new technology in recent memory. LLMs like ChatGPT and Bard are being integrated across all levels of education for various purposes (Skates, 2023). These tools are paving the way for one-on-one education models to become mainstream, as AI technology widens access to personalized services including tutoring, coaching, mentorship, and even therapy (Hernandez et al., 2023; Irby et al., 2023). This alignment demonstrates a serendipitous convergence of technological advancement with educational needs and aspirations.

In fact, generative AI offers a novel solution to the longstanding challenge in education known as Bloom's 2 Sigma Problem, which has persisted for nearly four decades (Bloom, 1984). This problem emerged from a comparison of student performance across different instructional approaches, including traditional classroom instruction, mastery learning, and one-to-one tutoring. The study found that students who received individualized, one-on-one tutoring significantly outperformed those taught in conventional group settings (Sayed et al., 2023). This difference equated to two standard deviations (or two sigma), marking a substantial improvement in learning outcomes. This discovery led to a pivotal question in educational practice: how could the success of one-to-one tutoring be emulated within group instruction environments, considering the limited resources and practical limitations typical of most schools and educational institutions?

Since the framing of the dilemma of the Bloom's 2 Sigma Problem, there has been a concerted effort by educators and researchers to create individualized tutoring strategies through methods like differentiated instruction, adaptive learning technologies, and the integration of active learning techniques (Alarmi et al., 2021; Dejene, 2019; Mulwa et al., 2010). Although these methods enhanced learning outcomes, the obstacles of scaling within a group instruction model and the associated costs of instruction have continued to be challenges—until now. The advent of generative AI and other cutting-edge technologies are bridging this divide, facilitating more personalized and accessible educational experiences for students, even within group environments (Mallik & Gangopadhyay, 2023). Furthermore, AI-powered personalization is not a novel concept confined to the educational sphere. In fact, industry has been leveraging AI for decades to deliver personalized content and recommendations, tailoring services and products to individual user behavior and preferences (Haleem et al., 2022). This approach, which has been employed extensively in marketing and customer service, is now being adapted and refined to meet the unique needs and challenges of modern education.

In solving Bloom's 2 Sigma Problem, therefore, AI has the potential to act as a live tutor for anyone, allowing human experts to focus on providing in-depth subject knowledge and emotional support to learners (Hu et al., 2023). Solutions such as Numerade's AI tutor, Ace, have already begun to demonstrate this, generating tailored study plans based on individual student skill levels and utilizing popular textbooks (https://www.numerade.com/). Trumbore (2023) has built upon this by arguing that the lessons learned from early computer-assisted instruction (CAI) systems like PLATO, as well as intelligent AI tutors like Ace, can inform the current use of digital assistants like ChatGPT as tutors across various levels of education.

Examining what CAI like PLATO has achieved in providing individualized and self-paced instruction in classrooms helps to delineate the learning design possibilities for the newest generation of widely available AI tools. For example, CAI allowed for the automated presentation of instructional material to learners, monitoring their progress, and guiding them to resources or feedback based on immediate needs. This enabled students to work independently and progress at their own rate, while obtaining real-time feedback on their understanding (Cope & Kalantzis, 2023). If a student's response was incorrect, the system encouraged them to revisit the content and make another selection, a feature that was also integrated into electronic textbooks by publishers like Cengage and McGraw Hill in the early 2000s (Brown, 2012). Presently, LLMs are poised to fulfill the role of personal tutors, supplying personalized instruction to a diverse array of learners (Kasneci et al., 2023). By challenging students to revise and expand their work, these digital assistants can boost learning outcomes. Their ability to engage in detailed dialogue and deliver extensive information makes them apt tutors for students of varying skill levels (Pedro et al., 2019).

AI is already well-studied to personalize learning with individualized learning pathways, and this expertise is expanding into various aspects of education. Through precise evaluation of students' abilities and areas needing improvement, AI-powered tools can tailor instructional methods, content formats, and curricula to suit each learner's unique needs (Al-Badi & Khan, 2022). Whether catering to advanced students, those struggling with specific concepts, introverted learners, or individuals with unique learning requirements, LLM can be strategically deployed to support a more diverse and effective educational experience. This transformation goes beyond simple customization, the expanded role of AI in personalization is also leading to innovative approaches to humanizing online instruction. Emotionally intelligent AI are emerging, offering not just tailored content, but a more empathetic and engaging learning environment. This transition represents a substantial advancement in deepening the relationship between learners and their educational journeys. Moving past traditional methods, AI and LLM can now adopt different personalities, emotions, and personas, creating a more nuanced and responsive approach. This not only recognizes but actively engages with the uniqueness of each student, reflecting a more human-centered and individualized way of learning.

EMOTIONALLY INTELLIGENT AI

Central to personalizing and humanizing online learning with AI is the need to first define what we mean by "human." In the traditional physical classroom, the nuanced verbal and non-verbal interactions between students and instructors create a dynamic and engaging environment. These interactions are colored by emotional states, personalities, and personas, leading to unexpected responses and a rich, multifaceted educational experience. In an innovative stride, generative AI now possesses the potential to replicate these emotionally engaging exchanges within the virtual world. This means that the complexities and organic interplay typical of face-to-face communication can be woven into standard online course structures, such as discussion boards, recorded lectures, and assessments.

By imbuing AI with the ability to recognize and respond to emotional cues, and in turn give it a personality with emotional responses, the door is opened to a more connected and humanized form of online learning that echoes the richness of traditional education. This new paradigm promises to bridge the gap between the cold, mechanical nature often associated with virtual learning and the warm, personalized experience that characterizes effective teaching and learning. In the following section, we will explore how emotionally intelligent AI can be utilized to achieve this transformation, focusing on practical applications and the broader implications for the future of education.

Emotionally intelligent AI is a burgeoning field that emphasizes the critical role of emotions in intelligent behavior and decision-making (Duan et al., 2019; Mahmud et al., 2022; Strich et al., 2021). Scholars have underscored the necessity of weaving emotions into artificial cognitive processes, asserting that artificial emotional intelligence is vital for enhancing social interactions (Zall & Kangavari, 2022). The multifaceted exploration in this domain includes research into creating machines capable of empathy, developing AI-enabled systems for emotional communication, and investigating the complex challenges and opportunities associated with artificial emotions in diverse sectors like healthcare and online marketing (Budhwar et al., 2022; Liu-Thompkins et al., 2022; Singh & Chouhan, 2023). Such groundbreaking work has facilitated the infusion of emotions into AI technology, setting the stage for interactions that are more nuanced, sensitive, and aligned with human contexts (Ray, 2023).

The domain of emotionally intelligent AI has opened up multifaceted avenues for exploration, underlining the integral role emotions play in intelligent behavior, decision-making, and the inherent opportunities and obstacles in weaving emotions into artificial intelligence. Research has accentuated the significance of emotions in sculpting human cognition and has called for a more extensive acknowledgment within engineering and computer science disciplines. Insights into the part emotions play in intelligent behavior and decision-making (Selvaraj et al., 2021), along with the vital role emotions hold in enhancing artificial cognitive processes (Jeste et al., 2020), underscore this call.

Conceptual frameworks revolving around socially emotional AI (Samsonovich, 2020) and the endeavor to program machines to display empathy and emotional intelligence (Picard et al., 2004) further emphasize the requisite for artificial emotional intelligence in enabling human-like social interactions. Progress in areas such as AI-driven emotional communication systems (Li et al., 2019) and breakthroughs in synthetic emotional intelligence (Khachane, 2017) reveal the vast application scope, including innovative developments like emotionally aware chatbots. Scrutiny of the ethical dimensions and practical challenges in crafting emotionally intelligent AI (Pusztahelyi, 2020), along with work in bio-inspired social and emotional cognitive systems (Cominelli et al., 2021), illuminate the complex considerations involved.

Recent dialogues on the evolution from emotional AI to cognitive AI (Liu et al., 2019), as well as the importance of robust emotion models (Wortman & Wang, 2022), add further layers to understanding this field's intricacies. In practical applications, proposals to incorporate emotion recognition tools in healthcare (Marcos et al., 2021), and debates regarding the decision-making autonomy of emotional AI systems (Huh & Seo, 2019), mirror the prospective influence and ethical questions in areas like healthcare. The legal and ethical hurdles (Andersson, 2022) further stress the imperative to contemplate foundational rights such as freedom of thought within this framework.

Collectively, this overview of academic insights paints a rich and diverse picture of the emotionally intelligent AI field. It encompasses an array of research interests and thrusts, from understanding emotions' role in cognition to the creation of empathetic machines, and the ethical dimensions that these new frontiers in AI introduce. It encapsulates the transformative potential of emotionally intelligent AI and the nuanced challenges that must be navigated as we seek to harness this potential across various sectors of society.

Socially Emotional AI for Learning

The exploration of emotionally intelligent AI has spanned across diverse domains and has showcased its versatility and impact in various fields. As this burgeoning technology continues to evolve, its potential is now being more purposefully harnessed for educational applications. Leveraging the insights gleaned from research and development in other sectors, the integration of socially emotional AI in learning environments is opening new horizons for enhancing educational experiences and outcomes. This shift not only recognizes the complex interplay of emotions in learning but also introduces innovative methods for personalizing and humanizing education in the digital age.

One approach that can be considered in the realm of Socially Emotional AI for Learning is the Six Emotional Dimension model, or 6DE model, an innovative framework geared toward the in-depth analysis and quantification of human emotions. The 6DE model, developed by Power (2006), encapsulates six emotional dimensions that encompass various facets of emotional experiences. These dimensions not only provide a thorough and nuanced comprehension of emotions but also pave the way for precise examination and replication of emotional states.

By employing this 6DE model, an intricate perspective on emotional experiences can be attained. It facilitates a meticulous analysis of emotional states within text-based interactions, even in the absence of sensory data. This granular approach, taking into consideration these subdimensions, augments the

Table 1. 6DE model, or six emotional dimension model (after Ratican & Hutson, 2023)

Dimension	Description
Arousal	This dimension gauges the activation or energy level connected with an emotion. It fluctuates between low arousal, manifesting in calmness and relaxation, to high arousal, characterized by excitement and anticipation. Arousal primarily focuses on the intensity and physiological reactions tied to emotions, like heart rate or breathing patterns.
Valence	Valence describes the positive or negative essence of an emotion. The spectrum ranges from negative valence, with feelings like sadness and frustration, to positive valence, marked by joy and contentment. It effectively captures the emotional polarity or the affective quality of an experience.
Dominance	Dominance illustrates the control or influence linked with an emotion. It moves from low dominance, signifying submission or passivity, to high dominance, denoting assertiveness. It defines the degree of influence and mastery an individual senses over their emotions.
Agency	This dimension reflects the extent of control one possesses over an emotion. Agency extends from no control, seen in reflexive and involuntary emotions, to full control, where emotions are under conscious choice. It seizes the level of personal command and independence individuals discern over their emotional encounters.
Fidelity	Fidelity evaluates how accurately an emotion mirrors the event or circumstance that induced it. It spans from low fidelity, indicating a mismatch between the emotion and its cause, to high fidelity, showing a strong alignment. It assesses the precision and suitability of emotional reactions to particular triggers.
Novelty	Novelty represents the freshness or unfamiliarity linked with an emotion, ranging from no novelty, typical to habitual emotions, to high novelty, linked with surprising or unprecedented experiences. It captures the surprise factor in emotional reactions.

capability of AI systems to comprehend and produce fitting emotional responses. In turn, this contributes to enhanced user experiences and fosters more effective human-AI dialogues in the educational context (de Carvalho, 2019).

Ratican and Hutson explore (2023) the potential for integration of emotions into AI, particularly with the utilization of the 6DE model, relating the possibilities for the educational sector. The first potential area is in the analysis of the emotional experiences of students. Imagine a classroom where students have just received feedback on their recent exams. The teacher wants to understand how each student feels about their results to provide personalized support and guidance. Using a prompt like "Please describe how you feel about your exam results, and try to express any emotions you're experiencing related to your performance," the teacher gathers responses from the students. The 6DE model can then be used to analyze the emotions expressed. For instance, should a student who describes feelings of excitement and anxiety, the teacher may discern high arousal and possibly negative valence. The teacher might then schedule a one-on-one meeting to discuss strategies to manage anxiety with that student. In another case, a student who feels a mismatch between their emotions and their results may have low fidelity in their emotional response. In response, the teacher could explore whether there were any misunderstandings about the exam content or grading with that student, ensuring that they are aligned with the learning objectives.

Along with this ability to first ascertain emotional states of students, crafting activities and scenarios to generate desired emotional responses is possible. Imagine a history teacher wants to teach a lesson about the American Civil War. They recognize that simply providing facts and dates may not fully engage the students. To create a more immersive and relatable experience, the teacher decides to design an emotionally charged scenario. The teacher selects a specific event from the Civil War, such as a famous battle, and constructs a hypothetical situation where the students must assume the roles of individuals who were part of that event. The prompt might be: "Imagine you are a soldier in the Battle of Gettysburg. You're away from home for the first time, and the sounds of cannons are echoing in the distance. How do you feel? What emotions are you experiencing? Consider factors like arousal, valence, dominance, agency, fidelity, and novelty as you describe your feelings." The students then respond to this prompt, placing themselves in the shoes of a soldier and considering their emotions from the perspective of the 6DE model. Some might focus on the high arousal of anticipation and fear, while others might consider the negative valence of sadness or homesickness. The teacher then engages the students in a discussion about their responses, connecting the emotional experiences to the historical context. This approach transforms the lesson from a dry recitation of facts into a vivid, emotionally resonant experience.

Beyond instructor-student interaction, the integration of AI-assisted learning opens a new frontier in education that can transform the way students interact with content, teachers, and the learning process itself. By personalizing emotional responses, the AI system can become a more responsive and empathetic tutor that caters to the unique emotional profiles of individual students. For example, consider a scenario where an AI tutor is used in a mathematics classroom. Using data and student feedback, the AI can detect a student's frustration with a particular concept, such as algebra. Recognizing the negative valence and potentially low dominance in the student's emotional state, the AI might adapt its teaching approach. An individualized learning pathway can be created, slowing the pace, simplifying the content, and offering more encouraging feedback. A specific prompt from the AI might be: "I see that this concept is a bit challenging. Let's take a step back and go through the basics again. Remember, it's okay to take your time."

In another context, the AI could be employed to teach a more complex subject like philosophy. Recognizing that this subject requires precise alignment and deep engagement, the AI might adopt a personality with higher fidelity, ensuring that the content is presented with accuracy and relevance. A tailored interaction could be: "Let's explore Plato's Allegory of the Cave. Consider how the concept of reality is portrayed and how it resonates with your own understanding of the world." The ability to adapt teaching styles and provide real-time personalized content based on the student's emotional state can create a more resonant and engaging learning experience. It makes the learning process more dynamic and responsive, meeting students where they are emotionally.

Further, by designing AI personalities with varying emotional dimensions, educators can craft unique learning experiences that align with different subjects and learning styles. An AI personality that exudes calmness and high agency might be suitable for meditation and mindfulness training, while an AI with higher arousal and excitement might be ideal for physical education or creative arts. In essence, the potential of integrating the 6DE model with AI in education offers a pathway to a more intuitive, empathetic, and engaging learning environment. It paves the way for education that's not only intellectually stimulating but emotionally resonant, recognizing the importance of emotions in the learning process and using technology to enrich that connection.

STRATEGIES FOR HUMANIZING ONLINE LEARNING

With the emergence of what Clark (2023) termed 'PedAIgogy,' technology has evolved beyond mere access to knowledge and now encompasses creating, modifying, organizing, synthesizing, and evaluating it. This innovative pedagogical method encourages co-creation of multimedia content and fosters complex relationships through collaborative virtual agents. These new automatable capabilities herald a revival of the Socratic approach to knowledge acquisition and application, cultivating the development, analysis, and evaluation of collaboratively created literature, imagery, audio, and video. Moreover, this approach paves the way for novel, interactive learning methods (Pal, 2022). These new AI tools, with their capacity to promote understanding and productivity in relation to emerging technologies, are proving to have a humanizing potential in online education. While the applicability across various domains is evident, a more engaged approach focusing on inquiry, co-creation, and collaboration is essential. Educators and learners alike must actively engage with these AI tools, delving into their capabilities and constraints to extract maximum benefit.

In the quest to humanize online learning environments, integrating AI and collaborative technologies stands as a beacon of innovation and effectiveness. Liang (2022) introduces AI-Enabled SPOC Teaching Strategies, which encapsulate human-machine integration, optimization of teaching resources, and multi-platform collaborative experiences. These strategies are designed to enrich the learning process by leveraging the unique capabilities of both educators and AI technologies, ensuring a more engaging and tailored educational experience.

Another vital aspect of modern online learning is the utilization of machine learning techniques to enhance collaborative learning. Maina, Wagacha, and Oboko (2015) emphasize that these techniques can significantly improve collaborative learning with minimal instructor involvement. By adapting to the needs of students and facilitating a more personalized learning journey, machine learning stands as a cornerstone for developing efficient and responsive educational environments. In the realm of collaborative strategies, Cooper and Burford (2010) highlight the significance of internet technologies like communication tools and discussion forums. These tools are instrumental in fostering student-to-student interaction and are crucial for a dynamic and interactive online learning environment. By encouraging dialogue and collaboration, these strategies not only enrich the learning experience but also contribute to the development of critical thinking and problem-solving skills.

The effectiveness of online collaborative learning is also contingent upon the optimization of course design and teaching methods. Li, Wei, and Zhuo (2022) advocate for a multifaceted approach involving the strengthening of teacher intervention, focus on formative feedback, and adoption of contingency teaching methods. These strategies are geared towards enhancing student satisfaction and maximizing the teaching impact, thus making the learning process more responsive and student-centered. Moreover, the incorporation of digital storytelling into online collaborative learning environments offers a compelling avenue for enhancing student engagement. Nam (2017) discusses how digital storytelling-based strategies can significantly improve aspects of communication, interactivity, and social presence. These strategies not only make the learning experience more engaging but also foster a sense of community and collaboration among learners, effectively bridging the gap between technology and human interaction. Lastly, the role of online collaborative writing in enhancing learning experiences cannot be overstated. Koonj (2020) highlights that collaborative writing not only improves writing skills in L2 learners but also fosters a more profound understanding compared to traditional classroom settings. This strategy exemplifies the power of collective effort and peer interaction in creating a more inclusive and effective learning environment, thereby humanizing the digital educational experience.

This section builds on this research and proposes practical strategies aimed at enhancing personalized engagement in online education and fostering a collaborative exchange between technology and learners. It emphasizes stimulating curiosity in both educators and students, dedicating time to explore, question, and understand AI tools. This includes experimenting with different ways of posing the same question to gather varying perspectives, always acknowledging when an AI tool has been utilized, and never accepting initial results without thorough examination, evaluation, and scrutiny. This approach encourages a deeper exploration of questions that yield both unexpected and anticipated results and promotes an ability to articulate and justify preferences for certain outcomes over others. The emphasis on human engagement, critical thinking, and mindful interaction with AI tools underscores the humanizing potential of these technologies within the educational landscape.

Sample Lessons

In the rapidly evolving educational landscape, the integration of AI offers a unique opportunity to reshape online learning experiences. However, this incorporation brings its set of challenges and considerations. One of the main concerns revolves around the tendency for assignments to fall into a "closed loop" scenario. In such situations, the AI tool provides a prompt, the student responds, and the AI evaluates or generates a response — all without the meaningful involvement of classmates, instructors, or even the deeper cognitive faculties of the student. This leads to a superficial engagement with the material and risks turning educational processes into transactional ones. To avoid this pitfall, assignments must be consciously designed to break this cycle and encourage continuous, iterative engagement with the material or problem at hand. Rather than being the endpoint, AI-generated responses should act as a catalyst, sparking further inquiry and deeper exploration.

In addressing the "closed loop" scenario in AI-integrated assignments and fostering deeper learning, recent research offers a variety of insightful strategies and examples. Daryanavard and Porr (2020) propose embedding deep learning into closed-loop systems while preserving continuous processing, enabling faster and more profound learning experiences. This approach ensures that learning is a dynamic, ongoing process rather than a static loop, fostering continuous engagement and deeper cognitive activity in students. Saunders et al. (2017) emphasize the significance of human oversight or "human-in-the-loop" in AI-integrated learning environments. This strategy involves active participation and intervention by instructors or peers, ensuring that AI does not replace but rather enhances the learning experience by preventing isolation and promoting collaboration and deeper understanding.

Moreover, Parsons and Faubert (2021) discuss the use of EEG-neurofeedback in perceptual-cognitive training paradigms to substantially improve learning speed and degree. This example highlights the potential of integrating biometric feedback mechanisms in AI-integrated assignments to monitor and promote deeper cognitive engagement, thus breaking the closed loop by making learners more aware of their learning processes. Rodríguez et al. (2020) suggest that decision-making systems based on fuzzy logic and machine learning can solve complex management problems, indicating a direction for creating more sophisticated, adaptive AI-integrated learning environments. Such systems can dynamically adjust learning paths based on performance and engagement, ensuring that students are continuously challenged and engaged. Additionally, Bolton, Campbell, and Schmorrow (2007) propose using physiological measures to inform automated decision processes in closed-loop training systems. By understanding the learner's physical responses to various tasks, AI systems can adapt in real-time, providing a more personalized and deeper learning experience.

Lastly, Chen et al. (2018) highlight the importance of privacy-preserving data analysis, knowledge transfer, and machine learning for causal inference in preventing closed-loop scenarios. By ensuring that learning environments are not only adaptive but also secure and responsible, educators and technologists can foster an atmosphere where AI assists in cultivating critical thinking and deeper learning. Together, these strategies and examples from recent research demonstrate a multifaceted approach to breaking the "closed loop" in AI-integrated assignments, emphasizing continuous adaptation, human oversight, biometric feedback, complex decision-making systems, and secure data analysis. By incorporating these elements, educators can ensure that AI serves as a dynamic tool for deepening and enhancing the learning experience.

One primary approach to achieving an engaging assignment is by emphasizing critical thinking, analysis, and metacognitive skills. In the age of information, where AI can generate vast amounts of data and answers, the ability to critically assess and analyze that information becomes paramount. Students should be equipped not just with the knowledge to understand a topic but with the tools to question, evaluate, and interrogate information critically. Swart (2016) emphasizes that technology-enhanced learning environments, such as classroom response systems and online discussion forums, can significantly support students' development of critical thinking and engagement. This implies that assignments in AI-integrated learning should not just be about interaction with AI, but also involve technologies that prompt deeper thinking and interaction with content.

To illustrate, consider a lesson where students are asked to interact with an AI model to generate potential solutions to a contemporary global challenge, such as climate change. Instead of accepting the AI-generated solutions at face value, students could be tasked with:

1. **Comparative Analysis:** Compare and contrast the solutions provided by the AI model with those proposed by human experts in recent articles or publications. This analysis should delve into the strengths, weaknesses, feasibility, and potential impacts of each solution.

2. **Bias Identification:** Investigate and report on any potential biases in the AI's suggestions. Are there certain solutions that seem favored? If so, why might that be the case?

3. **Credibility Assessment:** Using their research skills, students could evaluate the credibility of the sources the AI model might have drawn from. This would involve checking the veracity of facts, understanding the methodology behind studies, and discerning any vested interests or biases in the source material.

4. **Metacognitive Reflection:** Encourage students to reflect on their thought processes throughout this exercise. How did they approach the problem? What biases did they bring into their analysis, and how did they work to mitigate them?

5. **Innovative Assessment Design:** Finally, the assessment should not just evaluate the conclusions the students draw but also the process they used to arrive at those conclusions. By focusing on the journey as well as the destination, educators can foster higher-level thinking skills.

In the midst of an AI-driven era, the role of education must shift from mere knowledge acquisition to skill development. These skills, especially critical thinking, analysis, and metacognition, will prepare students to excel in an increasingly complex world, ensuring that they remain not just consumers of information but also discerning and engaged participants in global dialogues.

Emotionally Intelligent AI Peer Reviewer: A Narrative Example

The preceding offers general considerations in crafting assignments to engage students with AI, but now consider the task of essay feedback – an essential aspect of the academic experience. Traditional AI can correct grammar and structure but lacks the depth to initiate reflective conversations about the content. emotionally intelligent AI, on the other hand, can act as a nurturing tutor, stimulating introspection and guiding students towards better articulation of their ideas. Therefore, this section will present a detailed scenario where students can employ such an intelligent agent, equipped with the 6DE model, as a peer reviewer for their written assignments.

Instead of using AI as a mere search engine that dispenses information, students are instead encouraged to interact with it as they would with a patient tutor, whose goal is to foster enduring, self-sustaining interactions. Berry and Kowal (2022) suggest the role-play strategy in online discussions to support student engagement and critical thinking. By placing students in authentic, real-world contexts and enabling exploration of different perspectives, role-playing can be an effective method to ensure that AI tools are used to stimulate, rather than limit, the learning experience, thereby cultivating a deeper, more engaged learning process. Boothe (2019) further supports the idea that well-designed online discussion groups can enhance learning, critical thinking, and increase student engagement in AI-integrated online learning environments. This implies the need for careful design and implementation of discussion prompts and activities that require critical analysis and creative thinking, making the AI a part of the learning journey rather than the entire path (Boothe, 2019). Such interactions enable students to critically analyze their work, delve deeper into their arguments, and most importantly, reflect on their writing process. Through a series of associated prompts, students are not only asked initial questions about their work but are also prompted to answer follow-up questions. This iterative process mimics the depth and flow of human conversations, ensuring students do not just get feedback but engage in a dialogue about their work.

In the proposed scenario, we will consider a student named Alex who is feeling nervous and unsure about his writing abilities in an online class. He has just finished writing an essay for his course and is unsure of its quality. The instructor of the class, however, has prepared a prompt that students can use at any time day or night to assist in engaging in the task- an AI tutor designed with the innovative 6DE model, imparting it with a semblance of emotional intelligence. The AI, named "Aria," wasn't just any machine given that it was crafted to understand and evaluate not just the content, but also the emotions behind the work of students. Its primary objective? To facilitate introspective, critical, and sustained conversations about a student's work, much like a compassionate peer-reviewer or tutor would. First, the student would paste into a LLM like ChatGPT the prompt found in Table 2.

The student then initiated the conversation and the following conversation unfolds.

Alex: Hey Aria, can you help me review my essay?

Aria: Of course, Alex! I'm here to help. Please paste your essay, and I'll act as a peer-reviewer. Remember, my goal is to guide you in critically analyzing your work, so I'll be asking some questions along the way. Let's embark on this journey together.

[Alex pastes their essay].

Aria: Thank you for sharing, Alex. Before we dive in, could you explain to me the central argument or thesis of your essay? I'd like to understand your perspective better.

[Sustained Interaction]

Alex: Well, I argued that the symbolism in the novel represents the protagonist's internal struggle with identity.

Aria: That's an intriguing perspective. Let's delve deeper. How have you connected the symbolism in the novel to the protagonist's internal struggles? Can you cite specific instances from your essay where you've made this connection?

Alex: I mentioned the recurring motif of the shattered mirror and related it to the protagonist's fragmented sense of self.

Aria: The shattered mirror as a symbol of fragmented identity is a powerful imagery. However, have you provided sufficient context in your essay for readers unfamiliar with the novel to understand this connection? And are there other symbols in the narrative that could further support your thesis?

Alex: I did touch upon the stormy weather mirroring his tumultuous emotions.

Table 2. Emotionally intelligent AI peer reviewer prompt using 6DE model (after Ratican & Hutson, 2023)

Emotionally Intelligent AI Peer Reviewer: Using "Aria" With 6DE Model	
Objective:	**Facilitate Introspective, Critical, and Sustained Conversations About a Student's Work, Similar to a Compassionate Peer-Reviewer or Tutor.**
Instructions:	
1. Start the Conversation	Begin by addressing Aria and expressing your intent, e.g., "Hey Aria, can you help me review my essay?"
2. Share Your Essay	Aria will prompt you to share your essay. Paste your complete essay in response.
3. Explain Your Argument	Aria will then ask for a brief explanation of the central argument or thesis of your essay. Provide a concise summary.
4. Engage with Aria	The AI will ask probing questions about symbols, context, supporting examples, and essay structure.
5. Respond and Reflect	Engage in the iterative conversation. Respond to Aria's queries and anticipate follow-up questions that drive introspection and refinement.
6. Make Revisions	Reflect upon feedback and insights received and revise your essay accordingly.
Note:	Treat Aria not just as a search engine but as a tutor, initiating interactions that are self-sustaining and designed for critical introspection. The aim is deep understanding and work refinement, not quick answers.

Aria: Great! Weather as a reflection of emotional turmoil is a classic literary device. With these symbols in mind, do you think you've provided enough examples and analyses to help your readers fully grasp your point? And how about the structure and formatting of your essay? Is it in the proper APA citation style as required?

The preceding back-and-forth with Aria provided the example student in question revelations about their essay through a series of interactions. The student was prompted to realize that while he had some strong arguments, there were areas where he could provide more depth and context. The iterative and introspective conversation with Aria was not about getting immediate answers but about refining their thought process, evaluating their arguments, and ensuring that their work was presented in the best possible manner. In essence, Aria, with its 6DE model foundation, became more than just a tool; it became a partner in the student's educational journey, challenging them, supporting them, and pushing them to achieve their best.

In considering the experience outlined above, it becomes evident that the potential of emotionally intelligent AI extends far beyond mere transactional interactions. For educators navigating the realm of online instruction, there lies a profound opportunity to harness the capabilities of AI like Aria, rooted in the 6DE model. By carefully curating prompts infused with diverse emotions and tasks, educators can create engaging AI tutors tailored to a myriad of student needs. Such tutors do not just provide feedback; they facilitate profound, introspective dialogues that enable students to confront their assumptions, refine their ideas, and embark on a journey of self-improvement. These dynamic AI-driven conversations can be a cornerstone of modern education, transforming passive learning experiences into active dialogues.

CONCLUSION

The journey towards humanizing online learning demands an innovative and holistic approach that recognizes the centrality of emotions in the educational experience. The traditional model of online education, often criticized for its lack of personal touch and emotional connection, is ripe for transformation. Examples provided by Ratican and Hutson (2023) and others demonstrate the potential use of various emotional models to infuse AI with emotional intelligence presents a path towards this much-needed change. Furthermore, this exploration underlines the importance of understanding, responding to, and even generating emotional states in learners. Analyzing emotional dimensions can provide educators with insights into the needs of students in various learning contexts, enabling more effective and personalized teaching strategies. Creating emotionally responsive scenarios can make learning more immersive and relatable. Integrating AI with the ability to tailor responses and even personalities according to the emotional landscape of the students can make education more engaging and empathetic.

The promise held by emotionally infused AI is demonstrable, but it is only the beginning. The next steps should involve rigorous research to ensure the ethical use of emotional data, the development of reliable models for emotional analysis, and continuous refinement of AI teaching strategies. There must be collaborations between educators, technologists, psychologists, and other stakeholders to ensure that the technology is aligned with educational goals and human values. In the classroom, educators must be trained to utilize these tools effectively, and students must be engaged in a way that respects their autonomy and individuality. Experimentation with different AI personalities, emotional responsiveness, and content tailored to emotional states should be conducted with care, evaluation, and adaptiveness.

Ultimately, the aspiration to humanize online learning through emotionally infused AI transcends mere technological advancement. It reflects a deeper understanding of human nature, a recognition of the role of emotions in learning, and a commitment to creating educational environments where technology serves not just the mind, but the heart as well. By pursuing this path, the field is not just enhancing the efficacy of education; it is enriching its very essence, and in doing so, taking a significant step towards a more compassionate and connected future of learning.

REFERENCES

Addae, D. (2022). Online Student Engagement in Times of Emergency: Listening to the Voices of Students. *E-Learning and Digital Media*.

Adzima, K. (2020). Examining Online Cheating in Higher Education Using Traditional Classroom Cheating as a Guide. *Electronic Journal of e-Learning*, *18*(6), 476–493.

Al-Badi, A., Khan, A., & Eid-Alotaibi. (2022). Perceptions of Learners and Instructors towards Artificial Intelligence in Personalized Learning. *Procedia Computer Science*, *201*, 445–451. doi:10.1016/j.procs.2022.03.058

Alamri, H. A., Watson, S., & Watson, W. (2021). Learning Technology Models that Support Personalization within Blended Learning Environments in Higher Education. *TechTrends*, *65*(1), 62–78. doi:10.1007/s11528-020-00530-3

Alanzi, N. S. A., & Alhalafawy, W. S. (2022). A Proposed Model for Employing Digital Platforms in Developing the Motivation for Achievement Among Students of Higher Education During Emergencies. *Journal of Positive School Psychology*, *6*(9), 4921–4933.

Alenezi, M. (2023). Digital Learning and Digital Institution in Higher Education. *Education Sciences*, *13*(1), 88. doi:10.3390/educsci13010088

Andersson, R. (2022). The Bioeconomy and the Birth of a "New Anthropology". *Cultural Anthropology*, *37*(1), 37–44. doi:10.14506/ca37.1.06

Armellini, C. A., Dunbar-Morris, H., Barlow, A. E., & Powell, D. (2022). Student Engagement in Blended and Connected Learning and Teaching: A View from Students. *Student Engagement in Higher Education Journal*, *4*(2), 165–181.

Azmat, M., & Ahmad, A. (2022). Lack of Social Interaction in Online Classes During COVID-19. *Journal of Materials & Environmental Sciences*, *13*(2), 185–196.

Berry, L., & Kowal, K. (2022). Effect of Role-Play in Online Discussions on Student Engagement and Critical Thinking. *Online Learning : the Official Journal of the Online Learning Consortium*, *26*(3). Advance online publication. doi:10.24059/olj.v26i3.3367

Bishop, M. M. (2019). *Addressing the Employment Challenge: The Use of Postsecondary Noncredit Training in Skills Development*. American Enterprise Institute.

Bloom, B. S. (1984). The 2 Sigma Problem: The Search for Methods of Group Instruction as Effective as One-to-One Tutoring. *Educational Researcher, 13*(6), 4–16. doi:10.2307/1175554

Bolton, A., Campbell, G., & Schmorrow, D. (2007). *Towards a Closed-Loop Training System: Using a Physiological-Based Diagnosis of the Trainee's State to Drive Feedback Delivery Choices.* doi:10.1007/978-3-540-73216-7_47

Boothe, D. (2019). *Discussion Groups and Online Learning.* Cognitive Science – New Media – Education. doi:10.12775/CSNME.2018.005

Braumberger, E. (2021). Library Services for Autistic Students in Academic Libraries: A Literature Review. *Pathfinder: A Canadian Journal for Information Science Students and Early Career Professionals, 2*(2), 86-99.

Brown, B. W. (2012). Vision and Reality in Electronic Textbooks: What Publishers Need to Do to Survive. *Educational Technology,* 30–33.

Budhwar, P., Malik, A., De Silva, M. T., & Thevisuthan, P. (2022). Artificial Intelligence–Challenges and Opportunities for International HRM: A Review and Research Agenda. *International Journal of Human Resource Management, 33*(6), 1065–1097. doi:10.1080/09585192.2022.2035161

Chen, K., He, Z., Wang, S., Hu, J., Li, L., & He, J. (2018). Learning-based data analytics: Moving towards transparent power grids. *CSEE Journal of Power and Energy Systems, 4*(1), 67–82. doi:10.17775/CSEEJPES.2017.01070

Clark, D. (2023). PedAIgogy – New Era of Knowledge and Learning Where AI Changes Everything. *Plan B.* http://donaldclarkplanb.blogspot.com/2023/03/pedaigogy-new-era-of-knowledge-and.html?m=1

Cominelli, L., Hoegen, G., & De Rossi, D. (2021). Abel: Integrating Humanoid Body, Emotions, and Time Perception to Investigate Social Interaction and Human Cognition. *Applied Sciences (Basel, Switzerland), 11*(3), 1070. doi:10.3390/app11031070

Cooper, L., & Burford, S. (2010). Collaborative Learning: Using Group Work Concepts for Online Teaching. In Web-Based Education: Concepts, Methodologies, Tools and Applications (pp. 163-178). IGI Global.

Cope, B., & Kalantzis, M. (2023). A Little History of E-Learning: Finding New Ways to Learn in the PLATO Computer Education System, 1959–1976. *History of Education, 52*(6), 1–32. doi:10.1080/0046760X.2022.2141353

Counselman Carpenter, E. A., Meltzer, A., & Marquart, M. (2020). Best Practices for Inclusivity of Deaf/deaf/Hard of Hearing Students in the Synchronous Online Classroom. *World Journal of Education, 10*(4), 26–34. doi:10.5430/wje.v10n4p26

Daryanavard, S., & Porr, B. (2020). Closed-Loop Deep Learning: Generating Forward Models With Backpropagation. *Neural Computation, 32*(11), 2122–2144. doi:10.1162/neco_a_01317 PMID:32946708

de Carvalho, P. A. C. (2019). *Emojar: Collecting and Reliving Memorable and Emotionally Impactful Digital Content* [Doctoral dissertation]. Universidade de Lisboa.

Dejene, W. (2019). *The Practice of Modularized Curriculum in Higher Education Institution: Active Learning and Continuous Assessment in Focus. Cogent Education, 6(1).*

Duan, Y., Edwards, J. S., & Dwivedi, Y. K. (2019). Artificial Intelligence for Decision Making in the Era of Big Data–Evolution, Challenges and Research Agenda. *International Journal of Information Management, 48*(1), 63–71. doi:10.1016/j.ijinfomgt.2019.01.021

Evans, A. Z., Adhaduk, M., Jabri, A. R., & Ashwath, M. L. (2023). Is Virtual Learning Here to Stay? A Multispecialty Survey of Residents, Fellows, and Faculty. *Current Problems in Cardiology, 48*(6), 101641. doi:10.1016/j.cpcardiol.2023.101641 PMID:36773945

Fung, C. Y., Su, S. I., Perry, E. J., & Garcia, M. B. (2022). Development of a Socioeconomic Inclusive Assessment Framework for Online Learning in Higher Education. In *Socioeconomic Inclusion During an Era of Online Education* (pp. 23–46). IGI Global. doi:10.4018/978-1-6684-4364-4.ch002

Gherheș, V., Stoian, C. E., Fărcașiu, M. A., & Stanici, M. (2021). E-Learning vs. Face-to-Face Learning: Analyzing Students' Preferences and Behaviors. *Sustainability (Basel), 13*(8), 4381. doi:10.3390/su13084381

González Rodríguez, G., Gonzalez-Cava, J. M., & Méndez Pérez, J. A. (2020). An intelligent decision support system for production planning based on machine learning. *Journal of Intelligent Manufacturing, 31*(5), 1257–1273. doi:10.1007/s10845-019-01510-y

Gorgosz, J., & Murphy, M. T. (2021). Making the Impersonal, Personal: Remote Learning During the COVID-19 Pandemic. *American Educational History Journal,* 109-116.

Haleem, A., Javaid, M., Qadri, M. A., Singh, R. P., & Suman, R. (2022). Artificial Intelligence (AI) Applications for Marketing: A Literature-Based Study. *International Journal of Intelligent Networks, 3*(1), 119–132. doi:10.1016/j.ijin.2022.08.005

Hernandez, P. R., Ferguson, C. F., Pedersen, R., Richards-Babb, M., Quedado, K., & Shook, N. J. (2023). Research Apprenticeship Training Promotes Faculty-Student Psychological Similarity and High-Quality Mentoring: A Longitudinal Quasi-Experiment. *Mentoring & Tutoring, 31*(1), 163–183. doi:10.1080/13611267.2023.2164973

Hu, Y. H., Fu, J. S., & Yeh, H. C. (2023). Developing an Early-Warning System Through Robotic Process Automation: Are Intelligent Tutoring Robots as Effective as Human Teachers? *Interactive Learning Environments,* ●●●, 1–14. doi:10.1080/10494820.2022.2160467

Huh, J. H., & Seo, Y. S. (2019). Understanding Edge Computing: Engineering Evolution with Artificial Intelligence. *IEEE Access : Practical Innovations, Open Solutions, 7*(1), 164229–164245. doi:10.1109/ACCESS.2019.2945338

Hutson, J., Steffes, R., & Weber, J. (2023). Virtual Learning Environments and Digital Twins: Enhancing Accessibility, Diversity, and Flexibility in Training Secondary Educational Administrators. *Metaverse, 4*(1), 1–16. doi:10.54517/m.v4i1.2165

Irby, B. J., Pashmforoosh, R., Lara-Alecio, R., Tong, F., Etchells, M. J., & Rodriguez, L. (2023). Virtual Mentoring and Coaching Through Virtual Professional Leadership Learning Communities for School Leaders: A Mixed-Methods Study. *Mentoring & Tutoring*, 31(1), 6–38. doi:10.1080/13611267.2023.2 164971

Janke, S., Rudert, S. C., Petersen, Ä., Fritz, T. M., & Daumiller, M. (2021). Cheating in the Wake of COVID-19: How Dangerous is Ad-Hoc Online Testing for Academic Integrity? *Computers and Education Open*, 2, 100055. doi:10.1016/j.caeo.2021.100055

Jeste, D. V., Graham, S. A., Nguyen, T. T., Depp, C. A., Lee, E. E., & Kim, H. C. (2020). Beyond Artificial Intelligence: Exploring Artificial Wisdom. *International Psychogeriatrics*, 32(8), 993–1001. doi:10.1017/S1041610220000927 PMID:32583762

Jones, T., Ramirez-Mendoza, J., & Jackson, V. (2020). *A Promise Worth Keeping: An Updated Equity-Driven Framework for Free College Programs*. Education Trust.

Kasneci, E., Seßler, K., Küchemann, S., Bannert, M., Dementieva, D., Fischer, F., Gasser, U., Groh, G., Günnemann, S., Hüllermeier, E., Krusche, S., Kutyniok, G., Michaeli, T., Nerdel, C., Pfeffer, J., Poquet, O., Sailer, M., Schmidt, A., Seidel, T., ... Kasneci, G. (2023). ChatGPT for Good? On Opportunities and Challenges of Large Language Models for Education. *Learning and Individual Differences*, 103, 102274. doi:10.1016/j.lindif.2023.102274

Khachane, M. Y. (2017). Organ-Based Medical Image Classification Using Support Vector Machine. [IJSE]. *International Journal of Synthetic Emotions*, 8(1), 18–30. doi:10.4018/IJSE.2017010102

Kim, K., de Melo, C. M., Norouzi, N., Bruder, G., & Welch, G. F. (2020, March). Reducing Task Load with an Embodied Intelligent Virtual Assistant for Improved Performance in Collaborative Decision Making. In *2020 IEEE Conference on Virtual Reality and 3D User Interfaces (VR)* (pp. 529-538). IEEE. 10.1109/VR46266.2020.00074

Koonj, N. (2020). The Impact of E-learning on L2 Learning: A Paradigm of Action Research. *Journal of Literature. Language and Linguistics (Taipei)*. Advance online publication. doi:10.7176/JLLL/68-02

Li, X., Wei, M., & Zhuo, Y. (2022, January). Online Collaborative Learning: Main Forms, Effect Evaluation and Optimization Strategies. In *Proceedings of the 2022 13th International Conference on E-Education, E-Business, E-Management, and E-Learning* (pp. 138-142). 10.1145/3514262.3514322

Li, Y., Jiang, Y., Tian, D., Hu, L., Lu, H., & Yuan, Z. (2019). AI-Enabled Emotion Communication. *IEEE Network*, 33(6), 15–21. doi:10.1109/MNET.001.1900070

Liang, G. (2022, November). Research on SPOC-based Effective Teaching by Artificial Intelligence Technology. In *2022 2nd International Conference on Social Sciences and Intelligence Management (SSIM)* (pp. 99-103). IEEE. 10.1109/SSIM55504.2022.10047942

Liu-Thompkins, Y., Okazaki, S., & Li, H. (2022). Artificial Empathy in Marketing Interactions: Bridging the Human-AI Gap in Affective and Social Customer Experience. *Journal of the Academy of Marketing Science*, 50(6), 1198–1218. doi:10.1007/s11747-022-00892-5

Lytras, M. D., Serban, A. C., Ruiz, M. J. T., Ntanos, S., & Sarirete, A. (2022). Translating Knowledge into Innovation Capability: An Exploratory Study Investigating the Perceptions on Distance Learning in Higher Education During the COVID-19 Pandemic-The Case of Mexico. *Journal of Innovation & Knowledge*, 7(4), 100258. doi:10.1016/j.jik.2022.100258

Mahmud, H., Islam, A. N., Ahmed, S. I., & Smolander, K. (2022). What Influences Algorithmic Decision-Making? A Systematic Literature Review on Algorithm Aversion. *Technological Forecasting and Social Change*, 175, 121390. doi:10.1016/j.techfore.2021.121390

Maina, E. M., Wagacha, P. W., & Oboko, R. O. (2015). A model for improving online collaborative learning through machine learning. In *Models for improving and optimizing online and blended learning in higher education* (pp. 204–219). IGI Global. doi:10.4018/978-1-4666-6280-3.ch011

Malik, K. M., & Zhu, M. (2023). Do Project-Based Learning, Hands-On Activities, and Flipped Teaching Enhance Student's Learning of Introductory Theoretical Computing Classes? *Education and Information Technologies*, 28(3), 3581–3604. doi:10.1007/s10639-022-11350-8 PMID:36189191

Mallik, S., & Gangopadhyay, A. (2023). Proactive and Reactive Engagement of Artificial Intelligence Methods for Education: A Review. *Frontiers in Artificial Intelligence*, 6, 1151391. doi:10.3389/frai.2023.1151391 PMID:37215064

Marcos, S., García Peñalvo, F. J., & Vázquez Ingelmo, A. (2021, October). Emotional AI in Healthcare: A Pilot Architecture Proposal to Merge Emotion Recognition Tools. In *Ninth International Conference on Technological Ecosystems for Enhancing Multiculturality (TEEM'21)* (pp. 342-349). 10.1145/3486011.3486472

May, D., Morkos, B., Jackson, A., Hunsu, N. J., Ingalls, A., & Beyette, F. (2022). Rapid Transition of Traditionally Hands-On Labs to Online Instruction in Engineering Courses. *European Journal of Engineering Education*, 1 19.

McKenzie, L. (2021). Students Want Online Learning Options Post-Pandemic. *Inside Higher Ed.* https://www.insidehighered.com/news/2021/04/27/survey-reveals-positive-outlook-online-instruction-post-pandemic#:~:text=The%20majority%20of%20students%2C%2073%20percent%2C%20%22somewhat%22%20or,offering%20a%20combination%20of%20in-person%20and%20online%20instruction

Montagnino, C. (2023). *Six Ways to Maximize Authentic Learning in the AI Era*. Fierce Education. https://www.fierceeducation.com/student-engagement/six-ways-maximize-authentic-learning-ai-era

Mulwa, C., Lawless, S., Sharp, M., Arnedillo-Sanchez, I., & Wade, V. (2010, October). Adaptive Educational Hypermedia Systems in Technology Enhanced Learning: A Literature Review. In *Proceedings of the 2010 ACM Conference on Information Technology Education* (pp. 73-84). 10.1145/1867651.1867672

Nam, C. (2017). The effects of digital storytelling on student achievement, social presence, and attitude in online collaborative learning environments. *Interactive Learning Environments*, 25(3), 412–427. doi:10.1080/10494820.2015.1135173

Noorbehbahani, F., Mohammadi, A., & Aminazadeh, M. (2022). A Systematic Review of Research on Cheating in Online Exams from 2010 to 2021. *Education and Information Technologies*, 27(6), 8413–8460. doi:10.1007/s10639-022-10927-7 PMID:35283658

Pal, K. (2022). Evaluation of a Scenario-Based Socratic Style of Teaching and Learning Practice. In Enhancing Teaching and Learning With Socratic Educational Strategies: Emerging Research and Opportunities (pp. 121-144). IGI Global. doi:10.4018/978-1-7998-7172-9.ch007

Parsons, B., & Faubert, J. (2021). Enhancing learning in a perceptual-cognitive training paradigm using EEG-neurofeedback. *Scientific Reports*, *11*(1), 4061. Advance online publication. doi:10.1038/s41598-021-83456-x PMID:33602994

Patra, S., & Sahu, K. K. (2020). Digitalisation, Online Learning and Virtual World. *Horizon Journal of Humanities and Social Science*, *2*(1), 45–52.

Pedro, F., Subosa, M., Rivas, A., & Valverde, P. (2019). *Artificial Intelligence in Education: Challenges and Opportunities for Sustainable Development*. Academic Press.

Picard, R. W., Papert, S., Bender, W., Blumberg, B., Breazeal, C., Cavallo, D., Machover, T., Resnick, M., Roy, D., & Strohecker, C. (2004). Affective Learning—A Manifesto. *BT Technology Journal*, *22*(4), 253–269. doi:10.1023/B:BTTJ.0000047603.37042.33

Power, M. J. (2006). The Structure of Emotion: An Empirical Comparison of Six Models. *Cognition and Emotion*, *20*(5), 694–713. doi:10.1080/02699930500367925

Pozo-Rico, T., Gilar-Corbí, R., Izquierdo, A., & Castejón, J. L. (2020). Teacher Training Can Make a Difference: Tools to Overcome the Impact of COVID-19 on Primary Schools. An Experimental Study. *International Journal of Environmental Research and Public Health*, *17*(22), 8633. doi:10.3390/ijerph17228633 PMID:33233750

Pusztahelyi, R. (2020). Emotional AI and Its Challenges in the Viewpoint of Online Marketing. *Curentul Juridic*, *81*(2), 13–31.

Ratican, J., & Hutson, J. (2023). The Six Emotional Dimension (6DE) Model: A Multidimensional Approach to Analyzing Human Emotions and Unlocking the Potential of Emotionally Intelligent Artificial Intelligence (AI) via Large Language Models (LLM). *Journal of Artificial Intelligence and Robotics*, *1*(1), 44–52.

Rippy, M., & Munoz, M. (2021). Designing Authentic Online Courses Intra-and Post-Pandemic. *Online Teaching and Learning in Higher Education During COVID-19*, 13–27.

Samsonovich, A. V. (2020). Socially Emotional Brain-Inspired Cognitive Architecture Framework for Artificial Intelligence. *Cognitive Systems Research*, *60*(1), 57–76. doi:10.1016/j.cogsys.2019.12.002

Saunders, W., Sastry, G., Stuhlmüller, A., & Evans, O. (2017). Trial without Error: Towards Safe Reinforcement Learning via Human Intervention. *ArXiv, abs/1707.05173*.

Sayed, W. S., Noeman, A. M., Abdellatif, A., Abdelrazek, M., Badawy, M. G., Hamed, A., & El-Tantawy, S. (2023). AI-Based Adaptive Personalized Content Presentation and Exercises Navigation for an Effective and Engaging E-Learning Platform. *Multimedia Tools and Applications*, *82*(3), 3303–3333. doi:10.1007/s11042-022-13076-8 PMID:35789938

Selvaraj, C., Chandra, I., & Singh, S. K. (2021). Artificial Intelligence and Machine Learning Approaches for Drug Design: Challenges and Opportunities for the Pharmaceutical Industries. *Molecular Diversity*, 1–21. PMID:34686947

Shulock, N., & Offenstein, J. (2012). *Career Opportunities: Career Technical Education and the College Completion Agenda. Part I: Structure and Funding of Career Technical Education in the California Community Colleges*. Institute for Higher Education Leadership & Policy.

Singh, A., & Chouhan, T. (2023). Artificial Intelligence in HRM: Role of Emotional–Social Intelligence and Future Work Skill. In The Adoption and Effect of Artificial Intelligence on Human Resources Management, Part A (pp. 175-196). Emerald Publishing Limited.

Singh, A., & Sharma, A. (2021). Acceptance of MOOCs as an Alternative for Internship for Management Students During COVID-19 Pandemic: An Indian perspective. *International Journal of Educational Management*, *35*(6), 1231–1244. doi:10.1108/IJEM-03-2021-0085

Skates, A. (2023). Five Predictions for the Future of Learning in the Age of AI. *Everyday AI*. https://a16z.com/2023/02/08/the-future-of-learning-education-knowledge-in-the-age-of-ai/?utm_campaign=GSVN2K&utm_medium=email&_hsmi=245282162&_hsenc=p2ANqtz-

Stöhr, C., Demazière, C., & Adawi, T. (2020). The Polarizing Effect of the Online Flipped Classroom. *Computers & Education*, *147*(1), 103789. doi:10.1016/j.compedu.2019.103789

Strich, F., Mayer, A. S., & Fiedler, M. (2021). What Do I Do in a World of Artificial Intelligence? Investigating the Impact of Substitutive Decision-Making AI Systems on Employees' Professional Role Identity. *Journal of the Association for Information Systems*, *22*(2), 9. doi:10.17705/1jais.00663

Sutiah, S., Slamet, S., Shafqat, A., & Supriyono, S. (2020). Implementation of Distance Learning During the COVID-19 Pandemic in Faculty of Education and Teacher Training. *Cypriot Journal of Educational Science*, *15*(1), 1204–1214. doi:10.18844/cjes.v15i5.5151

Swart, R. (2016). Critical thinking instruction and technology enhanced learning from the student perspective: A mixed methods research study. *Nurse Education in Practice*, *23*, 30–39. doi:10.1016/j.nepr.2017.02.003 PMID:28213153

Tangermann, V. (2023). Get a Load of This New Job: "Prompt Engineers" Who Act as Psychologists to AI Chatbots. *Futurism*. https://futurism.com/prompt-engineers-ai

Teng, Y., Zhang, J., & Sun, T. (2023). Data-Driven Decision-Making Model Based on Artificial Intelligence in Higher Education System of Colleges and Universities. *Expert Systems: International Journal of Knowledge Engineering and Neural Networks*, *40*(4), e12820. doi:10.1111/exsy.12820

Trumbore, A. (2023). ChatGPT Could be an Effective and Affordable Tutor. *The Conversation*. https://theconversation-com.cdn.ampproject.org/c/s/theconversation.com/amp/chatgpt-could-be-an-effective-and-affordable-tutor-198062

Vlasova, H. (2022). Online Education Statistics – How COVID-19 Changed the Way We Learn? *Admissionly*. https://admissionly.com/online-education-statistics/

Whalen, J. (2020). Should Teachers be Trained in Emergency Remote Teaching? Lessons Learned from the COVID-19 Pandemic. *Journal of Technology and Teacher Education, 28*(2), 189–199.

White, S. (2023). *2023 Trends in Online College Education.* https://study.com/resources/online-education-trends

Wingard, D. (2019). Data-Driven Automated Decision-Making in Assessing Employee Performance and Productivity: Designing and Implementing Workforce Metrics and Analytics. *Psychosociological Issues in Human Resource Management, 7*(2), 13–18. doi:10.22381/PIHRM7220192

Wortman, B., & Wang, J. Z. (2022). HICEM: A High-Coverage Emotion Model for Artificial Emotional Intelligence. *arXiv preprint arXiv:2206.07593.*

Zall, R., & Kangavari, M. R. (2022). Comparative Analytical Survey on Cognitive Agents with Emotional Intelligence. *Cognitive Computation, 14*(4), 1223–1246. doi:10.1007/s12559-022-10007-5

Chapter 12
Humanizing Online Instruction With AI–Powered Chatbots and Multimedia Introduction:
Empirical Advice for Online College Classrooms

Lucas John Jensen
ⓘ https://orcid.org/0000-0003-0552-1430
Georgia Southern University, USA

Jackie HeeYoung Kim
Georgia Southern University, USA

ABSTRACT

Given ongoing issues with a lack of humanization in online classroom settings, this chapter shares insights gained through failed implementations of social media, the use of various multimedia introductions, and the utilization of a chatbot to humanize online classrooms. The chapter will discuss why participants did not feel a connection to each other when social networks were used in the classroom and how multimedia introductions built on Web 2.0 tools might increase relatedness among participants. Moreover, it discusses how AI-powered tools provide personalized assistance, such as meeting notes and summarizations, in promoting humanization, increased participation, and a sense of community. The chapter further highlights influential factors in both the failure and success of using multimedia introductions and AI-powered tools in the humanization of online learning, based on authors' experiences, backed by self-determination theory and social presence theory. This chapter concluded with guidelines on how to use these innovative tools to humanize online learning environments.

INTRODUCTION

Online education provides great benefits for learners with regards to flexibility and convenience, capable of delivering content to learners around the globe, as long as they have access to the internet and

DOI: 10.4018/979-8-3693-0762-5.ch012

internet-enabled devices, such as smartphones, tablets, and laptops. As more and more courses offered by post-secondary higher education institutions become asynchronous online experiences, learners are able to access course materials on their own timetables from their own locations. However, the convenience and flexibility offered by online education comes with its trade-offs, particularly in the realms of motivation and engagement. Research on the topic of motivation and engagement in online classes, including that from the authors, indicates that online learners can feel isolated and dehumanized, where they are only a set of names on a screen to either their instructors or their fellow students (Rovai, 2002a; 2002b; Rovai & Jordan, 2004; Philangee & Malec, 2017). This inability to create human connections in the online educational space is a challenge that faces many online instructors and learners alike, and there is evidence that this lack of humanization and human interaction has deleterious effects on learners' ability to engage with online courses. Face-to-face courses often provide the ability for learners to interact with one another and, to a lesser extent, with the instructors, allowing everyone to see each other as fellow human beings with interests and wants. To those in online spaces, and especially asynchronous courses, the learners only know each other from the names and profile pictures provided and whatever tiny amounts of context are doled out via discussion forums and in-course interactions. These limited opportunities for human interaction relegate the learners to passengers on separate parallel vessels, rather than passengers on a single ship, so to speak.

Online Learning and a Lack of Humanization

Though whether it is anomalous compared to traditional face-to-face education is of some question, the perception of online learning is one of high attrition rates (Phirangee & Malec, 2017). Early attempts to explain these attrition rates in online learning environments highlighted a number of factors, including that students felt disconnected from online learning and isolated from each other (Rovai, 2002a; 2002b; Rovai & Jordan, 2004), in part because of a lack of communication and interaction between peers (Carr, 2000). This inability to foster interaction and communication between students can leave students feeling divorced from their online community, lacking the necessary feelings of social presence and being seen as an intellectual equal (Leh, 2001; Tu, 2002; Dunlap & Lowenthal, 2010). One barrier to communication online, according to Kear et al. (2014) is that text-based online environments can be impersonal, lacking in typical face-to-face human interaction cues like "facial expression and tone of voice" (p.1). These human interactions can provide a necessary human connection for online learners, particularly those in asynchronous online environments like online discussion forums, where learners are communicating mostly by text (Kear et al., 2014). Asynchronous online environments and activities can also add time delays between content posting and responses, which further exacerbates a lack of human connection. Philangee & Malec (2017) note that online learning can lead to the othering of other students because students do not see each other as fully-formed human beings, focusing on differences between them rather than similarities. This can have negative effects, especially in terms of building a community: "When online learners perceive or experience feelings of otherness they may encounter identity incongruence, may feel a lack of social presence, and may have a weak sense of community with their peers" (Philangee & Malec, 2017, p. 2). Typical online learning environments are housed in Learning Management Systems (LMSs) and built out of text, lacking much in the way of visual aesthetics. These stand in contrast to the current world of social media like Instagram, Facebook, and TikTok, with their rampant sharing of videos, pictures, and personal information. In a world where some people primarily act through apps built on sharing multimedia content, receiving near-immediate replies from others, these can feel out of step and "school-y," so to speak. As will be discussed later, this lack of connection, social presence, and being understood by others can depress learner motivation and participation. Additionally, the relatedness piece, one of the driving forces of motivation in self-determination theory, might explain why the certain way of technology use resulted in failure. Two theories related to motivation and learning engagement might highlight the importance of humanization and human interaction: Self-Determination Theory and the Theory of Social Presence. In the next section, we will briefly introduce these two theories related to the use of innovative technologies in fostering humanization in online learning.

Theory of Social Presence

Social presence is the degree to which a person is perceived as "real" in mediated communication (Gunawardena & Zittle, 1997; Tu, 2002; Yen & Tu, 2011). In other words, social presence relates to whether participants feel they are interacting with real people in online learning environments, which could be one explanation for the isolation and disconnection from others that learners feel in online courses, as interactions lack facial expressions and body language (Yang et al., 2016). This geographical separation and reduced physical presence involves learners' ability to share who they are both socially and emotionally online, and, similarly to relatedness, have the people on the other side of the computer screen perceive them as "real people" (Boston et al., 2010, p. 68). Online social presence is a significant factor contributing to the improvement of humanization in online learning environments.

According to numerous researchers (Salazar, 2013; Arbaugh & Hwang, 2006; Garrison et al., 2009; Yang et al., 2016), it is adamant that the elements of creating "real people" is not centered on a single focus, rather it is multifaceted. Salazar (2013) previously mentioned that humanizing education is not merely about transferring knowledge, but also ensuring the students' well-being by providing the positive and conducive learning environment where the students feel welcomed, comfortable, accompanied, heard, safe and connected to their peers and teachers. The lesson, then, is conducive to a more humanized learning experience. To achieve students' well-being, Van Houtte (2005) emphasized that interpersonal competence is necessary. In the online learning context, the main actor that should perform interpersonal competence is the teacher, because they are the significant adult in the online circumstance. Thus, creating harmony is a huge task for teachers during online learning. The teacher should be able to create a comforting classroom climate. Thus, we defined students' well-being during online learning as the presence of positive emotions and cognition and the presence of dialog when the students experience negative emotions and cognition. Pacansky-Brock et al. (2020) mention that to be able to establish humanizing online teaching, teachers should have more empathy toward students, provide adjustable teaching and syllabus and provide a secure and judgment-free online learning environment for all students.

Lowenthal and Snelson (2017) found that the term social presence is connected to the actions, such as being salient, being real, being there, projecting oneself, connection, belonging and community. Social presence has three essential aspects, all of which the two featured assignments attempt to elicit: emotional expression, open communication, and group cohesion. Without this sort of expression, the connections between the instructors and students, and between the students themselves, might weaken, resulting in the deterioration of online classroom climate. Many researchers investigated how to foster social presence perceptions among users trying to understand how to optimize opportunities for social presence within the online classroom. A significant portion of this research has centered on enhancing social presence by leveraging features such as the incorporation of personal profiles (Kear et al., 2014), text messages

(DuVall et al., 2007), individualized video feedback (Lowenthal & Dunlap, 2011), and one-on-one email communication (Dunlap & Lowenthal, 2010). Pacansky-Brock et al. (2020) also emphasized instructors' role in social presence, which has a direct connection to humanizing online learning.

Instructor strategies concern specific ways in which an instructor can create social presence (Aragon, 2003). Garrison et al. (2000) coined the term as teaching presence, the preparedness of the teacher to deal with the learning materials, lesson planning and learning assessment (Garrison et al., 2000). Teaching presence is a complex construct that bridges the sense of distance between instructor and student. By scaffolding, modeling, and coaching students, instructors create an environment conducive to the cognitive and social processes required for learning (Arbaugh & Hwang, 2006; Garrison et al., 2009; Yang et al., 2016). Establishing a teaching presence is not only limited to direct instruction, but also through design and organization, and facilitation of discourse, making themselves visible as the instructor in the online learning environment from the student's perspective. The visibility of instructors in any stages of instruction is closely connected to creating "real people." Creating teaching presence requires multimodal instructional methods using a variety of instructional tools, such as videos, audios, that caters to diverse learning styles and needs. Another way of fostering teaching presence is flexibility and adaptability to students' needs (Akyol & Garrison, 2008; Arbaugh, 2008; Saint-Jacques, 2013; Shea & Bidjerano, 2009; Sheridan et al., 2013).

While artificial intelligence (AI) tools are becoming increasingly available, there has been a body of research that found a role of artificial intelligence (AI) tools in establishing social presence. In order to truly understand the ways to enhance *instructor* social presence, it is imperative to know if AI would enhance social presence. Researchers have found the concept of social presence important (Oh et al., 2018), particularly in humans' perceptions about machine agents (Spence et al., 2014). Social presence is not limited to being aware of the other agent; rather, it is a perception of socially and psychologically being involved in the interaction (Biocca et al., 2003). For example, Shin and Choo (2011) note that social presence intensifies the effects of perceived usefulness of robot interactions on favorable attitudes toward the robot.

Self-Determination Theory

In this section, we will discuss the motivational theory Self-Determination Theory, typically associated with the psychologists Edward Deci and Richard Ryan. This theory holds that there are three basic human psychological needs that support intrinsic motivation: autonomy, competency, and relatedness (Ryan & Deci, 2000; Deci & Ryan, 2000; Adams et al., 2017). Intrinsic motivation is the motivation that comes from within because of interest and enjoyment, contrasted with extrinsic motivation, where someone does something because of external rewards or factors (Ryan & Deci, 2000). Extrinsic motivation is guided by external rewards, which diminishes people's autonomy and thus their intrinsic motivation (Ryan & Deci, 2000; Deci & Ryan, 2000; Adams et al., 2017). Self-Determination Theory holds that intrinsic motivation is powerful, and it comes from satisfying these three needs in conjunction with one another.

As mentioned above, *autonomy* is an important component of self-determination, as it means feeling in control over one's goals, outcomes, and behaviors (Ryan & Deci, 2020). People feel motivated when they have a sense that what they are doing matters and will lead to real change. For example, if a student in a class gets to choose the subject of a project versus being assigned it, that might have a motivational effect.

Competency works closely with autonomy (Ryan & Deci, 2000) in influencing intrinsic motivation. When people feel competent, like they have the skills and/or the knowledge to achieve their goals, they will be more intrinsically motivated. For example, learners struggling with online course technology might disengage from the whole course, demotivated because of their lack of technology skills regarding the Learning Management System made them feel less competent.

While all three are important to intrinsic motivation, it is the *relatedness* component–the intrinsic "desire to be connected to others" (Deci and Ryan, 2000, p.231) that will be the focus of this chapter. If humans lose the ability to feel this connection and be related to, then that can have a negative effect on their intrinsic motivation, the powerful kind of motivation that comes from within, eschewing external goals (Ryan & Deci, 2000; Deci & Ryan, 2000; Adams et. al, 2017). These assignments offer a chance for students to gain relatedness to their instructors and/or other classmates, a chance for them to share who they are as humans and recognize the humanity of others.

Humanizing in this context might be described as adding a human face to the online course in order to increase personal connections between learners and between learners and the instructor. This humanizing might be seen as an attempt to increase relatedness, to feel understood and connected by others. In the authors' research and in their observation after decades of online teaching, they have observed that without relatedness among students, participation, motivation, and engagement are low. Online instruction, typically housed within aesthetically plain and sometimes confusing Learning Management Systems (LMSs), can feel more like filling out digital gradebooks than platforms for communication between students and instructors. Knowing that the other names in this digital gradebook are fellow human beings with similar interests, career goals, locations, sports teams, pets, and more might make the students feel more connected to one another, possibly increasing relatedness and thus intrinsic motivation. Greater relatedness could mean the possibility for greater willingness to participate in course behaviors that require more communication, such as discussions, reaching out for help, finding collaborators, and accomplishing group tasks.

Twitter Failure and Humanization

The authors arrived at this issue based on the failure of previous attempts to ameliorate the problems of motivation, engagement, and humanization in classroom settings, both face-to-face and online (Kim & Jensen, 2019). In one case, one of the authors oversaw a failed implementation of social media into the classroom: an attempt to use Twitter and its hashtag functionality to connect students from multiple classes in a larger discussion was met with indifference, if not outright hostility, from students, even though most of them were social media users (Jensen, 2015). Five courses of the same section used a communal hashtag on each one of their tweets, which was meant to make it easier for the students in the course to find individual posts. Even though the assignment was worth five points, most students failed to even tweet the relatively low requirement of ten tweets with the hashtags. Most tweets were short, superficial, and preferred pictures over substantive text. The engagement between students was even more non-existent than the content quality, as the only interaction between them was in the form of retweets, where a Twitter user posts another tweet to their feed. In fact, not a single student in the five courses used Twitter's reply functionality during the course of the research. While this was supposed to replace the often stilted conversations in typical online discussion forums, it failed to generate any discussion at all. The single tweet with the most engagement in terms of likes and retweets begged "let's get this trending" and hashtagged the university and its football mascot. By any measure, this attempt to replace online discussion forums with Twitter hashtags was a failure in terms of meeting its instructional goals (Jensen, 2015; Kim & Jensen, 2019).

This research project made a few miscalculations, most notably the assumption that Twitter was much more popular than it was with these undergraduate students than it was. Though they were surveyed on their preferences at the beginning of the course, showing that Facebook, Snapchat, and Instagram were all more popular, the decision to move forward with Twitter as the social media platform was made by the researchers and instructors. The research was built on the notion of Personal Learning Environments, wherein students might be more engaged by online course materials if they are more congruent with their own personal technology use, allowing some autonomy in how they built their own digital learning environment (Martindale & Dowdy, 2010; Sclater, 2008; Van Harmelen, 2008). At the very least, they should feel some ownership over the technology integrated into the course.

By choosing a platform that was not amenable to a large majority of the students, the project stripped them of this autonomy and ownership. And it was not just being unfamiliar with Twitter. A few students even felt antipathy toward Twitter, including some who had already used it and subsequently rejected it. There was a sense that many students did not like their educational sphere invading their personal space, and this was evident in the fact that many students created new Twitter accounts for this project, removing all personal information and tweets about their own interests outside of school. This had the effect of making all social media profiles fairly anonymous, and all tweets were obligatory and related to the course. This attempt at humanization was actually dehumanizing, in that it stripped away the personality and depth from each user, turning them into names and not much more, cyphers that portrayed little of their interests and hobbies through Twitter. Unlike a face-to-face course, where students might learn bits of information about each other over the course of a semester, no one interacted with each other online, so little was learned about each other. Nobody engaged in a conversation with another student on the hashtag during the semester, in an assignment that was meant to supplant a more typical online discussion forum.

One of the issues that emerged from research was that the participants did not feel a connection to each other because the Twitter accounts were only used for school purposes. Relatedness, a sense of connectedness and belongingness, is an innate psychological need and a necessary component of intrinsic motivation (Ryan & Deci, 2000). This lack of a relatedness and failed attempts at humanization possibly decreased intrinsic motivation. The anonymous profiles and tweets only related to class did little to humanize other students, and they related with little of the content that they saw on the hashtag, usually pictures. In fact, pictures of the classroom and classmates were usually the most popular posts, in terms of likes and retweets, suggesting the importance of seeing another student, in the flesh, so to speak. While it could be argued that retweeting pictures is one of the easiest interactions to do on Twitter, it demonstrates, in our view, the fact that seeing each other and relating to one another was important in terms of what content they allowed to enter their own Twitter feeds. This aligns with the general lack of relatedness that arose in interviews, surveys, and the nature and lack of Twitter activity itself.

Maximizing Element of Humanization in the Classroom Through Multimedia Introductions

The aforementioned failure to integrate a social media platform, Twitter (now known as X), into the online portions of a classroom, replacing typical online discussion forums, highlights the possible importance of relatedness in motivating students to participate in online course activities. Given this failure, plus the authors' years of teaching online and observing student demotivation through lack of humanization, the authors have attempted to mitigate the issue of student dehumanization in their own online classes through a number of activities, which will be elucidated in this chapter.

The first thing that the one of the authors did to address the problem of lack of humanization and isolation was to take the time to humanize themselves at the beginning of the course. It may sound simple and common sense, but taking the time to show that the instructor, the person behind the curtain, so to speak, is a human, too, will make the instructor and course more approachable, lowering the barriers students often have in communicating their needs and struggles. This humanizing exercise should be more than a visual syllabus or welcome video, though those can be very helpful, too. The tools and methods of delivery, while important, are not so important as demonstrating self-expression through technology. The author modeled this assignment in Adobe Express by creating a multimedia narrative of their life as both an academic and a person outside the classroom and academic life, including previous unique jobs (e.g., crawfish cook and paper delivery person), pets, artistic and musical interests, and sports team fandoms. Copious amounts of photos, links to external sites, and videos were used, all accompanied by commentary from the instructor. The attempt here is to show that the instructor is more than a person who grades assignments and manages course materials, whose hand in administering the course is largely unseen. The author has received feedback from students that this multimedia sharing of personal information brings something of a simulacrum of face-to-face interaction, and the reactions have been uniformly positive, usually expressing excitement to learn from someone who has human traits like them. Conversations have arisen between student and instructor over subjects like favorite bands, video games, raising chickens, and so much more, all spurred on by taking the time to create an in-depth, humanizing profile.

While the discussion of pets with students might seem banal, there is some evidence that creating a personal profile can increase social presence with students. For example, in two separate studies, Kear et al. (2014) found that creating personal profiles, complete with self-descriptions and accompanying pictures, caused some students to feel more connected to one another, though some worried about privacy issues and breaking the boundaries between the personal and the professional. Skeels and Grudin (2009) looked to existing social media sites like Facebook and LinkedIn, where every user has a personal profile of sorts, as a way of building rapport. In interviewing 105 community college instructors, Li et al. (2021) found that instructors, when asked how they might improve their teaching, considered increasing communication and "humanizing student-instructor interaction" (p. 19) a way to increase personal connection for the students to the course, with responses such as "I think it is very important to make personal contact with students" (p.19-20) and "[students want] instructors who are open to letting their students know them as people" (p. 20).

This assignment spurs the students on as they are asked to create their own multimedia introductions, using sites like Canva, Adobe Express, Animaker, Powtoon, Storyjumper, and Google Sites. Similar to the instructor, they discuss their work, families, pets, interests, and more. Generally, they are asked to discuss their previous experience with the course subject, but there are few limitations or instructions given. The instructor's rather long multimedia narrative does tend to set the tone for the student responses, but students are encouraged to be creative and, if at all possible, use a technology that is new to them. Students do everything from videos to screencasts to single-subject websites to infographics. These are expected to be detailed, personalized multimedia introductions at the beginning of the course, attaching their personalities and experiences to their names, which benefits both fellow students and the instructor in terms of relatedness and social presence. It is important to note that tudents are not asked to share more than they are comfortable sharing.

The online instructor often has little to distinguish students beyond their names and, though it might not substitute for the face-to-face classroom, this does give them greater distinguishing characteristics, in addition to learning things about each one of them that might come in useful during instruction. The authors can learn about the fears of online students from these introductions, quite often fears of technology usage and online education, which are helpful to know about and fairly common. These can help the instructor identify and pay special attention to those students who need more guidance through the sometimes overwhelming learning environment of an LMS.

Similarly, for students, learning that other students have the same fears and interests often serves a comforting factor for the anxiety that affects some online learners, especially new students, who can be confused by navigation of an LMS. The authors have observed students striking up quick acquaintance-ships with one another in the forum posts underneath each multimedia introduction, guided to another student based on shared hobbies and interests, closeness in geography, musical tastes, professional concerns, and more. In classes with group projects, many of the groups are formed in these moments, as students identify peers whose goals, professional and/or personal, align with theirs. Though there is no way to prove this, this method of group formation based on these humanizing presentations, while rather unstructured, seems to produce mostly viable groups in terms of internal dynamics, certainly no worse than previous experiences in that arena.

This has an additional pedagogical benefit in that it gets students creating and sharing instructional technology products early in the semester, getting comfortable with the technology, the design process, and being creative–and sharing creative products. Many of the students, undergraduate and graduate alike, are relatively new to online education, and online students can be overloaded with information, the LMS interface, and the lack of community, diminishing participation (Vonderwell & Zachariah, 2005). This view toward meeting the three central needs of Self-Determination Theory extends throughout many of the authors' courses, which often feature constructionist assignments, where students build artifacts of their learning and share them, usually in the form of multimedia, like animations, videos, online courses, infographics, interactive quizzes, video games, and more.

Another method with which the authors have attempted to address dehumanization in the online classroom is through the use of Otter.AI. The author initially observed that only a few people attended the Zoom office hours, despite the instructor's efforts to create an inviting environment. However, the introduction of Otter.AI has apparently changed this trend and improved attendance. In this chapter, the authors will explore how exactly it influenced the attendance and how its specific features make the Zoom office experience more humanizing.

AI-powered Tools and Humanization

AI can be considered a system, machine, or computer that imitates human intelligence (Muggleton, 2014) in complex processes such as learning and problem-solving (Russell & Norvig, 2010). It is also defined as operating like human intelligence for learning, cognitive problem-solving, and model recognition (Ma et al., 2014). AI-powered tools provide personalized and flexible learning environments, which are among the most important advantages of artificial intelligence in education (Chounta et al., 2022; Pokrivčáková, 2019). The personalization process involves specific mechanisms that enable interaction with the learner by differentiating the process, feedback, and outcomes. Students generate new information through mutual feedback interaction (Jou et al., 2016). Three categories of educational AI technologies were established by Baker and Smith (2019): learner-facing, teacher-facing, and system-facing AI. Learner-facing AI tools encompass tools that students utilize to study any subject. Teacher-facing AI tools are for teachers who employ artificial intelligence (AI) systems to make evaluation, feedback, and administration. System-facing AI tools are preferred by administrators and principals for institutional process monitoring. Considering AI-powered tools, Diffusion of Innovation Theory (Berger, 2005) helps us think differently with innovative tools when generating alternative solutions to problems to meet individual and institutional needs. Many times innovation makes us think to utilize a previously unknown concept or design that an individual or organization has not used before (Berger, 2005). Use of innovation can generate alternative options to meet student needs and interests. The following section discusses how a professor used the innovative tool to offer an alternative way, which became an effective tool for increased participation and adaptability, which are key elements of humanization.

Experiences With an AI-Powered Tool to Humanize Online Instruction

Student attendance during college professor office hours can vary widely depending on various factors, such as the size of the class, the professor's popularity, the relevance of the office hour topic, and the overall engagement and motivation of students. It may be that the popular professors have a higher attendance rate, but the authors' office hour attendance rate has been relatively low, or even zero, in both in-person and virtual with only a small percentage of students taking advantage of the opportunity to meet with me. Being online students, the authors' students were challenged with conflicting schedules and hesitance to seek help or engage in additional discussions. The authors actively advocated for and encouraged student participation, crafting topics that are both challenging and relevant. Until recently, it had not occurred to me that some students may prefer alternative forms of communication or seek assistance through generative AI. However, recently, the authors' Zoom office hours attracted more than eight students at a time. One of the students plugged Otter.AI into the Zoom office hour session, and others joined Otter.ai. From that moment, the office hours proliferated, with more than 13 students at a time attending. The introduction of generative AI, a novel addition to the authors; technological repertoire, offered a fresh perspective to the use of technology in teacher-student interactions, notably increasing participation in the virtual environment.

Otter.ai is an AI-powered transcription service that converts spoken content such as meetings, interviews, lectures, and other spoken interaction, into written text. It utilizes machine learning and speech recognition technology to transcribe audio in real-time, providing accurate and searchable transcripts. It has recording capability for live conversation as well as storing pre-recorded audio files to obtain written transcriptions for various purposes, including note-taking, documentation, accessibility, and more. The range of the use of Otter.ai is wide from personal use for assisting with their daily tasks, work, and personal activities as well as professional use for transcribing business meetings, conferences, and seminars. It helps capture and organize key points, action items, and discussions. Individuals with hearing disabilities use Otter.ai to transcribe audio content, making it accessible and allowing them to read conversations. People using English as a second language can use Otter.ai to learn languages by transcribing spoken conversations.

The most effective feature of this chatbot is to capture and organize key points. This chatbot's functions, quick summarization and delivery of key points, allows students to participate in meetings easily and to achieve the purpose with a blink of time. The economy of these functions, the comprehensive overview of the class content in a brief moment of time, efficiently serves students who are in the constant chase of time in the hectic schedules. With the ability to provide time-stamped references, the chatbot enables participants to navigate directly to specific points in recorded meetings or lessons, making it efficient to locate and review relevant information.

Otter.AI provides a convenient alternative to attending a scheduled office hour meeting, particularly when faced with conflicting commitments in students' calendar. This alternative not only boosts participation rates but also contributes to heightened social presence by fostering communication, engagement, and a sense of community among students. In contrast to full virtual participation, it represents a form of partial, delayed, or focused engagement. This is facilitated through the chatbot, which generates personalized and indirect participation opportunities. This approach allows students to interact in a manner that suits their schedules and preferences.

Given the features and functions that allow participants to make up the lost time, the chatbots offer personalized assistance. Students who may have missed the live session or need a quick review can easily catch up, reducing the risk of anxiety of potentially missing out information. Knowing that meeting notes will be summarized and shared, students may feel more encouraged to actively attend the Zoom office hour. The economy of online classes, least effort and greater outcomes, lure students who are constrained by time and limited by hectic schedules due to other personal and professional commitments. Shared access to summarize meeting notes creates a sense of community among students.

In this regard, the chatbot's assumed role as the means that can increase adaptability of learning mechanisms to meet students' needs or ease anxiety of potential information gaps. This chapter argues that one of the main features of AI-powered tools is that they provide personalized results, such as the meeting notes and summarizations, which would promote teaching presence in many ways. The support and interaction that results from a robust teaching presence can improve the sense of social community in the classroom, improving student satisfaction and learning (Liaw & Huang, 2013; Skylar, 2009). As students refer to the same set of notes, they develop a shared experience, reinforcing the idea that they are part of a larger academic community despite the virtual nature of the classroom. For students who miss a class, having summarized meeting notes ensures they can catch up on the class information efficiently.

This support reduces feelings of isolation for absent students and maintains their connection to the ongoing discussions in the online classroom. It contributes to an inclusive and collaborative learning environment, ultimately enriching the overall educational experience for students in the virtual classroom setting. The use of chatbot has a great potential to unleash social presence by improving participants' chances to identify with the community and communicate purposefully (Garrison, 2009), being a regular attendees of the scheduled meetings indirectly.

Guidelines for Curbing Dehumanizing Factors With Technology Tools

Throughout this chapter, we summarized the theories and our experiences related to humanizing technology tools. Thus, we would like to offer overarching guidelines in this section, using insights learned from our experiences with these tools.

- Whenever possible, lean towards self-expression and letting students choose what (relatedness) and how (competency) to share it.
- Self-expression might increase relatedness by sharing and viewing what others are sharing. It makes it a more human, less isolated, space.

- Using Web 2.0 technology tools such as Canva, Adobe Express, and Google Sites also increases autonomy and competency in that the learners have control over how they express themselves, using the tools that they know best.
- Recognize the crucial role of AI tools in fostering teaching presence, one of humanizing elements in the online settings, by facilitating communication, engagement, and a sense of community in an online learning environment.
- From the planning stage of the course construction, consider integrating AI-powered tools, such as chatbots or transcription services, for virtual office hours and online lectures to increase teaching presence by offering multimodality of participation.
- Use AI tools to ensure inclusivity by providing alternative ways for students to participate. Recognize that not all students may prefer or be able to attend the scheduled live sessions. AI-generated summaries offer an inclusive solution, which will increase the participant rate and the sense of belonging.
- Acknowledge the role of AI tools in supporting students with conflicting schedules. The efficiency of AI-generated summaries has the ability to address the needs of students managing busy schedules and other personal or professional commitments.

CONCLUSION

Humanizing online learning environments involves multifaceted elements, ranging from various teacher and student discourse styles to teaching presence to ways of course facilitation. As outlined in this chapter, emerging technology tools, whether AI-powered or multimedia Web 2.0 tools used for introduction, should be considered in any attempt to humanize online learning, recognizing their roles in different contexts from traditional learning settings. Given the magnitude of theories on humanizing online learning, we argue that a positive social-emotional climate (Garrison, 2017) and teaching presence (Anderson et al., 2001) are significant factors to humanizing online learning. These tools can be instrumental to increase comfortability in social-emotional climate (Parker & Herrington, 2015) and teaching presence. Furthermore, these tools can be used to break down barriers between instructors and students and between students themselves. These innovative tools create a user-friendly learning environment, build positive rapport between teachers and students, give students a sense of belonging, and promote a sense of purpose. Moreover, these tools can play a critical role in "the design, facilitation, and direction of cognitive and social processes (Anderson et al., 2001, p.5)" while increasing teaching presence, which bridges the sense of distance between instructor and student (Arbaugh & Hwang, 2006; Garrison et al., 2009; Yang et al., 2016).

This more welcoming environment, one where students and instructors share aspects of their lives via multimedia introductions at the beginning of the course, might fulfill students' innate need for relatedness within the online classroom, hopefully increasing intrinsic motivation, according to Self-Determination Theory (Deci & Ryan, 2000; Ryan & Deci, 2000). Sharing personal profiles and interests at the beginning of the course can break down communication barriers between students and between students and instructors, making it easier for students to ask for help and collaborate with one another (Kear et al., 2014). Traditionally text-based online environments in LMSs can be overwhelming and isolating for students, so this added dose of personhood can humanize the online course, allowing everyone in the course to relate to one another on a human level, beyond a list of names in the course. The authors' courses are project-based technology courses, so the creation of these multimedia introductions have the knock-on effect of providing an early use of technology, to help the students feel comfortable with the tools that will be used in the courses.

As the advent of AI-powered tools, the integration of AI-powered tools emerges as a strategic approach to elevate connection, inclusion, and the enriched sense of purpose by providing a multimodal avenue for student participation. The utilization of AI tools increase the probability to attend the meetings and lectures by offering an alternative means of participation for online students who may face constraints in attending live sessions. This inclusive solution not only increases participant rates but also fosters a deeper sense of belonging among students, contributing to building a learning community. In embracing the multifaceted benefits of AI tools, educators are poised to create a more dynamic and inclusive online learning environment. The strategic incorporation of these tools during the planning phase not only amplifies teaching presence but also aligns with the principles of humanizing education in the digital era. As we continue to navigate the landscape of virtual education, the thoughtful integration of AI tools stands as a key element in cultivating engaging, accessible, and student-centric online learning experiences.

By using these guidelines and suggestions provided in this chapter to inform their instructional practices, educators will be able to improve social presence and relatedness, providing educators with meaningful opportunities to learn and explore new ways to instruct online courses, motivating and engaging students in the process. Our hope is that this information will be used to inform practice and to stimulate future research into best practices for humanizing in online classrooms in the postsecondary education.

REFERENCES

Adams, N., Little, T. D., & Ryan, R. M. (2017). Self-Determination Theory. In M. Wehmeyer, K. Shogren, T. Little, & S. Lopez (Eds.), *Development of Self-Determination Through the Life-Course*. Springer. doi:10.1007/978-94-024-1042-6_4

Akyol, Z., & Garrison, D. R. (2011). Understanding cognitive presence in an online and blended community of inquiry: Assessing outcomes and processes for deep approaches to learning. *British Journal of Educational Technology*, *42*(2), 233–250. doi:10.1111/j.1467-8535.2009.01029.x

Anderson, T., Liam, R., Garrison, D. R., & Archer, W. (2001). Assessing teaching presence in a computer conferencing context. *Journal of Asynchronous Learning Networks*, *2*(5), 1–17.

Aragon, S. R. (2003). Creating social presence in online environments. *New Directions for Adult and Continuing Education*, *100*(100), 57–68. doi:10.1002/ace.119

Arbaugh, J. B. (2008). Does the community of inquiry framework predict outcomes in online MBA courses? *International Review of Research in Open and Distance Learning*, *9*(2), 1–21. doi:10.19173/irrodl.v9i2.490

Arbaugh, J. B., & Hwang, A. (2006). Does "teaching presence" exist in online MBA courses? *The Internet and Higher Education*, *9*(1), 9–21. doi:10.1016/j.iheduc.2005.12.001

Baker, T., & Smith, L. (2019). *Educ-AI-tion rebooted? Exploring the future of artificial intelligence in schools and colleges*. Nesta. https://media.nesta.org.uk/documents/Future_of_AI_and_education_v5_WEB.pdf

Berger, S. (2005). *How we compete: What companies around the world are doing to make it in today's global economy.* Crown Currency.

Biocca, F., Harms, C., & Burgoon, J. K. (2003). Toward a more robust theory and measure of social presence: Review and suggested criteria. *Presence (Cambridge, Mass.)*, *12*(5), 456–480. doi:10.1162/105474603322761270

Boston, W., Diaz, S., Gibson, A., Ice, P., Richardson, J., & Swan, K. (2010). An exploration of the relationship between indicators of the Community of Inquiry framework and retention in online programs. *Journal of Asynchronous Learning Networks*, *14*(1), 67–83.

Carr, S. (2000). As Distance Education Comes of Age, the Challenge Is Keeping the Students. *The Chronicle of Higher Education*, *46*(23).

Chounta, I. A., Bardone, E., Raudsep, A., & Pedaste, M. (2022). Exploring teachers' perceptions of Artificial Intelligence as a tool to support their practice in Estonian K-12 education. *International Journal of Artificial Intelligence in Education*, *32*(3), 725–755. doi:10.1007/s40593-021-00243-5

Deci, E. L., & Ryan, R. M. (2000). The" what" and" why" of goal pursuits: Human needs and the self-determination of behavior. *Psychological Inquiry*, *11*(4), 227–268. doi:10.1207/S15327965PLI1104_01

Dringus, L. P., Snyder, M. M., & Steven, R. T. (2010). Facilitating discourse and enhancing teaching presence: Using mini audio presentations in online forums. *The Internet and Higher Education*, *13*(1-2), 75–77. doi:10.1016/j.iheduc.2009.11.001

Dunlap, J. C., & Lowenthal, P. R. (2009). Tweeting the Night Away: Using Twitter to Enhance Social Presence. *Journal of Information Systems Education*, *20*(2), 129–135.

DuVall, J. B., Powell, M. R., Hodge, E., & Ellis, M. (2007). Text messaging to improve social presence in online learning. *EDUCAUSE Quarterly*, *30*(3), 24.

Garrison, D. R., Anderson, T., & Archer, W. (1999). Critical Inquiry in a Text-Based Environment: Computer Conferencing in Higher Education. *The Internet and Higher Education*, *2*(2–3), 87–105. doi:10.1016/S1096-7516(00)00016-6

Garrison, D. R., Anderson, T., & Archer, W. (2000). Critical inquiry in a text-based environment: Computer conferencing in higher education. *The Internet and Higher Education*, *2*(2), 87–105.

Gunawardena, C. N., & Zittle, F. J. (1997). Social presence as a predictor of satisfaction within a computer-mediated conferencing environment. *American Journal of Distance Education*, *11*(3), 8–26. doi:10.1080/08923649709526970

Jensen. (2015). *Building relatedness through hashtags: social influence and motivation within social media-based online discussion forums* [Doctoral dissertation]. University of Georgia.

Jou, M., Lin, Y. T., & Wu, D. W. (2016). Effect of a blended learning environment on student critical thinking and knowledge transformation. *Interactive Learning Environments*, *24*(6), 1131–1147. doi:10.1080/10494820.2014.961485

Kear, K., Chetwynd, F., & Jefferis, H. (2014). Social presence in online learning communities: The role of personal profiles. *Research in Learning Technology*, *22*, 22. doi:10.3402/rlt.v22.19710

Kim & Jensen. (2019). Pedagogical cases in integrating technology into instruction: What can we do to celebrate failure? In S. Keengwe & Bull, H. (Eds.), *Handbook of Research on Innovative Pedagogies and Best Practices in Teacher Education*. Hershey, PA: IGI Global.

Leh, A. S. C. (2001). Computer-Mediated Communication and Social Presence in a Distance Learning Environment. *International Journal of Educational Telecommunications*, *7*(2), 109–128.

Li, Q., Zhou, X., Bostian, B., & Xu, D. (2021). How Can We Improve Online Learning at Community Colleges?: Voices from Online Instructors and Students. *Online Learning : the Official Journal of the Online Learning Consortium*, *25*(3). Advance online publication. doi:10.24059/olj.v25i3.2362

Liaw, S. S., & Huang, H. M. (2013). Perceived satisfaction, perceived usefulness and interactive learning environments as predictors to self-regulation in e-learning environments. *Computers & Education*, *60*(1), 14–24. doi:10.1016/j.compedu.2012.07.015

Lowenthal, P. R., & Dunlap, J. C. (2018). Investigating students' perceptions of instructional strategies to establish social presence. *Distance Education*, *39*(3), 281–298. doi:10.1080/01587919.2018.1476844

Lowenthal, P. R., & Snelson, C. (2017). In search of a better understanding of social presence: An investigation into how researchers define social presence. *Distance Education*, *38*(2), 141–159. doi:10.1080/01587919.2017.1324727

Ma, W., Adesope, O. O., Nesbit, J. C., & Liu, Q. (2014). Intelligent tutoring systems and learning outcomes: A meta-analysis. *Journal of Educational Psychology*, *106*(4), 901–918. doi:10.1037/a0037123

Martindale, T., & Dowdy, M. (2010). Personal Learning Environments. *Emerging Technologies in Distance Education*, 177–193.

Muggleton, S. (2014). Alan Turing and the development of Artificial Intelligence. *AI Communications*, *27*(1), 3–10. doi:10.3233/AIC-130579

Oh, C. S., Bailenson, J. N., & Welch, G. F. (2018). A systematic review of social presence: Definition, antecedents, and implications. *Frontiers in Robotics and AI*, *5*, 409295. doi:10.3389/frobt.2018.00114 PMID:33500993

Pacansky-Brock, M., Smedshammer, M., & Vincent-Layton, K. (2020). Humanizing online teaching to equitize higher education. *Current Issues in Education (Tempe, Ariz.)*, *21*(2), 1–21. https://cie.asu.edu/ojs/index.php/cieatasu/article/view/1905

Parker, J., & Herrington, J. (2015). *Setting the Climate in an Authentic Online Community of Learning*. Australian Association for Research in Education.

Pokrivčáková, S. (2019). Preparing teachers for the application of AI-powered technologies in foreign language education. *Journal of Language and Cultural Education*, *7*(3), 135–153. doi:10.2478/jolace-2019-0025

Rovai, A. P. (2002a). Sense of community, perceived cognitive learning, and persistence in asynchronous learning networks. *The Internet and Higher Education, 5*(4), 319–332. doi:10.1016/S1096-7516(02)00130-6

Rovai, A. P. (2002b). Building sense of community at a distance. *International Review of Research in Open and Distance Learning, 3*(1), 1–16. doi:10.19173/irrodl.v3i1.79

Rovai, A. P., & Jordan, H. M. (2004). Blended learning and sense of community: A comparative analysis with traditional and fully online graduate courses. *International Review of Research in Open and Distance Learning, 5*(2), 1–13. doi:10.19173/irrodl.v5i2.192

Russell, S. J., & Norvig, P. (2010). *Artificial Intelligence: A Modern Approach* (3rd ed.). Prentice Hall.

Ryan, R. M., & Deci, E. L. (2000). Intrinsic and Extrinsic Motivations: Classic Definitions and New Directions* 1. *Contemporary Educational Psychology, 25*(1), 54–67. doi:10.1006/ceps.1999.1020 PMID:10620381

Saint-Jacques, A. (2013). Effective teaching practices to foster vibrant communities of inquiry in synchronous online learning. In *Educational communities of inquiry: Theoretical framework, research and practice* (pp. 84–108). IGI Global. doi:10.4018/978-1-4666-2110-7.ch006

Salazar, M. (2013). A humanizing pedagogy: Reinventing the principles and practices of education as a journey towards liberation. *Review of Research in Education, 37*(1), 121–148. doi:10.3102/0091732X12464032

Sclater, N. (2008). Web 2.0, personal learning environments, and the future of learning management systems. *Research Bulletin (International Commission for the Northwest Atlantic Fisheries), 13.*

Shea, P., & Bidjerano, T. (2009). Community of inquiry as a theoretical framework to foster "epistemic engagement" and "cognitive presence" in online education. *Computers & Education, 52*(3), 543–553. doi:10.1016/j.compedu.2008.10.007

Sheridan, K., Kelly, M. A., & Bentz, D. T. (2013). A follow-up study of the indicators of teaching presence critical to students in online courses. In *Educational communities of inquiry: Theoretical framework, research and practice* (pp. 67–83). IGI Global. doi:10.4018/978-1-4666-2110-7.ch005

Shin, D. H., & Choo, H. (2011). Modeling the acceptance of socially interactive robotics: Social presence in human–robot interaction. *Interaction Studies: Social Behaviour and Communication in Biological and Artificial Systems, 12*(3), 430–460. doi:10.1075/is.12.3.04shi

Skeels, M. M., & Grudin, J. (2009, May). When social networks cross boundaries: a case study of workplace use of Facebook and LinkedIn. In *Proceedings of the 2009 ACM International Conference on Supporting Group Work* (pp. 95-104). 10.1145/1531674.1531689

Skylar, A. A. (2009). A comparison of asynchronous online text-based lectures and synchronous interactive web conferencing lectures. *Issues in Teacher Education, 18*(2), 69–84.

Spence, P. R., Westerman, D., Edwards, C., & Edwards, A. (2014). Welcoming our robot overlords: Initial expectations about interaction with a robot. *Communication Research Reports, 31*(3), 272–280. doi:10.1080/08824096.2014.924337

Van Harmelen, M. (2008). Design trajectories: Four experiments in PLE implementation. *Interactive Learning Environments, 16*(1), 35–46. doi:10.1080/10494820701772686

Van Houtte, M. (2005). Climate or culture? A plea for conceptual clarity in school effectiveness research. *School Effectiveness and School Improvement, 16*(1), 71–89. doi:10.1080/09243450500113977

Vonderwell, S., & Zachariah, S. (2005). Factors that influence participation in online learning. *Journal of Research on Technology in Education, 38*(2), 213–230. doi:10.1080/15391523.2005.10782457

Yang, J. C., Quadir, B., Chen, N.-S., & Miao, Q. (2016). Effects of online presence on learning performance in a blog-based online course. *The Internet and Higher Education, 30*, 11–20. doi:10.1016/j.iheduc.2016.04.002

Yang, Y.-T. C., Newby, T. J., & Bill, R. L. (2005). Using Socratic questioning to promote critical thinking skills through asynchronous discussion forums in distance learning environments. *American Journal of Distance Education, 19*(3), 163–181. doi:10.1207/s15389286ajde1903_4

Yen, C., & Tu, C. (2011). A multiple-group confirmatory factor analysis of the scores for online presence: Do they measure the same thing across cultural groups? *Journal of Educational Computing Research, 44*(2), 219–242. doi:10.2190/EC.44.2.e

Chapter 13
Exploring Embodied Learning and XR Technologies in Online Education

Sunok Lee
Chonnam National University, South Korea

Daeun Kim
https://orcid.org/0009-0006-4821-9302
Chonnam National University, South Korea

Yura Jeong
Chonnam National University, South Korea

Jeeheon Ryu
Chonnam National University, South Korea

ABSTRACT

The concept of embodiment has been central to the design of extended reality (XR) technologies and is one of the keys to immersive learning. However, there is still a need for further conceptual frameworks to aid developers, practitioners, and educators in comprehending the various facets of embodiment and their impact on learning. This gap becomes apparent when examining the revised taxonomy that includes layers for interactive learning experiences in digital technologies. In this context, this chapter aims to address this deficiency by presenting a design case focused on a digital art application leveraging XR technology. By integrating sensorimotor information based on kinetic movements, the application aims to enrich the tactile painting experience within liberal arts education. Developed for Hololens2, the XR art application incorporates interactive elements such as avatars, narratives, multi-sensory features, and tools for creating artifacts. Throughout the chapter, the authors offer insights into the considerations taken during the interface and interaction design phases, particularly emphasizing the promotion of immersive engagement.

DOI: 10.4018/979-8-3693-0762-5.ch013

INTRODUCTION

Many online learners frequently express a sense of disconnection from their educational journey despite the rapid expansion of online learning to enhance higher education accessibility (Xu & Xu, 2020). This perceived isolation not only hinders effective communication but also contributes to feelings of alienation and a lack of engagement in online courses (Berge & Collins, 1995; Chen & Wu, 2015; Yamada, 2009). According to recent studies, learners often experience distractions, lack of motivation, frustration, and discouragement, thereby leading to reduced participation (Cesari et al., 2021; Pregowska et al., 2021). In response, scholars, exemplified by Muir et al. (2020), consistently stress the importance of adopting a pedagogical approach that "humanizes" online learning, treating the learner as a genuine social participant who feels connected to the learning community. This concept of "humanizing learning" underscores the importance of crafting online learning experiences that are not only technologically advanced but also sensitive to the learner's perspective, aiming to enhance the quality and effectiveness of online education (Muir et al., 2020). This perspective necessitates further exploration to better understand how to create engaging and effective online learning experiences.

Digital technologies and resources have the potential to personalize learning experiences, offer greater choices to learners, facilitate engagement with real-world issues, and provide meaningful learning opportunities (Alaghbary, 2021). In essence, technology-assisted instructional learning can leverage technology's educational capabilities to achieve intended learning outcomes by designing learning experiences that are authentic for learners. The human-centered design of instructional strategies is crucial to fully exploit the potential of digital technologies. Gilly Salmon's five-stage model (Salmon, 2002) serves as a valuable framework for guiding the seamless progression and comprehensive explanation of online course design. However, Salmon's approach predominantly focuses on social interaction and social knowledge construction rather than individual cognitive processing.

Moreover, a recent meta-analysis (Wu et al., 2020) highlights the need for new frameworks to address the challenge faced by numerous studies utilizing modern technologies and tools. Recognizing the potential of technology-based theoretical models for teaching and learning, researchers are developing frameworks that establish connections between digital tools and Bloom's (Revised) Taxonomy (Park et al., in press). This instructional design model is structured around the various levels of knowledge within the Taxonomy, integrating layers for interactive learning experiences using digital tools and resources. The outcomes derived from these layers can influence learner behavior, thereby improving the overall learning experience and facilitating the achievement of learning objectives. Consequently, the application of appropriate instructional design strategies in online learning is considered essential.

A critical aspect of designing learning experiences in online settings is to ensure learners are actively engaged cognitively. This approach acknowledges the importance of fostering a sense of presence, described as the feeling of "being there" in an online learning environment. According to Yamada (2009), the presence of learning plays a pivotal role in enhancing learner engagement and positively impacting student performance in online courses. The inclusion of interactive tools in online learning has been shown to enhance presence positively in terms of media characteristics (Chou & Min, 2009; Joyce & Brown, 2009; Mykota & Duncan, 2007; Weinel et al., 2011; Wise et al., 2004). The unique capabilities of immersive technologies, such as Virtual Reality (VR), Augmented Reality (AR), and Mixed Reality (MR), suggest that learners' sense of presence, influenced by immersion and interaction, is heightened when using these technologies. Consequently, integrating immersive technologies, along with effective pedagogy and social interactions, can generally enhance the overall sense of presence in online learning.

XR technologies, which encompass VR, AR, and MR, are revolutionizing online learning environments. Through XR-based devices like HoloLens, reality is extended by adding digital elements to the real world or incorporating digital materials into the physical world in real-time (Morimoto et al., 2022). By utilizing XR technology to simulate real-world experiences, learners can engage in physically implausible activities (Suh & Prophet, 2018). The specialized features of XR sensors significantly contribute to enhancing interactive learning experiences (Liu et al., 2016), ultimately providing learners with a heightened sense of reality (Witmer & Singer, 1998). This heightened presence has been linked to various positive outcomes, including improved learning abilities, work efficiency, and users' intention to use a system (Bower et al., 2014; Radu et al., 2021; Salar et al., 2020; Zinchenko et al., 2020). These findings suggest that immersive technologies can facilitate active participation in educational settings, both formal and informal.

XR technology plays a vital role in enabling embodied experiences through physical movement within networked learning environments. It supports the integration of learning with meaningful experiences and guides the design of learning environments accordingly (Black et al., 2012). Embodied learning acknowledges the interplay between cognitive processes, the body, emotions, and the environment, establishing a meaningful connection between body movements and the content being learned (Duijzer et al., 2019; Lindgren & Johnson-Glenberg, 2013; Skulmowski & Rey, 2018). Multiple frameworks, such as the Cognitive Affective Model of Immersive Learning (Makransky & Petersen, 2021), and instructional design models (Park et al., in press), highlight that XR can provide students with interactive and meaningful learning experiences (Wyss et al., 2021).Top of Form This approach acknowledges students' agency in their learning experiences, enabling the design of learning activities that effectively align physical modes of interaction with targeted concepts (Kang et al., 2021). Diverse strategies have emerged to integrate multimodal data sources with layers of digital content projected into learners' surrounding environments (Birt et al., 2018), thereby expanding our comprehension of learning within an embodied context (Prieto et al., 2018). Among these methods is the use of AR, holographic imaging, and VR technologies to present virtual images, including avatars that blend seamlessly with the real world (Alnagrat et al., 2014). The multifaceted applications of XR technology, encompassing interactive learning experiences, embodied connections, and innovative modalities such as AR, holographic imaging, and VR, underscore its transformative potential in shaping a dynamic and immersive educational landscape.

The interactive nature of avatars within 3D spaces holds promise for enhancing learner agency in online learning. Moreover, avatars inherently offer affordances that establish implicit connections to embodiment. Research consistently supports the notion that gesture-based interaction can effectively stimulate learning and allow learners to express their evolving comprehension of ideas in ways conducive to new learning (Gallaher & Lindgren, 2015; Lindgren, 2014). This personalized interaction fosters a sense of agency, allowing learners to actively engage with the educational content and express their understanding through gestures within the immersive digital space. The incorporation of avatars, coupled with XR technologies, not only enhances the interactive learning experiences but also contributes to the embodiment of knowledge, bridging the gap between virtual and physical realms.

This chapter introduces the development and implementation of XR-based liberal arts learning applications that integrate Bloom's Revised Taxonomy to emphasize higher-order thinking skills and embodied learning experiences. Our approach involved applying the cognitive affective model (Makransky & Petersen, 2021) and an instructional design model (Park et al., in press). We focused on refining media interactions and instructional methods to enhance presence and agency in immersive technology-based learning. Importantly, we integrated features for embodied learning, facilitating meaningful connections through gestures and learning artifacts within the online learning environment. Through the utilization of these immersive learning environments, learners can enrich their experiential learning, which may be less attainable in a traditional educational setting. Additionally, we described how instructional designers can create and develop XR-based learning applications to facilitate a humanized learning experience.

THEORETICAL FRAMEWORK

Humanizing Online Learning and Learning Experience

Lately, great attention has been paid to online learning, typically defined as web-based instruction, owing to its potential for providing flexible access to content and instruction at anytime and anywhere (Carliner, 2004; Kim et al., 2021; Seo et al., 2020). Online learning, a contemporary adaptation of distance education, utilizes technology to facilitate the educational process (Carliner, 2004). Typically, a course is considered online when 70 to 80 percent of its content is delivered digitally (Lim et al., 2005). Regarded as a modern iteration of distance education, online learning is perceived to broaden learners' access to educational opportunities (Benson, 2002; Conrad, 2002). With the continual advancements in technology, online learning has diversified to include various formats such as e-learning, blended learning, and cyber-learning (Sun & Chen, 2016). The widespread availability of the Internet has made these learning modalities prevalent in education, incorporating tools like video conferencing, web-based platforms, massive open online courses (MOOCs), instant messaging, and educational apps. MOOCs, for instance, provide a scalable and accessible means for learners to enroll in courses from different institutions (Calvo et al., 2020). The advantages of online learning, such as flexibility and accessibility, gained significant recognition during the COVID-19 pandemic, leading to a considerable surge in distance learning usage (Adedoyin & Soykan, 2023). This global event also spurred further research into online learning, confirming its efficacy in digital education.

However, the quality of online courses may be compromised by institutions or instructors' reluctance to embrace digital learning tools that align with the course objectives (Rapanta et al., 2020). Online learning heavily relies on computer-mediated textual or graphical communication, occasionally impeding effective interaction. This limitation can result in feelings of isolation and reduced student engagement (Berge & Collins, 1995; Chen & Wu, 2015; Yamada, 2009). Learners often express a sense of detachment, perceiving their interactions as confined to the virtual realm rather than with real individuals (Rush, 2015). The absence of physical interaction and peer presence in online environments can exacerbate feelings of isolation (Coman et al., 2020). Additionally, the digital environment may lead to distractions and a loss of focus for learners. These perceived sentiments of alienation not only impede effective communication but also contribute to frustration and discouragement experienced in online courses (Berge & Collins, 1995; Cesari et al., 2021; Chen & Wu, 2015; Pregowska et al., 2021; Yamada, 2009). Ayu (2020) found that some online learners required the format to better support their understanding of the learning environment, indicating a mismatch between their needs and the online learning setting. These factors underscore the significance of designing online learning experiences that treat the learner as a genuine social participant who feels connected to the learning community (Muir et al., 2020). Addressing the challenges associated with online learning requires a proactive approach to embrace digital tools that align with course objectives, fostering effective communication and engagement. Recognizing the potential for feelings of isolation and detachment in the digital realm, educators should prioritize creating online environments that promote a sense of connection and belonging among learners.

Previous research has laid the foundation for instructors to implement humanized learning in online courses. For instance, Gilly Salmon's five-stage model (Salmon, 2002) offers a valuable framework for guiding online course design. It begins with the access and motivation stage, where learners gain personalized access to digital resources, fostering motivation. The subsequent online socialization stage emphasizes creating a virtual community to promote learner interaction and collaboration. Transitioning to the information exchange stage, the model facilitates effective content dissemination using various digital tools. In the knowledge construction stage, learners are encouraged to engage deeply in exploration and analysis, utilizing digital resources to construct knowledge. Finally, the development stage encourages learners to self-assess and apply acquired knowledge in real-world contexts, emphasizing a comprehensive learning experience.

While Salmon's model provides a comprehensive framework for designing and delivering online courses, there remains a need for a clear framework organized in a learner-centered manner. Notably, Salmon's approach focuses less on individual cognitive processing and more on social interaction and knowledge construction. A recent meta-analysis (Wu et al., 2020) highlights the need for new frameworks to guide research and application development in light of the challenges posed by modern technologies and tools.

Theoretical and empirical studies have underscored the importance of Learning Experience Design (LXD) in online learning. Floor (2016) defines LXD as creating learning experiences that enable learners to achieve desired outcomes in a human-centered and goal-oriented manner. A notable shift in LXD involves redefining it through the lens of User Experience Design (UXD), particularly in educational settings (Schmidt & Huang, 2021). Several studies advocate for student agency and presence to humanize online learning experiences. Park (2022) emphasizes the necessity of cognitive presence in facilitating meaningful learning experiences online.

Existing literature suggests promoting presence in online courses through media-rich multi-modes, such as audio and video, in content delivery, and actively facilitating learning activities (Borup et al., 2012; Clark & Mayer, 2011; Mandernach et al., 2006). Muir et al. (2020) stress the importance of a pedagogical approach that humanizes online learning by considering each learner's unique needs, interests, and abilities, fostering an inclusive learning environment that promotes full engagement. This holistic approach prioritizes learners' needs, goals, and motivations to craft engaging and effective learning experiences.

Adopting an LXD perspective in online learning design enhances learner engagement and positively influences students' social-cognitive motivational characteristics and learning behaviors (Quintana & Quintana, 2023; Wong & Hughes, 2022). By centering on holistic, human-centered design principles, LXD can generate more vibrant, interactive, and meaningful learning experiences that resonate deeply with learners. This study aims to design and develop instructional resources that humanize online learning, drawing on these literatures.

Extended Reality Based Learning

XR technologies, comprising VR, AR, and MR, are transforming the landscape of online education, enhancing reality by integrating digital components into physical environments or overlaying digital content onto real-world settings in real-time (Morimoto et al., 2022). These technologies facilitate multimodal learning experiences, enabling learners to grasp concepts through sensory engagement (Prieto et al., 2018). XR technology provides two crucial benefits for learning. To begin with, it is known to generate a sense of presence, fundamental for immersive learning, grounded in place illusion and plausibility (Slater, 2017). Secondly, XR also allows embodiment, which enables learners to interact with content in three dimensions, incorporating both visual and physical engagement. Thus, as a matter of fact, significantly enhances content retention (Johnson-Glenberg, 2019; Goldin-Meadow, 2011). The transformative impact of XR technologies on online education is evident, as they enhance reality by seamlessly integrating digital components into physical environments and facilitate multimodal learning experiences, allowing learners to grasp concepts through sensory engagement.

XR-based learning environments, which are known to merge real and virtual experiences, offer unprecedented potential for reshaping education and practice. These environments offer a scaffolded learning context that caters to individual needs while enriching sensorial and embodied experiences (Aguayo & Eames, 2023). XR capabilities can enhance comprehension of intricate subjects such as marine science, fostering ecological literacy and behavioral change (Aguayo & Eames, 2023). Lindgren et al. (2016) found that participants who fully engaged their bodies in mixed-reality simulations exhibited enhanced learning and positive attitudes toward the learning environment compared to those using desktop versions.

Despite the promising potential of XR technologies, their integration into online education faces challenges and has not yet gained widespread acceptance (Alalwan et al., 2020; Baniasadi et al., 2020; Cook et al., 2019; Velev & Zlateva, 2017). A primary technical impediment is the need for advanced hardware and software infrastructure, including high-quality VR headsets, AR devices, and MR systems, which may not be universally accessible or affordable (Doolani et al., 2020). Furthermore, consistent high-speed internet connectivity is essential for seamless XR experiences, posing a barrier in areas with connectivity issues. At the same time, the complexity of developing and maintaining XR content requires expertise in both educational content creation and XR technology, thereby stymieing its adoption to specific subject areas or courses (Doolani et al., 2020). Institutional inertia and traditional teaching methods also hinder XR adoption in university settings (Kavanagh et al., 2017), with educators often favoring established practices over technology-driven approaches. The lack of clear evidence demonstrating XR's superiority over traditional online learning methods further hampers its integration into university settings.

There is a recognized necessity for more appropriate frameworks to guide the design of educational XR systems (Yang et al., 2020). While the educational potential of XR is evident, its effective utilization relies on meticulous design to align with the intricacies of the learning experience itself. Addressing this requirement, Park et al. (2022) introduced an instructional design model comprising layers aimed at crafting interactive learning experiences within XR environments. This framework consists of four layers that synergistically merge to deliver an immersive user experiences (Park et al., in press). Foundational to this model is the instructional approach of Immersive Learning, which delineates the cognitive-emotional impact of immersive learning, guiding the design of XR learning experiences. Both models highlight that the benefits of XR are maximized when harmoniously integrated with effective instructional design. In other words, learning significantly improves when instructional methods in immersive learning align with the distinctive features of the medium.

These models identify presence and agency as overarching psychological benefits of immersive learning, demonstrating how factors like immersion level, control mechanisms, and representational fidelity contribute to augmenting these benefits. According to the models, instructional methods that enhance learning through increased presence or agency specifically amplify learning via immersive technology. Moreover, the models elucidate that enhancing presence and agency positively influences learning outcomes by promoting learner embodiment. In summary, considering the embodied experience of immersive learning is crucial in the design of effective learning experiences

Embodied Learning Experience

The concepts of embodiment and embodied learning, deeply rooted in theories of embodied cognition, are increasingly gaining traction in the field of education (Georgiou & Ioannou, 2019). Embodied cognition posits that cognitive processes are influenced by the body's interactions with the world (Margaret Wilson, 2002). Recent foundational research in embodied cognition offers a fresh outlook on learning, providing insights for crafting learning environments that intertwine learning with experiences to enhance their significance and utility (Black et al., 2012). Barsalou et al. (2003), prominent researchers in grounded cognition and embodiment, discovered a compatibility effect between an individual's physical state and mental state. Barsalou (2008) further elaborated that bodily-rooted knowledge encompasses perceptual processes that fundamentally influence conceptual thinking.

XR technology presents a promising avenue for supporting embodied experiences with physical movement in networked learning environments. As highlighted by Jacob Fortman and Rebecca Quintana (2023), XR environments offer tremendous opportunities for learners to connect with new representations and modes of interaction, thereby enriching learning experiences through embodiment. They open up possibilities for learners to utilize movement, gesture, and gaze to support learning while co-located within virtual learning environments (Coban et al., 2022; Yu & Xu, 2022). Researchers and practitioners could incorporate more gestures and body movements into their learning experience designs, thereby creating immersive and gesture-rich learning environments. Such embodied environments, according to Georgiou and Ioannou (2019), should facilitate multi-modal and multi-sensory forms of interaction, encompassing gestures, bodily movement, tactile sensations, and auditory experiences.

The experience of embodiment further enhances the affordances of the XR medium. Embodied experiences allow students to play an active role in their learning, fostering a sense of agency (Kang et al., 2021). According to the embodiment principle, people tend to learn more deeply when on-screen agents display human-like gestures, movements, eye contact, and facial expressions (Mayer, 2014a). Therefore, integrating elements of embodiment into XR-based learning environments not only enhances engagement but also promotes deeper learning experiences by tapping into fundamental cognitive processes influenced by embodiment.

Researchers are integrating concepts from embodied cognition into the design of learning environments within the realm of education employing immersive technology. "Embodied learning" involves creating meaningful connections between body movements, artifacts, and learning content (Duijzer et al., 2019; Lindgren & Johnson-Glenberg, 2013; Skulmowski & Rey, 2018). Kang et al. (2021) delve into the exploration of gesture patterns and learning within an embodied XR science simulation. Their groundbreaking ELASTIC3S system facilitates learners' interaction with diverse science simulations through whole-body gestures, such as hand waving and kicking. The study's outcomes offer valuable insights into the potential of integrating real-time assistance within embodied simulations, thereby fostering adaptive learning experiences.

In a similar vein, Yiannoutsou et al. (2021) expand on the pedagogical design of embodied mathematical experiences tailored for visually impaired children. Their system creates avenues to anchor mathematical concepts in audition and bodily experience. Their findings underscore the effectiveness of bodily movement and positioning in enhancing engagement among visually impaired children, while also discussing the prerequisites for implementing immersive VR in educational settings. These examples, particularly pertinent in functional subjects like art, dance, and physical education, underscore the significance of embodied experiences in education.

In summary, further research is imperative to leverage embodied experiences alongside the affordances of XR, especially in functional subjects, to engage learners effectively and optimize learning outcomes. The integration of embodied experiences within XR environments holds immense promise for creating immersive and inclusive educational experiences across diverse learning contexts.

Research Questions

The research explores the content design theory focused on the experiential embodiment of learners when utilizing HoloLens 2 as a learning tool. Therefore, the present study undertakes an examination of the embodied cognitive theories embedded in the design elements of HoloLens education experiences. This involves exploring the types of bodily activities recommended by embodied cognition theories, the functionalities enabled by HoloLens and its content, as well as the design elements and attributes applicable to general art education content categorized based on art education objectives.

The specific research questions that this study addresses are as follows:

(1) What are the design and development processes to create an Extended Reality (XR)-based art education content for embodied learning?

(2) What are the learning experiences concerning the embodied learning in Extended Reality (XR)-based art education?

DESIGN AND DEVELOPMENT OF EMBODIED XR APPLICATION

This section delineates the methodology employed in this research, offering insight into the process of XR design and the formulation of application requirements aimed at humanizing learning. The development of the Art Education XR application adhered to the framework delineated by Allen and Sites (2012) (see Figure 1). The methodology adopted the Successive Approximation Model (SAM), which is deeply ingrained in ongoing and iterative agile processes, prioritizing collaboration and partnership among university students, experts, and developers (Sears et al., 2007; Vasilchenko et al., 2020).

Designing Art Education XR

In this section, the design and development procedures followed will be mapped on the Allen and Sites' (2012) process displayed in Figure 1.

Preparation Phase: Goal-Setting

Ahead of the design interview involving five university students, two art education instructors and one faculty expert diligently chronicled the process of art education following established practice guidelines. In South Korea, the General Art Education framework serves as the cornerstone for all registered

Figure 1. Successive Approximation Model (SAM) (Source: Allen & Sites, 2012)

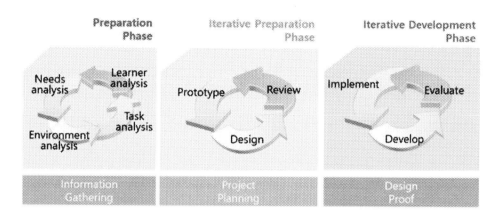

education aims in art education courses, outlining the expected competencies and skills. In addition to these standards, there are best practice guidelines and frameworks for digital literacy in XR technologies, aimed at guiding the design and development of XR-based learning content. The interviews with students thus delved into their digital literacy, specifically regarding XR technologies. The analysis of these interviews forms the bedrock for determining the direction of learning content design.

The initial documentation phase primarily focused on identifying the problem and exploring the learning and teaching objectives within the current curriculum. This process established a framework of decision points and stages to guide the student interviews. The interviews kicked off with an introduction to XR technologies and the overarching goal of the XR application project, aimed at enhancing embodied and experiential learning in general art education. Individual interviews were conducted to gain insights into the perceptions and requirements for XR-based art education content. Five university students with prior experience in art education participated in these interviews. Given that the primary objective was to develop XR-based learning content, the interviews covered topics such as technology literacy, with a specific focus on XR technologies. The questionnaire encompassed inquiries about memorable art education experiences, perceptions of art classes, knowledge of art and artists, preferred art teaching methods, experience with advanced technology, understanding of XR, and opinions on implementing XR in art classes. All interviews were recorded, transcribed, and subjected to content analysis, forming the basis for guiding the design of learning content.

During the analysis phase, the instructional problem was explicated, and the instructional goals and objectives were established. Furthermore, the learning environment, along with the learners' existing knowledge and skills, was identified. The students highlighted a lack of hands-on skills as a central challenge in art education. They emphasized the importance of engaging in XR scenario design to develop the knowledge, skills, and confidence necessary to immerse themselves in authentic situations and paint proficiently under supervision. The students expressed that the project's objective was groundbreaking and held significant potential in enhancing their learning engagement, particularly through the application of embodied cognition in the online learning environment. The findings that were addressed during the analysis phase are as follows:

The objectives of art education inherently call for a hands-on, experiential learning approach, placing a strong emphasis on practical experience to enhance retention and memorization of knowledge (Kang, 2013). It is widely acknowledged that actively utilizing materials and tools is more effective than passively receiving instructions on their usage. This underscores the significance of embodiment through hands-on experience in art education.

Incorporating an individual's body into the process of knowledge acquisition and understanding can provide students with personalized and individualized learning experiences. This approach closely aligns with the fundamental principles of embodied learning, facilitating students' connection with and internalization of knowledge in real-world contexts. In higher education, art as general education extends beyond merely appreciating aesthetic objects and their enjoyment; it plays a central role in the broader humanities curriculum, focusing on aesthetic experiences (Jin & Ye, 2022). This integration is vital for enhancing artistic competencies, such as aesthetics, and fostering a comprehensive set of cultural and creative skills in students. As highlighted by Aziz (2023) and Shih (2019), arts education can enrich learners' understanding of diverse cultural expressions and their creative thinking skills. To accommodate the diverse skill levels of learners in higher education, art programs can be designed to offer both introductory courses for beginners and more advanced, specialized options for those with prior exposure to or specific interests in the arts. This ensures that all students, regardless of their initial level of artistic skill or knowledge, can deeply engage with and benefit from the arts, enhancing their overall learning experience.

In an introductory painting course, the topic of color schemes holds particular importance in art education, as it allows learners to grasp the fundamental features of visual arts and express their creativity (Salazar, 2021). Color schemes play a crucial role in conveying emotions and moods within artwork, and their harmonious combination optimizes the aesthetics of the piece (Choudhury & Kumar, 2023). Additionally, mastering the proper usage of art tools is essential for learners to effectively express their artistic ideas (Wang, 2022). These foundational topics enable students to understand the fundamental principles of art and establish a basis for developing their artistic style and abilities.

Iterative Preparation Phase: Design

The preparatory efforts undertaken through the interview process in the preparatory phase were instrumental in delineating the procedural steps and decision-making criteria for the design and development phase. Moreover, this preparatory endeavor laid the foundation for conceptualizing scenarios and crafting three-dimensional spaces and interactions within the XR application, leveraging the advanced capabilities of the high-fidelity HoloLens 2. The specific content design was executed using flow charts and storyboards. A highly immersive and meticulously researched scenario was developed, enabling students to assume the role of Van Gogh's apprentices within a virtual environment (Canabal et al., 2020). The scenario was intricately designed with a branching narrative structure, empowering learners to explore a variety of actions and controls, resulting in a diverse learning experience.

Significantly, this study adopted the framework of interactive learning experience in the XR environment (Park et al., in press). In humanizing the learning experience within an XR learning environment, Layer 1, rooted in Bloom's revised taxonomy, establishes instructional objectives by integrating cognitive processes with knowledge domains. In an immersive learning environment like XR, as previously noted, embodied experiences enable direct interaction, fostering deeper knowledge acquisition. Learning through real-world actions and movements aids in developing practical skills beyond theoretical understanding. This embodied learning process plays a crucial role in helping learners acquire new skills, solve complex problems, and materialize creative ideas. Hence, it is essential to consider both the cognitive dimension of knowledge and the psychomotor domain. Consequently, this present study revised the existing framework of interactive learning experience by incorporating the psychomotor domain into Layer 1 of the framework (see Figure 2).

The learning objectives are categorized into two cognitive domains. Firstly, learners will recognize the features of color schemes and art tools, which involves conceptual and procedural knowledge. Secondly, learners will practice conceptual and procedural knowledge about color schemes and art tools by mimicking Van Gogh's "Sunflowers." This learning application also incorporates a cover story that actively engages learners throughout the learning process. Based on this narrative, learners assume the role of Van Gogh's apprentices, immersing themselves in studying art techniques and organizing an exhibition alongside fellow apprentices. This approach enhances engagement while simultaneously deepening the understanding of art through practical application.

The learning activities are structured around the psychomotor domains, aiming to engage learners in active, hands-on experiences. Initially, learners engage in listening to Van Gogh's explanations about color schemes and exploring the characteristics of various art tools to fulfill the first learning objective. This interactive dialogue with Van Gogh provides learners with valuable insights into color theory and tool usage, setting the stage for practical application. Subsequently, learners participate in exercises where they utilize these tools to create basic color schemes. This hands-on approach ensures that learners move beyond passive reception of information, actively engaging in activities like blending and applying colors. By immersing themselves in these tasks, learners solidify their understanding of fundamental concepts while honing their artistic skills.

To achieve the second learning objective, learners are challenged with the hands-on task of recreating Van Gogh's renowned masterpiece, "Sunflowers." This painting is particularly well-suited for practicing color blending due to its intricate use of similar hues, including various shades of yellows and golds. The complexity of "Sunflowers" offers learners a stimulating yet rewarding opportunity to discern and blend colors effectively. Furthermore, the painting's widespread recognition enhances learner engagement and fosters a deeper interest in the learning process.

Figure 2. Revised Framework of Interactive Learning Experience (Park et al., in press)

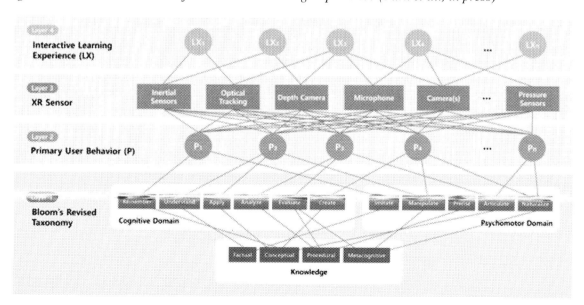

The process begins with learners carefully analyzing the painting's color palette before utilizing provided art materials to mix and match colors, striving for an accurate rendition of the artwork. Each step in this process contributes to refining learners' color-mixing skills and familiarizing them with the unique properties of different art tools. These elements are crucial to shaping learning behaviors, which are delineated in Layer 2 of the framework. Layer 2 focuses on primary user behavior, encompassing specific actions and interactions undertaken by learners during the learning process, particularly within an XR environment. These behaviors include listening to explanations, selecting tools, choosing colors, blending colors, applying paint, and evaluating artistic choices. For a comprehensive breakdown of these behaviors, refer to Table 1. This integrated approach ensures that learners actively participate in the learning process, ultimately enhancing their comprehension and retention of artistic principles.

The *Layer 3* is the XR sensors, which are critical for designing primary user interactions in XR environments. In this research, Microsoft's HoloLens 2 emerges as the preferred headset for developing immersive XR-based learning environments, primarily owing to its unparalleled sensor capabilities. The sensors integrated into HoloLens 2 are meticulously designed to enhance user interaction, offering a seamless blend of the physical and digital realms. Notably, these sensors excel in spatial recognition, enabling the device to seamlessly overlay digital content onto the real world with remarkable precision. Moreover, HoloLens 2's sensors possess the remarkable ability to recognize physical objects in real-time, adjusting the digital overlay accordingly. This user-centric design extends to responsiveness to hand gestures and gaze direction, facilitating intuitive control and navigation within the XR environment. Collectively, these unique features of HoloLens 2 contribute to a more natural, intuitive, and interactive learning experience for users.

Layer 4, an interactive learning experience within the XR environment, holds immense potential for fostering new insights and knowledge. In this context, the concept of LX combines experiential learning with transformative processes. Kolb's (1984) theory underscores the significance of concrete experiences, followed by reflective observation, abstract conceptualization, and active experimentation. LX, in essence, embodies learning linked to sensory perception, motor skills, past experiences, intuition, or implicit rules of thumb (Nonaka et al., 2009). In the context of HoloLens 2, LX is manifested through hand gestures, head movements, and sensory engagement, allowing users to manipulate virtual objects within the XR environment, thereby gaining practical knowledge and skills. This approach aligns with kinesthetic learning principles, highlighting the importance of physical interaction in learning and retention of new information.

Table 1. Primary User Behavior

Primary User Behavior	Specific Action in XR Environment
Listening to Explanations	Engaging with audio-visual explanations on color theory and tool usage.
Selecting Tools	Pointing at and selecting a brush or palette knife using hand gestures.
Choosing Colors	Indicating desired colors by pointing at them with hand gestures
Blending Colors	Executing brushing motions on the virtual canvas through hand movements
Applying Paint	Selecting a brush or palette knife using hand gestures in the Hololens2 interface and applying paint to the virtual canvas.
Inspecting and Evaluating Choices	Assessing and making artistic decisions by visually inspecting and evaluating choices

Furthermore, the immersive nature of XR, driven by the advanced sensor capabilities of HoloLens 2, facilitates personalized adaptive learning experiences. Learners have the freedom to explore and interact with educational material at their own pace, tailored to their individual learning styles. This adaptability amplifies the effectiveness of the educational experience, ensuring that learners engage deeply with the content and maximize their learning outcomes.

Development

Crafting Immersive Learning Experience Based on Technology Factors

This chapter utilized two instructional design frameworks to shape the learning experience within educational XR systems (Yang et al., 2020). One of these frameworks is the Interactive Learning Experience in the XR Environment (Park et al., in progress). This framework comprises four layers that interactively integrate to deliver an immersive user experience. Additionally, the theoretical framework developed by Makransky serves as the foundation for designing XR learning experiences. These two models work together to create an interactive learning environment in XR, providing users with an embodied experience within the designed content. Both models emphasize the importance of seamlessly integrating the affordances of XR with effective instructional design to optimize learning outcomes. Essentially, learning becomes significantly more effective when instructional methods in immersive learning align with the unique capabilities of the medium. In our implementations, the Interactive Learning Experience framework is guided by three critical technical factors: immersion, control factors, and representational fidelity (Makransky & Petersen, 2021; Park et al., in progress).

Immersion

First, by combining an individual's psychological state with the technology's properties that enable a particular experience, *immersion* leads to a presence in the learning environment (Agrewal et al., 2020). Learners can seamlessly observe and interact with 3D virtual objects integrated into their real-world environment by wearing the HoloLens 2 headset. The degree of immersion experienced is closely tied to the level of engagement with the narrative and its portrayal. To enhance the level of immersion, the application introduces a compelling storyline, casting learners in specific roles as students under a master artist, collaborating to organize an exhibition with their peers. This narrative structure is intentionally crafted to immerse learners in the scenario, fostering a more profound connection to the learning experience.

Moreover, immersion is heightened when a life-size Van Gogh avatar appears, providing explanations of the learning content and engaging directly with learners (refer to Figure 3). Avatars of this nature play a pivotal role in enhancing immersion and significantly contribute to enriching the overall learning experience. The life-size Van Gogh avatar exemplifies the concept of embodied learning through its physical representation and spatial awareness. This immersive approach facilitates a more natural and interactive learning experience, where educational content is not merely observed but encountered in an intuitive and engaging manner. Avatars transcend their role as information conduits; they act as guides and interactive agents, assisting learners in establishing profound connections with content by shaping the learning context. Through these elements, the application can deliver an authentic, engaging, immersive, and embodied learning experience.

Figure 3. Interacting With a Full-Scale Virtual Avatar for an Immersive Learning Experience

Control Factors

Second, *control factors* denote the autonomy learners can exercise in a virtual environment. As Witmer and Singer (1998) highlight, this concept encompasses several dimensions, including the degree, immediacy, and mode of control. The degree of control pertains to the extent of influence learners wield over their actions within the virtual setting. In this application, learners are empowered with significant control, allowing them to independently manage their tasks within the confines of the prescribed narrative. This approach fosters a sense of ownership and boosts engagement with the learning content.

Furthermore, immediacy of control refers to the speed at which learners' actions manifest within the virtual environment. Emphasizing immediacy, this application ensures that learners can manipulate virtual objects, such as painting tools, in real-time. They can freely manipulate, adjust, and resize these objects, receiving instant feedback from their interactions. This immediate responsiveness bridges the gap between the physical and virtual realms, enhancing the intuitiveness of interactions and enriching the overall learning experience.

Regarding the mode of control, learners interact with the virtual environment in a manner akin to real-world interactions. For example, when a learner picks up a virtual brush to paint a canvas green, the system replicates real-world dynamics by tracking their hand movements as if they were handling a physical brush (refer to Figure 4). This mode of control makes the virtual environment more accessible and intuitive, thereby encouraging active participation. By integrating the essence of embodied learning with natural movements, this control mode creates a virtual environment that is not only navigated but also experienced, facilitating a more instinctive and immersive learning process closely aligned with real-world experiences.

Representational Fidelity

Last, *representational fidelity* refers to the level of realism in representing the interactive features within the virtual environment (Brkic´ et al., 2016). This fidelity encompasses various aspects, including graph-

Figure 4. Creating a Virtual Painting Using Hand Gesture Interaction

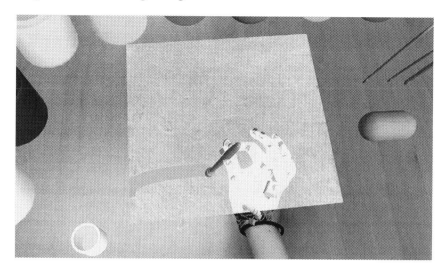

ics, sounds, and physics realism, all of which contribute to creating a lifelike virtual world. Key elements of representational fidelity include realistic environment rendering, smooth transitions in viewpoint, and consistent behavior of virtual objects (Dalgarno & Lee, 2010). In this program, enhancing representational fidelity is crucial for maximizing realism and immersion. For example, the program meticulously simulates the dripping effect when a learner dips a brush into paint, thereby augmenting the authenticity of the learning experience (refer to Figure 5).

The application leverages the capabilities of the HoloLens 2 device, which prioritizes intuitive hand interaction, allowing learners to interact with objects naturally. While a slight delay is intentionally incorporated to ensure a smooth user experience, this default setting may hinder precise interactions, especially during activities such as painting with a brush. To address this issue, we have minimized the delay and meticulously optimized virtual objects, such as the paintbrush, to accurately and promptly respond to the learner's hand movements. This optimization enhances the overall user experience and facilitates seamless interaction with virtual elements, thereby enhancing the effectiveness of the learning environment.

In the development phase of this XR-based application, the emphasis was strongly placed on integrating technical factors such as immersion, control factors, and representational fidelity. These elements are crucial in creating a sense of learner presence and agency. Immersion draws the learner into the virtual environment, control factors empower them with the ability to manipulate and interact within this setting, and representational fidelity ensures presence and agency. Ultimately, these components can induce an embodied experience by enhancing the learner's engagement and interactive learning experience in the XR-based learning environment.

Avatar Development

The development of the XR-based learning environment placed significant emphasis on crafting a lifelike and interactive avatar. This avatar, representing the renowned artist Van Gogh, underwent meticulous creation using Reallusion's Character Creator 3 and additional enhancements in Adobe Photoshop.

Figure 5. Representation Fidelity of Virtual Painting Experience

Through this amalgamation of tools, a life-sized Van Gogh avatar was realized, boasting both visual realism and dynamic interaction capabilities with students. The avatar's design was carefully orchestrated to align seamlessly with educational content and historical accuracy. Every aspect, from attire to facial features and gestures, was meticulously chosen to evoke the essence of Van Gogh's era and artistic style, thereby enhancing the immersive learning experience. Beyond serving as a mere visual aid, the avatar was engineered to offer multifaceted functionality. Employing advanced animation and rigging techniques in iClone 7, the avatar was programmed to perform a myriad of movements and interactions, encompassing gestures, facial expressions, and actions relevant to the conveyed narrative.

By emulating human-like interactions, the avatar played a pivotal role in captivating learners, fostering a more relatable and effective learning journey. Integrating the avatar into the XR environment necessitated meticulous attention to ensure seamless interaction. Animated content was choreographed using universally recognizable gestures and synchronized with voice recordings from a professional actor. This process involved aligning the avatar's movements and interactions with learners' actions and responses within the virtual realm. Special care was taken to synchronize the avatar's speech with precise lip movements, ensuring a seamless audio-visual experience. The intricate design and functionality of the avatar significantly enriched the overall immersion and interactivity of the learning environment, allowing learners to feel as though they were genuinely engaging with the persona of Van Gogh himself.

System Development and Integration

The development of the XR-based learning environment primarily relied on Unity 2020.3.2.7, complemented by Microsoft's Mixed Reality Toolkit (MRTK) 2.7.3 to enhance interaction capabilities. Unity serves as a robust game engine, proficient in integrating various components such as 3D models, animations, and interactive features, thus facilitating the creation of a cohesive learning environment. MRTK, an open-source SDK tailored for mixed reality applications, played a crucial role in bridging the functionalities of HoloLens 2 with the Unity development environment. Its versatility extends to crafting interactive learning experiences that capitalize on HoloLens' distinctive features, including spatial awareness, hand interaction, and eye tracking.

Ensuring smooth and realistic interactions between learners and virtual elements posed a major challenge. Addressing this challenge involved implementing advanced physics simulations and authentic object behaviors to enhance the user experience's authenticity. For instance, when learners interacted with virtual painting tools, the system responded realistically to their movements, mimicking the process of painting in a physical setting.

Additionally, the incorporation of haptic feedback, where feasible, provided visual and auditory cues, enriching the overall sense of immersion. Integrating the avatar system with the main application emerged as a crucial aspect, necessitating precise synchronization of the avatar's animations and interactions with other system components. This synchronization ensured a seamless and uninterrupted learning experience for users. Moreover, the user interface of the system was thoughtfully designed to be intuitive and user-friendly, enabling learners to focus on educational content without being encumbered by technical intricacies. In essence, the system development phase was characterized by meticulous attention to detail in crafting an immersive, interactive, and user-friendly learning environment. By leveraging advanced technologies and employing thoughtful design principles, the application aimed to deliver an engaging and effective educational experience within the realm of XR.

CONCLUSION

In this chapter, we outlined an approach to design and develop XR-based applications, with a specific focus on immersive and embodied technologies utilizing HoloLens 2. Our design strategy emphasized strategically arranging and integrating XR-based embodied learning experiences to heighten users' sense of presence and agency. The complexity of designing and developing XR content necessitates knowledge from various disciplines, including interaction design, user experience, programming, and content creation. This complexity is further compounded in educational XR, where additional competencies in learning objectives are required to ensure that designed activities align with intended educational outcomes (Gilardi et al., 2021). By incorporating frameworks such as the Interactive Learning Experience into the development process, practitioners can work towards overcoming these challenges. The primary contribution of this chapter lies in its potential to aid LXD designers and developers in addressing the isolation challenges often encountered in online learning environments.

The significance of XR content in arts education lies in its acknowledgment of the importance of sensorimotor processes, bodily experience, creativity, and representation in human cognition (Corcoran, 2018). Our study has demonstrated that XR paintings can leverage an expanded sensorium to dynamically communicate concepts through a broader range of bodily movements compared to traditional drawing methods. Guided by principles of embodied cognition rooted in Bloom's revised taxonomy, online art education underscores the notion of "embodied cognition," which is pivotal in comprehending art education from a connectivist standpoint. Additionally, our research has identified extensive bodily, haptic, and locomotive resources for designing and representing immersive virtual environments. XR technologies for embodied cognition are projected to be among the fastest-growing technologies of this decade (Fernandez, 2017).

As evidenced by our study, XR holds significant promise in revolutionizing teaching and learning methodologies, particularly in higher online education settings. However, it is crucial to acknowledge that many of these solutions entail substantial costs, rendering them inaccessible to certain teachers, instructors, and educational institutions. Moreover, a systematic review conducted by Alnagrat et al. (2022) has raised pertinent questions regarding equity in XR usage. The "bring-your-own-device" (BYOD) philosophy and personal prerequisites for head-mounted displays, such as the HoloLens 2, can significantly impact the learning experiences of students, particularly those from disadvantaged backgrounds. Additionally, the predominance of XR learning content providers in English-speaking countries limits access for learners in non-English-speaking regions and international schools that do not follow English-speaking curricula. Addressing these equity issues is paramount in designing future XR educational technologies. Inclusive design should be prioritized to ensure that these emerging technologies can serve as mainstream educational tools in real classroom settings.

Additionally, it is crucial to acknowledge a potential limitation in this chapter, which revolves around the predominantly hand-gesture nature of the stimuli provided. Technological advancements should take into account the necessity of accommodating learners with physical disabilities, cognitive impairments, or other accessibility challenges, thereby addressing the needs of the disabled community. Previous research underscores that users engage with virtual environments and objects through multiple sensory channels during XR interactions. Hence, forthcoming studies should explore stimuli incorporating haptic and auditory feedback, expanding the investigation into how various senses influence the perceived learning experience in XR environments. Within the realm of educational XR, systems could adopt similar strategies as an initial step towards fostering inclusive experiences by integrating multisensory cues and promoting embodied learning to cater to a diverse range of abilities.

Furthermore, future research endeavors should integrate collaborative learning as an integral component of learning content within XR environments. Collaborative social experiences play a pivotal role in facilitating effective immersive learning within XR settings. As previously mentioned, theoretical underpinnings such as social presence theory and computer-mediated collaborative learning emphasize the significance of fostering a sense of presence and a collaborative environment to yield positive learning outcomes. To foster spontaneous collaborative social environments within XR, users should be afforded the capability to interact with individuals or XR content naturally, utilizing gestures, speech, haptic touch, or other forms of interaction. Consequently, educators and instructional designers must exercise greater caution when designing and implementing XR technologies within authentic online classrooms.

REFERENCES

Adedoyin, O. B., & Soykan, E. (2023). Covid-19 pandemic and online learning: The challenges and opportunities. *Interactive Learning Environments, 31*(2), 863–875. doi:10.1080/10494820.2020.1813180

Agrewal, S., Simon, A. M. D., Bech, S., Bærentsen, K. B., & Forchammer, S. (2020). Defining immersion: Literature review and implications for research on audiovisual experiences. *Journal of the Audio Engineering Society, 68*(6), 404–417. doi:10.17743/jaes.2020.0039

Aguayo, C., & Eames, C. (2023). Using mixed reality (XR) immersive learning to enhance environmental education. *The Journal of Environmental Education, 54*(1), 58–71. doi:10.1080/00958964.2022.2152410

Alaghbary, G. S. (2021). Integrating technology with Bloom's revised taxonomy: Web 2.0-enabled learning designs for online learning. *Asian EFL Journal, 28*(1), 10–37.

Alalwan, N., Cheng, L., Al-Samarraie, H., Yousef, R., Alzahrani, A. I., & Sarsam, S. M. (2020). Challenges and prospects of virtual reality and augmented reality utilization among primary school teachers: A developing country perspective. *Studies in Educational Evaluation*, *66*, 100876. doi:10.1016/j. stueduc.2020.100876

Alavi, S. M., & Taghizadeh, M. (2013). Cognitive presence in a virtual learning community: An EFL Case. *International Journal of E-Learning & Distance Education/Revue internationale du e-learning et la formation à distance*, *27*(1).

Alnagrat, A., Ismail, R. C., Idrus, S. Z. S., & Alfaqi, R. M. A. (2022). A review of extended reality (xr) technologies in the future of human education: Current trend and future opportunity. *Journal of Human Centered Technology*, *1*(2), 81–96. doi:10.11113/humentech.v1n2.27

Alnagrat, A. J. A., Zulkifli, A. N., & Yusoff, M. F. (2014). Evaluation of UUM mobile augmented reality based i-brochure application. *International Journal of Computing. Communication and Instrumentation Engineering*, *2*(2), 92–97.

Aziz, A. (2023). The importance of art implementation in college general education. *Policy Futures in Education*. Advance online publication. doi:10.1177/14782103231172818

Baniasadi, T., Ayyoubzadeh, S. M., & Mohammadzadeh, N. (2020). Challenges and practical considerations in applying virtual reality in medical education and treatment. *Oman Medical Journal*, *35*(3), e125. doi:10.5001/omj.2020.43 PMID:32489677

Benson, A. D. (2002). Using online learning to meet workforce demand: A case study of stakeholder influence. *Quarterly Review of Distance Education*, *3*(4), 443–452.

Berge, Z. L., & Collins, M. P. (Eds.). (1995). Computer mediated communication and the online classroom: distance learning. Academic Press.

Birchfield, D., & Megowan-Romanowicz, C. (2009). Earth science learning in SMALLab: A design experiment for mixed reality. *International Journal of Computer-Supported Collaborative Learning*, *4*(4), 403–421. doi:10.1007/s11412-009-9074-8

Black, J. B., Segal, A., Vitale, J., & Fadjo, C. L. (2012). Embodied cognition and learning environment design. *Theoretical Foundations of Learning Environments*, *2*, 198–223.

Bower, M., Howe, C., McCredie, N., Robinson, A., & Grover, D. (2014). Augmented reality in education—Cases, places and potentials. *Educational Media International*, *51*(1), 1–15. doi:10.1080/09523 987.2014.889400

Brkić, V. K. S., Putnik, G. D., Veljkovic, Z. A., & Shah, V. (2016). Interface for distributed remote user controlled manufacturing: manufacturing and education sectors led view. In Handbook of Research on Human-Computer Interfaces, Developments, and Applications (pp. 363-391). IGI Global. doi:10.4018/978-1-5225-0435-1.ch015

Calvo, S., Lyon, F., Morales, A., & Wade, J. (2020). Educating at scale for sustainable development and social enterprise growth: The impact of online learning and a massive open online course (MOOC). *Sustainability (Basel)*, *12*(8), 3247. doi:10.3390/su12083247

Canabal, J. A., Otaduy, M. A., Kim, B., & Echevarria, J. (2020, May). Simulation of Dendritic Painting. *Computer Graphics Forum, 39*(2), 597–606. doi:10.1111/cgf.13955

Cesari, V., Galgani, B., Gemignani, A., & Menicucci, D. (2021). Enhancing qualities of consciousness during online learning via multisensory interactions. *Behavioral Sciences (Basel, Switzerland), 11*(5), 57. doi:10.3390/bs11050057 PMID:33919379

Chen, C. M., & Wu, C. H. (2015). Effects of different video lecture types on sustained attention, emotion, cognitive load, and learning performance. *Computers & Education, 80*, 108–121. doi:10.1016/j.compedu.2014.08.015

Chou, S. W., & Min, H. T. (2009). The impact of media on collaborative learning in virtual settings: The perspective of social construction. *Computers & Education, 52*(2), 417–431. doi:10.1016/j.compedu.2008.09.006

Choudhury, N., & Kumar, J. (2023, July). Investigation of Chromatic Perception of School Children During HCI in Computer-Supported Collaborative Learning. In *International Conference on Human-Computer Interaction* (pp. 225-230). Cham: Springer Nature Switzerland. 10.1007/978-3-031-35998-9_31

Coban, M., Bolat, Y. I., & Goksu, I. (2022). The potential of immersive virtual reality to enhance learning: A meta-analysis. *Educational Research Review, 36*, 100452. doi:10.1016/j.edurev.2022.100452

Coman, C., Țîru, L. G., Meseșan-Schmitz, L., Stanciu, C., & Bularca, M. C. (2020). Online teaching and learning in higher education during the coronavirus pandemic: Students' perspective. *Sustainability (Basel), 12*(24), 10367. doi:10.3390/su122410367

Conrad, D. (2002). Deep in the hearts of learners: Insights into the nature of online community. *Journal of Distance Education, 17*(1), 1–19.

Cook, M., Lischer-Katz, Z., Hall, N., Hardesty, J., Johnson, J., McDonald, R., & Carlisle, T. (2019). Challenges and strategies for educational virtual reality. *Information Technology and Libraries, 38*(4), 25–48. doi:10.6017/ital.v38i4.11075

Corcoran, R. P., Cheung, A. C., Kim, E., & Xie, C. (2018). Effective universal school-based social and emotional learning programs for improving academic achievement: A systematic review and meta-analysis of 50 years of research. *Educational Research Review, 25*, 56–72. doi:10.1016/j.edurev.2017.12.001

Dalgarno, B., & Lee, M. J. (2010). What are the learning affordances of 3-D virtual environments? *British Journal of Educational Technology, 41*(1), 10–32. doi:10.1111/j.1467-8535.2009.01038.x

Doolani, S., Wessels, C., Kanal, V., Sevastopoulos, C., Jaiswal, A., Nambiappan, H., & Makedon, F. (2020). A review of extended reality (xr) technologies for manufacturing training. *Technologies, 8*(4), 77. doi:10.3390/technologies8040077

Fernandez, M. (2017). Augmented virtual reality: How to improve education systems. *Higher Learning Research Communications, 7*(1), 1–15. doi:10.18870/hlrc.v7i1.373

Flavián, C., Ibáñez-Sánchez, S., & Orús, C. (2021). The influence of scent on virtual reality experiences: The role of aroma-content congruence. *Journal of Business Research, 123*, 289–301. doi:10.1016/j.jbusres.2020.09.036

Floor, N. (2016, September 28). *This is learning experience design.* LinkedIn. https://www.linkedin.com/pulse/learning-experience-design-niels-floor

Fortman, J., & Quintana, R. (2023). Fostering collaborative and embodied learning with extended reality: Special issue introduction. *International Journal of Computer-Supported Collaborative Learning, 18*(2), 145–152. doi:10.1007/s11412-023-09404-1

Fotaris, P. (2020). *ECGBL 2020 14th European Conference on Game-Based Learning.* Academic Conferences limited.

Fransson, G., Holmberg, J., & Westelius, C. (2020). The challenges of using head mounted virtual reality in K-12 schools from a teacher perspective. *Education and Information Technologies, 25*(4), 3383–3404. doi:10.1007/s10639-020-10119-1

Gallagher, S., & Lindgren, R. (2015). Enactive metaphors: Learning through full-body engagement. *Educational Psychology Review, 27*(3), 391–404. doi:10.1007/s10648-015-9327-1

Georgiou, Y., & Ioannou, A. (2019). Embodied learning in a digital world: A systematic review of empirical research in K-12 education. *Learning in a digital world: Perspective on Interactive Technologies for Formal and Informal Education,* 155-177.

Gilardi, M., Hainey, T., Bakhshi, A., Rodriguez, C., & Walker, A. (2021, September). XR Maths: Designing a Collaborative Extended Realities lab for Teaching Mathematics. *Proceedings of the 15th European Conference on Game Based Learning (ECGBL),* 277-286. https://doi.org/10.34190/GBL.21.115

Goldin-Meadow, S., & Beilock, S. L. (2010). Action's influence on thought: The Case of gesture. *Perspectives on Psychological Science, 5*(6), 664–674. doi:10.1177/1745691610388764 PMID:21572548

Grassini, S., Laumann, K., & Rasmussen Skogstad, M. (2020). The use of virtual reality alone does not promote training performance (but sense of presence does). *Frontiers in Psychology, 11,* 1743. doi:10.3389/fpsyg.2020.01743 PMID:32765384

Ip, H. H. S., Li, C., Wong, Y. W., Leoni, S., Ma, K. F., Wong, H. T., & Sham, S. H. (2016). Delivering Immersive Learning Experience for Massive Open Online Courses (MOOCs). In D. Chiu, I. Marenzi, U. Nanni, M. Spaniol, & M. Temperini (Eds.), *Advances in Web-Based Learning – ICWL 2016.* Springer. doi:10.1007/978-3-319-47440-3_12

Jin, X., & Ye, Y. (2022). Impact of fine arts education on psychological wellbeing of higher education students through moderating role of creativity and self-efficacy. *Frontiers in Psychology, 13,* 1–13. doi:10.3389/fpsyg.2022.957578 PMID:36017422

Johnson-Glenberg, M. C. (2019). The necessary nine: Design principles for embodied VR and active stem education. *Learning in a digital world: Perspective on interactive technologies for formal and informal education,* 83-112.

Joyce, K. M., & Brown, A. (2009). Enhancing social presence in online learning: Mediation strategies applied to social networking tools. *Online Journal of Distance Learning Administration, 12*(4), n4.

Kang, B. (2013). Implication of Embodied Cognition for Art Education. *Journal of Research in Art & Education, 14*(1), 73–94. doi:10.20977/kkosea.2013.14.1.73

Kang, J., Diederich, M., Lindgren, R., & Junokas, M. (2021). Gesture patterns and learning in an embodied XR science simulation. *Journal of Educational Technology & Society*, *24*(2), 77–92.

Kavanagh, S., Luxton-Reilly, A., Wuensche, B., & Plimmer, B. (2017). A systematic review of virtual reality in education. *Themes in Science and Technology Education, 10*(2), 85-119. https://eric.ed.gov/?id=EJ1165633

Kolb, D. A. (2014). *Experiential learning: Experience as the source of learning and development*. FT Press.

Lindgren, R. (2014). Getting into the cue: Embracing technology-facilitated body movements as a starting point for learning. In *Learning Technologies and the Body* (pp. 39–54). Routledge.

Lindgren, R., & Johnson-Glenberg, M. (2013). Emboldened by embodiment: Six precepts for research on embodied learning and mixed reality. *Educational Researcher*, *42*(8), 445–452. doi:10.3102/0013189X13511661

MacKenzie, A., Bacalja, A., Annamali, D., Panaretou, A., Girme, P., Cutajar, M., Abegglen, S., Evens, M., Neuhaus, F., Wilson, K., Psarikidou, K., Koole, M., Hrastinski, S., Sturm, S., Adachi, C., Schnaider, K., Bozkurt, A., Rapanta, C., Themelis, C., ... Gourlay, L. (2022). Dissolving the dichotomies between online and campus-based teaching: A collective response to the manifesto for teaching online (Bayne et al. 2020). *Postdigital Science and Education*, *4*(2), 271–329. doi:10.1007/s42438-021-00259-z

Makransky, G., & Petersen, G. B. (2021). The cognitive affective model of immersive learning (CAMIL): A theoretical research-based model of learning in immersive virtual reality. *Educational Psychology Review*, *33*(3), 1–22. doi:10.1007/s10648-020-09586-2

Mayer, R. E. (2014). Principles based on social cues in multimedia learning: Personalization, voice, image, and embodiment principles. The Cambridge Handbook of Multimedia Learning, 16, 345-370.

Morimoto, T., Hirata, H., Ueno, M., Fukumori, N., Sakai, T., Sugimoto, M., Kobayashi, T., Tsukamoto, M., Yoshihara, T., Toda, Y., Oda, Y., Otani, K., & Mawatari, M. (2022). Digital transformation will change medical education and rehabilitation in spine surgery. *Medicina*, *58*(4), 508. doi:10.3390/medicina58040508 PMID:35454347

Muir, T., Douglas, T., & Trimble, A. (2020). Facilitation strategies for enhancing the learning and engagement of online students. *Journal of University Teaching & Learning Practice, 17*(3), 8. doi:10.53761/1.17.3.8

Mykota, D., & Duncan, R. (2007). Learner characteristics as predictors of online social presence. *Canadian Journal of Education*, *30*(1), 157–170. doi:10.2307/20466630

Nonaka, I., & Von Krogh, G. (2009). Perspective—Tacit knowledge and knowledge conversion: Controversy and advancement in organizational knowledge creation theory. *Organization Science*, *20*(3), 635–652. doi:10.1287/orsc.1080.0412

Park, D., Lee, G., Kang, S., Kim, S., Ahn, E., & Jang, S. (2022). Deriving Improvement Measures for University Teaching and Learning Following the Implementation of Online Classes in the Post-COVID-19 Era. *Industrial Convergence Research*, *20*(3), 11–21. doi:10.22678/JIC.2022.20.3.011

Park, S., Jeong, Y., Kim, D., & Ryu, J. (in press). Cultivating Cultural Immersion Through an Extended Reality-based Digital Board Game in Social Studies. In M. Schmidt, B. Hokanson, M. Exter, A. Tawfik, & Y. Earnshaw (Eds.), *Transdisciplinary Learning Experience Design: Futures, Synergies, and Innovation*. Springer.

Pregowska, A., Masztalerz, K., Garlińska, M., & Osial, M. (2021). A worldwide journey through distance education—From the post office to virtual, augmented and mixed realities, and education during the COVID-19 pandemic. *Education Sciences*, *11*(3), 118. doi:10.3390/educsci11030118

Prieto, L. P., Sharma, K., Kidzinski, Ł., Rodríguez-Triana, M. J., & Dillenbourg, P. (2018). Multimodal teaching analytics: Automated extraction of orchestration graphs from wearable sensor data. *Journal of Computer Assisted Learning*, *34*(2), 193–203. doi:10.1111/jcal.12232 PMID:29686446

Ruzmetova, M. (2018). Applying Gilly Salmon's five stage model for designing blended courses. *Dil ve Edebiyat Araştırmaları*, *17*(17), 271–290. doi:10.30767/diledeara.418085

Salar, R., Arici, F., Caliklar, S., & Yilmaz, R. M. (2020). A model for augmented reality immersion experiences of university students studying in science education. *Journal of Science Education and Technology*, *29*(2), 257–271. doi:10.1007/s10956-019-09810-x

Salazar, S. (2021). *A Guide to Teaching Art at the College Level*. Teachers College Press.

Salmon, G. (2002). Approaches to Researching Teaching and Learning Online. In C. Steeples & C. Jones (Eds.), *Networked Learning: Perspectives and Issues*. Springer., doi:10.1007/978-1-4471-0181-9_11

Saul Carliner. (2004). *An Overview of Online Learning*. Human Resource Development.

Schmidt, M., & Huang, R. (2021). Defining learning experience design: Voices from the field of learning design & technology. *TechTrends*, *66*(2), 141–158. doi:10.1007/s11528-021-00656-y

Shih, Y. H. (2019). An examination of the functions of a general education art curriculum in universities. *Policy Futures in Education*, *17*(3), 306–317. doi:10.1177/1478210318811012

Slater, M. (2017). Implicit learning through embodiment in immersive virtual reality. *Virtual, Augmented, and Mixed Realities in Education*, 19-33.

Suh, A., & Prophet, J. (2018). The state of immersive technology research: A literature analysis. *Computers in Human Behavior*, *86*, 77–90. doi:10.1016/j.chb.2018.04.019

Sun, A., & Chen, X. (2016). Online education and its effective practice: A research review. *Journal of Information Technology Education*, *15*, 15. doi:10.28945/3502

Velev, D., & Zlateva, P. (2017). Virtual reality challenges in education and training. *International Journal of Learning and Teaching*, *3*(1), 33–37. doi:10.18178/ijlt.3.1.33-37

Wang, B. (2022). The Application of Modern Computer-Aided Technology in Fine Art Education. *Security and Communication Networks*, *2022*, 1–10. doi:10.1155/2022/8288855

Wilson, M. (2002). Six views of embodied cognition. *Psychonomic Bulletin & Review*, *9*(4), 625–636. doi:10.3758/BF03196322 PMID:12613670

Witmer, B. G., & Singer, M. J. (1998). Measuring presence in virtual environments: A presence questionnaire. *Presence (Cambridge, Mass.)*, *7*(3), 225–240. doi:10.1162/105474698565686

Wu, B., Yu, X., & Gu, X. (2020). Effectiveness of immersive virtual reality using head-mounted displays on learning performance: A meta-analysis. *British Journal of Educational Technology*, *51*(6), 1991–2005. doi:10.1111/bjet.13023

Wyss, C., Bührer, W., Furrer, F., Degonda, A., & Hiss, J. A. (2021). Innovative teacher education with the augmented reality device Microsoft Hololens—Results of an exploratory study and pedagogical considerations. *Multimodal Technologies and Interaction*, *5*(8), 45. doi:10.3390/mti5080045

Xu, D., & Xu, Y. (2020). The ambivalence about distance learning in higher education: Challenges, opportunities, and policy implications. Higher Education: Handbook of Theory and Research, 35, 351-401.

Xu, W., Xing, Q. W., Zhu, J. D., Liu, X., & Jin, P. N. (2023). Effectiveness of an extended-reality interactive learning system in a dance training course. *Education and Information Technologies*, *28*(12), 1–31. doi:10.1007/s10639-023-11883-6

Yamada, M. (2009). The role of social presence in learner-centered communicative language learning using synchronous computer-mediated communication: Experimental study. *Computers & Education*, *52*(4), 820–833. doi:10.1016/j.compedu.2008.12.007

Yang, K., Zhou, X., & Radu, I. (2020). XR-ed framework: Designing instruction-driven and learner-centered extended reality systems for education. *arXiv preprint arXiv:2010.13779*.

Yiannoutsou, N., Johnson, R., & Price, P. (2021). Non-visual virtual reality: Considerations for the pedagogical design of embodied mathematical experiences for visually impaired children. *Journal of Educational Technology & Society*, *24*(2), 151–163.

Zinchenko, Y. P., Khoroshikh, P. P., Sergievich, A. A., Smirnov, A. S., Tumyalis, A. V., Kovalev, A. I., & Golokhvast, K. S. (2020). Virtual reality is more efficient in learning human heart anatomy especially for subjects with low baseline knowledge. *New Ideas in Psychology*, *59*, 100786. doi:10.1016/j.newideapsych.2020.100786

Compilation of References

75% of College Students Unhappy with Quality of eLearning During Covid-19 . (2020). https://oneclass.com/blog/featured/177356-7525-of-college-students-unhappy-with-quality-of-elearning-during-covid-19.en.html

Abacioglu, C. S., Volman, M., & Fischer, A. H. (2020). Teachers' multicultural attitudes and perspective-taking abilities as factors in culturally responsive teaching. *The British Journal of Educational Psychology, 90*(3), 736–752. doi:10.1111/bjep.12328 PMID:31814111

Adams, N., Little, T. D., & Ryan, R. M. (2017). Self-Determination Theory. In M. Wehmeyer, K. Shogren, T. Little, & S. Lopez (Eds.), *Development of Self-Determination Through the Life-Course*. Springer. doi:10.1007/978-94-024-1042-6_4

Addae, D. (2022). Online Student Engagement in Times of Emergency: Listening to the Voices of Students. *E-Learning and Digital Media*.

Adedoyin, O. B., & Soykan, E. (2023). Covid-19 pandemic and online learning: The challenges and opportunities. *Interactive Learning Environments, 31*(2), 863–875. doi:10.1080/10494820.2020.1813180

Adzima, K. (2020). Examining Online Cheating in Higher Education Using Traditional Classroom Cheating as a Guide. *Electronic Journal of e-Learning, 18*(6), 476–493.

Agrawal, S., Simon, A. M. D., Bech, S., Bærentsen, K. B., & Forchammer, S. (2020). Defining immersion. Literature review and implications for research on audiovisual experiences. *Journal of the Audio Engineering Society, 68*(6), 404–417. doi:10.17743/jaes.2020.0039

Aguayo, C., & Eames, C. (2023). Using mixed reality (XR) immersive learning to enhance environmental education. *The Journal of Environmental Education, 54*(1), 58–71. doi:10.1080/00958964.2022.2152410

Aivo. (2020). *How universities are using education chatbots to enhance the system*. Retrieved January 15, 2024, https://www.aivo.co/blog/how-universities-are-using-education-chatbots-to-enhance-the-system

Akcaoglu, M., & Lee, E. (2016). Increasing social presence in online learning through small group discussions. *The International Review of Research in Open and Distributed Learning, 17*(3).

Akyol, Z., & Garrison, D. R. (2011). Understanding cognitive presence in an online and blended community of inquiry: Assessing outcomes and processes for deep approaches to learning. *British Journal of Educational Technology, 42*(2), 233–250. doi:10.1111/j.1467-8535.2009.01029.x

Akyol, Z., Garrison, D., & Ozden, M. (2009). Online and blended communities of inquiry: Exploring the developmental and perceptional differences. *International Review of Research in Open and Distance Learning, 10*(6), 65–83. doi:10.19173/irrodl.v10i6.765

Alaghbary, G. S. (2021). Integrating technology with Bloom's revised taxonomy: Web 2.0-enabled learning designs for online learning. *Asian EFL Journal, 28*(1), 10–37.

Alalwan, N., Cheng, L., Al-Samarraie, H., Yousef, R., Alzahrani, A. I., & Sarsam, S. M. (2020). Challenges and prospects of virtual reality and augmented reality utilization among primary school teachers: A developing country perspective. *Studies in Educational Evaluation, 66*, 100876. doi:10.1016/j.stueduc.2020.100876

Alamri, H. A., Watson, S., & Watson, W. (2021). Learning Technology Models that Support Personalization within Blended Learning Environments in Higher Education. *TechTrends, 65*(1), 62–78. doi:10.1007/s11528-020-00530-3

Alanzi, N. S. A., & Alhalafawy, W. S. (2022). A Proposed Model for Employing Digital Platforms in Developing the Motivation for Achievement Among Students of Higher Education During Emergencies. *Journal of Positive School Psychology, 6*(9), 4921–4933.

Alavi, S. M., & Taghizadeh, M. (2013). Cognitive presence in a virtual learning community: An EFL Case. *International Journal of E-Learning & Distance Education/Revue internationale du e-learning et la formation à distance, 27*(1).

Al-Badi, A., Khan, A., & Eid-Alotaibi. (2022). Perceptions of Learners and Instructors towards Artificial Intelligence in Personalized Learning. *Procedia Computer Science, 201*, 445–451. doi:10.1016/j.procs.2022.03.058

Alenezi, M. (2023). Digital Learning and Digital Institution in Higher Education. *Education Sciences, 13*(1), 88. doi:10.3390/educsci13010088

Ali, W. (2020). Online and remote learning in higher education institutes: A necessity in light of COVID-19 pandemic. *Higher Education Studies, 10*(3), 16–25. doi:10.5539/hes.v10n3p16

AlJeraisy, M. N., Mohammad, H., Fayyoumi, A., & Alrashideh, W. (2015). Web 2.0 in education: The impact of discussion board on student performance and satisfaction. *Turkish Online Journal of Educational Technology-TOJET, 14*(2), 247–258.

Allen, S. J. (2020). On the cutting edge or the chopping block? Fostering a digital mindset and tech literacy in business management education. *Journal of Management Education, 44*(3), 362–393. doi:10.1177/1052562920903077

Alnagrat, A. J. A., Zulkifli, A. N., & Yusoff, M. F. (2014). Evaluation of UUM mobile augmented reality based i-brochure application. *International Journal of Computing. Communication and Instrumentation Engineering, 2*(2), 92–97.

Alnagrat, A., Ismail, R. C., Idrus, S. Z. S., & Alfaqi, R. M. A. (2022). A review of extended reality (xr) technologies in the future of human education: Current trend and future opportunity. *Journal of Human Centered Technology, 1*(2), 81–96. doi:10.11113/humentech.v1n2.27

Aloni, M., & Harrington, C. (2018). Research based practices for improving the effectiveness of asynchronous online discussion boards. *Scholarship of Teaching and Learning in Psychology, 4*(4), 271–289. doi:10.1037/stl0000121

Alon, L., Sung, S., Cho, J., & Kizilcec, R. F. (2023). From emergency to sustainable online learning: Changes and disparities in undergraduate course grades and experiences in the context of COVID-19. *Computers & Education, 203*, 104870. doi:10.1016/j.compedu.2023.104870

Alyahyan, E., & Dustegor, D. (2020). Predicting academic success in higher education: Literature review and best practices. *International Journal of Educational Technology in Higher Education, 17*(3), 1–21. doi:10.1186/s41239-020-0177-7

Amichai-Hamburger, Y., Gazit, T., Bar-Ilan, J., Perez, O., Aharony, N., Bronstein, J., & Sarah Dyne, T. (2016). Psychological factors behind the lack of participation in online discussions. *Computers in Human Behavior, 55*, 268–277. doi:10.1016/j.chb.2015.09.009

Anagnostopoulos, D., Basmadjian, K. G., & McCrory, R. S. (2005). The decentered teacher and the construction of social space in the virtual classroom. *Teachers College Record*, *107*(8), 1699–1729. doi:10.1111/j.1467-9620.2005.00539.x

Anderson, T., Liam, R., Garrison, D. R., & Archer, W. (2001). Assessing teaching presence in a computer conferencing context. *Journal of Asynchronous Learning Networks*, *2*(5), 1–17.

Anderson, T., Rourke, L., Garrison, D. R., & Archer, W. (2001). Assessing teaching presence in a computer conferencing environment. *Journal of Asynchronous Learning Networks*, *5*(2), 1–17.

Anderson, T., Rourke, L., Garrison, D. R., & Archer, W. (2001). Journal of asynchronous learning networks. *Journal of Asynchronous Learning Networks*, *5*(2), 1–17. doi:10.24059/olj.v5i2.1875

Anderson, W. L., Mitchell, S. M., & Osgood, M. P. (2008). Gauging the gaps in student problem-solving skills: Assessment of individual and group use of problem-solving strategies using online discussions. *CBE Life Sciences Education*, *7*(2), 254–262. doi:10.1187/cbe.07-06-0037 PMID:18519617

Andersson, R. (2022). The Bioeconomy and the Birth of a "New Anthropology". *Cultural Anthropology*, *37*(1), 37–44. doi:10.14506/ca37.1.06

Andrews, J. (1980). The verbal structure of teacher questions: Its impact on class discussion. POD Quarterly. *Journal of Professional and Organizational Development Network in Higher Education*, *2*(3 & 4), 129–163.

An, H., Shin, S., & Lim, K. (2009). The effects of different instructor facilitation approaches on students' interactions during asynchronous online discussions. *Computers & Education*, *53*(3), 749–760. doi:10.1016/j.compedu.2009.04.015

Aragon, S. R. (2003). Creating social presence in online environments. *New Directions for Adult and Continuing Education*, *100*(100), 57–68. doi:10.1002/ace.119

Arbaugh, J. B. (2008). Does the community of inquiry framework predict outcomes in online MBA courses? *International Review of Research in Open and Distance Learning*, *9*(2), 1–21. doi:10.19173/irrodl.v9i2.490

Arbaugh, J. B., & Hwang, A. (2006). Does "teaching presence" exist in online MBA courses? *The Internet and Higher Education*, *9*(1), 9–21. doi:10.1016/j.iheduc.2005.12.001

Ariely, D., & Wertenbroch, K. (2002). Procrastination, deadlines, and performance: Self-control by precommitment. *Psychological Science*, *13*(3), 219–224. doi:10.1111/1467-9280.00441 PMID:12009041

Armellini, C. A., Dunbar-Morris, H., Barlow, A. E., & Powell, D. (2022). Student Engagement in Blended and Connected Learning and Teaching: A View from Students. *Student Engagement in Higher Education Journal*, *4*(2), 165–181.

Aronson, B., & Laughter, J. (2016). The theory and practice of culturally relevant education: A synthesis of research across content areas. *Review of Educational Research*, *86*(1), 163–206. doi:10.3102/0034654315582066

Asino, T. I., Giacumo, L. A., & Chen, V. (2017). Culture as design "next": Theoretical frameworks to guide new design, development, and research of learning environments. *The Design Journal*, *20*(1), 875–885. doi:10.1080/14606925.2017.1353033

Azevedo, P. C., Hauth, C., Macedonia, A., Marotta, J., & Thompson, J. (2023). Retreating: The gift of time and community to write [Research Presentation]. Carnegie Project on the Education Doctorate (CPED) Convening, Pensacola, FL.

Aziz, A. (2023). The importance of art implementation in college general education. *Policy Futures in Education*. Advance online publication. doi:10.1177/14782103231172818

Azmat, M., & Ahmad, A. (2022). Lack of Social Interaction in Online Classes During COVID-19. *Journal of Materials & Environmental Sciences*, *13*(2), 185–196.

Baaki, J., & Maddrell, J. (2020). Building empathy and developing instructional design experience and skills: A case study using personas to design open education resources. *The Journal of Applied Instructional Design, 9*(3), 1–14. https://edtechbooks.org/jaid_9_3/building_empathy

Baaki, J., Maddrell, J., & Stauffer, E. (2017). Designing authentic personas for open education resources designers. *International Journal of Designs for Learning, 8*(2), 110–122. doi:10.14434/ijdl.v8i2.22427

Bahadır, E. (2016). Using neural network and logistic regression analysis to predict prospective mathematics teachers' academic success upon entering graduate education. *Educational Sciences: Theory & Practice, 16*(3), 943–964. doi:10.12738/estp.2016.3.0214

Bair, C., Grant Haworth, J., & Sandfort, M. (2004). Doctoral student learning and development: A shared responsibility. *NASPA Journal, 41*(3), 709–727. doi:10.2202/1949-6605.1395

Baker, T., & Smith, L. (2019). *Educ-AI-tion rebooted? Exploring the future of artificial intelligence in schools and colleges.* Nesta. https://media.nesta.org.uk/documents/Future_of_AI_and_education_v5_WEB.pdf

Baker, T., & Smith, L. (2019). *Educ-AI-tion rebooted? Exploring the future of artificial intelligence in schools and colleges.* Retrieved from Nesta Foundation website: https://media.nesta.org.uk/documents/Future_of_AI_and_education_v5_WEB.pdf

Bandura, A. (1977). *Social learning theory.* General Learning Press.

Bangert, A. (2008). The influence of social presence and teaching presence on the quality of online critical inquiry. *Journal of Computing in Higher Education, 20*(1), 34–61. doi:10.1007/BF03033431

Baniasadi, T., Ayyoubzadeh, S. M., & Mohammadzadeh, N. (2020). Challenges and practical considerations in applying virtual reality in medical education and treatment. *Oman Medical Journal, 35*(3), e125. doi:10.5001/omj.2020.43 PMID:32489677

Baran, E., & Correia, A. P. (2009). Student-led facilitation strategies in online discussions. *Distance Education, 30*(3), 339–361. doi:10.1080/01587910903236510

Batson, C. D. (2009). These things called empathy: Eight related but distinct phenomena. In J. Decety & W. Ickes (Eds.), *The social neuroscience of empathy* (pp. 3–15). The MIT Press. doi:10.7551/mitpress/9780262012973.003.0002

Battaglia, D., & Battaglia, J. (2016). Faculty mentoring in communication sciences and disorders: Case study of doctoral teaching practicum. *Academy of Educational Leadership Journal, 20*(3), 1–11.

Battarbee, K., & Koskinen, I. (2005). Co-experience: User experience as interaction. *CoDesign, 1*(1), 5–18. doi:10.1080/15710880412331289917

Baumeister, R. F., & Leary, M. R. (1997). Writing narrative literature reviews. *Review of General Psychology, 1*(3), 311–320. doi:10.1037/1089-2680.1.3.311

Bawa, P. (2016). Retention in online courses: Exploring issues and solutions-A literature review. *SAGE Open, 6*(1), 1–11. doi:10.1177/2158244015621777

Bayne, H., Neukrug, E., Hays, D., & Britton, B. (2013). A comprehensive model for optimizing empathy in person-centered care. *Patient Education and Counseling, 93*(2), 209–215. Advance online publication. doi:10.1016/j.pec.2013.05.016 PMID:23769885

Beaudoin, M. F. (2015). Distance education leadership in the context of digital change. *Quarterly Review of Distance Education, 16*, 33–44.

Becker, S. (2022, October 28). *Enrollment in this doctorate program is surging–here's why.* Fortune. https://fortune.com/education/articles/enrollment-in-this-doctorate-program-is-surging-heres-why/

Bégin, C., & Géarard, L. (2013). The role of supervisors in light of the experience of doctoral students. *Policy Futures in Education, 11*(3), 267–276. doi:10.2304/pfie.2013.11.3.267

Beltramo, J. L. (2018). Developing Mutual Accountability between Teachers and Students through Participation in Cogenerative Dialogues. *International Journal of Student Voice, 3*(1). https://ijsv.psu.edu/?article=developing-mutual-accountability-between-teachers-and-students-throughparticipation-in-cogenerative-dialogues

Benson, A. D. (2002). Using online learning to meet workforce demand: A case study of stakeholder influence. *Quarterly Review of Distance Education, 3*(4), 443–452.

Berge, Z. L., & Collins, M. P. (Eds.). (1995). Computer mediated communication and the online classroom: distance learning. Academic Press.

Berger, S. (2005). *How we compete: What companies around the world are doing to make it in today's global economy.* Crown Currency.

Berner, R. T. (2003). *The benefits of bulletin board discussion in a literature of journalism course.* The Technology Source. Accessed Oct 2, 2023. http://technologysource.org/article/313/

Berry, S. (2017). Student support networks in online doctoral programs: Exploring nested communities. *International Journal of Doctoral Studies,* (12), 33-48. doi:10.28945/3676

Berry, S. (2019). Teaching to connect: Community-building strategies for the virtual classroom. *Online Learning, 23*(1), 164–183. doi:.v23i1.1425 doi:10.24059/olj

Berry, L., & Kowal, K. (2022). Effect of Role-Play in Online Discussions on Student Engagement and Critical Thinking. *Online Learning : the Official Journal of the Online Learning Consortium, 26*(3). Advance online publication. doi:10.24059/olj.v26i3.3367

Bin Mubayrik, H. F. (2020). New trends in formative-summative evaluations for adult education. *SAGE Open, 10*(3). Advance online publication. doi:10.1177/2158244020941006

Biocca, F., Harms, C., & Burgoon, J. K. (2003). Toward a more robust theory and measure of social presence: Review and suggested criteria. *Presence (Cambridge, Mass.), 12*(5), 456–480. doi:10.1162/105474603322761270

Birchfield, D., & Megowan-Romanowicz, C. (2009). Earth science learning in SMALLab: A design experiment for mixed reality. *International Journal of Computer-Supported Collaborative Learning, 4*(4), 403–421. doi:10.1007/s11412-009-9074-8

Bishop, M. M. (2019). *Addressing the Employment Challenge: The Use of Postsecondary Noncredit Training in Skills Development.* American Enterprise Institute.

Black, A. (2005). The use of asynchronous discussion: Creating a text of talk. *Contemporary Issues in Technology & Teacher Education, 5*(1), 5–24.

Black, J. B., Segal, A., Vitale, J., & Fadjo, C. L. (2012). Embodied cognition and learning environment design. *Theoretical Foundations of Learning Environments, 2,* 198–223.

Bloom, B. (1956). *Taxonomy of educational objectives.* David McKay.

Bloom, B. S. (1984). The 2 Sigma Problem: The Search for Methods of Group Instruction as Effective as One-to-One Tutoring. *Educational Researcher, 13*(6), 4–16. doi:10.2307/1175554

Bolliger, D. U., & Halupa, C. (2019). Culturally Responsive Teaching in online learning environments: A faculty development intervention. *The Internet and Higher Education, 40*, 11–19.

Bolton, A., Campbell, G., & Schmorrow, D. (2007). *Towards a Closed-Loop Training System: Using a Physiological-Based Diagnosis of the Trainee's State to Drive Feedback Delivery Choices.* doi:10.1007/978-3-540-73216-7_47

Bong, W. K., & Chen, W. (2021). Increasing faculty's competence in digital accessibility for inclusive education: A systematic literature review. *International Journal of Inclusive Education, 25*, 1–17. doi:10.1080/13603116.2021.1937344

Bonner, E. P. (2014). Investigating practices of highly successful mathematics teachers of traditionally underserved students. *Educational Studies in Mathematics, 86*(3), 377–399. doi:10.1007/s10649-014-9533-7

Bonner, F. A. (2013). *The role of faculty in multicultural initiatives: A critical policy analysis of teaching and learning.* Stylus Publishing.

Boothe, D. (2019). *Discussion Groups and Online Learning.* Cognitive Science – New Media – Education. doi:10.12775/CSNME.2018.005

Borgatti, S. P., Mehra, A., Brass, D. J., & Labianca, G. (2009). Network analysis in the social sciences. *Science, 323*(5916), 892–895. doi:10.1126/science.1165821 PMID:19213908

Borrego, M. L. (2022). *The relationship between culturally engaging campus environments and sense of belonging among Hispanic students* [Unpublished doctoral dissertation]. University of Miami.

Borrego, E. (2017). *Cultural competence for public managers: Managing diversity in today's world.* Routledge. doi:10.4324/9781315095219

Boston, W., Diaz, S., Gibson, A., Ice, P., Richardson, J., & Swan, K. (2010). An exploration of the relationship between indicators of the Community of Inquiry framework and retention in online programs. *Journal of Asynchronous Learning Networks, 14*(1), 67–83.

Bowen, J. A., & Watson, C. E. (2017). *Teaching Naked Techniques: A practical guide to designing better classes.* Jossey-Bass.

Bower, M., Howe, C., McCredie, N., Robinson, A., & Grover, D. (2014). Augmented reality in education—Cases, places and potentials. *Educational Media International, 51*(1), 1–15. doi:10.1080/09523987.2014.889400

Bradley, M. E., Thom, L. R., Hayes, J., & Hay, C. (2008). Ask and you will receive: How question type influences quantity and quality of online discussions. *British Journal of Educational Technology, 39*(5), 888–900. doi:10.1111/j.1467-8535.2007.00804.x

Braumberger, E. (2021). Library Services for Autistic Students in Academic Libraries: A Literature Review. *Pathfinder: A Canadian Journal for Information Science Students and Early Career Professionals, 2*(2), 86-99.

Brinkerhoff, J., & Koroghlanian, C. M. (2007). Online students' expectations: Enhancing the fit between online students and course design. *Journal of Educational Computing Research, 36*(4), 383–393. doi:10.2190/R728-28W1-332K-U115

Brkić, V. K. S., Putnik, G. D., Veljkovic, Z. A., & Shah, V. (2016). Interface for distributed remote user controlled manufacturing: manufacturing and education sectors led view. In Handbook of Research on Human-Computer Interfaces, Developments, and Applications (pp. 363-391). IGI Global. doi:10.4018/978-1-5225-0435-1.ch015

Broadbent, J., & Poon, W. L. (2015). Self-regulated learning strategies & academic achievement in online higher education learning environments: A systematic review. *The Internet and Higher Education, 27*, 1–13. doi:10.1016/j.iheduc.2015.04.007

Broderick, M. (2020). Representation in 21st century online higher education: How the online learning culture serves diverse students. In *Socioeconomics, diversity, and the politics of online education* (pp. 165–183). IGI Global. doi:10.4018/978-1-7998-3583-7.ch010

Brooks, D., & Jeong, A. (2006). The effects of pre-structuring discussion threads on group interaction and group performance in computer-supported collaborative argumentation. *Distance Education, 27*(3), 371–390. doi:10.1080/01587910600940448

Brown, B. (2021). *Atlas of the heart: Mapping meaningful connection and the language of human experience.* Random House.

Brown, B. A., Boda, P., Lemmi, C., & Monroe, X. (2019). Moving culturally relevant pedagogy from theory to practice: Exploring teachers' application of culturally relevant education in science and mathematics. *Urban Education, 54*(6), 775–803. doi:10.1177/0042085918794802

Brown, B. W. (2012). Vision and Reality in Electronic Textbooks: What Publishers Need to Do to Survive. *Educational Technology*, 30–33.

Brown, S., & Burdsal, C. (2012). An exploration of sense of community and student success using the national survey of student engagement. *The Journal of General Education, 61*(4), 433–460. doi:10.5325/jgeneeduc.61.4.0433

Bruner, J. S. (1961). The act of discovery. *Harvard Educational Review, 31*(1), 21–32.

Budhwar, P., Malik, A., De Silva, M. T., & Thevisuthan, P. (2022). Artificial Intelligence–Challenges and Opportunities for International HRM: A Review and Research Agenda. *International Journal of Human Resource Management, 33*(6), 1065–1097. doi:10.1080/09585192.2022.2035161

Bueno, D. C. (2020). *The "New Normal": Consolidated plans, practices, policies, and procedures on flexible instructional management and supervision.* Graduate school for Professional Advancement and Continuing Education (G-SPACE), Columban College Inc.

Buss, R. R. (2018). How CPED guiding principles and design concepts influenced the development and implementation of an EdD program. *Impacting Education: Journal on Transforming Professional Practice, 3*(2). Advance online publication. doi:10.5195/ie.2018.57

Bye, L., Smith, S., & Rallis, H. M. (2009). Reflection using an online discussion forum: Impact on student learning and satisfaction. *Social Work Education, 28*(8), 841–855. doi:10.1080/02615470802641322

Byrd, J. (2016). Understanding the online doctoral learning experience: Factors that contribute to students' sense of community. *The Journal of Educators Online, 13*(2), 102–135. doi:10.9743/JEO.2016.2.3

Calderon, O., & Sood, C. (2020). Evaluating learning outcomes of an asynchronous online discussion assignment: A post-priori content analysis. *Interactive Learning Environments, 28*(1), 3–17. doi:10.1080/10494820.2018.1510421

Calvo, S., Lyon, F., Morales, A., & Wade, J. (2020). Educating at scale for sustainable development and social enterprise growth: The impact of online learning and a massive open online course (MOOC). *Sustainability (Basel), 12*(8), 3247. doi:10.3390/su12083247

Canabal, J. A., Otaduy, M. A., Kim, B., & Echevarria, J. (2020, May). Simulation of Dendritic Painting. *Computer Graphics Forum, 39*(2), 597–606. doi:10.1111/cgf.13955

Carnegie Project on the Education Doctorate. (2019). *CPED Framework.* https://www.cpedinitiative.org/assets/images/cped_infographic_5.png

Carroll, M., & Mcbain, L. (2021). Where empathy meets learning: Exploring design abilities in K-12 classrooms. *Voices from the Middle, 29*(1), 14–17. doi:10.58680/vm202131424

Carr, S. (2000). As Distance Education Comes of Age, the Challenge Is Keeping the Students. *The Chronicle of Higher Education, 46*(23).

Caskurlu, S., Maeda, Y., Richardson, J., & Lu, J. (2020). A meta-analysis addressing the relationship between teaching presence and student's satisfaction and learning. *Computers & Education, 157*, 103966. doi:10.1016/j.compedu.2020.103966

CAST. (2018). *Universal design for learning guidelines version 2.2* [graphic organizer]. CAST.

CAST. (2018). *Universal design for learning guidelines version 2.2.* http://udlguidelines.cast.org

CAST. (2018). *Universal Design for Learning Guidelines Version 2.2.* http://udlguidelines.cast.org

CAST. (2018). *Universal Design for Learning Guidelines version 2.2.* Retrieved from http://udlguidelines.cast.org

Castellanos-Reyes, D. (2020). Years of the Community of Inquiry Framework. *TechTrends, 64*(4), 557–560. doi:10.1007/s11528-020-00491-7

Castro, M. D. B., & Tumibay, G. M. (2021). A literature review: Efficacy of online learning courses for higher education institution using meta-analysis. *Education and Information Technologies, 26*(2), 1367–1385. doi:10.1007/s10639-019-10027-z

Cayanus, J. L., & Martin, M. M. (2008). Teacher self-disclosure. Amount, relevance and negativity. *Communication Quarterly, 56*(3), 325–341. doi:10.1080/01463370802241492

Center for Digital Dannelse. (2023). *The digital competence wheel.* https://digital-competence.eu/dc/en/front/what-is-digital-competence/#:~:text=Digital%20competence%20is%20a%20combination,to%20the%20use%20of%20technology

Cesari, V., Galgani, B., Gemignani, A., & Menicucci, D. (2021). Enhancing qualities of consciousness during online learning via multisensory interactions. *Behavioral Sciences (Basel, Switzerland), 11*(5), 57. doi:10.3390/bs11050057 PMID:33919379

Chen, C. M., & Wu, C. H. (2015). Effects of different video lecture types on sustained attention, emotion, cognitive load, and learning performance. *Computers & Education, 80*, 108–121. doi:10.1016/j.compedu.2014.08.015

Chen, C., Landa, S., Padilla, A., & Yur-Austin, J. (2021). Learners' experience and needs in online environments: Adopting agility in teaching. *Journal of Research in Innovative Teaching & Learning, 14*(1), 18–31. doi:10.1108/JRIT-11-2020-0073

Chen, K., He, Z., Wang, S., Hu, J., Li, L., & He, J. (2018). Learning-based data analytics: Moving towards transparent power grids. *CSEE Journal of Power and Energy Systems, 4*(1), 67–82. doi:10.17775/CSEEJPES.2017.01070

Cheung, W. S., Hew, K. F., & Ng, C. L. (2008). Toward an understanding of why students contribute in asynchronous online discussions. *Journal of Educational Computing Research, 38*(1), 29–50. doi:10.2190/EC.38.1.b

Chiu, T. K. F. (2022). Applying the self-determination theory (SDT) to explain student engagement in online learning during the COVID-19 pandemic. *Journal of Research on Technology in Education, 54*(sup1, S1), S14–S30. doi:10.1080/15391523.2021.1891998

Choudhury, N., & Kumar, J. (2023, July). Investigation of Chromatic Perception of School Children During HCI in Computer-Supported Collaborative Learning. In *International Conference on Human-Computer Interaction* (pp. 225-230). Cham: Springer Nature Switzerland. 10.1007/978-3-031-35998-9_31

Chounta, I. A., Bardone, E., Raudsep, A., & Pedaste, M. (2022). Exploring teachers' perceptions of Artificial Intelligence as a tool to support their practice in Estonian K-12 education. *International Journal of Artificial Intelligence in Education, 32*(3), 725–755. doi:10.1007/s40593-021-00243-5

Chou, S. W., & Min, H. T. (2009). The impact of media on collaborative learning in virtual settings: The perspective of social construction. *Computers & Education, 52*(2), 417–431. doi:10.1016/j.compedu.2008.09.006

Chu, S. K. W., Zhang, Y., Chen, K., Chan, C. K., Lee, C. W. Y., Zou, E., & Lau, W. (2017). The effectiveness of wikis for project-based learning in different disciplines in higher education. *The Internet and Higher Education, 33*, 49–60. doi:10.1016/j.iheduc.2017.01.005

Cipresso, P., Giglioli, I., Raya, M., & Rivan, G. (2018). The Past, Present, and Future of Virtual and Augmented Reality Research: A Network and Cluster Analysis of the Literature. *Frontiers in Psychology, 9*, 1–20. doi:10.3389/fpsyg.2018.02086 PMID:30459681

Clark, D. (2023). PedAIgogy – New Era of Knowledge and Learning Where AI Changes Everything. *Plan B*. http://donaldclarkplanb.blogspot.com/2023/03/pedaigogy-new-era-of-knowledge-and.html?m=1

Clark, R. C., & Mayer, R. E. (2016). e-Learning and the science of instruction: Proven guidelines for consumers and designers of multimedia learning. Wiley.

Cleveland Clinic. (2021). *How Box Breathing Can Help You Destress*. https://health.clevelandclinic.org/box-breathing-benefits

Cliffordson, C. (2002). The hierarchical structure of empathy: Dimensional organization and relations to social functioning. *Scandinavian Journal of Psychology, 43*(1), 49–59. doi:10.1111/1467-9450.00268 PMID:11885760

Coban, M., Bolat, Y. I., & Goksu, I. (2022). The potential of immersive virtual reality to enhance learning: A meta-analysis. *Educational Research Review, 36*, 100452. doi:10.1016/j.edurev.2022.100452

Cole, A. W., Lennon, L., & Weber, N. L. (2021). Student perceptions of online active learning practices and online learning climate predict online course engagement. *Interactive Learning Environments, 29*(5), 866–880. doi:10.1080/10494820.2019.1619593

Collins, J. A., & Fauser, B. C. J. M. (2005). Balancing the strengths of systematic and narrative reviews. *Human Reproduction Update, 11*(2), 103–104. doi:10.1093/humupd/dmh058 PMID:15618290

Comadena, M. E., Hunt, S. K., & Simonds, C. J. (2007). The Effects of Teacher Clarity, Nonverbal Immediacy, and Caring on Student Motivation, Affective and Cognitive Learning. *Communication Research Reports, 24*(3), 241–248. doi:10.1080/08824090701446617

Coman, C., Țîru, L. G., Meseșan-Schmitz, L., Stanciu, C., & Bularca, M. C. (2020). Online teaching and learning in higher education during the coronavirus pandemic: Students' perspective. *Sustainability (Basel), 12*(24), 10367. doi:10.3390/su122410367

Cominelli, L., Hoegen, G., & De Rossi, D. (2021). Abel: Integrating Humanoid Body, Emotions, and Time Perception to Investigate Social Interaction and Human Cognition. *Applied Sciences (Basel, Switzerland), 11*(3), 1070. doi:10.3390/app11031070

Conrad, D. (2002). Deep in the hearts of learners: Insights into the nature of online community. *Journal of Distance Education, 17*(1), 1–19.

Cook, M., Lischer-Katz, Z., Hall, N., Hardesty, J., Johnson, J., McDonald, R., & Carlisle, T. (2019). Challenges and strategies for educational virtual reality. *Information Technology and Libraries, 38*(4), 25–48. doi:10.6017/ital.v38i4.11075

Cooper, L., & Burford, S. (2010). Collaborative Learning: Using Group Work Concepts for Online Teaching. In Web-Based Education: Concepts, Methodologies, Tools and Applications (pp. 163-178). IGI Global.

Cooper, A., Reimann, R., Cronin, D., & Noessel, C. (2014). *About face: The essentials of interaction design* (4th ed.). John Wiley & Sons, Inc.

Cope, B., & Kalantzis, M. (2023). A Little History of E-Learning: Finding New Ways to Learn in the PLATO Computer Education System, 1959–1976. *History of Education, 52*(6), 1–32. doi:10.1080/0046760X.2022.2141353

Corcoran, R. P., Cheung, A. C., Kim, E., & Xie, C. (2018). Effective universal school-based social and emotional learning programs for improving academic achievement: A systematic review and meta-analysis of 50 years of research. *Educational Research Review, 25*, 56–72. doi:10.1016/j.edurev.2017.12.001

Corp, I. B. M. (2020). *IBM SPSS Statistics for Windows (Version 27.0)* [Computer software]. IBM Corp.

Counselman Carpenter, E. A., Meltzer, A., & Marquart, M. (2020). Best Practices for Inclusivity of Deaf/deaf/Hard of Hearing Students in the Synchronous Online Classroom. *World Journal of Education, 10*(4), 26–34. doi:10.5430/wje.v10n4p26

Craig, L., & Kuykendall, L. (2020). Fostering an inclusive classroom environment with evidence-based approaches. *Industrial and Organizational Psychology: Perspectives on Science and Practice, 13*(4), 482–486. doi:10.1017/iop.2020.85

Cruz, R. A., Manchanda, S., Firestone, A. R., & Rodl, J. E. (2020). An examination of teachers' culturally responsive teaching self-efficacy. *Teacher Education and Special Education, 43*(3), 197–214. doi:10.1177/0888406419875194

Crystle, J., Boyd, R., Melideo, S., & Hauth, C. (2024). *Faculty mentors' perceptions: Evidence of applied practitioner research by EdD candidates. In Impacting Education.* CPED.

Cunha, F. R. Jr, van Kruistum, C., & van Oers, B. (2016). Teachers and Facebook: Using online groups to improve student's communication and engagement in education. *Communication Teacher, 30*(4), 228–241. doi:10.1080/17404622.2016.1219039

Daigle, D. T., & Stuvland, A. (2021). Social presence as best practice: The online classroom needs to feel real. *PS, Political Science & Politics, 54*(1), 182–183. doi:10.1017/S1049096520001614

Dalgarno, B., & Lee, M. J. (2010). What are the learning affordances of 3-D virtual environments? *British Journal of Educational Technology, 41*(1), 10–32. doi:10.1111/j.1467-8535.2009.01038.x

Dalton, A. (2023). Hollywood actors' union board approves strike-ending deal as leaders tout money gains and AI rights. *WHYY.* Retrieved on January 15, 2024, https://whyy.org/articles/hollywood-actors-union-board-strike-ending-deal-money-gains-ai-rights/

Darby, F., & Lang, J. M. (2019). *Small teaching online: Applying learning science in online classes.* John Wiley & Sons.

Darling-Hammond, L., Hyler, M. E., & Gardner, M. (2017). *Effective teacher professional development.* Learning Policy Institute. doi:10.54300/122.311

Daryanavard, S., & Porr, B. (2020). Closed-Loop Deep Learning: Generating Forward Models With Backpropagation. *Neural Computation, 32*(11), 2122–2144. doi:10.1162/neco_a_01317 PMID:32946708

David, F.D. (1989). Perceived usefulness, perceived ease of use and user acceptance of information technology. *MIS Quarterly, 13*.

Davis, M. H. (1994). *Empathy: A social psychological approach.* Westview Press.

Day, L., & Beard, K. V. (2019). Meaningful inclusion of diverse voices: The case for culturally responsive teaching in nursing education. *Journal of Professional Nursing, 35*(4), 277–281. doi:10.1016/j.profnurs.2019.01.002 PMID:31345507

de Carvalho, P. A. C. (2019). *Emojar: Collecting and Reliving Memorable and Emotionally Impactful Digital Content* [Doctoral dissertation]. Universidade de Lisboa.

de Lima, D. P., Gerosa, M. A., & Conte, T. U., & de M. Netto, J. F. (2019). What to expect, and how to improve online discussion forums: The instructors' perspective. *Journal of Internet Services and Applications, 10*, 1–15. doi:10.1186/s13174-019-0120-0

De Oliveira, A. S., Silva, M. A. R., Da Silva, D., & Borges, R. C. (2021). Quality Assessment of Online Discussion Forums: Construction and Validation of a Scale That Values Student Perception. *Turkish Online Journal of Distance Education, 22*(4), 43–57. doi:10.17718/tojde.1002759

De Wever, B., Schellens, T., Valcke, M., & Van Keer, H. (2006). Content analysis schemes to analyze transcripts of online asynchronous discussion groups: A review. *Computers & Education, 46*(1), 6–28. doi:10.1016/j.compedu.2005.04.005

Dearing, V. A. (2023). *Manual of textual analysis*. Univ of California Press. doi:10.2307/jj.8306194

Deaton, S. (2015). Social learning theory in the age of social media: Implications for educational practitioners. *Journal of Educational Technology, 12*(1), 1–6.

Deci, E. L., & Ryan, R. M. (2000). The" what" and" why" of goal pursuits: Human needs and the self-determination of behavior. *Psychological Inquiry, 11*(4), 227–268. doi:10.1207/S15327965PLI1104_01

DeCuir, J. T., & Dixson, A. D. (2004). So when it comes out, they aren't that surprised that it is there: Using Critical Race Theory as a tool of analysis of race and racism in education. *Educational Researcher, 33*(5), 26–31. doi:10.3102/0013189X033005026

Dede, C. (2006). *Online professional development for teachers: Emerging models and methods*. Harvard Education Press.

Dejene, W. (2019). *The Practice of Modularized Curriculum in Higher Education Institution: Active Learning and Continuous Assessment in Focus. Cogent Education, 6(1)*.

Delahunty, J. (2018). Connecting to learn, learning to connect: Thinking together in asynchronous forum discussion. *Linguistics and Education, 46*, 12–22. doi:10.1016/j.linged.2018.05.003

Dell, C. A., Dell, T. F., & Blackwell, T. L. (2015). Applying universal design for learning in online courses: Pedagogical and practical considerations. *The Journal of Educators Online, 12*(2), 166–192. doi:10.9743/JEO.2015.2.1

Dennen, V. P. (2005). From message posting to learning dialogues: Factors affecting learner participation in asynchronous discussion. *Distance Education, 26*(1), 127–148. doi:10.1080/01587910500081376

Devecchi, A., & Guerrini, L. (2017). Empathy and design. A new perspective. *The Design Journal, 20*(1), 4357–4364. doi:10.1080/14606925.2017.1352932

Dewey, J. (1910). *How we think*. D.C. Heath and Company. doi:10.1037/10903-000

Dewey, J. (1959). My pedagogic creed. In J. Dewey (Ed.), *Dewey on education* (pp. 19–32). Teachers College, Columbia University. (Original work published 1897)

Dias, B., & Boulder, T. (2023). Toward Humanizing Online Learning Spaces. *The Journal of Applied Instructional Design, 12*(4). https://edtechbooks.org/jaid_12_4/toward_humanizing_online_learning_spaces

Dick, W., Carey, L., & Carey, J. O. (2015). *The systematic design of instruction* (8th ed.). Pearson.

Ding, L., Er, E., & Orey, M. (2018). An exploratory study of student engagement in gamified online discussions. *Computers & Education*, *120*, 213–226. doi:10.1016/j.compedu.2018.02.007

Discord. (2023, November 26). https://discord.com/

Dixson, M. (2015). Measuring student engagement in the online course: The Online Student Engagement Scale. *Online Learning : the Official Journal of the Online Learning Consortium*, *19*(4). Advance online publication. doi:10.24059/olj.v19i4.561

Dixson, M. D., Greenwell, M. R., Rogers-Stacy, C., Weister, T., & Lauer, S. (2017). Nonverbal immediacy behaviors and online student engagement: Bringing past instructional research into the present virtual classroom. *Communication Education*, *66*(1), 37–53. doi:10.1080/03634523.2016.1209222

Dohrenwend, A. M. (2018). Defining empathy to better teach, measure, and understand its impact. *Academic Medicine*, *93*(12), 1754–1756. doi:10.1097/ACM.0000000000002427 PMID:30134271

Doolani, S., Wessels, C., Kanal, V., Sevastopoulos, C., Jaiswal, A., Nambiappan, H., & Makedon, F. (2020). A review of extended reality (xr) technologies for manufacturing training. *Technologies*, *8*(4), 77. doi:10.3390/technologies8040077

Douglas, T., James, A., Earwaker, L., Mather, C., & Murray, S. (2020). Online discussion boards: Improving practice and student engagement by harnessing facilitator perceptions. *Journal of University Teaching & Learning Practice*, *17*(3), 7. doi:10.53761/1.17.3.7

Doyle, N., Jacobs, K., & Ryan, C. (2016). Faculty mentors' perspectives on e-mentoring postprofessional occupational therapy doctoral students. *Occupational Therapy International*, *23*(4), 305–317. doi:10.1002/oti.1431 PMID:27250596

Dringus, L. P., Snyder, M. M., & Steven, R. T. (2010). Facilitating discourse and enhancing teaching presence: Using mini audio presentations in online forums. *The Internet and Higher Education*, *13*(1-2), 75–77. doi:10.1016/j.iheduc.2009.11.001

Dron, J. (Ed.). (2007). *Control And constraint in e-learning: Choosing When to choose: choosing when to choose*. IGI Global. doi:10.4018/978-1-59904-390-6

Dron, J., & Anderson, T. (2014). *Teaching crowds: Learning and social media*. Athabasca University Press.

Duan, Y., Edwards, J. S., & Dwivedi, Y. K. (2019). Artificial Intelligence for Decision Making in the Era of Big Data–Evolution, Challenges and Research Agenda. *International Journal of Information Management*, *48*(1), 63–71. doi:10.1016/j.ijinfomgt.2019.01.021

Dudek, J., & Heiser, R. (2017). Elements, principles, and critical inquiry for identity-centered design of online environments. *International Journal of E-Learning and Distance Education*, *2*(32), 1–18. https://www.ijede.ca/index.php/jde

Duffy, J., Wickersham-Fish, L., Rademaker, L., & Wetzler, E. (2018). Using collaborative autoethnography to explore online doctoral mentoring: Finding empathy in mentor/protégé relationships. *American Journal of Qualitative Research*, *2*(1), 57–76. doi:10.29333/ajqr/5794

Duffy, M. C., & Azevedo, R. (2015). Motivation matters: Interactions between achievement goals and agent scaffolding for self-regulated learning within an intelligent tutoring system. *Computers in Human Behavior*, *52*, 338–348. doi:10.1016/j.chb.2015.05.041

Du, J., Havard, B., & Li, H. (2005). Dynamic online discussion: Task-oriented interaction for deep learning. *Educational Media International*, *42*(3), 207–218. doi:10.1080/09523980500161221

Du, J., & Xu, J. (2010). The quality of online discussion reported by graduate students. *Quarterly Review of Distance Education*, *11*(1), 13–24.

Dumford, A. D., & Miller, A. L. (2018). Online learning in higher education: Exploring advantages and disadvantages for engagement. *Journal of Computing in Higher Education, 30*(3), 452–465. doi:10.1007/s12528-018-9179-z

Dunlap, J. C., & Lowenthal, P. R. (2009). Tweeting the Night Away: Using Twitter to Enhance Social Presence. *Journal of Information Systems Education, 20*(2), 129–135.

DuVall, J. B., Powell, M. R., Hodge, E., & Ellis, M. (2007). Text messaging to improve social presence in online learning. *EDUCAUSE Quarterly, 30*(3), 24.

Edmunds, J. A., Gicheva, D., Thrift, B., & Hull, M. (2021). High tech, high touch: The impact of an online course intervention on academic performance and persistence in higher education. *The Internet and Higher Education, 49*, 100790. Advance online publication. doi:10.1016/j.iheduc.2020.100790

Elmore, R. (2021). Reflections on mentoring online doctoral learners through the dissertation. *Christian Higher Education, 20*(1-2), 57-68.

Emdin, C. (2007). Exploring the contexts of urban science classrooms: Part 1: Investigating corporate and communal practice. *Cultural Studies of Science Education, 2*(2), 319–350. doi:10.1007/s11422-007-9055-z

Emdin, C. (2016). *For White folks who teach in the hood... and the rest of y'all too: Reality pedagogy and urban education*. Beacon Press.

Endmann, A., & Keßner, D. (2016). User journey mapping–A method in user experience design. *i-com, 15*(1), 105-110.

Engbers, R. (2019). Students' perceptions of interventions designed to foster empathy: An integrative review. *Nurse Education Today, 86*, 104325. doi:10.1016/j.nedt.2019.104325 PMID:31926381

Englund, C., Olofsson, A., & Price, L. (2017). Teaching with technology in higher education: Understanding conceptual change and development in practice. *Higher Education Research & Development, 36*(1), 73–87. doi:10.1080/0729436 0.2016.1171300

Ertmer, P. A., & Koehler, A. A. (2014). Online case discussions: Examining coverage of the afforded problem space. *Educational Technology Research and Development, 62*(5), 617–636. Advance online publication. doi:10.1007/s11423-014-9350-9

Ertmer, P. A., & Koehler, A. A. (2015). Facilitated versus non-facilitated online case discussions: Comparing differences in problem space coverage. *Journal of Computing in Higher Education, 27*(2), 69–93. doi:10.1007/s12528-015-9094-5

Ertmer, P. A., & Koehler, A. A. (2018). Facilitation strategies and problem space coverage: Comparing face-to-face and online case-based discussions. *Educational Technology Research and Development, 66*(3), 639–670. doi:10.1007/s11423-017-9563-9

Ertmer, P. A., Sadaf, A., & Ertmer, D. (2011). Designing effective question prompts to facilitate critical thinking in online discussions. *Design Principles & Practices, 5*(4), 1–10. doi:10.18848/1833-1874/CGP/v05i04/38121

Esterhuizen, H. D., Blignaut, S., & Ellis, S. (2013). Looking out and looking in: Exploring a case of faculty perceptions during e-learning staff development. *International Review of Research in Open and Distance Learning, 14*(3), 59–80. doi:10.19173/irrodl.v14i3.1358

Evans, A. Z., Adhaduk, M., Jabri, A. R., & Ashwath, M. L. (2023). Is Virtual Learning Here to Stay? A Multispecialty Survey of Residents, Fellows, and Faculty. *Current Problems in Cardiology, 48*(6), 101641. doi:10.1016/j.cpcardiol.2023.101641 PMID:36773945

Fandos-Herrera, C., Jiménez-Martínez, J., Orús, C., Pérez-Rueda, A., & Pina, J. M. (2023). The influence of personality on learning outcomes and attitudes: The case of discussants in the classroom. *International Journal of Management Education, 21*(1), 100754. doi:10.1016/j.ijme.2022.100754

Farris, S. (2015). Think "e" for engagement: Use technology tools to design personalized professional e-learning. *Journal of Staff Development, 36*(5), 54–58.

Fernandez, M. (2017). Augmented virtual reality: How to improve education systems. *Higher Learning Research Communications, 7*(1), 1–15. doi:10.18870/hlrc.v7i1.373

Ferrari, R. (2015). Writing narrative style literature reviews. *Medical Writing, 24*(4), 230–235. doi:10.1179/2047480615Z.000000000329

Figueras-Maz, M., Grandío-Pérez, M.-M., & Mateus, J.-C. (2021). Students' perceptions on social media teaching tools in higher education settings. *Communicatio Socialis, 34*(1), 15–28. doi:10.15581/003.34.1.15-28

Finn, A. N., Schrodt, P., Witt, P. L., Elledge, N., Jernberg, K. A., & Larson, L. M. (2009). Meta-analytical review of teacher credibility and its associations with teacher behaviors and student outcomes. *Communication Education, 58*(4), 516–537. doi:10.1080/03634520903131154

Fiock, H. (2020). Designing a community of inquiry in online courses. *International Review of Research in Open and Distance Learning, 21*(1), 135–153. doi:10.19173/irrodl.v20i5.3985

Fiock, H., Maeda, Y., & Richardson, J. C. (2021). Instructor Impact on Differences in Teaching Presence Scores in Online Courses. *International Review of Research in Open and Distance Learning, 22*(3), 55–76. doi:10.19173/irrodl.v22i3.5456

Fishman, B., Konstantopoulos, S., Kubitskey, B. W., Vath, R., Park, G., Johnson, H., & Edelson, D. C. (2013). Comparing the impact of online and face-to-face professional development in the context of curriculum implementation. *Journal of Teacher Education, 64*(5), 426–438. doi:10.1177/0022487113494413

Fitton, I. S., Finnegan, D. J., & Proulx, M. J. (2020). Immersive virtual environments and embodied agents for e-learning applications. *PeerJ. Computer Science, 6*, e315–e315. doi:10.7717/peerj-cs.315 PMID:33816966

Fitzsimons, G. M., & Finkel, E. J. (2018). Transactive-goal-dynamics theory: A discipline-wide perspective. *Current Directions in Psychological Science, 27*(5), 332–338. doi:10.1177/0963721417754199

Flavián, C., Ibáñez-Sánchez, S., & Orús, C. (2021). The influence of scent on virtual reality experiences: The role of aroma-content congruence. *Journal of Business Research, 123*, 289–301. doi:10.1016/j.jbusres.2020.09.036

Floor, N. (2016, September 28). *This is learning experience design.* LinkedIn. https://www.linkedin.com/pulse/learning-experience-design-niels-floor

Fluckiger, J. (2010). Single Point Rubric: A Tool for Responsible Student Self-Assessment. *Teacher Education Faculty Publications, 5*. https://digitalcommons.unomaha.edu/tedfacpub/5

Fortman, J., & Quintana, R. (2023). Fostering collaborative and embodied learning with extended reality: Special issue introduction. *International Journal of Computer-Supported Collaborative Learning, 18*(2), 145–152. doi:10.1007/s11412-023-09404-1

Fotaris, P. (2020). *ECGBL 2020 14th European Conference on Game-Based Learning.* Academic Conferences limited.

Fourtane, S. (2021). *Classroom 3.0: Instructors Leveraging Augmented Reality, Holograms.* https://www.fierceeducation. com/best-practices/classroom-3-0-instructors-leveraging-augmented-reality-holograms?mkt_tok=Mjk0LU1RRi0w NTYAAAF8S27cvLN_H0BnxdR0Okpqoe3kPO9pi4XLwvifPXcyKmlP2BX6SiumorSRu_qzBcTTzCvUFtjc5SWu6qjP- c9F-4X3ol5cAiNmKmolKekwTA8afj5odD3E&mrkid=144996160

Fransson, G., Holmberg, J., & Westelius, C. (2020). The challenges of using head mounted virtual reality in K-12 schools from a teacher perspective. *Education and Information Technologies, 25*(4), 3383–3404. doi:10.1007/s10639-020-10119-1

Freed, A., Huffling, L. D., Benavides, A., & Scott, H. (2023). *Engage students in real science using simple virtual tools* [Interactive Webinar]. University of Central Arkansas summer professional development, Virtual. https://www.youtube. com/watch?v=2YaFtexWJZ0&list=PLMhw_-NyMrSzCIbLUBxhF6bG6RRfvhgDU&index=6

Frieder, S., Pinchetti, L., Griffiths, R. R., Salvatori, T., Lukasiewicz, T., Petersen, P.C., Chevalier, A., Berner, J. (2023). Mathematical Capabilities of ChatGPT. *arXiv, 2301.13867.*

Fruchterman, T. M. J., & Reingold, E. M. (1991). Graph drawing by force-directed placement. *Software, Practice & Experience, 21*(11), 1129–1164. doi:10.1002/spe.4380211102

Fuentes, M. A., Zelaya, D. G., & Madsen, J. W. (2021). Rethinking the course syllabus: Considerations for promoting equity, diversity, and inclusion. *Teaching of Psychology, 48*(1), 69–79. doi:10.1177/0098628320959979

Fung, C. Y., Su, S. I., Perry, E. J., & Garcia, M. B. (2022). Development of a Socioeconomic Inclusive Assessment Framework for Online Learning in Higher Education. In *Socioeconomic Inclusion During an Era of Online Education* (pp. 23–46). IGI Global. doi:10.4018/978-1-6684-4364-4.ch002

Gallagher, S., & Lindgren, R. (2015). Enactive metaphors: Learning through full-body engagement. *Educational Psychology Review, 27*(3), 391–404. doi:10.1007/s10648-015-9327-1

Galustyan, O. V., Borovikova, Y. V., Polivaeva, N. P., Kodirov, B. R., & Zhirkova, G. P. (2019). Elearning within the field of andragogy. *International Journal of Emerging Technologies in Learning, 14*(9), 148–156. doi:10.3991/ijet.v14i09.10020

García-Morales, V. J., Garrido-Moreno, A., & Martín-Rojas, R. (2021). The transformation of higher education after the COVID disruption: Emerging challenges in an online learning scenario. *Frontiers in Psychology, 12*, 616059. doi:10.3389/ fpsyg.2021.616059 PMID:33643144

García-Peñalvo, F. J. (2023). The Perception of Artificial Intelligence in Educational Contexts after the Launch of Chat-GPT: Disruption or Panic? *Education in the Knowledge Society, 24*, 1–9. doi:10.14201/eks.31279

Gardner, S. K. (2010). Keeping up with the Joneses: Socialization and culture in doctoral education at one striving institution. *The Journal of Higher Education, 81*(6), 658–679. doi:10.1080/00221546.2010.11779076

Garrison, D. R., Anderson, T., & Archer, W. (2001). Critical Thinking, Cognitive Presence, and Computer Conferencing in Distance Education. *American Journal of Distance Education, 15*, 7–23. doi:10.1080/08923640109527071

Garrison, D. R., Anderson, T., & Archer, W. (1999). Critical Inquiry in a Text-Based Environment: Computer Conferencing in Higher Education. *The Internet and Higher Education, 2*(2–3), 87–105. doi:10.1016/S1096-7516(00)00016-6

Garrison, D. R., Anderson, T., & Archer, W. (2000). Critical inquiry in a text-based environment: Computer conferencing in higher education. *The Internet and Higher Education, 2*(2), 87–105.

Garrison, D. R., Anderson, T., & Archer, W. (2010). The first decade of the community of inquiry framework: A retrospective. *The Internet and Higher Education, 13*(1), 5–9. doi:10.1016/j.iheduc.2009.10.003

Garrison, D. R., & Baynton, M. (1987). Beyond independence in distance education: The concept of control. *American Journal of Distance Education, 1*(3), 3–15. doi:10.1080/08923648709526593

Garrison, D. R., & Cleveland-Innes, M. (2005). Facilitating cognitive presence in online learning: Interaction is not enough. *American Journal of Distance Education, 19*(3), 133–148. doi:10.1207/s15389286ajde1903_2

Garrison, D., & Arbaugh, J. (2007). Researching the Community of Inquiry Framework: Review, issues, and future directions. *The Internet and Higher Education, 10*(3), 157–172. doi:10.1016/j.iheduc.2007.04.001

Gautam, A., Williams, D., Terry, K., Robinson, K., & Newbill, P. (2018). *Mirror Worlds: Examining the Affordance of a Next Generation Immersive Learning Environment.* Tech Trends.

Gay, G. (2002). Preparing for culturally responsive teaching. *Journal of Teacher Education, 53*(2), 106–116. doi:10.1177/0022487102053002003

Gay, G. (2015). The what, why, and how of culturally responsive teaching: International mandates, challenges, and opportunities. *Multicultural Education Review, 7*(3), 123–139. doi:10.1080/2005615X.2015.1072079

Gay, G. (2018). *Culturally responsive teaching: Theory, research, and practice.* Teachers College Press.

Gayon, R., & Tan, D. (2021). Experiences of higher education institution (HEI) teachers in the implementation of flexible learning. *Science International (Lahore), 33*(1), 47–52.

Gee, J. P. (2000). Chapter 3: Identity as an analytic lens for research in education. *Review of Research in Education, 25*(1), 99–125. doi:10.3102/0091732X025001099

George, B. H. (2017). A study of traditional discussion boards and social media within an Online landscape architecture course. *Review of Applied Socioeconomic Research, 13*(1), 16–25.

Georgiou, Y., & Ioannou, A. (2019). Embodied learning in a digital world: A systematic review of empirical research in K-12 education. *Learning in a digital world: Perspective on Interactive Technologies for Formal and Informal Education,* 155-177.

Gherheș, V., Stoian, C. E., Fărcașiu, M. A., & Stanici, M. (2021). E-Learning vs. Face-to-Face Learning: Analyzing Students' Preferences and Behaviors. *Sustainability (Basel), 13*(8), 4381. doi:10.3390/su13084381

Gierdowski, D. C. (2019). *ECAR Study of Undergraduate Students and Information Technology, 2019.* https://www.educause.edu/ecar/research-publications/ecar-study-of-undergraduate-students-and-information-technology/2019/technology-use-in-the-classroom

Gilardi, M., Hainey, T., Bakhshi, A., Rodriguez, C., & Walker, A. (2021, September). XR Maths: Designing a Collaborative Extended Realities lab for Teaching Mathematics. *Proceedings of the 15th European Conference on Game Based Learning (ECGBL),* 277-286. https://doi.org/10.34190/GBL.21.115

Gilbert, P. K., & Dabbagh, N. (2005). How to structure online discussions for meaningful discourse: A case study. *British Journal of Educational Technology, 36*(1), 5–18. doi:10.1111/j.1467-8535.2005.00434.x

Gkrimpizi, T., Peristeras, V., & Magnisalis, I. (2023). Classification of Barriers to Digital Transformation in Higher Education Institutions: Systematic Literature Review. *Education Sciences, 13*(7), 746. doi:10.3390/educsci13070746

Glazier, R. A. (2021). *Connecting in the online classroom: Building rapport between teachers and students.* JHU Press. doi:10.1353/book.98266

Gleason, B., & Heath, M. K. (2021). Injustice embedded in Google Classroom and Google Meet: A techno-ethical audit of remote educational technologies. *Italian Journal of Educational Technology, 29*(2), 26–41. doi:10.17471/2499-4324/1209

Glynn, K., & Tolsma, D. (2017). Design thinking meets ADDIE. *Learning and Development, 34*(1714), 1-20. https://www.td.org/td-at-work/design-thinking-meets-addie

Goldin-Meadow, S., & Beilock, S. L. (2010). Action's influence on thought: The Case of gesture. *Perspectives on Psychological Science, 5*(6), 664–674. doi:10.1177/1745691610388764 PMID:21572548

González Rodríguez, G., Gonzalez-Cava, J. M., & Méndez Pérez, J. A. (2020). An intelligent decision support system for production planning based on machine learning. *Journal of Intelligent Manufacturing, 31*(5), 1257–1273. doi:10.1007/s10845-019-01510-y

Gorgosz, J., & Murphy, M. T. (2021). Making the Impersonal, Personal: Remote Learning During the COVID-19 Pandemic. *American Educational History Journal*, 109-116.

Govindaraju, V., & Seruji, Z. (2022). Interpersonal communication and relationship: A conceptual review between educators and undergraduate students. *Multicultural Education, 8*(6), 30–37.

Graham, C. R., Henrie, C. R., & Gibbons, A. S. (2014). Developing models and theory for blended learning research. In A. G. Picciano, C. D. Dzuibun, & C. R. Graham (Eds.), *Blended Learning: Research Perspectives* (Vol. 2, pp. 13–33). Routledge.

Graham, K., Rios, A., & Viruru, R. (2023). Constructing radical community: An ecological model for shifting from an EdD to a We-dD in online doctoral programs. *Higher Education, 85*(2), 301–323. doi:10.1007/s10734-022-00834-8 PMID:35287377

Graham, L. (Ed.). (2020). *Inclusive education for the 21st century: Theory, policy, and practice.* Routledge. doi:10.4324/9781003116073

Grassini, S., Laumann, K., & Rasmussen Skogstad, M. (2020). The use of virtual reality alone does not promote training performance (but sense of presence does). *Frontiers in Psychology, 11*, 1743. doi:10.3389/fpsyg.2020.01743 PMID:32765384

Gray, C. M. (2015). Critiquing the role of the learner and context in aesthetic learning experiences. In B. Hokanson, G. Clinton, & M. Tracey (Eds.), The design of learning experience. Educational communications and technology: Issues and innovations (pp. 199-213). Springer International Publishing. doi:10.1007/978-3-319-16504-2_14

Gray, J. & DiLoreto, M. (2016). The effects of student engagement, student satisfaction and perceived learning in online learning environments. *NCPEA International Journal of Educational Leadership, 11*(1).

Green, B. N., Johnson, C. D., & Adams, A. (2006). Writing narrative literature reviews for peer-reviewed journals: Secrets of the trade. *Journal of Chiropractic Medicine, 5*(3), 101–117. doi:10.1016/S0899-3467(07)60142-6 PMID:19674681

Greenfield, N. (2024). Facing Facts: ChatGPT can be a tool for critical thinking. *University World News.* Retrieved on January 15, 2024, https://www.universityworldnews.com/post.php?story=20230222131416630

Greenhill, K., & Wiebrands, C. (2008). The unconference: a new model for better professional communication. In *LIANZA Conference 2008: Poropitia Outside the Box.* LIANZA.

Groen, J. (2021). Student engagement in doctoral programs: Principal factors that facilitate learning. *New Directions for Teaching and Learning, 167*(167), 77–84. doi:10.1002/tl.20461

Gunawardena, C. N., & Zittle, F. J. (1997). Social presence as a predictor of satisfaction with a computer-mediated conferencing environment. *American Journal of Distance Education, 11*(3), 8–26. doi:10.1080/08923649709526970

Guo, P., Ren, D., & Admiraal, W. (2022). The community of inquiry perspective on teachers' role and students' evaluations of online project-based learning. *Online Learning : the Official Journal of the Online Learning Consortium, 26*(4), 259–280. doi:10.24059/olj.v26i4.3193

Gupta, S., & Jagannath, K. (2019). Artificially intelligently (AI) tutors in the classroom: A need assessment study of designing chatbots to support student learning. *Twenty-third Pacific Asia Conference on Information Systems.*

Haag, M., & Marsden, N. (2019). Exploring personas as a method to foster empathy in student IT design teams. *International Journal of Technology and Design Education, 29*(3), 565–582. doi:10.1007/s10798-018-9452-5

Hacker, P., Engel, A., & Mauer, M. (2023). Regulating ChatGPT and other large generative AI models. *2023 ACM Conference on Fairness, Accountability, and Transparency,* 1112-1123. 10.1145/3593013.3594067

Hackman, M. Z., & Walker, K. (1990). Instructional communication in the televised classroom: The effects of system design and teacher immediacy on student learning and satisfaction. *Communication Education, 39*(3), 196–206. doi:10.1080/03634529009378802

Hadwin, A., & Oshige, M. (2011). Self-regulation, coregulation, and socially shared regulation: Exploring perspectives of social in self-regulated learning theory. *Teachers College Record, 113*(2), 240–264. doi:10.1177/016146811111300204

Haleem, A., Javaid, M., Qadri, M. A., Singh, R. P., & Suman, R. (2022). Artificial Intelligence (AI) Applications for Marketing: A Literature-Based Study. *International Journal of Intelligent Networks, 3*(1), 119–132. doi:10.1016/j.ijin.2022.08.005

Hamilton, E. R., Rosenberg, J. M., & Akcaoglu, M. (2016). The substitution augmentation modification redefinition (SAMR) model: A critical review and suggestions for its use. *TechTrends, 60*(5), 433–441. doi:10.1007/s11528-016-0091-y

Hammond, Z. (2014). *Culturally responsive teaching and the brain: Promoting authentic engagement and rigor among culturally and linguistically diverse students.* Corwin Press.

Hao, K. (2019). *China has started a grand experiment in AI education. It could reshape how the world learns.* MIT Technology Review.

Harasim, L. (2017). *Learning theory and online technologies.* Routledge. doi:10.4324/9781315716831

Hargittai, E. (2002). Second-Level Digital Divide: Differences in People's Online Skills. *First Monday, 7*(4). Advance online publication. doi:10.5210/fm.v7i4.942

Harris, J., Mishra, P., & Koehler, M. (2009). Teachers' technological pedagogical content knowledge and learning activity types: Curriculum-based technology integration reframed. *Journal of Research on Technology in Education, 41*(1), 393–416. doi:10.1080/15391523.2009.10782536

Haydon, T., Macsuga-Gage, A. S., Simonsen, B., & Hawkins, R. (2012). Opportunities to respond: A key component of effective instruction. *Beyond Behavior, 22*(1), 23–31. doi:10.1177/107429561202200105

Hendricks, G. P. (2019). Connectivism as a learning theory and its relation to open distance education. *Progressio, 41*(1). Advance online publication. doi:10.25159/2663-5895/4773

Henry, D. (2008). Changing classroom social settings through attention to norms. *Toward positive youth development: Transforming schools and community programs,* 40-57. doi:10.1093/acprof:oso/9780195327892.003.0003

Herman, W., & Pinard, M. (2015). *Critically examining inquiry-based learning: John Dewey in theory, history, and practice.* doi:10.1108/S2055-36412015000000301

Hernández, L. E., Darling-Hammond, L., Adams, J., & Bradley, K. (2019). *Deeper Learning networks: Taking student-centered learning and equity to scale. Deeper Learning Networks Series*. Learning Policy Institute.

Hernandez, P. R., Ferguson, C. F., Pedersen, R., Richards-Babb, M., Quedado, K., & Shook, N. J. (2023). Research Apprenticeship Training Promotes Faculty-Student Psychological Similarity and High-Quality Mentoring: A Longitudinal Quasi-Experiment. *Mentoring & Tutoring*, *31*(1), 163–183. doi:10.1080/13611267.2023.2164973

Hew, K. F., & Cheung, W. S. (2003). Evaluating the participation and quality of thinking of pre-service teachers in an asynchronous online discussion environment: Part 1. *International Journal of Instructional Media*, *30*(3), 247–262.

Hew, K. F., & Cheung, W. S. (2008). Attracting student participation in asynchronous online discussions: A case study of peer facilitation. *Computers & Education*, *51*(3), 1111–1124. doi:10.1016/j.compedu.2007.11.002

Hew, K. F., & Cheung, W. S. (2014). *Student participation in online discussions: Challenges, solutions, and future research*. Springer Science & Business Media. doi:10.1007/978-1-4614-2370-6

Hew, K. F., Cheung, W. S., & Ng, C. S. L. (2010). Student contribution in asynchronous online discussion: A review of the research and empirical exploration. *Instructional Science*, *38*(6), 571–606. doi:10.1007/s11251-008-9087-0

Hew, K. F., Huang, W., Du, J., & Jia, C. (2023). Using chatbots to support student goal setting and social presence in fully online activities: Learner engagement and perceptions. *Journal of Computing in Higher Education*, *35*(1), 40–68. doi:10.1007/s12528-022-09338-x PMID:36101883

Heyman, E. (2010). *Overcoming student retention issues in higher education online program: A delphi study* [Doctoral dissertation]. ProQuest document ID:748309429.

Hiebert, J., & Grouws, D. A. (2007). The effects of classroom mathematics teaching on students' learning. Second handbook of research on mathematics teaching and learning, 1(1), 371-404.

Ho, C. H., & Swan, K. (2007). Evaluating online conversation in an asynchronous learning environment: An application of Grice's cooperative principle. *The Internet and Higher Education*, *10*(1), 3–14. doi:10.1016/j.iheduc.2006.11.002

Holder, B. (2007). An investigation of hope, academics, environment, and motivation as predictors of persistence in higher education online programs. *The Internet and Higher Education*, *10*(4), 245–260. doi:10.1016/j.iheduc.2007.08.002

Hoskins, C., & Goldberg, A. (2005). Doctoral student persistence in counselor education programs: Student-program match. *Counselor Education and Supervision*, *44*(3), 175–188. doi:10.1002/j.1556-6978.2005.tb01745.x

Hostetter, C., & Busch, M. (2013). Community matters: Social presence and learning outcomes. *The Journal of Scholarship of Teaching and Learning*, *13*(1), 77–86.

Howard, T. C. (2021). Culturally responsive pedagogy. In J. A. Banks (Ed.), *Transforming Multicultural Education Policy and Practice: Expanding Educational Opportunity* (p. 137). Teachers College Press.

Huffling, L. D., Freed, A., Scott, H. C., Benavides, A., & Ward, J. L. (2024). *Template for Humanizing Online PD Development*. Department of Middle Grades and Secondary Education Faculty Publications, Paper 215. https://digitalcommons.georgiasouthern.edu/teach-secondary-facpubs/215

Huh, J. H., & Seo, Y. S. (2019). Understanding Edge Computing. Engineering Evolution with Artificial Intelligence. *IEEE Access : Practical Innovations, Open Solutions*, *7*(1), 164229–164245. doi:10.1109/ACCESS.2019.2945338

Husain, H., Bais, B., Hussain, A., & Samad, S. A. (2012). How to construct open-ended questions. *Procedia: Social and Behavioral Sciences*, *60*, 456–462. doi:10.1016/j.sbspro.2012.09.406

Hutson, J., Steffes, R., & Weber, J. (2023). Virtual Learning Environments and Digital Twins: Enhancing Accessibility, Diversity, and Flexibility in Training Secondary Educational Administrators. *Metaverse*, *4*(1), 1–16. doi:10.54517/m. v4i1.2165

Hu, Y. H., Fu, J. S., & Yeh, H. C. (2023). Developing an Early-Warning System Through Robotic Process Automation: Are Intelligent Tutoring Robots as Effective as Human Teachers? *Interactive Learning Environments*, ●●●, 1–14. doi:1 0.1080/10494820.2022.2160467

Hyatt, L., & Williams, P. E. (2011). 21st century competencies for doctoral leadership faculty. *Innovative Higher Education*, *36*(1), 53–66. doi:10.1007/s10755-010-9157-5

International Society for Technology in Education. (2023). *ISTE standards for students*. https://iste.org/standards/students

Ip, H. H. S., Li, C., Wong, Y. W., Leoni, S., Ma, K. F., Wong, H. T., & Sham, S. H. (2016). Delivering Immersive Learning Experience for Massive Open Online Courses (MOOCs). In D. Chiu, I. Marenzi, U. Nanni, M. Spaniol, & M. Temperini (Eds.), *Advances in Web-Based Learning – ICWL 2016*. Springer. doi:10.1007/978-3-319-47440-3_12

Irby, B. J., Pashmforoosh, R., Lara-Alecio, R., Tong, F., Etchells, M. J., & Rodriguez, L. (2023). Virtual Mentoring and Coaching Through Virtual Professional Leadership Learning Communities for School Leaders: A Mixed-Methods Study. *Mentoring & Tutoring*, *31*(1), 6–38. doi:10.1080/13611267.2023.2164971

Jahromi, V. K., Tabatabaee, S. S., Abdar, Z. E., & Rajabi, M. (2016). Active listening: The key to successful communication in hospital managers. *Electronic Physician*, *8*(3), 2123–2128. doi:10.19082/2123 PMID:27123221

Jameson, C., & Torres, K. (2019). Fostering motivation when virtually mentoring online doctoral students. *Journal of Educational Research and Practice*, *9*(1). Advance online publication. doi:10.5590/JERAP.2019.09.1.23

Janke, S., Rudert, S. C., Petersen, Ä., Fritz, T. M., & Daumiller, M. (2021). Cheating in the Wake of COVID-19: How Dangerous is Ad-Hoc Online Testing for Academic Integrity? *Computers and Education Open*, *2*, 100055. doi:10.1016/j. caeo.2021.100055

Jensen. (2015). *Building relatedness through hashtags: social influence and motivation within social media-based online discussion forums* [Doctoral dissertation]. University of Georgia.

Jeong, A. C. (2004). The combined effects of response time and message content on growth patterns of discussion threads in computer-supported collaborative argumentation. *International Journal of E-Learning & Distance Education/Revue Internationale du e-learning et la formation à distance*, *19*(1).

Jeste, D. V., Graham, S. A., Nguyen, T. T., Depp, C. A., Lee, E. E., & Kim, H. C. (2020). Beyond Artificial Intelligence: Exploring Artificial Wisdom. *International Psychogeriatrics*, *32*(8), 993–1001. doi:10.1017/S1041610220000927 PMID:32583762

Jin, X., & Ye, Y. (2022). Impact of fine arts education on psychological wellbeing of higher education students through moderating role of creativity and self-efficacy. *Frontiers in Psychology*, *13*, 1–13. doi:10.3389/fpsyg.2022.957578 PMID:36017422

Ji, Y., & Han, Y. (2019). Monitoring Indicators of the Flipped Classroom Learning Process based on Data Mining: Taking the Course of "Virtual Reality Technology" as an Example. *International Journal of Emerging Technologies in Learning*, *14*(3), 166–176. doi:10.3991/ijet.v14i03.10105

Johnson, A. (2013). *Excellent! Online Teaching: Effective strategies for a successful semester online*. Aaron Johnson.

Johnson, A. L., & Nino, M. (2022). Gaining "empathy" for the online learner with instructional design and design thinking strategies (V). In E. Langran (Ed.), *Proceedings of Society for Information Technology & Teacher Education International Conference* (pp. 1304–1308). https://www.learntechlib.org/primary/p/220884/

Johnson, D., & Johnson, R. (1996). Conflict resolution and peer mediation programs in elementary and secondary schools: A review of the research. *Review of Educational Research, 66*(4), 459–506. doi:10.3102/00346543066004459

Johnson-Glenberg, M. C. (2019). The necessary nine: Design principles for embodied VR and active stem education. *Learning in a digital world: Perspective on interactive technologies for formal and informal education,* 83-112.

Jones, T., Ramirez-Mendoza, J., & Jackson, V. (2020). *A Promise Worth Keeping: An Updated Equity-Driven Framework for Free College Programs.* Education Trust.

Jou, M., Lin, Y. T., & Wu, D. W. (2016). Effect of a blended learning environment on student critical thinking and knowledge transformation. *Interactive Learning Environments, 24*(6), 1131–1147. doi:10.1080/10494820.2014.961485

Joyce, K. M., & Brown, A. (2009). Enhancing social presence in online learning: Mediation strategies applied to social networking tools. *Online Journal of Distance Learning Administration, 12*(4), n4.

Kang, B. (2013). Implication of Embodied Cognition for Art Education. *Journal of Research in Art & Education, 14*(1), 73–94. doi:10.20977/kkosca.2013.14.1.73

Kang, J., Diederich, M., Lindgren, R., & Junokas, M. (2021). Gesture patterns and learning in an embodied XR science simulation. *Journal of Educational Technology & Society, 24*(2), 77–92.

Kanuka, H., & Garrison, D. R. (2004). Cognitive presence in online learning. *Journal of Computing in Higher Education, 15*(2), 21–39. doi:10.1007/BF02940928

Kanwar, A. (2021). *Building resilient education systems for the future: Role of ODL.* http://hdl.handle.net/11599/3869

Kasneci, E., Seßler, K., Küchemann, S., Bannert, M., Dementieva, D., Fischer, F., Gasser, U., Groh, G., Günnemann, S., Hüllermeier, E., Krusche, S., Kutyniok, G., Michaeli, T., Nerdel, C., Pfeffer, J., Poquet, O., Sailer, M., Schmidt, A., Seidel, T., ... Kasneci, G. (2023). ChatGPT for Good? On Opportunities and Challenges of Large Language Models for Education. *Learning and Individual Differences, 103,* 102274. doi:10.1016/j.lindif.2023.102274

Kauffman, H. (2015). A review of predictive factors of student success in and satisfaction with online learning. *Research in Learning Technology, 23,* 1–13. doi:10.3402/rlt.v23.26507

Kaufmann, R., Sellnow, D. D., & Frisby, B. N. (2016). The development and validation of the online learning climate scale (OLCS). *Communication Education, 65*(3), 307–321. doi:10.1080/03634523.2015.1101778

Kavanagh, S., Luxton-Reilly, A., Wuensche, B., & Plimmer, B. (2017). A systematic review of virtual reality in education. *Themes in Science and Technology Education, 10*(2), 85-119. https://eric.ed.gov/?id=EJ1165633

Kear, K., Chetwynd, F., & Jefferis, H. (2014). Social presence in online learning communities: The role of personal profiles. *Research in Learning Technology, 22,* 22. doi:10.3402/rlt.v22.19710

Khachane, M. Y. (2017). Organ-Based Medical Image Classification Using Support Vector Machine. [IJSE]. *International Journal of Synthetic Emotions, 8*(1), 18–30. doi:10.4018/IJSE.2017010102

Kieran, L., & Anderson, C. (2019). Connecting universal design for learning with culturally responsive teaching. *Education and Urban Society, 51*(9), 1202–1216. doi:10.1177/0013124518785012

Kilgore, W. (2016). Humanizing online instruction in undergraduate business education. In *Humanizing Online Teaching and Learning.* https://pressbooks.pub/humanmooc/

Kim & Jensen. (2019). Pedagogical cases in integrating technology into instruction: What can we do to celebrate failure? In S. Keengwe & Bull, H. (Eds.), *Handbook of Research on Innovative Pedagogies and Best Practices in Teacher Education*. Hershey, PA: IGI Global.

Kim, G., & Gurvitch, R. (2020). Online education research adopting the community of inquiry framework: A systematic review. *Quest*, *72*(4), 395–409. doi:10.1080/00336297.2020.1761843

Kim, K., de Melo, C. M., Norouzi, N., Bruder, G., & Welch, G. F. (2020, March). Reducing Task Load with an Embodied Intelligent Virtual Assistant for Improved Performance in Collaborative Decision Making. In *2020 IEEE Conference on Virtual Reality and 3D User Interfaces (VR)* (pp. 529-538). IEEE. 10.1109/VR46266.2020.00074

Kim, Y., Thayne, J., & Wei, Q. (2017). An embodied agent helps anxious students in Mathematics learning. *Educational Technology Research and Development*, *65*(1), 219–235. doi:10.1007/s11423-016-9476-z

King, M. R. (2023). A conversation on artificial intelligence, chatbots, and plagiarism in higher education. *Cellular and Molecular Bioengineering*, *16*(1), 1–2. doi:10.1007/s12195-022-00754-8 PMID:36660590

Kinzie, J., & Kuh, G. (2017). Reframing Student Success in College: Advancing Know-What and Know-How. *Change*, *49*(3), 19–27. doi:10.1080/00091383.2017.1321429

Klapwijk, R., & Van Doorn, F. (2015). Contextmapping in primary design and technology education: A fruitful method to develop empathy for and insight in user needs. *International Journal of Technology and Design Education*, *25*(2), 151–167. doi:10.1007/s10798-014-9279-7

Klebig, B., Goldonowicz, J., Mendes, E., Miller, A. N., & Katt, J. (2016). The combined effects of instructor communicative behaviors, instructor credibility, and student personality traits on incivility in the college classroom. *Communication Research Reports*, *33*(2), 152–158. doi:10.1080/08824096.2016.1154837

Klein, A. (2013). Who Is in the Community of Inquiry? *Transactions of the Charles S. Peirce Society*, *49*(3), 413–423.

Klisc, C., McGill, T., & Hobbs, V. (2009). The effect of assessment on the outcomes of asynchronous online discussion as perceived by instructors. *Australasian Journal of Educational Technology*, *25*(5). Advance online publication. doi:10.14742/ajet.1114

Knowles, M. S., Holton, E. F. III, Swanson, R. A., & Robinson, P. A. (1973). *The adult learner: A neglected species*. Gulf Publication Company.

Koehler, A. A. (2023). Planning and facilitating case-based learning in online settings. In G. Quek (Ed.), *Designing technology-mediated case learning in higher education - a global perspective* (pp. 215–237). Springer.

Koehler, A. A., Cheng, Z., Fiock, H., Janakiraman, S., & Wang, H. (2020). Asynchronous online discussions during case-based learning: A problem-solving process. *Online Learning : the Official Journal of the Online Learning Consortium*, *24*(4), 64–92. doi:10.24059/olj.v24i4.2332

Koehler, A. A., Cheng, Z., Fiock, H., Wang, H., Janakiraman, S., & Chartier, K. (2022). Examining students' use of online case-based discussions to support problem solving: Considering individual and collaborative experiences. *Computers & Education*, *179*, 104407. Advance online publication. doi:10.1016/j.compedu.2021.104407

Koehler, A. A., & Meech, S. (2022). Ungrading learner participation in a student-centered learning experience. *TechTrends*, *66*(1), 78–89. doi:10.1007/s11528-021-00682-w

Koehler, M. J., & Mishra, P. (2009). What is technological pedagogical content knowledge? *Contemporary Issues in Technology & Teacher Education*, *9*(1), 60–70. https://www.learntechlib.org/primary/p/29544/

Kolb, D. A. (2014). *Experiential learning: Experience as the source of learning and development.* FT Press.

Kolomitz, K., & Cabellon, E. T. (2016). A strategic necessity: Building senior leadership's fluency in digital technology. *New Directions for Student Services, 2016*(155), 47–57. doi:10.1002/ss.20182

Kooli, C. (2023). Chatbots in education and research: A critical examination of ethical implications and solutions. *Sustainability (Basel), 15*(7), 5614. doi:10.3390/su15075614

Koonj, N. (2020). The Impact of E-learning on L2 Learning: A Paradigm of Action Research. *Journal of Literature. Language and Linguistics (Taipei).* Advance online publication. doi:10.7176/JLLL/68-02

Koranteng, F. N., Wiafe, I., & Kuada, E. (2019). An empirical study of the relationship between social networking sites and students' engagement in higher education. *Journal of Educational Computing Research, 57*(5), 1131–1159. doi:10.1177/0735633118787528

Kouprie, M., & Visser, F. S. (2009). A framework for empathy in design: Stepping into and out of the user's life. *Journal of Engineering Design, 20*(5), 437–448. doi:10.1080/09544820902875033

Krasnova, T., & Ananjev, A. (2015). Students' perception of learning in the online discussion environment. *Mediterranean Journal of Social Sciences, 6*(6 S1), 202. DOI: doi:10.5901/mjss.2015.v6n6s1p202

Kuh, G. (2001, May - June). Assessing what really matters to student learning: Inside the national survey of student engagement. *Change, 33*(3), 10–17. https://www.jstor.org/stable/40165768. doi:10.1080/00091380109601795

Kuh, G. D., Kinzie, J., Schuh, J. H., & Whitt, E. J. (2010). *Student success in college: Creating conditions that matter.* Jossey-Bass.

Kuhn, D. (2015). Thinking together and alone. *Educational Researcher, 44*(1), 46–53. doi:10.3102/0013189X15569530

Kulik, J. A., & Fletcher, J. D. (2016). Effectiveness of intelligent tutoring systems: A meta-analytic review. *Review of Educational Research, 86*(1), 42–78. doi:10.3102/0034654315581420

Kumar, S., Dawson, K., Black, E. W., Cavanaugh, C., & Sessums, C. D. (2011). Applying the community of inquiry framework to an online professional practice doctoral program. *International Review of Research in Open and Distance Learning, 12*(6), 126–142. doi:10.19173/irrodl.v12i6.978

La Fleur, J., & Dlamini, R. (2022). Towards learner-centric pedagogies: Technology-enhanced teaching and learning in the 21st century classroom. *Journal of Education (University of KwaZulu-Natal),* (88), 4-20. doi:10.17159/2520-9868/i88a01

Ladson-Billings, G. (1995a). Toward a theory of culturally relevant pedagogy. *American Educational Research Journal, 32*(3), 465–491. doi:10.3102/00028312032003465

Ladson-Billings, G. (1995b). But that's just good teaching! The case for culturally relevant pedagogy. *Theory into Practice, 34*(3), 159–165. doi:10.1080/00405849509543675

Ladson-Billings, G. (2021a). *Culturally relevant pedagogy: Asking a different question.* Teachers College Press.

Ladson-Billings, G. (2021b). I'm here for the hard re-set: Post-pandemic pedagogy to preserve our culture. *Equity & Excellence in Education, 54*(1), 68–78. doi:10.1080/10665684.2020.1863883

Ladson-Billings, G. (2023). "Yes, but how do we do it?": Practicing culturally relevant pedagogy. In *White teachers/diverse classrooms* (pp. 33–46). Routledge. doi:10.4324/9781003448709-6

Lammers, J. (2021, June 17-18). *Empathy mapping: Bridging cultural and linguistic divides in international online education* [Symposium presentation]. Teaching Culturally and Linguistically Diverse International Students in Open or Online Learning Environments: A Research Symposium, Windsor, Ontario, Canada. https://scholar.uwindsor.ca/itos21/?_gl=1*1n7hgas*_ga*MTAyMTEyODQ1LjE2OTg2MDgxODY.*_ga_TMHVD0679R*MTY5ODYwODg3N S4xLjAuMTY5ODYwODg3NS42MC4wLjA

Lapointe, D. K., & Gunawardena, C. N. (2004). Developing, testing, and refining of a model to understand the relationship between peer interaction and learning outcomes in computer-mediated conferencing. *Distance Education*, *25*(1), 83–106. doi:10.1080/0158791042000212477

LaRose, R., Mastro, D., & Eastin, M. S. (2001). Understanding Internet usage: A social-cognitive approach to uses and gratifications. *Social Science Computer Review*, *19*(4), 395–413. doi:10.1177/089443930101900401

Laurillard, D. (2002). *Rethinking university teaching: A framework for the effective use of learning technologies* (2nd ed.). Routledge. doi:10.4324/9780203160329

Lave, J., & Wenger, E. (1996). *Communities of practice*. doi:10.1007/978-3-642-28036-8_644

Lay, C. D., Allman, B., Cutri, R. M., & Kimmons, R. (2020). Examining a decade of research in online teacher professional development. *Frontiers in Education*, *5*, 573129. doi:10.3389/feduc.2020.573129

Lee, N., Ray, R., Lai, S., & Tanner, B. (2022). *Ensuring equitable access to AR/VR in higher education.* The Brookings Institution. Retrieved on January 11, 2024, https://www.brookings.edu/articles/ensuring-equitable-access-to-ar-vr-in-higher-education/#:~:text=To%20improve%20student%20access%20to,of%20high%2Dspeed%20broadband%20networks

Lee, K. M., Jeong, E. J., Park, N., & Ryu, S. (2011). Effects of interactivity in educational games: A mediating role of social presence on learning outcomes. *International Journal of Human-Computer Interaction*, *27*(7), 620–633. doi:10.1080/10447318.2011.555302

Leh, A. (2002). Action research on hybrid courses and their online communities. *Educational Media International*, *39*(1), 31–38. doi:10.1080/09523980210131204

Leh, A. S. C. (2001). Computer-Mediated Communication and Social Presence in a Distance Learning Environment. *International Journal of Educational Telecommunications*, *7*(2), 109–128.

Leonard, D., & Rayport, J. F. (1997). Spark innovation through empathic design. *Harvard Business Review*, *75*(6), 102–108. PMID:10174792

Li, C., & Lalani, F. (2020). The COVID-19 pandemic has changed the world forever: This is how. *World Economic Forum*. https://www.weforum.org/agenda/2020/04/coronavirus-education-global-covid19-online-digital-learning/

Liang, G. (2022, November). Research on SPOC-based Effective Teaching by Artificial Intelligence Technology. In *2022 2nd International Conference on Social Sciences and Intelligence Management (SSIM)* (pp. 99-103). IEEE. 10.1109/SSIM55504.2022.10047942

Liaw, S. S., & Huang, H. M. (2013). Perceived satisfaction, perceived usefulness and interactive learning environments as predictors to self-regulation in e-learning environments. *Computers & Education*, *60*(1), 14–24. doi:10.1016/j.compedu.2012.07.015

Li, F. (2022). "Are you There?": Teaching presence and interaction in large online classes. *Asian-Pacific Journal of Second and Foreign Language Education*, *7*(1), 45. doi:10.1186/s40862-022-00180-3

Lilley, M., Pyper, A., & Attwood, S. (2012). Understanding the student experience through the use of personas. *Innovation in Teaching and Learning in Information and Computer Sciences*, *11*(1), 4–13. doi:10.11120/ital.2012.11010004

Lin, J., & Tallman, J. (2006). A theoretical framework for online inquiry-based learning. In C. Crawford, R. Carlsen, K. McFerrin, J. Price, R. Weber & D. Willis (Eds.), *Proceedings of SITE 2006--Society for Information Technology & Teacher Education International Conference* (pp. 967-974). Association for the Advancement of Computing in Education (AACE).

Li, N., & LeFevre, D. (2020). Holographic teaching presence: Participant experiences of interactive synchronous seminars delivered via holographic videoconferencing. *Research in Learning Technology*, 28(0), 2265. doi:10.25304/rlt.v28.2265

Lindgren, R. (2014). Getting into the cue: Embracing technology-facilitated body movements as a starting point for learning. In *Learning Technologies and the Body* (pp. 39–54). Routledge.

Lindgren, R., & Johnson-Glenberg, M. (2013). Emboldened by embodiment: Six precepts for research on embodied learning and mixed reality. *Educational Researcher*, 42(8), 445–452. doi:10.3102/0013189X13511661

Lindo, E. J. (2020). Committed to advancing cultural competence and culturally sustaining pedagogy. *Teaching Exceptional Children*, 53(1), 10–11. doi:10.1177/0040059920945644

Linn, R. L., Baker, E. L., & Dunbar, S. B. (1991). Complex, performance-based assessment: Expectations and validation criteria. *Educational Researcher*, 20(8), 15–21. doi:10.2307/1176232

Li, Q., Zhou, X., Bostian, B., & Xu, D. (2021). How Can We Improve Online Learning at Community Colleges?: Voices from Online Instructors and Students. *Online Learning : the Official Journal of the Online Learning Consortium*, 25(3). Advance online publication. doi:10.24059/olj.v25i3.2362

Liu, S. (2007). Assessing Online Asynchronous Discussion in Online Courses: An Empirical Study. In *Proceedings of TCC 2007* (pp. 24-32). TCCHawaii.

Liu-Thompkins, Y., Okazaki, S., & Li, H. (2022). Artificial Empathy in Marketing Interactions: Bridging the Human-AI Gap in Affective and Social Customer Experience. *Journal of the Academy of Marketing Science*, 50(6), 1198–1218. doi:10.1007/s11747-022-00892-5

Li, X., Wei, M., & Zhuo, Y. (2022, January). Online Collaborative Learning: Main Forms, Effect Evaluation and Optimization Strategies. In *Proceedings of the 2022 13th International Conference on E-Education, E-Business, E-Management, and E-Learning* (pp. 138-142). 10.1145/3514262.3514322

Li, Y., Jiang, Y., Tian, D., Hu, L., Lu, H., & Yuan, Z. (2019). AI-Enabled Emotion Communication. *IEEE Network*, 33(6), 15–21. doi:10.1109/MNET.001.1900070

Lo, C. K. (2023). What is the impact of ChatGPT on education? A rapid review of the literature. *Education Sciences*, 13(4), 410. doi:10.3390/educsci13040410

Loncar, M., Barrett, N. E., & Liu, G. Z. (2014). Towards the refinement of forum and asynchronous online discussion in educational contexts worldwide: Trends and investigative approaches within a dominant research paradigm. *Computers & Education*, 73, 93–110. doi:10.1016/j.compedu.2013.12.007

Long, Y., & Koehler, A. A. (2021). Student participation and interaction in online case-based discussions: Comparing expert and novice facilitation. *Online Learning*. https://olj.onlinelearningconsortium.org/index.php/olj/article/view/2901

Loom. (n.d.). *Free screen recorder for Mac and PC*. https://www.loom.com/

Lopez-Littleton, V., & Blessett, B. (2015). A framework for integrating cultural competency into the curriculum of public administration programs. *Journal of Public Affairs Education*, 21(4), 557–574. doi:10.1080/15236803.2015.12002220

Lovitts, B. E. (2001). *Leaving the ivory tower: The causes and consequences of departure from doctoral study*. Rowman & Littlefield.

Lowenthal, P. R., & Dunlap, J. C. (2018). Investigating students' perceptions of instructional strategies to establish social presence. *Distance Education*, *39*(3), 281–298. doi:10.1080/01587919.2018.1476844

Lowenthal, P. R., Humphrey, M., Conley, Q., Dunlap, J. C., Greear, K., Lowenthal, A., & Giacumo, L. A. (2020). Creating accessible and inclusive online learning: Moving beyond compliance and broadening the discussion. *Quarterly Review of Distance Education*, *21*(2), 1–22.

Lowenthal, P. R., & Snelson, C. (2017). In search of a better understanding of social presence: An investigation into how researchers define social presence. *Distance Education*, *38*(2), 141–159. doi:10.1080/01587919.2017.1324727

Luévano, E., DeLara, E. L., & Castro, J. E. (2015). Use of telepresence and holographic projection mobile device for college degree level. *Procedia Computer Science*, *75*, 339–347. doi:10.1016/j.procs.2015.12.256

Lundine, T. (2022). *How dissertation faculty leaders develop dissertation chairs using the knowledge creation process*. https://www.proquest.com/docview/2725223042?pq-origsite=gscholar&fromopenview=true

Lytras, M. D., Serban, A. C., Ruiz, M. J. T., Ntanos, S., & Sarirete, A. (2022). Translating Knowledge into Innovation Capability: An Exploratory Study Investigating the Perceptions on Distance Learning in Higher Education During the COVID-19 Pandemic-The Case of Mexico. *Journal of Innovation & Knowledge*, *7*(4), 100258. doi:10.1016/j.jik.2022.100258

MacKenzie, A., Bacalja, A., Annamali, D., Panaretou, A., Girme, P., Cutajar, M., Abegglen, S., Evens, M., Neuhaus, F., Wilson, K., Psarikidou, K., Koole, M., Hrastinski, S., Sturm, S., Adachi, C., Schnaider, K., Bozkurt, A., Rapanta, C., Themelis, C., ... Gourlay, L. (2022). Dissolving the dichotomies between online and campus-based teaching: A collective response to the manifesto for teaching online (Bayne et al. 2020). *Postdigital Science and Education*, *4*(2), 271–329. doi:10.1007/s42438-021-00259-z

Maddox, S. (2017), *Did not finish: Doctoral attrition in higher education and student affairs* [Doctoral dissertation, University of Northern Colorado]. https://digscholarship.unco.edu/cgi/viewcontent.cgi?article=1434&context=dissertations

Mahmud, H., Islam, A. N., Ahmed, S. I., & Smolander, K. (2022). What Influences Algorithmic Decision-Making? A Systematic Literature Review on Algorithm Aversion. *Technological Forecasting and Social Change*, *175*, 121390. doi:10.1016/j.techfore.2021.121390

Maina, E. M., Wagacha, P. W., & Oboko, R. O. (2015). A model for improving online collaborative learning through machine learning. In *Models for improving and optimizing online and blended learning in higher education* (pp. 204–219). IGI Global. doi:10.4018/978-1-4666-6280-3.ch011

Makransky, G., & Lilleholt, L. (2018). A structural equation modeling investigation of the emotional value of immersive virtual reality in education. *Educational Technology Research and Development*, *66*(5), 1141–1164. doi:10.1007/s11423-018-9581-2

Makransky, G., & Petersen, G. B. (2021). The cognitive affective model of immersive learning (CAMIL): A theoretical research-based model of learning in immersive virtual reality. *Educational Psychology Review*, *33*(3), 1–22. doi:10.1007/s10648-020-09586-2

Malik, K. M., & Zhu, M. (2023). Do Project-Based Learning, Hands-On Activities, and Flipped Teaching Enhance Student's Learning of Introductory Theoretical Computing Classes? *Education and Information Technologies*, *28*(3), 3581–3604. doi:10.1007/s10639-022-11350-8 PMID:36189191

Mallik, S., & Gangopadhyay, A. (2023). Proactive and Reactive Engagement of Artificial Intelligence Methods for Education: A Review. *Frontiers in Artificial Intelligence*, *6*, 1151391. doi:10.3389/frai.2023.1151391 PMID:37215064

Marcos, S., García Peñalvo, F. J., & Vázquez Ingelmo, A. (2021, October). Emotional AI in Healthcare: A Pilot Architecture Proposal to Merge Emotion Recognition Tools. In *Ninth International Conference on Technological Ecosystems for Enhancing Multiculturality (TEEM'21)* (pp. 342-349). 10.1145/3486011.3486472

Marotta, J. A. (2023). It's time to make more room for program evaluation in the education doctorate program. *Impacting Education: Journal on Transforming Professional Practice*, *8*(4), 50–56. doi:10.5195/ie.2023.335

Martindale, T., & Dowdy, M. (2010). Personal Learning Environments. *Emerging Technologies in Distance Education*, 177–193.

Martin, F., & Bolliger, D. U. (2018). Engagement matters: Student perceptions on the importance of engagement strategies in the online learning environment. *Online Learning : the Official Journal of the Online Learning Consortium*, *22*(1), 205. doi:10.24059/olj.v22i1.1092

Martin, F., Pirbhai-Illich, F., & Pete, S. (2017). Beyond culturally responsive pedagogy: Decolonizing teacher education. In F. Pirbhai-Illich, S. Pete, & F. Martin (Eds.), *Culturally responsive pedagogy: Working towards decolonization, indigeneity and interculturalism* (pp. 235–256). Palgrave. doi:10.1007/978-3-319-46328-5_11

Martin, F., Wu, T., Wan, L., & Xie, K. (2022). A meta-analysis on the community of inquiry presences and learning outcomes in online and blended learning environments. *Online Learning : the Official Journal of the Online Learning Consortium*, *26*(1), 325–359. doi:10.24059/olj.v26i1.2604

Martin, J. (2019). Building relationships and increasing engagement in the virtual classroom: Practical Tools for the Online Instructor. *The Journal of Educators Online*, *16*(1). Advance online publication. doi:10.9743/jeo.2019.16.1.9

Martin, J. P., Choe, N. H., Halter, J., Foster, M., Froyd, J., Borrego, M., & Winterer, E. R. (2019). Interventions supporting baccalaureate achievement of Latinx STEM students matriculating at 2-year institutions: A systematic review. *Journal of Research in Science Teaching*, *56*(4), 440–464. doi:10.1002/tea.21485

Marymount University. (2021, September 1). Ed.D. in education leadership and organizational innovation handbook [Unpublished manuscript]. School of Education, Marymount University.

Matthews, M. T., Williams, G. S., Yanchar, S. C., & McDonald, J. K. (2017). Empathy in distance learning design practice. *TechTrends*, *61*(5), 486–493. doi:10.1007/s11528-017-0212-2

Matthews, M. T., & Yanchar, S. C. (2018). Instructional design as manipulation of, or cooperation with, learners? *TechTrends*, *62*(2), 152–157. doi:10.1007/s11528-017-0245-6

Ma, W., Adesope, O. O., Nesbit, J. C., & Liu, Q. (2014). Intelligent tutoring systems and learning outcomes: A meta-analysis. *Journal of Educational Psychology*, *106*(4), 901–918. doi:10.1037/a0037123

Ma, X., Yue, Z., Gong, Z., Duan, N., Shi, Y., Wei, G., & Li, Y. (2017). The effect of Diaphragmatic Breathing on Attention, Negative Affect and Stress in Healthy Adults. *Frontiers in Psychology*, *8*, 874. doi:10.3389/fpsyg.2017.00874 PMID:28626434

May, D., Morkos, B., Jackson, A., Hunsu, N. J., Ingalls, A., & Beyette, F. (2022). Rapid Transition of Traditionally Hands-On Labs to Online Instruction in Engineering Courses. *European Journal of Engineering Education*, 1–19.

Mayer, R. E. (2014). Principles based on social cues in multimedia learning: Personalization, voice, image, and embodiment principles. The Cambridge Handbook of Multimedia Learning, 16, 345-370.

Mayer, R. E. (2017). Using multimedia for e-learning. *Journal of Computer Assisted Learning*, *33*(5), 403–423. doi:10.1111/jcal.12197

McCleskey, J. A., & Gruda, D. (2021). The New Normal: Student Views of Higher Education During the COVID-19 Pandemic. *Southwest Academy of Management 2021 Virtual Conference.*

McDonagh, D. C. (2006). *Empathic design: emerging design research methodologies* [Doctoral dissertation]. Loughborough University.

McKenzie, L. (2021). Students Want Online Learning Options Post-Pandemic. *Inside Higher Ed*. https://www.insidehighered.com/news/2021/04/27/survey-reveals-positive-outlook-online-instruction-post-pandemic#:~:text=The%20majority%20of%20students%2C%2073%20percent%2C%20%22somewhat%22%20or,offering%20a%20combination%20of%20in-person%20and%20online%20instruction

McKinney, B. K. (2018). The impact of program-wide discussion board grading rubrics on students and faculty satisfaction. *Online Learning : the Official Journal of the Online Learning Consortium*, *22*(2), 289–299. doi:10.24059/olj.v22i2.1386

McKinney, P., & Sen, B. (2016). *The use of technology in group work: A situational analysis of students' reflective writing*. Education for Information.

McMurtrie, B. (2023, January 5). Teaching: Will ChatGPT change the way you teach? *The Chronicle of Higher Education*. https://www.chronicle.com/newsletter/teaching/2023-01-05

Megahed, F. M., Chen, Y., Ferris, J. A., Knoth, S., & Jones-Farmer, L. A. (2023). How generative AI models such as ChatGPT can be (mis)used in SPC practice, education, and research? An exploratory study. Quality Engineering, 1–29. doi:10.1080/08982112.2023.2206479

Mehrabian, A. (1971). *Silent messages: implicit communication of emotions and attitudes*. Wadsworth.

Mehta, R., & Aguilera, E. (2020). A critical approach to humanizing pedagogies in online teaching and learning. *The International Journal of Information and Learning Technology*, *37*(3), 109–120. doi:10.1108/IJILT-10-2019-0099

Mehta, R., & Gleason, B. (2021). Against empathy: Moving beyond colonizing practices in educational technology. *Educational Technology Research and Development*, *69*(1), 87–90. doi:10.1007/s11423-020-09901-2

Melideo, S. (2023, July 3-5). *Constituting community: A heuristic examination of tools and opportunities for deepening connectivity and engagement of asynchronous doctoral students* [Paper presentation]. 15th annual International Conference on Education and New Learning Technologies, Palma de Mallorca, Spain. https://library.iated.org/view/MELIDEO2023CON

Mensah, F. M. (2021). Culturally relevant and culturally responsive. *Science and Children*, *58*(4), 10–13. doi:10.1080/00368148.2021.12291647

Mercader, C., & Gairin, J. (2020). University teachers' perception of barriers to the use of digital technologies: The importance of academic discipline. *International Journal of Educational Technology in Higher Education*, *17*(1), 4. doi:10.1186/s41239-020-0182-x

Merrill, M. D. (1996). What new paradigm of ISD? *Educational Technology*, *36*(4), 57–58. https://www.jstor.org/stable/44428351

MhlandaD. (2023). Open AI in Education, the Responsible and Ethical Use of ChatGPT Towards Lifelong Learning. SSRN. doi:10.2139/ssrn.4354422

Miller, A. N., Katt, J. A., Brown, T., & Sivo, S. A. (2014). The relationship of instructor self-disclosure, nonverbal immediacy, and credibility to student incivility in the college classroom. *Communication Education, 63*(1), 1–16. doi:10.1080/03634523.2013.835054

Miller, M., Hahs-Vaughn, D., & Zygouris-Coe, V. (2014). A confirmatory factor analysis of teaching presence within online professional development. *Online Learning : the Official Journal of the Online Learning Consortium, 18*(1). Advance online publication. doi:10.24059/olj.v18i1.333

Mishra, P., & Koehler, M. (2006). Technological pedagogical content knowledge: A framework for teacher knowledge. *Teachers College Record, 108*(6), 1017–1054. doi:10.1111/j.1467-9620.2006.00684.x

Montagnino, C. (2023). *Six Ways to Maximize Authentic Learning in the AI Era*. Fierce Education. https://www.fierce-education.com/student-engagement/six-ways-maximize-authentic-learning-ai-era

Moon, J., Passmore, C., Reiser, B. J., & Michaels, S. (2014). Beyond comparisons of online versus face-to-face PD: Commentary in response to Fishman et al., "Comparing the impact of online and face-to-face professional development in the context of curriculum implementation". *Journal of Teacher Education, 65*(2), 172–176. doi:10.1177/0022487113511497

Moore, M. G. (2013). The theory of transactional distance. In M. G. Moore (Ed.), *Handbook of Distance Education* (2nd ed., pp. 84–103). Routledge. doi:10.4324/9780203803738.ch5

Morimoto, T., Hirata, H., Ueno, M., Fukumori, N., Sakai, T., Sugimoto, M., Kobayashi, T., Tsukamoto, M., Yoshihara, T., Toda, Y., Oda, Y., Otani, K., & Mawatari, M. (2022). Digital transformation will change medical education and rehabilitation in spine surgery. *Medicina, 58*(4), 508. doi:10.3390/medicina58040508 PMID:35454347

Moses, T. (2020, August 17). *5 reasons to let students keep their cameras off during Zoom classes*. The Conversation. https://theconversation.com/5-reasons-to-let-students-keep-their-cameras-off-during-zoom-classes-144111

Muggleton, S. (2014). Alan Turing and the development of Artificial Intelligence. *AI Communications, 27*(1), 3–10. doi:10.3233/AIC-130579

Muhammad, G. (2023). *Unearthing joy: A guide to culturally and historically responsive curriculum and instruction*. Scholastic.

Muir, T., Douglas, T., & Trimble, A. (2020). Facilitation strategies for enhancing the learning and engagement of online students. *Journal of University Teaching & Learning Practice, 17*(3), 8. doi:10.53761/1.17.3.8

Mukhtar, K., Javed, K., Arooj, M., & Sethi, A. (2020). Advantages, limitations and recommendations for online learning during COVID-19 pandemic era. *Pakistan Journal of Medical Sciences, 36*(COVID19-S4), S27.

Mullen, C. A. (2021). Online doctoral mentoring in a pandemic: Help or hindrance to academic progress on dissertations? *International Journal of Mentoring and Coaching in Education, 10*(2), 139–157. doi:10.1108/IJMCE-06-2020-0029

Mulwa, C., Lawless, S., Sharp, M., Arnedillo-Sanchez, I., & Wade, V. (2010, October). Adaptive Educational Hypermedia Systems in Technology Enhanced Learning: A Literature Review. In *Proceedings of the 2010 ACM Conference on Information Technology Education* (pp. 73-84). 10.1145/1867651.1867672

Murphy, E., & Coleman, E. (2004). Graduate students' experiences of challenges in online asynchronous discussions. *Canadian Journal of Learning and Technology/La revue canadienne de l'apprentissage et de la technologie, 30*(2).

Mykota, D., & Duncan, R. (2007). Learner characteristics as predictors of online social presence. *Canadian Journal of Education, 30*(1), 157–170. doi:10.2307/20466630

Naisbitt, J., & Bisesi, M. (1983). Megatrends: Ten new directions transforming our lives. *Sloan Management Review, 24*(4), 69. doi:10.1016/0007-6813(83)90036-8

Nam, C. (2017). The effects of digital storytelling on student achievement, social presence, and attitude in online collaborative learning environments. *Interactive Learning Environments, 25*(3), 412–427. doi:10.1080/10494820.2015.1135173

National Center for Education Statistics. (2020). *Table 311.15. Digest of Education Statistics (NCES 2017–094)*. Author.

National Center for Education Statistics. (2023). Undergraduate Enrollment. In *Condition of Education*. U.S. Department of Education, Institute of Education Sciences. Retrieved January 11, 2024, from https://nces.ed.gov/programs/coe/indicator/cha

Neale-McFall, C. W. (2011). *Perceived satisfaction of counseling doctoral students with their dissertation chairperson: Examining selection criteria and chairperson behaviors* [Doctoral dissertation, Old Dominion University]. https://digitalcommons.odu.edu/cgi/viewcontent.cgi?article=1080&context=chs_etds

Neale-McFall, C., & Ward, C. A. (2015). Factors contributing to counselor education doctoral students' satisfaction with their dissertation chairperson. *The Professional Counselor, 5*(1), 185. https://digitalcommons.wcupa.edu/cgi/viewcontent.cgi?article=1001&context=counsed_facpub

Neubauer, D., Paepcke-Hjeltness, V., Evans, P., Barnhart, B., & Finseth, T. (2017). Experiencing technology enabled empathy mapping. *The Design Journal, 20*(1), S4683–S4689. doi:10.1080/14606925.2017.1352966

Newman, D. R., Johnson, C., Webb, B., & Cochrane, C. (1997). Evaluating the quality of learning in computer supported cooperative learning. *Journal of the American Society for Information Science American Society for Information Science, 48*, 484-495. doi: 1097-4571 (199706)48:6<484::AID-ASI2>3.0.CO;2-Q. doi:10.1002/(SICI)

Ngoc, H., Hoang, L., & Hung, V. (2020). Transforming education with emerging technologies in higher education: A systematic literature review. *International Journal of Higher Education, 9*(5), 252–258. doi:10.5430/ijhe.v9n5p252

Nielsen, L. (2019). *Personas: User focused design* (2nd ed.). Springer. https://link.springer.com/content/pdf/10.1007/978-1-4471-7427-1.pdf doi:10.1007/978-1-4471-7427-1

Nolan-Grant, C. R. (2019). The community of inquiry framework as learning design model: A case study in postgraduate online education. *Research in Learning Technology, 27*(0). Advance online publication. doi:10.25304/rlt.v27.2240

Nonaka, I., & Von Krogh, G. (2009). Perspective—Tacit knowledge and knowledge conversion: Controversy and advancement in organizational knowledge creation theory. *Organization Science, 20*(3), 635–652. doi:10.1287/orsc.1080.0412

Nonnecke, B., & Preece, J. (2000, April). Lurker demographics: Counting the silent. In *Proceedings of the SIGCHI conference on Human factors in computing systems* (pp. 73-80). 10.1145/332040.332409

Noorbehbahani, F., Mohammadi, A., & Aminazadeh, M. (2022). A Systematic Review of Research on Cheating in Online Exams from 2010 to 2021. *Education and Information Technologies, 27*(6), 8413–8460. doi:10.1007/s10639-022-10927-7 PMID:35283658

Novak, K., & Thibodeau, T. (2016). *UDL in the cloud: How to design and deliver online education using universal design for learning*. CAST Professional Publishing.

NSSE. (2014). *Promoting student learning and institutional improvement: Lessons from NSSE at 13*. Indiana University for Postsecondary Research.

Nye, B. D. (2016). ITS, the end of the world as we know it: Transitioning AIED into a service-oriented ecosystem. *International Journal of Artificial Intelligence in Education, 26*(2), 756–770. doi:10.1007/s40593-016-0098-8

O*Net. (2024a). *Business Teachers, Postsecondary*. Retrieved on January 19, 2024, https://www.onetonline.org/link/summary/25-1011.00

O*Net. (2024b). *Chief Executives*. Retrieved on January 19, 2024, https://www.onetonline.org/link/summary/11-1011.00

O*Net. (2024c). *Child, Family, and School Social Workers*. Retrieved on January 19, 2024, https://www.onetonline.org/link/summary/21-1021.00

O*Net. (2024d). *Registered Nurse*. Retrieved on January 19, 2024, https://www.onetonline.org/link/summary/29-1141.00

O'Doherty, D., Dromey, M., Lougheed, J., Hannigan, A., Last, J., & McGrath, D. (2018). Barriers and solutions to online learning in medical education – an integrative review. *BMC Medical Education, 18*(130), 130. doi:10.1186/s12909-018-1240-0

Oh, C. S., Bailenson, J. N., & Welch, G. F. (2018). A Systematic Review of Social Presence: Definition, Antecedents, and Implications. *Frontiers in Robotics and AI, 5*, 5. doi:10.3389/frobt.2018.00114 PMID:33500993

Oje, A., Hunsum, N., & May, D. (2023). Virtual Reality assisted engineering education: a multimedia learning perspective. Computers & Education: X Reality, 3.

Orús, C., Barlés, M. J., Belanche, D., Casaló, L., Fraj, E., & Gurrea, R. (2016). The effects of learner-generated videos for YouTube on learning outcomes and satisfaction. *Computers & Education, 95*, 254–269. doi:10.1016/j.compedu.2016.01.007

Osatuyi, B. (2013). Information sharing on social media sites. *Computers in Human Behavior, 29*(6), 2622–2631. doi:10.1016/j.chb.2013.07.001

Osborne, D. M., Byrne, J. H., Massey, D. L., & Johnston, A. N. (2018). Use of online asynchronous discussion boards to engage students, enhance critical thinking, and foster staff-student/student-student collaboration: A mixed method study. *Nurse Education Today, 70*, 40–46. doi:10.1016/j.nedt.2018.08.014 PMID:30145533

Ouyang, F., & Pengcheng, J. (2021). Artificial intelligence in education: The three paradigms. *Computers and Education: Artificial Intelligence, 2*, 1–6. doi:10.1016/j.caeai.2021.100020

Pacansky-Brock, M. (2020). *How to humanize your online class, version 2.0* [Infographic]. https://brocansky.com/humanizing/infographic2

Pacansky-Brock, M., (2020). *How and why to humanize your online course*. Academic Press.

Pacansky-Brock, M. (2022). Reflections on inclusive teaching. *Journal of Educational Research and Practice, 12*(0), 1. doi:10.5590/JERAP.2022.12.0.01

Pacansky-Brock, M., Smedshammer, M., & Vincent-Layton, K. (2020). Humanizing online teaching to equitize higher education. *Current Issues in Education (Tempe, Ariz.), 21*(2), 1–21.

Pacansky-Brock, M., Smedshammer, M., & Vincent-Layton, K. (2020). Humanizing online teaching to equitize higher education. *Current Issues in Education (Tempe, Ariz.), 21*(2), 1–21. https://cie.asu.edu/ojs/index.php/cieatasu/article/view/1905

Pacansky-Brock, M., Smedshammer, M., & Vincent-Layton, K. (2023). In search of belonging online: Achieving equity through transformative professional development. *Journal of Educational Research and Practice, 12*(0), 39–64. doi:10.5590/JERAP.2022.12.0.04

Page, K., & Nowak, M. (2002). Empathy leads to fairness. *Bulletin of Mathematical Biology, 64*(6), 1101–1116. Advance online publication. doi:10.1006/bulm.2002.0321 PMID:12508533

Pal, K. (2022). Evaluation of a Scenario-Based Socratic Style of Teaching and Learning Practice. In Enhancing Teaching and Learning With Socratic Educational Strategies: Emerging Research and Opportunities (pp. 121-144). IGI Global. doi:10.4018/978-1-7998-7172-9.ch007

Palloff, R., & Pratt, K. (2007). *Building online learning communities: Effective strategies for the virtual classroom.* Wiley.

Papanastasiou, G., Drigas, A., Skianis, C., Lytras, M., & Papanastasiou, E. (2019). Virtual and augmented reality effects on K-12, higher and tertiary education students' twenty-first century skills. *Virtual Reality (Waltham Cross), 23*(4), 425–436. doi:10.1007/s10055-018-0363-2

Papert, S., & Harel, I. (Eds.). (1991). *Constructionism.* Ablex Publishing.

Paré, G., Trudel, M. C., Jaana, M., & Kitsiou, S. (2015). Synthesizing information systems knowledge: A typology of literature reviews. *Information & Management, 52*(2), 183–199. doi:10.1016/j.im.2014.08.008

Paris, D., & Alim, H. (2014). What are we seeking to sustain through culturally sustaining pedagogy? A loving critique forward. *Harvard Educational Review, 84*(1), 85–100. doi:10.17763/haer.84.1.982l873k2ht16m77

Park, D., Lee, G., Kang, S., Kim, S., Ahn, E., & Jang, S. (2022). Deriving Improvement Measures for University Teaching and Learning Following the Implementation of Online Classes in the Post-COVID-19 Era. *Industrial Convergence Research, 20*(3), 11–21. doi:10.22678/JIC.2022.20.3.011

Parker, J., & Herrington, J. (2015). *Setting the Climate in an Authentic Online Community of Learning.* Australian Association for Research in Education.

Parker, N., Mahler, B. P., & Edwards, M. (2021). Humanizing online learning experiences. *The Journal of Educators Online, 18*(2), 119–129.

Park, S., Jeong, Y., Kim, D., & Ryu, J. (in press). Cultivating Cultural Immersion Through an Extended Reality-based Digital Board Game in Social Studies. In M. Schmidt, B. Hokanson, M. Exter, A. Tawfik, & Y. Earnshaw (Eds.), *Transdisciplinary Learning Experience Design: Futures, Synergies, and Innovation.* Springer.

Parrish, P. (2006). Design as storytelling. *TechTrends, 50*(4), 72–82. doi:10.1007/s11528-006-0072-7

Parrish, P. (2014). Designing for the half-known world: Lessons for instructional designers from the craft of narrative fiction. In B. Hokanson & A. Gibbons (Eds.), *Design in educational technology: Design thinking, design process, and the design studio* (pp. 261–270). Springer International. doi:10.1007/978-3-319-00927-8_15

Parrish, P., & Linder-VanBerschot, J. (2010). Cultural dimensions of learning: Addressing the challenges of multicultural instruction. *International Review of Research in Open and Distance Learning, 11*(2), 1–19. doi:10.19173/irrodl.v11i2.809

Parsons, B., & Faubert, J. (2021). Enhancing learning in a perceptual-cognitive training paradigm using EEG-neurofeedback. *Scientific Reports, 11*(1), 4061. Advance online publication. doi:10.1038/s41598-021-83456-x PMID:33602994

Patch, W. (2020). *Impact of Coronavirus on Students' Academic Progress and College Plans.* https://www.niche.com/about/enrollment-insights/impact-of-coronavirus-on-students-academic-progress-and-college-plans#college

Patra, S., & Sahu, K. K. (2020). Digitalisation, Online Learning and Virtual World. *Horizon Journal of Humanities and Social Science, 2*(1), 45–52.

Paulsen, M. F. (2003). *Online education and learning management systems: Global e-learning in a Scandinavian perspective.* NKI Forlaget.

Peacock, S., & Cowan, J. (2019). Promoting sense of belonging in online learning communities of inquiry at accredited courses. *Online Learning : the Official Journal of the Online Learning Consortium, 23*(2), 67–81. doi:10.24059/olj.v23i2.1488

Peacock, S., Cowan, J., Irvine, L., & Williams, J. (2020). An exploration into the importance of a sense of belonging for online learners. *International Review of Research in Open and Distance Learning, 21*(2), 18–35. doi:10.19173/irrodl.v20i5.4539

Pedro, F., Subosa, M., Rivas, A., & Valverde, P. (2019). *Artificial Intelligence in Education: Challenges and Opportunities for Sustainable Development.* Academic Press.

Pereira Nunes, B., Kawase, R., Fetahu, B., Casanova, M. A., & de Campos, G. H. (2014). Educational forums at a glance: Topic extraction and selection. *Web Information Systems Engineering – WISE 2014*, 351–364. doi:10.1007/978-3-319-11746-1_25

Picard, R. W., Papert, S., Bender, W., Blumberg, B., Breazeal, C., Cavallo, D., Machover, T., Resnick, M., Roy, D., & Strohecker, C. (2004). Affective Learning—A Manifesto. *BT Technology Journal, 22*(4), 253–269. doi:10.1023/B:BTTJ.0000047603.37042.33

Picciano, A. G. (2002). Beyond student perceptions: Issues of interaction, presence and performance in an online course. *Journal of Asynchronous Learning Networks, 6*(1), 21–40.

Pinkus, E. (2020). *SurveyMonkey poll: Distance learning for college students during the Coronavirus outbreak.* https://www.surveymonkey.com/curiosity/surveymonkey-poll-distance-learning-college-students-covid/

Pitchford, A., Owen, D., & Stevens, E. (2020). *A handbook for authentic learning in higher education: Transformational learning through real-world experiences.* Routledge. doi:10.4324/9780429242854

Pokrivčáková, S. (2019). Preparing teachers for the application of AI-powered technologies in foreign language education. *Journal of Language and Cultural Education, 7*(3), 135–153. doi:10.2478/jolace-2019-0025

Poll, K., Widen, J., & Weller, S. (2014). Six Instructional Best Practices for Online Engagement and Retention. *Journal of Online Doctoral Education, 1*(1), 56–72.

Portman, S. (2020). Reflective journaling: A portal into the virtues of daily writing. *The Reading Teacher, 73*(5), 597–602. doi:10.1002/trtr.1877

Powell, R. M., & Murray, O. (2012). Using storytelling strategies to improve student comprehension in online classes. *The Journal of Effective Teaching, 12*(1), 46–52.

Power, M. J. (2006). The Structure of Emotion: An Empirical Comparison of Six Models. *Cognition and Emotion, 20*(5), 694–713. doi:10.1080/02699930500367925

Pozo-Rico, T., Gilar-Corbí, R., Izquierdo, A., & Castejón, J. L. (2020). Teacher Training Can Make a Difference: Tools to Overcome the Impact of COVID-19 on Primary Schools. An Experimental Study. *International Journal of Environmental Research and Public Health, 17*(22), 8633. doi:10.3390/ijerph17228633 PMID:33233750

Pregowska, A., Masztalerz, K., Garlińska, M., & Osial, M. (2021). A worldwide journey through distance education—From the post office to virtual, augmented and mixed realities, and education during the COVID-19 pandemic. *Education Sciences, 11*(3), 118. doi:10.3390/educsci11030118

Preisman, K. (2014). Teaching Presence in Online Education: From the Instructor's Point of View. *Online Learning : the Official Journal of the Online Learning Consortium, 18*(3), 1–16. doi:10.24059/olj.v18i3.446

Prestridge, S., Main, K., & Schmid, M. (2023). (2023). Identifying how classroom teachers develop presence online: Breaking the fourth wall in online learning. *Education and Information Technologies*. Advance online publication. doi:10.1007/s10639-023-11714-8 PMID:37361763

Prieto, L. P., Sharma, K., Kidzinski, Ł., Rodríguez-Triana, M. J., & Dillenbourg, P. (2018). Multimodal teaching analytics: Automated extraction of orchestration graphs from wearable sensor data. *Journal of Computer Assisted Learning*, *34*(2), 193–203. doi:10.1111/jcal.12232 PMID:29686446

Project Squirrel. (2018). *Project Squirrel*. https://projectsquirrel.org/index.shtml

Project Zero. (2023, July 12). *Project Zero's Thinking Routine Toolbox*. https://pz.harvard.edu/thinking-routines

Pruitt, J., & Grudin, J. (2003, June). Personas: practice and theory. In *Proceedings of the 2003 conference on Designing for user experiences* (pp. 1-15). Academic Press.

Purdue University. (2024). *Student accountability in online environments*. Retrieved on January 15, 2024, https://onlineteachinghub.education.purdue.edu/wp-content/uploads/2022/11/student_accountability_in_online_environments_summary.pdf

Pusztahelyi, R. (2020). Emotional AI and Its Challenges in the Viewpoint of Online Marketing. *Curentul Juridic*, *81*(2), 13–31.

Radu, I. (2014). Augmented reality in education: A meta-review and cross-media analysis. *Personal and Ubiquitous Computing*, *18*(6), 1533–1543. doi:10.1007/s00779-013-0747-y

Rahman, M. M., & Watanobe, Y. (2023). ChatGPT for education and research: Opportunities, threats, and strategies. *Applied Sciences (Basel, Switzerland)*, *13*(9), 5783. doi:10.3390/app13095783

Rajeswaran, P., Hung, N., Kesavadas, T., Vozenilek, J., & Kumar, P. (2018). AirwayVR: learning endotracheal intubation in virtual reality. *2018 IEEE Conference on Virtual Reality and 3D User Interfaces (VR)*, 669–670. 10.1109/VR.2018.8446075

Ramlatchan, M., & Watson, G. S. (2019). Enhancing instructor credibility and immediacy in online multimedia designs. *Educational Technology Research and Development*, *68*(1), 511–528. doi:10.1007/s11423-019-09714-y

Ramlatchan, M., & Watson, G. S. (2020). Enhancing Instructor Credibility and Immediacy in the Design of Distance Learning Systems and Virtual Classroom Environments. *The Journal of Applied Instructional Design*, *9*(2). Advance online publication. doi:10.51869/92mrgsw

Rapanta, C., & Cantoni, L. (2014). Being in the users' shoes: Anticipating experience while designing online courses. *British Journal of Educational Technology*, *45*(5), 765–777. doi:10.1111/bjet.12102

Ratican, J., & Hutson, J. (2023). The Six Emotional Dimension (6DE) Model: A Multidimensional Approach to Analyzing Human Emotions and Unlocking the Potential of Emotionally Intelligent Artificial Intelligence (AI) via Large Language Models (LLM). *Journal of Artificial Intelligence and Robotics*, *1*(1), 44–52.

Rawas, S. (2023). ChatGPT: Empowering lifelong learning in the digital age of higher education. *Education and Information Technologies*. Advance online publication. doi:10.1007/s10639-023-12114-8

Razzouk, R., & Shute, V. (2012). What is design thinking and why is it important? *Review of Educational Research*, *82*(3), 330–348. doi:10.3102/0034654312457429

Reeve, J., & Jang, H. (2022). Agentic engagement. In *Handbook of research on student engagement* (pp. 95–107). Springer International Publishing. doi:10.1007/978-3-031-07853-8_5

Reigeluth, C. M. (1996). A new paradigm of ISD? *Educational Technology, 36*(3), 13–20. https://www.jstro.org/stable/44428335

Replication and extension in the online classroom. (2020). *Journal of Research on Technology in education,* 1-17. doi: 10.1080/15391523.2020.1766389

Richardson, J. C., Ice, P., & Swan, K. (2009). *Tips and techniques for integrating social, teaching, & cognitive presence into your courses.* Poster session presented at the Conference on Distance Teaching & Learning, Madison, WI.

Richardson, J. C., Maeda, Y., Lv, J., & Caskurlu, S. (2017). Social presence in relation to students' satisfaction and learning in the online environment: A meta-analysis. *Computers in Human Behavior, 71,* 402–417. doi:10.1016/j.chb.2017.02.001

Richardson, J., Koehler, A., Besser, E., Caskurlu, S., Lim, J., & Mueller, C. (2015). Conceptualizing and Investigating Instructor Presence in Online Learning Environments. *International Review of Research in Open and Distance Learning, 16*(3), 256–297. doi:10.19173/irrodl.v16i3.2123

Richardson, J., Koehler, A., Besser, E., Caskurlu, S., Lim, J., & Mueller, C. (2016). Instructor's perceptions of instructor presence in online learning environments. *International Review of Research in Open and Distance Learning, 17*(4), 82–104. doi:10.19173/irrodl.v17i4.2330

Richardson, J., & Swan, K. (2003). *An Examination of Social Presence in Online Courses in Relation to Students' Perceived Learning and Satisfaction* (Vol. 7). Research Gate.

Rico, R., & Ertmer, P. A. (2015). Examining the role of the instructor in problem-centered instruction. *TechTrends, 59*(4), 96–103. doi:10.1007/s11528-015-0876-4

Rigler, K. L., Jr., Bowlin, L. K., Sweat, K., Watts, S., & Throne, R. (2017). *Agency, socialization, and support: A critical review of doctoral student attrition* [Paper presentation]. International Conference on Doctoral Education, University of Central Florida. https://files.eric.ed.gov/fulltext/ED580853.pdf

Rippy, M., & Munoz, M. (2021). Designing Authentic Online Courses Intra-and Post-Pandemic. *Online Teaching and Learning in Higher Education During COVID-19,* 13–27.

Roberts, C., & Hyatt, L. (2018). *The dissertation journey* (3rd ed.). Corwin Press.

Rockinson-Szapkiw, A. J., Holmes, J., & Stephens, J. S. (2019). Identifying significant personal and program factors that predict online EdD students' program integration. *Online Learning : the Official Journal of the Online Learning Consortium, 23*(4), 313–335. doi:10.24059/olj.v23i4.1579

Roddy, C., Amiet, D. L., Chung, J., Holt, C., Shaw, L., McKenzie, S., Garivaldis, F., Lodge, J. M., & Mundy, M. E. (2017). Applying best practice online learning, teaching, and support to intensive online environments: An integrative review. *Frontiers in Education, 2,* 59. Advance online publication. doi:10.3389/feduc.2017.00059

Roll, I., Russell, D. M., & Gašević, D. (2018). Learning at scale. *International Journal of Artificial Intelligence in Education, 28*(4), 471–477. doi:10.1007/s40593-018-0170-7

Ross, J. D. (2011). *Online professional development: Design, deliver, succeed!* Corwin Press.

Roumeliotis, K. I., & Tselikas, N. D. (2023). ChatGPT and open-AI models. A preliminary review. *Future Internet, 15*(6), 192. doi:10.3390/fi15060192

Rovai, A. (2007). Facilitating online discussions effectively. *The Internet and Higher Education, 10*(1), 77–88. doi:10.1016/j.iheduc.2006.10.001

Rovai, A. P. (2002). Sense of community, perceived cognitive learning, and persistence in asynchronous learning networks. *The Internet and Higher Education*, 5(4), 319–332. doi:10.1016/S1096-7516(02)00130-6

Rovai, A. P. (2002b). Building sense of community at a distance. *International Review of Research in Open and Distance Learning*, 3(1), 1–16. doi:10.19173/irrodl.v3i1.79

Rovai, A. P. (2007). *Facilitating online discussions effectively. Internet and Higher Education, 10(1), 77-88.*

Rovai, A. P., & Jordan, H. M. (2004). Blended learning and sense of community: A comparative analysis with traditional and fully online graduate courses. *International Review of Research in Open and Distance Learning*, 5(2), 1–13. doi:10.19173/irrodl.v5i2.192

Ruan, S., Willis, A., Xu, Q., Davis, G. M., Jiang, L., Brunskill, E., & Landay, J. A. (2019). BookBuddy. *Proceedings of the Sixth (2019) ACM Conference on Learning @ Scale - L@S '19.*

Rudolph, J., Tan, S., & Tan, S. (2023). ChatGPT: Bullshit spewer or the end of traditional assessments in higher education? *Journal of Applied Learning and Teaching*, 6(1).

Russell, S. J., & Norvig, P. (2010). *Artificial Intelligence: A Modern Approach* (3rd ed.). Prentice Hall.

Ruzmetova, M. (2018). Applying Gilly Salmon's five stage model for designing blended courses. *Dil ve Edebiyat Araştırmaları*, 17(17), 271–290. doi:10.30767/diledeara.418085

Ryan, R. M., & Deci, E. L. (2000). Intrinsic and Extrinsic Motivations: Classic Definitions and New Directions* 1. *Contemporary Educational Psychology*, 25(1), 54–67. doi:10.1006/ceps.1999.1020 PMID:10620381

Sadaf, A., Richardson, J., & Ertnmer, P. (2011). Relationship between question prompts and critical thinking in online discussions. In *Annual Meeting of the Association for Educational Communications and Technology* (Vol. 10). Academic Press.

Saint-Jacques, A. (2013). Effective teaching practices to foster vibrant communities of inquiry in synchronous online learning. In *Educational communities of inquiry: Theoretical framework, research and practice* (pp. 84–108). IGI Global. doi:10.4018/978-1-4666-2110-7.ch006

Salar, R., Arici, F., Caliklar, S., & Yilmaz, R. M. (2020). A model for augmented reality immersion experiences of university students studying in science education. *Journal of Science Education and Technology*, 29(2), 257–271. doi:10.1007/s10956-019-09810-x

Salazar, M. (2013). A humanizing pedagogy: Reinventing the principles and practices of education as a journey towards liberation. *Review of Research in Education*, 37(1), 121–148. doi:10.3102/0091732X12464032

Salazar, M., Norton, A., & Tuitt, F. (2017). Weaving promising practices for inclusive excellence into the higher education classroom. *To Improve the Academy*, 28(1), 208–226. doi:10.1002/j.2334-4822.2010.tb00604.x

Salazar, S. (2021). *A Guide to Teaching Art at the College Level*. Teachers College Press.

Salmon, G. (2002). Approaches to Researching Teaching and Learning Online. In C. Steeples & C. Jones (Eds.), *Networked Learning: Perspectives and Issues*. Springer., doi:10.1007/978-1-4471-0181-9_11

Salmon, G. (2003). *E-moderating: The Key to teaching and learning online*. Routledge.

Saltan, F., & Arslan, Ö. (2017). The use of augmented reality in formal education: A scoping review. *Eurasia Journal of Mathematics, Science and Technology Education*, 13(2), 503–520.

Samsonovich, A. V. (2020). Socially Emotional Brain-Inspired Cognitive Architecture Framework for Artificial Intelligence. *Cognitive Systems Research*, *60*(1), 57–76. doi:10.1016/j.cogsys.2019.12.002

San Diego State University (SDSU). (2023). *The Empathy Lens*. Retrieved on January 15, 2024, from https://its.sdsu.edu/innovation/empathy-lens

Sanders, C., & Scanlon, E. (2021). The digital divide is a human rights issue: Advancing social inclusion through social work advocacy. *Journal of Human Rights and Social Work*, *6*(2), 130–143. doi:10.1007/s41134-020-00147-9 PMID:33758780

Sanders, K., & Lokey-Vega, A. (2020). K-12 Community of Inquiry: A case study of the applicability of the Community of Inquiry framework in the K-12 learning environment. *Journal of Online Learning Research*, *6*(1), 35–56.

Santos, J. P., Abana, E. C., Tindowen, D. J. C., Mendezabal, M. J. N., & Pattaguan, E. J. P. (2020). *Perceptions and readiness of USL stakeholders on flexible learning*. http://119.92.172.179/papers/dafun/dafun_vol3_s2020_p3.pdf

Saul Carliner. (2004). *An Overview of Online Learning*. Human Resource Development.

Saunders, W., Sastry, G., Stuhlmüller, A., & Evans, O. (2017). Trial without Error: Towards Safe Reinforcement Learning via Human Intervention. *ArXiv, abs/1707.05173*.

Savery, J. R. (2006). Overview of problem-based learning: Definitions and distinctions. *The Interdisciplinary Journal of Problem-Based Learning*, *1*(1), 9–20. doi:10.7771/1541-5015.1002

Saxena, M. (2011). Learner analysis framework for globalized e-learning: A case study. *International Review of Research in Open and Distance Learning: A Case Study*, *12*(5), 93-107. doi:10.19173/irrodl.v12i5.954

Sayed, W. S., Noeman, A. M., Abdellatif, A., Abdelrazek, M., Badawy, M. G., Hamed, A., & El-Tantawy, S. (2023). AI-Based Adaptive Personalized Content Presentation and Exercises Navigation for an Effective and Engaging E-Learning Platform. *Multimedia Tools and Applications*, *82*(3), 3303–3333. doi:10.1007/s11042-022-13076-8 PMID:35789938

Schiff, D. (2021). Out of the laboratory and into the classroom: The future of artificial intelligence in education. *AI & Society*, *36*(1), 331–348. doi:10.1007/s00146-020-01033-8 PMID:32836908

Schmidt, M., & Huang, R. (2021). Defining learning experience design: Voices from the field of learning design & technology. *TechTrends*, *66*(2), 141–158. doi:10.1007/s11528-021-00656-y

Schroeder, N. L., & Adesope, O. O. (2015). Impacts of pedagogical agent gender in an Accessible learning environment. *Journal of Educational Technology & Society*, *18*(4), 401–411.

Schwalbe, M. L. & Mason Schrock, D. (1996). Identity work as group process. *Advances in Group Processes, 13*(113), 113-147. https://www.researchgate.net/publication/284293040_Identity_work_as_group_process

Sclater, N. (2008). Web 2.0, personal learning environments, and the future of learning management systems. *Research Bulletin (International Commission for the Northwest Atlantic Fisheries)*, 13.

Scott, D. E., & Scott, S. (2010). Innovation in the use of technology and teacher professional development. In A. D. Olofsson & J. O. Lindberg (Eds.), *Online learning communities and teacher professional development: Methods for improved education delivery* (pp. 169–189). Information Science Reference. doi:10.4018/978-1-60566-780-5.ch010

Scott, H., & Huffling, L. D. (2022). Going with the flow: Shifting Fface-to-Fface PD to Ffully Oonline in the Eera of COVID-19. *International Journal for the Scholarship of Teaching and Learning*, *16*(1), 6. doi:10.20429/ijsotl.2022.160106

Seaman, J. E., Allen, I. E., & Seaman, J. (2018). *Grade increase: Tracking distance education in the United States*. Babson Survey Research Group.

Seifert, T. (2016). Involvement, collaboration, and engagement—Social networks through a pedagogical lens. *Journal of Learning Design*, 9(2), 31–45. doi:10.5204/jld.v9i2.272

Selvaraj, C., Chandra, I., & Singh, S. K. (2021). Artificial Intelligence and Machine Learning Approaches for Drug Design: Challenges and Opportunities for the Pharmaceutical Industries. *Molecular Diversity*, 1–21. PMID:34686947

Seo, K. (2007). Utilizing peer moderating in online discussions: Addressing the controversy between teacher moderation and nonmoderation. *American Journal of Distance Education*, 21(1), 21–36. doi:10.1080/08923640701298688

Seo, K., Tang, J., Roll, I., Fels, S., & Yoon, D. (2021). The impact of artificial intelligence on learner-instructor interaction in online learning. *International Journal of Educational Technology in Higher Education*, 18(1), 54. doi:10.1186/s41239-021-00292-9 PMID:34778540

Shaffer, D. (2017). *Quantitative ethnology*. Cathcart Press.

Shaul, M. (2007). Assessing online discussion forum participation. *Information Communication Technologies*, 1459–1467. doi:10.4018/978-1-59904-949-6.ch099

Shea, P., & Bidjerano, T. (2009). Community of inquiry as a theoretical framework to foster "epistemic engagement" and "cognitive presence" in online education. *Computers & Education*, 52(3), 543–553. doi:10.1016/j.compedu.2008.10.007

Shea, P., Richardson, J., & Swan, K. (2022). Building bridges to advance the community of inquiry framework for online learning. *Educational Psychologist*, 57(3), 148–161. doi:10.1080/00461520.2022.2089989

Sheridan, K., & Kelly, M. (2010). The indicators of instructor presence that are important to students in online courses. *Journal of Online Learning and Teaching*, 6(4), 767–779.

Sheridan, K., Kelly, M. A., & Bentz, D. T. (2013). A follow-up study of the indicators of teaching presence critical to students in online courses. In *Educational communities of inquiry: Theoretical framework, research and practice* (pp. 67–83). IGI Global. doi:10.4018/978-1-4666-2110-7.ch005

Shih, Y. H. (2019). An examination of the functions of a general education art curriculum in universities. *Policy Futures in Education*, 17(3), 306–317. doi:10.1177/1478210318811012

Shin, D. H., & Choo, H. (2011). Modeling the acceptance of socially interactive robotics: Social presence in human–robot interaction. *Interaction Studies: Social Behaviour and Communication in Biological and Artificial Systems*, 12(3), 430–460. doi:10.1075/is.12.3.04shi

Short, J., Williams, E., & Christie, B. (1976). *The Social Psychology of Telecommunications*. Wiley.

Shulock, N., & Offenstein, J. (2012). *Career Opportunities: Career Technical Education and the College Completion Agenda. Part I: Structure and Funding of Career Technical Education in the California Community Colleges*. Institute for Higher Education Leadership & Policy.

Siemens, G. (2005). Connectivism: A learning theory for the digital age. *International Journal of Instructional Technology and Distance Learning*, 2(1).

Silge, J., & Robinson, D. (2017). *Text mining with R: A tidy approach*. O'Reilly Media, Inc.

Silver, N., Kaplan, M., LaVaque-Manty, D., & Meizlish, D. (Eds.). (2023). *Using reflection and metacognition to improve student learning: Across the disciplines, across the academy*. Taylor & Francis.

Sinclair, S., & Rockwell, G. (2016). *Voyant Tools*. https://voyant-tools.org/

Singh, A., & Chouhan, T. (2023). Artificial Intelligence in HRM: Role of Emotional–Social Intelligence and Future Work Skill. In The Adoption and Effect of Artificial Intelligence on Human Resources Management, Part A (pp. 175-196). Emerald Publishing Limited.

Singh, A., & Sharma, A. (2021). Acceptance of MOOCs as an Alternative for Internship for Management Students During COVID-19 Pandemic: An Indian perspective. *International Journal of Educational Management, 35*(6), 1231–1244. doi:10.1108/IJEM-03-2021-0085

Singh, J., Singh, L., & Matthees, B. (2022). Establishing Social, Cognitive, and Teaching Presence in Online Learning-A Panacea in COVID-19 Pandemic, Post Vaccine and Post Pandemic Times. *Journal of Educational Technology Systems, 51*(1), 568–585. doi:10.1177/00472395221095169

Skates, A. (2023). Five Predictions for the Future of Learning in the Age of AI. *Everyday AI.* https://a16z.com/2023/02/08/the-future-of-learning-education-knowledge-in-the-age-of-ai/?utm_campaign=GSVN2K&utm_medium=email&_hsmi=245282162&_hsenc=p2ANqtz-

Skeels, M. M., & Grudin, J. (2009, May). When social networks cross boundaries: a case study of workplace use of Facebook and LinkedIn. In *Proceedings of the 2009 ACM International Conference on Supporting Group Work* (pp. 95-104). 10.1145/1531674.1531689

Skylar, A. A. (2009). A comparison of asynchronous online text-based lectures and synchronous interactive web conferencing lectures. *Issues in Teacher Education, 18*(2), 69–84.

Slater, M. (2017). Implicit learning through embodiment in immersive virtual reality. *Virtual, Augmented, and Mixed Realities in Education*, 19-33.

Smeenk, W., Sturm, J., Terken, J., & Eggen, B. (2018). A systematic validation of the Empathetic Handover approach guided by five factors that foster empathy in design. *International Journal of CoCreation in Design and the Arts, 15*(4), 308–328. https://doi-org.ezproxy.lib.purdue.edu/10.1080/15710882.2018.1484490

Smith, B. (2010). *E-learning technologies: A comparative study of adult learners enrolled on blended and online campuses engaging in a virtual classroom* [Doctoral dissertation].

Soffer, T., & Yaron, E. (2017). Perceived learning and students' perceptions toward using tablets for learning: The mediating role of perceived engagement among high school students. *Journal of Educational Computing Research, 55*(7), 951–973. doi:10.1177/0735633117689892

Solan, A. M., & Linardopoulos, N. (2011). Development, implementation, and evaluation of a grading rubric for online discussions. *Journal of Online Learning and Teaching, 7*(4).

Sotirou, S., & Bogner, F. (2008). Visualizing the Invisible: Augmented Reality as an Innovative Science Education Scheme. *Advanced Science Letters, 1*(1), 114–122. doi:10.1166/asl.2008.012

Spence, P. R., Westerman, D., Edwards, C., & Edwards, A. (2014). Welcoming our robot overlords: Initial expectations about interaction with a robot. *Communication Research Reports, 31*(3), 272–280. doi:10.1080/08824096.2014.924337

St. Clair, D. (2015). A simple suggestion for reducing first-time online student anxiety. *Journal of Online Learning and Teaching, 11*(1), 129–135.

Stefaniak, J. E., & Baaki, J. (2013). A layered approach to understanding your audience. *Performance Improvement, 52*(6), 5–9. doi:10.1002/pfi.21352

Stephens, M., & Jones, K. M. (2015). Emerging roles: Key insights from librarians in a massive open online course. *Journal of Library & Information Services in Distance Learning, 9*(1-2), 133–147. doi:10.1080/1533290X.2014.946353

Stöhr, C., Demazière, C., & Adawi, T. (2020). The Polarizing Effect of the Online Flipped Classroom. *Computers & Education, 147*(1), 103789. doi:10.1016/j.compedu.2019.103789

Stone, C., & Springer, M. (2019). Interactivity, connectedness and teacher-presence': Engaging and retaining students online. *Australian Journal of Adult Learning, 59*(2), 146–169.

Street, B. V. (2006). Autonomous and ideological models of literacy: Approaches from new literacy studies. *Media Anthropology Network, 17*(1), 1–15.

Strich, F., Mayer, A. S., & Fiedler, M. (2021). What Do I Do in a World of Artificial Intelligence? Investigating the Impact of Substitutive Decision-Making AI Systems on Employees' Professional Role Identity. *Journal of the Association for Information Systems, 22*(2), 9. doi:10.17705/1jais.00663

Studebaker, B., & Curtis, H. (2021). Building community in an online doctoral program. *Christian Higher Education, 20*(1–2), 15–27. doi:10.1080/15363759.2020.1852133

Student Engagement and Community-Building | Barnard Center for Engaged Pedagogy. (n.d.). https://cep.barnard.edu/student-engagement-and-community-building

Sugar, W. (2014). Analysis. In *Studies of ID practices: A review and synthesis of research on ID current practices.* Springer. doi:10.1007/978-3-319-03605-2_2

Suh, A., & Prophet, J. (2018). The state of immersive technology research: A literature analysis. *Computers in Human Behavior, 86*, 77–90. doi:10.1016/j.chb.2018.04.019

Suk, H., & Laine, T. H. (2023). Influence of avatar facial appearance on users' perceived embodiment and presence in immersive virtual reality. *Electronics (Basel), 12*(3), 583. doi:10.3390/electronics12030583

Sun, A., & Chen, X. (2016). Online education and its effective practice: A research review. *Journal of Information Technology Education, 15*, 15. doi:10.28945/3502

Sung, E., & Mayer, R. E. (2012). Five facets of social presence in online distance education. *Computers in Human Behavior, 28*(5), 1738–1747. doi:10.1016/j.chb.2012.04.014

Sutiah, S., Slamet, S., Shafqat, A., & Supriyono, S. (2020). Implementation of Distance Learning During the COVID-19 Pandemic in Faculty of Education and Teacher Training. *Cypriot Journal of Educational Science, 15*(1), 1204–1214. doi:10.18844/cjes.v15i5.5151

Sutton, K. K., & DeSantis, J. (2017). Beyond change blindness: Embracing the technology revolution in higher education. *Innovations in Education and Teaching International, 54*(3), 223–228. doi:10.1080/14703297.2016.1174592

Swan, K. P., Richardson, J. C., Ice, P., Garrison, D. R., Cleveland-Innes, M., & Arbaugh, J. B. (2008). Validating a measurement tool of presence in online communities of inquiry. *E-Mentor, 2*(24), 1–12.

Swan, K., Garrison, D. R., & Richardson, J. C. (2009). A constructivist approach to online learning: the Community of Inquiry framework. In C. R. Payne (Ed.), *Information Technology and Constructivism in Higher Education: Progressive Learning Frameworks* (pp. 43–57). IGI Global. doi:10.4018/978-1-60566-654-9.ch004

Swan, K., & Ice, P. (2010). The community of inquiry framework ten years later: Introduction to the special issue. *The Internet and Higher Education, 13*(1–2), 1–4. doi:10.1016/j.iheduc.2009.11.003

Swart, R. (2016). Critical thinking instruction and technology enhanced learning from the student perspective: A mixed methods research study. *Nurse Education in Practice, 23*, 30–39. doi:10.1016/j.nepr.2017.02.003 PMID:28213153

Taft, H. (2023, December 27). *Example biology discussion prompt*. Taft Portfolio, Blogspot. https://taftportfolio.blogspot.com/p/example-biology-discussion-prompts.html

Tamtik, M., & Guenter, M. (2019). Policy analysis of equity, diversity, and inclusion strategies in Canadian universities–How far have we come? *Canadian Journal of Higher Education*, *49*(3), 41–56. doi:10.47678/cjhe.v49i3.188529

Tangermann, V. (2023). Get a Load of This New Job: "Prompt Engineers" Who Act as Psychologists to AI Chatbots. *Futurism*. https://futurism.com/prompt-engineers-ai

Tatum, B. D. (2019). Together and alone? The challenge of talking about racism on campus. *Daedalus*, *148*(4), 79–93. doi:10.1162/daed_a_01761

Tatum, B. D. (2021). What is racism anyway? In S. M. McClure & C. A. Harris (Eds.), *Getting real about race* (p. 17). SAGE.

Tegos, S., Psathas, G., Tsiatsos, T., & Demetriadis, S. (2019, May 20–22). Designing Conversational Agent Interventions that Support Collaborative Chat Activities in MOOCs. *EMOOCs 2019: Work in Progress Papers of the Research, Experience and Business Tracks*. https://ceur-ws.org/Vol-2356/

Teng, Y., Zhang, J., & Sun, T. (2023). Data-Driven Decision-Making Model Based on Artificial Intelligence in Higher Education System of Colleges and Universities. *Expert Systems: International Journal of Knowledge Engineering and Neural Networks*, *40*(4), e12820. doi:10.1111/exsy.12820

Terrell, S. R., Snyder, M. M., & Dringus, L. P. (2009). The development, validation, and application of the doctoral student connectedness scale. *The Internet and Higher Education*, *12*(2), 112–116. doi:10.1016/j.iheduc.2009.06.004

Terry, C., & Cain, J. (2016). The emerging issue of digital empathy. *American Journal of Pharmaceutical Education*, *80*(4), 58. Advance online publication. doi:10.5688/ajpe80458 PMID:27293225

Teven, J. J., & McCroskey, J. C. (1997). The relationship of perceived teacher caring with student learning and teacher evaluation. *Communication Education*, *46*(1), 1–9. doi:10.1080/03634529709379069

Theodosiou, N. A., & Corbin, J. D. (2020). Redesign your in-person course for online: Creating connections and promoting engagement for better learning. *Ecology and Evolution*, *10*(22), 12561–12572. doi:10.1002/ece3.6844 PMID:33250995

Thomas, G., & Thorpe, S. (2019). Enhancing the facilitation of online groups in higher education: A review of the literature on face-to-face and online group-facilitation. *Interactive Learning Environments*, *27*(1), 62–71. doi:10.1080/10494820.2018.1451897

Thompson, K., deNoyelles, A., Chen, B., & Futch, L. (2016). Create effective discussion prompts. In B. Chen & K. Thompson (Eds.), *Teaching Online Pedagogical Repository*. University of Central Florida Center for Distributed Learning. https://topr.online.ucf.edu/discussion-prompts/

Thorpe, S. J. (2016). Online facilitator competencies for group facilitators. *Group Facilitation*, (13), 79.

Tlili, A., Shehata, B., Adarkwah, M. A., Bozkurt, A., Hickey, D. T., Huang, R., & Agyemang, B. (2023). What if the devil is my guardian angel: ChatGPT as a case study of using chatbots in education. *Smart Learning Environments*, *10*(1), 15–24. doi:10.1186/s40561-023-00237-x

Top Hat Staff. (2020). *Adrift in a Pandemic: Survey of 3,089 Students Finds Uncertainty About Returning to College*. https://tophat.com/blog/adrift-in-a-pandemic-survey-infographic/

Tracey, M. W., & Baaki, J. (2022). Empathy and empathic design for meaningful deliverables. *Educational Technology Research and Development*, *70*(6), 2091–2116. doi:10.1007/s11423-022-10146-4

Tracey, M. W., & Hutchinson, A. (2019). Empathic design: Imagining the cognitive and emotional learner experience. *Educational Technology Research and Development*, *67*(5), 1259–1272. doi:10.1007/s11423-019-09683-2

Trinter, C. P. & Hughes, H. E. (2021) Teachers as Curriculum Designers: Inviting Teachers into the Productive Struggle. *RMLE Online*, *44*(3), 1-16. doi:10.1080/19404476.2021.1878417

Trumbore, A. (2023). ChatGPT Could be an Effective and Affordable Tutor. *The Conversation*. https://theconversation-com.cdn.ampproject.org/c/s/theconversation.com/amp/chatgpt-could-be-an-effective-and-affordable-tutor-198062

Twenty to Nine LLC. (2023). Delve [online qualitative analysis software]. Available from delvetool.com

UNESCO. (2021). *Supporting learning recovery one year into COVID-19: The Global Education Coalition in action.* https://unesdoc.unesco.org/ark:/48223/pf0000376061

Vallade, J. I., & Kaufmann, R. (2020). *Instructor misbehavior and student outcomes*. Academic Press.

Valverde-Berrocoso, J., Garrido-Arroyo, M. C., Burgos-Videla, C., & Morales-Cevallos, M. B. (2020). Trends in educational research about e-learning: A systematic literature review (2009–2018). *Sustainability (Basel)*, *12*(12), 5153. doi:10.3390/su12125153

Van Boven, L., & Lowenstein, G. (2005). Empathy gaps in emotional perspective taking. In B. F. Malle & S. D. Hodges (Eds.), *Other minds: How humans bridge the divide between self and others* (pp. 284–297). The Guilford Press.

Van Harmelen, M. (2008). Design trajectories: Four experiments in PLE implementation. *Interactive Learning Environments*, *16*(1), 35–46. doi:10.1080/10494820701772686

Van Houtte, M. (2005). Climate or culture? A plea for conceptual clarity in school effectiveness research. *School Effectiveness and School Improvement*, *16*(1), 71–89. doi:10.1080/09243450500113977

vanDijk, J. (2006). Digital divide research, achievements, and shortcomings. *Poetics*, *34*(4-5), 221–235. doi:10.1016/j.poetic.2006.05.004

Vann, L. (2015). Demonstrating empathy: A phenomenological study of instructional designers making instructional strategy decisions for adult learners. *International Journal on Teaching and Learning in Higher Education*, *29*, 233–244. https://files.eric.ed.gov/fulltext/EJ1146186.pdf

Velev, D., & Zlateva, P. (2017). Virtual reality challenges in education and training. *International Journal of Learning and Teaching*, *3*(1), 33–37. doi:10.18178/ijlt.3.1.33-37

Ventayen, R. J. M. (2023, March). OpenAI ChatGPT Generated Results: Similarity Index of Artificial Intelligence-Based Contents. *SSRN 4332664*. https://ssrn.com/abstract=4332664

Vijayakumar, R., Bhuvaneshwari, B., Adith, S., & Deepika, M. (2019). AI-Based Student Bot for Academic Information System using Machine Learning. *International Journal of Scientific Research in Computer Science, Engineering, and Information Technology*, *5*(2), 590–596. https://doi-org.ezproxy.liberty.edu/10.32628/CSEIT1952171

Violanti, M. T., Kelly, S. E., Garland, M. E., & Christen, S. (2018). Instructor clarity, humor, immediacy, and student learning: Replication and extension. *Communication Studies*, *69*(3), 251–262. doi:10.1080/10510974.2018.1466718

Virtual Speech. (2024). *Job Interview Preparation*. Retrieved on January 14, 2024, from https://virtualspeech.com/courses/interview-vr

Vlasova, H. (2022). Online Education Statistics – How COVID-19 Changed the Way We Learn? *Admissionsly*. https://admissionsly.com/online-education-statistics/

Vonderwell, S., & Zachariah, S. (2005). Factors that influence participation in online learning. *Journal of Research on Technology in Education*, *38*(2), 213–230. doi:10.1080/15391523.2005.10782457

Vos, L. (2023). How to correctly use ChatGPT for essay writing. *E School News*. Retrieved on January 15, 2024, https://www.eschoolnews.com/digital-learning/2023/09/20/how-to-correctly-use-chatgpt-for-essay-writing/

Vygotsky, L. S., & Cole, M. (1978). *Mind in society: Development of higher psychological processes*. Harvard University Press. doi:10.2307/j.ctvjf9vz4

Wang, B. (2022). The Application of Modern Computer-Aided Technology in Fine Art Education. *Security and Communication Networks*, *2022*, 1–10. doi:10.1155/2022/8288855

Wang, Q. Y. (2008). Student-facilitators' roles of moderating online discussions. *British Journal of Educational Technology*, *39*(5), 859–874. doi:10.1111/j.1467-8535.2007.00781.x

WangX.GongZ.WangG.JiaJ.XuY.ZhaoJ.FanQ.WuS.HuW.LiX. (2023). ChatGPT Performs on the Chinese National Medical Licensing Examination. *Journal of Medical Systems*. doi:10.21203/rs.3.rs-2584079/v1

Wasik, B. A., & Hindman, A. H. (2013). Realizing the promise of open-ended questions. *The Reading Teacher*, *67*(4), 302–311. doi:10.1002/trtr.1218

Watson, S. L., Koehler, A. A., Ertmer, P. A., Rico, R., & Kim, W. (2018). An expert instructor's use of social congruence, cognitive congruence, and expertise in an online case-based instructional design course. *The Interdisciplinary Journal of Problem-Based Learning*, *12*(1). Advance online publication. doi:10.7771/1541-5015.1633

Watson, S., Sullivan, D., & Watson, K. (2023). Teaching Presence in Asynchronous Online Classes: It's Not Just a Façade. *Online Learning : the Official Journal of the Online Learning Consortium*, *27*(2), 288–303. doi:10.24059/olj.v27i2.3231

Weave Media Team. (2023, July 24). *Your user personas are biased*. https://medium.com/kubo/your-user-personas-are-biased-ac7280f9e222

Weisz, E., & Cikara, M. (2020). Strategic Regulation of Empathy. *Trends in Cognitive Sciences*, *25*(3), 213–227. . doi:10.1016/j.tics.2020.12.002 PMID:33386247

Weizenbaum, J. (1966). ELIZA—A computer program for the study of natural language communication between man and machine. *Communications of the ACM*, *9*(1), 36–45. doi:10.1145/365153.365168

Weltzer-Ward, L. (2011). Content analysis coding schemes for online asynchronous discussion. *Campus-Wide Information Systems*, *28*(1), 56–74. doi:10.1108/10650741111097296

West, C. (2021). *12 ways to use social media for education*. https://sproutsocial.com/insights/social-media-for-education/

Western Governors University. (2023). *Annual Report for 2022*. Retrieved on January 15, 2024, https://www.wgu.edu/about/annual-report.html

Whalen, J. (2020). Should Teachers be Trained in Emergency Remote Teaching? Lessons Learned from the COVID-19 Pandemic. *Journal of Technology and Teacher Education*, *28*(2), 189–199.

White, S. (2023). *2023 Trends in Online College Education*. https://study.com/resources/online-education-trends

Whiteside, A. L., Garrett, D. A., & Swan, K. (Eds.). (2017). *Social presence in online learning: Multiple perspectives on practice and research*. Stylus Publishing.

Wicks, D. A., Craft, B. B., Mason, G. N., Gritter, K., & Bolding, K. (2015). An investigation into the community of inquiry of blended classrooms by a faculty learning community. *The Internet and Higher Education*, *25*, 53–62. doi:10.1016/j.iheduc.2014.12.001

Williams van Rooij, S. (2012). Research-based personas: Teaching empathy in professional education. *The Journal of Effective Teaching*, *12*(3), 77–86.

Williams, F. (2021). Flexible learning design: A turning point for resilient adult education. *Journal of Adult Education in Tanzania*, *23*(1), 165–191.

Williams, R. (2021). Concerns of Socially Interactive Technologies' Influence on Students: Digital Immigrant Teachers' Perspectives. *Ingenta Connect*, *141*(3), 109–122.

Williams, S. S., Jaramillo, A., & Pesko, J. C. (2015). Improving depth of thinking in online discussion boards. *Quarterly Review of Distance Education*, *16*(3), 45.

Willis, J. (1998). Alternative instructional design paradigms: What's worth discussing and what isn't. *Educational Technology*, *38*(3), 5–16. https://www.jstor.org/stable/44428983

Will, M., & Najarro, I. (2022). What is culturally responsive teaching? *Education Week*, *41*(33), 16–18. https://www.edweek.org/teaching-learning/culturally-responsive-teaching-culturally-responsive-pedagogy/2022/04

Wilson, B. G. (2013). A practice-centered approach to instructional design. In J. M. Spector, B. B. Lockee, S. Smaldino, & M. Herring (Eds.), *Learning, problem solving, and mindtools: Essays in honor of David H. Jonassen* (pp. 35–54). Routledge.

Wilson, M. (2002). Six views of embodied cognition. *Psychonomic Bulletin & Review*, *9*(4), 625–636. doi:10.3758/BF03196322 PMID:12613670

Wingard, D. (2019). Data-Driven Automated Decision-Making in Assessing Employee Performance and Productivity: Designing and Implementing Workforce Metrics and Analytics. *Psychosociological Issues in Human Resource Management*, *7*(2), 13–18. doi:10.22381/PIHRM7220192

Witmer, B. G., & Singer, M. J. (1998). Measuring presence in virtual environments: A presence questionnaire. *Presence (Cambridge, Mass.)*, *7*(3), 225–240. doi:10.1162/105474698565686

Witt, P. L., Wheeless, L. R., & Allen, M. (2004). A meta-analytical review of the relationship between teacher immediacy and student learning. *Communication Monographs*, *71*(2), 184–207. doi:10.1080/036452042000228054

Wlodkowski, R. J., & Ginsberg, M. B. (2017). *Enhancing adult motivation to learn: A comprehensive guide for teaching all adults*. John Wiley & Sons.

Wombacher, K. A., Harris, C. J., Buckner, M. M., Frisby, B., & Limperos, A. M. (2017). The effects of computer-mediated communication anxiety on student perceptions of instructor behaviors, perceived learning, and quiz performance. *Communication Education*, *66*(3), 299–312. doi:10.1080/03634523.2016.1221511

Woodley, X., Hernandez, C., Parra, J., & Negash, B. (2017). Celebrating difference: Best practices in culturally responsive teaching online. *TechTrends*, *61*(5), 470–478. doi:10.1007/s11528-017-0207-z

Woods, K., & Bliss, K. (2016). Facilitating successful online discussions. *The Journal of Effective Teaching*, *16*(2), 76–92.

Wortman, B., & Wang, J. Z. (2022). HICEM: A High-Coverage Emotion Model for Artificial Emotional Intelligence. *arXiv preprint arXiv:2206.07593*.

Wright, P., & McCarthy, J. (2005). The value of the novel in designing for experience. In A. Pirhonen, C. Roast, P. Saariluoma, & H. Isom (Eds.), *Future interaction design* (pp. 9–30). Springer-Verlag. doi:10.1007/1-84628-089-3_2

Wu, B., Yu, X., & Gu, X. (2020). Effectiveness of immersive virtual reality using head-mounted displays on learning performance: A meta-analysis. *British Journal of Educational Technology*, *51*(6), 1991–2005. doi:10.1111/bjet.13023

Wu, D., & Hiltz, S. R. (2004). Predicting learning from asynchronous online discussions. *Journal of Asynchronous Learning Networks*, *8*(2), 139–152. https://doi.og/10.1142/S1609945104000115

Wu, S. Y., Hou, H. T., Hwang, W. Y., & Liu, E. Z. F. (2013). Analysis of learning behavior in problem-solving-based and project-based discussion activities within the seamless online learning integrated discussion (SOLID) system. *Journal of Educational Computing Research*, *49*(1), 61–82. doi:10.2190/EC.49.1.c

Wyss, C., Bührer, W., Furrer, F., Degonda, A., & Hiss, J. A. (2021). Innovative teacher education with the augmented reality device Microsoft Hololens—Results of an exploratory study and pedagogical considerations. *Multimodal Technologies and Interaction*, *5*(8), 45. doi:10.3390/mti5080045

Xie, J. A. G., Rice, M. F., & Griswold, D. E. (2021). Instructional designers' shifting thinking about supporting teaching during and post-COVID-19. *Distance Education*, *42*(3), 331–351. doi:10.1080/01587919.2021.1956305

Xie, K. (2013). What do the numbers say? The influence of motivation and peer feedback on students' behaviour in online discussions. *British Journal of Educational Technology*, *44*(2), 288–301. doi:10.1111/j.1467-8535.2012.01291.x

Xie, K., DeBacker, T. K., & Ferguson, C. (2006). Extending the traditional classroom through online discussion: The role of student motivation. *Journal of Educational Computing Research*, *34*(1), 68–78. doi:10.2190/7BAK-EGAH-3MH1-K7C6

Xu, D., & Xu, Y. (2020). The ambivalence about distance learning in higher education: Challenges, opportunities, and policy implications. Higher Education: Handbook of Theory and Research, 35, 351-401.

Xu, W., Xing, Q. W., Zhu, J. D., Liu, X., & Jin, P. N. (2023). Effectiveness of an extended-reality interactive learning system in a dance training course. *Education and Information Technologies*, *28*(12), 1–31. doi:10.1007/s10639-023-11883-6

Yadav, R., Tiruwa, A., & Suri, P. K. (2017). Internet based learning (IBL) in higher education: A literature review. *Journal of International Education in Business*, *10*(2), 102–129. doi:10.1108/JIEB-10-2016-0035

Yamada, M. (2009). The role of social presence in learner-centered communicative language learning using synchronous computer-mediated communication: Experimental study. *Computers & Education*, *52*(4), 820–833. doi:10.1016/j.compedu.2008.12.007

Yang, K., Zhou, X., & Radu, I. (2020). XR-ed framework: Designing instruction-driven and learner-centered extended reality systems for education. *arXiv preprint arXiv:2010.13779.*

Yang, D., Richardson, J. C., French, B. F., & Lehman, J. D. (2011). The development of a content analysis model for assessing students' cognitive learning in asynchronous online discussions. *Educational Technology Research and Development*, *59*(1), 43–70. doi:10.1007/s11423-010-9166-1

Yang, J. C., Quadir, B., Chen, N.-S., & Miao, Q. (2016). Effects of online presence on learning performance in a blog-based online course. *The Internet and Higher Education*, *30*, 11–20. doi:10.1016/j.iheduc.2016.04.002

Yang, Y.-T. C., Newby, T. J., & Bill, R. L. (2005). Using Socratic questioning to promote critical thinking skills through asynchronous discussion forums in distance learning environments. *American Journal of Distance Education*, *19*(3), 163–181. doi:10.1207/s15389286ajde1903_4

Yen, C., & Tu, C. (2011). A multiple-group confirmatory factor analysis of the scores for online presence: Do they measure the same thing across cultural groups? *Journal of Educational Computing Research, 44*(2), 219–242. doi:10.2190/EC.44.2.e

Yengin, İ., Karahoca, D., Karahoca, A., & Yücel, A. (2010). Roles of teachers in e-learning: How to engage students & how to get free e-learning and the future. *Procedia: Social and Behavioral Sciences, 2*(2), 5775–5787. doi:10.1016/j.sbspro.2010.03.942

Yiannoutsou, N., Johnson, R., & Price, P. (2021). Non-visual virtual reality: Considerations for the pedagogical design of embodied mathematical experiences for visually impaired children. *Journal of Educational Technology & Society, 24*(2), 151–163.

Yin, J., Goh, T., Yang, B., & Xiaobin, Y. (2021). Conversation technology with micro-learning: The impact of chatbot-based learning on students' learning motivation and performance. *Journal of Educational Computing Research, 59*(1), 154–177. doi:10.1177/0735633120952067

Yuan, Q., & Gao, Q. (2023). Being there, and being together: Avatar appearance and peer interaction in VR classrooms for video-based learning. *International Journal of Human-Computer Interaction,* 1-21. doi:10.1080/10447318.2023.2189818

Zall, R., & Kangavari, M. R. (2022). Comparative Analytical Survey on Cognitive Agents with Emotional Intelligence. *Cognitive Computation, 14*(4), 1223–1246. doi:10.1007/s12559-022-10007-5

Zawacki-Richter, O., Marín, V. I., Bond, M., & Gouverneur, F. (2019). Systematic review of research on artificial intelligence applications in higher education – where are the educators? *International Journal of Educational Technology in Higher Education, 16*(1), 1–27. doi:10.1186/s41239-019-0171-0

Zeichner, K., Payne, K. A., & Brayko, K. (2015). Democratizing teacher education. *Journal of Teacher Education, 66*(2), 122–135. doi:10.1177/0022487114560908

Zhang, Y., Stohr, C., Jamsvi, S., & Kabo, J. (2023). Considering the Community of Inquiry Framework in online engineering-a literature review. *Journal of Higher Education Theory and Practice, 23*(6), 55–68.

Zhou, L., Xue, S., & Li, R. (2022). Extending the Technology Acceptance Model to explore students' intention to use an online education platform at a University in China. *SAGE Open, 12*(1). doi:10.1177/21582440221085259

Zinchenko, Y. P., Khoroshikh, P. P., Sergievich, A. A., Smirnov, A. S., Tumyalis, A. V., Kovalev, A. I., & Golokhvast, K. S. (2020). Virtual reality is more efficient in learning human heart anatomy especially for subjects with low baseline knowledge. *New Ideas in Psychology, 59*, 100786. doi:10.1016/j.newideapsych.2020.100786

About the Contributors

Laura E. Gray, a Southern gal, was born and raised in Louisiana and on the Mississippi Gulf Coast. Laura grew up in Long Beach, Mississippi, and graduated from Long Beach High School in 1988. From there, she went on to college at the University of Louisiana at Monroe where she earned her Bachelor's degree in secondary education with credentials in social studies and English for grades 7-12. She taught a year of junior high in Louisiana, a year of Job Corps in Gulfport, MS, and four years at Hancock High School in Kiln, MS (most famous for being the home of Bret Favre of Green Bay Packers football fame). After finishing her master's degree in school counseling, she spent the next 8 years as the counselor of a large K-5 school back in Long Beach and was there when Hurricane Katrina blew the school away in 2005. By 2007, Laura was able to take early retirement, where she stayed home with her 3 children and worked on her doctorate in Instructional Design for Online Learning, which was completed in 2015. Since then, she has taught both undergraduate and graduate courses in instructional design and has developed a variety of courses and trainings. In the summer of 2019, after having lived in Belize for 2 1/2 years and the Yucatan for 6 years, Laura and her family moved back to the States where they chose the Treasure Valley near Boise, Idaho as their home. Since then, both of their sons, ages 25 and 27, have left Mississippi and joined them, and their daughter, who is 22, is going to college and figuring out what she wants to do. When she's not working and doing family things with the husband and kids, Laura enjoys traveling, shopping, reading, watching shows on Netflix, and spending time with friends and her two dogs, Dany and Lucy, as well as her cat Xander. Laura currently works remotely as a full-time faculty member and research methodologist in the Ed.D. program at South College.

Shernette D. Dunn is a four time graduate of Florida Atlantic University earning her bachelors, masters, specialist, and Ph.D degrees all from the College of Education. She is also the first to earn the Instructional Designer Certificate offered by the College of Education. 'When I moved to the United States in 1997 from Jamaica, like most immigrants, I wanted to achieve the 'American Dream' and I chose education as my path," said Dr. Dunn, who earned her doctorate in 2020. After graduating with her bachelor's degree, Dr. Dunn began working for Broward County Schools teaching various grade levels. While working in the school system she also gained the coveted National Board Certification. She was also an adjunct instructor at Broward College for over 10 years where she taught Reading, English for Academic Purposes and College Success Skills. She has worked in various other educational sectors in Broward County supporting children and their families. While attending FAU, Dr. Dunn was a commuter student and considered the Davie campus her home campus. "It was easy and convenient to attend the Davie campus because it was a stone's throw from Nova Eisenhower Elementary where I worked for over 10 years," she said. Dr. Dunn has also worked as a part time instructor for FAU to help first year students get familiar with college courses, and expectations. She said that was one of the highlights of her career where she felt like she came full circle by helping other students to grow and develop educationally. Dr. Dunn supports education both at the local and nation level. She previously worked at one of the Nation's Military Academies where she served in an administrative role to promote student success. She is now working on a project for the National Academies of Science where she is helping to write a report for education practices for adult learners in the military context. Dr. Dunn also supported education and technology ventures by being part of the National Technology Leadership Summit and other organizations that promotes education and technology.

* * *

Aerin Benavides is an Associate Research Professor at the University of North Carolina Greensboro. Her teaching and research focus on using sustainable development goals in science teacher education and expansive learning in preparing pre-service and in-service teachers to teach science.

Ruth Boyd began her teaching career in elementary education, teaching third grade for 13 years. After transitioning to higher education, she expanded her practice to teacher preparation, specifically in the fields of early childhood education, elementary education, and literacy instruction. Dr. Boyd has enjoyed serving as university supervisor for teacher candidates, at both the undergraduate and graduate level, and developing graduate program options in Reading Specialist and Instructional Coaching. As Vice President for Student Affairs, she served as the senior student affairs officer, overseeing and managing institutional effectiveness through strategic planning, recruitment, admissions, registration, and retention initiatives. Dr. Boyd held direct supervisor responsibility over the Dean of Students, Student Activities, Title IX, Enrollment Management, Career Services, International Student Affairs, Registrar's Office, Student Counseling Service, Student Health Services, Upward Bound, Wellness Center and Intramural Activities, Public Safety, and the Student Government Association.

Jen Crystle joined Marymount in 2017 and most recently served as the head of the Office of Global Learning, Engagement, and Research. Throughout her career in international education, Jen has conducted research on international education policy, ethical issues in education abroad, and fostering global and social responsibility among students. Jen has extensive experience in higher education administration and leadership, with experience at both public and private institutions. She has served on several strategic committees, including committees on high-impact practices, curriculum development, and diversity and inclusion initiatives. Jen has presented at numerous local and national conferences and has conducted many international site visits. Jen is a member of the Marymount Inclusion Network and she is a certified administrator of the Intercultural Development Inventory. Her academic and professional interests include global education policy, intercultural and career competencies, experiential learning, and school leadership.

Liu Dong is a doctoral student in the Learning Design and Technology program at Purdue University. Currently, she focuses on learning and exploring the interaction between learners in online communities through learning analytics. She is also interested in how emerging technologies (e.g., VR, MR) can support language learning.

Allison Freed is an Assistant Professor of Instructional Technology and coordinator of the Instructional Technology Graduate Program at the University of Central Arkansas. Her teaching and research interests include global learning, technology integration, blended learning, and Collaborative Online International Learning (COIL).

Jana Gerard is an adjunct instructor and the Coordinator of The EDvolution Center, College of Education, Health, and Human Studies at Southeast Missouri State University. She ensures teacher candidates at Southeast Missouri State are prepared to effectively and appropriately implement educational technology in their future classrooms. This is accomplished through providing instruction on digital literacy, digital competency, and digital citizenship through the lens of the ISTE Standards for Educators. Jana also provides students, faculty, and staff professional development on design thinking, coding, 3D printing, and virtual and augmented reality. In addition, she presents nationally and internationally on a variety of educational technology topics. Her research interests include AI in language learning, how preservice educators learn educational technology skills, and ways to incorporate education professionals in interprofessional education with health professions.

Trudy C. Giasi is currently the Principal of Valle Catholic Grade School within the Archdiocese of St. Louis. Prior to this role she served as an Assistant Professor of STEM Education at Southeast Missouri State University. She has designed and facilitated undergraduate and graduate-level education courses and serves the university, community, and beyond through participation in various educational committees and organizations. In addition, she conducts educational research and presents on topics related to STEM/STEAM education, educational technology, program sustainability and leadership, and professional development. Throughout her career, she has been involved with program, curriculum, standards, assessment, and partnership development at the school, district, state, and national levels. She is nationally-recognized as a leader of STEM curriculum and has collaborated with several school districts throughout the country as well as state-level education departments to develop cohesive and integrated STEM programming. She has a Ph.D. in STEM Education, M.A. in Educational Administration, M.Ed. in Science Education, and B.F.A. in Dance from The Ohio State University.

Noël Gieringer is a clinical instructor at the University of Central Arkansas.

Clara Hauth joined Marymount in 2014. Her academic experience includes teaching both graduate and undergraduate online instruction at George Mason University and James Madison University. Prior to her work at Marymount, she spent 5 years in the broadcasting industry, training and leading teams in program content, and 10 years as a secondary special education teacher and chair leading teacher training. She serves as a liaison with state and national programs supporting students with disabilities and is an active member of AERA, ASCD, CEC, and divisions CCBD, CLD, DISES, and TED. She serves as the past president of the DISES board, collaborating with global educational organizations on teacher development and leadership. Dr. Hauth's transformational leadership in preparing teachers and administrators for careers in the critical field of special education is noted through her co-authored book The Survival Guide for New Special Education Teachers. Her research agenda includes interventions in schools, teacher and school leadership, and global education. In 2020 she became Program Coordinator for the EdD in Educational Leadership and Organizational Innovation.

Jessica Herring Watson is an assistant professor in the College of Education and the University of Central Arkansas. With over a decade of teaching experience, Jessica focuses her work on cultivating meaningful relationships between technology-enabled learning and engaging pedagogy. Her research investigates preservice and in-service teachers' development and persistent use of technology-enabled learning to cultivate more inclusive, creative, and engaging learning environments and to transform educational cultures.

Lacey D. Huffling is an Associate Professor of Science Education in the Department of Middles and Secondary Education at Georgia Southern University. Her research interests include agency, equity, and identity in environmental education, science education, and teacher education. She is currently an Early Career Research Fellow for the Gulf Research Program of the National Academies of Science, Engineering, and Medicine.

James Hutson is an administrator and researcher in higher education specializing in artificial intelligence, neurohumanities, neurodiversity, immersive realities, digital humanities, and gamification of education. He received his BA in Art from the University of Tulsa, MA in Art History from Southern Methodist University, and his PhD in Art History from the University of Maryland, College Park. He has also received his MA in Leadership and MA in Game Design at Lindenwood University and is now pursuing his PhD in Artificial Intelligence at Capitol Technology University. Dr. Hutson has taught at five universities across the country since 2006 and has served as chair of Art History and program manager of Pre-Art Therapy and Pre-Art Conservation, Assistant Dean of Graduate and Online Programs for the School of Arts, Media, and Communication, and now serves as Lead XR Disruptor and Department Head of Art History and Visual Culture for the College of Arts and Humanities. His scholarship focuses on the intersections of art, culture, and technology.

Anthony Ilobinso is a PhD student in the Learning Design and Technology Program at Purdue University.

Lucas John Jensen is an Associate Professor of Leadership, Technology, and Human Development at Georgia Southern University. His work focuses on social media and education, motivation, video games and education, and online instruction. Much of his research has examined youth game design activities in informal learning environments.

Jackie HeeYoung Kim, Ed.D., is a Professor in the College of Education at Georgia Southern University. Dr. Jackie Kim has rich experiences in teaching pre-service teachers and working with Georgia teachers through the Teacher Quality Grant and other statewide grants. Dr. Kim's areas of expertise are in educational technology (particularly technology integration into curriculum) and curriculum and instruction. Her research interest includes the transformation of K-12 classrooms with digital technology, professional development for technology integration into differentiated instruction, and flipped learning in K-8 and higher education.

Adrie A. Koehler is an associate professor at Purdue University in the Learning Design and Technology program. Her professional interests include the consideration of instructional strategies in teaching and learning processes. Specifically, she researches ways emerging technologies, specifically social media, can be used for instructional purposes; how instructors develop a presence in online settings and the impact of this presence; and methods to best facilitate case-based instruction. Additionally, she is interested in discovering techniques for improving the transition of pre-service teachers into the education profession.

Jim A. McCleskey is a Senior Faculty Instructor at Western Governors University. He holds a Ph.D. in Organization and Management with an emphasis in Leadership Studies and an MBA in Management and Marketing. His research areas of interest include leadership emergence, attachment, dark leadership, leadership efficacy, emotional labor, and affect in organizations. He is a native Texan who lives in the Houston area. He is a husband, a father of three sons, and a grandfather. When he is not working, he enjoys reading and martial arts.

Sally Meech is a doctoral candidate in the Learning Design and Technology program at Purdue University. Her research interests are broadly focused on the area of online teaching and learning, specifically exploring instructor leadership, empathy, and technology affordances. She currently works in the consulting industry as a Learning Evaluation Advisor.

Shannon Melideo joined Marymount in 2004. She currently serves as a teaching faculty member and a Lead Doctoral Faculty Mentor for students in the EdD program. Throughout her career, she has presented and collaborated extensively on schoolwide, districtwide, campuswide, statewide, national, and international committees, research projects, and task forces. She taught grades 1, 3, 4, 5, ESOL grades K-5, music grades K-8, and 7th-12th grade biology in high needs schools. She has served as a mentor teacher, cooperating teacher, elementary administrator, and district coordinator of ESOL. On the university level, she has served as university department chairperson, supervisor, and associate dean. She recently returned to the elementary classroom as a lead teacher, and was nominated as teacher of the year thrice at her school.

Rebecca Melton serves as Faculty in the School of Business at Western Governors University, teaching courses in Human Resources and Business. She earned a Ph.D. in Business Psychology from the Chicago School of Professional Psychology, and a Masters in Business Administration (MBA) and Bachelors in Psychology from Bowling Green State University. With more than 25 years of experience in Leadership, Operations and Human Resources, she holds the SHRM-SCP and SPHR certifications. Further, she is a certified Vocational Expert in the Franklin County Domestic Courts. At the university level, she serves on the Student Conduct Board and the Faculty Learning Community.

Michael Mills, Interim Dean of the Graduate School and Associate Dean of the College of Education at the University of Central Arkansas, is a leading expert on assessment accountability and the practical uses of mobile technology, with a particular focus on ensuring educational equity and designing strategies for effectively integrating mobile devices in the classroom. He is an SXSWedu, ISTE, and SITE presenter, has been recognized as an Apple Distinguished Educator and Google Education Trainer, and has served on the advisory boards for SXSWedu and the Apple Distinguished Educator Program for the Americas. Feel free to follow him on Twitter (@MichaelSMills).

Daniel Plate earned his B.A. in English and philosophy from Taylor University in Indiana; an M.F.A. in creative writing from the University of Arkansas; and a Ph.D. in literature from Washington University in St. Louis. He teaches creative writing, literature, and composition at Lindenwood University. He has published poetry and research in artificial intelligence and pedagogy and splits his time between developing code to support his teaching and doing research in the overlap between AI and innovative pedagogy.

Heather C. Scott is an Assistant Professor of science education in the Department of Middles and Secondary Education at Georgia Southern University. Her research interests include environmental education, science education, and teacher education. She is the program director for the Master of Arts in Teaching for Middle Grades and Secondary Education.

Jennifer Thompson has been working with children and families in a variety of settings since her undergraduate days at Tulane University, where she received her bachelors in Sociology and a minor in Psychology. She has also gained experience in opening and operating a boutique real estate brokerage as an operations manager and real estate agent as a top producer. She returned to school to gain her Masters of Education in Curriculum and Instruction while working full time at Marymount as an administrative assistant and LDFM coordinator in the School of Education. She has since enjoyed contributing to research projects globally and nationally with the School of Education faculty.

Jodie Ward is currently pursuing her Master of Education in Counseling at Georgia Southern University.

Stuart White is a biology lecturer and PhD student in the Learning Design and Technology program at Purdue University.

Florence Williams is an accomplished instructional designer at the University of Central Florida. She has over two decades of experience in Education and a background of working in both public and private university environments. In her role, Florence focuses on enhancing course design and instructional methods for faculty. She provides pedagogical support to faculty members, offering coaching and mentoring for creating online and blended courses. Fondly referred to as "Flo," this Jamaican national has held various leadership and faculty development positions, consistently advocating for excellence through technology integration and curriculum enhancement. Florence shares her work nationally and internationally on her research interests of inclusive excellence and the potential benefits of emerging technologies in teaching and learning. Beyond her professional commitments, she dedicates her time to volunteering with professional organizations in her field and Big Brother Big Sister of Tampa Bay. An avid enthusiast of outdoor pursuits, Florence finds joy in camping, hiking, and kayaking in the scenic state parks of Florida's Adventure Coast.

Qian Xu, a Ph.D. candidate in Learning Design and Technology, specializes in self-regulated learning, mobile learning, and second language acquisition. As an instructional designer at Eli Lilly and Company, she applies her research expertise in a corporate setting. At Purdue University, Qian has taught/co-taught various courses, including Chinese Language, Introduction to Educational Technology, and the graduate-level Foundations of Instructional Design Theory.

Weijian Yan is a doctoral student in the Learning Design and Technology program at the College of Education at Purdue University. She is interested in instructional design, and immersive technologies, especially applying VR-enhanced instruction to the teaching and learning of foreign languages.

Zhuo Zhang is a Ph.D. candidate in the Learning Design and Technology program at Purdue University. He teaches an undergraduate course titled "Introduction to Educational Technology & Computing." His research focuses on preservice teachers' motivation for technology integration, online learning, and the use of research methodologies to explore these areas further.

Index

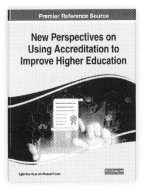

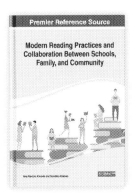
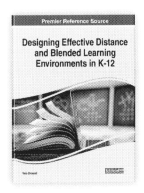

 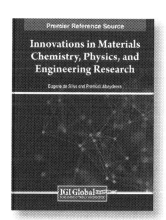 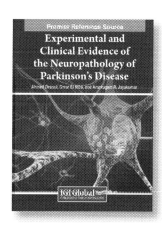 

Submit an Open Access Book Proposal

Have Your Work Fully & Freely Available Worldwide After Publication

Seeking the Following Book Classification Types:

Authored & Edited Monographs • Casebooks • Encyclopedias • Handbooks of Research

Gold, Platinum, & Retrospective OA Opportunities to Choose From

Easily Track Your Work in Our Advanced Manuscript Submission System With **Rapid Turnaround Times**

Double-Blind Peer Review by Notable Editorial Boards (*Committee on Publication Ethics* (COPE) Certified

Publications Adhere to All **Current OA Mandates & Compliances**

Affordable APCs *(Often 50% Lower Than the Industry Average)* Including Robust Editorial Service Provisions

Direct Connections with **Prominent Research Funders** & OA Regulatory Groups

Institution Level OA Agreements Available (Recommend or Contact Your Librarian for Details)

Join a **Diverse Community of 150,000+ Researchers Worldwide** Publishing With IGI Global

Content Spread Widely to Leading Repositories (AGOSR, ResearchGate, CORE, & More)

Retrospective Open Access Publishing

DID YOU KNOW?

You Can Unlock Your Recently Published Work, Including Full Book & Individual Chapter Content to Enjoy All the Benefits of Open Access Publishing

Learn More

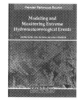

Printed in the United States
by Baker & Taylor Publisher Services